To Neal —
Christmas 1970
from Dot & Dick
Uhle

ROOSEVELT:
THE SOLDIER OF FREEDOM

Other books by James MacGregor Burns

PRESIDENTIAL GOVERNMENT: THE CRUCIBLE OF LEADERSHIP

THE DEADLOCK OF DEMOCRACY: FOUR-PARTY POLITICS IN AMERICA

JOHN KENNEDY: A POLITICAL PROFILE

ROOSEVELT: THE LION AND THE FOX

GOVERNMENT BY THE PEOPLE (with Jack W. Peltason)

CONGRESS ON TRIAL

OKINAWA: THE LAST BATTLE (co-author)

GUAM: OPERATIONS OF THE 77TH DIVISION

JAMES MacGREGOR BURNS

Roosevelt:
THE SOLDIER OF FREEDOM

HARCOURT BRACE JOVANOVICH, INC.
New York

FOR Joan
David
Stewart and Sally
Deborah
Trienah
Becky
Peter

First edition

ISBN 0-15-178871-5

Library of Congress Catalog Card Number: 71-95877

Printed in the United States of America

A prince must have no other object and no other thought than war and its methods and conduct . . . for this is the only branch of knowledge that is required of him who governs. . . . The prince should read history, and give attention to the actions of great men related to it, and to examine the cause of their victories and defeats. . . . A wise prince should practice such habits as these . . . so that when Fortune grows contrary he may be found ready to assist her.

—Machiavelli, *The Prince,* 1532

History with its flickering lamp stumbles along the trail of the past, trying to reconstruct its scenes, to revive its echoes, and kindle with pale gleams the passion of former days. What is the worth of all this? The only guide to a man is his conscience; the only shield to his memory is the rectitude and sincerity of his actions. It is very imprudent to walk through life without this shield, because we are so often mocked by the failure of our hopes and the upsetting of our calculations; but with this shield, however the Fates may play, we march always in the ranks of honour.

—Winston Churchill to the House of Commons, November 9, 1940

. . . Do you realize that there is no definitive (I hate the word) short history of any of our past wars? . . . We ought . . . to capture or recapture the public pulse as it throbs from day to day—the effect on the lives of different types of citizens—the processes of propaganda—the parts played by the newspaper emperors. . . . It is war work of most decided value. It is not dry history. . . . It is trying to capture a great dream before it dies.

—Franklin D. Roosevelt to Archibald MacLeish, June 9, 1943

PREFACE

THE PROPOSITION of this work is that Franklin D. Roosevelt as war leader was a deeply divided man—divided between the man of principle, of ideals, of faith, crusading for a distant vision, on the one hand; and, on the other, the man of *Realpolitik,* of prudence, of narrow, manageable, short-run goals, intent always on protecting his power and authority in a world of shifting moods and capricious fortune. This dualism cleft not only Roosevelt, but also his advisers, separating Henry Stimson and others who acted consciously on the basis of the "righteousness" of their cause from those who followed the ancient practices of the Prince. And it divided the American people themselves, who were vacillating between the evangelical moods of idealism, sentimentalism, and utopianism of one era and older traditions of national self-regard, protectiveness, and prudence of another.

This dualism between the prophet and the prince was not clearcut; nothing could be neat or tidy in the complexity of Roosevelt's mind and heart or in the fuzzy ideology and volatile politics of Americans. Nor is it the only key to understanding Roosevelt's war leadership. Several subthemes run through his war administration.

One such theme is the origin of the Cold War. While the roots of post-World War II hostility between Russia and the West are of course multifold, lying deep in Russian, European, and American history, I have concluded that the decisive turn toward the Cold War came during the war, at the very time when Anglo-American-Soviet relations were, on the surface, almost euphoric—indeed, partly because they did seem euphoric.

Another theme is the transformation of the presidency. It was during World War II, in Roosevelt's third term, rather than in the earlier New Deal years, that the foundations of modern presidential government were laid. The courts sustained presidential curtailment of liberties, such as those of the Japanese-Americans. Congress was surly and prickly on minor issues, generally acquiescent on the big. Under the pressure of war, the presidential staff proliferated:

the "presidential press" had a wider role; the bureaucracy was refashioned for war.

A third theme is the alteration in American society. War is the forcing house of social change; World War II cut deep into the bone and marrow of American life. The vast migration of whites and blacks, the growth of a new culture of war at home and overseas, the creation of novel and ominous war industries, especially the atomic and electronic—these and other developments set off revolutions in the interstices of American society.

But always one must return to the division in the war strategy of Franklin Roosevelt and in the moods and practices of the American people, for that division informs all the lesser issues of the war. It was because Roosevelt acted both as a soldier bent on a military victory at minimum cost to American lives and as an ideologue bent on achieving the Four Freedoms for peoples throughout the world that his grand strategy was flawed by contradictions that would poison American relations with Russia and with Asia. It was in part because he ran the White House as a personal agency that subsequent Chief Executives had to deal with the acute problem of how the White House could master the bureaucratic giants springing up on the banks of the Potomac. It was in part because federal power during the war, especially over such matters as race relations. could not channel the fast-running social and economic currents that the war seemed to release, and bring them into balance with crucial sectors of life that burst out of control.

None of this, however, need diminish the stature of Roosevelt the man. He picked up Woodrow Wilson's fallen banner, fashioned new symbols and programs to realize old ideals of peace and democracy, overcame his enemies with sword and pen, and died in a final exhausting effort to build a world citadel of freedom. He deserves renewed attention today especially from those who reject the old ways of princes and demand that people and nations base their relations on ideals of love and faith. He was indeed, in all the symbolic and ironic senses of the term, a soldier of freedom.

J. M. B.

CONTENTS

PART TWO · DEFEAT

PART THREE · STRATEGY

PART FIVE • THE LAST HUNDRED DAYS

ILLUSTRATIONS

following page 338

(Cartoons depicting the Roosevelt era, interspersed throughout the book, are not listed here.)

PROLOGUE *Fall 1940*

THE GLEAMING lights of the house shone against the dark that enveloped the south lawn and the woods and the Hudson below. Inside, a host of family and friends celebrated over scrambled eggs as the final clinching returns came in through the chattering teletype machines. The President sat with a small group in the dining room, his coat off and his necktie loosened, tally sheets spread out before him. It was election night, November 5, 1940.

Toward midnight the guests rushed to the windows at the sound of a commotion outside. Franklin Delano Roosevelt's neighbors were straggling down the entrance road and mustering in a singing, jostling crowd before the portico. Their torches threw dancing tongues of red light onto the ancient trees, the thick hemlock hedge around the rose garden, the long white balustrade. A drum-and-bugle corps blared out victory tunes. An exuberant banner proclaimed SAFE ON THIRD.

A door opened. Franklin Roosevelt moved haltingly to the balustrade. He leaned on a son's arm, his face full and ruddy in the glow of the cameramen's flares. Arrayed with him were his mother, Sara, his wife, Eleanor, his sons Franklin and John and their wives. At the rear of the portico, standing alone, his face exultant, Harry Hopkins smacked his fist into his palm as he performed a little pirouette of triumph. Out front a boy darted forward with a placard on which the words SAFE ON THIRD had been clearly printed over OUT STEALING THIRD, and the President laughed with the crowd.

It was a moment of enormous relief for Roosevelt. Earlier in the evening he had been upset by early election returns from New York; but far more important, he had been worried for weeks about the ominous forces that seemed to be lining up with the opposition. There were altogether too many people, he felt, who thought in terms of appeasement of Hitler—honest views, most of them, he granted, but views rising out of materialism and selfishness. Vague reports had come in of obscure fifth-column activities.

Speaking to Joseph Lash that election night, Roosevelt was blunt: "We seem to have averted a *Putsch,* Joe."

But now, standing before the crowd, Roosevelt could forget the stress of the campaign. He joked with his neighbors and reminisced about this "surprise" celebration—actually an old election-night tradition at Hyde Park.

"A few old greybeards like me," he said, "go back to 1912 and 1910. But I think that, except for a very few people in Hyde Park, I go back even further than that. I claim to remember—but the family say that I do not—and that was the first election of Grover Cleveland in 1884.

"I was one and a half years old at that time, and I remember the torchlight parade that came down here that night. . . .

"And this youngster here, Franklin Roosevelt, Jr., was just saying to me that he wondered whether Franklin, 3rd, who is up there in that room, will also remember tonight. He also is one and a half years old. . . .

"We are facing difficult days in this country, but I think you will find me in the future just the same Franklin Roosevelt you have known a great many years.

"My heart has always been here. It always will be."

HYDE PARK

"The same Franklin Roosevelt you have known . . ." A few in the crowd must have remembered Franklin as a small boy snowshoeing across the fields, shooting birds for his collection, skating and iceboating on the Hudson. Then Hyde Park had not seen much of him for a time. Fall after fall he had left for school—for four years at Groton and for another four at Harvard.

He had returned to settle down with his widowed mother, but not for long; soon he made a suitable marriage with his distant cousin Eleanor Roosevelt, a niece of President Theodore Roosevelt. Again he had left Hyde Park—this time for Manhattan, where he studied and practiced law. Hyde Park had seen a good deal of him in the fall of 1910 when he campaigned strenuously to capture a seat in the New York Senate. But then he was off again—to Albany, where he spent two years as an anti-Tammany Democrat; to Washington, where he served Woodrow Wilson as Assistant Secretary of the Navy; to the political crossroads of the nation, as he campaigned in 1920 for the vice presidency.

Then suddenly he was home again, his body seemingly shrunken, his long legs inert, his political career in ruins. For seven years he had searched for a cure for the effects of infantile paralysis, resting at Hyde Park, crawling around lonely beaches in Florida, swimming in the buoyant waters of Warm Springs, in Georgia. He never found the cure. But he had found himself, steadied his political course, struck out for the highest stakes in the nation's politics. In 1928 his neighbors had helped send him to Albany, where he governed New York for four years. In March 1933 he had left Hyde Park for Washington, amid a numbing depression, to preside exuberantly for eight years over a nation in upheaval and regeneration.

And then 1940. He had broken tradition to win a third-term nomination, taken on a formidable adversary in Wendell Willkie, and plunged into the maelstrom of shifting political alliances and seething political reactions to events abroad. He had faced isolationists in both parties, a labor turncoat in John L. Lewis, a bleak

"LOOK! I'M AN ARTIST!"

September 18, 1940, Rollin Kirby, reprinted by permission of the New York *Post*

October 14, 1940, Rollin Kirby, reprinted by permission of the New York *Post*

parting with his old campaign manager, James A. Farley. Hitler dominated events in America. The presidential politician who above all had sought to keep his choices wide and his timing under control had had, at the height of the campaign, to send destroyers to England and to draft American boys.

The pursuit of victory had exacted a heavy price. In the last desperate days, Roosevelt had made some fearsome concessions to the isolationists. After Willkie hurled the flat prediction that a third term would mean dictatorship and war, Roosevelt had assured the "mothers of America" categorically that "your boys are not going to be sent into any foreign wars." Yet his whole posture toward Hitler for months had been founded on the assumption that fascism was a menace to democracy everywhere, that the Nazis would not be content with the conquest of Europe but, with their junior partners, Italy and Japan, would ultimately carve up the world. Still, there was this flat pledge to the mothers of America.

And now he was back, at the height of his power and prestige. Who was this Franklin Roosevelt? The master campaigner who had evaded the Republican attack and then outflanked and beaten his enemies in the last two weeks of the campaign? The son of Hyde Park who had never really left home, who had measured men and events by old-fashioned standards of *noblesse oblige,* aristocratic responsibility, inconspicuous consumption? The graduate of Groton who was still inspired by Rector Endicott Peabody's admonitions about honesty, public morality, fair play? The state legislator who had embraced an almost radical farm-laborism at the height of Bull Moose reform? The Democratic-coalition politician who had learned to barter and compromise with Tammany chiefs, union leaders, city bosses, Western agrarians, Republican moderates, and isolationist Senators? The Wilson internationalist who had fought for the League of Nations but then abandoned it? The humanitarian who could spend billions for relief and recovery but almost obsessively preach the need for a balanced budget? The foe of totalitarianism who had stood by, vocal but inactive, during the agony of Munich? Could he be all these things?

No one—certainly not his Hyde Park neighbors—could have answered such questions this election night of 1940. They might have seen some significance, however, in the people gathered around Roosevelt on that mild November evening.

There was his mother, still active and bustling in her eighty-seventh year. A belle of the 1870's, later a young wife to a much older man, she had been the dominating influence on Franklin's early character. She had struggled to keep her son in his Hyde Park frame. Politics, she felt, was for vulgar men. But she was proud of her son's success, and a little defensive. This very election night she was confiding to a reporter that she could not understand why businessmen hated her son so. "They say he has been stirring up class hatred, but there is nothing in his heart to justify that. We were not brought up to consider whether people were rich or poor."

There was Eleanor Roosevelt, radiant and vivacious tonight in a red chiffon dress, so busy entertaining forty or so guests that she hardly paused to hear the election returns. A tortured childhood had seemed to make her sensitive to misfortune and, though this ugly duckling had made a fine marriage, her private troubles had not ceased. She had had to endure Sara's benevolent dictatorship at Hyde Park, years of supervising five young children—and then the discovery that her gay, handsome husband was in love with another woman. This was Lucy Mercer, whom Eleanor had brought into the family as a part-time social secretary. Almost ten years younger than Roosevelt, she was a Catholic, and poor but of a noted Maryland family. She had won Roosevelt's heart with her pretty face, artless, beguiling way, and her touching love for him. The affair had ended, Eleanor must have realized, mainly because Franklin feared his mother's reaction and the political cost. But had the affair really ended? Certainly it had seemed so during Roosevelt's invalidism, but one evening during her husband's convalescence Eleanor had talked about it to her daughter, Anna, and had broken down and cried.

Now, facing her third term in the White House, she was no

longer the controversial First Lady of the mid-thirties. Most people had come to accept—many had come to admire—her endless travels and her championship of youth, Negroes, sharecroppers, the poor in general. Out of her private sufferings had emerged an indomitable public lady, compassionate, gracious, even gay, but also imposing, a bit didactic, tenacious, sometimes hard as steel. But the private woman was still sensitive and vulnerable. She and her husband had the kind of affection and mutual consideration that temper a long marriage; but she was an ever-present conscience. "When you take a position on an issue," Roosevelt once protested, "your backbone has no bend!" In many respects she was but a member of the President's staff. Perhaps in a sense she willed it this way; Joan Erikson concluded that Eleanor Roosevelt had first become a decisive woman when, remembering how as a girl she had been unable to prevent the father she adored from being institutionalized, she resolved to help her polio-stricken husband to stay active in public life.

There was Henry Morgenthau, Jr., a Dutchess County neighbor for many years. The Secretary of the Treasury was virtually a member of the Roosevelt family, with an especially close relation to Roosevelt's sons. Fussy, thin-skinned, morose, he was sometimes a bother to the Roosevelts, but the President prized him for his absolute loyalty, his solid convictions, and, perhaps most of all, his fellow feeling for Dutchess County, its trees and land and crops.

And there was Harry Hopkins, by 1940 the President's chief aide. On the surface Hopkins was still the keen, casual, tough-talking New Dealer who had infuriated the conventional with his outspoken distaste for conservatives, his frequenting of race tracks, his jabbing attacks at friend and foe alike. But underneath, Hopkins had changed since the heady days of the New Deal. Scourged by illness, steadied by relentless demands, he had lost some of his "gee whiz" attitude toward rubbing shoulders with celebrities. He had given up the Secretaryship of Commerce in August 1940 to work and live in the White House as Roosevelt's eyes, ears, and legs. Instantly empathetic to the President's needs and moods, broadly educated by his chief in the ways and wiles of bureaucratic politics, he was essentially a means of presidential management and manipulation.

Others were at Hyde Park that night: Missy LeHand and Grace Tully, both gay, devoted, long-time presidential secretaries who laughed at their boss's endlessly repeated stories and gave him the relaxed after-dinner companionship that was so hard for Eleanor Roosevelt to provide; Samuel Rosenman, an old friend from gubernatorial days, now the President's chief speech writer; Stephen Early, a florid, sometimes suave, sometimes bristling Virginian, in charge of the President's press relations; Marvin McIntyre, a former newspaperman and a friend of Roosevelt's since Navy Department days; General Edwin Watson, known as "Pa" in the White House, another Southerner, genial, bluff, adept at letting the right people see his chief and mollifying the disappointed; Robert Sherwood, a playwright and eloquent liberal, who had been drafted to help with the 1940 campaign speeches and who had stayed on.

And Roosevelt himself? People were still trying to take the measure of the man. By the end of his second term his bewildering complexity had become his most visible trait. He could be bold or cautious, informal or dignified, cruel or kind, intolerant or long-suffering, urbane or almost rustic, impetuous or temporizing, Machiavellian or moralistic. Most political leaders embody contrasting traits; the baffling question about Roosevelt was what kind of internal standard, if any, determined which of his qualities would appear in what situations.

And always there was his mercurial capacity to move from one mood to another, to deal with portentous public events with little private evasions, to lose himself as a political leader, at least for a moment, in some strange or funny role. For instance, shortly before Christmas 1940—at a time when Roosevelt was working on one of the momentous speeches of his presidency—a letter arrived for Fala from Henrik Van Loon's dog Noddle. Back went a letter to Noddle from Fala. "The cookies were grand and I am glad you like me and I am glad, too, that you have never been on a train because the long rides on swaying cars over rolling wheels—just like five thousand mile cruises to see a lot of islands—ain't no fun for us folks. . . . P.S. I prefer to walk in the yard where trees grow and there is some place to scratch."

Was there a discernible core of ideas and values behind the glittering façades? What kind of crucible would prove the iron in the man?

LONDON

At the moment Roosevelt was greeting his Hyde Park neighbors, Luftwaffe bombers were dumping their loads onto London and turning back toward the Continent. It was almost dawn; all-clear sirens wailed, and groggy Londoners stumbled out of their shelters after the fiftieth consecutive night of Nazi bombing. Great craters pocked the heart of the ancient capital; buildings stood like skeletons; much of the dock area was rubble. Tiny paper Union Jacks fluttered on top of Londoners' homes.

Winston Churchill exulted over Roosevelt's re-election. He had not dared to speak his mind before, "but now," he wrote to the

President on this day, "I feel you will not mind my saying that I prayed for your success and that I am truly thankful for it." That did not mean, he added guardedly, "that I seek or wish for anything more than the full, fair, and free play of your mind upon the world issues now at stake. . . . We are entering upon a sombre phase of what must evidently be a protracted and broadening war. . . . Things are afoot which will be remembered as long as the English language is spoken in any quarter of the globe. . . ." Unaccountably Roosevelt never acknowledged this message; perhaps his silence was eloquent.

It *was* a somber time for Churchill. Resolute in war, defiant in defeat, he was impatient and fretful in these days of delay and uncertainty, when eddies and crosscurrents were cleaving the great tides of war. Britain had stood alone; the Royal Air Force had ground down the Luftwaffe; Hitler had postponed and then called off the cross-channel invasion; defenses in Britain and in Africa had been bolstered. But now sinkings in the Atlantic were increasing at a sickening rate; Germany was putting pressure on Vichy France and Franco Spain; the Free French had just fumbled a plan to seize Dakar. At home, production was lagging and the politicians were bickering.

The old landmarks were vanishing. Bombs pitted famous London monuments; old clubs simply disappeared between teatime and supper. Often, Churchill was compelled to quit 10 Downing Street for a headquarters thirty-five feet below ground. There, in a monastic bedroom, he carried on his work, dictating clear, witty, marvelously precise instructions; attaching red labels reading ACTION THIS DAY to his orders and queries; and presiding over meetings in a cavernous yellow chamber protected by steel girders. He was restless underground. When he heard heavy bombing he climbed painfully to a rooftop, where, in his Air Force overcoat and cap, thick siren suit, with gas mask and steel helmet, he puffed stolidly on a long cigar and watched London burning. His daily schedule was quite different from Roosevelt's. He started work in midmorning in a bed strewn with cables and reports, met with his aides later in the morning, presided exuberantly over a staff luncheon, took a long nap in the afternoon whenever the spirit moved him, conferred further or toured a blitzed section of the city, and then went through a strenuous evening of dictation, conferences, and idle talk until far past midnight—often to the dismay of his colleagues.

By the end of 1940 these colleagues were acquiring the professionalism, steadfastness under pressure, and mild cynicism of old war hands. Churchill's compact, nonpartisan War Cabinet comprised the Labour party's leader, Clement Attlee, as Lord Privy Seal; Herbert Morrison, a long-time Cockney trade-union boss, as

Home Secretary; Sir Kingsley Wood, as Chancellor of the Exchequer; Lord Halifax, as Foreign Secretary. Churchill was his own Minister of Defence. General Sir Hastings L. Ismay, a highly professional soldier who somehow coped with Churchill petulant as well as Churchill puckish, headed the Defence Secretariat; Sir John Dill presided over the Imperial General Staff; Lord Louis Mountbatten was Chief of Combined Operations. The death of Neville Chamberlain in early November 1940 and the return of Anthony Eden to the Foreign Office at year's end (with Halifax shifted to the British Embassy in Washington) seemed to symbolize the final triumph of the Churchill men. The Prime Minister, at the height of his powers in his mid-sixties, drove them remorselessly, in turn infuriated, inspired, confounded, and consoled them.

By this time Churchill was on terms of slightly circumspect but close familiarity with Roosevelt, even though they had met only once, during World War I—a meeting Roosevelt professed to remember and Churchill did not. Their messages flowed back and forth freely. The Former Naval Person, as he still signed himself, could send as late as 2:00 A.M. a cable that would go directly to the American Embassy in London, which would flash it to the White House through special coding machines; often Roosevelt would have it before he went to bed. Sometimes the President's reply was awaiting Churchill when he awoke in the morning.

Churchill had looked on with admiration as Roosevelt defied the Nazis abroad and the isolationists at home. He had rejoiced when Roosevelt trounced his opposition at the polls. Now—presumably—the President would act.

There were subdued differences between the two, however, even at this early stage. Each was his nation's agent; each was a patriot. The interests of their nations, so closely intertwined during these months, could always branch off; they could even break apart, as had those of Vichy and London. Roosevelt had turned away Churchill's plea for destroyers in May, when they were most needed; the deal in September, though warmly greeted in London, would bring only half a dozen of the old craft into action by the end of 1940. The destroyers themselves had been the lesser stakes in the game. Churchill's main goal had been to entangle the two nation's affairs and interests beyond possibility of separation and divorce. Roosevelt had wanted instead a straight *quid pro quo* that he could present to a wary Congress as a simple Yankee horse trade. The two leaders had compromised: Churchill had treated the exchange of destroyers and leased bases as a "parallel transaction" reflecting the mutual interests of the two countries; Roosevelt had presented it to Congress as the *quid* and *quo* of a deal.

Churchill had won his main goal. "I have no doubt," he told the

House of Commons, "that Herr Hitler will not like this transfer of destroyers, and I have no doubt that he will pay the United States out, if he ever gets the chance."

But now, with Roosevelt's trial by votes over, there was a curious lull and resistance in Washington. Where were the stepped-up actions and bold new departures that the election returns seemed to warrant? The Roosevelt administration seemed to be following a clear policy of "America First." Washington was still demanding "cash and carry"; increasingly, London was finding it hard to supply either.

A month after the election Churchill wrote perhaps the most important letter of his life. "My Dear Mr. President," it began. "As we reach the end of this year, I feel you will expect me to lay before you the prospects for 1941. I do so with candour and confidence, because it seems to me that the vast majority of American citizens have recorded their conviction that the safety of the United States, as well as the future of our two Democracies and the kind of civilisation for which they stand, is bound up with the survival and independence of the British Commonwealth of Nations. Only thus can those bastions of sea-power, upon which the control of the Atlantic and Indian Oceans depend, be preserved in faithful and friendly hands. . . ."

He went on to assess the strategic situation. Britain could not match the immense armies of the Germans, but through air and sea power it could meet the Nazis where only comparatively small forces could be brought into action. To defend Africa and southern Asia, as well as the home islands, Britain was forming between fifty and sixty divisions. "Even if the United States were our ally, instead of our friend and indispensable partner, we should not ask for a large American expeditionary army." Shipping was the limiting factor. "The decision for 1941 lies upon the seas." Here Churchill revealed recent shipping losses: over 400,000 tons in the five weeks ending November 3. "The enemy commands the ports all around the northern and western coasts of France. He is increasingly basing his submarines, flying-boats, and combat planes on these ports and on the islands off the French coast. We are denied the use of the ports or territory of Eire in which to organize our coastal patrols by air and sea. In fact, we have now only one effective route of entry to the British Isles, namely, the northern approaches, against which the enemy is increasingly concentrating, reaching ever farther out by U-boat action and long-distance aircraft bombing." Britain's battleship strength, even with the *King George V* and the *Prince of Wales* coming into action, provided a dangerously small margin of safety.

Churchill touched on the fields of danger. At any point Vichy could go over to Hitler; if the French Navy were to join the Axis, "the control of West Africa would pass immediately into their hands, with the gravest consequences to our communications between the Northern and Southern Atlantic, and also affecting Dakar and of course thereafter South America." It seemed clear that in the Far East Japan was thrusting southward through Indochina to Saigon and other naval and air bases, thus threatening Singapore and the Dutch East Indies.

What did Churchill ask the United States to do? Item by item he laid out his requests: 1. reassertion by the United States of the doctrine of the freedom of the seas, so that American ships could trade with countries against which there was not an effective legal blockade; 2. protection of this lawful trading by American warships ("I think it is improbable that such protection would provoke a declaration of war by Germany upon the United States, though probably sea incidents of a dangerous character would from time to time occur. Herr Hitler has shown himself inclined to avoid the Kaiser's mistake. . . . His maxim is 'One at a time' "); 3. failing these the gift, loan, or supply of a large number of American warships, especially destroyers, to help maintain the Atlantic route, and extension by the United States Navy of its sea control of the American side of the Atlantic; 4. "good offices" to induce Eire to co-operate on such matters. A shopping list of specific needs followed. Then finance: "The moment approaches when we shall no longer be able to pay cash for shipping and other supplies. . . . I believe you will agree that it would be wrong in principle and mutually disadvantageous in effect if at the height of this struggle Great Britain were to be divested of all saleable assets, so that after the victory was won with our blood, civilisation saved, and the time gained for the United States to be fully armed against all eventualities, we should stand stripped to the bone." Such a course, he said, would not be in the moral or the postwar economic interest of either country.

"If, as I believe, you are convinced, Mr. President, that the defeat of the Nazi and Fascist tyranny is a matter of high consequence to the people of the United States and to the Western Hemisphere, you will regard this letter not as an appeal for aid, but as a statement of the minimum action necessary to achieve our common purpose."

BERLIN

News of Roosevelt's re-election came to Adolf Hitler in his modern Reichskanzler's palace on the Wilhelmstrasse. The Führer made no public statement; he allowed no provocative remarks. But two days later he gave an answer of sorts—to Roosevelt, to Churchill, to all his enemies—in Munich, on the seventeenth anniversary of the Beer Hall Putsch.

"I am one of the hardest men Germany has had for decades, perhaps for centuries, equipped with the greatest authority of any German leader," Hitler gasconaded to his old comrades, jammed around him in the swastika-bedecked hall. "But above all, I believe in my success. I believe in it unconditionally. . . ." He evoked his comrades' memories of World War I. Germany had been poorly armed when war broke out, but it had held for four years. For four years the Allies strained themselves, "and then they had to get the American magician-priest, who found a formula that took in the German nation, trusting in the word of honor of a foreign President."

He had wanted the closest friendship with England, Hitler went on. "If England had agreed, good. They did not agree. Also good."

He turned to Britain's ally—and made a curious concession. "As far as American production figures are concerned, they cannot even be formulated in astronomical figures. In this field, therefore, I do not want to be a competitor. But I can assure you of one thing: German production capacity is the highest in the world. . . . Germany today, in any case, is, together with her Allies, strong enough to oppose any combination of powers in the world. . . ."

The world listened; this was the man who, between one summer and the next, had overwhelmed six nations; the man who was now threatening to invade Britain, seize Gibraltar, and overrun the Balkans. Yet November 1940 was a time of frustration and indecision for Hitler, just as it was for Churchill. The conqueror of Europe had journeyed across France to persuade Spain's Francisco Franco to allow Nazi troops to take Gibraltar and other strategic outposts in the western Mediterranean. Impressed by Britain's survival and pressed by Churchill, the Caudillo had bickered and shilly-shallied through nine hours of tortuous talk with Hitler; rather than go through that again, Hitler said later, he would prefer to have four or five teeth taken out. Vichy was also an irritation. On the way back to Berlin, Hitler had met with Marshal Henri Pétain; the old man had been courteous and reserved, but made only vague promises about collaborating with the New Order.

But it was Mussolini—Hitler's old comrade in arms—who had been most vexing of all. Il Duce was one of the few persons Hitler really admired; even so he had not been willing to take his junior partner into his full confidence. Piqued in turn by Hitler's coups and *faits accomplis,* Mussolini had ordered his troops to invade Greece on October 28, with the least and latest possible notice to Berlin. The Führer got the news on the way back from his talks with Franco and Pétain. He was almost beside himself. Fall was the wrong time to attack through the mountains; the fragile balance of power in the Balkans would be upset; Mussolini was supposed to conserve his troops for his main thrust against the British in North Africa. Abruptly, Hitler ordered his train south to Florence to meet and deter the Duce. Too late; Mussolini greeted him on the platform with the announcement—almost as though mimicking Goebbels in Berlin—"Victorious Italian troops crossed the Greco-Albanian frontier at dawn today."

And then—most galling of all—the invasion had floundered. Greek soldiers, waiting in mountain recesses, had routed the Italians and sent them back into Albania. The British took the opportunity to occupy Crete and Lemnos, greatly strengthening their position in the eastern Mediterranean. Now the Rumanian oil fields were threatened by the RAF. Now Hitler would have to send divisions south. Was Mussolini an ally or an embarrassment?

Yet, all these were pinpricks compared with Hitler's main concern during the dark November days of 1940. He was approaching a momentous strategic decision: whether to risk a two-front war.

Nothing had proved Hitler's military genius more strikingly than his capacity to isolate his foe diplomatically and militarily and then dispose of him: thus Austria, Czechoslovakia, Poland, France. Was Britain next? If things had gone according to tentative plan, German forces would have been invading Britain by the fall of 1940, while Russia stood by, wary but inactive, and the United States looked on, concerned but impotent. Britain, however, had refused to co-operate. It would be spring before a heavy invasion smash could be mounted, but by then British resistance would be tougher, and the German admirals were still dubious about the operation. Aside from the tactical risks of a cross-channel invasion, there was always the enigma of Roosevelt. What would the meddlesome President do? He had sent destroyers and munitions at the height of an election campaign; was it conceivable that he would let his Navy stand by idle while German troops poured across the Channel?

Then there was Russia. Hitler had long planned to crush the despised Bolshevik-Slav-Jewish regime to the east; this was probably the most fixed part of his world plan. But when? The nonaggression pact of 1939 had been merely a device to gain time and leverage. Stalin had not only taken every jot of his share of the booty while Hitler was busy attacking Frenchmen and Englishmen in the west, but he had calmly occupied the Rumanian lands of northern Bukovina and Bessarabia and seized Estonia, Latvia, and Lithuania as well. Russian behavior was unbearable. But it posed a harsh dilemma. Should Hitler turn east before disposing of

Britain? Could he manage a two-front war—with the ever-increasing likelihood of massive American aid to the English? At a conference in mid-November Admiral Erich Raeder, Commander in Chief of the Navy and a more maritime-minded strategist than the Führer, once again warned him against a showdown with Russia before Britain was finished off.

Hitler looked yearningly east, but he paused. Was an alternative possible—a repetition of the strategy of 1939, but on a continental scale? The Tripartite Pact, signed by Germany, Italy, and Japan in September 1940 in the great Hall of Ambassadors, had been aimed mainly at facing Roosevelt with the prospect of a strengthened Japan and diverting him from aid to Britain. What if Moscow could now be induced to join the pact? Would this not discourage Roosevelt and demolish Churchill's last hope of aid from either Washington or Moscow? With this heady aim in mind Hitler had invited the Russian Foreign Minister to Berlin.

Vyacheslav Molotov arrived on November 12. A band played the march of welcome; an honor guard strutted; there were even Russian flags, with the long-hated hammer and sickle. But surrounding everything was a glacial atmosphere, which seemed to deepen as Molotov was driven through silent crowds under leaden skies to his apartment in the Tiergarten.

Foreign Minister Joachim von Ribbentrop lost no time in confronting his guest with the cardinal issue. Britain was beaten, he declared flatly, and would be begging for peace. Churchill, to be sure, was depending on aid from America, but, he proclaimed, "the entry of the United States into the war is of no consequence at all for Germany." Germany would never again allow an Anglo-Saxon to land on the European Continent. While Molotov listened with poker face, Ribbentrop pumped up his trial balloon. The British Empire would be carved up. "Everything turns to the south"—Germany to its former colonies in central Africa; Italy to the African Mediterranean coast; Japan to Southeast Asia and the western Pacific. What about Russia? Would not Moscow want access to the open seas through the Dardanelles? Molotov was silent, except to ask about specifics with an annoying literalness of mind.

Molotov was just as cool and reserved when he met with Hitler later in the day. The Führer rambled, in his talk, across the face of the globe, dividing real estate. Britain was through. The United States could not be a threat for decades—"not in 1945 but at the earliest in 1970 or 1980." Molotov patiently waited out Hitler's harangue; then he again turned to specifics. The questions were steady and remorseless. Just what would the New Order mean? What part would the Soviet Union play? Exactly what areas was Japan promised? What about Moscow's interest in Turkey and the

Balkans? "The questions rained down upon Hitler," his interpreter later remembered. "No foreign visitor had ever spoken to him in this way in my presence."

Hitler could barely keep his temper in the presence of this icy Bolshevik with old-fashioned pince-nez perched below a bulging forehead and with his jabbing questions. The Führer suggested that the talks be recessed, since an air raid was possible. The next day's discussion was even more strained. The two men jousted over the same issues: Finland, the Baltic, the Balkans, Turkey. In vain the Führer tried to divert Molotov from Europe and toward the south with vague suggestions of a "purely Asiatic territory in the South"—presumably India. During the afternoon the talks degenerated into a spate of petty broils.

Hitler gave up. He again turned Molotov over to Ribbentrop, who, in diplomatic line of duty, had to attend a gala banquet at the Russian Embassy. Winston Churchill, lacking an invitation to the Berlin festivities, sent his greetings in the form of RAF bombers. Ribbentrop was just about to reply to Molotov's toast when the air-raid sirens wailed and the guests fled. He escorted Molotov to a shelter, where he made another effort to convince him to seize this last chance to remount the Nazi world band wagon. Again and again, while the explosions rumbled, Ribbentrop asserted that Britain was through. Molotov looked at him. "If that is so, why are we in this shelter, and whose are those bombs that fall?"

The thwarted Führer still did not make a final decision to turn against Russia. He ordered planning and preparations against the East to continue, but for a while kept open various alternatives to the foreboding prospect of a second front.

In December he set off a propaganda barrage aimed at arousing the workers of the world against the plutocrats in Britain and America. Standing on a platform in the Rheinmetall-Borsig Works of Berlin, with a bristling artillery piece as a backdrop, he proclaimed that the stakes were far greater than the fate of one nation: "It is rather a war of two opposing worlds." Britain, he said, had seized control of sixteen million square miles of the surface of the earth.

"All my life I have been a 'have-not.' At home I was a 'have-not.'" He rambled on, flaying the capitalists of the world, their kept press and political parties. "If in this world everything points to the fact that gold is fighting against work, capitalism against peoples, and reaction against the progress of humanity, then work, the peoples, and progress will be victorious. Even the support of the Jewish race will not avail the others. . . .

"Who was I before the Great War? An unknown, nameless individual. What was I during the war? A quite inconspicuous, ordinary soldier. I was in no way responsible for the Great War. However, who are the rulers of Britain today? They are the same people who were warmongering before the Great War, the same Churchill who was the vilest agitator among them during the Great War. . . ." Hitler was now in his second hour of oratory. He roamed further through history and across the globe—but with no mention of America or Russia. He pictured the New Order of which he dreamed—a new order of peace, reconstruction, the supremacy of work over capitalism—"the Great German Reich of which great poets have dreamed. . . .

"Should anyone say to me: 'These are mere fantastic dreams, mere visions,' I can only reply that when I set out on my course in 1919 as an unknown, nameless soldier I built my hopes of the future upon a most vivid imagination. Yet all has come true. . . ."

TOKYO

Official Japan feigned a posture of indifference toward Roosevelt's re-election; hostility was allowed to show only in the lower echelons. The President must now reorient his Far Eastern policy, said a Foreign Office spokesman; his present attitude was "unfeasible and too far-fetched." A newspaper recalled Roosevelt once saying "I hate war," but now he seemed to be leading his country directly into one. The only hope was that Americans would overcome their misunderstanding of Japan's New Order. Comment soon died away; a more pleasing event was at hand in Tokyo—two days of celebrating the founding of the Japanese Empire twenty-six centuries before.

The ceremony fused ancient and modern Japan. In dead silence a huge crowd awaited the Emperor beneath the gray walls of the ancient military camp that had become the Imperial Palace. Chrysanthemums stood in martial rows around dazzling floral designs. Precisely on time, the imperial standard could be seen moving slowly through the trees, followed by a crimson Rolls-Royce. The caravan crept across the double bridge spanning the moat; bands played the national anthem; the Emperor and Empress disembarked and seated themselves behind a table covered with brocade.

The notables of Japan flanked Hirohito; his brothers and other nobility, old statesmen and warriors who still had access to the throne, and his Cabinet stood rigid and solemn in their frock coats. Here was the Foreign Minister, Yosuke Matsuoka, brilliant, mercurial, talkative, unpredictable, a graduate of the University of Oregon, where he had suffered the real and imagined humiliations of a hotel busboy to put himself through college; the Minister of War, Hideki Tojo—"Fighting Tojo," to his young schoolmates—now a brusque, sharp-minded army general who had built his reputation in governing the Emperor's troops in Manchuria; Navy Minister Zengo Yoshida, the tireless agent of his service; the Premier, Prince Fumimaro Konoye, a handsome aristocrat, towering over his colleagues only in height, adroit, versatile, but also irresolute and hypochondriacal, lacking both the means and the will to bridle his military colleagues.

The Emperor arose; Prince Konoye shouted the banzais; 50,000 people bobbed in rippling waves, and throughout Japan millions of villagers, assembled before their elders, bowed to their Emperor. In front of the palace all eyes fastened on Hirohito, man, god, high priest, symbol, and emperor. He looked every inch not an emperor, but he played the part destined for him: a patient ceremonialist, dutiful family man, titular autocrat with influence over the drift of affairs through a look or a gesture but without decisive control over major decisions.

Next day, at an equally stately ceremony, Roosevelt's old friend and fellow Grotonian Ambassador Joseph C. Grew spoke for the diplomatic corps. He faced the Emperor, bowed, got out spectacles and manuscript, read, bowed, replaced his manuscript and spectacles, bowed again, turned backward, and paced solemnly to his place. It was a bland address, calling for peace and mutual cooperation and new contributions by Japan to culture, but the Ambassador was pleased that Hirohito seemed to nod vigorous approval of his main points. Was this a sign to the military? Grew could not tell.

Now in his eighth year in Tokyo, he had reported to Washington a series of dismal events: assassinations of key government leaders by army fanatics; the tightening grip on Manchuria; Tokyo's joining with Berlin in the Anti-Comintern Pact of 1936; the move into China, with the capture of Shanghai and the rape of Nanking; the ever-heightening pressure on Chiang Kai-shek's government; the fierce, furtive clashes of Japanese and Russian troops in Asia. The military clearly had been given its head, but there were times of hesitation, when the moderates seemed to have their chance, especially after the shocking news—at least to genuinely anti-Communist military chiefs—of the Russo-German Pact of 1939. Patient, correct, polished, outwardly imperturable but inwardly mystified and anguished, Grew had counseled moderation, in the hope that the military's fortune would run out.

Adolf Hitler's blitz through the Low Countries, the fall of France, the threatened invasion of Britain had echoed thunderously in the councils of Tokyo. Dutch, French, even British possessions seemed ready to be plucked. Impatient to seize the opportunity, military leaders in July 1940 had forced a moderate government to quit and had established a new government under Konoye. A hard line was then set. In order to settle the "China incident," Nationalist China's supply lines were to be severed, which would mean a flanking move through Indochina. Such a move would in turn antagonize Washington and London and would require offsetting support in the West. Hitler and Mussolini, eager to divert American efforts into the Pacific, would readily accept a stronger Axis coalition.

Late in August, Tokyo extracted from Vichy an accord that recognized Japan's immediate military interest in Indochina. In this pinch the French had turned to Roosevelt for help, but the administration, deep in a political contest, offered nothing but moralisms. Washington's attitude was hardening, however—as was that of its man in Tokyo. In a cable that was to become famous as the "Green Light" message, Grew stated that "Japan today is one of the predatory powers; she has submerged all moral and ethical sense and has become unashamedly and frankly opportunist, seeking at every turn to profit by the weakness of others. Her policy of southward expansion definitely threatens American interests in the Pacific." Japan must be deterred no longer by words, but by American power.

Grew's views strengthened the hands of those advisers who were urging Roosevelt to use his only immediate weapon. Late in September the administration decided on a complete embargo on all types of iron and steel scrap—but not on oil—to Japan and announced a new loan to China.

By now Tokyo was fishing in deep waters. For several weeks Matsuoka had been negotiating with the Germans over a tripartite pact. The burning question was the extent to which Berlin would recognize Japan's sphere of interest. A hopeful list of acquisitions under Japan's New Order had been drawn up: Indochina, Thailand, British Malaya, British Borneo, the Dutch East Indies, Burma, Australia, New Zealand, India, "etc.," with Japan, Manchuria, and China as the New Order's heartland. To Tokyo's surprise and delight Hitler's envoy had gone along with this list, except possibly for India, which might be reserved for Russia. The Germans made clear, however, that Japan must help them keep America out of the European war.

Supporting the treaty, Matsuoka stated flatly to the Privy Council: "Germany and Japan have a common aim in concluding this pact. Germany wants to prevent America's entry into the war, and Japan a Japanese-American conflict." But the elder statemen pondered Article 3 of the pact: "Germany, Italy and Japan agree . . . to assist one another with all political, economic and military means if one of the three Contracting Powers is attacked by a Power at present not involved in the European War or in the Chinese-

Japanese conflict." Could war be prevented better by appeasing Roosevelt or through a show of coalition power? But it was too late for second thoughts; in September the Japanese signed the Tripartite Pact.

Publicly the United States had responded calmly to the news of the pact but an intense struggle over policy continued. The pact had bolstered the position of the hawks, who wanted a tougher line against Japan. The administration was divided, some members fearing that stronger measures—especially an embargo on oil—would precipitate a war that the country was not yet ready to fight. The President considered a number of alternatives, including a shift of naval strength westward, even to Singapore, or a naval patrol, but he decided to play for time.

"Now we've stopped scrap iron," Eleanor Roosevelt wrote him a week after Election Day, "what about oil?"

"The real answer which you *cannot* use," he replied "is that if we forbid oil shipments to Japan, Japan will increase her purchases of Mexican oil and furthermore, may be driven by actual necessity to a descent on the Dutch East Indies." And that, he added, might encourage the spread of war in the Far East.

Tokyo, for its part, was quiet. Matsuoka insisted that the pact was not directed against the United States; he even invited Washington to join the pact and to help the Axis make the world into one big family. It was this kind of bravado that led Cordell Hull to say that Matsuoka was as crooked as a basket of fishhooks.

In mid-December Grew sent "Dear Frank" a personal year-end assessment of the Pacific situation. After eight years of effort, he told the President, he found that diplomacy had been defeated "by trends and forces utterly beyond its control, and that our work has been swept away as if by a typhoon. . . ." He put the main problem directly to the President: "Sooner or later, unless we are prepared . . . to withdraw bag and baggage from the entire sphere of 'Greater East Asia including the South Seas' (which God forbid), we are bound eventually to come to a head-on clash with Japan.

"A progressively firm policy on our part will entail inevitable risks—especially risks of sudden uncalculated strokes, such as the sinking of the *Panay*, which might inflame the American people—but in my opinion these risks are less in degree than the far-greater future dangers which we would face if we were to follow a policy of *laissez faire*. . . .

"It is important constantly to bear in mind the fact that if we take measures 'short of war' with no real intention to carry those measures to their final conclusion if necessary, such lack of intention will be all too obvious to the Japanese, who will proceed undeterred and even with greater incentive, on their way. Only if they become certain that we mean to fight if called upon to do so will our preliminary measures stand some chance of proving effective and of removing the necessity for war—the old story of Sir Edward Grey in 1914. . . .

"You are playing a masterly hand in our foreign affairs," he concluded, "and I am profoundly thankful that the country is not to be deprived of your clear vision, determination, and splendid courage in piloting the old ship of state." These remarks were pleasing and barbed; the pilot in the White House, who had stayed on the bridge in part by promising to keep the American people out of war, now had to face *Realpolitik.*

WASHINGTON

Two days after the election Franklin Roosevelt's train rolled slowly south along the Hudson River, was shunted through New York City, and then bore him through the long night to Washington. In the morning Eleanor Roosevelt, Vice President-elect Henry A. Wallace, and several thousand Washingtonians greeted him at Union Station. Two hundred thousand people lined Pennsylvania Avenue. The returning hero, back from the wars like some conqueror of old, jubilantly doffed his familiar campaign fedora as the limousine inched its way to the White House. Thousands followed the car, poured through the open White House gates, swarmed over the lawn, and chanted "WE WANT ROOSEVELT!" until the President and the First Lady appeared on the north portico.

And now the daily routine, fashioned during eight years in office, began again in the famous old mansion. Around 8:30 A.M. the President, a cape thrown around his shoulders, breakfasted in bed while he skimmed rapidly through dispatches and newspapers—usually the New York *Times* and the *Herald Tribune* (especially flown from New York), the Washington papers, the Baltimore *Sun,* and the Chicago *Tribune*—his eyes lighting with radar speed on presidential and political items. Eleanor might come in at this point with an urgent plea, and then presidential aides—Hopkins, Watson, Early, McIntyre, the old White House hand William D. Hassett, presidential physician Ross T. McIntyre for a brief check-up. Around 10:00 A.M. the President's valet, Arthur Prettyman, trundled him into the White House elevator in his small armless wheel chair, lowered him to the ground floor, and wheeled him through the colonnade to his office, now accompanied by Secret Service men with baskets of presidential papers. Fala might meet his master on the way and receive a presidential caress. After the President's return to his study around 5:30 came a relaxed and garrulous cocktail hour, as the President painstakingly measured out the liquor and dominated the conversation at the same time. Usually he dined with immediate members of his family and staff, and in the evening variously worked on speeches, leafed through reports, reminisced with his secretaries, or toyed with his collections of stamps and naval prints.

Friday was usually Cabinet day; on the Friday after the election the President met with his official family for the first time since he had left for the campaign battles. The Cabinet of November 1940 was ripe in years, experience—and disagreements. The members with the greatest political weight, measured either by formal authority or by easy access to the President and *his* influence, were (along with Morgenthau) Secretary of State Cordell Hull, courtly, conspicuously patient and long-suffering until the point when he could explode under pressure with a mule skinner's temper and damn his enemies, foreign and domestic; Secretary of War Henry L. Stimson, no intimate of the President, but a man of such moral stature in American politics and strong and plain opinions that he exerted a constant, if unseen, influence on his chief; Secretary of Labor Frances Perkins, the first woman Cabinet member in American history, utterly loyal to the President and to Eleanor Roosevelt, a sweet-talking conciliator of rival politicians and labor leaders, her official mien hardly concealing a sensitive feminine personality; and, oddly, Secretary of the Interior Harold L. Ickes, the Eeyore of the Cabinet if Morgenthau was its Rabbit, a prowling defender of his bureaucratic turf, prickly and petty but insufferably right-minded on the big issues, a host to his chief for poker and a grumpy guest of the President for fishing.

The Cabinet was a brier patch of rivalries and differences. Stimson and most of the others fretted over Hull's procrastinations and precautions; Hull, for his part, suspected, sometimes rightly, that certain of his colleagues would be happy to take over some of his department's responsibilities; Morgenthau, in moving ahead on aid to Britain, jousted with both the State and War Departments; Ickes had battled with virtually all his colleagues, and pursued his most passionate determination, next to thwarting Hitler, to filch the Forest Service from the Department of Agriculture.

But the Cabinet was broadly united on the cardinal issue of 1940. Hull had warned Latin-American diplomats of a wild runaway race by "certain rulers" bent on conquest without limit. Stimson was gradually becoming convinced that war was not only inevitable but also necessary to clear the field for a decisive effort. Morgenthau feared and hated the Nazis and yearned to help Britain as fully as American resources allowed. Ickes for years had been publicly reviling Hitler and for months urging a full embargo against Japan. The others were strong interventionists.

Every ounce of the Cabinet's talent and militance was needed in the fall of 1940. It was clear that Britain faced a crisis of shipping, supply, and money. There were rumors of mighty strategic decisions being made in enemy capitals. Interventionists were demanding action; the President had a mandate for all aid to Britain short of war—why didn't he deliver? But nothing seemed to happen. When Lord Lothian, the British Ambassador, returned from London late in November with a warning that his nation was nearing the end of its financial resources, Roosevelt told him that London must liquidate its investments in the New World before asking for money.

While official Washington waited for marching orders, the President took a four-day cruise down the Potomac to catch up on his sleep. Then he upset press predictions by making no changes in his Cabinet, tried unsuccessfully to persuade the aged General John J. Pershing to serve as ambassador to Vichy France, asked Librarian of Congress Archibald MacLeish to find out if the Cherable Islands, which he had once told reporters he would visit, could be found in poetry or fiction (they could not), and called for an annual Art Week under White House sponsorship. The President made it clear that he would not ask for repeal or modification of the Neutrality Act, which forbade loans to belligerents, or of the Johnson Act, which forbade loans to countries that had defaulted on their World War I debts.

At a press conference, the President fended off reporters who were looking for big postelection decisions on the war. It was all very good-natured. Asked by a reporter whether his economy ban on civilian highways included parking shoulders for defense highways, the President could not resist the opening.

"Parking *shoulders*?"

"Yes, widening out on the edge, supposedly to let the civilians park as the military go by."

"You don't mean necking places?"

The reporters roared, but they got precious little news. The administration seemed to be drifting. Then on December 3 the President boarded the cruiser *Tuscaloosa* for a ten-day cruise through the Caribbean. Besides his office staff he took only Harry Hopkins.

While Roosevelt fished, watched movies, entertained British colonial officials—including the Duke and Duchess of Windsor—and looked over naval bases, Cabinet officers back in Washington struggled with the dire problem of aid to Britain. Production officials agreed that American industry could produce enough for both countries, and army chiefs were happy to supply British as well as American needs, for this would require an enormous expansion of defense production facilities, but what about the financing? The

British in Washington contended that they could not possibly pay for such a huge program. Morgenthau asked Jesse Jones, head of the Reconstruction Finance Corporation, if he could legally use its funds to build defense plants. For the War Department, yes, said Jones, but not for the British. Stimson argued that the administration must no longer temporize, but present the whole issue to Congress, and the others agreed. But this seemed a counsel of despair; everyone could imagine the explosion on Capitol Hill if the issues were clearly drawn. And would the President risk a legislative defeat of this magnitude?

A thousand miles south, Navy seaplanes were bringing the President daily reports on these anxious searchings. Then, as the *Tuscaloosa* sat off Antigua in the bright sun, a seaplane arrived with Churchill's fateful postelection letter. No one remembered later that Roosevelt seemed especially moved by it. "I didn't know for quite a while what he was thinking about, if anything," Hopkins said later. "But then—I began to get the idea that he was refueling, the way he so often does when he seems to be resting and carefree. So I didn't ask him any questions. Then, one evening, he suddenly came out with it—the whole program. He didn't seem to have any clear idea how it could be done legally. But there wasn't a doubt in his mind that he'd find a way to do it."

The "whole program" was Lend-Lease—the simple notion that the United States could send Britain munitions without charge and be repaid not in dollars, but in kind, after the war was over.

This was no rabbit pulled out of a presidential hat. Churchill's letter had acted merely as a catalyst. A British shipbuilding mission had recently arrived in Washington to contract for ships to be built in the United States. For weeks, perhaps months, the President had been thinking of building cargo ships and leasing them to Britain for the duration. Why not extend the scheme to guns and other munitions? This apparently simple extension, however, represented a vast expansion and shift in the formula. There was no way that Britain could return thousands of planes and tanks after the war; there was no way that Americans could use them if it did. Maritime Commission officials had opposed even the leasing of ships, on the ground that the United States would not need a large fleet after the war and would be stuck with a lot of useless vessels. If this was true of ships, it was doubly true of tanks and guns. But so adroitly and imaginatively did Roosevelt handle the matter that for a long time its critics made every objection except the crucial one.

Armed with his formula, restored and buoyant after his trip, the President returned to Washington on December 16 and plunged into a series of conferences with his anxious advisers. The next two weeks were one of the most decisive periods in Roosevelt's presidency. His foxlike evasions were put aside; now he took the lion's role.

In one of the surprises he enjoyed engineering he sprang his plan at a press conference. Though he disclaimed at the start that there was "any particular news," the reporters could tell from his airs—the uptilted cigarette holder, rolled eyes, puffing cheeks, bantering tone—that something was up. He began casually. He had been reading a good deal of nonsense, he said, about finances. The fact was that "in all history no major war has ever been won or lost through lack of money." He scornfully recalled meeting his banking and broker friends on the Bar Harbor Express at the outset of World War I and their telling him that the war could not last six months because the bankers would stop it. Some "narrow-minded people" were talking now about repealing the Neutrality Act and the Johnson Act and about lending money to Britain. That was "banal." Others were talking about sending arms, planes, and guns to Britain as a gift. That was banal, too. The best idea—talking selfishly, from the American point of view, "nothing else"—was to build production facilities and then "either lease or sell the materials, subject to mortgage," to the people on the other side.

"Now what I am trying to do is to eliminate the dollar sign. That is something brand new in the thoughts of practically everybody in this room, I think—get rid of the silly, foolish old dollar sign.

"Well, let me give you an illustration: Suppose my neighbor's home catches on fire, and I have a length of garden hose four or five hundred feet away. If he can take my garden hose and connect it up with his hydrant, I may help him to put out his fire. Now what do I do? I don't say to him before that operation, 'Neighbor, my garden hose cost me $15; you have to pay me $15 for it.' What is the transaction that goes on? I don't want $15—I want my garden hose back after the fire is over. All right. If it goes through the fire all right, intact, without any damage to it, he gives it back to me and thanks me very much for the use of it." If his neighbor smashed it up he could simply replace it.

The reporters pressed him. Would this mean convoying? No. The Neutrality Act would not need to be amended? Right! Was congressional approval necessary? Yes. Would such steps bring a greater danger of getting into war than the existing situation? No, of course not. Nobody asked the President what use repayment "in kind" would be after the war, and hence why his plan was not an outright gift of munitions.

By now Berlin could no longer remain quiet. Fearing that Roosevelt would turn over to Britain 70,000 tons of German shipping in American ports, and that the United States Navy might begin to escort cargo ships, a Wilhelmstrasse spokesman

FULL PRESSURE

January 8, 1941, Ernest H. Shepard, © Punch, London

warned that Roosevelt's policy of "pinpricks, challenges, insults, and moral aggression" had become "insupportable."

But the climax of Roosevelt's year-end effort was yet to come. On the evening of December 29 he was wheeled into the diplomatic reception room and seated in front of a plain desk covered with microphones indicating their networks: NBC, CBS, MBS. Around him in the hot little room was jammed a small and mixed group: Cordell Hull and other Cabinet members, Sara Roosevelt, Clark Gable and his wife, Carole Lombard. The President, wearing pince-nez and a bow tie, seemed grave but relaxed.

"This is not a fireside chat on war," he began in his smooth, resonant voice. "It is a talk on national security; because the nub of the whole purpose of your President is to keep you now, and your children later, and your grandchildren much later, out of a last-ditch war for the preservation of American independence and all the things that American independence means to you and to me and to ours. . . .

"Never before since Jamestown and Plymouth Rock has our American civilization been in such danger as now. . . .

"The Nazi masters of Germany have made it clear that they intend not only to dominate all life and thought in their own country, but also to enslave the whole of Europe, and then to use the resources of Europe to dominate the rest of the world."

Roosevelt quoted Hitler's statement of three weeks earlier: " 'There are two worlds that stand opposed to each other.' "

"In other words, the Axis not only admits but *proclaims* that there can be no ultimate peace between their philosophy of government and our philosophy of government."

The President then reviewed the history of Nazi aggression and the Nazis' attempts to justify it by "various pious frauds." He charged that Americans in high places were "unwittingly, in most cases," aiding foreign agents. "The experience of the past two years has proven beyond doubt that no nation can appease the Nazis. No man can tame a tiger into a kitten by stroking it. . . . The American appeasers . . . tell you that the Axis powers are going to win anyway; that all this bloodshed in the world could be saved; that the United States might just as well throw its influence into the scale of a dictated peace, and get the best out of it that we can.

"They call it a 'negotiated peace.' Nonsense! Is it a negotiated peace if a gang of outlaws surrounds your community and on threat of extermination makes you pay tribute to save your own skins?"

Then the President renewed his pledge to keep out of war. "Thinking in terms of today and tomorrow, I make the direct statement to the American people that there is far less chance of the United States getting into war, if we do all we can now to support the nations defending themselves against attack by the Axis than if we acquiesce in their defeat, submit tamely to an Axis victory, and wait our turn to be the object of attack in another war later on.

"If we are to be completely honest with ourselves, we must admit that there is risk in any course we may take. But I deeply believe that the great majority of our people agree that the course that I advocate involves the least risk now and the greatest hope for world peace in the future. . . ." The government did not intend to send an American expeditionary force outside its borders. "You can, therefore, nail any talk about sending armies to Europe as deliberate untruth."

"Our national policy is not directed toward war. Its sole purpose is to keep war away from our country and our people."

He appealed to the nation to put every ounce of its effort into producing munitions swiftly and without stint. "We must be the great arsenal of democracy. For us this is an emergency as serious as war itself. . . .

"There will be no 'bottlenecks' in our determination to aid Great Britain. No dictator, no combination of dictators, will weaken that determination by threats of how they will construe that determination. . . ."

The speech was sending a thrill of hope across the anti-Nazi world. Londoners, crouching by their radios, listened avidly to the now reedy, now vibrant voice coming across the Atlantic. On this night the Nazis were fire-bombing London in the heaviest attack the city had known. Far away in Tokyo, Grew felt that the speech marked a turning point in the war; he read it so often he came to know it almost by heart. Telegrams began streaming into the White House; later, secretaries reported that the letters and wires had run a hundred to one in support.

The speech had the bracing tonic of conviction and faith. "I believe that the Axis powers are not going to win this war," the President said. "I base that belief on the latest and best information." Actually, Roosevelt's only information was his faith that Lend-Lease would pass Congress and make an Axis victory impossible.

He concluded with a plea for the mightiest production effort in American history: "As President of the United States I call for that national effort. I call for it in the name of this nation which we love and honor and which we are privileged and proud to serve. I call upon our people with absolute confidence that our common cause will greatly succeed."

PART 1 *The Miscalculated War*

ONE *The Struggle to Intervene*

On the eve of the New Year of 1941 Franklin and Eleanor Roosevelt entertained a small group of family and friends at the White House. It was the kind of affair the President liked most—acquaintances who could talk about the old days, an orchestra serving up old favorites, the White House at its gayest and most relaxed. Toward midnight the group broke into "Auld Lang Syne." Then the President, eggnog glass in hand, offered his annual toast: "To the United States of America."

It was a moment for remembrance of the dying year—the dull winter months of the phony war; the lightning attack on Norway; the remorseless impalement of Belgium, Holland, and France; the third-term nomination struggle; the mounting air attack on Britain; the draft; the Willkie challenge; the gathering Nazi invasion fleet; the destroyer deal; the election victory; the lull; and the letter from Churchill.

A time for remembrance—and now a time for action. Next day the President sat in his study with his speech writers, Hopkins, Sherwood, and Rosenman, working on his annual message to Congress. He studied a sheaf of rough drafts. The speech had been well laid out; now it needed a peroration. Dorothy Brady, a stenographer, waited, pencil in hand, as the President leaned far back in his swivel chair, gazed at the ceiling, suddenly leaned forward, and, mimicking George M. Cohan in *I'd Rather Be Right,* trumpeted: "Dorothy, take a law."

The President at this moment may have remembered a press conference the previous July, when a reporter had asked him to spell out his long-range peace objectives. Slowly the President had listed them: freedom of information and of religion and of self-expression and freedom from fear. Wasn't there a fifth freedom, a reporter asked—freedom from want? Yes, he had forgotten it, Roosevelt said. In the ensuing six months he had been saving in his speech file ideas for an economic bill of rights—ideas gathered from administration officials, personal advisers, newspapers, religious leaders. Now he dictated his own formulation, pausing to find the right phrases.

Six days later the President stood before Congress. The floor and galleries were crowded with legislators, Cabinet members, diplomats. Eleanor Roosevelt, accompanied by Princess Martha of Norway, scrutinized the congressional reaction. Roosevelt waited for the applause to die down. The moment was unprecedented, he began, "because at no previous time has American security been as seriously threatened from without as it is today." Then he ripped off some telling sentences:

"In times like these it is immature—and incidentally, untrue—for anybody to brag that an unprepared America, singlehanded, and with one hand tied behind its back, can hold off the whole world.

"No realistic American can expect from a dictator's peace international generosity, or return of true independence, or world disarmament, or freedom of expression, or freedom of religion—or even good business.

"Such a peace would bring no security for us or for our neighbors. 'Those, who would give up essential liberty to purchase a little temporary safety, deserve neither liberty nor safety.'

"As a nation, we may take pride in the fact that we are softhearted; but we cannot afford to be soft-headed.

"We must always be wary of those who with sounding brass and tinkling cymbal preach the 'ism' of appeasement."

Then came the presidential call for a world founded upon the Four Freedoms. Roosevelt gave the concept sharper meaning by spelling out an economic bill of rights:

Equality of opportunity for youth and for others
Jobs for those who can work
Security for those who need it
The ending of special privilege for the few
The preservation of civil liberties for all
The enjoyment of the fruits of scientific progress in a wider and constantly rising standard of living.

"In the future days, which we seek to make secure, we look forward to a world founded upon four essential human freedoms:

"The first is freedom of speech and expression—everywhere in the world.

"The second is freedom of every person to worship God in his own way—everywhere in the world.

"The third is freedom from want—which, translated into world terms, means economic understandings which will secure to every nation a healthy peacetime life for its inhabitants—everywhere in the world.

"The fourth is freedom from fear—which, translated into world terms, means a world-wide reduction of armaments to such a point and in such a thorough fashion that no nation will be in a position to commit an act of physical aggression against any neighbor—anywhere in the world.

"That is no vision of a distant millennium. It is a definite basis for a kind of world attainable in our own time and generation. . . ."

So stirring was this message, following so quickly on the "Arsenal of Democracy" fireside chat, that the grandest moment of all—the third-term inaugural—was almost anticlimactic. Judging that the people had had enough of warnings and proposals, the President devoted his Inaugural Address to a ringing but rather abstract affirmation of faith in democracy. He had always loved to sermonize; while he had had help from his friend Archibald MacLeish, the President himself insisted on a high-toned speech. "It is not enough to clothe and feed the body of this Nation," he intoned in his clear, beautifully modulated voice. "For there is also the spirit. And of the three the greatest is spirit." To perpetuate democracy "we muster the spirit of America, and the faith of America."

The words fell hollowly on the shivering throng in the Capitol Plaza, and the President felt later that he had failed to rouse his audience. But the inaugural as a whole was a triumph. There was the presidential procession down flag-bedecked Pennsylvania Avenue, as Roosevelt waved his top hat jubilantly at the crowds; the democratic flavor of the hosts of party faithful who crowded into the White House for their moment of recognition; the martial pomp and pageantry of the Inaugural Parade, as the services showed off their finest marching men; the fragment of the New Deal represented by the uniformed youths of the Civilian Conservation Corps doggedly trying to order their ranks; the glitter of the showy Inaugural Ball. And there was humor, too, when Fala jumped into the President's seat for the inaugural ride and had to be ousted; when the borrowed top hat of retiring Vice President John N. Garner kept falling off his patch of white hair; and when the Supreme Court clerk holding Roosevelt's worn and heavy old family Bible dropped it after the oath-taking, picked it up—and dropped it again.

All these doings were mirrored in Roosevelt's face—in his grave expression while attending service at St. John's in the morning, in his wide grin as he nodded and waved to the crowds, in the set of his jaw as he affirmed his faith in democracy, in his eager interest in the guns, scout cars, and tanks that rolled by in front of his stand. They were reflected in the faces of the people, too, as they stood deep along Pennsylvania Avenue, climbed on trees and boxes to get a better view, and yelled "Atta boy, Franklin!" as the presidential limousine rolled by.

THE NEW COALITION AT HOME

At the start of his third term Franklin Roosevelt seemed to be reaching a peak in his political prestige and reputation. In 1940 he had put down his adversaries in the Democratic party and beaten the keenest competition the Republicans could offer. He had challenged and overcome one of the oldest and most potent political bugaboos —the no-third-term tradition. He had won virtually every major piece of foreign-policy legislation he had requested since the start of the war in Europe. His standing in the polls—on the question "If you were voting today, would you vote for or against Roosevelt?" —was rising toward the mid-seventy percentile, after running in the fifties during 1938 and 1939 and the sixties during 1940 (except during the campaign period, when it dropped).

If presidential power turns as much on the appearance of power as on direct control of the mechanisms of power, Roosevelt's capacity to mobilize influence in national politics was probably greater in early 1941 than it had been at the height of the euphoria of 1933. The "Ace Power Politician of the World," a Republican Senator termed him—in his diary.

He seemed to have reached a peak of personal efficacy, too. His long, rubbery face was more deeply lined and jowly than eight years before, his hair a bit thinner, but he seemed on Inauguration Day as keen and zestful as his friends could ever remember. On the eve of the third term Dr. Ross McIntire, who examined him about twice a week, diagnosed his health as the best in many years. His weight was a near-perfect 187½, he was still managing to swim several times a week in the White House pool; he had his old buoyancy and resiliency and, above all, the ability to put his burdens aside. "We are looking ahead to the next four years without any apprehension," said Admiral McIntire.

Beyond all this, the President was now presiding over and ruling through a new coalition, which undergirded his national and world leadership with a structure of political authority. It was a coalition of three of the four parties that dominated American politics by the end of the 1930's.

The strongest of these parties was the national Democratic party, which Roosevelt had reshaped in gaining and holding the presidency in 1932 and in 1936. This party embraced a restless collection of industrial workers, reliefers, Western farmers, city machines, elements of the old Border State Democracy, and middle-income and even upper-income groups that had turned against the Republicans. Roosevelt's party was closely allied with a second party, comprising Deep South interests, which had controlled the machinery of the "Solid South" in Congress, to a degree far beyond what its numbers would warrant, by gaining seniority on committees in both chambers and thereby controlling congressional machinery and organization. The two Democratic parties—one centered in the Northeast and the other in the Southeast; one liberal and the other moderate to conservative; one wielding influence largely through the executive and the other through the legislature—fought with each other over domestic policy, but they tended to agree on a low-tariff, pro-British, generally interventionist foreign policy. In 1938 Roosevelt had battled month after month with Senator Carter Glass of Virginia and other Southern conservatives—even to the point of trying to purge Southern obstructionists from their congressional seats—and had mainly failed. But as the decade waned, Roosevelt Democrats reunited with their Southern brethren against the isolationist forces.

By early 1941 Roosevelt was losing no opportunity to butter up old Carter Glass, whom he had fought in the late thirties for control of Virginia patronage. He wrote to him that the Nazis had described Glass, the President, and President Nicholas Murray Butler, of Columbia University, as Jewish Freemasons. "I can understand it in your case and mine on account of our noses but I do not quite see where Nicholas Miraculous Butler comes in."

The Republicans were as divided as the Democrats. After eight years out of power, the national organization had fallen partly into the hands of such congressional nabobs as Senators Charles McNary of Oregon, Robert A. Taft of Ohio, already a rising young fogy, Arthur H. Vandenberg of Michigan, and others, mainly Midwesterners, in the Senate; and of such as Joseph W. Martin of Massachusetts and John Taber of New York in the House. Cautious toward innovations, prudent in public finance, tending toward isolationism in foreign policy, the Republican congressional leadership had allied with its ideological counterparts in the Southern Democracy to hamstring the New Deal during Roosevelt's second term. Symbolic of this party to the President, but actually in the party's right wing, was his own Congressman, Hamilton Fish, fellow Harvard man, fellow mid-Hudson politician, and ex-football great. Roosevelt had barred him from the White House because, he told friends, he had made a knowingly false attack on the President's mother years before.

Flanking the congressional Republicans was the presidential Republican party, more liberal in economic and social policy, far more international-minded, rooted more in the urban areas of the Northeast, and imbued with memories of its great days in the past. This party, led in past years by a string of New Yorkers including Theodore Roosevelt, Elihu Root, Charles Evans Hughes, had been headless and disorganized in the 1930's. Then in 1940 it suddenly found a dramatic champion in Wendell Willkie, of Indiana and New York. For four months the Taft-Martin Republicans papered over their differences with the presidential party in a frantic effort to overcome the "third-term candidate"; then, with Willkie beaten, the election coalition began to break up again.

The plight of the Republican presidential party was due in part to Roosevelt's skill at not challenging but infiltrating it. At just what point he decided to win over some of the presidential Republican leadership is still hard to say. Perhaps he was tempted by immediate advantages and only later saw the strategic possibilities, for he had always stepped easily back and forth between his roles as party leader and as bipartisan chief of state. When war broke out in Europe in September 1939 he had sought to achieve a political coup by bringing into his Cabinet the 1936 Republican ticket of Alf Landon and Frank Knox. Landon declined, fearing that he might become a cat's-paw for Roosevelt's third-term ambitions. Roosevelt let the matter lie until the spring of 1940, when Felix Frankfurter and others urged him to draft Stimson. Reassured that Stimson, at seventy-two, was still keen and resilient, the President telephoned him on a day in June 1940 just after Stimson, over the radio, called for repeal of the Neutrality Act, compulsory military service, and stepped-up aid to Britain and France even if it required Navy convoys.

In drafting Stimson, Roosevelt had gained an indomitable, world-minded, richly experienced war administrator. Equally significant was the fact that Stimson brought into his administration a symbol and rallying point for a host of Republicans who since Hoover's time, and even since Teddy Roosevelt's, had felt cut off from the nation's service—cut off by the stultifying Harding and Coolidge administrations, by the congressional Republicans, by Roosevelt and the national Democracy. These men came mainly from the larger cities, especially in the Northeast; attended old preparatory schools and Ivy League universities and took on a speech and a set of airs with a slightly alien, British tinge; fanned out into law firms and banks and brokerage houses; worked smoothly together in clubs, foundations, and on boards of trustees; read the New York *Times* or the *Herald Tribune* or their moderate, internationalist counterparts in Boston, Philadelphia, or a dozen other cities. Experienced in managing or advising big enterprises, cosmopolitan in their national and international travels and contacts, accustomed to dealing with governmental bureaucracy even while denouncing it, these Republicans, along with their opposite numbers in the Democratic party, were anti-Hitler, pro-British, and defense-minded.

Frank Knox represented a somewhat different sector of Republicanism. A Rough Rider who had backed Teddy Roosevelt in the great schism of 1912, while Stimson, as a member of William Howard Taft's Cabinet, had stayed with his chief, Knox had been a newspaperman and politician in both New Hampshire and Michigan before becoming publisher of the Chicago *Daily News* in 1931. In the Chicagoland of Colonel Robert R. McCormick's *Tribune,* he had been a voice for moderate, internationalist Republicanism, especially in more recent years.

The two presidential parties supplied Roosevelt with public servants as well as political support. Stimson and Knox, along with old New Dealers Hopkins, Justice Frankfurter, and others, served as recruiting sergeants for the host of lawyers and businessmen who were taking posts in Washington—including Robert Patterson, Union College 1912, Harvard Law School, and infantry officer in World War I, and a federal judge until coming to Washington; James V. Forrestal, a Princetonian who had seen naval service during the first war and had later worked his way up to the presidency of Dillon, Read; John J. McCloy, a graduate of Amherst, Harvard Law School, and prestigious New York law firms, who became Assistant Secretary of War in the spring of 1941; Robert Lovett, Yale University, Harvard graduate school, and long a banker. These men had the defects of their virtues; they were sometimes narrow in vision and conventional in outlook, but few challenged their public spirit—or their usefulness to Roosevelt as the nation mobilized for defense.

If Stimson and others provided Roosevelt's coalition with authentic Republican credentials, Cordell Hull and the new Secretary of Commerce, Jesse Jones, spoke for the old and the new South. After eight years in office Hull was still the Wilsonian idealist and moralizer, still the advocate of world trade as the long-run solution to world conflict, still a link between the White House and the old Southerners on Capitol Hill. Jones was cut from different calico. A towering, white-thatched Texan, long hostile to Wall Street finance, he had built a small bureaucratic empire in alien New Deal soil just as he had once built a financial empire in Texas. Part capitalist, part populist, but always a Houston Texan, the "Emperor Jones" wielded wide influence because of his control of both Commerce and the Federal Loan Agency, and because of his ties with Southerners on the Hill.

The rest of the Cabinet seemed to reflect all the main elements of the New Deal Democratic party: Morgenthau, who could speak for Eastern financial, philanthropic interests; Frances Perkins, for the labor, humanitarian, social-welfare groups; Harold Ickes, for the old Bull Moose, clean-government, conservation elements; Attorney General Robert Jackson, for the urban, partisan, liberal Democratic party; Claude Wickard, for the new agriculture subsidized by the

New Deal. The new Postmaster General, Frank Walker, who had taken Jim Farley's place after Farley quit on the third-term issue, carried on the old urban-immigrant-Catholic traditions of the party. Vice President Henry Wallace, a baffling combination of agrarian, progressive, administrative politician, scientific agriculturalist, and philosophical mystic, had emerged from the progressive wing of Midwestern agriculture and still spoke for it, but he was a man of parts, as liberal in domestic policy as Ickes or Perkins, as internationalist as Hull or Stimson. Indeed, all the Cabinet members were far more than brokers of group interests. Most by now were veteran administrators and hardy survivors of bureaucratic infighting. In their experience, drive, political skills, breadth of outlook, and sheer diversity they made up by 1941 one of the ablest Cabinets in American history—though Roosevelt dealt with them far more as individuals than as a collective organism.

The President's three-party coalition also embraced key enclaves of Capitol Hill. The President's men—Speaker Sam Rayburn, of Texas, and Majority Leader John W. McCormack, of Massachusetts, in the House, and Senate Majority Leader Alben W. Barkley, of Kentucky, and James F. Byrnes, of South Carolina—were party, and partisan, leaders in the two houses. Southerners chaired most of the important committees in both chambers; the Deep South bloc, though occasionally divided, formed the most cohesive of the party voting blocs on Capitol Hill, especially on foreign policy. This bloc, allied with conservative, mainly rural Republicans, had harassed the New Deal, but as the axis of national priority shifted from domestic to foreign policy, the Southern bloc was becoming a legislative bastion for the White House. Senator Walter George of Georgia symbolized the shift. The prime target—and survivor—of Roosevelt's unsuccessful purge of conservative Southerners, George was now supporting Roosevelt's interventionist policies from his high post on the Foreign Relations Committee. The Southerners, in any event, did not wholly monopolize the committee chairmanships. Urban Democrats, slowly building seniority after the cities had begun to go heavily Democratic twenty years before, were now crowding toward the top. Robert F. Wagner, of New York, presided over the Senate Banking and Currency Committee; David I. Walsh, of Massachusetts—no friend of the President—over Naval Affairs; and, in the House, Sol Bloom, of uptown Manhattan, over the Foreign Affairs Committee; Mary T. Norton, of New Jersey, over Labor; and Adolph J. Sabath, of Chicago, over the Southern-dominated Rules Committee.

Formidable though it was, this three-party coalition of Franklin Roosevelt's depended in the end on the votes and voices of the people. And as the nation turned to its great decisions of 1941, the President was taking his soundings of popular attitudes through his visitors, public-opinion polls, White House mail, fellow politicians, press opinion—and through his own extrasensory political perceptions.

Public opinion hunched strongly toward greater aid to Britain. Poll after poll in the early weeks of 1941 showed that by roughly two-to-one margins people supported not only the Lend-Lease bill but also controversial specifics, such as use by British warships of American ports to repair, refuel, and refit; and the lending of warplanes and any other war supplies belonging to the United States services if the President judged that such aid would help the defense of the United States. A strong majority would help England win even at the risk of getting into war. Such opinions had a markedly geographical cast. Polls showed isolationist feeling to be strongest in the nation's broad hinterland, the Midwest and the Plains states. Generally, younger people were more isolationist than older; lower-income than higher; less-informed than better-informed—differences that implied some weaknesses in the foundations of Roosevelt's three-party coalition.

Guiding and galvanizing interventionist attitudes was an energetic pressure group, the carefully named Committee to Defend America by Aiding the Allies. Organized in the wake of the Nazi invasion of Norway, the committee was headed by William Allen White, the shrewd old Kansas editor. The President, an old friend, enjoyed chiding him for being with the administration three and a half years out of every four, but White had retained his Republican credentials even while helping mobilize support for Roosevelt's foreign policy. Local chapters of the committee were so numerous and articulate that the national committee seemed, to many a friend and foe, to be the spearhead of a mighty army. Actually, its numbers were relatively few, and White, who kept in close touch with the White House, was almost as cautious on intervention as the President himself. He felt that his committee should not "get out ahead of the White House and the main body of troops." The committee had been rent by divisions between all-aid-short-of-war advocates and all-out interventionists, who were especially strong in the big Eastern cities. White resigned his chairmanship of the committee at the beginning of January 1941, not long after Fiorello La Guardia, the pugnaciously interventionist Mayor of New York, had accused him of "doing a typical Laval." Equally formidable in appearance but divided in fact were the isolationist groups, which stretched across a broad spectrum from the "respectable" Fight for Freedom Committee to the largest and most prestigious organization, America First, to Gerald L. K. Smith's Committee of One Million, along with a host of smaller, even more extreme groups.

There was, indeed, a curiously mottled, unstable quality to opinions on foreign policy, especially on the isolationist side. There were the ethnic isolationists—the German-Americans and Italian-Americans, who resented the ever-intensifying feeling against the old country (the German-Americans, moreover, remembered the anti-Hun hysteria of World War I); the Irish-Americans centered in the larger cities, who could not forget English excesses on the Ould Sod. There were the ideological isolationists, who felt that the United States had been sucked into the first war, bled white, and then rejected as Uncle Shylock, and who saw a diabolical motive and a cabalistic plot in every step toward intervention. There were the left-wing isolationists, who viewed the war as a struggle among imperialisms; right-wing isolationists, who feared intervention would mean more spending, heavier taxes, bigger government, less individual liberty, and an even more dictatorial Roosevelt; intellectual isolationists, who had little in common with one another except their fear of militarism, their reading of diplomatic history as the seduction of innocent Americans, and their vision of war as corrosive of civil liberties, social welfare, and the free play of the mind.

The interventionists were divided, too, and in much the same way. No group was monolithic. The division over foreign policy within business, labor, and liberal groups seemed as sharp as the divisions between them. And bit by bit alignments were changing under the impact of events abroad.

Behind this complex of slowly shifting attitudes was something far more powerful, more unreasoning, more awesome to the Washington politicians. This was not a program or group or opinion; it was a mood, expressed in the simple outcry "No Foreign Wars!" It was a mood compounded of fear of foreign involvement, cynicism toward other nations, pessimism about the possibilities of cooperation among the democracies. It was a mood fired by frustration, fear, disillusion, mingled feelings of superiority and inferiority toward other peoples. It took form in a simple, powerful, irresistible feeling against taking part in foreign wars. Defense, yes; aid to the Allies, perhaps; but foreign wars—never.

Roosevelt had not only recognized this mood; he had helped create it. In speech after speech he had made his obeisances to the God of No Foreign War. His protestations had reached a climax in the 1940 election campaign. Military action, he seemed to be saying, was no longer an alternative to be used prudently and sparingly as an instrument of foreign policy. It was flatly ruled out, except in case of outright invasion. But now this mood was confronting another mood, still of lesser sweep and intensity, but rising in the face of Nazi conquest, a mood resulting from indignation over fascist conquest and cruelty, hostility to Nazi racism, sympathy for afflicted peoples and occupied nations, concern for the Jews, admiration for the British.

Like a huge old sounding box, Congress picked up, amplified, and distorted this welter of ideologies, attitudes, and moods. With the more interventionist South and the more isolationist hinterland both overrepresented in the Senate, the extremes tended to dominate debate. It was an easy way to avoid the dilemmas of hard policy. Isolationist Congressmen could arouse emotional unity by spurning the horrors of war for American boys. Interventionist Senators, spread-eagling above the baffling choices and dilemmas, could appeal to sympathy for the heroic Allies and to fear of the Axis.

But the President could not elude the hard choices. The time for oratory alone was long past. It was a time for policies and programs, and for politicians who could work together. The crucial step for the President was to cement his alliance with the moderate, interventionist Republicans. Wendell Willkie, who had wasted little time nursing his election sores, had decided to visit embattled Britain. When in mid-January he came to Washington to pick up his passport, Hull took him to see the President. The two ex-candidates had a jocular meeting. The President handed Willkie a letter addressed to "Dear Churchill."

"Wendell Willkie is taking this to you. He is being a true help in keeping politics out of things.

"I think this verse applies to you people as well as to us:

> "Sail on, O Ship of State!
> Sail on, O Union, strong and great!
> Humanity with all its fears,
> With all the hopes of future years
> Is hanging breathless on thy fate!"

LEND-LEASE: THE GREAT DEBATE

The President now faced a daunting political problem: how to gain congressional and popular support for a measure strong enough to give decisive aid to the democracies—but a measure that would be unfamiliar to most voters, expensive to the taxpayers, and obviously unneutral; a measure that would so entangle the nation's military and diplomatic affairs with Britain's—and with other nations'—as to arouse the isolationists; a measure that, above all, would challenge the popular mood of No Foreign Wars. The President's solution to this problem was simple. The Lend-Lease bill was to be presented as a step not toward war but away from war. Roosevelt would not challenge the mood-god of America.

His foes suspected as much. "Never before," cried Senator Burton K. Wheeler, of Montana, over the radio, "has this nation resorted to duplicity in the conduct of its foreign affairs. Never before has the United States given to one man the power to strip this Nation of its defenses." Warming to the attack, Wheeler went on: "The lend-lease-give program is the New Deal's triple A foreign policy; it will plow under every fourth American boy." Roosevelt, who was usually an expert in remaining quiet under attack, saw his opening and struck back. He regarded Wheeler's statement, he told reporters, as the most untruthful, the most dastardly, unpatriotic thing that had ever been said. "Quote me on that. That really is the rottenest thing that has been said in public life in my generation."

As Congress convened and politicians prepared for the great debate, the President took charge of the shape and strategy of the bill. He sought advice and suggestions from a host of advisers and experts, including Supreme Court Justice Felix Frankfurter; tried—and failed—to bypass the isolationist-ridden Senate Foreign Rela-

April 17, 1941, C. D. Batchelor, *Times-Herald,* courtesy of *The News,* New York's Picture Newspaper

tions Committee; consulted the House and Senate leadership and some internationalist Republicans; counseled Morgenthau, with whom he was working closely, on his presentation to the House Foreign Affairs Committee; and even wrote part of Hull's opening testimony. The bill itself—happily given the number H.R. 1776—vested sweeping powers in the President to make or procure "any defense article for the government of any country whose defense the President deems vital to the defense of the United States"; to sell or transfer or exchange or lease or lend any such article to any such government; to repair or outfit any such defense article for any such government. The President would also have full authority over arranging terms, if any, with such governments.

"This is a bill for the destruction of the American Republic," thundered the Chicago *Tribune*. "It is a brief for an unlimited dictatorship with power over the possessions and lives of the American people, with power to make war and alliances forever." Interventionist papers answered Colonel McCormick; soon the debate was raging in the press. Messages to the White House reflected strong support for the bill, especially in the Middle Atlantic states, but Roosevelt knew the dangers of relying on mail as a measure of public opinion.

"Now don't be definite," he had cautioned Morgenthau about his testimony. The Secretary complied. So did Hull, Stimson, and Knox, in testifying before the House Foreign Affairs Committee. To the tune of four-column headlines in the New York *Times*, the Cabinet members warned of a likely invasion of Britain within three months, expressed fear of an invasion of the United States if the British Navy was beaten or taken, and asked for the widest executive discretion possible under the act. They were evasive on specifics, such as how much money Lend-Lease would require, and what nations besides Britain might be included. The committee members, flanking their chairman, the owlish Sol Bloom, pressed the notables on two key questions: Would not Lend-Lease, to be effective, require United States naval help in convoying munitions across the Atlantic? And would not convoying mean war?

These questions posed a moral problem for the Secretaries. All four were activists who, in their own ways, wanted to intervene more strongly than the President was yet willing to do. But all had to follow their chief's step-by-step tactics—and his claim that Lend-Lease would be a way of reducing the chances of war. Stimson's dilemma was especially painful. Given to blunt talk and direct action, he believed that the Navy must convoy merchant ships and that ultimately the United States would have to go to war. But he could not speak up. Sensing his dilemma, the congressional foes bore down on him—and none more than his old adversary Ham Fish.

Roosevelt managed to stay clear of the sharpening clashes on Capitol Hill. But when committee members repeatedly questioned his spokesmen as to whether the President under the bill could hand over part of the United States naval forces, the old Navy hand rebelled. "The President—being very fond of the American Navy—did not expect to get rid of that Navy," he remarked icily at his press conference. The bill did not prevent the President, he went on, "from standing on his head, but the President did not expect to stand on his head."

The first witness against the bill was also a member of the administration, but a departing one—Joseph P. Kennedy, Ambassador Extraordinary and Plenipotentiary to Great Britain. Kennedy proved to be a disconcerting witness. So divided was he between his skepticism over Britain's chances and his admiration for the nation he had seen under bombardment, between his loyalty to the President and his fear of presidential power, between his distaste for Nazism and his opposition to American involvement, that he ended by opposing the Lend-Lease bill while favoring all aid to Britain short of war. Norman Thomas, four-time Socialist candidate for President, spoke with his usual eloquence of the threat in the bill to American democracy and civil liberties, but the isolationist members found his articulate major premises so alien to their own that they took mixed comfort from his testimony.

The isolationists needed a national hero, a popular symbol, and a clear voice, and they found all three in their star witness, Charles A. Lindbergh. As slim and youthful-appearing as when he had flown the Atlantic fourteen years before, the "Lone Eagle" drove home his points before an applauding, neck-craning audience. Air power, he said, had made it impossible for Germany to conquer the United States, and vice versa. The nation should channel all its strength into hemispheric defense. The United States had no stake in victory for either side; it should seek a negotiated peace. H.R. 1776 would simply prolong the war and increase bloodshed on both sides. It was a step away from democracy and a step closer toward war. "We are strong enough in this nation and in this hemisphere to maintain our own way of life regardless of . . . the attitude . . . on the other side. I do not believe we are strong enough to impose our way of life on Europe and on Asia."

Roosevelt knew that he had the votes in the House committee and in the House itself, but to make doubly sure he readily agreed late in January to accept several amendments, including a limitation of the period during which he could authorize agreements; a requirement that he consult with the service chiefs before sending defense materials abroad; and a vague anticonvoy provision. On February

8 the House passed the revised bill, almost intact, 260 to 165. The four-party pattern was clear, with a large Democratic group and a small Republican contingent voting Yea, and most of the Republicans and only a few of the Democrats voting Nay.

The main test lay ahead, in the Senate. Waiting in the proud upper chamber was the high priestdom of American isolationism: Hiram Johnson, of California, the old Bull Mooser and League of Nations foe, pugnacity and independence stamped on his face; Robert M. La Follette, Jr., of Wisconsin, son and political heir of the progressive, isolationist "Fighting Bob"; Arthur Vandenberg, shrewd, observant, contemplative; Bennett Champ Clark, son of the great Champ Clark, of Missouri, a dogged cross-examiner; Gerald P. Nye, of North Dakota, captain and caretaker of the world-famous investigation of munitions makers as "merchants of death" in the mid-thirties. All these were members of the Foreign Relations Committee; they were supported in the chamber by a bipartisan faction headed by Burton Wheeler, a fiery speaker who was conducting a personal vendetta against the President, and by Robert Taft, elected only two years before but already gaining intellectual ascendancy on the Hill. Administration stalwarts were represented on the committee, too: Tom Connally, of Texas, Claude Pepper,

February 11, 1941, H. M. Talburt, courtesy of the Washington *Daily News*

of Florida, Theodore Francis Green, of Rhode Island, Barkley, and Byrnes.

Argument resounded throughout the land. Educators, lawyers, businessmen, ministers took to the rostrum, the microphone, and the soapbox. The America First Committee vied with the Committee to Defend America in disgorging pamphlets, broadsides, radio transcriptions, petitions, auto stickers, buttons, posters, news letters. The two groups fought a pitched battle in Chicago; America First amassed over half a million Illinois names on petitions, while the interventionists mailed 100,000 letters and distributed 30,000 handbills at mill gates. These were the "respectable" adversaries; flanking them were a host of extremist, demagogic groups that had reduced the whole debate to a contest between "defeatists and fascists" on one side and "Commies and warmongers" on the other.

The storm swept into Washington and into the Capitol itself. The Paul Revere Sentinels and the Women's Neutrality League marched in front of the British Embassy with their placards; one read BENEDICT ARNOLD HELPED ENGLAND TOO. They left a two-faced effigy of Roosevelt and Willkie hanging on the embassy gate. Mothers, real ones and not, were especially active. Elizabeth Dilling, author of *The Red Network,* led the Mothers' Crusade Against Bill 1776 into the Senate Office Building and staged a sit-down strike outside the office of outspoken interventionist Carter Glass. House debate was disrupted by a lady wearing a black cloak and death's-head mask and chanting "My Novena." Police stopped a large left-wing parade at the Capitol steps. The militants stayed in town for the next phase, the Senate hearings in the dim, ornate old Senate caucus room.

Once again Hull, Stimson, and the others argued the administration's case and played down the likelihood of war; once again Lindbergh and the other foes of the bill warned of war, dictatorship, bankruptcy, and postwar chaos and Communism. But now the White House had a new and powerful voice for the bill. Wendell Willkie was back from his triumphant visit to Britain. He appeared before the committee on February 11, just off the plane, as rumpled, genial, and fast-talking as ever. Twelve hundred people, packed deep against the marble walls, variously cheered and groaned as he broadly endorsed Lend-Lease. Again and again committee members quoted Willkie's campaign charges of Rooseveltian deviousness, secretiveness, and incitement to war.

Willkie hunched forward; he tried to explain, then broke off. "Again I protest. I struggled as hard as I could to beat Franklin Roosevelt, and I tried to keep from pulling any of my punches. He was elected President. He is my President now." The audience broke into applause; the chairman threatened to clear the room. A few minutes later Senator Nye picked up the line. He quoted candidate Willkie on Roosevelt: "On the basis of his past performance with pledges to the people, you may expect we will be at war by April 1941, if he is elected."

"You ask me whether or not I said that?"

"Do you still agree that that might be the case?"

"It might be. It was a bit of campaign oratory." Laughter swept the chamber. "I am very glad you read my speeches, because the President said he did not." More laughter. Nye desisted.

Once again the administration had the votes. In mid-February the Committee on Foreign Relations endorsed the bill in substance, 15 to 8, with one Republican supporting the measure and two Democrats opposing it. The isolationists made a final effort to weaken the bill by stalling it in the Senate. Nye alone spoke twelve hours. By now it was certain that the bill would pass; the question was how soon and with what changes. Working through his legislative leadership, Roosevelt was able to ward off an amendment designed to curb his use of naval or military forces outside the hemisphere. But the President, who had hoped that the bill would pass Congress by mid-February, was dispirited by the semifilibuster on the Hill and by an influenza attack.

At this juncture two influential Democratic Senators, Byrnes and Harry Byrd, of Virginia, combined with Taft to give Congress final control over Lend-Lease supplies by retaining for it close authority over appropriations. From the start Roosevelt had insisted on presidential discretion, but he felt that debate must not be prolonged. After strenuous efforts by the administration to block this change, the President accepted it. Congressional opposition now crumbled. The revised bill passed both houses by resounding majorities. Roosevelt, recovered in body and spirit, moved quickly. Within a few hours of signing 1776 on March 11, he sent lists of available weapons to British and Greek officials and asked Congress for an appropriation of seven billion dollars to carry out the new law.

Seven billion dollars—no one now could doubt the President's determination, or the nation's. After agonizing delays the United States had made a commitment to Atlantic unity and defense, a commitment that would hold for decades.

"Yes, the decisions of our democracy may be slowly arrived at," the President said a few days later at the dinner of the White House Correspondents' Association. "But when that decision is made, it is proclaimed not with the voice of one man but with the voice of one hundred and thirty million."

"SPEED—AND SPEED NOW"

Roosevelt had not thrown his full weight into the congressional struggle over Lend-Lease. He had readily compromised on several major amendments, declined to answer bitter personal attacks on him as a warmonger, and used his direct influence sparingly—though one pork-barrel-minded Western Senator did walk into the President's office hostile to Lend-Lease and walked out converted. Mostly the President suffered in silence. Once the struggle was over, however, he no longer contained himself.

It was the day after he had signed the Lend-Lease bill. Following dinner with Hopkins, Sherwood, and Missy LeHand, the President sat in the oval study ruminating over the speech he was to give to the White House Correspondents' Association. He had been gay at dinner; now as he went through the clippings in a speech folder on his lap he remembered all the bitter accusations. Announcing that he was going "to get really tough in this one," he proceeded to dictate one of the most scathing and vindictive speeches Sherwood had ever heard. A "certain Senator" had said this, a "certain Republican" had said that—now Roosevelt let his pent-up indignation lash back at them. For one endless hour he went on in this fashion. Appalled, Sherwood sought out Hopkins, who had left for his room down the corridor. How could the President be so irate in his hour of victory? Hopkins was reassuring. The boss would not use any of that tirade, he said; he was just getting it off his chest. Then Hopkins spoke of Roosevelt in a fashion that Sherwood had rarely heard before:

"You and I are for Roosevelt because he's a great spiritual figure, because he's an idealist, like Wilson, and he's got the guts to drive through against any opposition to realize those ideals. . . . Oh—there are a lot of small people in this town who are constantly trying to cut him down to their size, and sometimes they have some influence. But it's your job and mine—as long as we're around here—to keep reminding him that he's unlimited, and that's the way he's got to talk because that's the way he's going to act. . . ."

Hopkins was right about Roosevelt's blowing off steam. "Do not let us waste time in reviewing the past, or fixing or dodging the blame for it," Roosevelt told the White House correspondents once they had settled down from their annual skits and hijinks. ". . . The big news story of this week is this: The world has been told that we, as a united Nation, realize the danger that confronts us—and that to meet that danger our democracy has gone into action. . . .

"We believe firmly that when our production output is in full swing, the democracies of the world will be able to prove that dictatorships cannot win.

"But now, *now,* the time element is of supreme importance. Every plane, every other instrument of war, old and new, every instrument that we can spare now, we will send overseas because that is the common sense of strategy. . . ."

By now the reporters, normally so overexposed to Roosevelt as to seem almost apathetic, were cheering.

"Here in Washington, we are thinking in terms of speed and speed now. And I hope that that watchword—'Speed, and speed now'—will find its way into every home in the Nation. . . ."

It was one of Roosevelt's most stirring speeches, but his rhetoric was running far ahead of the nation's war capacity as of late winter 1941. Many officials were doubtful that the President's defense organization could perform the gigantic tasks of mobilizing a still-disorganized and strike-ridden economy. Production was uneven; in places there were miracles of output, but as over-all production rose by degrees, the demand—at home, in Britain, in Greece and the Near East and the Far East—was soaring above the highest earlier efforts and even predictions.

Late the previous year Roosevelt had been hotly criticized, especially by Willkie, for clinging to an old-fashioned defense organization. In the wake of the Nazi blitz in France the President had established the Advisory Commission to the Council of National Defense. A carry-over from World War I, the council lacked legal authority, adequate delegation of power from the President, or a single head. The NDAC was impressive less as an agency than as a collection of notable "advisers": William S. Knudsen, an immigrant's son who had risen through the assembly line to become famous as a General Motors production genius, was in charge of "advising" on industrial production; Edward R. Stettinius, son of a Morgan partner but friendly to the New Deal, on industrial materials; Sidney Hillman, another immigrant's son, a curious amalgam of driving union leader and labor-management diplomat, an old friend and supporter of the President, on manpower problems; Leon Henderson, a hard-driving, highly undiplomatic New Dealer, on materials and food prices. By the end of 1940 the advisers, still lacking clear leadership and authority, themselves were urging on Roosevelt a tighter and stronger organization.

Early in the new year the President set up the Office of Production Management, headed by Knudsen, Hillman, Stimson, and Knox, staffed with most of the old advisers, and granted, on paper, wider and clearer powers than the NDAC had enjoyed. The President explained the new setup to the press. The "Big Four" would make policy and Knudsen and Hillman would carry it out, "just like a law firm that has a case." The reporters groped for an understanding of the shape of this Hydra-headed agency. Would Knudsen and Hillman be equals?

Roosevelt: "That's not the point; they're a firm. Is a firm equals? I don't know. . . ."

Reporter: "Why is it you don't want a single, responsible head?"

"I have a single, responsible head; his name is Knudsen & Hillman."

"Two heads."

"No, that's one head. In other words, aren't you looking for trouble? Would you rather come to one law firm or two?"

"I don't think that's comparable."

"Just the same thing, exactly. Wait until you run into trouble."

"I would rather avoid trouble."

"I think they will. They think they will—that's an interesting thing. . . ."

"Wait until you run into trouble"—this might have been the motto of Roosevelt's defense mobilizers throughout 1941. By early spring they were running into serious matériel shortages. After much false optimism the OPM chiefs had to cope with a dearth of aluminum—so vital for planes—and with the near-monopoly of aluminum produced by the Aluminum Company of America. When the question rose of expanding supply more quickly through Alcoa or more slowly by a new and potentially competitive company, New Dealers opposed the aluminum "trust," but Stimson remarked: "I'd rather have some sinful aluminum now than a lot of virtuous aluminum a year from now." Machine tools, the cutting edge of any defense effort, were limited, and despite optimistic statements from the industry a shortage of electric power loomed. Coal reserves were vast, too, but here the problem was a threat of strike action by the United Mine Workers under John L. Lewis, who was still smarting from his vain election appeal to his miners to support Willkie over Roosevelt.

The President seemed to retain his usual debonair optimism about the nation's capacity to produce in the pinch. A crucial potential bottleneck was steel. Late in 1940 he had asked Stettinius to assess steel capacity; when Stettinius's man Gano Dunn, working with the steel industry, predicted a surplus of ten million tons of steel in 1942, Roosevelt canonized the report by devoting a whole press conference to it and accepting its findings. Dunn had to issue a more pessimistic report within five weeks.

Watching these happenings through skeptical pince-nez was a veteran of World War I mobilization struggles. Bernard Baruch had long enjoyed a friendly relation with the President, who paid the old Wilsonian every compliment except following his advice.

For months Baruch's advice had been simple and flat: centralize all controls—allocations, priorities, price-fixing—in one agency, with one boss. Many editorial writers agreed; so did many high administration officials. Stimson, too, had urged this move, on the ground that someone clearly in charge would feel the "sting of responsibility." Morgenthau wanted his chief to set up a Cabinet-level department of supply to run the whole mobilization program. Everyone seemed to want a czar—especially if he himself could be the czar.

Roosevelt would have none of it. It was impossible to find any one "Czar" or "Poohbah" or "Ahkoond of Swat," he had said in explaining the OPM to reporters, and only amateurs thought otherwise. Under the Constitution only one man—the President—could be in charge. But as spring 1941 approached, it was clear that the President, with his other multifarious responsibilities, could not be the co-ordinating head of defense production. Yet he would not budge. Clearly he had deeper reasons—reasons distilled from his diverse tactics of moving step by step, avoiding commitments to any one man or program, letting his subordinates feel less the sting of responsibility than the goad of competition, thwarting one man from getting too much control, preventing himself from becoming a prisoner of his own machinery, and, above all, keeping choices wide in a world full of snares and surprises—that prompted him to drive his jostling horses with a loose bit and a nervous but easy rein.

On the day after Roosevelt's inaugural in January 1941 the liberal newspaper *PM* in New York ran across its front page not an account of the Washington glitter but a picture of row upon row of men on the benches of a Bowery mission. They sat, their heads lowered, not in prayer, but on the hard narrow top of the bench ahead, their coats pulled up over their heads, babbling, coughing, snoring, scratching. They were part of an army of 7,000 homeless men in New York City—men who lived on handouts during the day and in missions, lodges, and flophouses at night. In the morning, young and old, amply nourished or not, well-clad or ill-dressed, able-bodied or lame, they would be turned out at 5:00 A.M. sharp, no matter how bitter the weather, to begin another day of aimless wandering.

It was a cruel comment on the end of two terms of "Relief, Recovery, and Reform" under Roosevelt. But it was not unfair. Four years after Roosevelt had pictured "one-third of a Nation ill-nourished, ill-clad, ill-housed," four years after he had demanded that "if we would make democracy succeed . . . we must act—NOW," economic and social conditions in the nation had not markedly improved. *Nourishment*: a national nutrition conference

HOW MANY TERMS FOR ME?

March 3, 1940, Daniel R. Fitzpatrick, St. Louis *Post-Dispatch*

for defense, meeting in Washington in the spring of 1941, reported that over 40 per cent of the people were not getting enough food or the right food. *Housing*: private construction was still lagging; in defense areas people were living in shacks, cabins, trailers, tent colonies, and "motor courts," often a whole family to a room, and towns were flooded by defense workers while rents soared. *Health*: of the first million men selected for the draft, almost 40 per cent were found unfit for general military service; one-third of the rejections were due directly or indirectly to poor nutrition. These were evils in themselves; they also showed marked social weaknesses in a nation girding for defense.

As usual, the plight of the Negro caricatured the social malaise of the whole people. A brilliant group of social scientists, under the leadership of the Swedish economist Gunnar Myrdal, was discovering that the percentage of Employment Service placements in major defense industries was actually declining for nonwhites during early 1941. Most of the big war plants had no blacks at all among their workers. Many unions discriminated against them, in part because of their fear that if Negroes came in, white workers might well go out. The future looked no more encouraging; in December 1940 less than 2 per cent of the trainees under defense pre-employment and refresher courses were black. Negroes could find opportunities for education and equal pay in the Army, but the services were still almost completely segregated, Negro trainees were concentrated mainly in the South, and as late as 1940 there were only two Negro combat officers in the Regular Army and none in the Navy. In the next year a detail of black soldiers, marching on an Arkansas highway, was pushed off the road by state troopers; when the white detail officer protested, he was called a "nigger lover."

It was not that the federal government lacked agencies to cope with this sharpening problem. The New Deal had immensely enlarged the machinery of action—perhaps too much so, in some sectors, considering the eleven federal agencies dealing with housing. But most of the programs were badly underfinanced; research and planning units had been starved by congressional conservatives; and the government was heavily dependent on state and local agencies and funds. Employment services, so crucial in a time of manpower mobility and mobilization, were an arresting example.

Confronting these problems almost daily in his double task of getting workers into the right jobs and keeping them there was the second half of the ungainly OPM leadership of "Knudsenhillman." Sidney Hillman was Roosevelt's kind of union man: opportunistic in meeting problems but principled in outlook; flexible in negotiations but right-minded in the final test; a tenacious defender of union rights who could also operate in the wider political arena; and with a solid and deliverable constituency in his Amalgamated Clothing Workers Union. Long accustomed to pacifying Communists, socialists, ethnic groups, hardboiled garment-industry bosses, "labor's politician" now had to thread his way between his old comrade in arms CIO chief John L. Lewis and William Green, of the AFL, between liberal labor ideologists all out for defense and pragmatic Washington politicians, between industry representatives in the defense establishment and New Dealers operating out of their old Washington enclaves.

Hillman needed all his rough-and-tumble union skills in Washington, for from the start he had to fight to maintain labor standards in the defense industry and his own influence among the loosely organized defense agencies in Washington. He got along with Knudsen—he could get along with almost anyone. They had easily agreed on their jurisdictions: Knudsen would concentrate on production and priorities, and Hillman on manpower supply, strike prevention and mediation, and safeguarding labor standards. But different constituencies, conflicting responsibilities and perceptions, and the pushing and hauling of interest groups and staff assistants around the two men brought constant strain. Racked by tension and illness, Hillman would turn to the White House for support.

He liked Roosevelt—he liked his cordiality, the very tilt of his cigarette holder; the man had style, Hillman told friends. But Roosevelt, too, had to bargain and conciliate and compromise, in a much wider orbit than Hillman did, and labor's politician was often left to build and repair his own fences in the Battle of Washington.

And so in early 1941 Hillman and Knudsen and their colleagues and rivals and clients carried on as best they could, coping with the social ills of twelve years of depression, partial recovery, and recession; often running separately under Roosevelt's loose rein; trying to convert men and plans to a war that was swiftly changing, to an American strategy that was obscure, to a leadership that delayed decisions for agonizing weeks and then moved overnight without warning. During the early weeks of 1941 a strike by thousands of workers at the Allis-Chalmers plant in Milwaukee—holder of a forty-million-dollar contract for turbines—seemed to symbolize OPM's problems. Hillman had to deal with left-wing union leaders, AFL and CIO factions, a company president who was antiunion and an isolationist, and a dispute over union status that was legally complex and ideologically explosive. He and his aides managed to get the workers back on the job, only to have the management in effect go on strike. As these and other disputes seized the nation's headlines, conservative Congressmen denounced Hillman as pro-Communist and prepared measures to limit the right to strike.

The President had called for "speed now"; in the late winter of 1941 everything seemed to conspire against action by a still-floundering democracy.

ROOSEVELT'S WHITE HOUSE

One morning early in April, John Gunther, already famous for his inside reports on Europe and Asia, visited Roosevelt to give his impressions from a recent tour of Latin America. Pa Watson told him that he could have only six or seven minutes; it was a crowded day, and the President was running behind. Gunther waited tensely. At the moment, Roosevelt was talking with the Commissioners of the District of Columbia; they took so long that Gunther's appointment had to be reset for the afternoon. When he finally was admitted to the oval office, the President was leaning back in his chair, Fala was biting a squealing doll, Missy LeHand was clearing up some papers. Roosevelt shoved himself forward. "Hello, how are you?" he called out brightly. Quickly put at ease, Gunther mentioned that he had visited all twenty Latin-American republics. The President asked one question: "What are the bad spots?" Panama, said Gunther, adding that its president was an adventurer —and also a Harvard man.

"My goodness," Roosevelt said. "Not really. Is he a *Harvard* man?" The President mentioned two other Latin-American dictators. "They're both bad men, really bad, shocking, but they've done good things."

Then, while Gunther sat in embarrassment thinking of the presidential time he was taking, his host began a monologue. The chatty, discursive talk went on and on—how the President had once met President Stenio Vincent, of Haiti; how Argentina really was a problem, but that one solution might be (Gunther shuddered) "colonizing" it; how Lend-Lease was going to help all along the line because (a big wink) "money talks"; how Iquitos, Peru, should become a free port; how he once told President Getulio Vargas, of Brazil, that if he were in his place he simply wouldn't stand for most Brazilian public utilities being owned outside Brazil; how the tourist business might be stimulated in Chile; how some foolish American politicians had opposed the Pan-American Highway because it might be a route for invasion of the United States ("as if a real enemy would use *roads*!"); how Gunther ought to have met a certain chap in Puerto Rico, who lived on Such-and-Such street, had once been married to So-and-So, and liked very dry Martinis; how he often made idealistic speeches but knew full well that what really counted in Latin America was power; and how (laughing) no Latin American knew how to sail a ship.

Suddenly a quick movement of the eyes, Gunther noticed, and the President began talking about Europe. Gunther's embarrassment grew, but now more because of the President's seeming indiscretions. We were not ready for convoys across the Atlantic "yet." Yes, the power of the Japanese was overestimated. Yes, we already had full plans to take over the whole Atlantic sphere, including Greenland. No, it would take about two months to get effective relief to Yugoslavia. Yes, Natal was necessary, but we could have it for the asking. Gunther got a remark in here; he said that he thought before the war was over the Union Jack and the Hammer and Sickle would be on the same side, and that the Red Army "might save us all." "Really! What makes you think that?" Roosevelt said, and laughed.

"The phone rang with a low buzz, and I made to go," Gunther wrote later. "He picked up the receiver, waving me to stay. Then began ten or eleven long minutes during which he said, 'Yes, Harry . . . No, Harry . . . Why, I thought that had been done, Harry!' He looked angry and nervously, forcefully, stabbed with a pencil at a pad. 'All right, I'll see to it, it's done now, thanks, Harry.' " Gunther thought this must be Harry Hopkins, but when Roosevelt leaned back in his chair, cupping the phone to his ear, and began a long discussion of the history of American foreign policy and of "your" Manchurian doctrine, Gunther realized it was Stimson. "Then I saw a quick rather hurt expression on FDR's face, and he laid the phone down suddenly. Obviously, Mr. Stimson had cut him off." Roosevelt stuck out his hand to Gunther and said, "So long! I've got to *run* along now!"

Scores of visitors had Gunther's experience: the long anxious wait outside, while Watson bustled around trying to keep a semblance of the agenda, the sudden admission to the ample room, the radiant smile and flung-up arm of welcome, the disconcerting use of the visitor's first name (disconcerting especially to Englishmen), and then the talk—bright, smooth, animated, discursive, but rarely on the purpose of the visitor's call. Many visitors felt cheated; they inferred that the President did not want to confront their problem, that he was deliberately diverting them. They were right only in part, perhaps the lesser part. Roosevelt had to talk, to laugh, to tell stories, to dramatize, to dominate the room, to exhibit his amazing array of information, to find bearings and moorings in his own experiences and recollections. But there were no histrionics; there was not even an attempt at grandeur. Sitting behind his desk, with its casual display of mementos, souvenirs, and gimcracks, the President put his visitors at ease with his expansiveness, openness, geniality.

The White House seemed to mirror its master's personality. By now journalists were picturing the President's home as the center of Free World decision making, the pivot of American power, the economic GHQ of the anti-Nazi coalition. Roosevelt had become President of the World, said the *New Republic*'s TRB after the passage of the Lend-Lease Act. Visitors from abroad, accustomed to showy palaces for even pip-squeak dictators, were astonished by the lack of front and ostentation in the President's home. Even more they were charmed by the simplicity and grace of the White House architecture, grounds, and some of its decor. And if they were important or lucky enough to visit the second floor of the house, they were surprised and a bit abashed by the casual appointments and cluttered quarters.

The second floor was pure Roosevelt; indeed, it seemed to Robert Sherwood that the President's and the First Lady's rooms had come almost to duplicate the rooms at Hyde Park. Bisecting the second floor was the same kind of long, narrow hall, haphazardly furnished with bookcases, photographs of crowned heads—most of them throneless, Sherwood noted—and prints. In 1941 Hopkins was living in a small suite in the southeast corner; Eleanor Roosevelt had a sitting room and bedroom in the southwest corner. Between them was the President's oval study, and off that were a bedroom and bath. The north side of the hallway was taken up mainly by guest rooms, large and small. In one of them hung Dorothy McKay's famous *Esquire* cartoon showing a moppet writing ROOSEVELT on the pavement in front of his house while his sister called out to their mother in the doorway: "Wilfred wrote a bad word."

The oval study—the decision-making center of the Free World—was actually a modest room, rather casually furnished, with naval prints and family phototgraphs pinned to the walls. Here Roosevelt liked to sit in the evening making an occasional phone call, sorting out his stamps, telling long anecdotes to his secretaries. On the third (and top) floor Missy LeHand, who was seriously ill by 1941, had a small sitting room and bedroom; the other rooms were used for overflow guests, especially for grandchildren at Christmastime. There was an air of small-town friendliness about the place extending through all the members of the staff, Sherwood remembered, and even to the Secret Service and White House police.

Washington reporters happily noted the symbolism: the President lodged in the center of the second floor, with Eleanor Roosevelt on his left and Harry Hopkins to his right. This was a comment on Hopkins's reputed desertion of the New Deal for the war, but actually both the First Lady and the First Assistant were committed liberals and internationalists. If they diverged in their approach to politics, much of their divergence was reflected in Roosevelt himself.

After eight years in White House service Eleanor Roosevelt was still the compassionate, idealistic, wholly engaged woman who had thrown herself into social welfare and liberal politics during the 1930's. Assisted by her faithful "Tommy," Malvina Thompson, she was still leading the seven lives of wife, mother, chief hostess, White House columnist, nationwide lecturer (one hundred lectures in 1940, about one-third of them paid), Democratic party voice and organizer, and spokeswoman in the White House for labor, Negroes, youth, tenant farmers, the poor, and women in general. If inevitably she could not wholly devote herself to any of these roles, she had learned to be well organized and efficient. And she still possessed the vigor that had awed and amused the country in the earlier White House years; in 1941, in her late fifties, she occasionally worked the whole night through and went right on the next day.

Hers was a conscience combined with an almost demonic commitment and tenacity. By now she had come to recognize that she could not have, even if she still wanted, a romantic or even close relation with her husband. Married now for thirty-six years, they treated each other with devotion, respect, and tolerance, but Roosevelt had learned how to withdraw into protective covering against his wife's importunings; and Eleanor had learned to accept her White House role as essentially a presidential aide, though a very special one, who was with the President far less than Grace Tully and Missy LeHand were. Often she was assailed by doubts; sometimes she was lonely in the White House crowd; but always there was the self-mastery and the passion that led her on to the next column, the next lecture, and the next cause.

Hopkins was made of quite different stuff. Years of growing power and racking illness had not changed him much; he was still the intense, brittle, tactless, irreverent operative who could prod defense bigwigs as mercilessly as he had once chastised state officials and relief administrators. Along with his chief he saw the New Deal as a source of strength to the nation at war, not a handicap to it, but now with a lower priority than defense preparation. He had become as intolerant of liberal ideologues as he had been of standpat businessmen. He had almost an extrasensory perception of Roosevelt's moods; he knew how to give advice in the form of flattery and flattery in the form of advice; he sensed when to press his boss and when to desist, when to talk and when to listen, when to submit and when to argue. Above all, he had a marked ability to plunge directly into the heart of a muddle or mix-up, and then to act. "Lord Root of the Matter," Churchill dubbed him.

By the spring of 1941 Hopkins had been living in the White House for a year, and was paying the price of standing and sleeping so close to throne and bedchamber. Ickes noted on a fishing trip with the President to the Everglades that Hopkins could walk into the President's cabin without being announced or even knocking, and that the President handed him apparently confidential papers that he showed no one else. "I do not like him," Ickes confided to his diary, "and I do not like the influence that he has with the President." Baruch complained that Hopkins was like a jealous woman in keeping others away from Roosevelt; everyone else had to "play him in a triangle."

Others were more charitable. Morgenthau found him deceptive and flamboyant but absolutely dedicated to the President. Stimson had his troubles with Hopkins but confided to *his* diary: "The more I think of it, the more I think it is a Godsend that he should be at the White House." But Roosevelt liked him—for his acute common sense, his humorous cynicism, his ability to cut through protocol, ignore old jurisdictions, straighten out tangled lines of administration. When Willkie, on visiting the White House after the election, asked the President why he kept Hopkins so close in view of the distrust and resentment people felt toward his aide, Roosevelt could speak his mind:

"I can understand that you wonder why I need that half-man around me. But—someday you may well be sitting here where I am now as President of the United States. And when you are, you'll be looking at that door over there and knowing that practically everybody who walks through it wants something out of you. You'll learn what a lonely job this is, and you'll discover the need for somebody like Harry Hopkins who asks for nothing except to serve you." The President was probably exaggerating for Willkie's benefit, but there was a ring of conviction to his words. In April he put his aide in charge of Lend-Lease and thus at the heart of economic, political, and military decision making.

Roosevelt's White House was a home inside a mansion inside an executive office. In 1941 the mansion was, to thousands of Americans, the first floor, with its Blue Room and Green Room and state dining room and all the rest, where the touring public could gawk during the day, and captains and kings were entertained at night. By 1941 the President was holding formal entertaining to a minimum; in wartime he would largely dispense with it. He spent most of his daytime working hours in the oval office in the southeast corner of the executive wing. Here he could look through the tall windows onto the hedges and garden outside.

Superficially there was a sort of pattern to Roosevelt's working day. Ensconced behind his big desk by 10:00 A.M. or so, he usually saw visitors through the rest of the morning, during the luncheon period (when a hot tray was brought in), and well into the afternoon. He spent the rest of the afternoon dictating letters and memos—most of them pithy but friendly little messages. His week had some pattern, too. He saw the congressional Big Four—the Vice President, the Speaker, and the majority leader of each chamber—on Monday or Tuesday; met with the press on Tuesday afternoons and Friday mornings; and presided over a Cabinet meeting on Friday afternoons.

This schedule could be easily upset by any kind of crisis, however, and there seemed to be no pattern at all in the way that Roosevelt actually did his work. Sometimes he hurried through appointments on crucial matters and dawdled during lesser ones. He ignored most letters altogether, sent many over to the agencies to be answered, turned over some to Watson or Early or Hopkins for reply, under their name or his. Sometimes he even wrote letters for an aide or secretary to sign. He took many phone calls (though few at night), refused others, saw inconsequential and even dull people and ignored others of apparently greater political or intellectual weight—all according to some mystifying structure of priorities known to no one, perhaps not even to himself.

Yet if Roosevelt's working habits lacked system and plan, they bespoke a habit of mind, a style of intellect, a *sens de l'état* that could be summed up in one word: accessibility. After eight years of pressure in the White House mold Roosevelt was still endlessly curious; he was still reaching out for ideas, open to innovation, willing to experiment. He corresponded and/or talked with an amazing variety of people: Supreme Court justices; royalty, including King George VI and King Haakon, of Norway; old family friends from Dutchess County; poets and novelists, including Carl Sandburg and Upton Sinclair; old political colleagues from Albany days; radicals, including Norman Thomas; journalists; old friends and diplomats, perhaps William Phillips, from Rome, Francis Sayre, from Manila, or Grew, from Tokyo; old Wilsonians, including Josephus Daniels; chiefs of government, including Canada's Mackenzie King; wise old men, including Grenville Clark, of New York and New Hampshire, and Bernard Baruch, of Lafayette Park; as well as Cabinet members, Senators, Representatives, undersecretaries, bureau and agency chiefs, governors, mayors, leaders of business, agriculture, and labor, veterans, and a host of other interest groups, with all their subleaders, opposition leaders, and rebels.

Inevitably this breadth and variety made for some superficiality of contact and probably of comprehension. No one—not even his wife or sons—felt that he could get close enough to the President to understand him. No one could assume that he himself was indispensable; Raymond Moley, Thomas Corcoran, and even his son James had moved in and out of the bright orbit of influence. Now that Hopkins was on top, people—Eleanor Roosevelt among them—were wondering how long the friendship would last, and whether Hopkins could stand the heartbreak if the time came when he might not be needed. Roosevelt was committed to no man or woman, nation or ally, cause or principle, but to some goal so deeply buried within himself and yet so transcendent that few could discern it amid the complex and turbulent events of the time.

But Roosevelt was not given to musing on such matters. He presided gaily over his White House. He kept channels open, fought routine, sabotaged institutionalization, knocked heads together, "locked people in rooms" until they agreed. He could confront with equal aplomb Ickes's obsessive efforts to wrest the Forest Service away from Agriculture, his son John's phone call asking his father to make arrangements for diaper service for a forthcoming visit of his wife and baby, the latest demand from Churchill for emergency aid, Eleanor's proddings to appoint liberals, and still cope with the voracious demands on his time and temperament. Amid emergencies he could pen joshing notes to his secretaries, challenge Ickes to catch bigger fish on the next expedition, record a memory of a long-forgotten episode of his childhood, and send

Mrs. Watson (with copies to the Secret Service and the FBI) a newspaper photo of Pa with an Apple Blossom Queen. On the eve of the greatest crisis of all, with Hitler turning to the most fateful venture in modern history, with Roosevelt leading an underprepared and undermobilized people at a moment of great peril, the "power center of the Western world" was a cluttered study or office inside an executive department inside a gracious home.

TWO *The Crucibles of Grand Strategy*

THE SPRING sun was rising earlier now, climbing higher, burnishing the compacted snow in Moscow streets, washing away the grimy slush of Berlin, starting freshets down the mountains of Greece and Yugoslavia, drawing up poppies in the London ruins and blossoms in the chestnut trees along the Seine, bringing cherry trees to bud along the Washington Tidal Basin and peonies to bloom in the Emperor's gardens in Tokyo. To soldiers this was fighting weather; along the endless war fronts and coastlines they redoubled their guard and lengthened their watches. Above all, this was Hitler's time, when he liked to prod and bully and attack. All through the early spring, rumors flashed from capital to capital about the Führer's next move.

It was a measure of Hitler's genius, as well as of his power, that in the spring of 1941 he seemed capable of striking in any or all of four directions. The British were still bracing themselves for the possibility of a tremendous onslaught across the Channel. The Spanish were wary; Hitler had been pressuring Franco to allow him to launch a blitz on Gibraltar and then sweep into Africa. The Caudillo had refused, but now it was rumored that the Nazis would invade Spain and stage their blitz anyway. Meanwhile, Hitler kept Vichy France on a tight bit. Then there were reports that the Nazis were concentrating armor and air power in Sicily in order to help the beaten Italians in Libya. And the Balkans, divided by ancient quarrels and racked by internal turmoil, were taut under Nazi pressure.

Roosevelt followed Hitler's chess moves with deepening anxiety. Encumbered by congressional resistance, inadequate arms, and by his own uncertainties, he tried nevertheless to throw his country's meager weight into the scales. When Churchill cabled him late in March that the battleship *Malaya* had been torpedoed while escorting a convoy and he would be "much obliged" if she could be repaired in American yards, the President replied that he would be delighted. When Hitler put pressure on Pétain to line up with the Axis, Roosevelt had his Ambassador in Vichy, Admiral William

D. Leahy, reaffirm America's faith in ultimate British victory. When Churchill warned the President that Vichy was planning to send the battleship *Dunkerque* from Oran to Toulon for repairs, and thus almost into the Nazi embrace, Roosevelt had Leahy lodge an emphatic and successful protest with Pétain. When the Greeks, fearful of Nazi invasion, begged the President to send thirty modern combat planes that he had long promised, the Commander in Chief pressed his Navy to provide the craft (but Greece would be overrun before they arrived). When Prince Paul, of Yugoslavia, showed signs of succcumbing to Nazi threats, Washington tried to persuade the Regent that the southern Balkans could be held against Hitler.

The President variously tried threats, bribes in the form of Lend-Lease goods, moral exhortation, and friendly counsel. But both his words and his actions had a hollow ring—for here was the most powerful democracy on earth urging small nations to resist the Nazi tide while it sat safely behind its Atlantic moat thousands of miles from the danger zone.

Amid these troubles the two great democracies occasionally found themselves at odds. The White House generally preferred to follow a conciliatory policy toward Pétain and a tough one toward Franco; the British tended to do the reverse. Churchill wanted Roosevelt to stage naval demonstrations in the East Atlantic to impress Portugal and other neutrals; the President was fearful of antagonizing Lisbon and reluctant to divert any of his fleet units from the Pacific. Churchill cabled that he would seize the Azores if Spain yielded to the Nazis or was overrun; Roosevelt cautioned him against such action unless Portugal was attacked, adding that if the British did seize the Azores they must make clear that it was not for permanent occupation. "We are far from wishing to add to our territory," the Prime Minister answered with hurt pride, "but only to preserve our life and perhaps yours."

If Washington at times was divided from London, it was also divided within itself. With Atlantic sinkings continuing at a horrifying rate, Stimson prodded the President early in the spring to seize the nettle and order the escorting of Allied ships by American warships and planes. His chief wanted to proceed more slowly—so slowly that some militants yearned for a scapegoat such as Hull, who also seemed cautious in both his Atlantic and his Pacific policy. Ickes barked into his diary: "Once again I say 'Goddamn the Department of State.' "

But most people close to the administration saw the main lack of leadership in Roosevelt himself. Frances Perkins and Frank Walker found alarming lethargy and ignorance about foreign policy in their trips across the country. Frankfurter told Ickes he was at a loss to understand the President's failure to take the initiative. Stimson bluntly warned his chief late in April that the political situation was deteriorating and that the administration must lead.

Roosevelt would lead—but not by more than a step. He seemed beguiled by public opinion, by its strange combinations of fickleness and rigidity, ignorance and comprehension, by rapidly shifting optimism and pessimism. If the reading and radio-listening public, he told reporters one day, "read history, they ought not to go up on a pinnacle of hope one day because of a sea battle off Italy, and go down to the depths of despair the next day because of an Axis advance in Greece." The war would be won, he went on, not by one sea fight "but by keeping the existence of the main defense of the democracies going—and, that is England—the British Empire."

The President was dismayed by the defeatism and fatalism in the country. Anne Morrow Lindbergh's *The Wave of the Future* had created a minor sensation with its picture of relentless—and seemingly authoritarian—forces at work. "These people," the President told reporters, "say out of one side of the mouth, 'No, I don't like it, I don't like dictatorship,' and then out of the other side of the mouth, 'Well, it's going to beat democracy, it's going to defeat democracy, therefore I might just as well accept it.' Now, I don't call that good Americanism. . . ."

Yet Roosevelt himself seemed irresolute. When Norman Thomas wrote that convoys would bring total war, Roosevelt sent him a rather wary reply: ". . . I wish you could be here for a week sitting invisibly at my side. It would not be a pleasant experience for you because you would get a shock every ten minutes.

"You and I are, I think, about the same age and certainly we had hoped to live out our own lives under conditions at least somewhat similar to the past. Today I am not sure that even you and I can do that."

But Roosevelt was facing an adversary who did understand the "complete change from older methods"—who, indeed, had helped produce the change. In the spring of 1941 Hitler was putting the final touches on his world strategy.

HITLER: THE RAPTURE OF DECISION

"Who was I before the Great War?" Adolf Hitler had demanded of the workers assembled before him at the Rheinmetall-Borsig Works in December. "An unknown, nameless individual." But who was Hitler in the spring of 1941? To his people he had become both messiah and miracle worker—a man who had somehow pulled off the great deeds he had promised. To Churchill he was a guttersnipe, a gangster, a "monstrous abortion of hatred and defeat," and while these epithets were for public consumption they did not much exaggerate Churchill's private view. To the Russians, despite the pact with Germany, Hitler personalized the final convulsions of capitalism and militarism. To millions of Americans and Britons he was a madman who went into frenzies, foamed at the mouth, fell to the floor, and chewed carpets.

To Roosevelt he was simply an enigma. There were odd resemblances between the two: both liked to talk, to dwell on old times with old friends, to act out roles, to be flattered, to play off friends as well as enemies against one another; they had both come to power at the same time. But the resemblances were superficial; the two men had emerged from different worlds, held almost opposite values.

Hitler as a boy had hated and feared his father and loved his mother, had moved repeatedly from place to place and from school to school, had a sense of self that was at once overblown and empty; Roosevelt loved his parents, had a strong feeling of family, place, identity. Hitler showed little ability to change and adjust; Roosevelt was growing and adapting throughout his life. Roosevelt had an average interest in sex and was restricted in part by lack of opportunity; Hitler had plenty of opportunity with women but was frustrated by his own inhibitions. Roosevelt loved to laugh; Hitler emitted at most a sort of barking gurgle. Roosevelt loved sun, water, and snow; Hitler hated them except at a distance. Roosevelt liked moderate amounts of tobacco, liquor, and meat; Hitler spurned all three. Hitler loved the grandiose, the morbid, the apocalyptic; Roosevelt, the tangible, the proximate, the concrete. Hitler was fascinated by blood, decapitation, by death in all its simplicity and finality; Roosevelt conducted a long love affair with life, with its endless complexity, surprises, and open-endedness.

Hitler was an ideologist. In his five decades of vagrancy, and of trench life, political combat, and finally the conquest of power, he had forged a system of values, a rigid theory of change, and a strategy of political action. The values were folkish, racist, xenophobic; they assaulted everything precious to the liberal mind—egalitarianism, altruism, tolerance, religion, individual liberty, internationalism. Hitler's theory of change was not of personal flexibility and adaptation, but of unremitting racial and national conflict and brutal violence, with the strong climbing to power over the bodies of the weak; there was no place for the flabby liberal notions of due process, minority rights, civil liberty, parliamentarianism, gradualism, accommodation. Hitler was a true ideologist in that his values, his theory of change, and his political strategy meshed perfectly. And as an ideologist he considered his adversaries not merely wrong or evil, but also mad. Roosevelt was simply crazy, he told his comrades; he behaved like a "tortuous, pettifogging Jew" because there was Jewish blood in his veins, and the "completely negroid appearance of his wife showed that she too was half-caste."

Hitler as a person was also beyond Roosevelt's ken. The President was long used to politicians grasping for influence, deserting old friends, breaking promises, nourishing grudges; he himself had done that kind of thing. But in Hitler he was dealing with a man possessed of a rage for recognition and deference far beyond that of a Huey Long or a John L. Lewis. Grounded in the security of doting parents, fixed home, social class, family traditions, Roosevelt could not easily gauge this product of social void and revolutionary turmoil. Hitler had lacked a home, but he found a new home in the Nazi party, in its ideas, and comradeship. Though he knew how to use the carrot as well as the stick, he had become a terrible simplifier. While Roosevelt proceeded by a series of knight's moves, bypassing, overleaping, encircling, Hitler went straight for his prey—opposition parties, Nazi dissidents, Jews, small nations.

And now in the early weeks of 1941 Hitler was facing the transcendent decision of his life, and of his time. In December he had ordered his high command to prepare a massive land assault against Russia, to take place in May. "The German Armed Forces must be prepared to *crush Soviet Russia in a quick campaign* (Operation Barbarossa) even before the conclusion of the war against England," the Führer's directive began. But the decision was not a final one. While his generals plotted supply routes and staging areas along the thousand-mile front, Hitler pondered his strategic situation.

That situation was stupendous in both promise and portent. Britain was not yet finished. America was giving it increasing support. The English had routed Mussolini's forces in Africa. The Western Front against Germany had been broken but it still existed at the Channel, and across it Anglo-Saxon power was growing. And if anything had been bred in the bone of every German statesman, strategist, even soldier, especially after 1918, it was this: never fight a two-front war. Hitler himself had stressed the point in *Mein Kampf.* The Führer had brilliantly mixed force and diplomacy—especially in crushing Poland before the West could intervene—to avoid this strategic vice. Such a principle could yield now to only the most overwhelming considerations. But so they seemed to Hitler.

Russia itself, to begin with, seemed a surly and cunning ally. After the Führer's generous invitation to Moscow to join the Tripartite Pact—along with spreading out the riches of India for Russia to feast on—Molotov had coolly demanded a free hand in Finland, Bulgaria, the Turkish straits, the Persian Gulf. Soon Hitler was calling Stalin a cold-blooded blackmailer. And what, he reasoned, did Moscow have to back up its claims? Russia was a giant with feet of clay. Its army had been weakened by a merciless purge of officers. Its frontier was vast and poorly defended. Its people, especially in the Ukraine, were eager to throw off the Bolshevik yoke.

The Führer knew, moreover, that Russia had its own dilemma of two fronts. On the east lay Japan, an old adversary, now united with Germany and Italy in a pact of steel. Here Hitler's surging strategic ambition conjured up global possibilities. "The *purpose* of the co-operation based on the Three Power Pact must be to *induce Japan to take action in the Far East* as soon as possible. This will tie down strong English forces and will divert the main effort of the United States of America to the Pacific. In view of the military unpreparedness of her enemies, the sooner Japan strikes, the greater her chances of success. . . ." He instructed his soldiers to respond generously to Tokyo's requests for military help.

The Führer pondered the interplay of nations' strategies. The United States in the long run was his most formidable adversary. It was big, rich, remote. He had not wanted to provoke Washington—at least not yet—but Roosevelt seemed to be girding the nation for military action. The destruction of Russia would enable Japan to turn all its strength against America. This in turn—combined with expanded U-boat warfare—would diminish Roosevelt's support for Churchill across the Atlantic. If American aid reached England, Hitler said, it would be "too little and too late." Britain, shorn of its present aid from America and of its potential help from Russia, would be forced to its knees. Meanwhile, he must refrain from provocative acts against American ships in the Atlantic.

So the attack on Russia, which to many at the time seemed like a lunatic lunge in the wrong direction, from Hitler's strategic view was the best way to break the growing global coalition against him. To turn east was really—on Hitler's very round globe—to turn west. Finally, he reasoned, the conquest of Russia would remove any threat to his rear when he re-engaged Britain, and it would insure vast supplies of raw materials. The timing was ripe, too, he felt. All nations were rearming, including Russia, but all were lagging. If he did not act on his own grand strategy quickly, the opposition coalition would be acting on its own. Were not Moscow and London already plotting against him?

Yet it was not an easy decision. Admiral Raeder opposed the eastern strategy and spoke of the glowing possibilities of action in the Mediterranean, in North Africa, in the Atlantic. Hitler demurred for two final reasons. One was the sheer complexity of operations in the West. Mussolini was proving more a drain than an ally; Vichy was controllable but evasive and inert; Franco was cautious as long as the British fleet dominated his coastline and meantime seemed eager only to drive a hard bargain. The Mediterranean, compared with the Russian heartland, was less a strategic entity than a collection of tactical opportunities—and pitfalls. Operations to the south and west called for consummate skill at mixing diplomacy, propaganda, pressure, and sea, air, and ground power. How much easier to mass his forces, crush Russia in a few tremendous blows, and topple the whole anti-Nazi combination.

The other reason was ideological. The one most powerful, consistent force in Hitler's thought had been mingled fear and loathing of the Slavic masses to the east, their "Jewish-Bolshevist leaders," and the huge Red Army. "We must never forget that the regents of present-day Russia are common blood-stained criminals; that here is the scum of humanity," he had raved on and on in *Mein Kampf*. "We must not forget that the international Jew, who today rules Russia absolutely, sees in Germany, not an ally, but a State marked for the same destiny." Contemptuous (and envious) of Britain but full of hatred toward Russia, he had negotiated with Moscow purely for reasons of state. In the long run, he believed, there could be only a death grapple between the two ideologies.

So Hitler confronted his sacred mission and wove his global tapestry of war as he stared out at the glistening Alps from his eyrie or bent over huge maps in his chancellery. Years later, even in the nuclear age of overkill, there was something awesome in the power of decision lodged in this one man. The actual authority of "absolute" monarchs and "totalitarian" dictators is usually exaggerated; the poor men are impeded at every step by suspicious allies, ambitious rivals, foot-dragging bureaucrats, demanding relatives, grasping wives or mistresses. But Hitler's personal power in 1941 was almost total. Between lunch and dinner he could make a decision that would topple governments, spill oceans of blood, desolate scores of cities, change the lives of literally millions of people in one quarter of the globe—and completely spare another corner. In one moment of frenzy or ideological rapture he could order a nation to die, a whole class of people to be exterminated. He was indeed the terrible simplifier.

By this time, moreover, Hitler's circle had been so narrowed that only a handful were privy to his fateful decisions. Goering, Goebbels, and Himmler vied with one another to carry out their Führer's orders, even to anticipate them. Ideologically at one with their leader, they had little reason to differ with him except over trifles or about their own power and jurisdiction. The natural sources of opposition—church, trade unions, political parties, intellectuals—had long been suppressed. As for allies, Mussolini had been reduced to the most junior partner; Hitler usually told him about major actions only on the eve. The heads of satellite nations did not dare cross the man whose soaring and shifting fortunes they must now share to the end.

Only the generals had the formal status, the *esprit,* the professional tradition, and the raw power to withstand him. But by this time they were almost impotent. Again and again proved wrong in their doubts about Hitler's gambles, hectored and bullied by him, fearful that if they thwarted him he would replace them with more fanatical soldiers or storm troopers, the generals largely stayed silent. They could not even take refuge in the bureaucrat's time-honored plea of ignorance or misunderstanding, for Hitler left nothing to chance. Hour after hour he lectured his silent generals, outlining his plans, the diplomatic parallel moves, the broader political context, their specific responsibilities.

Only the moral fervor of an independent nation could withstand Hitler in 1941. During the late winter and spring the Führer infiltrated the Balkans to block any show of independence or threat by the British, and to protect his right flank for the drive into Russia. One by one he outflanked and isolated his victims. Bulgaria, threatened by Nazi troops in Rumania and unresponsive to Russian proffers of support, adhered to the Tripartite Pact at the end of February. Turkey, terrified by Hitler's nearby divisions, was effectively neutralized. Greece, still beleaguered by Italian troops in the northwestern mountains, lay naked to Nazi attack from the northeast. Only Yugoslavia retained some freedom of action and will.

For a time it seemed that this small country, too, would submit to the genteel suffocation that Hitler reserved for nations that had not unduly provoked him. Prince Paul, conscious of his political and military weakness, spurned British invitations to form a common Balkan front against Germany. This was not enough for Hitler. In mid-March he summoned Paul to a secret meeting and demanded that Belgrade adhere to the pact. A week later, facing a final Nazi ultimatum, the Regent decided to comply. Then came an event that was not on Hitler's schedule—and would fatally alter it. Serbian army officers, outraged by Paul's capitulation, ousted him from office. Churchill announced elatedly that Yugoslavia had "found its soul" and urged Roosevelt to give the new government his fullest support.

The overturn in Belgrade threw Hitler into a boiling rage. Summoning the high command, he stormed that Yugoslavia must be beaten down once and for all, no matter what declaration of loyalty Belgrade might now make. Quietly and skillfully the generals regrouped their forces; then Nazi planes swooped down on the defenseless capital and almost obliterated the heart of it. Seventeen thousand people died. Nazi columns stabbed across the border from the north and east. Effective resistance was erased within ten days.

Hitler exulted over his devastating show of strength. He had taken some risks, since attack to the south had meant postponing his invasion of Russia by a good month. He was not unduly concerned. Success, like power, ennobles some men; others it emboldens and corrupts. The struggle with Russia, Hitler told his commanders, was one of ideologies and racial differences and would have to be conducted with unprecedented and unrelenting mercilessness. In particular, Soviet commissars—"bearers of an ideology directly opposed to National Socialism—must be shot out of hand." Schutzstaffel Chief Heinrich Himmler was given "special tasks" in the wake of the attack.

Toward the end of March Hitler summoned his generals again to stress the ideological—and hence ruthless and final—nature of the struggle ahead. "They sat there before him," an observer remembered, "in stubborn silence, a silence broken only twice—when the assembly rose first as he entered through a door in the rear and went up to the rostrum, and later when he departed the same way. Otherwise not a hand moved and not a word was spoken but by him."

At the end of April Hitler set June 22 as D day for BARBAROSSA—about five weeks later than the original plan. He was confident; so were his commanders. "We have only to kick in the door," Hitler said, "and the whole rotten structure will come crashing down."

CHURCHILL: THE GIRDLE OF DEFEAT

Nowhere did the pause of winter 1940-41 bring graver strategic reassessments than in the command posts in Whitehall. After the traumas of 1940 the British had, of course, much to celebrate. "We were alive," Churchill said later. "We had beaten the German Air Force. There had been no invasion of the island. The Army at home was now very powerful. London had stood triumphant through all her ordeals. Everything connected with our air mastery over our own island was improving fast. . . ." The British were winning a brilliant victory over the Italians in the Libyan desert. And "across the Atlantic the Great Republic drew ever nearer to her duty and our aid."

There was a much darker side. Sinkings along the Atlantic lifeline were still appalling, and the Germans would send out many more U-boats in the coming months. Britain's voracious war theaters were swallowing up the still-lagging war supply. Tokyo's intentions in the Orient remained ominously inscrutable. Most troubling of all was the strategic situation in the Mediterranean. Even in the flush of desert victories, Britain could not ignore the weaknesses in the balance of its Near Eastern obligations and power. Franco was still flirting with Hitler, though with the apparent reluctance of a suspicious señorita. Pétain seemed ever subject to collapse under Nazi pressure. German air power hovered over the Balkans. Turkey and other Near Eastern countries coldly measured nearby British strength. This was meager—50,000 British, Indian, and Commonwealth troops scattered across a broad area, six battleships divided between the eastern and western Mediterranean, two hundred planes in the Nile Valley.

What were the Germans planning? British Intelligence failed to divine Berlin's strategic intention, partly because Hitler had not come to a final decision. All his information indicated that the Germans were still preparing to invade Britain, Churchill wrote to Roosevelt late in January; he was getting ready to give them a reception worthy of the occasion. But there was news from the East that large Nazi air and ground forces were being established in Rumania and infiltrating into Bulgaria, with Sofia's connivance. "It would be natural for Hitler to make a strong threat against the British Isles in order to occupy us here and cover his Eastern designs." But, Churchill added with a shade of envy, the Nazi forces were so strong that they could mount both offensives at the same time.

Keeping Roosevelt informed and sympathetic was Churchill's cardinal policy. The two men still had not met as President and Prime Minister, but their correspondence was becoming frequent and far-ranging. Early in 1941 the President sent Hopkins to England as his personal representative. The British were put off a bit by his unkempt state and blunt talk, but soon they caught the measure of the man. "There he sat," Churchill remembered later, "slim, frail, ill, but absolutely glowing with refined comprehension of the Cause"—the Cause being the defeat of Hitler—"to the exclusion of all other purposes, loyalties, or aims." General Ismay, stiffly noting that Hopkins was deplorably untidy, soon decided that not even Churchill was more single-minded in his conviction that Nazism must be crushed.

Other Roosevelt men followed: W. Averell Harriman, to help expedite Lend-Lease at the British end; William J. Donovan, Roosevelt's old Republican adversary and personal friend, who conferred with Churchill's men in the Balkans and the Mediterranean area; and a new ambassador to the Court of St. James's—John G. Winant, former Republican governor of New Hampshire, slow of speech, Lincolnesque of mien, and as committed as Hopkins to Churchill's Cause.

To the dispatch of such emissaries Churchill responded in kind.

On the death of Lord Lothian he chose his Foreign Secretary, Halifax, as Ambassador to the United States, thus also making way for Anthony Eden at the Foreign Office. To signalize the appointment, Churchill sent Halifax across the Atlantic in his newest and mightiest battleship, the *King George V,* after journeying to Scapa Flow, with an ailing, shivering Hopkins in tow, to see him off. Roosevelt, at the other end, sailed out from Annapolis to greet the new Ambassador—and also got a chance to look over Churchill's newest dreadnaught.

But all turned on plans being shaped in London—and by March 1941 Churchill and his military chiefs were facing a dire strategic predicament. The Germans were threatening Greece from their Balkan enclaves. Britain, historically a patron of the ancient nation, was providing air support to the counterattack against the Italians. Some kind of Nazi assault was inevitable, British strategists felt, and hence it was crucial to organize an anti-Nazi bloc in the area; in this they had the support of Colonel Donovan, who went from capital to capital exhorting resistance on the natives' part and offering American aid in the long run but little at the moment. All through the winter London feverishly marshaled diplomatic and military pressure to win the support of Yugoslavia and Turkey. But Belgrade was too exposed to Axis attack, and too divided internally, to put up a resolute front against Hitler, and Ankara feared that acceptance of British aid would simply provoke a Nazi assault on its spirited but underarmed troops.

Amid all the murk and doubt only one nation seemed fixed in its purpose. Athens informed London categorically that it would resist German invasion, as it had Italian. Would the British help them?

Such a question was bound to excite Churchill's passion, sympathy, and proclivity toward certain strategies. He admired Greek courage; he wanted to set an example—especially for the United States—of British willingness to succor a besieged ally; and the Balkans had long seemed a likely avenue for an ultimate re-entry into the Continent. All this made his dilemma sharper: to send troops to Greece meant taking them away from his North African front. General Archibald Wavell had trounced the Italians; but how soon would Hitler send reinforcements down the Italian boot, across Sicily, and into Africa? Would Greece turn out to be a trap? But could Britain stand by idly, as Eden said, and see Hitler win a bloodless victory?

Some of Churchill's military men flatly opposed any drain from North Africa, which they viewed as second in importance only to the home islands themselves. "Why will politicians never learn the simple principle of concentration of force at the vital point and the avoidance of dispersal of effort?" General Alan Brooke wondered. Unlike Roosevelt, Churchill was not simply and neatly commander in chief. Unlike Hitler, he could not easily override his generals. He had assumed the post of Minister of Defence so that no intermediary would dilute his direct influence on generals and planners. He deluged them with politely worded minutes and chits that could cut like a lash. Hour by hour his orders, reminders, requests poured out of his office urging "action this day," overriding excuses, demanding reports. But his sheer vitality betrayed a basic lack of authority and control; he had to deal with professional soldiers who admired his strategic versatility and imagination but deplored his amateurism; he had to clear major decisions with his War Cabinet, which included Labourites as well as Tories; he was answerable to Parliament, which at any time could question his policies, express lack of confidence, and even—though it would be almost un-British—vote him out of office. Within this ancient constitutional system Churchill influenced men less by his formal authority than by his inexhaustible energy, sweeping imagination, popular standing, capacity to cajole, flatter, manipulate, and overwhelm.

And now the soldiers awaited the politicians' decision on Greece. For a time even Churchill drew back. Military co-ordination with the Greeks was faltering; the Balkan common front seemed less likely than ever; a German general named Erwin Rommel was building up striking power in Libya. "Do not consider yourselves obligated to a Greek enterprise if in your hearts you feel it will only be another Norwegian fiasco," Churchill wired to Eden in Cairo. But Eden, Dill, and Wavell favored standing by Greece, no matter how hazardous the course.

It was less Churchillian strategy than Churchillian temperament that decided the issue. For months his febrile eye had been sweeping the shores of Europe for openings. He had a leaning toward quick, daring assaults that would exploit Britain's sea power, keep the enemy off balance, minimize losses, and widen the role of heroism and dash. With all his bent for modern arms, he had a distaste for mass armies, for their heavy apparatus of mechanics, signalmen, lorries, supply depots, laundries, motor pools. War for him was still an enterprise for bravery and brawn, for mobile forces darting and feeling and jabbing. And behind his strategy and temperament was a sense of history—of the role of character and courage, of contingency and chance. One vast effort might fail and all would be lost. Many efforts by unflinching men along a broad periphery might fail, too, but one force might get through and open up a host of new opportunities.

So London stayed committed to Greece, and on April 6—the

same day they invaded Yugoslavia—the Germans smashed into the little country from the northeast.

There was something magnificent about a nation, itself beleagured, that stood by its commitment to a small ally despite a sinking realization of the hazards. It was magnificent—but it was not war. Hitler, as usual, followed the soldier's strategy of massing overwhelming force at the crucial points, and his strategic initiative gave him tactical flexibility. He marshaled fourteen divisions—four armored—for a quick assault. Gallantry and dash on the other side were not enough. Soon the British troops with their Greek comrades were streaming south in a nightmare of shrieking Stukas, burned-out vehicles, blocked one-lane mountain roads, dust, and mud. The British Navy rescued the survivors off the southern coasts of the Peloponnesus; 12,000 dead, wounded, and prisoners were left behind.

Meantime, in North Africa the other pincer was turning. Hitler had not planned a major offensive toward Cairo, but once again he was in the right place with the biggest battalions. Testing the British and Australian defenses, Rommel soon felt out the weaknesses resulting from the diversion to Greece. Then, in a series of nicely executed strokes, he turned Wavell's left flank, drove the British out of Benghazi, and put Tobruk under siege. Wavell's great turn-of-the-year victory over Italy was canceled out.

The third and cruelest chapter was to come: Crete. With Greece and Yugoslavia secured, Hermann Goering planned an audacious exercise for his pilots, glider men, and paratroops—the first large-scale air-borne attack in history. The Germans mobilized 16,000 paratroopers and mountain soldiers and about 1,200 planes. The blow fell on May 20. The defenders killed hundreds of Germans in the air and on the ground; the British Navy in one night destroyed a convoy, drowning 4,000 men. But the Germans kept coming by air. Within a week the British were performing another miracle of evacuation—and Hitler was celebrating his most daring victory of all.

By now Churchill's strategy was under heavy fire. Old David Lloyd George, his chief in World War I, rose in the House of Commons to flay the conduct of the war. He remembered passing through discouraging days in the first war. "But we have had our third, our fourth great defeat and retreat." There was no question about Churchill's brilliance, he went on. But he needed some "ordinary persons" around him—"men against whom he can check his ideas, who are independent, who will stand up to him and tell him really what they think. . . ." A dozen other members joined in the attack. Before a rapt house Churchill responded with spirit to Lloyd George's "not particularly exhilarating talk." So the former

Premier wanted the present one to "be surrounded by people who would stand up to me and say, 'No, No, No,' " Churchill declaimed. "Why, good gracious, has he no idea how strong the negative principle is in the constitution and working of the British war-making machine?" The problem was not more brakes, but more speed. "At one moment we are asked to emulate the Germans in their audacity and vigour, and the next moment the Prime Minister is to be assisted by being surrounded by a number of 'No-men'."

Only three Members voted against the government, but recriminations swelled after the debacle in Crete. Churchill grumbled in the House that neither Hitler nor Mussolini had been summoned before their parliaments to account for their mistakes. He reminded the Members that the Germans could readily shift air power along the interior railroads and airways of Europe, while Britain had to send aircraft "packed in crates, then put on ships and sent on the great ocean spaces until they reach the Cape of Good Hope, then taken to Egypt, set up again, trued up and put in the air when they arrive. . . ." He would not go into tactical details. "Defeat is bitter." The only answer to defeat was victory.

In Parliament Churchill overcame his foes; it was his friends who puzzled him. After Greece, Roosevelt wired him condolences on the loss, congratulations on British heroism in the "wholly justified delaying action," but added ominously: "Furthermore, if additional withdrawals become necessary, they will all be a part of the plan which at this stage of the war shortens British lines, greatly extends the Axis lines, and compels the enemy to expend great quantities of men and equipment. I am satisfied that both here and in Great Britain public opinion is growing to realize that even if you have to withdraw farther in the Eastern Mediterranean, you will not allow any great *debacle* or surrender, and that in the last analysis the naval control of the Indian Ocean and the Atlantic Ocean will in time win the war."

Churchill bridled at what seemed to be Roosevelt's counsel of despair. The loss of Egypt and the Middle East would be grave, he warned Roosevelt. In this war every post was a winning-post, "and how many more are we going to lose?" He would be frank. "The one decisive counterweight I can see to balance the growing pessimism in Turkey, the Near East, and in Spain would be if United States were immediately to range herself with us as a belligerent Power."

Defeat is bitter. After the loss of the Balkans, Churchill faced strategic bankruptcy. Where could he stop Hitler? During these anxious weeks his soldiers had mopped up Italians in East Africa and bested Vichy Frenchmen in Syria; but they had not beaten Nazis. By June he was reduced to the tactics of desperation: to bolster the defense against Rommel he took the terrible risk of sending ships loaded with tanks directly through Gibraltar to Wavell, depleting tank strength at home and risking sinkings in the Mediterranean. The gamble succeeded, but Wavell still could not force Rommel back. Reluctantly Churchill decided to shift Wavell out of the Mideast command. Nothing seemed to be going well. In May the Germans gave London its worst bombing yet and destroyed much of the House of Commons; Churchill stood in the wreckage and cried.

It was clearer to him than ever: America was his only hope. So far, he told the House of Commons in his May 7 speech, his government had made no serious mistakes in dealing with Washington. "Neither by boasting nor by begging have we offended them." Now must be awaited the full deployment of that mighty democracy of 130 million people. But everyone knew that time was getting short, and the mighty democracy was moving with awful deliberation. Churchill concluded a broadcast to his people:

> "For while the tired waves, vainly breaking,
> Seem here no painful inch to gain,
> Far back, through creeks and inlets making,
> Comes silent, flooding in, the main.
>
> "And not by eastern windows only,
> When daylight comes, comes in the light;
> In front the sun climbs slow, how slowly,
> But westward, look, the land is bright."

KONOYE: THE VIEW TOWARD CHUNGKING

Eastward the land was dark and disquieting. During the lull of 1940-41, London and Washington tried to divine Tokyo's next moves. Would the Japanese expand their drive into China, or turn north toward Soviet Siberia, or south toward the exposed colonies of France and Holland, or east toward the Philippines or even Hawaii? Step by step the soldiers and diplomats of Tokyo had been building the Greater East Asia Co-Prosperity Sphere; they had occupied Hainan, poured troops into northern French Indochina, signed the Tripartite Pact, set up a puppet government in Nanking, demanded oil and trade in the Dutch East Indies. What next?

Rumors drifted through Tokyo. ". . . There is a lot of talk around town to the effect that the Japanese, in case of a break with the United States, are planning to go all out in a surprise mass attack on Pearl Harbor," Ambassador Grew noted in his diary late in January 1941. "I rather guess the boys in Hawaii are not precisely asleep."

In fact the Japanese had no master plan, no global strategy, to guide their expansionist thrust. Hopes that had bloomed in mid-1940, after the fall of France and the air blitz on Britain, were ebbing. Tokyo had calculated that Axis power and unity might discourage British and American aid to China, attract Russia to the Tripartite Pact, and persuade Chiang to accept a settlement dictated by Japan. Instead, Russia, as well as Great Britain and the United States, was still giving aid and comfort to Chungking. Now the Japanese were waiting on the next move abroad—on Hitler's strategic decisions, Britain's capacity to survive, America's response to Axis moves.

No co-ordinated strategy at this point could have emerged from the unstable equilibrium over which Premier Konoye presided. Every week or so, in a small room at his residence, a "liaison conference" was held to link diplomatic and military policy. The meetings were dominated by the military—by Army and Navy Chiefs of Staff, and by young staff officers in close touch with extremist elements in the General Staff. But the division in Tokyo was not simply between the soldiers and the civilians. The military leaders, too, were divided—especially the Navy and the Army—and some of the civilians were more militant than some of the military. Foreign Minister Matsuoka startled even the saber-rattlers with his grandiose dreams of expansion.

Unsure of their strategy, divided in their councils, the Japanese tried to divine the inscrutable Occident. Would their German ally launch an invasion of Britain, or turn south, or even attack Russia? Could Britain maintain its power in the Pacific—in India, Singapore, Hong Kong—if the Nazis stepped up their pressure on the home islands, in Africa, or in the Atlantic? Above all, what about the United States? To Tokyo planners Roosevelt seemed the most baffling of Western leaders. He appeared to shift overnight from conciliation to threats to high-blown preaching to invitations to parley. But item by item—so gradually as to rob Tokyo of a dramatic issue—he was restricting the export of war materials to Japan.

In February Matsuoka left Tokyo on a good-will mission to Moscow and Berlin. He had a vaulting ambition—endorsed by many of his colleagues in the liaison conferences—both to tighten Japan's bonds with its Axis partners and to bargain for Soviet recognition of Japan's role in northern China, Manchuria, and the whole Co-Prosperity Sphere. Thus Japan's northern flank would be protected while its soldiers drove deeper toward Chungking—protected, too, in the event that its Navy and Army turned south.

In Washington, Roosevelt viewed the journey with wry detachment. "When it is announced that a certain gentleman starts for

Berlin and Rome," he wrote to Undersecretary of State Sumner Welles, "it might be possible for the Secretary or you to express a slight raising of the eyebrows in surprise that he is not also planning to visit Washington on his way home!"

Matsuoka's first stop after taking the slow train across Siberia was Moscow, where he offered Stalin a nonaggression pact. The Russians were cautious. Then on to Berlin, where Matsuoka was received with pomp and punctilio. Soon he was closeted with Hitler, who concentrated on impressing his visitor even though he was in the midst of the Yugoslav crisis. To his silent guest the Führer boasted of his war successes: how he had crushed sixty Polish divisions, six Norwegian, eighteen Dutch, and twenty-two Belgian, one hundred and thirty-eight French, all in a year and a half; how he had routed the British Army in France; how he was winning the Battle of the Atlantic and bailing out the unlucky Italians in North Africa. England had already lost the war and was now simply looking for any straw to grasp. It had only two—America and Russia.

He did not want to provoke Roosevelt into war, he went on, at least for the time being. America had three choices: it could arm itself, or it could assist England, or it could fight on another front. If it helped England it could not arm itself. If it abandoned England, the latter would be destroyed and America would be left isolated and facing the Axis. But in no case could America wage war on another front. As for Russia, the Reich had made treaties with that country, but far more important were the 160 to 180 German divisions for "defense" against Russia. Hitler said not a word to Matsuoka about his plans for its invasion.

Then Hitler dangled the bait before the Foreign Minister's gold spectacles. This, he said, was the perfect moment—indeed, it was unique in history—for Japanese action against Britain. Of course there was risk, but it was small now, with Russia immobilized by German divisions on its western border, Britain weak in the East, and America in only the early stages of rearming. The Axis, moreover, would suffer no division of interests; Germany, whose interest lay in Africa, was as little concerned with East Asia as Japan was with Europe. America would not dare move west of Hawaii.

At last Hitler stopped talking and looked challengingly at the Foreign Minister. Matsuoka spoke guardedly. He agreed with the Führer in principle, he said. He himself wanted to follow such a strategy—he had specifically favored an attack on Singapore—but he could not overcome the weak intellectuals, businessmen, court circles, and all the others who were balking him. He could make no commitment, but he would personally work for the goals he and the Führer shared. Hitler was visibly disappointed, and he decided to show his hand a bit. Bidding Matsuoka good-by, he said: "When you get back to Japan, you cannot report to your Emperor that a conflict between Germany and the Soviet Union is out of the question." But the Foreign Minister left Berlin, as Hitler carefully planned, without any definite knowledge of Nazi plans for Russia.

If Hitler deceived his Japanese ally on the most crucial question of the day, Matsuoka had an agreeable opportunity to turn the tables when he returned to Moscow. Not only had Hitler made clear that Russia would not be invited to join the Tripartite Pact, but Ribbentrop had advised Matsuoka not to get too involved with the Russians. Matsuoka still had his own game: settling his nation's differences with the Russians. Those differences were acute: Soviet aid to China, Japanese threats to Moscow's Far Eastern borders, and Russian demands that Japan sell the southern part of Sakhalin as against Tokyo's insistence on its oil and coal rights in the Soviet northern half. In several days of hard bargaining, Matsuoka won Stalin's approval of a simple neutrality agreement that avoided the basic issues. Stalin merely dropped his demand for southern Sakhalin in response to Matsuoka's promise that he would urge his government to ease its objectives in northern Sakhalin. The cardinal point was an agreement to maintain neutrality in case either party was attacked by a third.

Konoye welcomed Matsuoka home with his pact. The Japanese rejoiced; their Foreign Minister had managed—seemingly—to strengthen ties with Berlin and at the same time narrow the danger of Soviet pressure in Asia. There was some grumbling. The diplomatic and military situation in the southern seas was as awkward as ever. But now Tokyo could turn to its main goal: the final conquest of China through war and diplomacy. Now Chiang would see the futility of his efforts; now Washington would reconsider its aid to Chungking. All other considerations of strategy were subordinated to this transcendental goal. Japan's prestige and honor were too exposed, the military too entangled, the people too psychologically committed, the losses already suffered too great, the political repercussions of a withdrawal from China too dire, for Japan now to compromise its long struggle on the mainland.

In Chungking, a thousand miles up the Yangtze from the coast, the Nationalist government experienced neither the luxury nor the quandary of strategic choice. At the end of 1940, after three years of resistance, the Chinese faced a bellicose enemy holding almost all his seaports and the richer sections of the country. With insouciance, Japanese aircraft rained bombs on the capital; the Nationalists had neither planes nor guns to drive them away. People huddled in deep dugouts in the high cliffs of the city; any day correspondents could see bloated human corpses floating down the river, drifting against junks, and being pushed away by boatmen with long spiked poles.

In an unpretentious mansion called "Ying Wo" ("Eagle's Nest") lived Generalissimo and Madame Chiang Kai-shek and a small staff of servants and guards. With his wiry frame and lean chiseled features, the Generalissimo looked like the ascetic he was; he dressed in simple khaki uniforms, ate lightly, drank little, and smoked not at all. But in early 1941 he presided over a country with a horrifying contrast between rich and poor, even in wartime; a country becoming slowly more disorganized, demoralized, and even defeatist. Chiang was still the public symbol of national revolution, but by now he was as anti-Communist as he was anti-Japanese. His army, underfed and badly cared for, was barely able to stabilize the front; and the old admiration for the Nationalist leader was changing in some quarters to suspicion that he was far more anxious to protect his postwar position and bleed the Americans than to withstand the Japanese.

China's situation was in fact critical. Tokyo had set up a puppet regime in Nanking under Wang Ching-wei, and however much the Kuomintang railed at the "arch-traitor," he obviously presided over a widening suzerainty. In the northwest the Chinese Communists maintained a state within a state and an army within an army; while committed to the struggle against Japan, the Communists were demanding from Chungking concessions that could only bolster their position in the long run. With the Burma Road cut off for months, Nationalist China was almost isolated, and it was caught in a soaring inflation. The Army was vast but inefficient and underequipped, the generals often incompetent, the old war lords still undependable. Japan's Axis partner was trying to bully Chungking into accepting Tokyo's terms. Germany had won the war in Europe, Ribbentrop told the Chinese Ambassador in Berlin; clearly China could not hope for succor from Britain, or from the United States either.

In its extremity China had redoubled its appeals to Roosevelt. His nation was nearing collapse, Chiang had warned the President through the American Ambassador, Nelson Johnson. He particularly needed dollars and planes. His pleas brought a sympathetic answer from the President and a flurry of activity in Washington, but tangible aid was still low. The War Department opposed any more diversions of weapons from its already deprived forces, or from Britain's. By the end of 1940—after all the fervent appeals and fine responses—the United States had sent only nine million dollars in arms and munitions to the Nationalists.

In January 1941 Chiang did receive from Roosevelt an important emissary in the person of Lauchlin Currie, an administrative assistant to the President. Looking at China through an economist's eyes, Currie was pessimistic about helping Chungking overcome inflation, but he returned to Washington more sensitive to China's desperate needs. During the spring, while Matsuoka was known to be urging Moscow to abandon its aid to China, Chungking received promises from Washington that it would be eligible for aid under Lend-Lease, and that Currie himself would be in charge. The Generalissimo had a persuasive representative in Washington in his brother-in-law, T. V. Soong. By now Chiang was asking for over half a billion in aid, including over a thousand fighting planes and bombers.

And Russia? News of the Soviet-Japanese neutrality pact fell like a thunderbolt in Chungking. At first Chiang was convinced that Moscow would abandon him; surely Matsuoka must have exacted this as part of the bargain. But the mysterious Russians promptly got word to Chungking that the new pact did not affect the Chinese. The Soviets would help them as long as they kept on fighting the invaders. At the same time Washington, jarred by the pact, renewed its promises of assistance. Plans were quickly made to speed money and supplies. In mid-April Roosevelt signed an executive order, which he left unpublicized, authorizing American airmen to resign from their services for the specific purpose of forming a volunteer and "civilian" group in China. This was the beginning of the Flying Tigers, under Colonel Claire L. Chennault, who had been Chiang's adviser for air since leaving the United States Army. And the President, in response to Chiang's request for help in getting a political adviser, suggested a scholar named Owen Lattimore, who would soon be on his way to Chungking.

In May, as China approached its fifth year of struggle against invasion, Chiang was still lecturing his friends from his moral pinnacle as the first victim of aggression. At a farewell dinner for Ambassador Johnson he threw down his challenge to Washington. "We believe our ultimate victory can be secured on the mainland of Eastern Asia alone provided the American people second their government's policy without reserve and bring their full weight to bear in support of Chinese resistance. If, on the other hand, the nations of the Pacific are careless of their responsibilities, each waiting for others to move first, exhibiting afresh the *laissez-faire* and slothful conduct of the past, ignoring Japanese designs and ambitions and failing positively to assist Chinese resistance—then a great war involving the whole Pacific area will ensue with consequences that do not bear thinking about."

ROOSEVELT: THE CRISIS OF STRATEGY

While soldiers and statesmen around the world were calling in their final credits, making or renewing commitments, and finally choosing sides during the early months of 1941, Franklin Roosevelt remained the strategic enigma in the swaying balances of global power and purpose. His December 29 broadcast and the Lend-Lease Act had made clear his commitment to the survival of Great Britain. But what was his purpose beyond material aid to America's old partner? Some foreigners assumed that Roosevelt's wavering course actually cloaked a firm global strategy. At home the isolationists suspected that the President, despite his artless ways, was directing a Grand Conspiracy designed to plunge the country into war. Even some presidential subordinates, operating in their tiny enclaves, assumed that the Commander in Chief, with his spacious White House perspective, was forging some master plan.

They did not know their man. At this juncture Roosevelt was unable to pierce the fog of world battle, was still shying away from final commitments. ". . . We cannot lay down hard-and-fast plans," he wrote to Grew. Not only did he evade strategic decisions, but he refused to let his military chiefs commit themselves on the most compelling matters. When late in 1940 Knox submitted Navy estimates covering several years ahead, Roosevelt wrote to him: "The dear, delightful officers of the regular Navy are doing to you today just what other officers were trying to do to me a quarter of a century ago. If you and I were regular officers of the Navy, you and I would do the same thing!" The Navy was asking for too many men, he went on.

"This is a period of flux. I want no authorization for what may happen beyond July 1, 1941.

"All of us may be dead when that time comes!"

The admirals and the generals could not be so noncommittal. They had to plan across a longer span of time, for the decisions they made at any one point—about construction, supplies, equipment, training stations—would affect operational decisions for years. It was part of their doctrine that tactical decisions were feckless and self-defeating unless shaped by broad strategy. For years the military had been drawing up elaborate plans to vanquish all possible foes —including Britain—and combinations of foes. Dramatically labeled Red, Orange, Blue, and so on, these plans were tactically impressive but strategically almost worthless, for they existed in a political void that the Commander in Chief had no interest in filling. The fall of France and the investment of Britain had shaken the military men out of their abstractions. Two things were now imperative: closer liaison with the British and more realistic strategic assessments.

Roosevelt, despite his distaste for planning—especially with the election coming up—late in June 1940 had presented a "hypothesis" that six months later Britain would still be intact, the British and French still holding in the Middle East, and the United States "active in the war" but with naval and air forces only. It was a brilliant projection—and one that the President of course kept secret.

In mid-November, with the President safely re-elected, Admiral Harold ("Betty") Stark, Chief of Naval Operations, sent him a strategic appreciation outlining four basic alternatives in the event of United States involvement in the war: A. concentrate on hemisphere defense; B. concentrate on Japan, and only secondarily in the Atlantic; C. make an equal effort in both oceans; D. maintain the offensive in the Atlantic, culminating in a British-American land offensive, with the Pacific secondary. Alternative D—"Plan Dog"—assumed that even if "forced into" a war with Japan, the United States would avoid major operations in the Pacific until Britain was at least secure. Plan Dog—the "first attempt to deal with American military strategy as a whole"—called clearly for an "Atlantic First" policy that would cast a long shadow over later American strategy.

Roosevelt neither approved nor disapproved Plan Dog and its portentous order of priorities. He merely endorsed Stark's proposal of military conversations with a British staff group, provided, of course, that they were secret, purely exploratory, and without commitment. Under the pressure of having to present the British with agreed-on positions, the Army and Navy by 1941 were lined up solidly behind Plan Dog. The American choice of Atlantic First—which practically meant Britain First—would be hardly unwelcome to the visitors from London, who were to arrive in Washington late in January disguised as members of the civilian British Purchasing Commission.

The man most in need of a clear lead from the President was the Army's Chief of Staff, George C. Marshall. Sworn in on September 1, 1939, the day Hitler invaded Poland, Marshall was a protégé of General Pershing and a product of the Army's command and staff system. Quietly assured, stiff, courtly in a standoffish way, he was a planner and organizer who had managed to bring his own strong temper under control and was trying to apply logic and order to the building of an army in a context of unstable domestic politics and unpredictable global turmoil. Toward the President he was reserved even to the point of not laughing at his jokes; his passion for prudent planning and administrative order, as Forrest Pogue has noted, ran counter to Roosevelt's ways, but the two men got along well in their work, partly because of Hopkins's mediation.

By mid-January the President was willing to give some lead to

Marshall and the other planners. In a long meeting with Hull, Stimson, Knox, Marshall, and Stark he estimated that there was one chance in five that Germany and Japan might jointly launch a sudden attack on the United States. In that event Washington would notify London immediately that it would not curtail supplies to Britain. The British could survive for six months, the President estimated, and with another two months before the Axis could turn west, the United States would have eight months to gather strength. Roosevelt warned the group, however, that long-range military plans were unrealistic; the Navy and Army must be ready to act with what was available. He concluded the meeting with some cautious directives, as summarized by Marshall:

"That we would stand on the defensive in the Pacific with the fleet based on Hawaii; that the Commander of the Asiatic Fleet would have discretionary authority as to how long he could remain based in the Philippines and as to his direction of withdrawal—to the east or to Singapore; that there would be no naval reinforcement of the Philippines; that the Navy should have under consideration the possibility of bombing attacks against Japanese cities.

"That the Navy should be prepared to convoy shipping in the Atlantic to England, and to maintain a patrol off-shore from Maine to the Virginia Capes.

"That the Army should not be committed to any aggressive action until it was fully prepared to undertake it; that our military course must be very conservative until our strength had developed. . . .

"That we should make every effort to go on the basis of continuing the supply of matériel to Great Britain, primarily in order to disappoint what he thought would be Hitler's principal objective in involving us in a war at this particular time, and also to buck up England."

The President also took a hand in revising the formal American position to be presented to the parley. For the words "should the United States desire to resort to war" he carefully substituted "should the United States be compelled to resort to war." He also replaced the term "Allies" with "Associates."

In the two months of meetings that followed, the American and British staffs agreed that Britain's security must be maintained "in all circumstances," that the British Commonwealth must be ultimately secure, that the "Atlantic and European areas" were considered the decisive theater, though the "great importance of the Mediterranean and North African areas" was duly noted, and that the Associated Powers would "conduct a sustained air offensive to destroy Axis military power," eliminate Italy early, carry out raids, support underground groups, and, finally, capture positions from which to launch "the eventual offensive against Germany." Detailed plans were laid for full American participation in escorting convoys in the North Atlantic, for mobilizing heavy units of the American Navy in the eastern Atlantic, and even for deploying twenty-five or thirty American submarines "for operations against enemy shipping in the Bay of Biscay and the Western Mediterranean." Recognizing some of the global implications, the planners agreed that American concentration in Europe required augmented British effort in the Far East.

The staff meetings ended on March 29, 1941; the Commander in Chief took no formal position on the agreements then or for months afterward. In contrast to Hitler's penchant for seizing the strategic initiative and carefully indoctrinating his generals, Roosevelt had a strangely passive role. By spring 1941 his Navy and Army were all but committed to a strategy that had emerged largely from military leaders, many of whom deliberately tried to exclude political and diplomatic questions on the ground that they were questions for civilians. Military and civilian planners did not work closely together in the fragmentized system the President ran. There is little indication that the strategic possibilities of a "Pacific First" emphasis were ever fully confronted—for example, the importance of heavily bolstering the shaky Chinese defenses. Something could have been said for a decision to beat the weaker nation first and then close in on Germany. Atlantic First was adopted for compelling but essentially military reasons.

Roosevelt was following a simple policy: all aid to Britain short of war. This policy was part of a long heritage of Anglo-American friendship; it was a practical way of blocking Hitler's aspirations in the west; it could easily be implemented by two nations used to working with each other; it suited Roosevelt's temperament, met the needs and pressures of the British, and was achieving a momentum of its own. But it was not a grand strategy embracing the full range of world-wide diplomatic, political, and economic as well as military power, potential as well as existing. It did not emerge from clear-cut confrontation of political and military alternatives; and it concentrated on practical ways of winning military victory—or at least preventing Axis victories—rather than on the long-run war and postwar security needs of the United States.

Above all, this strategy was a negative one in that it could achieve full effect—that is, joint military and political action with Britain—only if the Axis took action that would force the United States into war. It was a strategy neither of war nor of peace, but a strategy to take effect (aside from war supply to Britain and a few defensive actions in the Atlantic) only in the event of war. Unless the President was willing and able to lead the nation into war—and he was not—the strategy was inoperative. All this Hitler understood —and hence it was largely his decision as to whether Roosevelt's strategy would come into operation at all.

Hitler's thunderous April blows in Greece, Yugoslavia, and North Africa resounded like a fire bell in Washington. There was a shiver of apprehension over Britain's capacity to wage war at all. Once again that country seemed to be showing military skill only in retreat and evacuation. Old differences surfaced; some of the military urged all-out war; others, withdrawal to the hemisphere; others remembered their troubles with the British in World War I. Many now doubted Britain's capacity to survive. London seemed at the end of its rope. "It has been as if living in a nightmare," Harriman later wrote to Hopkins, "with some calamity hanging constantly over one's head."

The President seized on every immediate means of helping Britain. He authorized British ships to be repaired in American docks, British pilots to be trained on American airfields. He transferred ten Coast Guard cutters to the Royal Navy. He widened the American neutrality patrol zone, putting Greenland and the bulge of Africa under Navy surveillance. And he announced the long-brewing agreement with the Danish Minister placing Greenland under the temporary guardianship of the United States and authorizing the construction of bases there.

Outwardly Roosevelt maintained his usual cheerful demeanor. On April 15—in the midst of gloomy conferences on Britain's crisis —he held an uproarious press conference. He opened by noting the "nice little coincidence" that on the first actual Lend-Lease list there really *had* been garden hose—actually fire hose, he admitted, after the laughter subsided. Would Hopkins be paid for his new Lend-Lease role? "Yes, sure. He's a Democrat! What a foolish question."

The President went on: "That was what I said to Bill Knudsen the other day. In about the fourth or fifth list of these dollar-a-year men, they were all listed as Republicans except a boy who had graduated from Yale last June and never voted, and I said, 'Bill, couldn't you find a Democrat to go on this dollar-a-year list anywhere in the country?' He said, 'I have searched the whole country over. There's no Democrat rich enough to take a job at a dollar a year.' " Again and again the reporters burst into laughter at Roosevelt's sallies—and then stood impressed while he went into the detailed historical background of Denmark and Greenland.

Actually the President was deeply concerned about Britain's position—even more so because he felt helpless to intervene with decisive effect. He asked Marshall and Stark to reassess the situation in the Middle East in the event of a British withdrawal from the eastern Mediterranean. And inexplicably he sent Churchill the long cable that upset the Prime Minister but that was evidently intended to solace Churchill if he had to pull out of the Middle East.

Of all the spikes of the global crisis the sharpest was in the North Atlantic. As the days lengthened, shipping losses mounted sharply again. The German battle cruisers *Scharnhorst* and *Gneisenau* were terrorizing the Atlantic, and the U-boats were perfecting new wolf-pack tactics. During one frightful night in early April a convoy lost ten of its twenty-two ships. The Atlantic was the one pivotal arena in which American intervention could be quick and crucial. Churchill was pleading for help. What could Roosevelt do?

For months the President had been tacking back and forth on the question of protecting British convoys. The administration had long before established patrols to observe and report on the movements of Axis raiders; they had even reported movements to the British. But naval escorts of convoys were a far more serious matter; such escorts would presumably attack nearby Axis ships or submarines on sight—and that was precisely why Churchill wanted Roosevelt to escalate from patrolling to escorting. The President fully saw the implications. In January he had said to reporters, as if to disarm his critics: "Obviously, when a nation convoys ships, either its own flag or another flag, through a hostile zone, just on the doctrine of chance there is apt to be some shooting—pretty sure that there will be shooting—and shooting comes awfully close to war, doesn't it?" The reporters agreed. The President continued: "You can see that that is about the last thing we have in our minds. If we did anything, it might almost *compel* shooting to start." In the following weeks Stimson, Knox, and Stark pressed Roosevelt to give British shipping the protection it needed; the President had been evasive and noncommittal. During this same period he was insisting publicly that Lend-Lease would help keep the nation out of war.

After the spring crises it seemed to many that the decision to escort convoys could no longer be put off. At a White House meeting Stimson, Knox, and now Hopkins urged the President to act. If the Navy was turned loose, Knox said, it "would clean up the Atlantic in thirty days." But forthright action in the Atlantic required in advance the transfer of a fleet from the Pacific, and the President quailed at this global redisposition. Here Hull affected the problem. For weeks he had been holding interminable discussions with Ambassador Kichisaburo Nomura, who had been presenting the more pacific face of Japan. Hull feared that Tokyo would misin-

Break It Up, Boys! There's Work To Do

Harold Carlisle, The Des Moines Register and Tribune Syndicate, from the Washington *Post,* April 29, 1941

"THE CAPITAL OF THE WORLD OF TOMORROW WILL BE EITHER BERLIN OR WASHINGTON."—WENDELL WILLKIE

May 5, 1941, Rollin Kirby, reprinted by permission of the New York *Post*

terpret withdrawal of fleet units from the Pacific as a sign of weakness. Stimson and Marshall tried to convince their chief that Hawaii was impregnable; but the President feared that Singapore, Australia, and the Dutch East Indies would be vulnerable without the American Navy. In vain Stimson urged on him that Britain could protect Singapore if the United States would reinforce the Atlantic. The President, backed by Hull and aware that the military itself was divided, would not move the fleet—and he would not order Atlantic escorts.

Roosevelt hoped that stepped-up patrolling would help in the Atlantic. Then, he told Stimson and Knox late in April, he could inform Latin-American capitals about Axis raiders. Stimson bridled. "But you are not going to report the presence of the German Fleet to the Americas. You are going to report it to the British Fleet." With his simplicity and directness and his narrower military responsibilities, he wanted Roosevelt to be honest with himself. The President must take the lead and also the risk, Stimson felt, for the public would not tell him ahead of time if they would follow him. But the President would not lead.

Was Roosevelt hoping that patrolling would trigger an incident that would dramatize Hitler's threat to the hemisphere and unite Americans behind a bolder strategy? Ickes and others were convinced that he was. But evidently no ordinary incident would do. On April 10 the American destroyer *Niblack,* while picking up survivors from a torpedoed Dutch merchantman, had made sound contact with a submarine and had driven it off with depth charges. This episode—the first military encounter between American and German armed forces—Roosevelt had not used to dramatize the emergency. What was he waiting for?

A deepening crisis of confidence enveloped the administration in May. No one knew what was going to be done, Stimson complained. Morgenthau, who had now concluded that the United States must go to war to save Britain, felt that both Roosevelt and Hopkins were groping as to what to do. Wallace wrote that the farm people of Iowa were ready for a "more forceful and definite leadership." Hopkins at one moment defended the President and in the next urged the military leaders to press their chief harder. In a tragicomic moment Stimson actually interrupted Hull's croquet game to enlist support for a changed policy. The croquet player continued his game. Roosevelt's personal friends—MacLeish, Frankfurter, William C. Bullitt—were deeply troubled. Ickes met secretly with Stimson, Knox, and Jackson to discuss ways of putting pressure on the President; all agreed that Roosevelt was failing to lead, that the country wanted more action and less talk, that something dramatic was needed to seize the attention of the world. It was Stimson who finally belled the cat. The people, he told the President to his face, must not be brought to combat evil through some accident or mistake, but through Roosevelt's moral leadership.

Why was Roosevelt so passive? His lieutenants searched for clues. He was in and out of bed with an enervating fever during much of May, but he seemed no more militant during his ups than his downs. He was watching Congress and public opinion warily—especially an anticonvoy resolution in the Senate—but he seemed no more purposeful after the resolution was blocked. Clearly he felt constrained by his peace pledges—to Stimson, he seemed "tangled up in the coils of his former hasty speeches on possible war and convoying as was Laocoön in the coils of the boa constrictors"—but the militants were not urging a declaration of war, but simply more drastic action. Bullitt perhaps came closest to understanding Roosevelt's mind at this point. The President realized that the United States would stand alone and vulnerable if Britain went down, Bullitt reported to Ickes after a long talk with Roosevelt, but he could not bring himself to go in simply and directly. He was still waiting for a major provocation from Hitler even while recognizing that it might not come at all. Above all, he was trusting to luck, to his long-tested flair for timing, and to the fortunes of war. He had no plans. "I am waiting to be pushed into the situation," he told Morgenthau in mid-May—and clearly it had to be a strong shove.

So the crisis of confidence was also a crisis of strategy. Roosevelt was still waiting on events. When he and Hull caviled at shifting fleet units from the Pacific, he was ultimately responding to Hitler's strategy of bolstering Tokyo in order to divert America from Europe. But the President had the virtues of his strategic defects; at least he would stay flexible, loose, ready to seize the opportunity. During May he agreed to shift about a quarter of the Hawaiian fleet to the Atlantic. And under pressure from the militants he considered making a major speech in which he would declare an unlimited national emergency—but then to their despair he delayed the speech.

The President wanted to move foot by foot. At a Cabinet meeting he had contended that patrolling was a step forward. Stimson burst out: "Well, I hope you will keep on walking, Mr. President. Keep on walking!"

STALIN: THE TWIST OF *REALPOLITIK*

Half a world away from Roosevelt—and a world away in mind and outlook—Joseph Stalin, too, was watching Adolf Hitler, playing for time, hoping for the best. If Hitler and Roosevelt were near-opposites in ideology and temperament, the Soviet dictator and the American President seemed almost polar opposites in personal style: the one hard, stolid, patient, granitic; the other dexterous, articulate, supple, noncommitted. Both were outlanders—Roosevelt the product of a graceful Hudson River culture; Stalin, of the violent, poverty-ridden, hate-seared land of Georgia—and both had moved into the political heartland and mastered it. But while Roosevelt had risen through the loose, fragmented politics of an open society, Stalin had played a different game, slowly amassing influence in a monolithic party structure, effacing himself to avoid the ripostes of Trotsky and other Bolshevik luminaries, building alliances, jockeying for key posts, and then, after acquiring the party leadership, coldly isolating and destroying his political adversaries.

Stalin was the supreme ideologue, calculating and acting within a closed logical system, viewing the world through vulgate-Marxist prisms. Roosevelt was the supreme opportunist, eschewing dogma, avoiding final commitments. They spoke different political languages. Stalin preferred the "practical arithmetic" of agreements to the "algebra" of declarations, as he once remarked to Eden, but Roosevelt preferred political algebra—the forms, symbols, devices that facilitated day-to-day compromise even at the risk of disagreement and misunderstanding.

Now, by a hard twist of fate, the ideologue was not controlling history, and the opportunist could not long evade it. Hitler had not only forced these disparate men into the same camp, but also forced them into a similar global stance. Strategically they were both marching to the Nazi drum beat.

As a strategist, Stalin had sought to combine ideology and *Realpolitik* in the service of Bolshevism and the motherland. His armies were to stand clear of the long-expected death struggle of fascist and bourgeois states; meanwhile they would prevent hostile encirclement of Mother Russia and avoid a two-front war. During the 1930's he had tried warily and sporadically through Foreign Minister Maxim Litvinov to join Western nations in efforts at collective security. The West, its leaders irresolute and divided, fearful of both fascism and Bolshevism, had temporized too long. Stalin's ideological radar picked up, amplified, and distorted the complex forces at work in the West, exaggerating the influence of Russophobes and Red baiters in Western chancelleries, assuming that "monopoly capitalism" would be bound by the ineluctable logic of history to attack Bolshevism, perceiving every conciliatory move toward Hitler as a capitalist plot to deflect Nazi expansion to the east. Munich was not only a surrender to Hitler but also a catalyst of fear and mutual suspicion between Moscow and the West. Within a year Stalin had replaced Litvinov with the glacial Molotov, signed a nonaggression pact with Hitler, and stunned the world with his ideological and military flip-flop.

Molotov rubbed the salt of *Realpolitik* into Western wounds. Only recently, he conceded before the Supreme Soviet, Germany and Russia had been enemies. "The situation has now changed," he went on blandly, "and we have stopped being enemies. The political art in foreign affairs is . . . to reduce the number of enemies of one's country, and to turn yesterday's enemies into good neighbors."

But how good were the good neighbors, now hundreds of miles closer to Moscow after the partition of Poland? Stalin had played the diplomatic game with Hitler, bargaining, pressuring, protesting, appeasing, and always hoping that Axis and Allies would bleed each other to debility if not death. As a strategist Stalin faced a dilemma like Roosevelt's. He led a people conditioned to wanting to stay out of other people's wars, namely "European" wars. Stalin knew that Russian soldiers would fight badly in the attack but defend their motherland tenaciously if invaded. He was almost as restricted as Roosevelt in seizing the strategic initiative; hence Hitler held it.

The fall of France, the siege of Britain, the accession of Japan to the Axis upset the balance of power and hostility on which Stalin had been counting. If Britain should go down and America stay neutral, Moscow would face the peril of isolation on a Nazi-dominated continent. A logical strategy might have been to build a global counter-coalition to the Axis, but the anti-Hitler leaders were crippled by suspicion and history. Britain had been cool to Moscow, especially over the Soviet attack on Finland and the Bear's swallowing up of the little Baltic states. The United States, remote and unfriendly, still maintained in 1940 the "moral embargo" placed on aircraft exports to Russia after the Soviet bombing of Finnish towns. "I shall not dwell on our relations with the U.S.A. If only because there is nothing good to report," Molotov told the Supreme Soviet, amid laughter, in August 1940.

Such was the course of affairs when Molotov journeyed to Berlin in November 1940. He returned with Hitler's vague proposals that Russia adhere to the Axis, be guaranteed existing frontiers, and receive a free hand in the south—toward the Indian Ocean. Stalin saw his chance to bargain. He would not join the Axis unless Hitler withdrew his troops from Finland, recognized Bulgaria as part of the Soviet sphere of influence, and supported Moscow's historic ambition to gain bases in the Dardanelles. Probably Stalin knew that these were impossible conditions for the Führer. At this juncture there was still a small possibility that Hitler would turn west rather than east. But during early 1941 events in the Balkans seemed to gather a momentum of their own. Helplessly Stalin watched the Germans infiltrate Bulgaria and crush Yugoslavia and Greece.

It was the eleventh hour for a counter-coalition to stop the surging Nazis. In January 1941 Roosevelt lifted the moral embargo against the Soviets; in February and March Welles informed the Kremlin of reports that Hitler planned to attack east. But Soviet ideology and narrow *Realpolitik* and American ideology and isolationism made a unified stand impossible. Britain remained hostile, partly because Moscow was still sending raw materials to Germany. By mid-June 1941 Washington was still sharply curbing economic intercourse with the Russians.

During the spring, rumors and reports of Hitler's intentions reached the Kremlin from many sources. Stalin did not ignore them or necessarily disbelieve them; he processed them through his ideological, *Realpolitik* mind. He was wary. Were the Nazis building up their eastern frontier and letting out rumors simply to camouflage their spring assault on England? Was Churchill—who had sent him an inconclusive warning that was delayed in the delivery—trying once again, like a typical imperialist and warmonger, to let Russia pull his chestnuts out of the fire? Was Hitler simply securing a position of strength from which he hoped to bargain harder with Moscow? Or could Hitler possibly be contemplating a war on two fronts?

At least Stalin could avert a second front against himself. The neutrality pact that he and Matsuoka had negotiated gave him a rare moment of relief—along with a moment of humor when the Japanese Foreign Minister said that the better elements in Japan were originally "moral Communists." In one stroke Stalin had minimized the chance of an eastern front and hence—presumably—a western one. In a surprise visit to Matsuoka's alcoholic, back-slapping send-off at the station, he embraced his guest, remarking, "We are Asiatics, too, and we've got to stick together." He went on: "Now that Japan and Russia have fixed their problems, Japan can straighten out the Far East; Russia and Germany will handle Europe. Later together all of them will deal with America." Seeking out the German Ambassador, he threw his arm around his shoulder and exclaimed: "We must remain friends and you must now do everything to that end."

For such friends time was running out. Early in May, Stalin spoke in the Kremlin to young officers just graduated from military academies. He told them bluntly that the situation was extremely serious, a German attack was possible; but that the Red Army was not strong enough to smash the Germans easily because of inadequate training, equipment, and defense lines. The government, he said, would try by all diplomatic means to put off a German attack until the fall; but even if this succeeded, almost inevitably there would be war with Germany in 1942, but under more favorable conditions for Russia. "Depending on the international situation, the Red Army will either wait for a German attack," Stalin went on, "or it may have to take the initiative, since the perpetuation of Nazi Germany as the dominant power in Europe is 'not normal.' "

Two days later Stalin made himself Chairman of the Council of People's Commissars, and thus the formal head of government. By now he seemed to be fighting for time, hoping Hitler would still turn west. He tried to appease Berlin by closing down embassies and legations of Nazi-occupied nations. He kept Russian oil and other supplies moving to Germany. He had TASS deny rumors that Berlin was putting pressure on Moscow—a denial that in fact was correct, because Hitler was now bound on annihilation, not bargaining—and imply that London was still trying to foment war between Russia and Germany.

Seven nights later the German Ambassador drove to the Kremlin shortly before dawn and read to Molotov a cable just received from Berlin. It was the same pack of Nazi lies and accusations a dozen nations had heard just before their doom.

"This is war," Molotov said. "Do you believe that we deserved that?"

At that moment—dawn of June 22, 1941—a tide of German troops, tanks, and guns was flooding across the open plains. The Wehrmacht struck with its usual deception, surprise, efficiency, and stunning force. In the north three Panzer divisions, with over six hundred tanks, simply swarmed over a weak Russian rifle division. In the center the Nazi spearhead—two Panzer groups comprising seven divisions and almost 1,500 tanks—burst through understrength Russian divisions. In the south another German army brushed aside Russian defenses—they might have been a row of glass houses, a German lieutenant observed—and soon was rolling along hard and intact roads with the sound of guns fading behind. By evening the leading Panzer divisions, stretched out over seven to ten miles—motorcyclists and armored cars scouting ahead, massed tanks following, and a "sandwich" of infantry and artillery in between—had pierced the Soviet border by almost twice their own length.

In East Prussia the night before, in his new underground headquarters, "Wolfsschanze" ("Wolf's Lair"), concealed in a dark forest, Hitler had dictated a letter. "DUCE! I am writing this letter to you at a moment when months of anxious deliberation and continuous nerve-wracking waiting are ending in the hardest decision of my life." He reviewed the situation. England had lost the war. It was trying to get Russia into it. "Behind these two countries stands the North American Union goading them on" and supplying them with war materials. If he had to send his Air Force against Britain, Russia would follow a strategy of extortion. So he would "cut the noose before it can be drawn tight." The war in the east would not be easy, but Germany and Italy would secure a common food-supply base in the Ukraine. He tried feebly to explain why he was notifying the Duce only at the last moment. The decision had been made. Now he felt spiritually free. "With hearty and comradely greetings. Your Adolf Hitler."

In London Churchill spoke over the radio to the people:

". . . No one has been a more consistent opponent of Communism than I have for the last twenty-five years. I will unsay no word that I have spoken about it. But all this fades away before the spectacle which is now unfolding. The past, with its crimes, its follies, and its tragedies, flashes away." He described the tranquil Russian villages, children playing, mothers and wives awaiting the return of their loved ones. "I see advancing upon all this in hideous onslaught the Nazi war machine, with its clanking, heel-clicking, dandified Prussian officers, its crafty expert agents fresh from the cowing and tying-down of a dozen countries. I see also the dull, drilled, docile, brutish masses of the Hun soldiery plodding on like a swarm of crawling locusts. . . . Behind all this glare, behind all this storm, I see that small group of villainous men who plan, organize, and launch this cataract of horrors upon mankind. . . ."

In Tokyo, officials reacted with shock and dismay. The Konoye government had had intelligence of the Nazi attack but could scarcely credit it. Now for a second time Hitler had presented a *fait accompli*. But Matsuoka was undaunted. Japan, he felt, now had a supreme opportunity to attack Soviet Siberia and destroy Russian power in the Far East. The man who had strolled with Stalin along the station platform exchanging felicities was ready two months later to scrap his agreement with the Soviet chief. He rushed to the Imperial Palace with his plan, but he met a cool reception. Russia was still formidable in Siberia, army chiefs contended; why not wait until it was bleeding so heavily from Nazi thrusts that its strength would be drained away from the east? Let Germans fight Russians; Japan could pursue its interests southward and later move north when the main job was done. Let Hitler undertake a two-front war; Tokyo would not.

In Moscow, Stalin waited two weeks—in a state of near-collapse, it was said later—before he spoke to his people. "Comrades, citizens, brothers and sisters, fighters of our Army and Navy! I am speaking to you, my friends." He described, and understated, the German advances. "A serious threat hangs over our country." He tried to justify the Nazi-Soviet Pact. "The enemy is cruel and merciless. He aims at grabbing our land, our wheat and oil. He wants to restore the power of the landowners, re-establish Tsarism, and destroy the national culture of the peoples of the Soviet Union . . . and turn them into slaves of German princes and barons." The writer Ilya Ehrenburg, sitting by the radio at the office of *Red Star,* had never heard Stalin sound so moved, so close to his people. The dictator warned against panic-mongers, called on the troops and the whole Soviet people to fight for every inch of Soviet soil, and leave not a single engine or railway track or pound of bread or pint of oil for the enemy.

"Comrades, our forces are immeasurably large. . . . All the strength of the people must be used to smash the enemy. Onward to victory!"

THREE *Cold War in the Atlantic*

THE WEEKS of May and early June 1941 had been among the most trying in Roosevelt's life. Although he, too, had had ample warning of Hitler's mobilization in the east, he could not be sure that this was not a massive feint for an attack on the British Isles or elsewhere. Britain's heavy needs, China's plaintive cries for help, Matsuoka's continental fence-mending, Pétain's and Franco's vulnerability in the Mediterranean, the isolationist clamor in Congress, the pressure of the militants around him—these and a host of other scourges put the President under heavy strain. His May cold dragged on. With the press he was less open and genial as the spring neared its end, with his subordinates less tolerant and patient.

". . . I wish to God," he wrote to Senator Josiah Bailey, of North Carolina, in regard to convoying, "I could make out what all this full-dress debate they are talking about in the Senate relates to. Why debate convoys?" Convoying was a matter for experts, not for "laymen like you or I." A few days later he burst out in a letter to an isolationist Congressman: ". . . When will you Irishmen ever get over hating England? Remember that if England goes down, Ireland goes down too. . . ." When former Congressman Bruce Barton wrote in to complain of inconsistent figures from the administration, the President replied: ". . . It is hard to explain technical problems either to the Congress or to the people in view of the distorted values which are promptly given to one phase or the other of a complete picture." The master interpreter to the American people of complex problems at this point seemed to have lost his touch.

As usual the President was trying to gauge public opinion, and as usual public opinion was blurred and drifting. Americans seemed fiercely protective of their own shores, very doubtful that Britain could survive without American aid, and very sure that American naval escort of war materials to Britain would put the country into war. In mid-May, Pa Watson got an advance tip on a Gallup Poll; the figures he gave his boss indicated that about a quarter of the respondents felt that the President had not gone far enough in helping Britain, almost a quarter thought he had gone too far, and about half answered "just about right." During the following weeks interventionist feeling seemed to run ahead of presidential action. A majority seemed to be in favor of convoying, for example. But what kind of convoying, where, at what risk of shooting? On the specific and crucial policy questions public opinion was, as usual, hazy and volatile.

Amid the impenetrable events of early 1941 people seemed to be waiting for some clarifying event or galvanizing incident—or at least for some clear lead from the top. Only the President could give such a lead. By late May the militants were putting heavy pressure on their chief to speak bluntly to the people and proclaim an unlimited national emergency. Stimson sensed that the President was waiting for the accidental shot of a German or American commander to move the country into war, when he should have been considering the "deep principles" underlying the question. Ickes wrote to the President that Hitler would not create an incident until he was ready, and he would strike when ready, incident or no incident. Morgenthau was still militant; Hull, still cautious of action, if not of word.

Finally deciding on a speech, the President went about its preparation in a curious way. He would not ask Sherwood or Rosenman to put in a declaration of unlimited emergency, and he professed surprise when he found it in a draft. High officials tussled over the text of the speech as if it were a declaration of war. Stimson wanted a statement about the transfer of fleet units to the Atlantic; Hull objected. Some favored a stark presentation of shipping losses in the Atlantic; the Chiefs of Staff objected. Roosevelt was set on two matters: he would not mention Japan, for fear of provoking that country toward war; he would mention Russia, in case Germany forced it into war.

The speech had a dramatic prelude. The German battleship *Bismarck* suddenly slipped through the North Sea fogs and headed into the North Atlantic. "We have reason to believe that a formidable Atlantic raid is intended," Churchill cabled to Roosevelt. "Should we fail to catch them going out, your Navy should surely be able to mark them down for us." The battle cruiser *Hood* and other mighty ships would be on its track, he added. "Give us the news and we will finish the job." But contrary news came to the White House: the *Bismarck* had sunk the *Hood* and was now on the loose. The President got the news while sitting behind his desk in the oval study, where he was working with Sherwood and others on his speech. He wondered whether the *Bismarck* would head straight toward Martinique. "Suppose she does show up in the Caribbean," he speculated almost casually. "We have some submarines down there. Suppose we order them to attack her and attempt to sink her?

Do you think the people would demand to have me impeached?" Two days later the President took a call from the Navy Department. The *Bismarck* had been cornered by British Navy units and blasted by shells and torpedoes. Roosevelt hung up and said exultantly, "She's sunk!"

After this prelude and all the rumors and anticipation, the final speech, on May 27, was somewhat anticlimactic. The setting was anomalous: inside the East Room, representatives of Latin-American republics sat uncomfortably on gilt ballroom chairs; outside, Communist pickets trudged up and down the sidewalk with their antiwar placards. The President began his address boldly with a flat declaration that the Nazis were bent on world domination. He was not speculating, he insisted; it was already in the "Nazi book of world conquest." The Nazis, he said, "plan to treat the Latin American Nations as they are now treating the Balkans. They plan then to strangle the United States of America and the Dominion of Canada." American labor would be oppressed, unions crushed, the farmer regimented and impoverished, churches threatened, children perhaps sent off "goosestepping in search of new gods."

Was the President picturing a Nazi-occupied nation, or a Nazi-besieged one? The speech was not clear on this and other matters. It seemed to reflect the struggle over its composition and the President's indecision over strategy. Roosevelt, though speaking in his usual arresting way, meandered on and on, from the geography of Nazi strategy, to the Battle of the Atlantic, to the need of responding to Hitler before he came too close—"Our Bunker Hill of tomorrow may be several thousand miles from Boston"—to a statement of national policy that offered little that was new, to a rebuttal of "sincere" pacifists and a denunciation of the "sinister" ones. He did release the alarming figures of the rate of German sinkings of merchant ships, and he made his strongest statement to date of his determination to deliver supplies to Britain by whatever means was necessary. But he did not say how he would do this beyond patrolling; he made no mention of transferring fleet units to the Atlantic, and he ignored the crucial question of actual escort of convoys. But toward the end he achieved a stirring climax:

"As the President of a united and determined people, I say solemnly:

"We reassert the ancient American doctrine of freedom of the seas.

"We reassert the solidarity of the twenty-one American Republics and the Dominion of Canada in the preservation of the independence of the hemisphere. . . .

"We in the Americas will decide for ourselves whether, and when, and where, our American interests are attacked or our security is threatened.

"We are placing our armed forces in strategic military positions.

"We will not hesitate to use our armed forces to repel attack. . . .

"Therefore . . . I have tonight issued a proclamation that an unlimited national emergency exists and requires the strengthening of our defense to the extreme limit of our national power and authority. . . ."

Soon after the talk, while Roosevelt happily listened to Irving Berlin play "Alexander's Ragtime Band" and other presidential favorites, telegrams began to come to the White House. Later in the evening Sherwood found the President immensely relieved. Sitting in bed surrounded by hundreds of wires he said: "They're ninety-five per cent favorable! And I figured I'd be lucky to get an even break in this speech." The newspapers in the morning gave him strong editorial support.

The militants were relieved, too; however lacking in specifics, the speech was a moving statement of national resolution and a call to vigorous action. But then came one of the Rooseveltian backtracks that had so often reduced his associates to despair. At a press conference next day, with plaudits still ringing in his ears, the President denied that he planned to use the Navy for convoying escorts, or to ask Congress to change the Neutrality Act, or to issue executive orders to effectuate his proclamation. These comments, Stimson lamented, almost undid the effect of his speech; even Hopkins was perplexed by the shift. The President's determination was soon put to the test. On June 11 reports began to arrive from survivors landing in Brazil of the torpedoing of their ship, the American freighter *Robin Moor,* by a U-boat in the South Atlantic three weeks earlier. Hopkins urged his chief to use the incident as reason to escalate from naval observation patrols to a security patrol to protect American-flag ships. After his first flush of anger, the President refused to do this; he was content to report the sinking to Congress as an example of the kind of Nazi threat he had pictured in his address.

The President still had no strategy except a strategy of no strategy. His main general policy was to wait on events—not any event, but one mighty event—to create the context for action. Such an event was Hitler's invasion of Russia. By the end of June the world was watching the Red Army at bay—and watching London and Washington, too.

ATLANTIC FIRST

So quick, eloquent, and audacious was Churchill's response to Russia's plight that for years his words distorted peoples' memories of the events of late June 1941. "We are resolved to destroy Hitler and every vestige of the Nazi regime," Churchill told the nation barely twelve hours after hearing of the invasion. "From this nothing will turn us—nothing. . . . It follows, therefore, that we shall give whatever help we can to Russia and the Russian people. . . ." Hitler's invasion of Russia, he said, was no more than a prelude to an assault on Britain itself.

Such was the steely rhetoric, but actually the first days of what would become the United Nations were marked by suspicion and near-paralysis. Communication between London and Moscow had been almost nonexistent during the spring months: Stalin and Molotov had kept a frosty distance from Sir Stafford Cripps, the British Ambassador; Churchill and Eden had doubted that Soviet Ambassador Ivan M. Maisky in London had the confidence of his chiefs. The Kremlin had smoldered over Britain's refusal to recognize its writ in the Baltic. Some Russians now wondered if Churchill had instigated the Nazi attack; certainly he wanted it, they judged, and was this the real purpose of the Rudolf Hess caper? Moscow seemed ominously quiet even after Churchill's address.

There were fears in London that the Red Army could not hold out for more than a few weeks. Would the Russians then surrender, or even join Hitler in an attack on Britain? A hundred Nazi divisions smashing and clawing their way east could not overcome years of mutual suspicion and hostility.

Washington had been even cooler than London in its formal posture toward the Soviets. For some weeks Hull and Welles had been parleying about relatively minor matters with the Russian Ambassador, Constantine Oumansky, whom they found fretful and stubborn. Only a week before the invasion the State Department had formalized a position of undertaking no approach to Moscow, treating Russian approaches with reserve, offering concessions only for a strict *quid pro quo,* and making clear to the Russians that improved relations were more important to Moscow than to Washington. Many in the American Army, as in the British, doubted Russia's capacity to stop the Wehrmacht.

Roosevelt's feelings toward Moscow were more mixed than his subordinates'. Often since the auspicious days of late 1933, when he had recognized the Bolshevik government, the President had been frustrated by Soviet policy; he positively disliked Oumansky and saw as little of him as possible. He had no illusions about the dictatorial nature of the Soviet regime, its secretiveness, rigidity, and greed for territory or satellites. On the other hand, he was somewhat optimistic about the Russians holding out—partly because of heartening words from former Ambassador Joseph E. Davies, at this time in Wisconsin. He was confident of his talent for working with any anti-Hitler government. He had a vague optimism about the Soviets' long-run potential for neighborly relations with the democracies. Above all, he feared the possibility of Communist expansion far less than the fact of fascist aggression, and hence wanted to buck up the Soviet defenders—at least with words.

He approved a limp State Department declaration that while fascism and Communism were both bad, fascism was so much worse that any assistance to the anti-Hitler forces, no matter what the source, would benefit American security. He told reporters that "of course we are going to give all the aid we possibly can to Russia," but he was vague as to when and how—and Britain still had priority on American arms production. When Fulton Oursler, of *Liberty,* sent him the draft of his first postinvasion editorial, on the theme "To Hell with Communism" and sharply attacking the Soviet regime, Roosevelt replied that "if I were at your desk I would write an editorial condemning the Russian form of dictatorship equally with the German form of dictatorship—but at the same time, I would make it clear that the immediate menace at this time to the security of the United States lies in the threat of Hitler's armies. . . ."

So Roosevelt's first reactions to Russia's plight were sympathetic, expedient, and cautious. Certainly he would issue no clarion call for a grand coalition against fascism or even for all-out aid to Russia.

He did take a couple of immediate steps, partly as trial balloons. He unfroze forty million dollars of Soviet funds in the United States, but made clear to the press that American aid to Russia would be effective only in the event of a long war, and he was not sure of Soviet needs anyway. His other action was a most effective piece of inaction: by failing to invoke the Neutrality law against Russia he insured that Vladivostok would stay open for American shipping. Otherwise he was content to let Churchill take the lead.

Paradoxically, at the time—and of the highest importance for the future—the first impact of the Nazi invasion of Russia was to push Washington and London closer together behind the Atlantic First strategy. In warning that Hitler's attack on Russia was no more than a prelude to his assault on Britain, Churchill was establishing an even heavier claim on American aid. In Washington, too, pressure on Roosevelt intensified less to send aid to Russia than to escalate naval operations in the Atlantic. Thirty hours after news of the invasion, Stimson wrote to Roosevelt that he had been doing little but reflecting on the implications of this "almost providential occurrence" for sharply stepped-up Anglo-American operations in the Atlantic. It would take Hitler six weeks to two months to clean up Russia, Knox told the President, and that time must not go by "without striking hard—the sooner the better." Within forty-eight hours of news of the attack Admiral Stark was telling the Commander in Chief that he should immediately seize the psychological opportunity to start escorting ships openly. Knox stated publicly that the nation had a "god-given chance" to "clear the path across the Atlantic." Like Stimson, he evidently felt that the Lord was against the Russians, perhaps because the Reds did not recognize Him.

For a moment the President veered toward such a direct approach. He authorized the Navy to escort American shipping, "including shipping of any nationality, which may join such convoys" west of Iceland. Here was a crucial step—the escorting of ships, inevitably including British ships, which would seek the shelter of a United States Navy-protected convoy. Then the President retreated. The actual operations orders of July 25 postponed the escorting of other than American ships.

Once again Knox and the other militants were in despair. Why did their chief not take the direct logical step of simply—and openly—protecting all friendly shipping in the West Atlantic? Their chief had his reasons. He was wary both of congressional opposition and of Far Eastern implications. But more than that, he was waiting on events to propel the nation toward full intervention in the Atlantic. Some events a President can create, however, and the biggest event of July was the American occupation of Iceland.

This project, long in the making, had glinted with complexities. The British had taken over Iceland—a pistol pointed at England, America, and Canada, as Churchill saw it—after its mother country, Denmark, had been overrun in 1940. The British and American military agreed early in 1941 that the United States would defend the island in the event of war. Later, Churchill, in the face of a feared Nazi attack, had hoped that Roosevelt would take it over, partly to relieve British forces, but mainly to hasten combined operations by his and Roosevelt's navies along the great supply routes of the North Atlantic. The President would act only on the invitation of the Icelandic Prime Minister, but this gentleman wanted American protection without having to embarrass his Nazi-supervised government in Copenhagen by asking for it. Patiently Roosevelt worked out a delicate minuet of invitation and acceptance; on July 7 he was ready to announce that the Navy had just arrived in Iceland in order to supplement and eventually replace the British.

Roosevelt could have had no doubt as to the seriousness of his move into Iceland. On June 17 Admiral Stark sent Hopkins a copy of his proposed instructions to the 1st Marine Brigade for "operations" in Iceland. The task: "IN COOPERATION WITH THE BRITISH GARRISON, DEFEND ICELAND AGAINST HOSTILE ATTACK." He wanted the President to approve the order, Stark told Hopkins, because there was so much "potential dynamite" in it. The normal thing to do, he went on, was to put the 4,000 American troops under British command, as the British wanted, but he could not go quite that far. "I have, however, as the President will note, ordered the force to cooperate with the British (in defending a British base operated by the British against the enemy). I realize that this is practically an act of war." Stark got the words he wanted at the bottom of the page—"OK FDR."

The American occupation of Iceland, Churchill told the House of Commons, was an event of "first-rate political and strategic importance"—one of the signal events of the war. Since large American and British traffic would now have to pass through those perilous waters, "I daresay it may be found in practice mutually advantageous for the two navies to assist each other. . . ." So they did, but the nature of the assistance was ambiguous. What were Roosevelt's ships and planes to do in "escorting, covering, and patrolling, as required by circumstances"? Were they to shoot first? On what grounds? At what targets? Or should they wait to be attacked? Decisive events seemed likely to turn on obscure and fugitive factors—visibility in the brumous Atlantic, communication in heavy seas, perceptions of the foe's intentions on the part of young commanders perhaps longing for action.

The uncertainty did not bother Roosevelt, who always thrived on disarray. At the very least he was realizing the simple aim of helping Britain in the North Atlantic; but much more, he was quietly challenging the Nazis on a crucial ocean front—one that they had taken up themselves when Hitler in the early spring had extended the German blockade and combat area to cover Iceland. Roosevelt would not yet order his Navy to shoot on sight; he would not yet openly escort British ships. He would let these things happen by day-to-day chance and necessity in the fog of Atlantic battle.

If ever there was a point when Roosevelt knowingly crossed some threshold between aiding Britain in order to stay out of war and aiding Britain by joining in the war, July 1941 was probably the time. Others, including Morgenthau and Ickes, had crossed this threshold earlier, and more decisively. If Roosevelt was still waiting on events, he was now nudging them in a direction that would deepen the cold war in the Atlantic and produce a crisis.

But his tactics were still at the mercy of Hitler's strategy. And the Führer still saw this situation with unblinking insight. For months Admiral Raeder, apprehensive about the flow of supplies across the Atlantic, had urged him to step up hostilities by seizing the Azores or by attacking American warships and merchantmen or by extending the blockade area. As if to goad his Führer, he drew up a list of twenty unneutral or hostile actions by Washington since the beginning of the war. Hitler was unruffled. Until Operation BARBAROSSA was well under way, he instructed Raeder, he wanted no provocative incident that Roosevelt could seize on to make war. Hitler not only refused to accelerate, but he decelerated. He insisted that Raeder take measures to insure that American vessels not be attacked by mistake—not that he would call a U-boat commander to account, he added, for an honest error.

Hitler had not been led afield by a passing whim of generosity. He reserved the right, he told Raeder, to deal with the United States "severely" after beating Russia. Meantime the Admiral must restrain his raiders and U-boats. Roosevelt must not have his incident.

While Hitler concentrated on Russia and played down the Atlantic in the early summer of 1941, Roosevelt concentrated on the Atlantic and played down the Pacific. Hitler was trying to avoid a showdown with the United States while he dealt with Russia; Roosevelt was trying to avoid a showdown with Japan while he engaged Hitler in the Atlantic. Churchill was dedicated to beating Germany—just how, he was not sure. And Japan wavered between moving north and driving south, all the while concentrating on its effort in China. Such were the main thrusts of the chief antagonists in the early summer of 1941, but in the ponderously swaying mobile of global strategies secondary stresses could throw the opposing weights out of balance.

It was no simple matter, Roosevelt knew, to be belligerent in the Atlantic and pacific in the Pacific. The two fronts were linked in numberless ways: Hitler's hope for Japanese action against Russia; Tokyo's stake in Hitler's attack east; Britain's eastern interests and obligations; Vichy's vulnerable authority over Indochina; the Dutch presence in the East Indies, all combined with the interests of secondary powers. The President had to calculate how these strains and thrusts were cantilevered by the complex and ever-shifting balances of military power and strategy. One blow could put the whole fragile mobile in motion, but in what direction neither he nor any other leader could foretell. He had to consider, too, the internal forces at work—the rivalries in Tokyo between diplomats and the military, between soldiers and sailors, even between sailors and sailors; the extent of the weariness and disarray of Chiang's armies; differences among the men of Vichy as to whether they should fight to hold Indochina. And always the differences at home, within Congress, within the administration, within the State Department and even the White House—and among the people, his constituents.

These were some of the imponderables in the global balance of mid-1941, but Roosevelt did not perceive them in this kind of systematic, categorized frame. He still preferred to deal with situations piecemeal, plucking the day's problem out of the tangle of events, turning it over, seeing its involvement in wider issues but not trying to deal with *them* as a whole. He was not seeking to be a grand strategist. In telling reporters one day that the country was not yet making the effort it should, he quoted with relish, from Sandburg, Lincoln's remarks to some visitors in 1862. The people, Lincoln had said, "have not buckled down to the determination to fight this war through; for they have got the idea into their heads that we are going to get out of this fix somehow by strategy! That's the word—*strategy*. . . ."

If Roosevelt was not making strategy, he was still recognizing priorities—especially the Atlantic over the Pacific. He felt that his policy of "babying" the Japanese along, of keeping them off balance, after two years was holding off a showdown in the Pacific. When Ickes pressed him to cut off oil to Japan, Roosevelt responded that "it is terribly important for the control of the Atlantic for us to help to keep peace in the Pacific. I simply have not got enough Navy to go round—and every little episode in the Pacific means fewer ships in the Atlantic." One trouble with this simple priority was that it could easily be disrupted by a turn of events. And in early summer 1941 Roosevelt's Atlantic First policy was nearly overturned, not by a hostile nation, but by Cordell Hull himself.

By mid-June Hull's long negotiations with Nomura were producing, phrase by phrase, an elaborate formulation for a détente in the Far East. Some of the most controversial points—especially the basis for a Japanese settlement with Chungking—were nebulous, but Tokyo seemed willing at least to discuss some kind of withdrawal from China. Hull's note late in June showed no sign of retreat from principles the Secretary had long preached: Wilsonian morality, international justice, equity, free trade, economic nondiscrimination, neighborly friendship.

All this was pure Hull, and surprised no one. But along with this moralistic note Hull gave Nomura an oral statement that had an unusually sharp edge. After a generous reference to the Ambassador himself it went on to assert that "some Japanese leaders in influential official positions are definitely committed to a course which calls for support of Nazi Germany and its policies of conquest." So long as Japanese leaders took such a position and aroused the people behind it, Hull went on indignantly, how could there be a settlement?

The Hull who asked this question was a tired, disappointed, and somewhat ailing man. After all his efforts to restore morality among nations he could not discern in Tokyo any real spirit of compromise. At times a terrible simplifier himself, he perceived Japanese leaders as neatly divided into two groups, one for peace, the other pro-German. Roosevelt, who had a strong streak of moralizing, too, but who coupled it with realistic and even Machiavellian attitudes, was content to let Hull sermonize to both the good guys and the bad guys in Tokyo while he played his main hand in the Atlantic.

Hull's note arrived in Tokyo during a sticky period for the Konoye government. Matsuoka, under pressure from Hitler and Ribbentrop, had been urging his colleagues to seize this supreme opportunity to erase the Russian menace in the north. Konoye and most of the military feared Russia's hardy Siberian troops and distrusted Hitler; why not wait until the Wehrmacht had broken Russia's back, they still argued, and then move in for the kill? But, insisted Matsuoka, "we can't take the fruits of victory without having done something. We have to either shed blood or engage in diplomacy. It's best to shed blood. . . ." First strike north, he urged, then go south. Nothing ventured, nothing gained. His skeptical colleagues preferred to reverse the order. The next objective, it was decided, was Indochina, with its tin and rubber, strategic relation to China, and fine possibilities as a jumping-off spot for further expansion south. On July 2 the Imperial Conference ratified this plan, at the same time deciding to prepare for—though it did not hope for—war with America and Britain.

". . . The Japs are having a real drag-down and knock-out fight among themselves," Roosevelt wrote to Ickes on July 1, "and have been for the past week—trying to decide which way they are going to jump—attack Russia, attack the South Seas (thus throwing in their lot definitely with Germany) or whether they will sit on the fence and be more friendly with us. No one knows what the decision will be. . . ."

At this point a desperate Matsuoka seized almost with relief on Hull's provocative words. An outrageous communication, he proclaimed to his colleagues. It was inexcusable for Nomura to transmit such a statement. America was seeking to destroy Japanese leadership in East Asia. Roosevelt was a demagogue; he was trying to lead his country into war.

The stage seemed set for a slandered Matsuoka to improve his shaky position through a bellicose policy north and south. But here surprising events intervened. By now Konoye and his colleagues had about enough of the impulsive, talkative Foreign Minister. His spring trip now seemed a fiasco. When Matsuoka stiffly rejected Hull's note without at the same time sending an agreed-on counterproposal, Konoye, playing his hand carefully, asked his

Cabinet to resign; the Prime Minister then reappointed the same members except for Matsuoka. The new Foreign Minister was Admiral Teijiro Toyoda, a friend of Nomura's who was expected to have Washington's confidence. Hull also eased matters by agreeing to the return of his note.

The moment seemed ripe for a détente, but it was already too late. Tokyo was still set on the seizure of Indochina. Washington knew of the planned move because its cryptographers, in a brilliant feat, had broken a key Japanese code. In mid-July Tokyo put pressure on Vichy to allow Japanese troops into Indochina, with the right to use airfields and naval bases at Saigon and elsewhere. Admiral Jean-François Darlan, lacking support from Berlin, capitulated. Forty thousand Japanese troops moved into southern Indochina and quickly took control of the country.

Now it was Washington's turn to wax indignant. Hull feared that Japan was breaking forth on a general program of expansion. Welles told Nomura to his face—and stated to the public next day—that Japan was bent on a policy of force and conquest. The Cabinet militants in Washington seized on Japan's move to urge drastic action.

Now the President intervened. Flanked by Welles and Stark, he told Nomura late in July that he had allowed the continued export of oil to Japan—despite the outcries of oil-starved motorists on the East Coast—in order to prevent a showdown in the Pacific; if Japan now tried to seize East Indies oil, the Dutch would resist, Britain would help them—and a grave situation would result. But if Japan would reconsider its occupation of Indochina, the United States would combine with other Western nations and with Japan to neutralize Indochina in the manner of Switzerland. Nomura, who had told Welles that he personally deplored the move into Indochina, was interested but pessimistic. Roosevelt ended by warning the envoy that Hitler was bent on conquering the world, not merely Europe or Africa.

The next day Roosevelt froze all Japanese assets in the United States, as well as all Chinese, the latter at Chiang's request. He notified Tokyo that the Panama Canal would be closed for repairs, and he took the long-planned step of mustering the Philippine military forces into United States service under Lieutenant General Douglas MacArthur. Newspapers rejoiced at the President's forthright action. Actually he planned to proceed cautiously in denying licenses; he would not cut off all gasoline, for example, but only high octane. His chief, Ickes grumbled, was still unwilling to draw the noose tight. He preferred "to slip the noose around Japan's neck and gave it a jerk now and then." To Stimson the President's fear that cutting off oil altogether would start a war was the "same old rot." Stark and the Navy planners, on the other hand, had warned Roosevelt that an embargo would probably bring more Japanese aggression. So if the President held a noose in one hand he still held out an olive twig in the other.

Tokyo's first reaction to the freeze was bellicose. Toyoda warned Grew that if the United States made any hostile move toward Indochina, "on the exclusively theoretical ground that it contradicts general doctrinaire principles which the American government embrace"—a slap at Hull—Tokyo would not be able to suppress an outburst of nationalist resentment, which was already aroused over American aid to China. Grew now saw the "vicious circle of reprisals and counter-reprisals" heading toward war. No response came to Roosevelt's neutralization proposal.

The crucial question always facing Roosevelt was whether firmness or conciliation would deter the Japanese. Now came a turn that seemed to justify the freeze. The moderates in Tokyo had been surprised by Washington's response to the move south. They, too, were waiting on events: America was angry, Russia was fighting hard, Britain was still intact. They knew that Japan could not desert the Axis, quit China, or pull back from Indochina, but were other compromises possible? The Emperor and his advisers, Konoye, and key Navy leaders began to press during August for serious counterproposals to Washington. Konoye toyed with the idea of a dramatic personal meeting with Roosevelt, perhaps in Hawaii.

Grave differences still separated the two nations, but at the very least these second thoughts in Tokyo would give Roosevelt another month to press his main efforts in the Atlantic.

RUSSIA SECOND

During the foreboding days of early summer 1941 conflict centered in two critical sectors: in the cold gray waters of the North Atlantic and on the vast plains of Mother Russia. And the nature of the struggle in each case would have gladdened the heart of Tolstoy's General Kutuzov.

In Russia the Red Army was reeling back as whole corps were fed piecemeal into the Nazi grinder and simply disappeared. Communications broke down; supply failed; soldiers moved blindly ahead and died; generals blundered and were shot for cowardice. The Russian front turned into an inferno of smashed roads, blazing dumps, crazed horses, blasted tank parks, milling officers and men. Yet in all the confusion and despair, heroism and funk, a General Kutuzov might have seen omens of the future: conscripts from all over the Soviet Union dumped out of freight trains and moving off, cardboard suitcases in hand, toward the front; long lines of Nazi tanks mired in the black mud and waiting for the earth to harden; Russians holding out in trenches, basements, burned-out tanks for days and weeks—and in the Wehrmacht the faint beginnings of doubt as the Russians, unlike Poles and Frenchmen earlier, showed signs of stiffening.

The North Atlantic presented a contrasting face of war. Moving in ten or twelve stately columns, a thousand yards apart, the great convoys of fifty or sixty merchantmen plowed slowly through summer seas. Speedy, sharply wheeling destroyers and corvettes darted back and forth on the ten-mile periphery. Everything was carefully planned: the assembling of the convoys, the evasive ocean routes, the elaborate zigzagging designed to outwit raiders without undue wasted motion. But in the thick, stormy nights, as the screening ships closed in to keep station, anything could happen—including a skirmish between an American destroyer captain, not sure of the application of his orders, and a German U-boat commander, impatient with his.

Ultimately these unlike fronts would become linked by the imperatives of global war, but for the moment all eyes were riveted on the Russian convulsion. By early July the military in both London and Washington were ready to write off the Red Army; it was only a matter of time, the experts said, and of how the West could exploit that time. There was fear that Stalin would quit—or even make another deal with Hitler. Churchill's position was one of pure expediency. He would never forget or excuse Russia's unconcern during the long months that the British alone were manning the ramparts against Germany. When Maisky pressed him for more aid Churchill burst out: "We never thought our survival was dependent on your action either way. . . . You have no right to make reproaches to us!" But there was no question of his immediate position; he would walk with the devil to beat Hitler.

Most Americans were less willing to walk with Satan. The isolationists were having a field day; frustrated by growing support for co-operation with Britain, they eagerly seized on a potent new reason to reject intervention in general and aid to Bolshevik, godless Russia in particular. "The heat is off," proclaimed the Chicago *Tribune* jubilantly. A Communist victory, said Senator Taft flatly, would be far more dangerous than a fascist one. John T. Flynn, columnist for the *New Republic,* demanded: "Are we going to fight to make Europe safe for Communism?" Herbert Hoover opposed any aid to the Soviets because it would simply help Russia seize more land and would make a "gargantuan jest" of fighting Hitler to save democracy. Senator Harry Truman struck a common note: "If we see that Germany is winning we ought to help Russia and if Russia is winning we ought to help Germany and that way let them kill as many as possible, although I don't want to see Hitler victorious under any circumstances. . . ."

Interventionists fell back on expediency. It was not time, warned the Committee to Defend America, to let ideology blind Americans to the need to counter Nazism. Walter Lippmann wrote that Americans should react to the new war as adult men, not as children quarreling over ideology. Many interventionists were pessimistic about Russia's chances of survival and urged that America seize the opportunity to redouble aid to Britain. It was argued, indeed, that such aid would prolong Soviet resistance, for American planes could enable the British to step up their bombing offensive against Germany. The single most important impact of the Nazi invasion, at least in the interventionist press, was to enhance the importance of the Atlantic Alliance and Atlantic First.

And Roosevelt? He had no yen to clash with the militant anti-Communists, the church groups, Polish-Americans, Finnish-Americans, patriotic societies, and a host of other ideological groups. He was trying to see through the clamor of the articulate groups on both sides and divine the feelings of a wider public. Within ten days of the invasion he had received from Hadley Cantril, a noted public-opinion analyst at Princeton, the summary results of recent polls. The Nazi attempt to enlist moral support for a holy war against Russia had so far completely failed with Americans, Cantril reported. The overwhelming majority of Americans wanted Russia to win the war against Germany. But most people opposed helping Russia to as great an extent as Britain; if the invasion produced any change in opinion it was toward more aid to *Britain*. For Roosevelt the policy implication must have been clear: he could aid Russia, but not at the expense of Atlantic First.

Everything depended, Roosevelt felt, on Russia's ability to hold out until winter, and hence on the masses of soldiers manning the long and precarious front, on their officers, on their leaders in the Kremlin—and on the long supply lines to Russia from outside. Could the Soviets hang on? As the Germans plunged deeper into Russia, the President received conflicting advice. The military were still dubious; Ambassador Laurence Steinhardt, in Moscow, was pessimistic at first; former Ambassador Davies remained more hopeful. Late in July a cable arrived from Hopkins, who had returned to London to iron out strategic and logistical questions. Would the President like him to go to Moscow? Stalin could be influenced to maintain a permanent front despite his losses, Hopkins suggested, and a personal envoy might convince him "that we mean business on a long term supply job." Roosevelt jumped at the chance to get his direct line into the Kremlin.

Hopkins, gaunt and ailing, traveled in a Catalina flying boat on the long route north of Norway to the Soviet port of Archangel. After a four-hour banquet and two hours' sleep, he flew on to Moscow, where Steinhardt briefed him on the situation there, grumbled about the Kremlin's secretiveness, and took him to see Stalin.

"I told Mr. Stalin that I came as personal representative of the President," Hopkins reported back to Roosevelt. ". . . I expressed to him the President's belief that the most important thing to be done in the world today was to defeat Hitler and Hitlerism. I impressed upon him the determination of the President and our Government to extend all possible aid to the Soviet Union at the earliest possible time." What did Russia need immediately, Hopkins asked, and what would it require for a long war? Immediately, antiaircraft guns, large machine guns, and rifles, Stalin said; later, high-octane aviation gas and aluminum. "Give us anti-aircraft guns and the aluminum and we can fight for three or four years."

After talks with Molotov and Cripps, Hopkins saw Stalin again. The President, he told Stalin, was anxious to have his analysis of the war. Stalin estimated that the German Army had 175 divisions on Russia's front when the invasion started, had increased this number to 232, and could mobilize a total of three hundred divisions. ". . . Mr. Stalin stated that he can mobilize 350 divisions and will have that many divisions under arms by the time the spring campaign begins in May 1942."

On and on Stalin had talked—about the need to blood his troops so they would realize Germans were not supermen; how Russians still kept fighting even when cut off and left far behind the lines; the impression he had of a slight decrease in German pressure; the quality—in great detail—of the opposing tanks and aircraft; how the Red Army discounted all divisions, whether Finnish, Rumanian, Italian, or Spanish, other than the German. Toward the end he asked Hopkins to give the President the following personal message: ". . . Hitler's greatest weakness was found in the vast numbers of oppressed people who hated Hitler and the immoral ways of his Government." These people could receive the kind of encouragement and moral strength they needed to resist Hitler from only one source, and that was the United States. "He stated that the world influence of the President and the Government of the United States was enormous."

It was inevitable, Stalin had gone on, that the United States "should finally come to grips with Hitler on some battlefield. The might of Germany was so great that, even though Russia might defend herself, it would be very difficult for Britain and Russia combined to crush the German military machine. He said that the one thing that could defeat Hitler, and perhaps without ever firing a shot, would be the announcement that the United States was going to war with Germany. Stalin said that he believed, however, that the war would be bitter and perhaps long; that if we did get in the war he believed the American people would insist on their armies coming to grips with German soldiers; and he wanted me to tell the President that he would welcome the American troops on any part of the Russian front under the complete command of the American Army." This last proffer was an astonishing concession from the ruler of Russia.

There had been no waste of word, gesture, or mannerism, Hopkins remembered later. "It was like talking to a perfectly coordinated machine, an intelligent machine. Joseph Stalin knew what he wanted, knew what Russia wanted, and he assumed that you knew. . . ."

Actually Stalin gave Hopkins a far more hopeful picture of Soviet resistance than the situation then warranted. But Hopkins's reports steeled Roosevelt's determination to speed all possible aid to Russia. During July that aid had been dismayingly low—less than seven million tons of materials—compared to Russia's enormous need. Aid had been caught in a quagmire of problems: the Russians were not exact as to what they needed; each Washington agency, anxious to hoard supplies for its own mission, passed the buck to other "shops"; State, Treasury, and the RFC bickered over measures to buy Russian gold and to extend credits to Moscow; Stimson hated to part with planes already assigned to Britain or to his own forces. Roosevelt had to admit that he could not spare some items—notably antiaircraft guns—because he did not have any himself. But he always had to worry that Stalin, feeling deserted by the perfidious West, might simply quit—or even go over to Hitler's side. And his enemies were becoming noisier at home.

"If somebody kidnaps Wheeler and shanghais him on board an outgoing steamer for the Congo," he wrote to Frankfurter, "can a habeas corpus follow him thither? You need not answer, if you don't want to because it would never get as far as the Supreme Court! Wheeler or I would be dead, first!"

Roosevelt's exasperation came to a head at a Cabinet meeting on August 1. He opened it with a pointed remonstrance on the "runaround" given the Russians during the previous month. "I am sick and tired of hearing that they are going to get this and they are going to get that." He did not want to hear what was on order; he wanted to hear what was on the water. The Cabinet sat agape at their chief's unusual performance; after half an hour of the lecture they tried to reply. Stimson, much annoyed, complained that he had not been informed as to Russia's actual needs. Morgenthau pointed out that with Hopkins away no one in town had authority to get the aid under way. Ickes had a helpful suggestion, too—that one of the newest bombers be sent to Russia by way of Japan, adding that it could set fire to Tokyo on the way by dropping a few incendiary bombs.

The President was not to be put off. He wanted a hundred or more fighters to go to the Soviets right away. "Get the planes right off with a bang next week," he told Stimson, even if they had to be taken from the American Army. He said that he would put one of the best administrators in Washington in charge of the Russian order. The President chose Wayne Coy right after the meeting and instructed him "with my full authority use a heavy hand and act as a burr under the saddle. . . . Step on it."

Coy tried to step on it, but he had a poor engine and a meager gas supply. It was weeks before total exports to Russia reached even thirty million dollars' worth. An air of expediency and feverish improvisation hung over the whole operation. Roosevelt could not make a clear moral issue of aid to Russia because of anti-Soviet attitudes; he could not make a strategic reformulation because he could not bank on Russian survival. His main goal was still simply to prolong Russian resistance. He was committed to a strategy of giving top priority to Britain and the Atlantic nations—a strategy shaped with his military chieftains over a long period and now encased in legislative, bureaucratic, financial, and political channels, interests, and expectations.

Hitler's lunge into Russia and the developing Soviet resistance were rapidly altering power balances around the world, with enormous implications for grand strategy; but the United States was still adhering to a strategy of Atlantic First.

GOVERNMENT AS USUAL

Speed, and speed now, the President had ordered in March, but neither the economy nor the ship of state responded briskly to this call from the bridge. Two months later, war supply was in a state of crisis in the face of voracious demands from Britain for its home defense, from the vast Middle East theater, from Roosevelt's generals and admirals for their own dire needs. In early summer the decision to aid Russia boosted demand once again. Outwardly the President seemed as confident as ever, even debonair, about his mobilization arrangements. Actually the delays and emergencies must have helped cause his occasional sullenness of the spring. No matter how much he improvised he could not overcome the deadly imbalance: war supply was increasing by small increments and break-throughs; war demand, by huge leaps and bounds.

The President put the best face on things even when he knew that progress was unsatisfactory. After giving out some hopeful defense-spending figures at a press conference in early April he jousted with the press.

Reporter: "How much do you think that this should be accelerated in your own mind? You say it is much too slow."

The President: "More."

"What is being done?"

"I can't give you a figure on that."

"What is being done to do that?"

"Well, we will just keep on using 'chestnut burs' all the time. You are familiar with the use of 'chestnut burs' to make a mule go."

"Can you identify the mule?" . . .

"You ought to, you come from Missouri, Frank."

"I came from Minnesota, sir." (By now much laughter)

"Mr. President, what are the main reasons why the progress is, as you say, much too slow?"

"Oh, thousands, thousands of reasons."

"I say the main."

"Individuals—mostly human beings."

"Can you break that down?"

"No."

"Mr. President, do you agree . . . that the next hundred days are going to be crucial in our production program?"

"Yes, and the next hundred after that"—laughing—"and the next hundred after that probably. I can't see as far ahead as that. . . ."

The President created some momentum simply by setting up new agencies. In March, faced with a doubling of strikes since December, he established a National Defense Mediation Board, of three members for the public and four each for labor and industry, to help keep labor peace through conciliation, voluntary arbitration, and fact-finding. In April he set up the Office of Price Administration and Civilian Supply—he had rather liked the term "price *adjustment*"—under Leon Henderson, who had become an increasingly vocal champion of the consumer. In May he created the Office of Civilian Defense, under an even shriller New Dealer and dynamic city administrator, Fiorello La Guardia, of New York, to serve as the co-ordination point for federal, state, and local efforts to protect civilians in emergencies. None of these agencies had much formal authority. The OPA held its breath waiting for its maximum price "schedule" to be challenged in the courts, but the threat of publicity and of denying government contracts enabled Henderson to improvise day by day until a price-control law could be passed. Roosevelt chose La Guardia for civilian defense more for his speechmaking and promotional than his executive abilities.

Conflict and tumult seemed to dog every step Roosevelt's defense chiefs took during this period. Old-line government officials, accustomed to administrative propriety and orderly procedures, sparred with dollar-a-year men who had not been anointed by civil service and were used to more direct action. Though there was never a clear-cut division between military and civilian officials, inevitably the military, under fierce pressure from the commanders down the line, fought for a larger share of the production cake, while civilians tried to protect the manpower and supply needs of farmers and manufacturers. Army and Navy procurement officials competed with one another and even among themselves for scarce items. Disputes broke out not only between agencies but also between different divisions of the same agency and even between hierarchies of the same division.

The loudest clamor rose from a familiar battleground, labor versus management, but now the issue was charged with emotional appeals to Patriotism and Victory. During most of April 400,000 of John L. Lewis's bituminous-coal miners were out on strike, and it took the combined efforts of Secretary Perkins, the NDMB, and the President to settle not only the main bread-and-butter issues but also the question of the forty-cent differential in the daily wage rates between the northern and southern regions. Contests between mine operators and Lewis's miners had become such standing operating procedure in Roosevelt's life as to be an almost comforting sign of normality. Far more distressing was a wildcat strike in early June at the Los Angeles plants of the North American Aviation Company, which was turning out military aircraft.

News of the walkout aroused indignation in the Cabinet next day. Stimson urged strong measures; Hull wanted the Justice Department to make an example of the labor agitators; Jackson raised the question of how aliens could be deported when their motherland—including Russia—would not receive them; Roosevelt suggested loading some of the worst of them onto ships and putting them off on some distant beach with just enough supplies to carry them for a while. Even Hillman, knowing that Communists had goaded the union membership to strike despite pleas from its own leadership, favored a showdown. On June 9 the President ordered the Secretary of War to take over the plant; soon troops mustered in front of it, fixed their bayonets, and drove back the unresisting pickets. But bayonets could not make planes, and it was some time—indeed, late June—before full production was assured. Roosevelt's action brought a flood of congratulatory mail to the White House, but it brought also many protests, especially from a wide range of union people, that this was a step toward fascism. And the episode fueled more charges from Lewis that Hillman was a betrayer of labor, and sharper demands in Congress for restrictive labor laws.

Cutting across most of the conflicts in Washington was one that combined old issues of ideology with urgent new issues of defense. This was expansionism versus "business as usual," as the liberals defined it. New Dealers—some of them in Roosevelt's defense agencies and in the White House itself—charged that big business was deliberately holding down defense production so that it could profit from the civilian sector, now swollen by defense spending; that it was monopolistic and restrictionist and hence unable to go all out for defense. Businessmen pointed to the extensive conversion that had taken place and contended that labor was unwilling to surrender its own restrictive practices and that New Dealers would not sacrifice labor and welfare policies that were a drain on the defense effort. Automobiles pinpointed the issue. With steel and aluminum and other metals in ever-shorter supply, the big auto plants at midyear were still turning out cars and trucks at the rate of four or five million a year. Knudsen as a symbol was an easy target for the liberals and expansionists—how could dollar-a-year men cut back their own industry?

By late spring the mobilization program seemed to be faltering. Economist John Maynard Keynes, in Washington, warned friends of the administration that it must ruthlessly convert to war production even if it meant two or three months of unemployment. There were shortages of such essential munitions as small-arms ammunition, antiaircraft guns and ammunition, and antitank guns. A private report to the President spelled out the bleak picture. Speed in placing ordnance contracts: of an eight-billion-dollar program, a little more than half contracted, and actual cash disbursements less than a billion. Lend-lease: program seven billion, contracts about two billion. Progress of heavy-bomber program: "peak production of 500 monthly not expected until middle of 1943 under present schedules." Even training of seamen for new merchant vessels had fallen behind by more than half. Each of these figures could be documented, the report noted. It was headed simply COULD BE BETTER.

The failures and setbacks were aired in the most visible of all arenas, a Senate investigating committee whose hearings were open to press and public. A Democratic Senator from Missouri, Harry S Truman, had become highly critical of the defense effort, partly because he had been rebuffed in trying to get defense contracts for small businessmen in his state. Re-elected to a second term in 1940, he had made a quiet tour of army camps, quizzed contractors, workers, and officials. After unearthing delays and makeshift he returned to Washington determined to launch an investigation that would expose the failures without emulating earlier Senate wartime committees, which, Truman knew as a student of American history, had infringed on executive power.

The administration was cool at first. Such a probe would be at least an embarrassment and, even under a good Roosevelt man like Truman, might be the entering wedge for a Senate effort to run defense; and Truman, then fifty-seven years old, seemed little more than a parochial politician with a mediocre record of achievement. The White House was far more concerned about the threat of another investigation, proposed by Representative Eugene Cox, of Georgia, a New Deal foe. So, through Byrnes, it was agreed that Truman could go ahead. Roosevelt was not averse to having one more separate source of information on the defense situation; indeed, he had already discussed with defense chiefs a proposal to set up a small organization to prepare data.

The Senate Special Committee to Investigate the Defense Program was approved without opposition from the sixteen Senators then on the floor, though Byrnes did have its appropriation cut to $15,000 and he flanked Truman with four Democrats and two Republicans. Soon the committee was busily delving into the defense effort and winning headlines across the nation. Under the committee's spotlight, officials conceded with unusual candor that sights had been set low, schedules had not been met, the nation had not been aroused to an all-out effort. At one point committee member Tom Connally was almost ready to ask for closed hearings. "We are just advertising to the world . . . that we are in a mess."

Once again clamor arose in the land for stronger leadership by the President. The American people, proclaimed Walter Lippmann, were not being treated as they deserved to be treated. "They are not being dealt with seriously, truthfully, responsibly and nobly. They are being dealt with cleverly, indirectly, even condescendingly and nervously." Frank Kent, in the Baltimore *Sun,* charged that the right kind of spirit did not exist among the people because it did not exist among the leaders. David Lilienthal, visiting Washington from Knoxville, where he ran the Tennessee Valley Authority, was reminded of the early days of 1933—the long hours, the excitement, the confusion, the griping about incompetence. He added in his diary: "But there are differences—the bold strokes of leadership, the clarion call, these aren't quite as fresh and invigorating as then. . . ."

How did the President react to these demands for leadership? Probably more than ever he felt that he understood pace and timing better than his critics did. They simply could not appreciate the web of restraints that surrounded him. It was not enough to cry out to high heaven for leadership and decisiveness. It was a matter of drawing millions of voters, thousands of opinion leaders, and hundreds of fellow politicians in Washington into a following that could be depended on both in the day-to-day exigencies of politics and at times of national crisis and decision making. The last group, the politicians, was the pivotal element. In midsummer the President experienced on Capitol Hill the kind of narrow escape that dramatized the divided government he was trying to lead and the dangers of sticking his chin out too far.

The Selective Service Act of 1940, enacted in the stress of an election year, had contained a politician's compromise—a twelve-month limitation on the selectees' period of service. By early summer 1941 Roosevelt and his defense chiefs faced the prospect of a disintegrating army during the critical months ahead. The President was reluctant to revive the draft debate. He could see all the ingredients for trouble: servicemen charging that a solemn promise had been violated; a new isolationist uproar; a panicky Congress; a possible defeat. His congressional leaders, Rayburn and McCormack, were gloomy over the prospects of a measure to extend the service. Polls showed people to be closely divided on the question. The President allowed Stimson and Marshall to take the initiative; finally, upon their urging, he sent Congress a strong appeal for extension.

Events proceeded more perilously than even Roosevelt could have foreseen. Ham Fish saw the measure as "part and parcel of a gigantic conspiracy" to put the country into war. America First chapters sprang into action. Under Senator Wheeler's frank a million antiwar postcards were sent out; some got into the hands of soldiers, prompting Stimson to accuse Wheeler of near-treason—a charge for which the Secretary later had to apologize. After the administration accepted a series of compromises—including an eighteen-month extension instead of an unlimited one—the bill passed the Senate handily, but the House by the closest shave—203 to 202. Defections took place in each sector of Roosevelt's three-party coalition.

One vote had saved the Army. The episode had been a sorry one for all concerned. Neither the White House nor the War Department had dealt with Congress expertly. The House was simply craven, with even supporters of extension hunting for some way to put the onus on the President. Selectees, openly denouncing their Commander in Chief and the Chief of Staff, began to scrawl OHIO on latrine walls—OVER THE HILL IN OCTOBER. Administration men found on the Hill not only marked opposition to White House policies but also a current of deep personal hostility to and resentment of Roosevelt himself.

Even in the top councils of the administration feeling was mounting that the President was not supplying clear, sustained, and purposeful leadership.

If government as a whole in Washington had not yet responded to the world crisis, "government as usual" almost literally dominated the nondefense effort. Even the White House had to follow customs and procedures inherited from fifteen decades of presidential routine. The Chief of State threw out the first baseball of the 1941 season and watched the Yankees—also following the custom of the day—beat the Senators. He spoke feelingly to the thousands crowding the White House lawn for the annual Easter egg rolling. He greeted the usual delegations and bestowed the usual medals and other honors despite Pa Watson's efforts to cut down on ceremonies. He received the usual tributes, serious and nonsensical; he had to accept a gorilla from Free French forces in Africa, and Fala was chosen president of Barkers for Britain. And he was the target of the usual death threats.

Like all chief executives, the President spent much of his time raising money and recruiting men. By the spring of 1941 soaring defense spending was putting heavy pressure on the peacetime tax structure. Actual spending was doubling and tripling over earlier months. There was a growing concern about equality of sacrifice during the crisis; a Treasury representative told the House Ways and Means Committee that one company with seventy million dollars' worth of defense orders was subject to no excess-profits tax on 1940 earnings, although its profits had multiplied thirty times over the preceding year.

The President blew hot and cold on tax reform, depending in part on his reading of the political thermometer. Both Morgenthau and the House Ways and Means Committee favored a provision to require married couples to file joint income-tax reports in order to end the abuse of the existing provisions by wealthy men in community-property states like California. But Rayburn felt that was "a damn dangerous thing. . . . All the married women and all the working women and all the Catholic priests and the Episcopalians" were against it. Roosevelt told the Treasury that for political reasons the provision must come out. But he pressed for a stronger excess-profits tax, and he astonished the Department by averring that he favored taxing all personal income above $100,000 a year at 99½ or 100 per cent.

"Why not?" he asked. "None of us is ever going to make $100,000 a year. How many people report on that much income?" But he did not press this confiscatory idea. The main need, in any event, was revenue. By summer the deficit was approaching the unprecedented figure of fourteen billion dollars. After asking in the spring for three and a half billion more in taxes, Roosevelt at the end of July recommended lowering exemptions for income-tax payers as a way to gain more revenue and also to let low-income-tax payers feel that they were making some contribution to the defense effort.

It fell to Roosevelt's lot during these months to make the most important of all appointments—and the rarest. On July 1 Charles Evans Hughes, at seventy-nine still the very figure of a Chief Justice, retired from the Supreme Court. The obvious man to succeed him seemed to be Attorney General Jackson, forty-nine, a tested New Dealer, a friend of the President, a good lawyer, and a skillful mediator and negotiator. The press and the organized bar, however, quickly registered their preferences for a sitting member of the high bench, Harlan Stone, sixty-eight, an independent-minded, moderate liberal who had helped lead the Court away from its judicial standpattism of the 1930's toward a recognition of the need for federal power.

For a few weeks suspense mounted as to whether the prize would go to Jackson or Stone—or to a dark horse. "We all think you should be C.J.," a noted lawyer wrote to Stone, "but who can predict what F.D.R. will do? He has not the faintest idea of what goes to make a judge. 'Views' are all he seems to value. . . ." The President consulted his old friend Felix Frankfurter, still a chief New Deal recruiting sergeant, who emphasized a point that was already clear to Roosevelt: the appointment of Stone, a Republican, would bolster the image of the President as a nonpartisan chief of state in time of emergency. The issue was not long in doubt; perhaps it never had been, for Roosevelt was able to give Stone's empty seat to Jackson and thus put him in the running as the new Chief Justice's likely successor.

Stone's appointment won plaudits from most quarters; it was "so clearly and certainly and surely right," said Archibald MacLeish, "it resounded in the world like the perfect word spoken at the perfect moment."

Not all the President's appointments were as easy or felicitous. The defense effort was creating an urgent demand for imaginative executives who could deal with business effectively without bending unduly to pressures. In April the President placed 85,000 additional positions under Civil Service. This action drew praise from "good-government" quarters, but it also betrayed weakness, for the Civil Service system that thwarted corruption and improper influence was also a shield for routineers lacking drive and imagination in the face of new defense needs, and hence for government as usual.

Roosevelt continued to be somewhat ambivalent about political appointments. In defense agencies he saw the need for nonpartisan policies. But he was under pressure from within the White House—even from his aides and secretaries, including Missy LeHand and Grace Tully—to crack down on appointments of lame-duck Republicans, or their assistants, to civilian agencies. He did not mind, he wrote to Jesse Jones, who was considered by New Dealers to be the most notorious offender, that in some of the defense agencies "we are employing dozens of men who have hated the Administration and fought all constructive change for years." But in the regular agencies "I honestly think that we ought to have people work for us who believe in us—not just lip-service. . . . What to do?" Jones stayed mute.

But amid "government as usual" one action of the President during these troubled days of mid-1941 was a sharp departure from tradition—a departure, indeed, that opened a shaft of broken light down the whole course of American life in the years to follow. By the spring of 1941 discrimination in defense industries and—ironically—in federally sponsored training and employment programs was stirring Negro leaders to a new militancy. In April the National Negro Council urged the President to abolish discrimination in all federal agencies by executive order. Meetings of Walter White and fellow black leaders with Hillman and other defense officials brought little but promises; the Negroes wanted an antidiscrimination program with teeth. As a last resort the militant A. Philip Randolph, head of the Brotherhood of Sleeping Car Porters, had proposed a march on Washington unless the administration took stronger action against discrimination. Now White and Lester Granger, of the Urban League, and other leaders picked up the idea. The threatened march would bring tens of thousands of blacks into Washington on July 1.

Roosevelt's attitude toward Negro rights had been a compound of personal compassion, social paternalism, political sensitivity to their increasing articulateness and to racism in Congress, and a practical realization of their importance to the defense effort. For years Eleanor Roosevelt had been trying to develop some rapport between Negro leaders and her husband and his staff; as early as 1935 she had tried to persuade Steve Early that Walter White did not mean to be rude and insulting, that if he was obsessed with the antilynching bill, "if I were colored, I think I should have about the same obsession that he has," that his martyr complex was typical of minority-group people and was "probably an inferiority complex." The general policy of the administration, if it had one, was separate but equal, in the armed forces, in civilian agencies, and—by exhortation—in defense industries, but the separation often thwarted the equality. Roosevelt had discouraged black militance and civil-rights controversy; he had reluctantly conferred with restless Negro leaders; he had also preached "equality of opportunity" again and again in speeches and in letters to Negro organizations. And in the campaign of 1940 he had made more definite pledges to black leaders than ever before. Now civil-rights spokesmen were asking him to deliver on both his principles and his promises.

He watched apprehensively the growing plan for the march. It seemed to offer a rude threat to the image of national unity he was carefully fostering. When direct but quiet pressure failed to budge the leaders, the President appealed to them through his wife. "I feel very strongly that your group is making a very grave mistake," Eleanor Roosevelt wrote to Randolph three weeks before the planned march. "I am afraid it will set back the progress which is being made, in the Army at least, towards better opportunities and less segregation." During this tense period, she went on, an incident might arouse in Congress "even more solid opposition from certain groups than we have had in the past." Crusades were successful sometimes—but not this time.

It was clearly a message from the President as well as the First Lady; still Randolph would not retreat without an executive order against discrimination. Roosevelt tried every compromise move he could: he met with Randolph and White along with his defense chiefs; he ordered the OPM to deal "effectively and speedily" with the problem; he tried all his arts of persuasion and conciliation. He still flatly opposed the march. "What would happen if Irish and Jewish people were to march on Washington?" he asked at the meeting, and answered the question himself: the American people would resent it as coercion.

But the President was beginning to weaken. In late June, with the march still scheduled, he sponsored a meeting of Mrs. Roosevelt, Aubrey Williams, head of the National Youth Administration, and Mayor La Guardia with the Negro leaders in New York. The meeting soon deadlocked, and Randolph and White threatened a march on the Little Flower's City Hall, too. "What for, what have I done?" the Mayor cried. But they managed to negotiate the draft of an executive order, and the President approved it. At almost the penultimate moment the march was called off.

Roosevelt's Executive Order 8802, issued on June 25, 1941, was a pontifical document with very small teeth. The duty of employers and labor unions was "to provide for the full and equitable participation of all workers in defense industries, without discrimination because of race, creed, color, or national origin." Defense contracts were to include such a provision, and federal agencies concerned with vocational and training programs for defense production were ordered to administer them without discrimination. A Committee on Fair Employment Practices was set up in OPM, but without any real policing power. The order—which someday would be called a landmark step in the nation's greatest internal struggle—was greeted with mixed feelings by Negro leaders and with subdued interest on the part of the big-city press. The President granted the committee limited funds, and it was slow to get under way. But it was a beginning.

RENDEZVOUS AT ARGENTIA

Late in the morning of Sunday, August 3, 1941, the presidential train pulled out of a muggy Washington and headed north. Franklin Roosevelt and a small group of friends were off on a boating and fishing expedition. Late in the day the presidential party arrived in New London, Connecticut. There the Commander in Chief was piped aboard his yacht *Potomac,* which in the afterglow of sunset headed into Long Island Sound.

Next morning the yacht, with her presidential banner flapping atop the mast, anchored off South Dartmouth, Massachusetts, in full view of hundreds on shore, took on Princess Martha, of Norway, and her two daughters, Prince Karl, of Sweden, and his party, and sailed out into Buzzards Bay, where the President and his royal guests bottom-fished from the stern of the yacht. They had only fair luck. In the evening the *Potomac* put back into South Dartmouth, the President taking the wheel of a Chris-Craft speedboat to land his guests at the yacht club. Next day the *Potomac,* still flying the presidential flag, proceeded north through the Cape Cod Canal, where onlookers gaped at the big figures of the President and his cronies sitting on the afterdeck.

But it was not the President they saw. Late the evening before, the *Potomac* had sped to the quiet waters off the western end of Martha's Vineyard, where seven darkened warships were waiting. Early the next morning the President and his mess crew were transferred to the heavy cruiser *Augusta.* His top military command were already on board. Soon the *Augusta* was steaming east past Nantucket Shoals Lightship; then it swung north. Admiral Ernest J. King, in command, had taken all precautions; destroyers were disposed ahead off both bows; swinging out from the prow of the *Augusta* were batteries of sharp steel knives to cut mine cables; recently installed radar peered through the mists. Two days later the little fleet sighted the coast of Newfoundland and soon put into Argentia Harbor, in a small bay rimmed by low hills covered by scrawny pines and brush. Here the Americans awaited Winston Churchill, who was proceeding west on the *Prince of Wales.*

It would be a meeting the President and the Prime Minister had long hoped for, a meeting that had been forced to wait on the tumultuous events of 1940 and 1941. As experts in the dramatic, they had set the stage carefully. To sharpen the suspense—and to discourage undue fears and expectations at home—Roosevelt had insisted on the tightest secrecy; even Grace Tully had had no hint of the trip. Such precautions meant hasty staff preparation and no agenda; the military chiefs were given the latest possible notice.

The President's son Franklin was ordered to report so abruptly to the "Commander in Chief" on the *Augusta* that he feared he was in for some kind of dressing down from Admiral King; Elliott Roosevelt, summoned from his air-reconnaissance squadron in Newfoundland, was equally mystified. Churchill had preferred a more publicized rendezvous; he wanted to dramatize Anglo-American unity, conduct meaningful discussions, plan definite steps, win major commitments. Roosevelt wanted merely to meet Churchill, feel him out, exchange ideas and information, and achieve a moral and symbolic unity.

Early on August 9 the huge battleship *Prince of Wales,* still scarred from her encounter with the *Bismarck,* loomed out of low-hanging mists and dropped anchor. Soon Churchill was clambering aboard the *Augusta,* while the President stood arm in arm with Elliott and the band played the national anthems. "At last," said Roosevelt, "we've gotten together." The Prime Minister handed the President a letter from the King; staffs were presented to each other; soon the two men were meeting alone, except for Hopkins, who had come over on the *Prince of Wales* with Churchill. By the time Elliott joined them after lunch the men were deep in problems of Lend-Lease, diplomacy, and American public opinion. In the evening, after the two leaders and their staffs shared broiled chicken, spinach omelet, and chocolate ice cream in the *Augusta*'s mess, Churchill, at Roosevelt's invitation, gave one of his enthralling appreciations of the military situation.

Rearing back in his chair, slewing his cigar around from cheek to cheek, hunching his shoulders forward, slashing the air with his hands, the Prime Minister described battles won and lost, spoke dourly of Russia's chances, and in his great rolling phrases conveyed all at the same time a sense of Britain's indomitability and its need for American intervention.

Roosevelt listened intently, fiddled with his pince-nez, doodled on the tablecloth with a burned match, occasionally put in questions. Next day, Sunday, he paid a return visit to the *Prince of Wales.* On the quarterdeck under the big guns President and Prime Minister attended religious services in the company of several hundred intermixed tars, bluejackets, and Marines spread out over the decks and turrets. It was another unforgettable ceremony, the Union Jack and Stars and Stripes draped side by side on the lectern, the President grave and attentive, Churchill, his Navy cap slightly askew, tearfully singing "Onward, Christian Soldiers," American and British chaplains sharing in the reading of the prayers. It was a time to live, Churchill later reflected; nearly half of those who sang were soon to die.

Then to the business at hand. As the President expected,

Churchill pressed from the start for stepped-up American action in the Atlantic and a stronger line in the Pacific. Despite the hopeful reports of Hopkins from Russia and continuing intelligence that the forces before Moscow were holding out, the two leaders evaluated aid to Russia on the basis of what could be spared from Atlantic and home needs. Churchill still was seeing Soviet aid as a temporary expedient; Roosevelt, more as a long-term enterprise; but neither was yet ready to gamble heavily on Soviet survival.

Roosevelt did not want to go, in the Atlantic, beyond the recently agreed-on policy of American escorts for all fast convoys between Newfoundland and Iceland. But his willingness to stretch neutrality past this breaking point was clear from his commitment on other Atlantic islands. Churchill told him that he planned to occupy the Canary Islands, perhaps even before a still-feared Nazi attack through Spain. Such a move, Churchill conceded, would inevitably cause a German-supported counterattack by Spain, in which case Britain could not live up to its promise to Portugal to defend the Azores. Would the United States do so instead? Roosevelt agreed, on the understanding that Portugal would make the request of him. Later Churchill called off the attack on the Canaries, but the incident showed how far Roosevelt was willing—given a crisis situation in Iberia—to allow a move as important as the occupation of the Azores to turn on Churchill's initiative.

Churchill was ready with a hard line on Japan, too. Following the Sunday services he proposed to Roosevelt a joint declaration to Tokyo that "any further encroachment by Japan in the Southwest Pacific" would produce a situation in which Britain and the United States "would be compelled to take counter measures even though these might lead to war" between Japan and the two nations. Churchill, under pressure from the Dutch and the Pacific Dominions to enlist American aid if Japan attacked, wanted to intertwine American and British efforts in the Pacific just as had been done in the Atlantic. Above all, Churchill feared a showdown that would leave Britain, with its weakened defenses in Southeast Asia, holding the fort alone against the Japanese. He was certain that only the stiffest warning from Washington would have any deterrent effect.

Roosevelt was more wary. Even less than Churchill did he seek a war with Japan, but while the Prime Minister thought a showdown could be avoided through firmness, the President preferred to drag things out, to parley, to stall the Japanese along, to let them save face, at least for a month or so. Hence, instead of sending off Churchill's near-ultimatum, he proposed to inform Nomura that if Tokyo would promise to pull out of Indochina, Washington would try to settle remaining issues with Japan, but that if the

Japanese failed to respond to this proposal and continued their military expansion, the President would then have to take steps that might result in war between the United States and Japan. Churchill went along with this procedure, which left the initiative wholly with the President.

By now both men must have seen the veiled but acute differences that separated them on Japan. Churchill could gamble on a strong line, for such a line would either compel Japan to give up China and Indochina and further expansion and take the pressure off the British in the Far East, or it would produce an explosion. An explosion that propelled the United States into a Pacific war would project it into the Atlantic war, too—Churchill's cardinal goal. The President preferred to delay any showdown until his Army and Navy were stronger, public opinion more receptive, and a two-front war more manageable. Meantime, he would follow his policy of Atlantic First.

While the two leaders agreeably negotiated and gently sparred, the military chiefs conducted almost wholly separate discussions on the *Prince of Wales*. First Sea Lord Sir Dudley Pound, Sir John Dill, and their cohorts tried to convince the Americans that increased aid and even intervention now would bring victory much sooner and more cheaply; the American Joint Chiefs tried to show the bareness of their cupboard, drained as it had been by the needs of Britain and other nations. Already in the discussions there were harbingers of future disagreement, as the British seemed bent on bombing, blockading, enveloping, and wearing out Germany, while the Americans—particularly Marshall—contended that it would be necessary for Allied ground forces to invade the Continent and close with the enemy. There were happier omens, too—especially the discovery that American and British officers could differ and occasionally clash, but also communicate, agree, and forge a closer working co-operation, each with considerable respect for the other side.

Strangely, the significance of the Argentia Conference would lie far less in strategic decisions and commitments, of which there were virtually none, than in a discussion of war aims toward which Roosevelt and Churchill had done little advance planning, but out of which came the Atlantic Charter, one of the most compelling statements of the war.

The President had discouraged open talk in the administration of specific postwar aims. It was all right to discuss lofty objectives, but debate over ways and means, he felt, might create dissension and divert attention from immediate diplomatic and military problems. Then, too, discussion of postwar matters assumed that there would be "war" first—which in turn could reopen old wounds from the League of Nations battle. "I have not the slightest objection toward your trying your hand at an outline of the post-war picture," he told Adolf A. Berle in June. "But for Heaven's sake don't ever let the columnists hear of it. . . ."

But events in 1941 forced Roosevelt's hand. The Russo-German war was already raising dire questions of the future of truncated Poland; the Polish government-in-exile in London had to be considered, as did the big Polish voting blocs at home. Roosevelt was concerned that London might be making secret territorial deals, as in days of yore. Hull and Welles were already pressing for nondiscriminatory postwar economic policies. And there was a large body of sentiment among both Roosevelt's and Churchill's constituents for an evocation of moral principles and a statement of war aims—especially as to a new League of Nations.

It was best, Roosevelt had decided, to stick to very general principles and to very realistic, functional institutions. Churchill, always eager to couple British and American policy more tightly, wanted to make more specific commitments. He and his aides produced a draft that started off with high-sounding promises and got down to business in a call for "fair and equitable distribution of essential produce" both between and within nations. Welles was disturbed by the vagueness of this economic plank. A Wilsonian himself, he could never forget that his chief back home would be acutely displeased if the way was left open for autarchy. After some sharp bargaining with Churchill, while Roosevelt looked on sympathetically, the Undersecretary gained as strong a statement as the Prime Minister felt would be acceptable to the Dominions, with their stake in imperial preference. There was no reference to trade liberalization, to Welles's keen disappointment.

The crucial discussion of war aims came late in the morning of August 11 in the Admiral's quarters on the *Augusta,* which served as Roosevelt's office and mess. Bright sunlight streamed through the portholes. Roosevelt sat in a gray suit, his shirt open at the collar; Churchill was still in naval uniform; Welles and Hopkins and one or two of the British staff sat by. The meeting was somewhat strained. Churchill was still upset by Welles's demand for free trade, and by Roosevelt's proposal that their joint statement make clear that there had been no commitments for the future between the two governments. Commitments were precisely what Churchill wanted to bring back to his country and to hearten the occupied nations. But the President feared the isolationist reaction to "secret agreements," and Churchill had to settle for only slightly stronger language.

It was on postwar international organization that the two leaders had their bluntest confrontation. Churchill asked the President if the charter could explicitly endorse some kind of "effective international organization." Roosevelt demurred; he said that he himself would not favor the creation of a new Assembly of the League of Nations, at least until after a period of time during which a British-American police force maintained security. Churchill warned that a vague plank would arouse opposition from strong internationalists. Roosevelt agreed, but he felt that he had to be politically realistic. Churchill gave in, with the understanding that he could add some language that would strengthen the plank without uttering the dread words "international organization" or invoking the ghost of Woodrow Wilson.

The final text of the Charter was agreed to on August 11. It read:

The President of the United States of America and the Prime Minister, Mr. Churchill, representing His Majesty's Government in the United Kingdom, being met together, deem it right to make known certain common principles in the national policies of their respective countries on which they base their hopes for a better future for the world.

FIRST—Their countries seek no aggrandizement, territorial or other;

SECOND—They desire to see no territorial changes that do not accord with the freely expressed wishes of the peoples concerned;

THIRD—They respect the right of all peoples to choose the form of government under which they will live; and they wish to see sovereign rights and self-government restored to those who have been forcibly deprived of them;

FOURTH—They will endeavor, with due respect for their existing obligations, to further the enjoyment by all states, great or small, victor or vanquished, of access, on equal terms, to the trade and to the raw materials of the world which are needed for their economic prosperity;

FIFTH—They desire to bring about the fullest collaboration between all Nations in the economic field with the object of securing, for all, improved labor standards, economic advancement, and social security;

SIXTH—After the final destruction of the Nazi tyranny, they hope to see established a peace which will afford to all Nations the means of dwelling in safety within their own boundaries, and which will afford assurance that all the men in all the lands may live out their lives in freedom from fear and want;

SEVENTH—Such a peace should enable all men to traverse the high seas and oceans without hindrance;

EIGHTH—They believe that all of the Nations of the world, for realistic as well as spiritual reasons, must come to the abandonment of the use of force. Since no future peace can be maintained if land, sea, or air armaments continue to be employed by Nations which threaten, or may threaten, aggression outside of their frontiers, they believe, pending the establishment of a wider and permanent system of general security, that the disarmament of such Nations is essential. They will likewise aid and encourage all other practicable measures which will lighten for peace-loving peoples the crushing burden of armaments.

[Signed] FRANKLIN D. ROOSEVELT
[Signed] WINSTON S. CHURCHILL

The *Prince of Wales* steamed out of Argentia Harbor late on the twelfth, as Roosevelt stood on the *Augusta* quarterdeck close by and the band played "Auld Lang Syne." The two leaders parted as friends and comrades. Roosevelt had learned something of Churchill's persuasiveness and persistence; Churchill had found how hard it was to commit the President when he refused to be cornered. Each had glimpsed the other's political problems—Churchill, the continuing threat of American isolationism, memories of World War I and the League, fear of binding commitments; Roosevelt, the claims of the Dominions and Empire on London, the Prime Minister's need to clear decisions with his War Cabinet within the hour, the hunger of the British for a far better postwar world than they had known. The two had amused, propagandized, flattered, annoyed, upstaged, and yielded to each other; their friendship had survived intact, deepened, and was ready for the heavier pressures to come.

The *Augusta* stood out to sea shortly after the British departed. It seemed as though history could not let go of the event. A journey that began in the company of old Scandinavian royalty and culminated in a convocation of the political and military leadership of the Atlantic world ended on the coast of Maine, with a visit from the President's old headmaster, Endicott Peabody. And as Roosevelt left Portland by train, a young assistant to Secretary Knox, referred to in the Navy log as "Adelai Stevenson," hurried in to see the President on an urgent strike matter.

It remained for Felix Frankfurter to take the full measure of the Atlantic meeting. The Justice was wont to write fulsome letters of praise to the President, but for once he did not rise above the occasion. Not even constant misuse could rob some phrases of their noble meaning, he wrote. Somewhere in the Atlantic, Roosevelt and Churchill *had* made history for the world.

"And like all truly great historic events, it wasn't what was said or done that defined the scope of the achievement. It's always the forces—the impalpable, the spiritual forces, the hopes, the purposes, the dreams and the endeavors—that are released that matter. . . .

"It was all grandly conceived and finely executed. . . . The deed and the spirit and the invigoration of a common human fraternity in the hearts of men will endure—and steel our will and kindle our actions toward the goal of ridding the world of this horror."

FOUR *Showdown in the Pacific*

NEWS OF Argentia broke up Washington's summer doldrums, at least for a time. Democratic leaders in Congress hailed the Atlantic Charter as a magnificent statement of war aims—indeed, as a signpost to "real and lasting peace." Hiram Johnson and Robert Taft accused Roosevelt of making a secret alliance and planning an invasion of Europe. The New York *Times,* billing the pledge to destroy Nazi tyranny in an eight-column headline, proclaimed that this was the end of isolationism, while the New York *Journal-American* accused the President of retracing, one by one, all the steps toward war taken by Wilson. Colonel McCormick's Chicago *Tribune,* irked by the Roosevelt-Churchill togetherness, reminded its readers that the President was "the true descendant of that James Roosevelt, his great-grandfather, who was a Tory of New York during the Revolution and took the oath of allegiance to the British King." Both friend and foe saw the meeting as a prelude to more aggressive action.

But not Roosevelt, evidently. Having taken a dramatic step forward, he executed his usual backward hop. Aside from a lackluster message to Congress incorporating the declaration, he took little action to follow it up. At the first press conference after the meeting, on the *Potomac,* reporters found him cautious. What about actual implementation of the broad declarations, he was asked. "Interchange of views, that's all. Nothing else." Were we any closer to entering the war? "I should say, no." Could he be quoted directly? "No, you can quote indirectly."

But the meeting at sea did seem popular with the people, according to the pollsters. Seventy-five per cent of those polled had heard about the eight-point credo, and of those about half indicated full or partial approval, while only a quarter of them were cool or hostile. Many were indifferent or uninformed, however, and this number grew as time passed. Five months later most people remembered the two men meeting, but few remembered anything about the Charter itself.

Nor did the conference seem measurably to change popular attitudes toward Roosevelt's aid-to-Britain program. Those attitudes seemed almost fixed during most of 1941. Asked in May, "So far as you, personally, are concerned, do you think President Roosevelt has gone too far in his policies of helping Britain?" about a quarter answered "too far," about a quarter "not far enough," and half "about right." This pattern persisted with remarkable stability into the fall; evidently the President was shifting step by step with the movement of opinion. On the face of it he was acting as a faithful representative of the people; a majority endorsed his policies and he fell evenly between the critics of both wings. As he took increasingly interventionist action "short of war," he was holding the great bulk of public support.

The troubling question remained whether, in view of the critical situation abroad, he should be more in advance of opinion than representative of it, more of a catalytic or even a divisive agent than a consensual one, more of a creator and exploiter of public feeling than a reflector and articulator of it.

This was the question Stimson kept raising. When the President phoned him early in the summer to tell him that he had some good news—that a forthcoming Gallup Poll was going to be much more favorable than the Gallup people had expected—Stimson reminded him again that all these polls omitted one factor which the President seemed to neglect—"the power of his own leadership." Roosevelt had not denied this but had complained that he simply did not feel peppy enough.

It was leadership and decision, after all, that American strategists needed, not merely symbol and pageantry. Early in July the President had asked Stimson to join with Knox and Hopkins in exploring over-all production needs in order to "defeat our potential enemies." For ten weeks the defense Secretaries had struggled with the question, and then given up. Everything depended on what assumptions they were working under, Stimson wrote to his chief—whether the United States promptly engaged in an avowed all-out military effort against Germany, or merely continued its present policy of helping nations fighting the Axis with munitions, transport, and naval help. The Army, Navy, and Air strategists were united in preferring active participation in the war against Germany, Stimson went on, but work could not be concluded until the President's views were known.

The military uncertainty was reflected right down the army line. A *Nation* reporter spent ten days in August tramping up and down Times Square talking with over three hundred Regular soldiers, draftees, National Guardsmen. They were a breezy, cocky lot, confident that any one of them could lick the Germans or an infinite number of Japanese. But, except for the Regulars, they hated the Army, Roosevelt, General Marshall, and Negroes in about equal degree. Few had any idea why they were in the Army or what the Army was for. Some were America Firsters—but they had little suspicion that the Commander in Chief was trying to drag the United States into war. They simply seemed confused. They neither attacked nor defended Roosevelt's foreign policy; they just did not seem to care.

But there was some logic to their position. They understood the President's policy of aid to Britain short of war, but if the nation was not preparing to fight Germany, "Why this Army?"

THE WINDS AND WAVES OF STRIFE

The President had promised Churchill at Argentia that he would use hard language in his message to Tokyo; the Prime Minister had feared that the State Department would try to water it down, and he was right. Hull and his aides felt that the warning might arouse the extremist wing in Japan, and by the time they finished massaging the message it was one more general warning. The President went along with the change. He decided that he could deliver the warning more effectively at a direct confrontation with Nomura. On Sunday afternoon, August 17, 1941, the Japanese Ambassador arrived at the White House.

The old Admiral was hard of hearing, had a glass eye, spoke English uncertainly, and was so fuzzy at times that Hull wondered if he understood his own government's position, let alone Washington's. But he was affable and had an encouraging way of nodding responsively, with an occasional mirthless chuckle, to Roosevelt's and Hull's main points. The President, in fine fettle after his two weeks at sea, made some pleasant remarks and then spoke gravely, contrasting his country's peaceful and principled record in the Far East, as he saw it, with Japan's conquests through force. Did the Admiral have any proposal in mind? Nomura did. Pulling a paper from his pocket, he said that his government was earnestly desirous of peaceful relations—and Premier Konoye proposed a meeting with the President midway in the Pacific.

The President seemed unperturbed at losing the initiative just as he was about to issue his warning. He read the watered-down statement anyway. Even this weak message Roosevelt presented almost defensively. Indeed—or so Nomura reported to Tokyo—the President finally handed him the oral remarks as a matter of information. The lion's roar of Argentia had become a lamb's bleat. Even so, Roosevelt reported to Churchill that his statement to Nomura was "no less vigorous" than the one they had planned.

Konoye's offer to meet Roosevelt was a weak card played from a shaky hand. Dropping Matsuoka had not eased the Premier's situation at home. Washington's reaction to the Indochina occupation had been sharper than Tokyo expected; the freeze seemed a direct threat to national survival. The Emperor, Konoye knew, was uneasy about the drift toward conflict with America. The Army under Tojo still took its old expansionist line, but now, to the Premier's alarm, the oil-conscious Navy was swinging to a more militant stance. The jingo press was attacking Washington for sending oil to Russia via Vladivostok and "Japanese" waters; officials lived under heavy police guard against assassination; extremists in the middle ranks of the Navy and Army were a constant threat. A dramatic meeting with Roosevelt might break the deepening spiral, Konoye calculated, arouse the moderates among the people, enlist the Emperor's backing, and present the militarists with a *fait accompli.* He won Tojo's grudging acquiescence to a parley on condition that if the meeting failed—as the War Minister expected it would—the Premier would return home not to resign but ready to lead the war against the United States.

Playing for the highest stakes, Konoye was so eager for a summit conference that he had Foreign Minister Toyoda sit down with Ambassador Grew and plead, on a long, stifling evening, for Grew's support for the idea. He prepared a special ship for the voyage to the conference and planned to take a brace of admirals and generals, all of them moderates, to "share responsibility" with him. In order to bypass Hull, Nomura would deliver Konoye's invitation to the President personally; a conciliatory note was prepared for Hull in a style calculated not to excite him.

The notes that Nomura handed Roosevelt on the morning of August 28 were full of benevolence and vague promises. Konoye renewed his invitation to meet—and to do so soon in the light of the present situation, which was "developing swiftly and may produce unforeseen contingencies." Roosevelt remarked that he liked the tone and spirit of Konoye's message. The note from the Japanese government indicated its willingness to withdraw from Indochina as soon as the China incident was settled, not to attack Russia, and indeed not to attack anyone, north or south. Roosevelt interrupted the reading of the note to offer some small rebuttals, and he could not resist the temptation, with what seemed to Nomura a cynical smile, to ask whether there would be an invasion of Thailand while he might be meeting with Konoye, just as Indochina had been invaded during Hull's conversations with Nomura.

Still, Roosevelt was sorely tempted to parley. A rendezvous in the Pacific would be a dramatic counterpart to his trip to Argentia; the Japanese seemed to be in a conciliatory mood; and he always had confidence in his ability to persuade people face to face. He even proposed Juneau as a place to confer, on the ground that it would require him to be away two weeks rather than three. But now the President ran into serious difficulties among his advisers.

Hull and the old Far Eastern hands in his Department opposed a conference unless the major questions were settled—and settled to Washington's liking—in advance. The Secretary seemed to take a mixed approach to Japan: he never tired of stating his principles and flailing Japan for not living up to them; he opposed conciliation because he had no faith in Konoye's ability to check the military; but he also opposed drastic action. He had both a devil theory of Japanese politics and an aversion to a showdown—an ambivalence that precluded any consistent policy except endless pieties, conversations, and delays. And Hull could hardly have welcomed another ocean conference where the President, off in the heady sea breezes with advisers like Welles and Hopkins, might take steps—like the warning to Japan drawn up at Argentia—that could upset Hull's patient diplomacy.

In Tokyo, Grew took the opposite stand. Though long a hard-liner toward Japan, he had seized on a Pacific rendezvous as the last-best hope of averting a showdown. He urged Hull not to reject the Japanese proposal "without very prayerful consideration." Konoye would not request such a meeting, he argued, unless he was willing to make concessions; he was determined to overcome the extremists, even at peril to his own life. At the most, Grew contended, Japan would make concessions on Indochina and China; at the very least a meeting would slow the growing momentum toward a head-on collision. He ended with a grim warning: if the meeting did not take place, new men would come to power and launch a do-or-die effort to take over all of Greater East Asia—which would mean war with the United States.

When faced with conflicting advice Roosevelt rarely made immediate clear-cut choices; in this case he took the expedient course of continuing to talk hopefully of a meeting while following Hull's advice to demand agreement on fundamental principles before consenting to a rendezvous. Calling Nomura to the White House on September 3, the President carefully dealt with the Japanese proposal of the week before. He appreciated Konoye's difficulties at home, he told the Ambassador, but he had difficulties, too. While Hull sat by, Roosevelt read the Secretary's four fundamental principles: respect for other nations' territorial integrity and sovereignty; noninterference in other nations' internal affairs; equality of commercial opportunity; nondisturbance of the *status quo* in the Pacific except through peaceful means. He was pleased, said the President, that Japan had endorsed these principles explicitly in its note of August 28. But, since there was opposition to such principles in certain quarters in Japan, what concrete concessions would Tokyo make in advance of the summit conference?

While Roosevelt played for time, other less visible decision makers in Japan were facing their own urgencies during August. Washington's freezing order of late July along with increasing indications that Russia would hold on were forcing Army and Navy planners in Tokyo to abandon thoughts of attacking the Soviets from the rear, at least during 1941, and to look south. The only way to overcome American, British, and Dutch power, it was decided, was through a series of lightning attacks. Such a plan would be heavily dependent on weather—on tides, phases of the moon, monsoons—and on moving fast, before oil gave out. On September 3 the military chiefs and the Cabinet met in a liaison conference. "We are getting weaker," Navy Chief of Staff Osami Nagano stated bluntly at the outset. "The enemy is getting stronger." A timetable must be set. Military preparations must get under way even while diplomacy continued. While Cabinet members sat by, Navy and Army chiefs soberly discussed plans. Finally it was agreed: "If, by the early part of October, there is still no prospect of being able to attain our demands, we shall immediately decide to open hostilities against the United States, Great Britain, and the Netherlands."

So a timetable had been set. In all the tortuous windings toward war, this was the single most crucial step. Why did Konoye agree? Partly because he had high hopes for his conference with Roosevelt—he would let the military play their game if they would let him play his. And partly because of the Emperor, who presumably could keep the military in line. On September 5 Konoye's Cabinet unanimously approved the action of the liaison conference. The Premier then hurried to the palace to inform the Emperor.

Hirohito was in an almost imperious mood. He listened to Konoye with apparently rising concern, then questioned him sharply. Were war preparations gaining precedence over diplomacy? Konoye said no, but suggested that the Emperor ask the military chiefs. Nagano and the Chief of the Army General Staff, Hajime Sugiyama, were summoned to the throne room. The Emperor questioned Sugiyama on military aspects of the plan. How long would a war with the United States last? For the initial phase about three months, the General said. The Emperor broke in: Sugiyama as War Minister in 1937 had said that the China incident would be over in a month; it was still going on. This was different, Sugiyama said; China was a vast hinterland, while the southern area was composed of islands. This only aroused the Emperor further. "If you call the Chinese hinterland vast would you not describe the

Pacific as even more immense?" Sugiyama looked down at his boots and was silent.

Next morning Hirohito called in his Lord Keeper of the Privy Seal, Koichi Kido. In a few minutes an imperial conference was to start; the Emperor had decided that he would speak out, he told Kido, and inform the military that he would not sanction war as long as the possibility of a settlement remained. Kido said smoothly that he had already asked Yoshimichi Hara, the President of the Privy Council, to ask the questions for the Emperor; it would be more appropriate for His Majesty to make any comments at the end.

Soon the Cabinet and the Chiefs of Staff were seated across from the Emperor on hard chairs in the east wing of the palace. One after another his ministers went through their carefully prepared recitations. The Empire would go to war by the end of October, declared Konoye, unless diplomacy had achieved its "minimum demands." These were: America and Britain should not hinder settlement of the China incident; they would cease helping the Chungking regime; they would not strengthen their military position in the Far East; they would co-operate with Japan economically. Japan's "maximum concessions" were: not to advance militarily from Indochina; to withdraw its forces from Indochina after peace was established; to guarantee the neutrality of the Philippines.

Nagano spoke next. Vital supplies—especially oil—were dwindling. Time was vital. He sketched the necessary strategy if war broke out. If the enemy aimed for a quick war and early decisions and dispatched their fleet, "this would be the very thing we hope for." With aircraft "and other elements" he could beat them in the Pacific. More likely, though, "America will attempt to prolong the war, utilizing her impregnable position, her superior industrial power, and her abundant resources." In a long war Japan's only chance, after the first quick strikes, was to seize the enemy's major military areas, establish an impregnable position, and develop military resources. Sugiyama then spoke up. He expressed the Army's complete agreement with Nagano. Japan must not mark time and be trapped by Anglo-American intrigue and delays. Intensive troop movements were required. If negotiations failed, a decision for war must be made within ten days of the failure at the latest. Others spoke, but there was no break in the united front.

The Emperor became flushed as Hara went through set questions and received set replies. A hush fell on the room. His Majesty was not satisfied with the assurances about diplomacy first. He drew a slip from his pocket and in his high voice read a poem composed by his grandfather the Emperor Meiji:

"All the seas, in every quarter,
are as brothers to one another,
Why, then, do the winds and waves of strife
rage so turbulently throughout the world?"

The Emperor's meaning was clear. All present were struck with awe, Konoye remembered, and there was silence throughout the hall. Nagano assured the Emperor that the whole Cabinet favored diplomacy first. The meeting adjourned in an atmosphere of unprecedented tension.

At just about this moment, on the other side of the world, the American destroyer *Greer* was speeding through North Atlantic waters on a mail run to Iceland. These waters were in both the German war zone and the American defense zone. A British patrol plane signaled her that a submerged U-boat lay athwart her course ten miles ahead. The *Greer* speeded up, sounded general quarters, zigagged toward the submarine, made sound contact, and began trailing the U-boat and reporting its exact position to the plane, but with no intention of attacking it. After an hour the plane dropped four depth charges without effect and turned back to refuel; the *Greer* hung on her quarry's trail. After two hours of this the submarine suddenly launched a torpedo at the *Greer,* and then one or two more. The *Greer* dodged them and began dropping a circle of depth charges, meantime losing contact. Over two hours later the *Greer* made contact again and dropped eleven more depth charges. The *Greer* trailed the U-boat a while longer, then broke off the pursuit, leaving it in the hands of British destroyers and planes in the area.

At last Roosevelt had his incident. It was not much of an incident, since the *Greer* had sought out the submarine and had jeopardized it by broadcasting its position; moreover, there was no indication (as the White House was informed) that the Germans even knew whether the destroyer was British or American. But shots had been exchanged in anger, and Roosevelt felt that here was his chance to dramatize the Nazi menace that he had long been picturing. He found Hull in an equally stern and even aggressive mood; the Secretary waxed so indignant about the situation that the President asked him to put it all in writing for a White House address. It was announced that the President would make a major statement the following Monday. Churchill wired that all were awaiting his speech with profound interest. The President went to Hyde Park for the weekend.

While he was there, on Saturday, September 6, his mother died, suddenly and peacefully, in her pleasant corner room looking out toward the Albany Post Road. What private grief Roosevelt felt at this loss, breaking his main link with his childhood, no one could tell, for he said little. But perhaps Mackenzie King was uttering Roosevelt's own thoughts when the Prime Minister wrote him later that one could not see "the main theatre of all one's actions since childhood's days" suddenly removed, "as Mrs. Roosevelt's passing must have been to you, without experiencing a sorrow much too great to express in words."

The President instructed Rosenman and Hopkins to continue work on his speech, which was now postponed to the eleventh. Back in Washington he read a draft of it to his Cabinet; all approved but Hull, who was now arguing for a strongly moralistic speech, though without threat of action. Roosevelt refused to tone it down.

"The Navy Department of the United States," he began his fireside chat, "has reported to me that on the morning of September fourth the United States destroyer *Greer,* proceeding in full daylight toward Iceland, had reached a point southeast of Greenland. She was carrying American mail to Iceland. She was flying the American flag. Her identity as an American ship was unmistakable.

"She was then and there attacked by a submarine. Germany admits that it was a German submarine. The submarine deliberately fired a torpedo at the *Greer,* followed later by another torpedo attack. In spite of what Hitler's propaganda bureau has invented, and in spite of what any American obstructionist organization may prefer to believe, I tell you the blunt fact that the German submarine fired first upon this American destroyer without warning, and with deliberate design to sink her.

"Our destroyer, at the time, was in waters which the Government of the United States had declared to be waters of self-defense—surrounding outposts of American protection in the Atlantic."

The President described these outposts and their role in protecting the lifelines to Britain. To people in the room with him, the mourning band for his mother showed somberly against his light-gray seersucker suit.

"This was piracy—piracy legally and morally." The President then reviewed a series of earlier incidents in the Atlantic, beginning with the *Robin Moor.* "In the face of all this, we Americans are keeping our feet on the ground. . . . It would be unworthy of a great Nation to exaggerate an isolated incident, or to become inflamed by some one act of violence. But it would be inexcusable folly to minimize such incidents in the face of evidence which makes it clear that the incident is not isolated, but is part of a general plan. . . . Hitler's advance guards—not only his avowed agents but also his dupes among us—have sought to make ready for him footholds and bridgeheads in the New World, to be used as soon as he has gained control of the oceans." Hitler was seeking world mastery, and Americans of all the Americas must give up the romantic delusion that they could go on living peacefully in a Nazi-dominated world.

"We have sought no shooting war with Hitler. We do not seek it now. But . . . when you see a rattlesnake poised to strike, you do not wait until he has struck before you crush him. . . .

"Do not let us be hair-splitters. Let us not ask ourselves whether the Americas should begin to defend themselves after the first attack, or the fifth attack, or the tenth attack, or the twentieth attack.

"The time for active defense is now." The President called the roll of early Presidents who had defended the freedom of the seas.

"My obligation as President is historic; it is clear. It is inescapable.

"It is no act of war on our part when we decide to protect the seas that are vital to American defense. The aggression is not ours. Ours is solely defense.

"But let this warning be clear. From now on, if German or Italian vessels of war enter the waters, the protection of which is necessary for American defense, they do so at their own peril. . . .

"The sole responsibility rests upon Germany. There will be no shooting unless Germany continues to seek it. . . .

"I have no illusions about the gravity of this step. I have not taken it hurriedly or lightly. It is the result of months and months of constant thought and anxiety and prayer. . . ."

Shoot on sight. Roosevelt was in effect declaring naval war on Germany, in response to the war of aggression he believed Germany was waging against his nation. The Atlantic cold war was over; now it was a hot war, limited only by America's neutrality laws and by Hitler's restraints on his submarine fleet. It was war nonetheless, and Roosevelt proceeded to act in those terms. Two days after his speech he ordered Admiral King officially to protect not only American convoys to Iceland but also shipping of any nationality that might join such convoys. A delighted Churchill at once diverted about forty destroyers and corvettes from the convoy area to duty elsewhere. If any doubt remained, Secretary Knox cleared it up at the American Legion convention in Milwaukee on September 15: "Beginning tomorrow . . . the Navy is ordered to capture or destroy by every means at its disposal Axis-controlled submarines or surface raiders in these waters.

"That is our answer to Mr. Hitler."

Mr. Hitler was infuriated by Roosevelt's escalation, but he was still playing it cool. Raeder made the long trip to the Führer's Wolfsschanze headquarters on the Eastern Front to protest that the

United States had declared war, that his U-boats either must be allowed to attack American warships or must be withdrawn, but Hitler insisted on no incidents—at least before about the middle of October. By that time the "great decision in the Russian campaign" would have been reached; and then, Hitler implied, he and Raeder could deal with the Americans. Glumly Raeder withdrew his proposal.

Roosevelt's fireside chat seemed to win wide support at home. In mid-September people favored "shoot on sight" by roughly two to one. The President had acted, indeed, on a foundation of public support; by even stronger ratios, polled Americans had favored American convoys for war goods at least as far as Iceland. But these polls could not measure intensity of feeling, and observers sensed a good deal of apathy among the public, or at least a feeling of fatalism. Opinion seemed to be volatile and moody, except when a question touched on the possibility of outright war. Then the people shrank from action. Clearly many Americans were still accepting at face value Roosevelt's promise that his defense measures would help America keep *out* of war.

The President judged opinion ripe for the next step—modification of the Neutrality Act, which was still barring the arming of American merchantmen and excluding them entirely from proclaimed combat zones. Interventionist newspapers were now in full cry against the act: it was worth a thousand submarines to the foe, declared the New York *Times*; it was a "hoary and decrepit antique," according to the New York *Post*; it had become a "stench in the nostrils" of the editors of the New York *Herald Tribune*. But the isolationists in Congress were not prepared to discard a measure that had been both an emblem of American virginity among world predators and a chastity belt to foil them. Senator Taft and others contended that repeal of the Neutrality Act would be equivalent to a declaration of war.

Remembering his one-vote margin on the draft-extension bill of August, the President decided against challenging the whole isolationist bloc. He would call for modification of neutrality rather than total repeal—above all, for authorization to arm American merchant ships. Soon his speech writers were at work on his proposals to Congress. The message was a direct and hard-hitting plea that Congress stop playing into Hitler's hands and that it untie Roosevelt's. But the President was adamant on the main tactic. Modification of neutrality must be presented to Congress not as any kind of challenge to the enemy but as a simple matter of the defense of American rights.

THE CALL TO BATTLE STATIONS

One could sense at the end of summer 1941 that the war was rushing toward another series of stupendous climacterics. German troops had isolated Leningrad and broken through Smolensk on the road to Moscow, had surrounded and overwhelmed four Russian armies in the Kiev sector; through the two-hundred-mile gap they had torn in the south the Nazis could see the grain of the eastern Ukraine and the oil of the Caucasus. Churchill was preparing a strong blow in North Africa and pressing for a bolder policy in Southeast Asia. Tokyo was vacillating between peace and war, under a dire timetable. Chungking's morale seemed to be ebbing away. Washington and London were stepping up the Battle of the Atlantic. And in Moscow, around the end of September, the first flakes of snow fell silently on the Kremlin walls.

Pressure from all these sectors converged on the man in the White House. Allies were stepping up their demands; enemies, their thrusts. His Cabinet war hawks battered him with conflicting advice. But Roosevelt under stress seemed only to grow calmer, steadier, more deliberate and even cautious. He joshed and jousted with the reporters even while artfully withholding news. He listened patiently while Ickes for the tenth time—or was it the hundredth?—maneuvered for the transfer of Forestry from Agriculture to Interior—an effort that the President might have found exquisitely irrelevant to the war except that he himself seemed excited by a plan to establish roe deer in Great Smoky Mountains National Park.

But Roosevelt was not impervious to the strain. More than ever before he seemed to retreat into his private world. He spent many weekends at Hyde Park, partly in settling his mother's estate. He devoted hours to planning a Key West fishing retreat for Hopkins and himself; he even roughed out a sketch for a hurricane-proof house. He found time to talk to the Roosevelt Home Club in Hyde Park, to Dutchess County schoolteachers, to a local grange. And always there were the long anecdotes about Washington during World War I days, about Campobello and Hyde Park.

Physically, too, the President was beginning to show the strain. Systolic hypertension had been noted four years earlier and not considered cause for concern; but—far more serious—diastolic hypertension was diagnosed during 1941. Dr. McIntire was no longer so rosily optimistic, though he said nothing publicly to temper his earlier statements. His patient was eating, exercising, and relaxing less, showing more strain, and carrying more worries to bed, than he had during the earlier years in the White House. But the President rarely complained and never seemed very curious about his health. Doubtless he felt that he had enough to worry about abroad.

Tension was rising, especially in the Far East. The imperial rebuke spurred Konoye to redoubled efforts at diplomacy even as the imperative timetable compelled generals and admirals to step up their war planning. The government seemed schizophrenic. All great powers employ military and diplomatic tactics at the same time; but in Japan the two thrusts were competitive and disjointed, with the diplomats trapped by a military schedule.

Subtly, almost imperceptibly, Konoye and the diplomats beat a retreat in the face of Washington's firm stand. Signals were confused: Nomura acted sometimes on his own; messages were also coming in via Grew and a number of unofficial channels; and Konoye and Toyoda had to veil possible concessions for fear extremists would hear of them and inflame the jingoes. The Japanese military continued to follow its own policies; amid the delicate negotiations, Washington learned that the Japanese Army was putting more troops into Indochina. The political chiefs in Tokyo, however, seemed willing to negotiate. On the three major issues Tokyo would: agree to follow an "independent" course under the Tripartite Pact—a crucial concession at this point, because America's widening confrontation with Germany raised the fateful possibility that Tokyo would automatically side with Berlin if a hot war broke out; follow co-operative, nondiscriminatory economic policies, a concession that was as salve to Hull's breast; and be willing to let Washington mediate a settlement between Japan and China.

Day after day Hull listened to these proposals courteously, discussed them gravely—and refused to budge. He insisted that Tokyo be even more specific and make concessions in advance of a summit conference. By now the Secretary and his staff conceded that Konoye was "sincere." They simply doubted the Premier's capacity to bring the military into line. That doubt did not end after the war when historians looked at the evidence, which reflected such a shaky balance of power in Tokyo that Konoye's parley might have precipitated a crisis rather than have averted it. Konoye had neither the nerve nor the muscle for a supreme stroke. Much would have depended on the Emperor, and the administration did not fully appreciate in September either his desire for effective negotiations or his ability to make his soldiers accept their outcome.

The mystery lay not with Hull, who was sticking to his principles, but with Roosevelt, who was bent on *Realpolitik* as well as morality. The President still had one simple approach to Japan—to play for time—while he conducted the cold war with Germany. Why, then, did he not insist on a Pacific conference as an easy way to gain time? Partly because such a conference might bring a showdown *too* quickly; better, Roosevelt calculated, to let Hull do the thing he was so good at—talk and talk, without letting negotiations either lapse or come to a head. And partly because Roosevelt was succumbing to his own tendency to string things out. *He* had infinite time in the Far East; he did not realize that in Tokyo a different clock was ticking.

Amid the confusion and miscalculation there was one hard, unshakable issue: China. In all their sweeping proposals to pull out of China, the Japanese insisted, except toward the end, on leaving some troops as security, ostensibly at least, against the Chinese Communists. Even the Japanese diplomats' definite promises on China seemed idle; it was as clear in Washington as in Tokyo that a withdrawal from a war to which Japan had given so much blood and treasure would cause a convulsion.

Washington was in almost as tight a bind on China as was Tokyo. During this period the administration was fearful of a Chinese collapse. Chungking was complaining about the paucity of American aid; some Kuomintang officials charged that Washington was interested only in Europe and hoped to leave China to deal with Japan. Madame Chiang at a dinner party accused Roosevelt and Churchill of ignoring China at their Atlantic meeting and trying to appease Japan; the Generalissimo chided his wife for her impulsive outburst but did not disagree. Every fragment of a report of a Japanese-American détente set off a paroxysm of fear in Chungking. Through all their myriad channels into the administration the Nationalists were maintaining steady pressure against compromise with Tokyo and for an immensely enlarged and hastened aid program to China.

Even the President's son James, as a Marine captain, urged his father to send bombers to China, in response to a letter from Soong stating that in fourteen months "not a single plane sufficiently supplied with armament and ammunition so that it could actually be used to fire has reached China." Chiang was literally receiving the run-around in Washington as requests bounced from department to department and from Americans to British and back again. Its very failure to aid China made the administration all the more sensitive to any act that might break Kuomintang morale.

So Roosevelt backed Hull's militant posture toward Tokyo. When the Secretary penciled a few lines at the end of September to the effect that the Japanese had hardened their position on the basic questions, Roosevelt said he wholly agreed with his conclusion—even though he must have known that Hull was oversimplifying the situation to the point of distortion. Increasingly anxious, Grew, in Tokyo, felt that he simply was not getting through to the President on the possibilities of a summit conference. On October 2 Hull again stated his principles and demanded specifics. The Konoye government in turn asked Washington just what it wanted Japan to do. Would not the Americans lay their cards on the table? Time was fleeting; the military now were pressing heavily on the diplomats. At this desperate moment the Japanese government offered flatly to "evacuate all its troops from China." But the military deadline had arrived. Was it too late?

Not often have two powers been in such close communication but with such faulty perceptions of each other. They were exchanging information and views through a dozen channels; they were both conducting effective espionage; there were countless long conversations, Hull having spent at least one hundred hours talking with Nomura. The problem was too much information, not too little—and too much that was irrelevant, confusing, and badly analyzed. The two nations grappled like clumsy giants, each with a dozen myopic eyes that saw too little and too much.

For some time Grew and others had been warning Washington that the Konoye Cabinet would fall unless diplomacy began to score; the administration seemed unmoved. On October 16 Konoye submitted his resignation to the Emperor. In his stead Hirohito appointed Minister of War Hideki Tojo. The news produced dismay in Washington, where Roosevelt canceled a regular Cabinet meeting to talk with his War Cabinet, and a near-panic in Chung-

October 13, 1941, Rollin Kirby, reprinted by permission of the New York *Post*

October 31, 1941, Rollin Kirby, reprinted by permission of the New York *Post*

king, which feared that the man of Manchuria would seek first of all to finish off the China incident. But reassurances came from Tokyo: Konoye indicated that the new Cabinet would continue to emphasize diplomacy, and the new Foreign Minister, Shigenori Togo, was a professional diplomat and not a fire-breathing militarist. As for Tojo, power ennobles as well as corrupts. Perhaps it had been a shrewd move of the Emperor, some of the more helpful Washingtonians reflected, to make Tojo responsible for holding his fellow mititarists in check.

So for a couple of weeks the President marked time. Since he was still following the diplomacy of delay, he could only wait for the new regime in Tokyo to take the initiative—and to wonder when the next clash would occur in the Atlantic.

That clash came on the night of October 16. About four hundred miles south of Iceland a slow convoy of forty ships, escorted by only four corvettes, ran into a pack of U-boats. After three ships were torpedoed and sunk, the convoy appealed to Reykjavik for help, and soon five American destroyers were racing to the scene. That evening the submarines, standing out two or three miles from the convoy and thus beyond the range of the destroyers' sound gear, picked off seven more ships. The destroyers, which had no radar, thrashed about in confusion in the pitch dark, dropping depth bombs; when the U.S.S. *Kearny* had to stop to allow a corvette to cross her bow, a torpedo struck her, knocked out her power for a time, and killed eleven of her crew. She struggled back to Iceland nursing some bitter lessons in night fighting.

At last the first blood had been drawn—and it was American blood (though the U-boat commander had not known the nationality of the destroyer he was firing at). News of the encounter reached Washington on the eve of a vote in the House on repealing the Neutrality Act's ban against the arming of merchant ships. Repeal passed by a handsome majority, 259 to 138. The bill had now to go to the Senate. On Navy Day, October 27, the President took up the incident. He reminded his listeners, packed into the grand ballroom of Washington's Mayflower Hotel, of the *Greer* and *Kearny* episodes.

"We have wished to avoid shooting. But the shooting has started. And history has recorded who fired the first shot. In the long run, however, all that will matter is who fired the last shot.

"America has been attacked. The U.S.S. *Kearny* is not just a Navy ship. She belongs to every man, woman, and child in this Nation. . . ."

The President said he had two documents in his possession: a Nazi map of South America and part of Central America realigning it into five vassal states; and a Nazi plan "to abolish all existing religions—Catholic, Protestant, Mohammedan, Hindu, Buddhist, and Jewish alike"—if Hitler won. "The God of Blood and Iron will take the place of the God of Love and Mercy." He denounced apologists for Hitler. "The Nazis have made up their own list of modern American heroes. It is, fortunately, a short list. I am glad that it does not contain my name." The President had never been more histrionic. He reverted to the clashes on the sea. "I say that we do not propose to take this lying down." He described steps in Congress to eliminate "hamstringing" provisions of the Neutrality Act. "That is the course of honesty and of realism.

"Our American merchant ships must be armed to defend themselves against the rattlesnakes of the sea.

"Our American merchant ships must be free to carry our American goods into the harbors of our friends.

"Our American merchant ships must be protected by our American Navy.

"In the light of a good many years of personal experience, I think that it can be said that it can never be doubted that the goods will be delivered by this Nation, whose Navy believes in the tradition of 'Damn the torpedoes; full speed ahead!' "

Some had said that Americans had grown fat and flabby and lazy. They had not; again and again they had overcome hard challenges.

"Today in the face of this newest and greatest challenge of them all, we Americans have cleared our decks and taken our battle stations. . . ."

It was one of Roosevelt's most importunate speeches, but it seemed to have little effect. After a week of furious attacks by Senate isolationists, neutrality revision cleared the upper chamber by only 50 to 37. In mid-November a turbulent House passed the Senate bill by a majority vote of only 212 to 194. The President won less support from Democrats on this vote than he had on Lend-Lease. It was clear to all—and this was the key factor in Roosevelt's calculations—that if the administration could have such a close shave as this on the primitive question of arming cargo ships, the President could not depend on Congress at this point to vote through a declaration of war. Three days after Roosevelt's Navy Day speech the American destroyer *Reuben James* was torpedoed, with the loss of 115 of the crew, including all the officers; Congress and the people seemed to greet this heavy loss with fatalistic resignation.

It was inexplicable. In this looming crisis the United States seemed deadlocked—its President handcuffed, its Congress irresolute, its people divided and confused. There were reasons running back deep into American history, reasons embedded in the country's Constitution, habits, institutions, moods, and attitudes. But the immediate, proximate reason lay with the President of the United States. He had been following a middle course between the all-out interventionists and those who wanted more time; he had been stranded midway between his promise to keep America out of war and his excoriation of Nazism as a total threat to his nation. He had called Hitlerism inhuman, ruthless, cruel, barbarous, piratical, godless, pagan, brutal, tyrannical, and absolutely bent on world domination. He had even issued the ultimate warning: that if Hitler won in Europe, Americans would be forced into a war on their own soil "as costly and as devastating as that which now rages on the Russian front."

Now—by early November 1941—there seemed to be nothing more he could say. There seemed to be little more he could do. He had called his people to their battle stations—but there was no battle. "He had no more tricks left," Sherwood said later. "The bag from which he had pulled so many rabbits was empty." Always a master of mass influence and personal persuasion, Roosevelt had encountered a supreme crisis in which neither could do much good. A brilliant timer, improviser, and manipulator, he confronted a turgid balance of powers and strategies beyond his capacity to either steady or overturn. Since the heady days of August he had lost the initiative; now he could only wait on events. And events with the massive impact that would be decisive were still in the hands of Adolf Hitler.

The crisis of presidential leadership mirrored the dilemma of national strategy in the fall of 1941. According to long-laid plans, the United States, in the event of war, would engage directly with Germany and stall off or conduct a holding action with Japan. Roosevelt was expecting a confrontation with Germany, probably triggered by some incident in the Atlantic, but he was evading a showdown with Japan. In his denunciations of Nazism he had been careful not to mention Nipponese aggression or imperialism. But Hitler still pointedly avoided final trouble in the Atlantic, while the Far Eastern front, instead of being tranquilized, was becoming the most critical one.

And if war did break out in the Pacific—what then? The chances seemed strong that the Japanese would strike directly at British or Dutch posssessions, not American. Sherwood posed the question well. If French isolationists had raised the jeering cry "Why die for Danzig?" why should Americans die to protect the Kra Isthmus, or British imperialism in Singapore or Hong Kong, or Dutch imperialism in the East Indies, or Bolshevism in Vladivostok? It would no longer be enough for the United States to offer mere aid. Doubtless Roosevelt could ram through a declaration of war—but how effective would a bitter and divided nation be in the crucible of total war? And if the United States did not forcibly resist Japanese aggression against Britain and Holland, what would happen to Britain's defenses in the Far East while so heavily committed at home, in the Middle East, in North Africa, and on the seven seas?

The obvious answer was to stall Tokyo as long as possible. Eventually an open conflict with Germany must come; if Japan had not yet entered the war, perhaps it would stay out for the same reason it had kept clear of the Russo-German conflict. By November 1941 Roosevelt needed such a delay not only because of Atlantic First, but also as a result of a shift in plans for the Philippines. Earlier, the archipelago had been assumed to be indefensible against a strong enemy assault, and hence the War and Navy Departments had not made a heavy commitment there. Now, with General MacArthur's appointment as commander of U.S. forces in the Far East and the development of the B-17 heavy bomber, the Philippines were once again considered strategically viable. But time was needed, at least two or three months.

So early hostilities with Japan would mean the wrong war in the wrong ocean at the wrong time. Yet it was clear by November 1941 that the United States was faced with the growing probability of precisely this war. Why did not the President string the Japanese along further, taking care not to get close to a showdown?

This is what he did try, at least until November. It was not easy. Every time reports spread that Washington had considered even a small compromise on the central issue of a Japanese withdrawal from China, frantic cries arose from Chungking. Churchill, too, pressed insistently for a harder line toward Tokyo. At home Roosevelt had to deal with public attitudes that turned more militantly against Japan than against Germany. In early August those opposing war with Japan outnumbered those favoring it by more than three to one, while by late November twice as many as not were *expecting* war between their country and Japan in the near future.

Doubtless the basic factor, though, was one of calculation, or analysis. Churchill, still responding to the bitter lessons of Munich, contended that a policy of firmness was precisely the way to earn peace; it was the democracies' vacillation that tempted aggressors to go to war. Roosevelt was not so sure that the Asiatic mind worked in just this way. Yet he went along with Churchill's theory of peace through firmness and with Hull's insistence on adherence to principles, rather than with Stimson's and Knox's urgent advice to stall the Japanese along in order not to be diverted from Atlantic First and in order to have time to prepare in the Pacific.

Later an odd notion would arise that the President, denied his direct war with Hitler, finally gained it through the "back door" of conflict with the Japanese. This is the opposite of what he was trying to do. He wanted to avoid war with Japan because—like all the grand strategists—he feared a two-front war, and American strategy was definitely set on fighting Hitler first. In another three or six months, after the Philippines and other Pacific outposts had been strengthened, the President might well have gone through the "back door" of war—but not in late 1941. Churchill's calculations, however, were more mixed. He could assume his stand-firm posture with far more equanimity than Roosevelt; the Prime Minister could reason that a Japanese-American break would probably bring the United States into the German war as well and thus realize London's burning hope of full American involvement. But much would depend on the strength of Berlin-Tokyo solidarity and on each nation's calculus of its interest. Churchill had to face the fearsome possibility that the United States might become involved *only* in the Pacific. Hence he, too, was following the Atlantic First strategy.

It was not Roosevelt's calculation that was at fault, but his miscalculation. And because he lacked the initiative, and was assuming the imperfect moral stand of condemning Hitlerism as utterly evil and bent on world domination without openly and totally combating it, he faced a thicket of secondary but irksome troubles. Labor was restive in the fall of 1941 as it saw its chance to get in on the war boom. For many businessmen it was still business as usual. The Supply Priorities and Allocations Board had been set up on top of OPM in August, but SPAB seemed to be working with little more effectiveness than its predecessors. Congress seemed incapable of passing an effective price-control bill. Military aid to Allies, though rising, was still inadequate in the face of gigantic demands, and the orderly flow of food and munitions was disrupted by sudden emergencies and shifting needs.

Stimson was still insisting that ills such as these could be remedied only if the President assumed clear moral leadership, took the initiative against Germany, and established definite priorities at home and abroad. But Roosevelt would not yet ask for a declaration of war. Rather, he would try by management and maneuver to swing his nation's weight into the world balance.

To relations with Moscow in particular Roosevelt applied his most delicate hand. Russia's sagging defenses in the Ukraine had produced no reversal of opinion among Congress and people, or of policy in the White House. The hard-core isolationists still opposed aid to the Soviet Union and expressed gratification that Russians and Germans were bleeding one another to death; that conflict, said the Chicago *Tribune,* was the only war for a century that civilized men could regard with complete approval. Roosevelt, who was holding all negotiations with the Kremlin tightly in his own hands, was granting dollars and other aid in small dabs while recognizing that Russia needed massive help. He took care not to propose—or even discuss—bringing the Soviets under Lend-Lease until after Congress passed a big fall appropriation for the program.

The President was showing his usual respect for public opinion, which as always was shrill, divided, inchoate, and waiting for leads. He was especially wary of Catholic feeling against involvement with Bolshevism. With his implicit encouragement, at least, his friend Supreme Court Justice Frank Murphy told fellow Catholics that Communism and Nazism were equally godless but the latter was godlessness plus ruthlessness. When the President, however, suggested to reporters that Russians had some freedom of religion under their constitution, religious leaders pounced on him for his "sophistry" and ignorance. Ham Fish proposed that the President invite Stalin to Washington and have him baptized in the White House pool. Roosevelt dispatched his envoy Myron Taylor back to Rome to sound out Pope Pius and to inform him that "our best information is that the Russian churches are today open for worship and are being attended by a very large percentage of the population." Taylor carried with him a letter from President to Pope granting that the Soviet dictatorship was as "rigid" as the Nazi, but that Hitlerism was more dangerous to humanity and to religion than was Communism. The Pope was little influenced by this view, and his doctrinal expert, Monsignor Domenico Tardini, bluntly stated that Communism was and always would be antireligious and militaristic and told the Pope privately that Roosevelt was apologizing for Communism. The Vatican did respond to Roosevelt a bit by restating doctrine in such a way as to enable Catholics to make a distinction between aiding Russians and aiding Communism. Roosevelt also tried to induce Moscow to relax its antireligious posture, but with little effect.

Clearly the great opportunist was having little impact on the great doctrinaire. But if the President hardly was leading a holy crusade for a full partnership of the antifascist forces, he was at least removing some of the roadblocks and allowing events to exercise their sway. Congress defeated moves to bar the President from giving Lend-Lease aid to Russia, and at the end of October the President without fanfare told Stalin that he could have one billion dollars in supplies. Yet the President paid a price for this success. He and his colleagues had to stress not the great ideals of united nations but the expedient need to help keep the Russian armies in the fight and thus to make American military intervention less necessary. Aid was extended for crass reasons of self-interest. The only link between Americans and Russians was a common hatred and fear of Nazism.

Stalin was not deceived. He wrote to Churchill in early November that the reasons for the lack of clarity in the relations of their nations were simple: lack of agreement on war and peace aims, and no second front. He could have said the same to Roosevelt.

The whole anti-Axis coalition, indeed, was in strategic disarray by late fall of 1941, even while it was co-operating on a host of economic, military, and diplomatic matters. Churchill was almost desperate over Washington's stubborn noninvolvement. He still had serious doubts about Russia's capacity to hold out; he had to face the nightmarish possibility of Britain alone confronting a fully mobilized Wehrmacht. As it was, he had to share American aid with Russia, and while he was eager to do anything necessary to keep the Bear fighting, he found it surly, snarling, and grasping. He still feared a Nazi invasion of Britain in the spring, and he was trying to build up his North African strength for an attack to the west. Stalin was always a prickly associate. A mission to Moscow led by Lord Beaverbrook and Averell Harriman had established closer working relations with the Soviets, but no mission could solve the basic problem that Russia was taking enormous losses while only a thin trickle of supplies was arriving through Archangel, Vladivostok, and Iran. As for China, which was at best third on the waiting list for American aid, feeling in Chungking ranged between bitterness and defeatism.

So if Roosevelt was stranded in the shoals of war and diplomacy, he was no worse off than the other world leaders in 1941. All had seen their earlier hopes and plans crumble. Hitler had attacked Russia in the expectation of averting a long war on two fronts; now he was engaged in precisely that. Churchill had hoped to gain the United States as a full partner, but had gained Russia; he had wanted to take the strategic initiative long before, but had failed; he doubted that Japan would take on Britain and America at the same time, but events would prove him wrong. Stalin had played for time and lost; now the Germans, fifty miles west of Moscow, were preparing their final attack on it.

All the global forces generated by raw power and resistance, by grand strategies and counter-strategies, by sober staff studies and surprise blows—all were locked in a tremulous world balance. Only some mighty turn of events could upset that balance and release Franklin Roosevelt from his strategic plight.

A TIME FOR WAR

On November 1, 1941, the new leaders of Japan met to decide the issues they had debated since assuming office two weeks before. Should they "avoid war and undergo great hardships"? Or decide on war immediately and settle matters? Or decide on war but carry on diplomacy and war preparations side by side? These were the alternatives as Premier Tojo framed them for his colleagues: Foreign Minister Togo, Finance Minister Okinori Kaya, Navy Minister Shigetaro Shimada, Navy Chief of Staff Osami Nagano, Planning Board Director Teiichi Suzuki. Also present were members of the military "nucleus": Army Chief of Staff General Sugiyama, the Army Vice Chief of Staff, the Navy Vice Chief of Staff, and others.

It was a long meeting—seventeen hours—and a stormy one. Pressed by a skeptical Togo and Kaya as to whether the American fleet would attack Japan, Nagano replied, "There is a saying, 'Don't rely on what won't come.' The future is uncertain; we can't take anything for granted. In three years enemy defenses in the South will be strong and the number of enemy warships will increase."

"Well, then," Kaya said, "when can we go to war and win?"

"Now!" Nagano exclaimed. "The time for war will not come later!"

The discussion went on. Finally it was agreed to pursue war preparations and diplomacy simultaneously. The burning issue was the timing of the two and their interrelation. The early deadline, said Tojo, was outrageous. A quarrel broke out so intense that the meeting had to be recessed; operations officers were called in to consider the timing question from a technical viewpoint. The military chiefs conceded that it would be all right to negotiate until five days prior to the outbreak of war. This would mean November 30.

"Can't we make it December 1?" asked Tojo. "Can't you allow diplomatic negotiations to go for even one day more?"

"Absolutely not," Army Vice Chief of Staff Tsukada said. "We absolutely can't go beyond November 30. Absolutely not."

"Mr. Tsukada," asked Shimada, "until what time on the 30th? It will be all right until midnight, won't it?"

"It will be all right until midnight."

Thus, as the army records of this session noted, a decision was made for war; the time for its commencement was set for the beginning of December; diplomacy was allowed to continue until midnight, November 30; and if diplomacy was successful by then, war would be called off. The conference then debated two alternative proposals for negotiation. The crucial point of Proposal A was that Japanese troops could be stationed in strategic areas of China until 1966. Proposal B would largely restore the *status quo ante* the July freeze: the two nations would undertake not to advance by force in Southeast Asia or the South Pacific; Japanese troops in Indochina would move to the northern part of the country; the United States would help Japan obtain resources in the Dutch East Indies and would supply annually a million tons of oil; the United States would not obstruct "settlement of the China incident." The military preferred A because it posed the crucial question of China and would settle it quickly one way or the other—but fearing that Tojo might resign and topple the whole Cabinet, they agreed also to support the broader, but hardly less severe, terms of B.

On November 5 Tojo presented this consensus to an imperial conference at the palace. All agreed that if the diplomats could not settle matters by December 1, Japan would go to war regardless of the state of negotiations at that time. The Emperor had nothing to offer on this occasion—not even verse.

It was another major step toward war, but the Japanese were still following their two-pronged approach. Nomura continued his discussions with Roosevelt and Hull and continued to receive sermons of peace, stability, and order in the Pacific. Roosevelt was still playing for time, but Hull's rigidity on principle was hardening as a result of MAGIC intercepts of Japanese coded messages indicating the dominance of the military and its timetable. Each side was now looking to its allies. Japan, which had edged away from Berlin as the Wehrmacht slowed in Russia, was now drawing closer to its partner in case of need. Hull told Nomura that he might be lynched if he made an agreement with Japan while Tokyo had a definite obligation to Germany.

The paramount issue was still China. When Nomura came back to the White House on November 17, this time with Saburo Kurusu, who had come from Tokyo as special ambassador to expedite the discussions, Roosevelt again urged the withdrawal of Japanese troops from China; once the basic questions were settled, he said, he would be glad to "introduce" Japan and China to each other to settle the details. After Kurusu failed to budge on this question Roosevelt retreated to homilies; there were no long-term differences preventing agreement, he said.

Empty words. It was becoming increasingly clear that there were few misunderstandings between the two countries, only differences. Despite much confusion the two governments understood each other only too well. Their interests diverged. They could not agree.

When the Tokyo diplomats in desperation presented Proposal B, now softened a bit but still providing an end to American aid to China, Hull dismissed the contents as "of so preposterous a character that no responsible American official could ever have accepted them"—even though Tokyo meant them only as a stopgap, and Stark and Marshall found them acceptable as a way to stave off war.

Word arrived from Chungking that Chiang was completely dependent on American support and was agitated about reports of temporizing in Washington.

Undaunted, Roosevelt by now was working up a truce offer of his own. Around the seventeenth he had penciled a note to Hull:

6 Months

1. U.S. to resume economic relations—some oil and rice now—more later.

2. Japan to send no more troops to Indo-China or Manchurian border or any place south (Dutch, Brit. or Siam).

3. Japan to agree not to invoke tripartite pact if U.S. gets into European war.

4. U.S. to *introduce* Japs to China to talk things over but U.S. take no part in their conversations. Later on Pacific agreements.

This was Roosevelt's most ambitious specific truce formula in the dying days of peace, and its short life and early death summed up the intractable situation. Hull combined Roosevelt's plan with other proposals, American and Japanese, and cut the period to three months. On the twenty-second a message from Tokyo to Nomura and Kurusu was intercepted; it warned that in a week "things are automatically going to happen." Cabling Churchill the essence of the American proposal, Roosevelt added that its fate was really a matter of internal Japanese politics. "I am not very hopeful and we must all be prepared for real trouble, possibly soon." On the same day the Chinese Ambassador, Dr. Hu Shih, objected vigorously to letting Tokyo keep 25,000 men in northern Indochina. Chiang was wondering, he said, whether Washington was trying to appease Japan at the expense of China. The Dutch and the Australians were dubious about concessions.

Churchill was worried, too. ". . . Of course, it is for you to handle the business," he cabled to Roosevelt, "and we certainly do not want an additional war. There is only one point that disquiets us. What about Chiang Kai-shek? Is he not having a very thin diet? Our anxiety is about China." If it collapsed, their joint dangers would enormously increase. "We are sure that the regard of the United States for the Chinese cause will govern your action. We feel that the Japanese are most unsure of themselves." Perhaps Roosevelt would have persevered. But on the morning of the twenty-sixth Stimson telephoned him an intelligence report of Japanese troop movements heading south of Formosa.

December 2, 1941, Rollin Kirby, reprinted by permission of the New York *Post*

The President fairly blew up—"jumped up into the air, so to speak," Stimson noted in his diary. To the President this changed the whole situation, because "it was evidence of bad faith on the part of the Japanese that while they were negotiating for an entire truce—an entire withdrawal (from China)—they should be sending their expedition down there to Indo-China." Roosevelt's truce formula died that day. In its stead Hull drew up a ten-point proposal that restated Washington's most stringent demands.

The whole matter had been broken off, Hull told Stimson. "I have washed my hands of it and it is now in the hands of you and Knox—the Army and the Navy." Shortly Stimson phoned the President again; the time had come, they agreed, for a final alert to MacArthur.

Diplomatic exchanges continued for a while, like running-down tops. On November 26 Hull presented Nomura and Kurusu with his ten points; Kurusu said that Japan would not take its hat off to Chiang—the proposals were not even worth sending to Tokyo. *November 27*—the President warned the two envoys at the White House that if Tokyo followed Hitlerism and aggression he was convinced beyond any shadow of a doubt that Japan would be the ultimate loser; but he was still ready to be asked by China and

Japan to "introduce" them for negotiations, just as he had brought both sides together in strike situations. *November 28*—Nomura and Kurusu received word from Tokyo that they would soon have an elaboration of its position and the discussions would then be "de facto ruptured"; but they were not to hint of this. *November 29* (Tokyo time) at the liaison conference: Togo: "Is there enough time left so that we can carry on diplomacy?" Nagano: "We do have enough time." Togo: "Tell me what zero hour is. Otherwise I can't carry on diplomacy." Nagano: "Well, then, I will tell you. The zero hour is"—lowering his voice—"December 8." *November 30*—at Warm Springs for a belated Thanksgiving with the patients, the President took a telephone call from Hull urging him to return to Washington because a Japanese attack seemed imminent; he left immediately. *December 1*—Premier Tojo at the Imperial Conference: "At the moment our Empire stands at the threshold of glory or oblivion." The Chiefs of Staff asked the Emperor's permission to make war on X day. Hirohito nodded his head. He seemed to the recorder to be at ease. *December 2*—Roosevelt, through Welles, demanded of Nomura and Kurusu why their government was maintaining such large forces in Indochina. *December 3*—Tokyo handed Berlin and Rome its formal request for intervention; Mussolini professed not to be surprised considering Roosevelt's "meddlesome nature." *December 4*—the President concluded a two-hour conference with congressional leaders with the request that Congress not recess for more than three days at a time. *December 5*—some in the White House were still considering reviving the ninety-day truce proposal, if only to gain time. *December 6*—Roosevelt worked on an arresting message to Hirohito urging a Japanese withdrawal from Indochina and the dispelling of the dark clouds over the Pacific.

Almost a century before, he reminded the Emperor, the President of the United States had offered the hand of friendship to the people of Japan and it had been accepted. "Only in situations of extraordinary importance to our countries need I address to Your Majesty messages on matters of state." Such a time had come. The President dwelt on the influx of Japanese military strength into Indochina. The people of the Philippines, the East Indies, Malaya, Thailand were alarmed. They were sitting on a keg of dynamite. The President offered to gain assurances from these peoples and even from China—and offered those of his own nation—that there would be no threat to Indochina if every Japanese soldier or sailor were to be withdrawn therefrom. Clearly the President was not engaging in serious negotiation here; it was one more effort to stall off a showdown.

"I address myself to Your Majesty at this moment in the fervent hope that Your Majesty may, as I am doing, give thought in this definite emergency to ways of dispelling the dark clouds. . . ."

It was like a gigantic frieze in which all the actors move and yet there is no motion. While diplomats were deadlocked, however, the military was acting with verve and precision. In September Japanese carriers and their air groups had started specific training for Pearl Harbor, with the help of a mock-up as big as a tennis court. On October 5 one hundred officer pilots of the carrier air groups got the heady news that they had been chosen to destroy the American fleet in Hawaii early in December. On November 7 Admiral Isoroku Yamamoto set December 8 as the likely date because it was a Sunday. During mid-November the striking force of six carriers, two battleships, two cruisers, and nine destroyers put out from Kure naval base and rendezvoused in the Kuriles. On November 25 Yamamoto, from his flagship in the Inland Sea, ordered the advance into Hawaiian waters, subject to recall. On December 2 he broadcast the phrase "NIITAKE-YAMA NOBORE" (Climb Mount Niitaka)—the code for PROCEED WITH ATTACK! Meantime, other Japanese fleet units and scores of transports were moving into positions throughout the southern seas.

And Roosevelt? In this time of diplomatic stalemate and military decision he was still waiting, now almost fatalistically. "It is all in the laps of the gods," he told Morgenthau on December 1. As late as December 6 he would tell Harold Smith that "we might be at war with Japan, although no one knew." The President was pinioned between his hopes of staving off hostilities in the Pacific and his realization that the Japanese might not permit it; between his promise to avoid "foreign" wars and his deepening conviction that Tokyo was following Nazi ways and threatened his nation's security; between his moral and practical desire to stand by the British and Dutch and Chinese and his worry that thereby he might be directly pulled into a Pacific war. He was pinioned, too, between people—between Hull, with his curious compound of moralizing and temporizing, and the militants, such as Morgenthau, who was pleading with the President not to desert China, and Ickes, who was ready to resign if he did; between the internationalists in the great metropolitan press and the isolationists in Congress; even between the "pro-Chinese" in the State Department and the "pro-Japanese," including Grew, and finally between the polled citizens who said he was going too far in intervening abroad and those who said he was doing too little.

Pinioned but not paralyzed. The President's mind was taken up by probabilities, calculations, guesses, alternatives. By the early days of December he felt that a Japanese attack south was probable.

It was most likely to come, he thought, in the Dutch East Indies; next most likely in Thailand, somewhat less likely in the Philippines, and least probable—to the extent he thought about it all—in Hawaii. If the Japanese attacked British territory he would give Churchill armed support, the nature and extent depending, much as in the Atlantic, on the circumstances; if the Japanese attacked Thailand or the East Indies, Britain would fight and Roosevelt would provide some kind of armed support; if the Japanese attacked China from Indochina, he would simply step up aid to Chungking.

At this penultimate hour Roosevelt was extending his Atlantic strategy to the Pacific. It was not a simple matter of "maneuvering the Japanese into firing the first shot," for the Japanese were probably going to fire the first shot; the question was where the United States could respond, how quickly, and how openly and decisively. What Roosevelt contemplated was a replica of his support of Britain in the Atlantic, a slow stepping-up of naval action in the southern seas, with Tokyo bearing the responsibility for escalation. He had asked and received permission from the British and Dutch to develop bases at Singapore, Rabaul, and other critical points—a repetition of his acquisition of Atlantic bases the year before. He did not concentrate on the Atlantic at the expense of the Pacific; he did not leave things unduly to Hull. He could not; the pressures were too heavy. But he did apply to the Pacific the lessons of his experience in the Atlantic.

It was a dangerous transfer, for it fostered Roosevelt's massive miscalculation as to where the Japanese would strike first. Since he had reason to believe that he was confronting another Hitlerite nation in the East, he assumed that Tokyo would follow the Nazi method of attacking smaller nations first and then isolating and encircling the larger ones. He told reporters, off the record, on November 28 that the Japanese control of the coasts of China and the mandated islands had put the Philippines in the middle of a horseshoe, that "the Hitler method has always been aimed at a little move here and a little move there," by which complete encirclement was gained. "It's a perfectly obvious historical fact today." But Roosevelt was facing a different enemy, with its own tempo, its own objectives—and its own way with a sudden disabling blow.

When general plans fail, lesser plans, miscalculations, technical procedures, and blind chance have a wider play. During the evening of December 6 the Japanese carriers reached the meridian of Oahu, turned south, and amid mounting seas sped toward Pearl Harbor with relentless accuracy. In Tokyo a military censor routinely held up the message from Roosevelt to Hirohito. If it had been in plain English he would not have dared hold up such an awesome communication; if it had been in top-priority code he would not have known enough to; but Roosevelt had sent it in gray code to save time, and it finally arrived too late. In the Japanese Embassy in Washington a many-part message began to come in from Tokyo; the parts were sent down to the coding room, but the cipher staff drifted off to a party, the fourteenth section was delayed, and the embassy closed down for the night. At the War and Navy Departments, signals experts received the first thirteen parts through their MAGIC intercept and swiftly decoded them; copies were rushed to the White House and to Knox and Navy chiefs, but not to Admiral Stark, who was at the theater, nor—inexplicably—to General Marshall, who was understood to be in his quarters.

At 9:30 P.M. a young Navy officer brought the thirteen parts to the oval study. The President was going over stamps, meanwhile chatting with Hopkins, who was sitting on the sofa. The President read rapidly through the papers. All day he had been receiving reports of Japanese convoy and ship movements in the Southwest Pacific.

"This means war," the President said as he handed the sheaf to Hopkins.

For a few moments the two men talked about likely Japanese troop movements out of Indochina. It was too bad, Hopkins said, that the Japanese could pick their own time and America could not strike the first blow.

"No, we can't do that," Roosevelt said. "We are a democracy and a peaceful people." Then he raised his voice a bit.

"But we have a good record."

RENDEZVOUS AT PEARL

In the dark early-morning hours scores of torpedo planes, bombers, and fighters soared off the pitching flight decks of their carriers to the sound of "Banzai!" Soon 183 planes were circling the carriers and moving into formation. At about 6:30 they started south. Emerging from the clouds over Oahu an hour later, the lead pilots saw that everything was as it should be—Honolulu and Pearl Harbor bathed in sunlight, quiet and serene, the orderly rows of barracks and aircraft, the white highway wriggling through the hills—and the great battlewagons anchored two by two along the mooring quays of Pearl Harbor. It was a little after 7:30 A.M., December 7, 1941. It was the time for war.

On the American ships this Sunday morning sailors were sleeping, eating breakfast, lounging on deck. Some could hear the sound of church bells. A bosun's mate noticed a flight of planes orbiting in the distance but dismissed it as an air-raid drill. Then the dive bombers screamed down, and the torpedo bombers glided in. Explosions shattered the air; klaxons squalled general quarters; a few antiaircraft guns began firing; colors were raised. Bombs and torpedoes hit the *West Virginia,* instantly knocking out power and light, disemboweling her captain, and soon sinking the ship to the shallow bottom. The *Tennessee,* protected by the *West Virginia* against torpedoes, took two bombs, each on a gun turret. The *Arizona* had hardly sounded general quarters when a heavy bomb plunged through the deck and burst in a forward magazine; more bombs rained down on the ship, one hurtling right down the stack; a thousand men burned to death or drowned as the ship exploded and listed. A torpedo tore a hole as big as a house in the *Nevada,* which nonetheless got under way to sortie, but then, under heavy bombardment, ran aground. Three torpedoes struck the *Oklahoma;* men scrambled over her starboard side as she rolled, only to be strafed and bombed. By now Japanese planes were attacking at will, pouring bombs and machine-gun fire on destroyers, seaplane tenders, minelayers, dry docks, ranging up and down the coast attacking airfields and infantry barracks.

The flash was received in Washington. AIR RAID PEARL HARBOR—THIS IS NO DRILL. "My God!" Knox exclaimed. "This can't be true, this must mean the Philippines!" He telephoned the President, who was sitting at his desk in the oval study talking with Hopkins about matters far removed from the war. There must be some mistake, Hopkins said; surely the Japanese would not attack Honolulu. The report probably was true, Roosevelt said; it was just the kind of unexpected thing the Japanese would do. The President was calm, almost relaxed; he seemed like a man who had just got rid of a heavy burden. He had hoped to keep the country out of war, he remarked to Hopkins, but if the report was true, Japan had taken the matter out of his hands. Then, just after 2:00 P.M., he telephoned the news to Hull.

The Secretary had been at his office all morning reading intercepts of Tokyo's message. Nomura and Kurusu, whose embassy was still struggling with the translation, were due in around two. Just as they arrived, Hull received Roosevelt's telephone call. In a steady, clipped voice the President advised Hull to receive the envoys, look at their statement as though he had not already seen it, and bow them out. Hull kept the Japanese standing while he pretended to read their note. Was Nomura, he asked, presenting this document under instructions from his government? Nomura said he was. Hull fixed him in the eye. "I must say that in all my conversations with you during the last nine months I have never uttered one word of untruth. . . . In all my fifty years of public service I have never seen a document that was more crowded with infamous falsehoods and distortions—infamous falsehoods and distortions on a scale so huge that I never imagined until today that any Government on this planet was capable of uttering them." Nomura seemed to struggle for words. Hull cut him off with a nod toward the door.

By now the President was getting first reports on losses, calling in the War Cabinet, dictating a news release to Early. Later Churchill telephoned. The Prime Minister had been sitting with Harriman and Winant at Chequers when a vague report came in over the wireless about Japanese attacks in the Pacific. A moment later his butler, Sawyers, had confirmed the news: "It's quite true. We heard it ourselves outside. . . ." It took two or three minutes to reach the White House. "Mr. President, what's this about Japan?" Yes, it was true. "They have attacked us at Pearl Harbor. We are all in the same boat now."

For Churchill it was a moment of pure joy. So he had won, after all, he exulted. Yes, after Dunkirk, the fall of France, the threat of invasion, the U-boat struggle—after seventeen months of lonely fighting and nineteen months of his own hard responsibility—the war was won. England would live; the Commonwealth and the Empire would live. The war would be long, but all the rest would be merely the proper application of overwhelming force. People had said the Americans were soft, divided, talkative, affluent, distant, averse to bloodshed. But he knew better; he had studied the Civil War, fought out to the last desperate inch; American blood flowed in his veins. . . . Churchill set his office to work calling Speaker and whips to summon Parliament to meet next day. Then, saturated with emotion, he turned in and slept the sleep of the saved and thankful.

In Washington the shattering specifics were now coming in. So noisy and confused was the President's study that Grace Tully moved into his bedroom, where she took the calls from an anguished Admiral Stark, typed each item while Pa Watson and the others looked over her shoulder, and rushed them to her boss. She would long remember the agony and near-hysteria of that afternoon. Roosevelt's early mood of relief was giving way to solemnity and anger. He was tense, excited, shaken. Stimson and Knox were incredulous; they could not understand why Pearl Harbor was sustaining such losses. During the evening, as reports of landings in Oahu came in, Marshall said the rumors reminded him of the last war. "We're now in the fog of battle."

The President found relief in action. He went over troop dispositions with Marshall; ordered Stimson and Knox to mount guards around defense plants; asked Hull to keep Latin-American republics informed and in line; ordered the Japanese Embassy protected and put under surveillance. When the room cleared he called in Grace Tully and began dictating a terse war message. He was calm but tired.

At 8:40 Cabinet members gathered in the study. Roosevelt nodded to them as they came in, but without his usual cheery greetings. He seemed solemn, his mind wholly concentrated on the crisis; he spoke to his military aides in a low voice, as if saving his energy. The group formed a small horseshoe around their chief.

It was the most serious such session, the President began, since Lincoln met with his Cabinet at the outbreak of the Civil War. He reviewed the losses at Pearl Harbor, which by now were becoming exaggerated in the shocked Navy reports. He read aloud a draft of his message to Congress. Hull urged that the message include a full review of Japanese-American relations, and Stimson and others wanted a declaration of war against Germany as well as Japan. The President rejected both ideas.

By now congressional leaders were crowding into the study: Speaker Sam Rayburn, Republican Leader Joseph Martin, Democrats Connally, Barkley, Bloom, Republicans McNary, Hiram Johnson, and others (but not Hamilton Fish, whom even at this juncture Roosevelt would not have in the White House). The newcomers gathered around the President's desk while the Cabinet members moved into outer seats. They sat in dead silence as the President went over the long story of negotiations with Japan. He mentioned the last Japanese note, full of "falsehoods."

"And finally while we were on the alert—at eight o'clock—half-past seven—about a quarter past—half past one [here]—a great fleet of Japanese bombers bombed our ships in Pearl Harbor, and bombed all of our airfields. . . . The casualties, I am sorry to say, were extremely heavy." Guam and Wake and perhaps Manila had been attacked, he went on. "I do not know what is happening at the present time, whether a night attack is on or not. It isn't quite dark yet in Hawaii. . . . The fact remains that we have lost the majority of the battleships there."

"Didn't we do anything to get—nothing about casualties on their side?" someone asked.

"It's a little difficult—we think we got some of their submarines but we don't know."

"Well, planes—aircraft?"

The President could offer no comfort. He seemed to Attorney General Francis Biddle still shaken, his assurance at low ebb.

The Navy was supposed to be on the alert, Connally burst out. "They were all asleep! Where were our patrols? They knew these negotiations were going on." The President did not know. But it was no time for recriminations. The fact was, he said again, that a shooting war was going on in the Pacific. When someone finally said, "Well, Mr. President, this nation has got a job ahead of it, and what we have got to do is roll up our sleeves and win the war," Roosevelt quickly seized on the remark. He arranged to appear before Congress the next day, without revealing what he would say.

People had been gathering around the White House all day, pressing against the tall iron fence in front, milling along the narrow street to the west, clustering on the steps of the old State Department Building and behind the green-bronze Revolutionary War cannon and anchor. They peered at the White House, incredulous, anxious, waiting for some sign or movement. Evening came, and a misty, ragged moon. People were now five deep behind the iron railings, their faces reflecting the glow of the brightly lighted mansion; trolleys ran back and forth on Pennsylvania Avenue behind them. Reporters at the front portico watched Cabinet members and Congressmen arrive. To correspondent Richard Strout they looked grim going in, glum coming out. He watched Hiram Johnson, stern, immaculate, stalk across the little stone stage of the portico, and all the ghosts of isolationism seemed to stalk with him. By now the moon was high and the crowd was thinning. From across the White House fountain and grounds a few high, cracked voices could be heard singing "God Bless America."

Inside, in his study on the second floor, Roosevelt was gray with fatigue when he finished his emergency conferences late that night. Edward R. Murrow had won an appointment long before and expected it to be canceled, but Roosevelt called for him to share sandwiches and beer. The President was still aroused, almost stunned, by the surprise attack. He poured out to Murrow the information he had on losses. Pounding his fist on the table, he exclaimed that American planes had been destroyed "on the ground, by God, on the ground!"

Next day, round after round of applause greeted the President as he slowly made his way to the rostrum of the House of Representatives.

"Yesterday, December 7, 1941—a date which will live in infamy—the United States of America was suddenly and deliberately attacked by naval and air forces of the Empire of Japan.

"The United States was at peace with that Nation and, at the solicitation of Japan, was still in conversation with its Government and its Emperor looking toward the maintenance of peace in the Pacific. Indeed, one hour after Japanese air squadrons had commenced bombing in the American Island of Oahu, the Japanese Ambassador to the United States and his colleague delivered to our Secretary of State a formal reply to a recent American message. And while this reply stated that it seemed useless to continue the existing diplomatic negotiations, it contained no threat or hint of war or of armed attack."

The chamber was dead quiet. The President was speaking with great emphasis and deliberateness.

"It will be recorded that the distance of Hawaii from Japan makes it obvious that the attack was deliberately planned many days or even weeks ago. During the intervening time the Japanese Government has deliberately sought to deceive the United States by false statements and expressions of hope for continued peace.

"The attack yesterday on the Hawaiian Islands has caused severe damage to American naval and military forces. I regret to tell you that very many American lives have been lost. In addition American ships have been reported torpedoed on the high seas between San Francisco and Honolulu.

"Yesterday the Japanese Government also launched an attack against Malaya.

"Last night Japanese forces attacked Hong Kong.

"Last night Japanese forces attacked Guam.

"Last night Japanese forces attacked the Philippine Islands.

"Lask night the Japanese attacked Wake Island.

"And this morning the Japanese attacked Midway Island."

A long pause. The chamber was still quiet.

"Japan has, therefore, undertaken a surprise offensive extending throughout the Pacific area. The facts of yesterday and today speak for themselves. The people of the United States have already formed their opinions and will understand the implications to the very life and safety of our Nation.

"As Commander in Chief of the Army and Navy I have directed that all measures be taken for our defense.

"But always will our whole Nation remember the character of the onslaught against us."

Applause broke out and quickly died away.

"No matter how long it may take us to overcome this premeditated invasion"—the President's voice was rising with indignation —"the American people in their righteous might will win through to absolute victory."

At last the chamber exploded in a storm of cheers and applause.

"I believe that I interpret the will of the Congress and of the people when I assert that we will not only defend ourselves to the uttermost but we will make it very certain that this form of treachery shall never again endanger us.

"Hostilities exist. There is no blinking at the fact that our people, our territory, and our interests are in grave danger.

"With confidence in our armed forces—with the unbounding

determination of our people—we will gain the inevitable triumph—so help us God.

"I ask that the Congress declare that since the unprovoked and dastardly attack by Japan on Sunday, December 7, 1941, a state of war has existed between the United States and the Japanese Empire."

PART 2 *Defeat*

FIVE *"The Massed Forces of Humanity"*

FOR Franklin Roosevelt there had been the shock of Pearl Harbor, then the sense of relief that the uncertainty was over at last, then the growing alarm and agony about the extent of the losses. All this had been followed by a calm acceptance of the fact of war. Congress voted for war thirty-three minutes after the President finished his address: only one Representative voted Nay. The Great Debate was adjourned, the isolationists suddenly stilled, the domestic strife seemingly over—as was the struggle within Roosevelt's mind and soul. No need now for misgivings or recriminations. Only one fact mattered: the United States was at war.

Yet it was only half a war. What would Germany do? The President would not take the initiative; here, too, he wanted the American people to be presented with the fact of war. But Berlin, aside from exultation in the press over the devastating Japanese blow, remained ominously quiet. Was it possible, after all Washington's elaborate efforts to fight first in Europe, with only a holding action in the Pacific, that the United States would be left with only a war in the Far East?

The answer lay mainly with one man: Adolf Hitler. He had hoped that Japan would join his war against Russia; failing that, he was eager that Japan go to war against the Anglo-Americans in the Pacific—in which event he would join that war, too. The crucial strategic question now was whether Japan in turn would attack the Soviet Union; otherwise Germany's mortal enemy, Russia, and Axis ally, Japan, would be left without a second front. For a quarter-century Hitler had warned against a two-front war; would he take on the most powerful democracy in the world and increase his own two-front gamble without pressuring Tokyo to help out against Russia? And if Tokyo resisted the idea, would Hitler honor his promise to intervene?

Britain's stand was never in doubt. Churchill leapt at the chance to fulfill his promise that if the United States and Japan went to war the British declaration would follow within the hour. It took the members of Parliament longer than that to return to London and take their seats, but on the afternoon of December 8 Churchill redeemed his promise. He warned Parliament of a long and hard ordeal. But "we have at least four-fifths of the population of the globe upon our side. We are responsible for their safety and for their future." Both houses of Parliament voted unanimously for war against Japan. Roosevelt had wanted Churchill to wait until Congress could act, but the Prime Minister moved so quickly that Roosevelt's message did not arrive in time. Britain was formally at war with Japan several hours before the United States was. The relations between the Atlantic Allies had already changed. When someone at a British staff meeting the day after Pearl Harbor took the same cautious approach to America as when its intervention was in doubt, Churchill spoke up with a wicked leer in his eye.

"Oh, that is the way we talked to her while we were wooing her; now that she is in the harem, we talk to her quite differently!"

While waiting tensely on Hitler, the President rallied his nation to the job ahead. Even under the pressure of crisis he would not abandon his regular press conference on the ninth—though the newspapermen would get "damn little" from him, he warned Early. The reporters filed in slowly because each one had to be checked by the Secret Service; during the lull Roosevelt joked with May Craig about her being "frisked" and announced he would hire a female agent to do the job.

He gave the hungry reporters a few tidbits. There had been an attack that morning on Clark Field in the Philippines, he told them, and he had met with SPAB and agreed on both a speeding up of existing production and an expansion of the whole program. The President saved his main remarks for a fireside chat that evening. He started by reviewing a decade of aggression, culminating in the Japanese attack. It was all of one pattern.

"We are now in this war. We are all in it—all the way. Every single man, woman, and child is a partner in the most tremendous undertaking of our American history. We must share together the bad news and the good news, the defeats and the victories—the changing fortunes of war.

"So far, the news has been all bad. We have suffered a serious set-back in Hawaii. Our forces in the Philippines, which include the brave people of that Commonwealth, are taking punishment, but are defending themselves vigorously. The reports from Guam and Wake and Midway Islands are still confused, but we must be prepared for the announcement that all these three outposts have been seized.

"The casualty lists of these first few days will undoubtedly be large. . . . It will not only be a long war, it will be a hard war." But the United States could accept no result but victory, final and complete.

Roosevelt still had to deal with the awkward fact that the Nazis had not yet declared war—and might not. He simply asserted that Germany and Italy "consider themselves at war with the United States at this moment just as much as they consider themselves at war with Britain or Russia." For weeks, the President said, Germany had been telling Japan that if it came in, it would receive the "complete and perpetual control of the whole of the Pacific area" and that if it did not, it would gain nothing.

"That is their simple and obvious grand strategy. And that is why the American people must realize that it can be matched only with similar grand strategy. We must realize for example that Japanese successes against the United States in the Pacific are helpful to German operations in Libya; that any German success against the Caucasus is inevitably an assistance to Japan in her operations against the Dutch East Indies; that a German attack against Algiers or Morocco opens the way to a German attack against South America, and the Canal. . . ."

Roosevelt's White House was now in battle uniform, but in its own casual way. The bright light under the portico no longer shone at night; Mrs. Henrietta Nesbitt, the housekeeper, went shopping for blackout curtains; gas masks were handed out and put aside. Morgenthau, who controlled the Secret Service, ordered the White House guard doubled. He also wanted to ring the grounds with soldiers and to place light tanks at the entrances, but Roosevelt demurred. No tanks, no men in uniform inside the fence, and only one soldier about every hundred feet outside it. Work was hastily begun on a special air-raid shelter in the vault of the Treasury, but the President did not take this seriously either. He told Morgenthau he would go down there only if he could play poker with the Secretary's hoard of gold.

Tuesday passed, and Wednesday—still no declaration from Berlin. But by now Hitler had made up his mind and was simply waiting to stage his announcement. After receiving the news of Pearl Harbor at his headquarters behind the bleeding Russian front, he had flown back to Berlin during the night of December 8-9. He would declare war on the United States; he would not demand that Japan intervene against Russia. His reasoning was, as usual, a combination of rational calculation and personal emotion. He could not bluff Tokyo, for Roosevelt had been so provocative that a German-American war was inevitable anyway. There was little that he could offer Japan in the Pacific struggle and hence little he could threaten to withhold. Japan could not wound the Soviet Union mortally from the east; Stalin had thousands of miles to trade off in Siberia. It was better that Japan focus its efforts in the Pacific, and since the war had become global anyway, the stronger the Japanese effort in that ocean, the better for Hitler in the Atlantic, where he hoped to cut off American war supply to Britain and Russia. Above and beyond all this, though, was Hitler's xenophobia and racism. He did not need the racially inferior Japanese to help him beat Russia, and he had only hatred and contempt for Americans, half Judaized, half Negrified, and certainly not a warrior race.

For months the Führer had publicly kept his temper in the face of Roosevelt's threats and name-calling. Now he could pour out his hatred. On December 11 he appeared before his puppet Reichstag, assembled in Berlin's Kroll Opera House. He began by denouncing "that man who, while our soldiers are fighting in snow and ice, very tactfully likes to make his chats from the fireside, the man who is the main culprit of this war. . . .

"I will pass over the insulting attacks made by this so-called President against me. That he calls me a gangster is uninteresting. After all, this expression was not coined in Europe but in America, no doubt because such gangsters are lacking here. Apart from this, I cannot be insulted by Roosevelt, for I consider him mad, just as Wilson was. . . . First he incites war, then falsifies the causes, then odiously wraps himself in a cloak of Christian hypocrisy and slowly but surely leads mankind to war, not without calling God to witness the honesty of his attack—in the approved manner of an old Freemason. . . .

"A world-wide distance separates Roosevelt's ideas and my ideas. Roosevelt comes from a rich family and belongs to the class whose path is smoothed in the democracies. I was only the child of a small, poor family and had to fight my way by work and industry." He dwelt on the contrast between them: in the Great War Roosevelt had a pleasant job, while the Führer had been an ordinary soldier; Roosevelt had remained in the Upper Ten Thousand, while Hitler had returned from the war as poor as before; after the war Roosevelt had tried his hand at financial speculation, while Hitler lay in the hospital. Roosevelt as President had not brought the slightest improvement to his country. Strengthened by the Jews all around him, he turned to war as a way of diverting attention from his failures at home.

The German nation wanted only its rights. "It will secure for itself this right even if thousands of Churchills and Roosevelts conspire against it. . . .

"I have therefore arranged for passports to be handed to the American chargé d'affaires today, and the following—" The rest of Hitler's words were drowned out in applause as the Deputies sprang to their feet. That afternoon Ribbentrop coldly handed the American Chargé d'Affaires Germany's declaration of war and dismissed him. Later in the day the three Axis nations declared their unshakable determination not to lay down arms until the Anglo-

Americans were beaten and not to make a separate peace. The President sent written messages to Congress asking that a state of war be recognized between Germany and Italy and the United States. Not one member of Congress voted against the war resolutions.

A CHRISTMAS VISITOR

The war news from the Pacific was almost all bad. The Japanese were following their Pearl Harbor strike with lightning thrusts in the Philippines, Guam, Midway, Wake Island, in Kota Bahru, Sing-

From the *Japan Times & Advertiser,* December 20, 1941, courtesy of the *Japan Times*

apore, Thailand, Hong Kong. The small, almost defenseless garrison on Guam faced impossible odds. Marines on Wake beat off the first Japanese landing, but the Pacific fleet was too crippled to send help, and it was clear that the Japanese would return. After smashing Clark Field, near Manila, enemy planes were striking at Cavite naval base. The Japanese, with nearly absolute freedom of naval and air movement, were rushing troops and arms west, south, and east.

The most crushing news of all arrived in Washington on the tenth. Japanese bombers from Saigon, catching the *Prince of Wales* and the *Repulse* at sea without air cover, had bombed and torpedoed the great ships to the bottom. In London, Churchill twisted and writhed in bed as the import of the news sank in on him: the Japanese Navy was supreme from the Indian Ocean to the eastern Pacific.

For Roosevelt and his military chiefs the long-dreaded predicament was now fact: cut to the bone to help its allies, the nation's Army and Navy suddenly had to guard dozens of vital sectors. Rumors spread that Japanese warships were headed back to Hawaii, to Panama, even to California. Frantic calls for protection came in from coastal cities. The Army and Navy dared not be caught napping a second time. For a while all was improvisation and inadequacy. Antiaircraft regiments had to be sent to the West Coast without most of their guns. Aviation schools were stripped to fill out combat groups. A convoy of five ships, halfway to the Philippines with infantry, artillery, munitions, and seventy dive bombers and pursuit planes, was ordered back to Hawaii. But Stimson and Marshall, anxious to buck up MacArthur in his travail, appealed to the President, who asked the Navy chiefs to reconsider their decision. The convoy was rerouted to Brisbane.

During these days Roosevelt was never seen to lose his air of grave imperturbability, punctuated by moments of relief and laughter. He not only kept cool; he watched himself keep cool. He took the time to write to Early a curious memo noting the many comments that "the President seems to be taking the situation of extreme emergency in his stride, that he is looking well and that he does not seem to have any nerves." People tended to forget, the memo went on, that the President had been through this kind of thing in World War I, that he had personally visited practically all defense activities throughout the United States and many abroad, that he had gone to Europe in the spring of 1918 on a destroyer and "probably saw a greater part of the war area than any other American." Roosevelt had long been defensive about his failure to don uniform in World War I; now he was in psychological uniform as Commander in Chief.

In this, the biggest crisis of his life, Roosevelt's first instinct was to unify the nation, his next to unify the anti-Axis world. Churchill had asked if he could come over to Washington at once, for military conferences, and Roosevelt gladly agreed. While Churchill sailed westward on his new battleship the *Duke of York,* Roosevelt took steps to solidify the spirit of unity that had swept the country after Pearl Harbor.

Party harmony was no problem; the President accepted pledges from the Democratic and Republican National Chairmen of cooperation during the war and suggested that the two party organizations could help civil defense. Nor did the Great Debate have to be adjourned; former isolationists were tumbling over themselves with promises of support. The most worrisome continuing division was between management and labor. The National Defense Mediation Board had been devastated by the resignation of the CIO representatives. Clearly new machinery was necessary for industrial peace. Shortly after Pearl Harbor the President asked union chiefs and the Business Advisory Council of the Commerce Department to designate representatives for a conference to draft a basic wartime labor policy. The first and essential objective of the conference, the President made clear, would be to reach a unanimous agreement to prevent strikes during the war period.

The President invited the conferees to the White House for a preliminary talk. In they came: industrialists who had hated Roosevelt; Lewis, who had broken with him in the 1940 election; Green, friendly but wary. The President greeted each delegate and then spoke to the group for almost half an hour—about the need to do "perfectly unheard of things" in war, about the need for a complete agreement quickly, for a time limit on conference speeches, for a self-imposed discipline. He had just been thinking of an old Chinese proverb, he said: "Lord, reform Thy world, beginning with me."

There was not much difference between labor and management, the President went on. "It's like the old Kipling saying about 'Judy O'Grady an' the Colonel's Lady.' They are both the same under the skin. That is true in this country, especially this country, and we want to keep it so." His manner, Frances Perkins noted, was both sober and buoyant, confident and serious, and even touched with humility. The shock of Pearl Harbor, she felt, the hazards ahead, had acted like a spiritual purge and left him simply stronger, more single-minded. The conferees went on to their labors moved by the President, if still unsure of finding common ground.

Christmas was nearing, but a strange Christmas for the nation and for the Roosevelts. Thousands of men were taking their last leaves before shipping out; other thousands had their Christmas furloughs canceled; whole outfits were pulled out of posts and bases overnight. The Roosevelts were not immune to the new anxieties of war. In New York a few days before Christmas Joseph Lash talked with Eleanor Roosevelt on the phone. He found her worried and despondent in her Sixty-fifth Street home; she mentioned having had a hard day and then burst into tears. Lash wondered if she was upset by some trouble in her work at the Office of Civilian Defense; but not so. She and the President, she told him, had said good-by to their son James, who was headed for Hawaii, and to Elliott. They had to go, of course, but it was hard; if only by the law of averages, not all her boys would return. She wept again, then steadied herself. No one saw the President weep. Probably he could not; on his desk awaiting his signature was a bill that could send seven million men, from twenty to forty-four years old, off to the battle fronts.

Only one sock—Fala's—would hang from the White House mantle, it was reported. But on December 22 Winston Churchill arrived in Washington, and life at the White House was instantly transformed.

Roosevelt was waiting, propped against his car, at the Washington airport as Churchill flew in from Hampton Roads, where he and his party had disembarked. With the usual plump cigar clamped in his teeth, the Prime Minister marched over to the President and "clasped his strong hand with comfort and pleasure," Churchill wrote later. After a semiformal dinner for seventeen the Prime Minister was installed in the big bedroom across from Hopkins's, with his cherished traveling map room nearby.

Suddenly the second floor of the White House was an imperial command post, with British officials hurrying in and out with their old red leather dispatch cases. The White House servants were soon agape at Churchill's drinking, eating, and sleeping habits. The President and the Prime Minister were together for several hours every day, with Hopkins often present. They worked together in the closest familiarity: sometimes after cocktails Churchill would wheel Roosevelt in his chair from the drawing room to the elevator, as a token of respect, but also with his image of Raleigh spreading his cloak before Elizabeth. Eleanor soon discovered with concern that her guest took a long nap in the afternoon while her husband worked—but that the President hated to miss any of Churchill's and Hopkins's talk in the evening, and stayed up much later than usual.

The two leaders and their staffs at once plunged into the business of war. Roosevelt's first priority, however, was not military strategy, but a declaration of the "associated nations" to symbolize the unity and aspirations of the anti-Axis coalition. The President and the Prime Minister, using a State Department draft and working much as they had at Argentia, each wrote a separate statement and then blended them together. Since many governments had to be consulted, further drafting went on while the two leaders turned to immediate military problems.

Christmas Eve they stood side by side on the south portico for the traditional ceremony of lighting the tree. A great throng waited in the cold blackness below. Addressing his listeners as "fellow workers for freedom," Roosevelt said: "Our strongest weapon in this war is that conviction of the dignity and brotherhood of man which Christmas Day signifies. . . ." He presented Churchill, who matched him in eloquence: "I have the honor to add a pendant to the necklace of that Christmas good will and kindness with which our illustrious friend, the President, has encircled the homes and families of the United States." Christmas Day was observed without a single son or grandchild in the house. Roosevelt and Churchill attended an interdenominational service, dined with a company of sixty, listened to Christmas carols by visiting carolers—and then worked on the war until long after midnight.

One paramount question had occupied Churchill and his colleagues as they plotted strategy in the ordered calm of the *Duke of York*. Would an aroused American people, venting its wrath over Pearl Harbor, force the President to turn the main weight of the nation against Japan, leaving Britain to cope alone with the Axis in Western Europe, Africa, and the Middle East? Had the carefully fashioned Atlantic First strategy collapsed when the first bombs were dropped in the Pacific? This cardinal question embraced numerous secondary ones. If Roosevelt stuck to Atlantic First—and it was Churchill's supreme aim to induce him to do so—what would be the plan of attack against Hitler? How could Japan be contained or at least slowed in the Pacific while the Allies concentrated on Germany? How would the Allied command be organized in the vast Pacific and Atlantic theaters? And how would new plans affect demand, supply, and transportation of munitions?

Atlantic First was not left long in doubt. Roosevelt and his military chiefs quickly made clear that—even under the frightful pressure of Pacific defeats—the Americans still saw Germany as the main enemy and victory in Europe as crucial to the whole global effort. Indeed, little time was spent during these tumultuous days on any fundamental reconsideration of the long-planned priority. The old Plan Dog was almost taken for granted. Reassured, Churchill, in the first evening's discussion, plunged into the next question—strategy for Europe.

The Prime Minister had rarely been in better form. He had carefully worked out his plans for Europe and cleared them with his military men on the way across the ocean. Now, flanked by Beaverbrook and Halifax, he presented his case to Roosevelt, Hull, Hopkins, and Welles. If the Germans were held in Russia, he said, they would try something else—probably an attack through Spain and Portugal into North Africa. It was vital to forestall such a move. He than presented his plan—GYMNAST. He proposed that American forces invade Northwest Africa in the Casablanca area, and later hook up with British troops renewing their drive along the North African coast from the east into Tunisia.

The eager Prime Minister wanted to launch the attack quickly—

in three weeks, he hoped. He had 55,000 troops ready to load onto ships at short notice. The actual plan of operation would depend largely on whether the French authorities in Northwest Africa co-operated or not. It seemed to Churchill—and so he reported confidently to his War Cabinet—that Roosevelt favored the plan "with or without invitation" from the French.

Perhaps Roosevelt was merely being the polite host this first evening; perhaps, as the absent Stimson and Marshall feared, he tended to be vulnerable to Churchill's eloquence and zeal when his military staff was not with him. In any event, Roosevelt's enthusiasm for a North African invasion had cooled markedly by next day, when the two leaders presided over a meeting of their staffs. The President now spoke on the basis of a War Department memorandum that stressed the safety of the British Isles as the central "fortress" and of Atlantic communications, but played down the value of American action anywhere in the Mediterranean. Stimson and Marshall had won the President's endorsement of this approach at a war conference the day before the British arrived; but the Secretary was as surprised as he was delighted when his chief now used the memorandum to brief Churchill and his party.

While Churchill's hopes for GYMNAST sank, the President posed other major possibilities. He was willing to take over the defense of Northern Ireland, thus freeing British troops for use elsewhere. He granted the importance of the islands in the eastern Atlantic, but inclined toward the Cape Verde Islands, rather than the Azores. He acclaimed the British successes in Libya but doubted the value of placing American troops there. He then moved across the globe to the Pacific. It was vital, he said, that Singapore be held; the United States would do its utmost to save the Philippines, or at least to help the defense of the Dutch East Indies.

By the time Churchill took over, the initiative had been gained by the President. The Prime Minister still clung to GYMNAST, emphasizing that British advances into Tunisia might arouse French support, or precipitate a showdown between Berlin and Vichy—and in either case Africa would be a fine opportunity. But Marshall remained cool to GYMNAST if it required a large American force.

The emergent difference between the Allies cast a long shadow on future strategy. In proposing GYMNAST Churchill had challenged the strategic assumptions and professional bias of Marshall and his fellow soldiers, and especially Stimson. The Americans were inclining toward a long build-up and then a massive, concentrated thrust toward the enemy center—Germany. Any other move was a dispersion of effort unless it directly supported this central thrust. The American mind in war planning, as well as in commerce and production, Churchill felt, ran to "broad, sweeping, logical conclusions on the largest scale," while the British allowed more for the role of opportunism and improvisation, trying to adjust to unfolding events rather than to dominate them. To the American military such strategic assumptions led to expediency, dispersion of effort, to that "peripheralism" that had marked so much of Churchill's thinking beginning with the Dardanelles in World War I. To the British, with their limited resources and perhaps more patient view of history, this kind of strategy was more supple, flexible, sophisticated. Churchill also feared that a long preparation for the final assault by the Americans would mean their hoarding the munitions and supplies that he had been planning on for the months directly ahead.

GYMNAST was also being strangled by the rush of events. While the planners talked in Washington, the Japanese hurricane was sweeping south and west. Some in the White House feared that the Japanese might bombard the West Coast, lay mines in the ports, or even land troops from the sea or air. Roosevelt and his staff still did not flinch from their strategic commitment to Atlantic First, but the crisis in the Pacific could demand day-to-day commitments that might erode that strategy. Even to slow up the Japanese, Washington had to support and strengthen its outposts, and the shipping requirements were appalling. The Japanese were carving an enormous salient into the direct route between the West Coast and Tokyo, which ordinarily would run just south of Alaska. The turnaround time between the East Coast and Australia was three months. Shipping had been short all along; now it would clog Allied strategy in both oceans.

The Pacific crisis also precipitated the whole problem of unified command. On Christmas afternoon, at a meeting of the American and British military chiefs in the Federal Reserve Building, across Constitution Avenue from the War and Navy buildings, Marshall seized the initiative. The Japanese could not be stopped, he said, unless there was complete unity of command over naval, land, and air forces. "With differences between groups and between services, the situation is impossible unless we operate on a frank and direct basis." He was no orator, but he was so earnest that his words became eloquent. "I am convinced that there must be one man in command of the entire theatre—air, ground, and ships." Cooperation was not enough; human frailties were such that local commanders would not put their troops under another service. He was ready to go the limit.

Marshall had a special reason to speak feelingly; at this point he was still smarting from a brief skirmish with the President. That morning he had heard that on Christmas Eve his Commander in

Chief had blithely discussed with Churchill the possibility that if American forces assigned to MacArthur were not able to get to the Pacific, they be turned over to the British. When Marshall and his colleagues took this report to Stimson, the Secretary became so heated over this threat to his precious reserves for MacArthur that he telephoned Hopkins that he would resign if the President persisted in this kind of thing. Hopkins raised this matter with Roosevelt and Churchill, who both denied that they had reached such an agreement—but Stimson cited the minutes that a British secretary had made of the evening meeting. The episode bolstered Marshall's view that only a unified Pacific Theater command would permit orderly planning and decision making.

That way of running things was not much to Roosevelt's taste. Typically he had not made basic changes in his own command arrangements. He had put the old Army-Navy Joint Board under the White House in 1939, but he preferred to deal informally and often separately with his military chiefs. His British guests were agog at the American command setup. "There are no regular meetings of their Chiefs of Staff," Dill wrote home to Brooke, "and if they do meet there is no secretariat to record their proceedings. They have no joint planners and executive planning staff. . . ." Simply informing the President was a problem. "He just sees the Chiefs of Staff at odd times, and again no record. There is no such thing as a Cabinet meeting. . . . The whole organization belongs to the days of George Washington. . . ."

In the press of crisis, though, Roosevelt was willing to change his ways—at least for a theater 8,000 miles away. He supported Marshall's specific proposal that the combined American, British, Dutch, and Australian—ABDA—sea, land, and air forces in the Southwest Pacific be placed at once under a single top commander with an inter-Allied staff. The huge theater would embrace not only the East Indies, Malaya, the Philippines, New Guinea, and Burma, but would also stretch limitlessly to New Britain, the Solomons, the Fijis, Samoa. Marshall won the grudging backing of Knox and some of the admirals. The main obstacle would be the British—and here Roosevelt tried some reverse English. "Don't be in a hurry to turn down the proposal the President is going to make to you," Hopkins said to Churchill, "before you know who is the man we have in mind." It was Wavell. Churchill was dubious about unity of command over such a vast expanse; some of his staff wondered whether Wavell was slated to be a British scapegoat who would preside over a rapidly disappearing command. But in the face of Roosevelt's and Marshall's persuasiveness, backed by Beaverbrook at a timely moment, Churchill agreed to the new command and commander.

This step in turn forced a far bigger decision on the structure of the top command. To whom was the ABDA commander to report? The British proposed a divided chiefs of staff committee, operating in both Washington and London and clearing with the Dutch, Australians, and New Zealanders. After some hesitation Roosevelt rejected this cumbersome arrangement and substituted a simple meeting in Washington between the American and British staffs, in turn reporting to the President and the Prime Minister, with the other nations consulted "if advisable." It was no embarrassment to Roosevelt that he had no joint chiefs in the British sense, and that he had no air chief as a counterpart to the head of Britain's RAF. He simply created, as the American component of the Combined Chiefs of Staff, a Joint Chiefs of Staff composed of Marshall, King, a hard-bitten old salt slated to replace Stark as Chief of Naval Operations, and General Henry H. ("Hap") Arnold, whose genial manner masked a flair for organization and management. In this rather backward fashion were the Allied and American command structures established.

"The Americans have got their way and the war will be run from Washington," wrote Churchill's observant personal physician, Sir Charles Wilson (later Lord Moran), doubtless reflecting feeling among the British chiefs, "but they will not be wise to push us so unceremoniously in the future." Churchill accepted the decision with good grace, largely because of his profound confidence in Roosevelt, Marshall, and Hopkins.

SENIOR PARTNERS, AND JUNIOR

During these days of long conferences in Washington and deepening crisis in the Pacific, the President continued work on the declaration of Allied unity. He was discovering that gaining agreement from a score of allies on even a simple proclamation was full of snares. One arose over a "freedom of religion" clause. The President, much to his later remorse, had left religion out of the Atlantic Charter; now surprisingly he left it out of his and Churchill's Christmas Day draft. Hopkins urged him to put it in—but this meant gaining the concurrence of the Russians. Litvinov had flown in; perhaps he could help.

The old Bolshevik had had his ups and downs since the cheerier days of 1933 when he was talking with Roosevelt about recognition. Dismissed by Stalin at the time of the Nazi-Soviet Pact, in 1939, the long-time proponent of collective security had faded into obscurity, only to be plucked out as Washington and Moscow were forced into partnership. From his war-stricken capital Litvinov had flown across the Pacific just in advance of the Japanese attack and had landed in a Washington still full of shiny cars, traffic jams, food, and parties.

The President found Litvinov notably less ebullient than in the old days. The envoy was clearly reluctant to urge Number One in Moscow to endorse a religious pledge, but Roosevelt was insistent. When Litvinov said that the Kremlin might agree to the phrase "freedom of conscience," Roosevelt assured him that it was exactly the same thing. Indeed, Roosevelt added expediently, the old Jeffersonian principle of religious freedom was so democratic that it included the right to have no religion at all; a person had the right to worship God or choose no god. Armed with this interpretation, Litvinov won the concurrence of Moscow.

The President took great pride in his feat. He regaled the White House company so often with his account of how he had talked with the Russian envoy about his own soul and the dangers of hell-fire, Churchill remembered later, that the Prime Minister promised to recommend him for appointment as Archbishop of Canterbury if he lost the next election.

The declaration ran into other obstacles, large and small. Roosevelt and Churchill wanted it to include "authorities" as well as "governments" as signatories, so that the Free French could sign, but Hull at this point had become indignant with the Free French to the verge of resignation over de Gaulle's unauthorized occupation of Saint Pierre and Miquelon, French islands south of Newfoundland, and Litvinov said that he could not agree to such a major change anyway. Churchill was annoyed at Hull's making so much of one small episode amid gigantic events, and contemptuous of Litvinov for acting like a frightened automaton. Roosevelt mediated the differences, but "authorities" stayed out. The Americans wanted India included in the signatories, but here Churchill resisted. The British wanted "social security" kept in the declaration, but Roosevelt dropped it, partly out of deference to congressional sensitivities. Another problem was Russia's relation with Japan; the declaration could call for victory only over Hitlerism, rather than over the Tripartite powers.

On New Year's Day, after a week of cabling among twenty-six countries, Roosevelt was wheeled into Churchill's room with the final version in hand. "I got out of my bath," Churchill said later, "and agreed to the draft." Roosevelt proposed at the last moment that the term "United Nations" replace "Associated Powers." Churchill was delighted; he showed his host the lines from Byron's *Childe Harold:*

> "Here, where the sword united nations drew,
> Our countrymen were warring on that day!"
> And this is much—and all—which will not pass away.

Roosevelt, Churchill, Litvinov, and T. V. Soong, the new Ambassador from China, gathered in the President's study on the evening of New Year's Day. The text lay before them.

DECLARATION BY UNITED NATIONS

A JOINT DECLARATION BY THE UNITED STATES OF AMERICA, THE UNITED KINGDOM OF GREAT BRITAIN AND NORTHERN IRELAND, THE UNION OF SOVIET SOCIALIST REPUBLICS, CHINA, AUSTRALIA, BELGIUM, CANADA, COSTA RICA, CUBA, CZECHOSLOVAKIA, DOMINICAN REPUBLIC, EL SALVADOR, GREECE, GUATEMALA, HAITI, HONDURAS, INDIA, LUXEMBOURG, NETHERLANDS, NEW ZEALAND, NICARAGUA, NORWAY, PANAMA, POLAND, SOUTH AFRICA, YUGOSLAVIA.

The Governments signatory hereto,

Having subscribed to a common program of purposes and principles embodied in the Joint Declaration of the President of the United States of America and the Prime Minister of the United Kingdom of Great Britain and Northern Ireland dated August 14, 1941, known as the Atlantic Charter,

Being convinced that complete victory over their enemies is essential to defend life, liberty, independence, and religious freedom, and to preserve human rights and justice in their own lands as well as in other lands, and that they are now engaged in a common struggle against savage and brutal forces seeking to subjugate the world, DECLARE:

(1) Each Government pledges itself to employ its full resources, military or economic, against those members of the Tripartite Pact and its adherents with which such Government is at war.

(2) Each Government pledges itself to cooperate with the Governments signatory hereto and not to make a separate armistice or peace with the enemies.

The foregoing declaration may be adhered to by other Nations which are, or which may be, rendering material assistance and contributions in the struggle for victory over Hitlerism.

Done at Washington
January First, 1942

The President signed first. Eleanor Roosevelt, Lash, and a few other onlookers watched from near the door, and Lash recorded the scene in his diary: Roosevelt observed that perhaps he should have signed as "Commander in Chief." " 'President ought to do,' Hopkins said dryly. Churchill then signed. The President looked and then called out, 'Hey, ought you not to sign 'Great Britain and Ireland?' Churchill agreed, corrected his signature and then stalked around the study, a look of great satisfaction on his face. Litvinov signed next, and finally T. V. Soong for China. While Soong was signing, Churchill asked Litvinov whether he had not seen him once on a plane to Paris. Litvinov looked blank and then said, betraying the tension he was under, 'It may have been my wife.' "

"Four fifths of the human race," Churchill remarked when Soong had finished signing.

Four-fifths of the human race. But on this New Year's Day at the White House, governments representing four-fifths of that four-fifths—hundreds of millions of Chinese, Indians, and Russians—were not given seats on the Combined Chiefs of Staff, which was to frame global strategy, and these governments had worries and forebodings about the shape of United Nations command and strategy.

The Kuomintang's elation at gaining two allies was soon offset by its growing fear that American aid, with many more mouths and guns to feed, might fall off rather than increase, at least for a time. Japan's invasion of Burma threatened to cut the Burma Road, along which a trickle of supplies was coming in. The great connecting points with the West—Singapore, the Philippines, the East Indies—were already under attack. Chiang accepted supreme command of Allied land and air forces in the theater he already commanded. The only other step Roosevelt felt able to take was to arrange for a "political loan" to Chungking. "I am anxious to help Chiang Kai-shek and his currency," he wrote to Morgenthau. "I hope you can invent some way of doing this." Reluctantly—because he had little confidence in China's capacity to fight—the Secretary obtained from Congress authorization for a half-billion-dollar loan to China, with repayment deferred until the end of the war. But Chiang still lacked what he wanted—massive aid in arms and a seat in the top strategic councils.

The Australians faced their own predicament. With three of its best divisions in North Africa and a fourth in Singapore, Canberra felt denuded in face of the Japanese thrust south. In ports along the northern coast, and even the eastern, Australians were preparing for attack. Within ten days of Pearl Harbor, Roosevelt had authorized Marshall to plan a major base in northern Australia—but would the Japanese get there first? The Dutch had a special grievance; in their haste Roosevelt and Churchill neglected to clear Wavell's appointment with them ahead of time, and Roosevelt felt constrained to salve wounded feelings by asking Marshall to release some war munitions to them "even though they be very modest." The Filipinos were beginning to doubt that the Americans would be able to save their country. And India, the second most populous nation in the world and also in the path of Japanese conquest, was hardly consulted at all.

But it was the place of Russia in the United Nations that raised the most fateful questions of all.

On New Year's Day the President was sitting with Churchill and the rest of the dinner company when the talk turned to Russia. At this point the Germans and Russians were locked in a critical struggle west of Moscow. Churchill, having served as War Secretary under Lloyd George in World War I, was not to be outdone by his host in tales of combat. Dispatches from the Russian front reminded him of the days when he was directing British military intervention against the new Bolshevik regime. His forces had got as far as Tula, just south of Moscow. But now, he said, he forgave the Russians "in proportion to the number of Huns they kill."

"Do they forgive you?" asked the brash Hopkins.

"In proportion to the number of tanks I send," Churchill said.

Roosevelt disagreed. He thought they did not forgive, he said. And he was probably right. Even in the first flush of United Nations collaboration, with Britain and the United States ranged solidly with Russia against the Axis, the fissures in the coalition were all too obvious. As the German armies had moved on his main cities, Stalin had complained about delays in arms shipments. Eden had been on his way to Moscow for conferences with Stalin and Molotov at the time of Pearl Harbor, and Churchill had been much disturbed by his ensuing reports from Moscow. Stalin had proposed to Eden an immediate secret agreement returning to Russia the Baltic states, the frontiers of 1941 with Finland and Rumania, and a frontier with Poland based on the old Curzon Line. Eden had demurred on the ground that Roosevelt had asked the British not to enter into any secret postwar reorganization of Europe without consulting him. Such an agreement would also be contrary to the Atlantic Charter.

Stalin had been annoyed and mystified. How could there be a wartime alliance if war aims differed? In Washington, Churchill was annoyed, too. Even now, after six months of brave Soviet resistance, he could not forget how Russia had been indifferent and even hostile to Britain's interests before June 1941, and had fought the Nazis only when attacked. But Churchill's opposition to making postwar agreements stemmed more from strategic calculations than either pique or principle. "No one can foresee how the balance of power will lie or where the winning armies will stand at the end of the war," Churchill counseled Eden. Britain and America would be economically and militarily strong; the Russians would need their aid. Churchill would defer postwar arrangements until he could move from a foundation of power.

The transcendental issue was the second front. In the critical days of late 1941 Stalin had pleaded for British action that could relieve the excrutiating pressure of the German war machine. Churchill had authorized Eden to discuss sending British troops into the Caucasus and into the Russian fighting line in the south. Nazi pressure in Africa, however, had led London to withdraw this offer, and a guarded proffer of RAF squadrons was dropped after Pearl Harbor. By late December the fortunes of war had changed. At just about the time the Japanese were smashing Pearl Harbor, the Russians were unleashing a tremendous counterattack on the Moscow front. For a few days the Red Army made spectacular progress.

Now it was Moscow's turn to announce tens of thousands of enemy soldiers encircled and trapped, vast war booty captured, key cities, including Kalinin and Tula, relieved or recaptured. After a few weeks Russian progress was slowed by the snow and cold, lack of transport, severe arms shortages, German tenacity, and sheer fatigue. But during the days when Eden and Stalin were meeting in Moscow, and Churchill and Roosevelt in Washington, Stalin was no longer in a begging mood. He could afford to look far into the future. No longer need he ask for American troops for the Russian front. But on one issue he would not change—would never change. He was still demanding a second front that might soften the tremendous blows that he knew Hitler would launch against him during the new year.

On the Far East, Stalin was coldly realistic. He was not ready to attack Japan. He reminded Eden that he had had to switch many divisions from Siberia to the Western Front. Moreover, war against Japan would be "unpopular with our people if the Soviet Government were to take the first step," he told Eden. "If, on the other hand, we were attacked, the feelings of the Soviet people would be strong." He even thought a Japanese attack on his country likely in the spring. Eden warned him that Japan would try to destroy its opponents one by one, including Russia, but Stalin commented that Britain was hardly fighting Japan alone.

Roosevelt had tried a more indirect approach. In mid-December he cabled to Stalin that he was suggesting to Chiang that he at once convene in Chungking a conference of Chinese, Soviet, British, Dutch, and American representatives to prepare for joint planning in the Far East. Stalin quickly answered that the President had not made clear the aims of such a conference and he wanted "elucidation," in effect putting the President off. But Stalin added: "I wish you success in the struggle against the aggression in the Pacific."

So committed was Roosevelt to Atlantic First strategy that never during these feverish days did he seriously consider the only alternative that might have brought Russia into the Far Eastern war—a Pacific First strategy that would have thrust American power on a direct axis across the northern Pacific, there to link up with the Soviets in a second front against Japan. Such a strategy would have faced formidable difficulties and represented a distinctly minority view. Yet it was some such plan as this that MacArthur had in mind when he cabled to the War Department that, with the Japanese so overextended to the south, a "golden opportunity" had arisen for a "master stroke" if Russia could be induced to enter the war against Japan and attack from the north. MacArthur did not explain how Russia was to be brought into the Pacific war. The President invited Stalin to discuss "joint planning" with the American, British, and Chinese Ambassadors in Moscow, but Stalin responded to this vague suggestion as coolly as he had to the idea of a Chungking conference.

So the Soviet Union remained half an ally—a member of the United Nations, the main foe of Germany, but not at war with the enemy in the Far East, and not a member of the Combined Chiefs of Staff. Roosevelt was satisfied with these arrangements, at least for the moment. He could understand Stalin's caution in Siberia; he felt that events would bring their own compulsion toward unity. The Soviet leader, he told friends at dinner on New Year's Day, had to rule a very backward people, which explained a good deal. Harry Hopkins, on his return from Moscow, had told him that Stalin had a sense of humor—which meant, the President said, that he also had a sense of proportion.

Clearly the President was bent less on setting grand strategy during these days than on establishing relationships, ordering priorities, soliciting views, laying immediate plans. The code name ARCADIA had been assigned to the Washington meetings, and a slightly idyllic atmosphere often seemed to surround the proceedings. The long-run decisions—aside from the reaffirmation of Atlantic First—were not to prove crucial. The importance of the conference lay in its certification of Anglo-American unity, establishment of joint machinery, and discussion of tactical plans. And ARCADIA left the two principals closer than ever in concord and comradeship.

The extent of Anglo-American co-operation, and indeed of the "industrial-military complex," was vividly shown later when Marshall came to Harvey Bundy with a rumor that Churchill was about to replace Dill in Washington. Dill had worked so closely with the administration that the Pentagon was dismayed at the thought of his leaving. Marshall suggested that Bundy arrange for Harvard to give Dill an honorary degree at a special convocation and thus raise him in London's estimation. Bundy tried with his friends in the Harvard establishment, but was told that Harvard never held special convocations. He then tried with his friends in the Yale establishment, only to be told the same thing. But then Yale thought of a way out: what about awarding Dill a prize for fostering Anglo-American co-operation? This was arranged, and the top Pentagon brass flew up to New Haven with Dill for the occasion. Dill's speech was given front-page treatment in the New York *Times*. Marshall told Bundy later that Churchill had been duly impressed; in any event, Dill stayed.

On January 14 the President and Hopkins drove with Churchill to his special train. Roosevelt sent with the Prime Minister's party some presents for Mrs. Churchill and a note:

"You would have been quite proud of your husband on this trip. . . . I didn't see him take anybody's head off and he eats and drinks with his customary vigor, and still dislikes the same people. . . ."

With his friend gone, the President could get more sleep. He could also devote more attention to the domestic state of the union.

THE SINEWS OF TOTAL VICTORY

"For the first time since the Japanese and the Fascists and the Nazis started along their blood-stained course of conquest they now face the fact that superior forces are assembling against them. Gone forever are the days when the aggressors could attack and destroy their victims one by one without unity of resistance. . . ."

It was January 6, 1942. The President was delivering his address on the state of the union—delivering it to Congress in person, as usual. He was in a militant mood.

"The militarists of Berlin and Tokyo started this war. But the massed, angered forces of common humanity will finish it."

The President proceeded to offer Congress a breath-taking set of production goals.

"First, to increase our production rate of airplanes so rapidly that in this year, 1942, we shall produce 60,000 planes, 10,000 more than the goal that we set a year and a half ago. This includes 45,000 combat planes—bombers, dive bombers, pursuit planes. The rate of increase will be maintained and continued so that next year, 1943, we shall produce 125,000 airplanes, including 100,000 combat planes.

"Second, to increase our production of tanks so rapidly that in this year, 1942, we shall produce 25,000 tanks; and to continue that increase so that next year, 1943, we shall produce 75,000 tanks.

"Third, to increase our production rate of anti-aircraft guns so rapidly that in this year, 1942, we shall produce 20,000 of them; and to continue that increase so that next year, 1943, we shall produce 35,000 anti-aircraft guns.

"And fourth, to increase our production rate of merchant ships so rapidly that in this year, 1942, we shall build 6,000,000 deadweight tons as compared with a 1941 completed production of 1,100,000. And finally, we shall continue that increase so that next year, 1943, we shall build 10,000,000 tons of shipping.

"These figures and similar figures for a multitude of other implements of war will give the Japanese and the Nazis a little idea of just what they accomplished in the attack at Pearl Harbor.

"And I rather hope that all these figures which I have given will become common knowledge in Germany and Japan. . . ."

The shipping goal was the most audacious of all. The President told reporters how he had called in Maritime Commission officials and put the problem to them.

"What are you making now?" he had said to them. " 'Well,' they said, 'we can step it up to five million tons.' I said, 'Not enough. Go back and sharpen your pencils.' . . . So they went back and sharpened their pencils, and they came back, and they said, 'It will hurt terribly, but we believe that if we are told to we can turn out six million tons of shipping this year.' I said, 'Now you're talking.' And I said, 'All right now, for '43 what can you do? Can you turn out four million more tons, to a total of ten million tons of shipping?' And they scratched their heads, and came back and said, 'Aye, aye, sir, we will do it.' . . ."

It was not quite so easy as all this. The ARCADIA Conference was making clear during these days that transports and merchantmen were now the worst bottleneck in all the war planning. Not only were the Allies scrambling for tonnage, but the President's services were competing fiercely over the building of warships versus army transports. Troop transports were so short, army planners concluded with dismay, that no other major troop movement could be undertaken in the Atlantic for at least three months if the North African operation was undertaken. Roosevelt had to raise his own sights. Within a few weeks of his January demands he was asking Chairman Emory S. Land, of the Maritime Commission, and Admiral Howard L. Vickery, of the Navy, to commission nine million tons in 1942 and fifteen million in 1943.

"I realize that this is a terrific directive," Roosevelt said, "but I feel certain that in this very great emergency we can attain it."

The nation must strain every existing arms-producing facility to the utmost, the President warned in his State of the Union message. In mid-January he established the War Production Board under the Office of Emergency Management in his Executive Office. The WPB was headed by the same eight officials who had manned SPAB, but with one major difference—the chairman would have unprecedented powers to "exercise general direction over the war procurement and production programs and determine plans and procedures for purchasing, contracting, building, requisitioning, plant expanding." OPM was put under the new board; SPAB was abolished. At last the President had responded to congressional and popular clamor to set up a czar of czars in production.

"Production for war is based on men and women—the human hands and brains which collectively we call Labor," the President told Congress in his message. "Our workers stand ready to work long hours; to turn out more in a day's work; to keep the wheels turning and the fires burning twenty-four hours a day, and seven days a week. . . ." A week later he established the National War Labor Board, with four public, four industry, and four labor members. In contrast to the old Defense Mediation Board, the new agency would have authority to take jurisdiction over a dispute on its own initiative; it would have major wage-stabilization responsibilities; and, above all, it could under its own rules impose arbitration rather than merely recommend it.

"War costs money," the President said in his State of the Union address. "So far, we have hardly even begun to pay for it. We have devoted only 15 per cent of our national income to national defense." The war program for the coming year, he said, would cost fifty-six billion dollars—more than half of the estimated annual national income. "That means taxes and bonds and bonds and taxes. It means cutting luxuries and other non-essentials. . . ."

In his budget message early in January the President urged that seven billion in additional taxes be collected during the fiscal year 1943 and that Social Security trust funds be raised by two billion. "An integrated program, including direct price controls, a flexible tax policy, allocations, rationing, and credit controls, together with producers' and consumers' cooperation will enable us to finance the war effort without danger of inflation." If inflation could be controlled during the war, a recession could be prevented after it.

". . . We are fighting, as our fathers have fought, to uphold the doctrine that all men are equal in the sight of God," Roosevelt concluded his message on the state of the union. "Those on the other side are striving to destroy this deep belief and to create a world in their own image—a world of tyranny and cruelty and serfdom.

"This is the conflict that day and night now pervades our lives. No compromise can end that conflict. There never has been—there never can be—successful compromise between good and evil. Only total victory can reward the champions of tolerance, and decency, and freedom, and faith."

It was one thing for the President to issue clarion calls for production, discipline, sacrifice—but something else to set up the necessary agencies and give them adequate powers. The impact of the new war agencies would depend on the kind of men he chose, the leadership he supplied them from the top, the power resources he could help them mobilize to carry out their programs in hostile terrain.

The bleak fact was that industrial mobilization had been faltering to the point of crisis during the weeks before Pearl Harbor. The priorities system—the heart of effective mobilization—was breaking down as manufacturers demanded and often received the highest ratings to obtain materials. Machinery and staff were inadequate for ordering priorities in terms of a comprehensive plan; there was, indeed, no real general plan. Disputes between civilian and war agencies, between New Dealers and conservative businessmen, between cautious expansionists and "all-outers" boiled beneath the surface and often erupted in the press—or at least in indignant memorandums to the Commander in Chief. SPAB and OPM could not program, allocate, order, deny, penalize; at best they could bargain, negotiate, mediate, persuade, and exhort.

Production figures were proof of the pudding. Aircraft production had soared; then the rate of increase fell off during 1941. Of 1,279 combat aircraft scheduled for production in October, Isador Lubin of OPM informed the President, war plants had turned out 923, most of which went to other countries. Fewer naval ships were produced in the third and fourth quarters of 1941 than in the second. Cargo-ship production declined during the last half of 1941; even more ominously, so did the production of copper, lead, and zinc. Steel production rose only a million tons between the first and last quarters.

The failures had a multitude of causes, but not least the President's reluctance to make strategic commitments, his determination not to plan ahead too far, his fear of vesting too much authority in one man or office. Pearl Harbor jarred these old predilections of his. The declared war not only gave him a plenitude of authority to clear the decks, boost production goals, and grant power; it also gave him the popular backing for crisis action and the self-assurance that he was acting for a consensus. He was aware, too, that events had dramatized the failures of SPAB and OPM. The Truman Committee was digging up production delays and muddles, and its chairman was urging that a strong man with full authority be placed at the head of the production effort.

Roosevelt was under pressure from within his administration, too: Stimson urged him to concentrate executive power into a single head on the business side of munitions making; Felix Frankfurter, who was still sending the President notes of unabashed admiration and praise, wrote him a long memo favoring the appointment of a man who would serve as the President's eyes and ears in overseeing the defense program and would be an instrument of the "centralized execution of the President's will—an instrument of dispatch, concentration and responsibility." The CIO was still pressing for faster conversion through the establishment of industry councils. Walter Reuther, of the Auto Workers, charged a week after Pearl

Harbor that his year-old plan to convert auto plants to airplane manufacture had been sabotaged by Knudsen.

Even with all this, Roosevelt took a gingerly approach. It was clear that Knudsen had to go; but the old GM boss had been so utterly loyal and had become such a symbol of mobilization that the President did not know how to let him go, until Hopkins came up with the idea of making him a lieutenant general and production expediter. For a time Roosevelt dallied with the notion of setting up a committee of Willkie, Donald M. Nelson, of OPM, and Justice William O. Douglas to "explore" the problem of defense organization for him; Hopkins talked him out of that notion. For a time he thought of making Douglas the new czar of czars, but Stimson felt that this would be a "hideous" appointment. In the end the job went to Nelson, who had proved himself no superczar, but a skilled conciliator, and had won the backing of most—or, at least, antagonized the fewest—of Roosevelt's defense chiefs.

"It took Lincoln three years to discover Grant, and you may not have hit on your production Grant first crack out of the box," Frankfurter wrote to him. "But the *vital* thing is that you have created the function—the function of one exclusive 'final' delegate of your authority . . . indispensable for *your* conduct of the war."

The labor situation before Pearl Harbor had been equally critical and far more visible. Four times as many workers struck during 1941 as in the year before. The defense boom and AFL-CIO rivalry were major causes, but the thorniest issue was union security. Labor chiefs contended that new workers flooding into the defense plants could not enjoy the benefits unions had fought for without joining; employers denounced any effort to use the defense crisis to boost union power. On this explosive issue the National Defense Mediation Board had followed a wavering course, always denying the union shop, once even granting a closed shop, and sometimes recommending maintenance of membership (under which all employees who were members of a union or who later became members must stay in the union for the life of the contract, or lose their jobs). The NDMB was under pressure to set a more definite policy, but, lacking clear direction from the President or credible authority of its own, the board continued to straddle the issue.

Roosevelt's old adversary John L. Lewis happily fished in these troubled waters. Wrangling in turn with employers, rival unionists, and the White House, he demanded a union shop for the "captive" miners working in pits controlled by Big Steel. In mid-September 1941 he pulled the captive mine workers out on strike. Fearful of strengthening his already powerful union, the Mediation Board

May 2, 1941, Hugh Hutton, by permission of the Philadelphia *Inquirer*

repeatedly denied him the union shop. In mid-November the two CIO members of the board denounced both the employer and the AFL members for opposing the union shop, and resigned. The miners kept striking, returning to work on the President's request, and then striking again. At the White House Roosevelt bluntly warned Lewis and CIO President Philip Murray that "the Government of the United States will not order, nor will Congress pass legislation ordering, a so-called closed shop."

Once again Roosevelt and Lewis were at loggerheads. When the President asked the union chief to let the question be arbitrated, Lewis replied loftily that the President was so prejudiced that no one he chose would be impartial.

The gauntlet had been thrown. By now—two weeks before Pearl Harbor—the Mediation Board was expiring. Its chairman, William H. Davis, was urging Roosevelt to request legislation authorizing the government to seize and operate the mines. Trouble flared on another labor front, as the five railway brotherhoods rejected the findings of an emergency presidential board. The White House asked both the miners and the railroad workers for further parleys, but clearly parleying was no longer enough. Both employers and union chiefs needed a command, and Roosevelt would not command them. Rather, he had become a one-man mediation appeals board. Pressure was applied on him directly from all sides. He had to devote hour after hour to negotiating, placating, maneuvering—and do so during the feverish days of rising military and diplomatic crisis of late November and early December.

But the President was still the master broker. While Lewis stalled on the question of arbitration, the President blandly went ahead and set up a tripartite board of arbitration, under John R. Steelman, head of the conciliation service of the Labor Department. The Mine Workers grumpily ordered its men back to work. The President's man was not as susceptible to Big Business blandishments as Lewis had charged, for Steelman promptly sided with labor to decide in favor of the union shop for the captive coal mines. That decision was handed down on December 7, and hence buried in the press—another bit of lucky timing for the President, and for Lewis.

After Pearl Harbor, in the exuberant new mood of national unity, the President convened his labor-management conference to reach agreement on basic policy for maintaining labor peace. The conferees labored five days. They agreed to discountenance all strikes and lockouts for the duration and to submit disputes to a new war labor board for binding settlements. But on the emotional issue of union security, the conference soon became deadlocked. Industry representatives wanted to freeze union status for the duration; labor would not have it. The session became tense.

Like an old stage manager, the President pulled down the curtain before the peace conference turned into a battle royal. He ingenuously accepted the no-strike pledge and announced that he would set up a new board to handle disputes. Since he did not exclude the union shop as an issue that the new board could properly arbitrate, the President in effect passed the spiky issue on to the new agency. This was a victory for laborites and liberals who wanted government to accept the challenge and opportunity of the union-security issue. Then in appointing men like Davis, Wayne Morse, long friendly to labor, and Frank P. Graham, a liberal educator, as public members, Roosevelt made an indirect commitment to some form of union security. With this lead from the White House everything would now turn on the decisions of the board under the day-to-day pressure of new disputes.

The President had long recognized that workers would not sacrifice wages and status unless the cost of living and industry profits were held down, but it was on this economic front that his power was most limited. He had had a price-control bill introduced in the House Banking and Currency Committee in August, only to open a Pandora's box of special interests. During three months of hearings, well-organized groups pressed for special exemptions; most vociferous and effective were the Farm Bureau Federation and other farm groups. Under their pressure Roosevelt and Henderson reluctantly went along with a provision for 110 per cent of parity. The bill that passed the House ten days before Pearl Harbor was already a tattered remnant of what Roosevelt had wanted. The Senate, even more vulnerable to farm pressures than the House, so riddled the bill with further concessions to cotton, wheat, oats, barley, and hog growers that Majority Leader Alben Barkley himself branded it a "farm relief" measure.

Thoroughly disappointed in the bill, the President took the unusual step of calling House members of the conference committee to his office to persuade them to moderate the farm provisions in the Senate version. Once again his persuasion seemed to work. After a long and bitter session, the conference committee agreed on a stiffer measure. Roosevelt's establishment of the new War Labor Board, with power to stabilize wages, mollified some Congressmen; even so, the price bill passed the House by a margin of only twenty-five votes over the opposition. Despite the negative recommendation of at least one OPA administrator, the President signed the bill. Perhaps he sensed even then that he would have to ask Congress for broader anti-inflation powers—a move that he did make within three months. Meanwhile, he would proceed one step at a time.

In a graceful statement on signing the compromise bill he concluded—perhaps a bit wryly after all the vexing delays—by quoting a remark of Woodrow Wilson: "The best form of efficiency is the spontaneous cooperation of a free people." But it was Wilson, too, who had extolled presidential leadership of a free people.

SIX *The Endless Battlefields*

GRADUALLY the White House changed into a military command post during the early weeks of 1942. Soldiers and heavy chains barred the gates. Listening devices lay in the grounds. Artillerymen manned antiaircraft guns on the roof of the mansion and behind false terraces on the lawns. The long line of tourists passing through the first-floor rooms came to an end by order of the Secret Service. Employees had to have passes; visitors had to be listed in advance and carefully checked through the gates. The President could no longer dine out at a hotel; the annual Cabinet dinner given to him and the First Lady had to be held at the White House.

The President was half-amused, half-exasperated by the precautions. What a wonderful opportunity, he speculated at the Cabinet dinner, for Hitler to drop a bomb and catch so many important people at one gathering. "If all of us except Frances were killed we would have a woman President!"

In his oval study on the second floor and in his oval office in the executive wing Roosevelt's routine was much the same as before. Now, however, he had a map room like Churchill's, and on his way to and from the office he liked to look in at the large charts with task forces and convoys clearly indicated, scan the latest bulletins, and chat with the young officer in charge. But the White House was a somewhat cheerless place, especially after Churchill left. Roosevelt had no family there. Eleanor was busier than ever with her work in the Office of Civilian Defense and in countless other activities. The burden of events—now most of it of a crisis nature—pressed harder than ever on staff and President alike. Evenings were less relaxed; there were more telephone calls, more messages and queries that could not wait.

He had occasional relief from pressure. At some point during the harrowing months just before or after Pearl Harbor, Franklin Roosevelt began seeing Lucy Mercer again. Their romance had seemed to be finished forever in 1920 when she had married Winthrop Rutherfurd, a well-to-do widower almost thirty years her senior, and even more the next year when Roosevelt had become an invalid and the ward of his mother and his wife. But some time later he managed to get back in touch with her, and she had shown up in Washington occasionally for official ceremonies during the first two terms. Her husband had recently suffered a stroke and was slowly dying, and the White House had become a lonelier place for Roosevelt than before. He found her the same poignant, diverting woman he had known a quarter-century earlier.

The revival of this *affaire de coeur* was well known to some in the White House but not to Eleanor Roosevelt. He would meet Lucy on a road beyond Georgetown and they would drive for a couple of hours; very occasionally friends arranged other meetings. When he once asked Anna whether she would mind if "an old friend" came to dinner, his daughter hesitated for two or three seconds, then said of course she would not. Doubtless the relationship was essentially temperamental rather than physical. Lucy Mercer still epitomized Roosevelt's ideal of womanliness. She had a charming smile, almost bittersweet features, and graceful, statuesque figure; she attracted him, too, with her relaxed vivacity, complete absorption in his talk of politics, people, and olden times, and her lack of demands on him—except to see him again.

But even more than Lucy's diversions, Roosevelt felt the pull to Hyde Park, to the place where he could throw off some of his cares and escape some of his burden, especially the burden of appointments. He firmly opposed his wife's suggestion that the big house there be turned into a convalescent home; he reminded her that he would not be able to cruise at sea and doubted that he could even use the *Potomac* because of the target she would make for planes from a hostile carrier. "O.K. My conscience is free," she wrote on the memo. So every two or three weeks during the winter and spring the President took the long slow train to Hyde Park for stays of five to ten days.

These trips were unpublicized, by the President's emphatic instructions. With his small party—Hassett, Grace Tully, one or two secretaries, a doctor, sometimes Hopkins, and always some Secret Service men—he would drive from the White House behind an army truck carrying his luggage and papers and board the presidential train at a secluded siding. On the B & O he slept, talked, sipped cocktails with his staff, watched the passing people and foliage, occasionally went over reports and signed executive orders. From Manhattan a New York Central locomotive would take him to Highland, across the river from Poughkeepsie and seven miles from Hyde Park. Soon the President would be happily installed in what was now his own home, with his staff in the Vanderbilt mansion three miles up the river. He had an intense interest in that mansion, its former owners, and present appointments; he quizzed Hassett and the others about their rooms and laughed with them over the Vanderbilts' effort to copy the decor of French royalty. He contrasted the artificial grandeur of the mansion with the plainer and simpler houses of the old Hudson Valley families; he was maintaining his own home as his mother had, he told Hassett, and as his family had for a century or more. What he really meant, Hassett concluded, was that old-fashioned families did not show off.

During these trips Hassett became in effect Roosevelt's first secretary. While sitting with the President on the train, or meeting him in the morning in the bedroom or even the bathroom—"Have a seat on the can, and remember your pants are up," Roosevelt told him once—or spreading documents out in the little study while the President's heavy signature dried, he and his chief talked about their common interests: old books and authors, old family friends and national personages, birds, trees—above all, Dutchess County politicians, places, and happenings. Roosevelt had a comfortable sense of ownership of the place; he happily listed for the authorities his possession of a farm truck, dump truck, station wagon, and his little Ford, though he was not sure whether he also owned a little garden truck. And he never lost his feeling for the local flora and fauna. He timed one of his Hyde Park visits to see his dogwood in bloom, and later the same May he left the house at four in the morning to go bird watching at Thompson's Pond in Pine Plains. His face lighted up later when he told how at daybreak he heard the note of a marsh wren, then a red-winged blackbird, then a bittern. He claimed to have identified the notes of twenty-two birds in all.

Roosevelt probably never had a "typical day" in his life, but a Saturday at Hyde Park late in March impressed people around him with the range of his interests and the continual flux of his mind. In the morning he chatted with Hassett about a variety of matters, including Sir Basil Zaharoff and American munitions makers who dealt with the Nazis. He then told Hassett of his plans to make a quick, unpublicized visit to New York City, without escort (a plan that failed). Later he discussed Pacific command problems with Hopkins. Then he motored over to the Vanderbilt mansion, called down Hackie (Louise Hackmeister, White House head telephone operator) and Hassett, whom he addressed as Empress Josephine and Cardinal Richelieu, and exchanged more Vanderbilt lore with them. Later he worked on antitrust matters and other affairs of state. In the evening he drove his old Ford, with its special hand levers, over to Eleanor's Val-Kill cottage for dinner, bringing with him Grace Tully, Hopkins, and Hopkins's daughter,

Diana. In front of the fireplace there was much talk of cousins, grandchildren, and friends. At dinner Eleanor peppered her husband with questions she had picked up in her travels—questions about destroyers being sent out without detectors, a rumored lack of incendiaries, the fall in bomb output resulting from a strike. Roosevelt dismissed the reports as "scuttlebutt." He talked about the clamor for a unified command but said Marshall knew nothing about ships and King nothing about the Army. He waxed indignant about isolationist newspapers that would not keep military secrets—and the failure of the Justice Department to crack down on them. He then admitted a certain affection for Arthur Krock and Mark Sullivan as ancient but dependable fixtures, claimed that he got along better with Stalin than the British did—this was only a hunch, he admitted, when challenged by his wife—discussed new methods of dental treatment in the Army, remembered the time he gave his dentist a "haymaker" by mistake when coming out of laughing gas, defended Walter Winchell, teased Grace Tully for allegedly snitching a piece of ham on Friday, then wondered what would be substituted for rubber girdles during the war shortage and was assured by the ladies that the problem had been solved. The President left for the big house about ten. It was a godsend that he could relax this way, Mrs. Roosevelt said to her guests afterward; otherwise he could not have stood three terms in office, especially this last one.

It was in these familiar and cheerful surroundings, in the serenity of Hyde Park, that the Commander in Chief received much of the shocking news from the Pacific.

DEFEAT IN THE PACIFIC

Rarely has a hemispheric strategy functioned so strikingly as did the Japanese grand offensive in the Pacific in the early months of 1942. The plan was audacious. Once the heavy units of America's Pacific fleet had been destroyed or neutralized at Pearl Harbor and westward, a task force would cut the Navy's line of communications across the Pacific by capturing Wake and Guam. Secured on their eastern flank, naval and army forces would then sweep south in a series of carefully phased movements.

In the first phase, lasting about seven weeks, one division from the army in South China would capture Hong Kong; two and a half divisions and one air division would assault the Philippines from Formosa; and in the southwest one army would occupy Thailand and then move into southern Burma, thus cutting the vital communications link between India and Malaya, while a larger army seized a bridgehead in northern Malaya and then drove south toward Singapore. In the second phase, taking another seven weeks, reinforced troops would advance south from the Philippines to capture key points in Borneo, the Celebes, and Timor, while the Guam-Wake task force moved on New Guinea and the Bismarck Archipelago. In the third phase, operations against Java and Sumatra would be completed, and in the fourth, the occupation of Burma and the seizure of the Andaman and Nicobar Islands in the Bay of Bengal. By this time Tokyo would have attained its strategic objective—a vast defense perimeter stretching from the India-Burma frontier, through the Bay of Bengal, Sumatra, Java, Timor, New Guinea, the Bismarck Archipelago, the Marshall and Gilbert Islands, and Wake, to the Kuriles.

That was the plan and that was what happened, though at different tempos. Seven hundred Japanese landed on the beaches of Agaña, in Guam, on December 10 and forced the tiny garrison's surrender after a half-hour fire fight. Wake took longer. A "fixed aircraft carrier" moored over a thousand miles from Midway, the little atoll was manned by about five hundred Marines, who had a few small artillery pieces and a dozen Grumman Wildcats lacking both armor and self-sealing fuel tanks. The first air attack knocked out most of the Wildcats on the ground. Bombing continued for three days, after which the Japanese tried a landing—only to be miraculously driven off by Wake's gun crews, with the loss of two destroyers. A relief expedition of carriers and support vessels was dispatched from Pearl Harbor but retired faintheartedly after a series of mishaps. After more air strikes had worn the defenders down, Japanese warships and transports returned on December 23 and overwhelmed the garrison in bloody fighting.

In the Philippines the Japanese planned to destroy America's Far East Air Force and then capture Luzon with a five-pronged ground assault, and that is what they did. Faulty communications and bad luck marked MacArthur's air defense. When the Zeroes roared down on Clark Field ten hours after the Pearl Harbor attack, they saw with surprise and relief B-17's and fighters nicely lined up, evidently preparing to take off.

In hardly more than an hour the Japanese knocked out thirty-five of the exposed planes and crippled American air power in the Philippines. MacArthur, who a day or two before had told military colleagues that he was absolutely secure against air attack, reported that the Japanese planes had been brilliantly handled and thought that some of them were perhaps handled by white pilots. Three hundred miles north, the Japanese, under Lieutenant General Masaharu Homma, were beginning their first landings on Luzon; in the next two weeks, in the face of harassment from the United States Navy, foul weather, and occasional communications failures of their own, they put thousands of troops on the northwestern, northern, and southeastern coasts of the long sprawl of Luzon, with the main concentration in Lingayen Gulf. In a final thrust—from the sea just before Christmas—twenty-four transports landed an infantry division in Lamon Bay, at the "rear entrance" to Manila.

For China, Tokyo planned a quick seizure of the foreign concessions in Shanghai and Tientsin as well as Hong Kong. The former had no chance to hold out; the crew of the river gunboat *Wake* had to surrender after failing to scuttle her—the only American ship to surrender in the whole war. The British and Canadian forces in Hong Kong put up unexpectedly strong resistance, but the increasingly familiar Japanese pattern—heavy bombing followed by overwhelming ground power—brought the surrender of the garrison on Christmas Day.

It was in Malaya, however, that Japanese Imperial Headquarters concentrated its main power. A naval force with nineteen transports headed up the Gulf of Siam, made a feint toward Bangkok, and then thrust its main force into the undefended port of Singora before dawn on December 8. The Japanese quickly won air command over the combat area and over the adjacent seas. In sinking the *Prince of Wales* and the *Repulse* they destroyed the only Allied battleship and battle cruiser west of Hawaii. Soon the ground forces were pushing down the length of Malaya and displaying the skill and versatility that would become a legend in the Pacific: turning strong points by quick amphibious hops, infiltrating the jungle, deftly employing light tanks and mobile forces, and always pressing the attack. By New Year's Day several columns were converging north of Singapore.

So quickly did the Japanese fan out across the South Pacific and knock their adversaries off balance that the Allies not only were unable to establish counterstrategy, but they were unable to set up effective command machinery to make such strategy. The new ABDA command under Wavell, embracing American, British, Dutch, and Australian forces spread out over vast areas of Burma, Malaya, the Dutch East Indies, and the Philippines, was disintegrating even as Wavell was trying to take control. Instructed to hold the Malay Barrier, Burma, and Australia, and even "to take the offensive at the earliest opportunity" against Japan, the British General found that even on paper he had no power to relieve subordinate commanders, who retained the right to appeal to their governments. It was a jerry-built structure that could not survive defeat, and perhaps not even victory.

Already Roosevelt's high goal of the militarily united nations was facing the splintering impact of defeat. As the Japanese drove south, Australia became more alarmed about its cities lying along the exposed seacoasts. Prime Minister John Curtin feared that the British would not be able to reinforce the defense of Malaya, which included Australian infantry units and air squadrons. Under heavy pressure, he communicated directly with Roosevelt, bypassing Churchill. "The army in Malaya must be provided with air support," he cabled to Washington the day after Christmas, "otherwise there will be a repetition of Greece and Crete, and Singapore will be grievously threatened." The fall of Singapore would leave Australia isolated from the mother country. Reinforcements marked by London for Malaya, he complained to Roosevelt, seemed utterly inadequate.

The next day Curtin made a declaration of military independence from Great Britain—and did so publicly. "Without any inhibitions of any kind, I make it quite clear that Australia looks to America, free of any pangs as to our traditional links with the United Kingdom."

Curtin's declaration put Roosevelt in a political vise between London and Canberra, but militarily he was able to reassure the apprehensive Australians. A week after Pearl Harbor, Marshall had called a fifty-one-year-old staff officer, Dwight D. Eisenhower, to Washington and asked him to work out a general plan of action for the Pacific. After a quick assessment Eisenhower concluded that while every effort should be made to help MacArthur on Luzon, the United States must keep open the Pacific line of communication with Australia and establish a base there. Stimson welcomed the plan, partly because he feared that the Navy was all too ready to abandon the Far East entirely while the admirals built up their battle power. If the Allies were driven out of the Philippines and Singapore, he calculated, they could fall back on the East Indies and Australia, "and with the cooperation of China—if we can keep that going—we can strike good counterblows at Japan." Roosevelt approved this plan, and soon was able to promise Curtin sizable reinforcements.

If we can keep China going—this was the cardinal problem in the Allied plan. Chungking emerged as both a demanding and a divisive factor in the United Nations within days of Pearl Harbor. Churchill found in Washington what he felt to be an exaggerated view of China's importance. Roosevelt, he sensed, believed that Chinese fighting power rivaled that of Britain and even of Russia. He warned Roosevelt that American opinion overestimated the contributions that China could make to the global war. The President strongly disagreed, Churchill remembered later. What would happen, Roosevelt asked him, if China's five hundred million population developed in the same way as Japan had and got hold of modern weapons? Churchill responded that he was more concerned with the present war. He assured Roosevelt that he would "of course always be helpful and polite to the Chinese, whom I admired and liked as a race"—but he still disagreed. If he could sum up in one word the lesson he had learned in the United States, he said later, it was "China."

Relations in the field between the Chinese and the British were already deteriorating. Immediately after Pearl Harbor, Chiang had grandly offered to hand over all Chinese resources unreservedly to the common cause, and he was disturbed that the British, even in their direst moment, seemed standoffish. Wavell would accept only two Chinese divisions for the defense of Burma—which was the defense also of the Burma Road, the only remaining supply route to Chungking. Chiang also suspected that in their extremity the British were filching supplies promised to China. But Wavell preferred to defend Burma with imperial troops, partly because the Burmese themselves, he felt, feared too many Chinese troops in their country. He asked Churchill to correct Roosevelt's erroneous impression of his attitude.

"I am aware of American sentiment about the Chinese," he added tartly, "but democracies are apt to think with their hearts rather than with their heads, and a general's business is, or should be, to use his head for planning."

By late January, American eyes riveted on Luzon. The ordeal of the jungle fighting was rivaled only by the bleakness of the choices facing the high command in Washington, and by the drama of the men caught in a huge trap from which they could not free themselves.

A more fitting hero for the drama could hardly have been contrived. By 1942 Douglas MacArthur's years stretched back over the great military events of the first half-century and a career of rare military virtuosity: observer with the Japanese Army in the Russo-Japanese War, aide-de-camp to President Theodore Roosevelt, assistant to Secretary of War Newton D. Baker, engineer officer in the Vera Cruz expedition, Chief of Staff of the 42nd (Rainbow) Division by the end of World War I, superintendent of West Point at the age of thirty-nine, Chief of Staff of the United States Army from 1929 to 1935, the third year of Roosevelt's first term, Field Marshal of the Philippine Army, recalled to active duty in 1941.

MacArthur and Roosevelt had long had the amicable, wary, and defensive relationship of two seasoned leaders who saw in each other something of the prima donna, the rival, and the expert in his own trade. Their relationship was now dominated by the dynamics of war. In wartime each military echelon tends to be generous and forgiving of the next echelon below, which is nearer the field of danger and heroism, and demanding and critical of the next echelon above. This was the case in the Philippines, but it was exacerbated by special conditions. MacArthur loved the Philippines like a second homeland. He had long been a personal friend as well as subordinate of Manuel Quezon, first President of the Philippine Commonwealth and a leader in its long fight for independence. Both men believed that Washington starved the Far East and Pacific commands in general and had neglected Philippine defenses in particular. Both saw the archipelago as the bastion of the Southwest Pacific.

MacArthur had worked out a plan for the best use of his limited strength. As the giant Japanese pincers converged on Manila from north and south, he declared the capital an open city and deftly sidestepped his forces, in a risky double retrograde movement, to the Bataan Peninsula. Homma now closed in for the siege of Bataan. With limited troops of his own, since Imperial Headquarters considered the Philippines a secondary objective, for six days he drove again and again at the improvised line of Americans and Filipinos across the northern part of the peninsula. Finding an opening, he forced MacArthur's troops down to the waist of Bataan. By now the main foe of both armies was not each other, but malaria, beriberi, dysentery, and deepening fatigue. Reluctantly Homma realized that he would have to call on Tokyo for more troops.

MacArthur by now was deep in another campaign—enlisting help from Washington. From the start he had rallied his forces with the promise that help was coming. The President's message of December 28 cheered the defenders, and the New York *Times* report of it even more: ALL AID PROMISED / PRESIDENT PLEDGES PROTECTION. Even in January MacArthur was assuring his forces that "thousands of troops and hundreds of planes" were on the way. But the hoped-for flood of supplies was actually a driblet. The embattled General had to deal not only with Washington but also with the United States Asiatic fleet, which was under the separate command of Admiral Thomas C. Hart. MacArthur wanted him to use his small fleet to protect the line of supply up the long string of islands, and even to ferry planes and supplies. Hart, with inadequate air cover, with a handful of ships all "old enough to vote," and with a new-found respect for Japanese striking power, would not risk his main strength; he agreed to commit only his large submarine fleet, but this was to prove inadequate. Commercial ships were hired to run the ever-tightening blockade, but only three small ships finally got through.

Unceasingly MacArthur called for a more aggressive strategy in the Southwest Pacific. "The Japanese are sweeping southward in a great offensive," he radioed to Marshall on February 4, "and the Allies are attempting merely to stop them by building up forces in their front." This method always failed in war and would be "a fatal mistake on the part of the Democratic Allies." The enemy could be defeated only by closing with him—and this meant striking with naval power at his 2,000 miles of weakly protected communications. A sea threat would at once relieve the pressure in the south. "I unhesitatingly predict that if this is not done the plan upon which we are now working, based upon the building up of air supremacy in the Southwest Pacific, will fail, the war will be indefinitely prolonged and its final outcome will be jeopardized. Counsels of timidity based upon theories of safety first will not win against such an aggressive and audacious adversary as Japan. . . ." United States High Commissioner Francis Sayre sent a similar plea.

Part of MacArthur's frustration was caused by the fear that his pleas and proposals were not getting through to the "highest authority." Marshall had to assure him that they were.

The Commander in Chief was indeed closely following MacArthur's plight and was eager to help him. But a difference of perspective and interest had separated the War Department and MacArthur from the start. MacArthur took—or professed to take—Stimson's and Marshall's decision to give him emergency support and to show loyalty to the Filipinos, and, above all, to slow down the enemy, as a willingness to make a major commitment in the Philippines. In fact, Marshall and Eisenhower did not propose to make this a strategic commitment; on the contrary, once they saw the weight of the Japanese assault in Luzon, assessed the full damage to the fleet after Pearl Harbor, and felt the sting of Japanese air power against warships and merchantmen, they prepared to write the archipelago off.

Well before Christmas, Stimson and the military leaders were expecting the loss of Luzon and the retreat into Bataan and even to Corregidor. By January 3 the army planners concluded that an offensive northward from Australia to Mindanao would require a fleet so huge that Navy units would have to be transferred from the Atlantic, and that this would constitute "an entirely unjustifiable diversion of forces from the principal theatre—the Atlantic." MacArthur kept up his pleas. As late as mid-February he was urging that time was growing short and that a "determined effort in force made now would probably attract the assistance of Russia." In vain. Deep in the jungles of Luzon, he was running into the citadel of Atlantic First.

Roosevelt's position was more ambiguous. His warm message to the Philippine people of December 28 had been reassuring about long-run protection of the Commonwealth but studiedly ambiguous as to immediate, all-out support. Fearing that both friend and foe might interpret his message as predicting a temporary loss of the archipelago, he had Hassett and Early deny that this was any kind of valedictory. But the more he stressed that he was *not* writing off MacArthur's forces, the more he aroused false expectations.

Now Quezon tried a desperate maneuver. Agonized by the Japanese advance, crippled by tuberculosis, enfuriated by Washington's refusal to act decisively, he proposed to Roosevelt that if the Philippines could not be saved, Washington should grant the country immediate independence and agree with Tokyo on a joint withdrawal of both forces; then the Philippines would be neutralized and spared the scourge of war and defeat. MacArthur had demurred at the step until Quezon told him that this was not a serious proposal; he hoped it might shock Washington into seeing the importance of the Far East.

Shock Washington it did. To Eisenhower it was a "bombshell." Stimson and Marshall were disturbed that MacArthur, in his accompanying message, did not disown the neutralization proposal; rather, he treated it seriously as an alternative. They took the message to Roosevelt. Standing before the President as if in a court, Stimson denounced the idea as a moral abdication. Roosevelt, far more than the War Department, had to think of all the political implications of allowing to die the commonwealth that his nation had promised independence.

But he did not hesitate to veto the plan. Watching him, Marshall decided that all his doubts about the President were negated—that here was a great man. Soon on the way from Roosevelt to MacArthur was a message free of reproach but clear in its summons:

"American forces will continue to keep our flag flying in the Philippines so long as there remains any possibility of resistance. I have made these decisions in complete understanding of your military estimate that accompanied President Quezon's message to me. The duty and necessity of resisting Japanese aggression to the last transcends in importance any other obligation now facing us in the Philippines.

"There has gradually been welded into a common front a globe encircling opposition to the predatory powers that are seeking the destruction of individual liberty and freedom of government. We cannot afford to have this line broken in any particular theatre. As the most powerful member of this coalition we cannot display weakness in fact or in spirit anywhere. . . .

"I therefore give you this most difficult mission in full understanding of the desperate situation to which you may shortly be reduced. . . ."

An accompanying message to Quezon struck the same note—and pledged ultimate liberation of the islands and independence for the Commonwealth.

Roosevelt could not save the Philippines, but he would save its President and its commander. On February 20, Quezon, his family, and his War Cabinet slipped away from Corregidor in a submarine. Three days later the President directed MacArthur to proceed to Mindanao, arrange for the prolonged defense of the southern Philippines, and then proceed to Australia, "where you will assume command of all United States troops." MacArthur stayed with his command at Corregidor for another two weeks; then he, his wife, his son, and a small staff left on a dark evening in four torpedo boats. Through hazards they made their way to Mindanao and then by plane and train to Melbourne, arriving to a hero's welcome and to the award by the Commander in Chief of the Congressional Medal of Honor.

"The President of the United States," MacArthur announced, "ordered me to break through the Japanese lines and proceed from Corregidor to Australia for the purpose, as I understand it, of organizing the American offensive against Japan, a primary object of which is the relief of the Philippines. I came through and I shall return."

By now, late March 1942, the whole Southwest Pacific defense was in disarray. Relying more on speed, surprise, and skill than massed strength, the Japanese had moved south and easily overpowered Singapore by mid-February; forced the British out of Rangoon and turned back the Chinese reinforcements; enveloped Borneo; and overrun the great Malay Barrier—4,000 miles long—stretching from northern Sumatra through Java and Timor to New Guinea, New Britain, and the Solomons. The Japanese claimed almost 100,000 prisoners, and their Navy took a heavy toll of cruisers and destroyers in the Java Sea. At the end of March, ABDA was in ruins; India and Australia lay open to invasion.

THIS GENERATION OF AMERICANS

During the early months of 1942 the President had to deal at home with one towering fact: for the first time in a century and a quarter Americans were experiencing wide and sustained military defeat at the hands of foreigners.

At first, even with the shocking news of Pearl Harbor and the other disasters, people had been excited and even titillated by the war, as with a new fad. The air-raid scares, the war rallies and bond drives, the exciting reports of Axis raiders off the coasts, the blossoming uniforms, the air-raid shelters and instructions, the first war jingles ("We're going to have to slap—the cheeky little Japs"), the roundup of aliens, the exhilarating sense of being part of a great national and world effort—all these, plus inexhaustible American optimism and the unquenchable sense of military superiority over all comers, seemed to obliterate the early bad news from the war fronts. Even the nuisances and shortages—cancellation of football games and other national ceremonies, tire rationing, endless lines—were submerged in the national mood of militancy, solidarity, purpose.

But as the weeks passed and the Japanese seemed to accelerate, rather than bog down, the mood changed. People seemed to be more querulous; they hunted for scapegoats; old differences burst through the screen of national unity; there was gambling, hoarding, profiteering. Roosevelt at this point was not much concerned about his personal popularity, which, indeed—in terms of answers to the query "Would you vote for Roosevelt today?"—spurted from the low 70 percentile in November 1941 to 84 in early January 1942, and then leveled off in the high seventies over the next six months. He was more concerned about the people's sense of confidence in their nation's effort and in themselves. The first three or four months of the war saw a steady decline in popular confidence that the nation was doing all it could to win the war, though there was little agreement about alternatives. Favorable press support of the President dropped on domestic affairs to 35 per cent, according to one February survey, and on his handling of foreign affairs to 52 per cent.

The President had helped create the early euphoria and he had to cope with the ensuing letdown. He had expressed the nation's optimism about victory, without the harsh warning of early defeats and blood and tears that Churchill had sounded; he had sent an ambiguously optimistic message to the Philippines; he had honored the fallen pilot Colin P. Kelly—by asking the President of 1956 to grant his son appointment as a West Point cadet—for a feat that was widely understood to be the sinking of a Japanese battleship, which in fact had been untouched. He could not overcome his invincible optimism about victory in the long run; and doubtless would not if he could—for that kind of optimism had helped unite and invigorate the nation in the dark days of 1933.

The most galling development for the President was that the isolationists of 1941 had become the guardhouse strategists of 1942. The war cry was no longer "Stay out of war," but "Pacific First." SEND SHIPS TO M'ARTHUR NOW was the banner headline across the front page of the New York *Journal-American* on March 10.

Why were war supplies still going to the Russians and British when American boys were desperately short in the Far East? Why weren't people like Colonel Lindbergh and Joseph P. Kennedy being used in the war administration? The Commander in Chief was rarely attacked personally, but, rather, through people close to him, including Eleanor Roosevelt. *Time* reported with a straight face a rumored "White House showdown" in which war chiefs said that Hopkins must quit or they would. Hugh Johnson said that nobody ever elected Harry Hopkins to any office and blamed him and his "palace janissariat" for the failure of war production.

All this was orthodox politics, however unpleasant. A more ominous note was struck by the radical right. Father Charles Coughlin was sticking to his old line as though Pearl Harbor had never happened. His journal, *Social Justice,* attacked Russia for not bombing Japan; charged that MacArthur was "thrown to the dogs"; implied that the battle for Malaya was really a battle for investment brokers holding tin and rubber interests there; and asked whether the common people's most dangerous enemies resided in Berlin, Rome, and Tokyo, or in Washington, New York City, London, and Moscow. During early 1942 the nation was reminded of the pre-Pearl Harbor connections between pro-Nazi isolationists and right-wing Congressmen by the conviction of one of Congressman Fish's secretaries for perjury in testifying about the franking of Nazi-inspired speeches by members of Congress.

The President was not in a wholly forgiving mood toward his old adversaries. He failed to acknowledge a Pearl Harbor day telegram from Joe Kennedy—"Name the battlefront. I'm yours to command"—and when Kennedy reminded him of it eight weeks later, the President answered him cordially, but Kennedy was never offered a major war post. The President and Stimson denied Lindbergh a combat post on the grounds that he had not wholly given up some of his old defeatist, or at least isolationist, views, and "evidently lacked faith," as the Secretary of War put it, "in the righteousness of our cause." Roosevelt was especially incensed by anti-British and anti-Russian criticism in the capital. "Washington is the worst rumor factory, and therefore the source of more lies that are spoken and printed throughout the United States, than any other community," he complained to reporters.

He was intrigued by Thomas E. Dewey's charge that an "American Cliveden set in Washington and other cities" was scheming to use the Republican party to achieve a negotiated peace with the Axis. "Who in the name of all that is mysterious are the members of the American 'Cliveden Set' in Washington or elsewhere?" he asked Myron Taylor. Politically he would have been delighted to have a Cliveden Set as a foil. Soon he decided that there was indeed a Cliveden Set—or a "Dower House Set," named for the country home of Eleanor ("Cissy") Patterson, publisher of the Washington *Times Herald,* and composed of Cissy, Joseph Patterson, of the New York *Daily News,* and Colonel McCormick, of the Chicago *Tribune,* with William Randolph Hearst and Roy Howard as associate members. The Commander in Chief laughed at McCormick's claim of having introduced ROTC into the schools and mechanization into the Army, and when Morris Ernst wrote to him that he was seeing Eleanor Patterson on behalf of his client Walter Winchell and proposed to "examine Cissy down to her undies," Roosevelt asked not to be present on that occasion—"I have a weak stomach."

To counter attitudes that he felt bordered on defeatism and disunity, the President decided late in February to make a major address on Washington's Birthday. He asked in advance that people listen with a world map in hand.

He began by reminding Americans of the formidable odds that Washington and his Continental Army had faced. "In a sense, every winter was a Valley Forge." Everywhere there had been fifth columnists, and selfish, jealous, fearful men who had proclaimed Washington's cause hopeless and demanded a negotiated peace.

"Washington's conduct in those hard times has provided the model for all Americans since then—a model of moral stamina."

The President stumbled a bit at the start of his talk, but soon reached his smooth, measured cadence.

"This war is a new kind of war. It is different from all other wars in the past, not only in its methods and weapons but also in its geography. It is warfare in terms of every continent, every island, every sea, every air lane in the world." He asked his listeners to take out their maps and follow with him the references to the world-encircling battlelines of the war.

He then launched into a blunt defense of his strategy. He warned against Axis efforts to isolate the United States, Britain, Russia, and China from one another through the old divide-and-conquer technique.

"There are those who still think in terms of sailing ships. They advise us to pull our warships and our planes and our merchant ships into our own home waters and concentrate solely on last-ditch defense. Look at your map. . . . It is obvious what would happen if all these great reservoirs of power were cut off from each other either by enemy action or by self-imposed isolation."

He then went into a detailed explanation of the interdependence of the reservoirs of power, beginning with China.

"From Berlin, Rome, and Tokyo we have been described as a Nation of weaklings—'playboys'—who would hire British soldiers, or Russian soldiers, or Chinese soldiers to do our fighting for us."

Now he spoke slowly and dramatically, with great pauses and emphases for effect.

"Let *them* repeat that *now!*

"Let them *tell* that to *General MacArthur* and his men.

"Let them tell *that* to the sailors who today are hitting *hard* in the far waters of the Pacific.

"Let them tell *that* to the boys in the Flying *For*tresses.

"Let them"—a long pause—"tell *that* to the Marines. . . ."

Up in the oval study after the speech the President learned that the Japanese had provided a dramatic accompaniment to his speech: while he was talking, a Japanese submarine surfaced off the coast near Santa Barbara and fired some shells, which landed on a ranch, inflicting no casualties or real damage. The shelling produced huge headlines next day—and taught Roosevelt, Sherwood said later, never again to announce his speeches more than two or three days ahead of time.

Even though the President was pleased by the reaction to his fireside chat, he realized that words, no matter how evocative, were idle unless backed by deeds, and that if he went on the air too often his talks would lose their impact. He felt that Churchill had suffered from too much personal leadership. The real trouble, he believed, lay not in the people or their elected leaders but in the former isolationists, who wanted disunity and even a negotiated peace—the publishers, columnists, radio commentators, the "KKK crowd" and "some of the wild Irish." But the only effective answer to them was victory—and victories were slow in coming in the winter and spring of 1942.

He could still exhibit a soldier's wry humor under fire. He enjoyed telling friends about Elmer Davis's comment following the Washington's Birthday speech:

"Some people want the United States to win so long as England loses. Some people want the United States to win so long as Russia loses. And some people want the United States to win so long as Roosevelt loses."

During these weeks of stinging defeat the President ratified an action that was widely accepted at the time but came to be viewed in later years as one of the sorriest episodes in American history. This was the uprooting of tens of thousands of Japanese-Americans from their homes on the West Coast and their incarceration in concentration camps hundreds of miles away.

Few Americans had paid more glowing homage than had Roosevelt to the democratic idea of individual liberty. A week after Pearl Harbor he had proclaimed Bill of Rights Day, on the hundred-and-fiftieth anniversary of the ratification of the Bill of Rights, and had taken the trouble, during those first harrowing days of war, to renew his and the nation's allegiance to the ancient liberties. After flaying Hitler for crushing individual liberty, he said: "We Americans know that the determination of this generation of our people to preserve liberty is as fixed and certain as the determination of those early generations of Americans to win it.

"We will not, under any threat, or in the face of any danger, surrender the guarantees of liberty our forefathers framed for us in the Bill of Rights.

"We hold with all the passion of our hearts and minds to those commitments of the human spirit. . . ."

The Bill of Rights seemed in little jeopardy at the time. Americans were treating German, Italian, and Japanese aliens in their midst with admirable restraint. There were only a few incidents, such as the sawing down by some fool or fanatic of four Japanese cherry trees in Washington's Tidal Basin. Oddly, one of the most tolerant areas with a large "foreign" population seemed to be California. The press there was restrained, even generous, as were letters to the editor. "The roundup of Japanese citizens in various parts of the country," declared the San Francisco *Chronicle*, ". . . is not a call for volunteer spy hunters to go into action." Other papers called for fairness toward Japanese aliens as well as toward Nisei—American-born citizens of Japanese parentage. "Let's not repeat our mistakes of the last war" was a refrain.

The new Attorney General, Francis Biddle, wished to avoid mass internment and any repetition of the persecution of aliens that occurred during World War I. Roosevelt's attitude was less clear. When Biddle brought him the proclamation to intern German aliens, Roosevelt asked him how many Germans there were in the country. Biddle thought about 600,000. "And you're going to intern all of them?" Roosevelt asked, as Biddle remembered later. Not quite all, Biddle said. "I don't care so much about the Italians," Roosevelt went on. "They are a lot of opera singers, but the Germans are different, they may be dangerous." Admiral McIntire was swabbing the President's nose during this colloquium, and Biddle hastily withdrew, with the impression that his chief was reacting more to his sinuses than to subversives.

During January the climate of opinion in California turned harshly toward fear, suspicion, intolerance. Clamor arose for mass evacuation and other drastic action. The causes of the change have long been studied and defy easy explanation. Partly it was the endless Japanese advance in the Pacific, combined with a spate of false alarms—aside from the Santa Barbara episode—of attacks on the coast, stories of secret broadcasting equipment, flashing signals, strange lights, and the like. In part it was a growing feeling that the Justice Department was pursuing half-measures; paradoxically, as the federal authorities became more energetic in sealing off sensitive zones and taking other precautions, the popular demand for drastic measures seemed to grow. But the main ingredient that fired and fueled the demand for "cleaning out the Japs" was starkly obvious. The old racism—economic, social, and pathological—toward Japanese on the West Coast simmered for a few weeks after Pearl Harbor and then burst into flames.

"Personally, I hate the Japanese," declared a prominent West Coast columnist on January 29, "and that goes for all of them." He called for immediate removal of every Japanese on the West Coast to the interior. "I don't mean a nice part of the interior either. Herd 'em up, pack 'em off and give 'em the inside room in the badlands. . . ."

More and more, Washington felt the heat. California officials—notably Governor Culbert L. Olson and Attorney General Earl Warren, working in close touch with sheriffs and district attorneys—threw their weight behind the campaign for evacuation. In Washington the West Coast congressional delegations put unrelenting pressure on the Justice and War Departments and on their regional officials. Congressmen denounced as "jackasses" those who had failed to deal with sabotage and espionage at Pearl Harbor and would fail again.

It was the old story of a determined and vocal minority group of regional politicians and spokesmen with a definite plan united against an array of federal officials who were divided, irresolute, and not committed against racism. General John De Witt, the Army's West Coast commander, after much vacillation finally gave his support to a general evacuation. For a while Stimson demurred on constitutional grounds. But during the first weeks of February—a time of frightful news from the war fronts—he gave way, partly because he had concluded that "their racial characteristics are such that we cannot understand or trust even the citizen Japanese."

Biddle held out longer. An aristocratic Philadelphian and Grotonian, proudly conscious of his inheritance from the Randolphs of Virginia and full of a fastidious *noblesse oblige,* he was not one to be swept off his feet by generals and regional politicians. But his political resources were small. He was a new member of the Cabinet, highly impressed by Stimson and somewhat mystified by Roosevelt. He did not enlist his potential Cabinet allies, Ickes and Morgenthau; indeed, there was no Cabinet discussion. Finding himself almost alone, he resorted to expedients and technicalities and was lost. Only a great outcry of protest on the highest moral grounds could have stopped the drift toward evacuation, and Biddle was neither temperamentally nor politically capable of it.

So the fate of 110,000 aliens and citizens was bucked over to the

White House—and into a void. Because there had been no clarion call of protest the President was never faced with a compelling set of alternatives and arguments. He confronted on February 11 a War Department memo that tried simply to put the onus of decision on him. The President would not have it. This was the same day he was answering Quezon's query about neutralization; Singapore was on the verge of surrendering. The evacuation may have seemed to him a tricky and second-level question. He told Stimson and McCloy to do whatever they thought necessary, and asked only that they be as reasonable as they could. Eight days later the President signed an order for evacuation prepared by Biddle and Stimson and their men. A month later Congress passed a bill supporting the President's action. During the debate Representative John Rankin, of Mississippi, demanded that Japanese in concentration camps be segregated by sex so that they would not multiply twenty-five times in two generations.

Hindsight would prove that there was little military necessity for mass evacuation. The American Civil Liberties Union would call it "the worst single wholesale violation of civil rights of American citizens in our history." Hindsight would also put responsibility not only on the obvious factors of racism and frustration, but also on a great negative factor—the opposition that never showed up. The liberal dailies and weeklies were largely silent. Walter Lippmann, so zealous of individual liberties back in New Deal days, urged strong measures because, he said, the Pacific Coast was officially a combat zone and no one had a constitutional right to "do business on a battlefield." Westbrook Pegler, citing Lippmann's argument, cried that every Japanese in California should be under guard, "and to hell with *habeas corpus* until the danger is over." A few Congressmen protested—most notably Senator Taft, in querying the congressional validation—but they were ineffectual. Doubting administration officials did not carry their protests to the Chief Executive.

Only a strong civil-libertarian President could have faced down all these forces, and Roosevelt was not a strong civil libertarian. Like Jefferson in earlier days, he was all for civil liberties in general but easily found exceptions in particular. He related to friends that at a Cabinet meeting (in March 1942) he had told Biddle that civil liberties were okay for 99 per cent but he ought to bear down on the rest. When Biddle pleaded that it was hard to get convictions, Roosevelt answered that when Lincoln's Attorney General would not proceed against Vallandigham, Lincoln declared martial law in that county and then had Vallandigham tried by a drumhead court-martial. Earlier he had treated Biddle's earnest support of civil liberties as a joking matter—in fact, had solemnly told him that he was planning to abrogate freedom of speech during the war and then he let Biddle declaim against the idea at length before telling him he was joking.

Indeed, Roosevelt seemed to enjoy shocking the shy Philadelphian. Once, when J. Edgar Hoover confessed to the President, in the Attorney General's presence, that an FBI agent had tried to tap the telephone wire of left-wing union leader Harry Bridges, and had been caught in the act, Roosevelt roared with laughter, slapped Hoover on the back, and shouted gleefully, "By God, Edgar, that's the first time you've been caught with your pants down!"

The President assumed that the German saboteurs who landed on the East Coast in June 1942 were guilty and should be executed. He liked the idea of quick drumhead courts in wartime. To be sure, Roosevelt's civil-liberties derelictions were not numerous, but certainly the wartime White House was not dependably a source of strong and sustained support for civil liberties in specific situations.

This expedient departure from principle was nothing new in American history, but it had a dangerous edge in 1942. The supreme irony of the evacuation was that while Germans and Italians offered the same alleged threats to military security as the Nisei and Issei, their guilt was established on an individual basis, not a racial basis. Roosevelt was quite aware of the distinction and supported it. Nor did he seem concerned that his friends the Chinese were part of the same yellow race against which he was discriminating. He was following unconsciously a kind of Atlantic First policy in civil liberties as well as military strategy. By allowing his subordinates to treat aliens and citizens on a racial basis, he was unwittingly validating the political strategy that Tokyo was directing during the early months of 1942.

THE WAR AGAINST THE WHITES

While Washington was interning over 100,000 American citizens and aliens mainly on racial grounds, Tokyo was conducting its main political offensive in Southeast Asia on largely the same basis.

The aims of the war, proclaimed the Imperial Rescript in December, were to insure the peace and stability of East Asia and to defend that region against Anglo-American exploitation. The struggle was named the Greater East Asia War; its aim was to build the Greater East Asia Co-Prosperity Sphere. Late in January 1942 Premier Tojo told the Diet that Japan would grant independence to South Pacific peoples who undertook to help build the new sphere. These plans were hoisted on a wave of popular exultation. Propagandists attacked white Western rule, its individualism, materialism, class and group strife. Soon newspapers were gleefully picturing white Europeans, naked to the waist, forced to do the physical labor once reserved for Asiatics. "Remember December Eighth!" proclaimed a Japanese poet:

> "This day world history has begun anew
> This day Occidental domination is shattered
> All through Asia's lands and seas.
> Japan, with the help of the gods
> Bravely faces white superiority."

The Japanese were shrewd enough to adapt their anti-Western strategy to specific situations. Tokyo signed an alliance with Thailand granting it sovereignty, independence, extensive assistance, and the return of lost territories; and promised Burma independence within the year. The Japanese interned the Dutch officials of Java, dismantled the colonial administrative system, rewrote the textbooks to champion anti-Western and pan-Asiatic doctrines, freed nationalist leaders, including Achmed Sukarno, who had been imprisoned by the Dutch, and promised political concessions.

But it was in the Philippines that the invaders found their most auspicious state of affairs. Proclaiming that they had come to emancipate the Filipinos from America's oppressive domination, they promised to set up the "Philippines for the Filipinos" as part of the Co-Prosperity Sphere. Collaborators were quickly found to adorn the new Japanese-controlled regime. American influence was denounced as hedonistic, materialistic, corrupting of the family. The local Japanese Commander in Chief admonished the Filipinos: "As a leopard cannot change its spots you cannot alter the fact that you are Orientals."

This imperious summons to an antiwhite, pan-Asiatic, nationalist crusade could not cloak potential weaknesses and divisions. Extremists in Tokyo made clear that while all the nations would be equal in the new Asia, Japan would be more so, as "center and leader." Indiscriminate cruelty was inflicted on native populations. Japan's long-term strategic stake in liberating colonial nations ran counter to the short-run needs of the Japanese military, which wanted to control and exploit local populations for immediate war needs. Still, the potential of an antiwhite, pan-Asiatic movement seemed almost limitless in the early months of 1942. Even more, the Japanese showed their skill in appealing to Moslem elements in Southeast Asia and thus raised the specter of an ultimate appeal to Islam and to antiwhite feeling in the Middle East.

Long critical of white colonial policies in Asia, Roosevelt did not underestimate the threat of Tokyo's war against the whites. With the Philippines and the other countries clamped firmly in the Japanese vise, there was little that he could do. But there was one potential battleground where he could try to wield influence—India. With the fall of Singapore in February and the impending overrunning of Rangoon, the subcontinent would soon lie almost naked before a Japanese advance.

Only a President with Rooseveltian self-confidence would have even dared touch the Indian cauldron in the early months of 1942. The looming threat from the east seemed to be sharpening all the old hopes, fears, and antagonisms in that steaming subcontinent. Indian nationalists saw their chance to win freedom from British rule, but they ranged from bitter pan-Asiatics willing to fight along with the Japanese against the whites to those who feared Japanese conquest even more than they hated British rule. Moslems dreaded a grant of independence that would inundate them in Hindu rule; a host of local princes depended on the British to help protect their accustomed prerogatives; separatist interests and sects throughout the country clamored for recognition; in the endless villages millions labored for their daily rice with only the haziest idea of the decisions of far-off London, Tokyo, or even Delhi.

Proud and powerful personalities stood amid the tumult: Jawaharlal Nehru, both a Western intellectual and an Indian patriot, anticolonial and antifascist, leader of Indian nationalists but also their agent; Mohammed Ali Jinnah, wary chief of the Moslem League; Subhas Chandra Bose, eager to form an Indian national army to help the Japanese throw the British out of India. And brooding over the scene was the gnarled, loinclothed figure of Mohandas Gandhi, leader of the Congress party, pacifist, vegetarian, the most powerful man in India, because of his ability to grip the attention of the masses.

Roosevelt had raised the question of India with Churchill in Washington after Pearl Harbor; the Prime Minister had reacted so hotly that the President never—or so Churchill later claimed—dared raise the matter to his face again. By late February the President was concerned with India more for military than ideological reasons. Along with influential Senators and administration officials he feared that the Indians would not rally in support of the British defenders. He asked his embassy in London to sound out Churchill anew, but the Prime Minister had not changed his views a whit. Most of the Indian troops, he said, were Moslems. The fighting people were mainly from the northern areas antagonistic to Congress party leaders. The big population of the low-lying center did not have the vigor to fight anybody. He would not risk alienating the Moslems or the princes.

Undaunted, the President now tried a different gambit. "With much diffidence," he wrote to Churchill, in making any suggestions on a subject which "of course, all of you good people know far more about than I do," he suggested that the American experience with the Articles of Confederation might be a helpful precedent. He presented in detail the idea that a temporary government in India, headed by a small group representing different castes, occupations, religions, regions, and princes, might direct the public services during the war, and at the same time plan for a more permanent government. "Perhaps the analogy of some such method to the travails and problems of the United States from 1783 to 1789 might give a new slant in India itself, and it might cause the people there to forget hard feelings, to become more loyal to the British Empire, and to stress the danger of Japanese domination, together with the advantage of peaceful evolution as against chaotic revolution. . . .

"For the love of Heaven don't bring me into this, though I do want to be of help. It is, strictly speaking, none of my business, except insofar as it is a part and parcel of the successful fight that you and I are making."

The President might well be diffident. Churchill rejected both the analogy and the proposal. He and George III, the Prime Minister felt, were facing altogether different problems. There was no time for a constitutional experiment and a period of trial and error. But because he was under intense pressure to try to break the developing deadlock in New Delhi, he decided to send Sir Stafford Cripps, now back from Moscow and a member of the War Cabinet, to India to make a last effort. Earlier the President had dispatched Louis Johnson, his former Assistant Secretary of War, to New Delhi on a vaguely defined military mission as his personal representative. The choice of Johnson seemed a curious one. A prosperous West Virginia lawyer and politico, he was a founder and onetime national commander of the American Legion, with no known views, if indeed he had any, on the great issues of colonialism, nationalism, and race that racked India.

For a brief moment events played a sardonic game of ducks and drakes with the visitors to New Delhi. Cripps, left-wing Labourite, vegetarian, anti-imperialist, friend of Nehru, acted essentially as an agent of Churchill's Cabinet and found the Congress leaders adamant. The Indians demanded a greater share in the conduct of the war than London would grant them, and they wanted at the end of the war a unified nation that would not be pulled to pieces by secessionist groups. The British feared that control of defense by Congress leaders would inflame the Moslem troops, fragmentize the conduct of the war, and convert Indian defense against the Japanese into a paltry guerrilla war at best. They would not renege on their old pledge to Moslems and princes; but neither would Nehru permit the Balkanization of India.

It was not Cripps the British radical but Johnson the West Virginia politician who for an intoxicating moment seemed about to break the deadlock. Undiscouraged by word from Welles that the President was now keeping hands off, Johnson hurried from Cripps to Nehru to Wavell and around the circle again to keep negotiations alive. Agreement seemed all the more imperative when word reached Delhi that the Japanese Navy in one foray had sunk 100,000 tons of shipping along India's east coast and was preparing to rout the small British fleet. Indians and British alike were turning to Washington for help.

"The magic name over here is Roosevelt," Johnson cabled to Hull, "the land, the people would follow and love, America."

Two days later Johnson's efforts collapsed. He suspected that Churchill was curbing Cripps. He was half right; Churchill was also curbing Johnson. Hopkins, in London, exposed to the Prime Minister's wrath, had urged Roosevelt to play down Johnson's mediatory role. In New Delhi, Cripps saw little hope; he cabled to Churchill that he was coming home. The Prime Minister replied that Cripps would be cordially welcomed for proving how great was the British desire to reach a settlement; the effect in Britain and America had been "wholly beneficial."

Roosevelt made a final effort. In one of the bluntest messages he ever sent to Churchill he urged him to postpone Cripps's departure to allow a final effort at negotiations. American public opinion was almost unanimous, he said, "that the deadlock has been caused by the unwillingness of the British Government to concede to the Indians the right of self-government" and could not understand why Britain was delaying it. The cable reached Churchill at Chequers at three in the morning, Sunday, April 12; Hopkins was still with him, despite Roosevelt's constant urging that his aide get his sleep. It was too late, Churchill cabled back; Cripps had already left, and, anyway, everything could not be thrown into the melting pot again.

"Anything like a serious difference between you and me would break my heart . . ." Churchill concluded. Privately he was bitter. He indicated to Hopkins that he would be ready to resign on the issue—but that if he did, the War Cabinet would continue his policy. Roosevelt had nothing more to say. In appealing to Churchill on the ground of American public opinion rather than of higher political, military, or even moral considerations, he had weakened his position, for Churchill must have known that in fact the American press, at least, broadly supported London's position. Roosevelt's next message was not to Churchill but to Marshall, who was in London:

"Please put Hopkins to bed and keep him there under 24-hour guard by Army or Marine Corps. Ask the King for additional assistance if required on this job."

A message arrived at the White House from Nehru. He only

wanted the President to know, he said, "how anxious and eager we were, and still are, to do our utmost for the defense of India and to associate ourselves with the larger causes of freedom and democracy. To us it is a tragedy that we cannot do so in the way and in the measure we would like to." Yet, he went on, India would not submit to Japanese aggression. "We, who have struggled for so long for freedom and against an old aggression, would prefer to perish rather than submit to a new invader." He concluded with a tribute to the President, "on whom so many all over the world look for leadership in the cause of freedom. . . ." The President did not reply directly; he had Welles ask Johnson to tell Nehru that the President was gratified by the pledge to resist Japan.

By mid-April the Japanese Navy had occupied India's Andaman Islands, smashed the harbor of Colombo, in Ceylon, and chased the crippled British fleet out of the Bay of Bengal and into East African waters.

For a century white rule had been symbolized and enforced by awesome battleships and gunboat diplomacy. Where was the United States Navy now? In hiding, said the Japanese. Rumors circulated that naval losses were much higher than reported. Willkie proclaimed that "we want our Navy seeking out the enemy, not hugging our shores. . . ."

In fact, most of the Pacific fleet was intact and by no means in hiding. On December 7 two forces had been out on mundane missions: the *Lexington,* with eight heavy cruisers and destroyers, delivering Marine bombers to Midway Island; the *Enterprise,* with twelve heavy cruisers and destroyers, returning to Pearl Harbor after ferrying a Marine fighter squadron to Wake Island. The carrier *Saratoga* was about to enter San Diego. After the jolting news from Hawaii, the *Lexington* and *Enterprise* task forces went hunting for the Japanese, but missed them in a tragicomedy of false alarms, erroneous intelligence, misidentification, and lesser blunders. Vice Admiral Chuchi Nagumo's striking force got away without a single encounter at sea by plane or ship—an outcome that was probably fortunate for the Americans, who might well have been annihilated by Nagumo's six carriers in a straight fight. A week later three carrier task forces were dispatched to the relief of beleaguered Wake, but this expedition withdrew as a result of more errors, stormy weather, undue caution, and bad luck.

For a Commander in Chief with a special pride and proprietary interest in the Navy he had built up during the previous decade, the President was remarkably calm about these setbacks. He grumbled at the Navy's lack of enterprise, but as an old mariner he knew the vagaries of wind and wave. Knox was less forbearing. The day Wake fell he complained to Churchill at the White House that the fleet had been ordered to fight the Japanese and after a few hours of steaming had turned back. "What would you do with your Admiral in a case like this?" Churchill replied mildly that it was "dangerous to meddle with Admirals when they say they can't do things. They have always got the weather or fuel or something to argue about." One thing Roosevelt and Knox could do was to reshuffle the shaken Navy command, making Admiral King Commander in Chief of the United States fleet. For some weeks King had an uneasy administrative relationship with Chief of Naval Operations Stark; then the President transferred Stark to London and gave King both jobs.

Far out in the central Pacific, fast American carrier forces were conducting hit-and-run raids during these early weeks of 1942. But the pivot of naval action had shifted west, as Japanese forces converged on the Malay Barrier. Defending the East Indies was a pick-up collection of Dutch, British, and American warships. To the continuing problems of inexperience were added those of a multinational command lacking in common training and even communications, and plagued by shortages of all kinds and by a sinking realization that the Allies could put up only a holding action at best. Despite small tactical victories and individual gallantry, the little Asiatic fleet was virtually destroyed and the Malay Barrier completely breached by early March. The Japanese were especially effective in protecting their ships and invasion forces with land- or carrier-based air power, while the American effort on this score was desperate. The Air Force actually had several hundred fighters accumulating in Australia, but ferrying them to Java via defenseless and unfamiliar fields was risky. One flight was smashed by the enemy over Bali. Another ran into foul weather, and all the planes crashed. Another turned back because of weather and was then destroyed in a heavy Japanese attack on Port Darwin. The aircraft tender *Langley* went down off Java with thirty-two P-40's on board; a cargo ship came through with twenty-seven crated fighters, but these had to be dumped, still crated, into the sea during the evacuation of Java.

"The Pacific situation is now very grave," Roosevelt cabled to Churchill after the fall of Java. It is doubtful, though, that, except for the few hours when the Pearl Harbor losses were coming in, he ever felt any sense of despair over the Pacific defeats. As he wrote to Churchill after the fall of Singapore, no matter how serious the setbacks "we must constantly look forward to the next moves that need to be made to hit the enemy." The sharper the challenge, indeed, the more direct the President's response, for feeling was rising in the administration that the people needed some dramatic feat of arms, even if the strategic value was small.

Such a feat was already in the works. In Florida, on an airstrip the size of a carrier's deck, army airmen under Colonel James Doolittle were practicing take-offs with fully loaded medium bombers. On April Fool's Day, sixteen of these B-25's were loaded onto the carrier *Hornet* and lashed down on the flight deck. Thirteen days later the *Hornet* rendezvoused in the northern Pacific with the *Enterprise,* flying the flag of Admiral William F. ("Bull") Halsey. The small fleet then sped west through heavy seas. These operations were carried out in the strictest secrecy; although this had been a pet project of the President, even he did not know the full details.

The plan was daring, almost foolhardy—to launch the bombers, which had a far longer range than carrier aircraft, about five hundred miles off the coast of Japan for raids on major cities, after which the planes would have barely enough fuel to fly on across the Sea of Japan and land on friendly Chinese airfields. The risk intensified when, about six hundred miles out from Japan, Halsey was discovered by Japanese picket boats; he chose to launch the bombers early instead of either retiring or running his carriers into a hornet's nest.

The army pilots had never flown off a flattop. Green water was breaking over the carrier's ramps. But Doolittle and all his men got off, and within four hours were dropping bombs on a surprised Tokyo and other cities. Not a plane was lost over Japan. One crew landed at Vladivostok and was interned by the neutral Russians; the Japanese captured two crews who went down short of China, and later executed three men for attacking civilian targets; three planes made crash landings; the other crews bailed out in the night over China. There were only five deaths. Behind them they left a mortified Imperial Headquarters and two exultant carriers streaking east.

"What's the news?" Roosevelt innocently asked Hassett the next morning in his Hyde Park bedroom. Hassett mentioned rumors of the bombing. "You know," Roosevelt said, "we have an airplane base in the Himalayas." Hassett looked skeptical. "The base is Shangri-La." The President got no rise from his aide, who had never read James Hilton's *Lost Horizon,* but Roosevelt liked his little joke and soon was telling reporters about the mythical base. The news of the bombing electrified the nation. Few cared that the bombers had done little damage, or that vengeance might be wreaked on the Chinese, or that the Japanese might even retaliate against the West Coast. At last something had been done to "remember Pearl."

The surprise raid, indeed, had a big and unexpected payoff. In the few months after Pearl Harbor the Japanese had destroyed five enemy battleships, one carrier, two cruisers, seven destroyers, and a host of merchant ships, all at the cost of twenty-three small ships—the largest a destroyer—and a sizable number of valuable but expendable planes. The Imperial Navy was riding high; where to turn next? To many in the high command, Australia and India were the most inviting targets. But Yamamoto was still insisting on the old strategy of crushing the American Navy and thus gaining time to build a western Pacific bastion. Pearl Harbor had failed to do the trick. Since the American bombers had obviously come from Midway, Yamamoto argued, the Japanese fleet must now turn east and capture both Midway and the western Aleutians—and draw into combat the carriers of Pacific fleet commander Admiral Chester W. Nimitz. With some doubt the high command approved this plan and began to assemble a huge fleet.

The Japanese at this point were still pressing their advance to the southwest, toward the Solomon Islands and into the Coral Sea. A clash here early in May gave a foretaste of the new kind of naval war—aerial combat at long distances, without direct engagements between surface vessels. The Americans drew first blood on May 7, sinking a small carrier. After much groping in the dark by both sides, planes next day from the *Lexington* and the *Yorktown* and from the *Shokaku* and the *Zuikaki* pummeled each other's carriers. The *Shokaku* was badly damaged, while the grand old *Lexington* caught fire and later went down, but not before every man was saved, and even the captain's dog. While the Japanese won the Battle of the Coral Sea, they pulled back from their drive on Port Moresby, and neither the *Shokaku* nor the *Zuikaki* was able to take part in the approaching showdown in the central Pacific.

But the Japanese felt that they had plenty of power left for the grand sortie against Midway. On May 27, anniversary of Admiral Togo's rout of the Russians in the Battle of Tsushima, the main striking force began to move out—first the screen of destroyers, then the cruisers, the battleships, headed by Admiral Yamamoto's flagship, the superdreadnaught *Yamato,* transports with troops for the seizure of Midway, a large covering force of submarines, and a great striking force of four carriers. To the northeast another attack group was heading toward the Aleutians. Yamamoto's design was bold and ambitious: to attack Dutch Harbor, in the eastern Aleutians, and to occupy the western islands in the chain; then to capture Midway, with the hope of drawing the American fleet to its defense and into a decisive battle. He did not plan to go on to Hawaii, at least for a time. These "Oriental disciples of Mahan," as Samuel Eliot Morison called them, knew that they could seize the military bastion of Oahu only by smashing America's Pacific fleet; if they failed, they could not even hold Midway.

Yamamoto's tactic depended on surprise as well as power, and surprise was denied him from the start. From early May 1942, the broken code and other sources had given Nimitz extensive intelligence of enemy plans. He had time to pack tiny Midway full of planes, to dispatch a small fleet of cruisers and destroyers off toward Alaska, and to mobilize his carriers for the main strike. The *Enterprise* and the *Hornet* sortied out of Pearl on May 28, under the command of Admiral Raymond A. Spruance. The heavily damaged *Yorktown*, patched up at Pearl Harbor in less than two days, pulled out on the thirtieth. The Japanese main fleet was now bearing down on its target.

The President followed the moves closely. "It looks, at this moment," he wrote to MacArthur on June 2, "as if the Japanese Fleet is heading toward the Aleutian Islands or Midway and Hawaii, with a remote possibility it may attack Southern California or Seattle by air."

Early on June 4 over one hundred planes soared off the four Japanese carriers and descended on Midway, while the *Enterprise* and the *Hornet*, unknown to the enemy, waited to pounce. So valiant was the island's defense that Nagumo, commanding the Japanese carrier forces, decided that a second softening-up was necessary before the invasion. Spruance's torpedo bombers caught him as he was busy recovering planes from the first strike and preparing planes for the second. By mischance the American torpedo bombers came in without fighter protection, and Zeroes knocked them down in a terrible slaughter; not a single torpedo reached the enemy flattops. But the intrepid torpedo bombers drew so much attention that American dive bombers were able to make their long plunges and rain their missiles on cluttered flight decks. In a few minutes three Japanese carriers were infernos of explosions and fire. Dive bombers got the fourth carrier later in the day. The *Yorktown*, too, was set afire in a counterstrike, and heeled badly; it was abandoned, then reboarded, and was being towed to safety when a Japanese submarine penetrated the screening warships and sank her and a destroyer with three torpedoes.

During the night, with his carriers burning or sunk, and his battleships never brought into play, Yamamoto ordered a withdrawal. Spruance considered pursuit but he feared running into the enemy's vastly superior gunpower and perhaps even more carriers. Each side had had enough. The Navy had made mistakes and enjoyed a good deal of luck in the encounter; yet in one carrier thrust Nimitz had broken the backbone of Japanese naval air power, turned the tide of battle in the central Pacific, and incidentally revealed, in Spruance, a commander with a fine balance of boldness and caution, intuition and realism.

The nation was elated by the victory, but Roosevelt did not

exaggerate its effect. The Japanese had won two footholds, Attu and Kiska, in the western Aleutians while Nimitz was occupied to the south, and all around its vast rim of advance and victory Japan was consolidating its grip. Bataan had long since fallen, and early in May the island fortress of Corregidor, pounded by massed artillery from only two miles across the water, had surrendered. The last message to the President from its commander, General Jonathan M. Wainwright, had epitomized the long string of defeats in the Southwest Pacific:

"With broken heart and head bowed in sadness but not in shame, with continued pride in my gallant troops, I go to meet the Japanese commander."

SEVEN *The Cauldron of War*

THE Commander in Chief had no direct part in either the dismal setbacks or the glittering victories of his Navy in the Pacific. He offered suggestions, approved the major decisions, and received a stream of reports during large engagements, but unlike Hitler, who constantly advised and pressed his generals on tactical matters, Roosevelt was content to leave such questions to Admiral King and his Navy headquarters down on Constitution Avenue, and to Admiral Nimitz in his command post at Pearl Harbor. The President occasionally got the same inflated reports of air victories over the Japanese that the public did; he happily informed Churchill that carrier planes in a surprise raid in New Guinea had sunk two heavy cruisers and probably a light cruiser, when actually only one light cruiser and a small transport had gone down. Tempted though he was to involve himself in the fascinating day-to-day moves of his services—especially the Navy—he knew that he must reserve himself for the overriding political and strategic problems. These were coming to a head in the early months of 1942.

For the third spring in a row Hitler was mobilizing for a vast offensive on his Eastern Front. During March the Russian counterattacks had ground down in the snow and mud. The invaders had suffered well over a million casualties—over 100,000 from frostbite alone—and new divisions had to be drawn from Germany and its junior partners. Hitler's aim was no longer the crushing of the Soviet colossus in great encircling movements, but attrition and defeat through close pincer actions.

"Our aim is to wipe out the entire defense potential remaining to the Soviets," he ordered in mid-April, "and to cut them off, as far as possible, from their most important sources of war industry." The Wehrmacht would hold in the center and seize Leningrad in the north, but put its main weight in the south to capture Sevastopol, immobilize Stalingrad, and break through into the Caucasus. Five armies, of one hundred divisions, and 1,500 aircraft were poised for the attack in the south. Hitler did not ignore the heady prospect below the Mediterranean of pushing the British east, opening up the Middle East for assault, and even driving on to a meeting with Japan in India. But, ever the proponent of concentrated strength and attack, he barred any strategic diversion from the eastern war.

The Kremlin still had little choice of strategy. "We want to rid our Soviet land of the German fascist scum," Stalin proclaimed on May Day 1942. "To achieve this aim we must smash the German fascist army and annihilate the German invaders to the last man if they do not surrender. There is no other way. . . ." The Kremlin, emboldened by its winter victories, was not relying on a passive defense; spoiling actions were planned against the expected Nazi assault. But to contain and hurl back the Nazi legions Stalin needed far more aid than he was receiving from the West. Above all, he wanted a direct attack across the English Channel that would create a major second front in France and ease the pressure.

The Kremlin was not reticent on the matter. *Pravda* complained about the inactivity in the west; to the Russians, who could lose whole divisions in a day, the Mediterranean and Pacific battles seemed little more than skirmishes. Litvinov, still the Kremlin's most persuasive commentator to the West, complained to American and British friends that only simultaneous offensives in the east and the west could vanquish Hitler. We hear much about the common efforts of the United Nations, he argued, but what were common efforts without common fighting?

The most powerful supporters of this point of view outside Russia were three politically conservative, anti-Communist, and militarily orthodox Americans: Henry Stimson, George Marshall, and Dwight Eisenhower. As the new head of the Army's revamped War Plans Division, Eisenhower had consistently urged the massing of American strength in Britain as the nearest, safest, most usable, best-located area to mount a concentrated attack against the German rear. "We've got to go to Europe and fight—and we've got to quit wasting resources all over the world—and still worse—wasting time," he argued. "If we're to keep Russia in, save the Middle East, India, and Burma, we've got to begin slugging by air at West Europe, to be followed by a land attack as soon as possible." Stimson and Marshall strongly concurred, despite some differences of opinion in the War Department. The plans for a North African invasion that had been tentatively worked up at the ARCADIA Conference were shelved for the time—a decision made easier by German successes in Libya. Late in March Stimson wrote to the President:

"John Sherman said in 1877, 'The only way to resume species payments is to resume.' Similarly, the only way to get the initiative in this war is to take it.

"My advice is: As soon as your Chiefs of Staff have completed the plans for the northern offensive to your satisfaction, you should send them by a most trusted messenger and advocate to Churchill and his War Council as the American plan which you propose and intend to go ahead with if accepted by Britain. . . . And then having done that, you should lean with all your strength on the ruthless rearrangement of shipping allotments and the preparation of landing gear for the ultimate invasion. That latter work is now going on at a rather dilettante pace. It should be pushed with the fever of war action, aimed at a definite rate of completion not later than September. . . ."

By the end of March, Stimson, Marshall, and Company had a double-pronged war plan for a second front. Between eighteen and twenty-one divisions, including armored, motorized, and one airborne, would be prepared for a massive assault across the Channel by April 1943. A contingency plan was also drawn for a more limited operation, employing a third as many men, for the fall of 1942. The purpose of the second plan betrayed the Army's concern that the Soviets might be either too weak or too strong. It would be employed only if the Russians faced imminent collapse without a second front—"In this case the attack should be considered as a sacrifice to the common good." Or it would be used if the German defenses in Western Europe became critically weakened.

On April 1, 1942, Stimson and Marshall took their plans to the White House. They were worried about the President's reaction. In past meetings he had shown, they felt, a tendency to respond too readily to the widely scattered needs of his allies and his area commanders. Stimson feared he might go in for another "dispersion debauch"; Marshall had tabbed the President's habit of "tossing out new operations" as his "cigarette-holder gesture." But this time they found their chief ready to be convinced. Whatever the difficulties, he recognized the importance of bolstering the Russians and keeping them in the war. Not only did he endorse a cross-channel attack, but he decided to send Hopkins and Marshall to London to consult Churchill. The President's decision "will mark this day as a memorable one in the war," Stimson noted in his diary for this April Fool's Day.

"What Harry and George Marshall will tell you all about has my heart and *mind* in it," Roosevelt wrote to Churchill three days later. "Your people and mine demand the establishment of a front to draw off pressure on the Russians, and these people are wise enough to see that the Russians are today killing more Germans and destroying more equipment than you and I put together. Even if full success is not attained, the *big* objective will be. . . ."

In London the Americans found Churchill surprisingly responsive to their plans. They sent optimistic reports to Roosevelt about the prospects for agreement. Actually Churchill was skeptical of an early large-scale invasion and downright hostile to an emergency landing in the fall of of 1942. All his old fears remained—of another desperate landing with a strong possibility of defeat and evacuation, as in Gallipoli, of a premature British commitment before the Americans could invest heavy ground and air power, of another blood bath in France like World War I. As always, he was playing with thoughts of peripheral operations; an invasion of northern Norway was the favorite at the moment. His military chiefs, notably Brooke, put their professional judgment behind his fears and doubts. Uncharacteristically, though, Churchill did not present his real views bluntly. He accepted the cross-channel attack in principle but lobbed up reservations and qualifications. At this juncture he wanted neither to discourage his ally Stalin, who, after all, could make some kind of deal with Hitler, nor to thwart his friend Roosevelt, who might give in to popular clamor to concentrate in the Pacific and abandon Atlantic First.

The London meetings took place during the Japanese naval victories in the Bay of Bengal. Again and again Churchill conjured up the dread picture of a Japanese conquest of India and a meeting with the Germans in the Middle East. In fact this picture was something of a bogy. The Japanese did not plan a strategic offensive against India. At this point they were heading in just the opposite direction—toward a naval attack in the central Pacific and the fateful showdown at Midway. Hitler was too involved in Russia to make a strategic commitment in the Middle East. The Germans and Japanese were not even conducting joint strategy.

But Churchill saw a mortal peril. To desert four hundred million of His Majesty's Indian subjects would be shameful; to let the Germans and Japanese join hands in India or the Middle East would be a "measureless disaster." Roosevelt doubted that the enemy would join hands—but he could not doubt the intensity of Churchill's feeling of imperial obligation to this huge, vulnerable area.

REPRISE: RUSSIA SECOND

Heartened by Churchill's apparent support of a cross-channel second front, the President turned to the ticklish job of involving the Kremlin in both the problems and the possibilities of the plan. It was unfortunate, he wrote to Stalin, that the distances were too great for them to meet; he hoped that next summer they could spend a few days together near their common border off Alaska, but in the meantime he hoped Stalin could promptly send Molotov and a general to discuss "a very important military proposal involving the utilization of our armed forces in a manner to relieve your critical Western Front."

A week later Stalin responded that he would send Molotov "for an exchange of views on the organization of a second front in Europe in the near future." He, too, hoped for a personal meeting. Roosevelt was pleased at the prospect of the Foreign Commissar's visit. As always, he felt that problems and misunderstandings could best be overcome by face-to-face talk. "I know you will not mind my being brutally frank," he had written to Churchill a few weeks before, "when I tell you that I think I can personally handle Stalin better than either your Foreign Office or my State Department. Stalin hates the guts of all your top people. He thinks he likes me better and I hope he will continue to do so. . . ."

Molotov arrived at the White House on the afternoon of May 29, 1942. He arrived in a state of uncertainty and apprehension, as symbolized by the pistol—along with a roll of sausage and a chunk of black bread—that he carried in his luggage. He had left a Kremlin still resentful over the lag in American military aid, the diversion of supplies to other battlefields, and the delay in planning for a second front. He had stopped in London on the way and signed with Eden a twenty-year peace treaty, but had found Churchill studiously vague about plans for an invasion of the Continent. At this point the Soviet spoiling attacks in the Crimea and south of Kharkov were going badly.

Soon the Foreign Commissar was installed, pistol and all, in a room on the family floor and then meeting with the President, Hull, Hopkins, Litvinov, and two interpreters. At first the discussion stumbled. For all his confidence in man-to-man talk, the President found Molotov stiff and reticent, and the translation delays were cramping. Seeking to establish common ground, Roosevelt ventured that the Soviets might work out some understanding with the Germans over prisoners of war. Molotov sharply dismissed any idea of treating with the treacherous Nazis, whereupon the President remarked that he had similar problems with Japanese treatment of American prisoners, who were fed on the Japanese army rations—"starvation for any white man." After desultory talk about other matters—but not the second front—Hopkins suggested that the Foreign Commissar might like to rest.

Things warmed up after cocktails and dinner that evening. The President talked at length about disarming after the war, policing Germany and Japan, guaranteeing peace for at least twenty-five years, or for as long as his and Stalin's and Churchill's generation could expect to live. Molotov seemed responsive, even amiable. Next day Roosevelt brought Marshall and King into the discussions and asked Molotov to brief them on the strategic situation.

The Russian drew a gloomy picture. Hitler might throw so many men and machines into the next general offensive that the Red Army might not be able to hold. The Nazis would be immensely strengthened, since they would then command food and raw materials in the Ukraine and oil in the Caucasus. This was the ominous prospect. But if the Americans and British were to create a new front and draw off forty German divisions in 1942, Russia could either beat Germany in 1942 or definitely insure its ultimate defeat. It must be 1942, not 1943, because in another year Hitler would be the undisputed master of the Continent and the job would be immeasurably more difficult.

He wanted a straight answer. What was the President's position on a second front?

Roosevelt was ready for the question, but he let Marshall answer it. Were developments clear enough, he asked the Chief of Staff, that we could tell Mr. Stalin that we were preparing a second front? Yes, said the General. Roosevelt then authorized Molotov to tell his government that it could expect the formation of a second front "this year." Disturbed by this apparent commitment, Marshall talked about the problems: the shipping shortage, getting enough men across the Channel, seizing air superiority. King stressed the frightful losses on the Murmansk route; only the day before, a destroyer and five ships out of a convoy of thirty-five had been lost. The Admiral hoped that the Soviet Air Force might bomb German air and submarine bases in northern Norway. Molotov favored a proposal by the President that twenty-four heavy bombers fly from Khartoum, bomb Rumanian oil fields, and land in Russia, but he was cool to a presidential tender that American fighter planes be delivered by air from Alaska to Siberia. The meeting recessed for an official lunch, at which Molotov reminisced about Hitler and Ribbentrop—"the two most disagreeable people he had ever had to deal with"—and the President toasted the masterful leadership of Joseph Stalin, whom he looked forward to meeting.

Thus Roosevelt made the fateful pledge. Later there would be controversy as to just what he had promised—what kind of second front, where, and when—but all the discussions with Molotov clearly implied a cross-channel attack by all the ground and air power Britain and the United States could muster, in August or September of 1942. Roosevelt's reasons seem equally clear in restrospect. He was affected by Molotov's dark picture of the Eastern Front, even though the Foreign Commissar stressed that Russia would never surrender. The news from that front seemed blacker day by day. It had long been agreed that a quick assault must be launched in the west if Russia seemed to be losing. Now the time seemed to have come.

The President, moreover, had an embarrassment on his hands.

He had recently promised the Russians 4.1 million tons of shipments, most of it general supplies but 1.8 million tons of it in planes, tanks, and guns. It was soon evident that the shipping shortage, production delays, and the stepped-up plans for supplies to Britain made such support impossible. Roosevelt decided to leave intact the military aid, which the Russians would need during the summer, and slash the general supplies by more than two-thirds. At his last meeting with Molotov he proposed this reduction on the ground that it would make available a large number of ships that could carry to Britain the munitions needed for the second front. Molotov reminded him that nonmilitary supplies like railroads had a direct bearing on maintaining the front.

A sharp exchange followed. Every ship shifted to England, Roosevelt repeated, brought the second front closer to realization; the Soviets could not eat their cake and have it, too. Molotov bristled at this. The second front would be stronger if the first front still stood. What would happen, he asked cuttingly, if the Soviets got less supply and then no second front eventuated? Evidently sensing a soft brokerage element in the President's proposal, Molotov became insistent. What answer should he take back about a second front? The President was placatory. He told his guest that the British and American military were already discussing practical invasion problems of landing craft and the like, although he knew at this time that Churchill was still worried about the difficulties of a 1942 invasion and was still eying Norway and French Africa.

A private promise was one thing, a public commitment something else. Molotov wanted the latter. He proposed a sentence to be included in a communiqué released in Washington and Moscow: "In the course of the conversations full understanding was reached with regard to the urgent tasks of creating a Second Front in Europe in 1942." Marshall felt that the statement was too strong and urged that there be no reference to 1942, but Roosevelt wanted it kept in. Molotov left Washington happy, the declaration in his pocket; the President wrote to Winant that his Russian visitor had "actually got chummy" toward the end.

Churchill watched these happenings with deepening anxiety. When Molotov returned to London with the communiqué, Churchill agreed to its publication in order to deceive the enemy, but he did not want to deceive his friends. He told Molotov both orally and in writing that although preparations were going forward, he could not promise a second front in 1942. When Molotov said that he had agreed to a reduction in supplies, the Prime Minister was unmoved; he could not see how Roosevelt's proposal to cut Russia's tonnage deliveries would help solve the problem of landing a small army on a heavily fortified coast. He was fully resolved on a big invasion in 1943, and if it was possible to do in 1942 what was planned for 1943, so much the better. With this vague reassurance Molotov flew back to Moscow and to a jubilant meeting of the Supreme Soviet, where in Stalin's presence he quoted the communiqué.

Churchill had sent to Washington Lord Louis Mountbatten, the youthful, adventurous Chief of Combined Operations, to present to Roosevelt some of the dire problems of staging a cross-channel attack in 1942; when Mountbatten reported to him that Roosevelt was talking about a "sacrificial landing" if Russia should be nearing collapse, the Prime Minister decided that he should fly to Washington to keep the President from "getting a little off the rails." His military staff continued to argue strongly against a 1942 assault, but he knew that Stimson and Marshall were pressing for it hard. Roosevelt, as usual, welcomed the visit and invited Churchill to see him first at Hyde Park. As the Prime Minister, Brooke, and Ismay left London on June 17, reports were coming in from Africa that the British were in full retreat and Rommel's forces were closing in around Tobruk.

Two days later the President was waiting in his car when Churchill came to a bumpy landing on a small airstrip near Hyde Park. He showed the Prime Minister his convertible and then drove him around the estate and out on the lawn overlooking the river. Churchill had some anxious moments as his host, using manual controls, turned and backed the car over the grassy bluffs and darted into thick woods to slip away from the Secret Service; the President tried to reassure him by inviting him to feel his biceps, which he said a famous prize fighter had envied. All the time they talked, with Churchill trying not to take Roosevelt's mind off his driving. After lunch the talk continued in Roosevelt's hot little study off the portico. Plans for a landing were going ahead, Churchill told the President, but not one of his commanders had been able to make a plan for September 1942 that had any chance of success. Had the American staff a plan? What would be required? Who would command? In the evening the two men boarded the presidential train for Washington.

Next day Churchill had hardly entered the President's study when a secretary came in with a telegram. Roosevelt read the pink slip and without a word handed it to Churchill. TOBRUK HAS SURRENDERED, WITH TWENTY-FIVE THOUSAND MEN TAKEN PRISONERS. Churchill visibly winced. Defeat he could take; this he felt was disgrace. There was a moment of silence. Then Roosevelt said:

"What can we do to help?"

"Give us as many Sherman tanks as you can spare, and ship them to the Middle East as quickly as possible."

The President sent for Marshall. The Chief of Staff had hardly been able to scrape together enough modern tanks to supply his armored units, after heartbreaking delays. But he rose to the occasion, too. "It is a terrible thing to take the weapons out of a soldier's hands," he said—but if Churchill needed them he could have them.

The fall of Tobruk clinched the British opposition to a European second front in 1942. The plan died hard. Churchill and his generals continued to pay lip service to a cross-channel attack in theory while finding numberless reasons to oppose or delay it in practice. Roosevelt continued to favor it in general while still allocating ships and supplies to other battle sectors across the vast fronts of Africa and Asia. Stimson kept pounding away at the President, as did Marshall, until Roosevelt sent him, along with Hopkins and King, to London for a showdown with the British. Roosevelt's instructions were ambivalent: to fight hard for an attack in France that year, but if that was "finally and definitely out of the picture," to determine upon another place for United States troops to fight in 1942. The three Americans found the British dead set against a second front in Europe. Other ways to commit American troops in 1942 were canvassed; attention turned more and more to Northwest Africa.

The President could hold out no longer, especially since he was somewhat ambivalent himself toward the cross-channel attack for 1942. Giving in to the British, he pressed for a decision on Africa, since time was getting short even for that lesser operation. When Hopkins cabled that the British were delaying a decision on that question, too, Roosevelt urged that planning proceed at once for African landings not later than October 20. He was relieved that a decision was finally in the works; tell Churchill, he said to Hopkins, that the orders now were "full speed ahead."

Who would tell the Bear in Moscow? After all the hopeful talk and half-promises, how would Stalin be informed that there would be no cross-channel attack in 1942? Churchill, who was headed for Cairo to deal directly with Middle Eastern command changes after Rommel's thrust east, glumly volunteered to go on to Moscow to impart the bad news. The President suggested he tell Stalin that a course of action had definitely been set for 1942 without informing him of its precise nature. "It is essential for us to bear in mind our Ally's personality," Roosevelt said, "and the very difficult and dangerous situation that he confronts. I think we should attempt to put ourselves in his place, for no one whose country has been invaded can be expected to approach the war from a world point of view."

Churchill left Cairo for Moscow on August 10 feeling as though he was carrying a large lump of ice to the North Pole. It was a terrible time for the Russians. German forces had taken Sevastopol and the whole Crimea, easily captured Rostov, crossed the Don, and were moving slowly toward Stalingrad. In the south they were racing toward the eastern shore of the Black Sea, penetrating the Caucasian foothills, and heading for the prized oil fields to the southeast. Once again Stalin faced desperate shortages, and he could not forget all the delays in shipments and all the diversions of supplies Churchill and Roosevelt had tolerated or effected—diversions to the Pacific, to the Middle East, even to Britain. After a convoy to Murmansk had been decimated, Churchill decided to suspend further such perilous expeditions during the long summer days; he told Stalin he could not defend the convoys with big warships because any major losses would jeopardize the "whole command of the Atlantic." Stalin had answered furiously late in July that wars could not be fought without losses, the Soviet Union was suffering far greater losses—and "I state most emphatically that the Soviet Government cannot tolerate the Second Front in Europe being postponed till 1943."

Harriman flew with Churchill to Moscow and cabled the proceedings to an anxious Roosevelt. On the first evening, Harriman reported, Stalin answered Churchill's arguments with a bluntness that approached insult. You cannot win wars, he said, if you are afraid of the Germans. He showed little interest in a 1943 second front. Churchill adroitly brought the discussion around to the increased heavy bombing of German cities—an agreeable topic to Stalin—and then to the plans for North Africa. Instantly Stalin showed an intense interest in these plans and before long was giving a masterly defense of them.

At the next evening's session, however, the atmosphere turned polar again. Stalin opened the meeting by handing Churchill and Harriman an *aide-mémoire* asserting that a 1942 second front had been "pre-decided" during Molotov's trip, that the Soviets had based their summer and fall plans on the assumption of such a front, that this failure not only inflicted a "moral blow on the whole of the Soviet foreign opinion" but would impair the Anglo-American military position as well. When Stalin said that if the British infantry would only fight the Germans as the Russians and indeed the RAF had done, it would not be so afraid of them, Churchill said: "I pardon that remark only on account of the bravery of the Russian troops." When Harriman asked about plans for ferrying American aircraft across Siberia the dictator turned on him: "Wars are not won with *plans.*"

Another strange shift of mood occurred the next evening, Harriman reported to the President. Stalin was in good spirits at the state dinner and seemed completely oblivious of the previous evening's unpleasantness. On the final evening Stalin invited Churchill to his apartment, and, after introducing his daughter, Svetlana, to his guest, talked with Churchill for six hours. "On the whole," Churchill cabled to Roosevelt, "I am definitely encouraged by my visit to Moscow." Roosevelt cabled Stalin that "we must bring our forces and our power against Hitler at the earliest possible moment."

Roosevelt, like the others, wondered why the Russians had blown so hot and cold during the short series of meetings. Both Harriman and Eden had encountered equally mystifying shifts in earlier conferences. There was speculation that Stalin on his own was friendly but had to take a harsher line in the presence of Politburo members or in reporting to them. Probably the truth was simpler. Frightful reports from the front, especially the Stalingrad sector, were arriving at the Kremlin during Churchill's visit.

Still, Stalin was profoundly ambivalent. Even as he denounced the lack of American and British help he must have reflected—for he never lost sight of the long-run, postwar implications of immediate decisions—on the strategic aspect of the Soviets' taking the brunt of the ground fighting in 1942. If the Anglo-Americans were tardy in returning to Europe, where would the various armies stand after the crushing of Germany?

ASIA THIRD

All the immediate decisions made in the crucible of crises and conflict, all the improvisations and expediencies, would have their long-run effects. Doubtless Hopkins was reflecting much of the President's feeling when he wrote to Winant after Molotov's departure from Washington in June: "We simply cannot organize the world between the British and ourselves without bringing the Russians in as equal partners. For that matter, if things go well with Chiang Kai-shek, I would surely include the Chinese too. The days of the policy of the 'white man's burden' are over. Vast masses of people simply are not going to tolerate it and for the life of me I can't see why they should. . . ." But the Soviets could hardly feel they were equal partners if they took an unequal share of the losses among the United Nations without an extra share of postwar compensation. Nor could the Chinese. Nor could the Indians.

While Churchill was dampening Soviet second-front hopes in Moscow, his political policy in Asia was facing its harshest test. The failure of the Cripps mission precipitated a crisis in the Indian

Congress. Gandhi and the other militants were urging civil disobedience. Nehru was in a dilemma. He abhorred any brand of fascism, supported the cause of the United Nations, and admired the Russian and Chinese defense against invaders. He believed, indeed, that a United Nations victory was necessary for Indian freedom. But he distrusted the British and wanted to stay abreast of his master, Gandhi, and the other nationalists as India marched toward independence. At a meeting of Congress leaders late in April Nehru supported a Gandhi-inspired resolution calling for a scorched-earth resistance to the Japanese while neither helping nor hindering Britain's war effort. "Quit India," Gandhi demanded of the British Raj; soon thousands were rallying to the call.

Early in the summer, as emotions were rising, Gandhi appealed to Roosevelt. "Dear Friend," he began.

"I twice missed coming to your great country. I have the privilege [of] having numerous friends there both known and unknown to me. . . . I have profited greatly by the writings of Thoreau and Emerson. I say this to tell you how much I am connected with your country." He went on to speak in the same vein of Great Britain; his plea that the British should unreservedly withdraw their rule, he said, was prompted by the friendliest intention.

"My personal position is clear. I hate all war. If, therefore, I could persuade my countrymen, they would make a most effective and decisive contribution in favour of an honourable peace. But I know that all of us have not a living faith in non-violence." So he proposed that if the Allies thought it necessary, they might keep their troops, at their own expense, in India, not for maintaining internal order but for preventing Japanese aggression and defending China. Then India must become free, even as America and Britain were. Only the full acceptance of his proposal could put the Allied cause on an unassailable basis.

"I venture to think that the Allied declaration, that the Allies are fighting to make the world safe for freedom of the individual and for democracy sounds hollow, so long as India and, for that matter, Africa are exploited by Great Britain, and America has the Negro problem in her own home. But in order to avoid all complications, in my proposal I have confined myself only to India. If India becomes free, the rest must follow, if it does not happen simultaneously. . . ."

It was a compelling appeal to the Roosevelt of the Four Freedoms, a bold linking of the aspirations of Indians, Chinese, Africans, and even American Negroes—but it produced no reply from Washington. In Chungking, now almost cut off from India by Japanese troops, Chiang somberly watched the growing crisis in the subcontinent. He had long felt a natural kinship with Indian nationalists. As the British position collapsed in Malaya and India he had talked with Gandhi in Calcutta and later had told Churchill and Roosevelt that he was shocked by the military and political situation in India and that, while he had tried to view the colonial problem objectively, he was certain that the political problem must be solved before Indian morale collapsed. In yielding to Churchill, Roosevelt had in effect repudiated Chiang's view. In their extremity the Chinese and Indian nationalists were drawing closer together. Late in June Gandhi wrote to Chiang.

"I can never forget the five hours close contact I had with you and your noble wife in Calcutta. I had always felt drawn towards you in your fight for freedom. . . ." He described his early friendships with Chinese in Johannesburg. Because of his warm feeling toward China he was anxious to make clear that his appeal to British power to withdraw from India was not meant in any way to weaken India's defense against the Japanese. "I would not be guilty of purchasing the freedom of my country at the cost of your country's freedom." Japanese domination of either country must be prevented. "I feel India cannot do so while she is in bondage. India has been a helpless witness of the withdrawal from Malaya, Singapore and Burma." The failure of the Cripps mission had left a deep wound that was still running.

Gandhi described to Chiang his overtures to the British. ". . . the Government of Free India would agree that the Allied powers might under treaty with us keep their armed forces in India and use the country as a base for operations against threatened Japanese attack." His heart went out to China in its heroic struggle and endless sacrifice. "I look forward to the day when Free India and Free China will cooperate together in friendship and brotherhood for their own good and for the good of Asia and the world."

Late the next month, with the situation degenerating as he had predicted, Chiang wrote a long letter to the President. "With both sides remaining adamant in their views, the Indian situation has reached an extremely tense and critical stage. . . . If India should start a movement against Britain or against the United Nations, this will cause deterioration in the Indian situation from which the Axis powers will surely reap benefit. Such an eventuality will seriously affect the whole course of the war and at the same time the world might entertain doubts as to the sincerity of the lofty war aims of the United Nations." The letter was rather repetitive, but Chiang put the matter squarely to the President. "Your country is the leader of this war of right against might and Your Excellency's views have always received serious attention in Britain." The Indians had long been expecting the United States to take a stand for justice and equality. The Indians were by nature a passive people, but likely to go to extremes. Repression would bring a violent reaction. The enlightened policy for Britain would be to grant complete freedom "and thus to prevent Axis troops from setting foot on Indian soil."

Chiang emphasized that this message was "strictly confidential . . . only for your Excellency's personal reference." But the day after receiving it Roosevelt, by telephone, instructed Welles to send the complete text of Chiang's cable to Churchill, with a covering message. Welles drafted the message, arguing that it would do no good. All State Department information, he told the President, confirmed Chiang's views that a desperately serious situation was at hand in India, of vital concern to American military interests in the Far East, and that Washington and Chungking should try to mediate between London and New Delhi. But the cable went to Churchill with a request for the Prime Minister's thoughts and suggestions. The reply came not from Churchill, but from Attlee for the War Cabinet. It was a stiff defense of the British position, plus a notification that stern measures would be taken in the event of mass civil disobedience.

Roosevelt sent a bland message to Chiang, stressing the need for

PEOPLE WE COULD DO WITHOUT

June 1, 1942, Rollin Kirby, reprinted by permission of the New York *Post*

military defense against Japan and declining to put pressure on the British. From New Delhi, Currie warned Roosevelt that Gandhi was accusing the United States of making common cause with Britain, and that this tendency "endangers your moral leadership in Asia and therefore America's ability to exert its influence for acceptable and just settlements in postwar Asia."

After Gandhi, Nehru, and other Indian leaders were arrested in early August, Chiang sent a final appeal to the President as "the inspired author of the Atlantic Charter." Roosevelt answered that neither he nor Chiang had the moral right to force their feelings on either the British or the Congress party, and that "irrespective of the merits of the case, any action which slows up the war effort in India results not in theoretical assistance, but in actual assistance to the armed forces of Japan."

Chiang had more than enough problems in his own country. China was nearing the end of its fifth year of war. The economy was steadily deteriorating. Artillery and aircraft were in desperately short supply. For months Washington had been promising military aid; much of it had been diverted to other, nearer fronts; some had been held in India; only a trickle had got through over the long, tortuous, and embattled supply lines. Chennault was still fighting gamely with his volunteer air group, and an army general, Joseph Stilwell, had been appointed commander of United States Army forces in China, Burma, and India, as well as Chief of Staff to Chiang, but neither officer had much to operate with. Roosevelt personally was the soul of graciousness to the Chinese, but also somewhat remote and evasive.

China simply had a low priority in Washington compared with other fronts. But Chiang at least had comrades in adversity. By a twist of fate Roosevelt, within the span of a few weeks, was the target of direct and moving appeals from the leaders of a billion people—Stalin and Molotov for a second front, Gandhi and Nehru for aid in their campaign for independence, Chiang for expanded military support to China and for moral support of Indian nationalists. Roosevelt had found it necessary to deny all these appeals.

There was a brief moment when the American military, galled by British rebuffs over the second front and other issues, flirted with the notion of repudiating Atlantic First and giving the Pacific top priority. MacArthur and King, both Pacific-oriented, favored heavy commitments to their respective theaters. The idea might have contained a bit of bluff; still, Marshall formally proposed to the Joint Chiefs of Staff that if the British prevailed on cross-channel postponement, "the U.S. should turn to the Pacific for decisive action against Japan." This would be a popular step with the

American public, he added, and the Chinese and Russians would be in accord.

Roosevelt would have none of it. To draw back from the Atlantic, he told Stimson, would be a little like taking up your dishes and going away. He stood fast for the basic plan of defeating Germany first, on the continuing assumption that trying to defeat Japan first would increase the chance of complete German domination of Europe and Africa. Defeat of Germany first, on the other hand, meant the defeat of Japan, probably without "firing a shot or losing a life."

THE LONG ARMS OF WAR

So it was still Atlantic First—but of all the Commander in Chief's battle efforts in the early months of the war, the most ineffective and humiliating occurred in the Atlantic itself. By spring 1942 the German submarine offensive against coastal shipping was scoring stunning triumphs. Within a day of declaring war Hitler had summoned Admiral Raeder to plan the offensive. Gone were the days when the Führer had to order his Navy to avoid provoking the Americans in the Atlantic. Now he could take the offensive. Raeder's and Karl Doenitz's U-boats were scattered from the Arctic to the South Atlantic, including a sizable fleet in the Mediterranean, but six large submarines were dispatched to the western Atlantic, with more to follow.

The German commanders found a U-boat paradise. Hundreds of Allied ships were beating along the great lanes that ran from off the coast of Nova Scotia down to Nantucket Shoals, to New York City, to the Chesapeake and Delaware Bays, to Florida, and thence to the rich oil ports of the Caribbean and the Gulf of Mexico. Few of the ships were armed; they did not sail in convoys; often they were silhouetted, a perfect target for German torpedoes, against the glowing shore lights of tourist cities like Miami and Atlantic City, whose neon signs were not doused until mid-April. The U-boats would strike without warning, sometimes blowing a tanker or cargo ship in two with one torpedo, usually rescuing survivors or letting them get away in lifeboats, sometimes offering provisions to survivors—"send the bill to Roosevelt"—but occasionally machine-gunning them. The young U-boat commanders sometimes had so many targets they would coolly let a ship in ballast pass by and wait for a laden freighter. In March the over-all toll was 788,000 tons of dry cargo shipping, 375,000 tons in tankers, mostly along the coast and in the Gulf. The loss in tankers was so severe they had to be withdrawn from the Atlantic coastal trade.

The Nazis were exultant. Raeder calculated that total Allied shipbuilding in 1942 would be seven million tons and that the Navy need sink only 600,000 tons a month to keep ahead; it was doing far better than that. Hitler, once so parsimonious with his Navy, played with the enticing hope that the offensive could slow down all Allied operations across the Atlantic or even stop them completely.

For a man who had dealt with a somewhat similar though far less critical problem during World War I, Roosevelt commanded a Navy that was surprisingly unprepared to cope with the fury and scope of the U-boat offensive. In part the problem was the usual one of scant equipment. Three months after Pearl Harbor the Navy had only eighty-six planes, sixty-seven Coast Guard cutters, and a motley collection of converted yachts and trawlers to cover the whole East Coast. The President had complained that it was hard to interest the Bureau of Ships in small vessels, but he merely ruffled the independent-minded admirals instead of commanding them. For a time the Navy tried aggressive patrolling, but as the sinkings mounted and ships had to run in and hole up in sheltered bays at night, King turned to ingenious combinations of convoys.

Not only was the Navy ill prepared and equipped when the U-boats first struck the coast in force; it also had virtually no plans to enlist, and co-operate with, the Army Air Force. The admirals became so desperate, however, that they turned to the Army as a temporary expedient. The Army Air Force was eager to help. It had been unable to close with the enemy in the Pacific, and its grandiose plans for the strategic bombing of Germany were still mere plans. Now it could fight Germans. By early spring a few score army bombers of any type that could be scratched up—one observer was reminded of Joffre's taxicab army—were running patrols out over the sea. The whole operation was gallant but amateurish. The pilots had not been trained for their work; indeed, under an old Army-Navy treaty, the Army controlled land-based and the Navy sea-based aviation. Army pilots had had little training in the fine art of hunting the U-boat; some of them first went out with demolition rather than depth bombs, ship identification was poor, and there was always the problem of co-ordinating with the Navy under harrowing conditions of shortages, faulty intelligence, and the constantly growing and moving packs of submarines.

The President was annoyed by the Navy's slow mobilization against the Nazi attack, Sherwood said later, but he took little direct hand, aside from suggesting to King on one occasion that a PBY be fit with a searchlight for night-hunting of submarines. In mid-April Hopkins cabled from London that losses were now running at more than half a million tons a month and that the need for ships over the next few months would be desperate. It was clear to the White House that the antisubmarine campaign would not succeed in time. The best way to overcome shipping losses was to outbuild them.

If there were any miracles in World War II, the shipbuilding spurt of 1942 would qualify. The President had set astronomical goals in January; he boosted these again the next month, and then again a few months later. Admiral Land and his Maritime Commission were aghast at these figures, which seemed to have been plucked out of nowhere. The commission had to compete for supplies against the Navy and Army, and the shipyards were plagued by machine-tool shortages, strikes, and poor planning of their own. Land demanded steel and more steel; he also urged the President to freeze labor-management relations in the industry so that the workers would not be distracted by union issues. During the first nine months of 1942, shipbuilding fell behind schedule and seemed unable either to meet Roosevelt's final goal or to offset Allied losses. But it was evident even during the output troughs that the curve of production would rise so high that by the end of 1942 the Commander in Chief's initial objective of eight million tons would be met. It was.

The near-miracle would become an American legend. It was achieved as much by flouting the rules as by observing them. Henry J. Kaiser, in particular, grabbed all the tools and materials he could lay his hands on, hired untrained workers recklessly on the theory that he could teach them, and was denounced for pirating labor and priority supplies. But he depended on American experience in standardization, prefabrication, and mass production, plus the happy protection of cost-plus. He had instinctively grasped Roosevelt's rule, Eliot Janeway noted, that energy was more efficient than efficiency. By spring of 1942 Kaiser's and other shipyards that had begun to build only the year before were breaking records by completing ships in sixty to seventy days rather than the anticipated 105. Deliveries rose from twenty-six in March to sixty-seven in June. Most of the credit for the feat went to the builders and doers. But the dreamer in the White House who had set the "impossible" goals in 1942 was also the signer of the Merchant Marine Act of 1936 and the launcher of a long-range shipbuilding program; he had stepped up the shipbuilding effort after the fall of France; he had put men like Land and Vickery in charge; and—perhaps hardest of all—despite his love for small graceful ships he had approved the design of a simple cargo vessel called the "Liberty ship" but known to Roosevelt and other sailors as the "Ugly Duckling."

Five months after Pearl Harbor war production had been lagging so badly that Roosevelt warned Nelson and others that his great goals for 1942 were not being met. War supply improved markedly during the spring, however, and by midsummer the toughest problem facing the administration was not so much production as planning the allocation of war supply to different services at home and to beseeching Allies abroad, in the face of ever-shifting strategic needs, as the fortunes of war rose and fell in distant battle theaters. This planning, of incredible magnitude and complexity, was putting heavy pressure on Roosevelt's war agencies and on his and Churchill's allied boards by late spring of 1942.

Part of the trouble lay in the sudden transition from cold to all-out war. Before Pearl Harbor the President had been cautious in his public projection of spending and in his requests to Congress, and Congress had been irresolute and at times niggardly. On December 7 everything instantly changed: Roosevelt set seemingly fantastic production goals, and Congress simply opened the floodgates, appropriating almost a hundred billion dollars in the first six months and adding another sixty billion in the next four.

Such was the case with fighting manpower, too. The Congress that had almost voted out the draft endorsed sudden huge expansions after Pearl Harbor. In January 1942 the President authorized an increase in army strength to 3.6 million by the end of the year. Four months later he boosted this goal to well over five million, but he would not approve Marshall's proposal to go to almost nine million by the end of 1943. To Marshall's chagrin, the President preferred to plan six months to a year ahead—and he made no secret of that preference. Roosevelt was sensitive to charges that more equipment was being bought than could be used or could be sent overseas—for example, a newspaper report that enough uniforms were on hand or on order for fifty million men.

Struggling to hold the colossal sums in some kind of balance was Donald Nelson and his WPB. In early spring he had to inform the President that the forty billion dollars' worth of production considered feasible for 1942 right after Pearl Harbor had become inflated to sixty-two billion, and the sixty billion for 1943 had swollen to 110 billion—and that the increases were physically not possible. Nelson was in an unhappy position of being the "production czar" without a czar's powers. The President had placed on him, he insisted to the War Department and other rivals, the duty of exercising direction over the entire war procurement and production program. But in fact he had to compete with General Brehon Somervell's huge new Services of Supply, with the Navy, with the international raw materials and allocations boards, and with a cluster of shipping and other czars. And Nelson himself was too much the conciliator and the negotiator to give driving leadership to the whole mobilization and allocation effort. The result was a procurement free-for-all. Merchant ships took steel from the Navy, the Navy took aluminum from aircraft, rubber took valves from escort vessels and from petroleum, the pipelines took steel from ships, new tools, and the railroads. "All semblance of balance in the production program disappeared," a Budget Bureau study revealed, "because of the different rates of contracting and of production that resulted from the scramble to place orders."

Roosevelt was still being urged to set up an integrated superagency under a real superczar, as Baruch had proposed long before the war, and he was still resisting. In the spring of 1942 strategic plans were still open; whether or not Russia could survive the gathering German offensive was still a burning question. The President still did not want to plan ahead more than six months or a year; he wanted, as always, to protect other options in case of a collapse in Russia or North Africa or the Pacific. He could not forget that the very strength of a production and allocation superczar might tie his hands in granting aid to other nations, especially Russia.

Always there were the frantic demands of Allied nations for supplies, and no one in authority in Washington was more sensitive to those demands than Roosevelt. The pressure from abroad itself was institutionalized; uneasily coexisting with United States agencies by this time were a host of international organizations for allocation. At the ARCADIA Conference Roosevelt and Churchill had set up the Combined Munitions Assignments Board (MAB) in Washington and London, operating under the Combined Chiefs of Staff; other combined boards were established for raw materials, production, shipping, and food during the first half of 1942. Despite some misgivings in Washington that the British would have an undue influence over the MAB pool of arms while making much the smaller contribution, the board worked reasonably well as a means of Anglo-American consultation and adjustment. But it was by no means a global agency. Its members were required only to "confer" with Russia, China, and other United Nations; when Chungking put out feelers for membership it was denied on the ground that only nations with disposable surpluses should be admitted.

Lend-Lease, now one of the veteran programs after a year of expansion and hard experience, had become a potent instrument of American foreign policy. It could set broad policy for programs in support of the civilian economy of beneficiary nations, but after Pearl Harbor it gave up to the War Department most of its control of military Lend-Lease. Military and civilian goods that could easily be segregated in theory could not be in practice—for example, when it came to shipping military equipment and nonmilitary supplies in one cargo vessel. For months after Pearl Harbor, military Lend-Lease was snarled by interagency conflict, administrative confusion, and innumerable crises.

The obvious questions were always there: who of the many claimants should get what, how much, and when? Those who lost out in the strenuous competition were sorely tempted to appeal to the White House—to Hopkins and even to Roosevelt. The elaborate and constantly expanding machinery set up to free the President from lesser problems could also jam and eject crises back into the White House, often at the most unpropitious moments. The Commander in Chief was not averse to shouldering this burden; he often seemed to welcome it. "Come to Poppa," he would tell the aggrieved. But there was always the possibility that the machinery would subvert or erode presidential purpose, especially when the machinery itself served narrower needs. Aid to Russia was a case in point.

Morgenthau came in to see the President in mid-March with some disturbing figures. Washington had agreed to deliver to the Soviets by April 1, 1942, 42,000 tons of steel wire, of which only 7,500 tons would have been shipped under existing schedules. The Secretary went down the gloomy list: 3,000 tools promised, 820 shipped; stainless steel—120 tons versus twenty-two; cold-rolled steel strips—48,000 tons versus 19,000; steel alloy tubes—1,200 tons versus none at all. . . .

"I do not want to be in the same position as the English," Roosevelt said as he contemplated these figures. "The English promised the Russians two divisions. They failed. They promised them help in the Caucasus. They failed. Every promise the English have made to the Russians, they have fallen down on. . . . The only reason we stand so well with the Russians is that up to date we have kept our promises. . . .

"I would go out and take the stuff off the shelves of the stores, and pay them any price necessary, and put it in a truck and rush it to the boat. . . . Nothing would be worse than to have the Russians collapse. . . . I would rather lose New Zealand, Australia or anything else than have the Russians collapse."

The President told Morgenthau to see to it personally that the "stuff" moved to Russia. He initialed a chit for his Secretary: "This is *critical* because (a) we *must* keep our word (b) because Russian resistance counts *most* today." Morgenthau told his staff that the President wanted him to get all concerned together, that the boss felt "they had made a perfect monkey of him" on Russian aid and he would not stand for it.

For weeks the President prodded his agencies, which had many excuses for delays and inaction, including failures at the Soviet end. By midsummer—a year after the original decision to aid Russia—deliveries were beginning to catch up with pledges. Through it all Roosevelt remained basically optimistic, even while the Russians were once again reeling back from German blows.

"The amusing thing about the President," Morgenthau noted in his diary in September after listening to the President discuss the holocaust in Russia, "is that he can state these facts coolly and calmly whether we win or lose the war, and to me it is most encouraging that he really seems to face these issues, and that he is not kidding himself one minute about the war. That, to me, seems to be the correct attitude for a commander-in-chief to take."

THE ALCHEMISTS OF SCIENCE

The Commander in Chief during these ominous summer weeks was worried by a prospect even more appalling than the overrunning of Russia—the possibility that the Nazis might have unlocked the secrets of the atomic bomb and might be building it.

It was now three years since Albert Einstein had written to the President to tell him that recent work by Enrico Fermi and Leo Szilard led him to expect that the element uranium might be turned into a new and important source of energy in the immediate future, that it might be possible to set up a nuclear chain reaction in a large mass of uranium to generate quantities of new radiumlike elements, and that it was "conceivable—though less certain—that extremely powerful bombs of a new type may thus be constructed"—bombs so powerful, Einstein added, that they could blow up a whole port and its environs. Einstein's letter was the culmination of passionate efforts by refugee scientists and others to press on the government their understanding of atomic energy, following Niels Bohr's announcement that Otto Hahn and Fritz Strassman in Berlin had achieved the fission of uranium atoms and the release of stupendous amounts of energy.

An atomic bomb in the hands of Hitler—this was unthinkable. How could the American government be alerted? After Fermi failed to interest the Navy Department early in 1939, it was decided that the President must be approached, and that this could best be done under the auspices of the celebrated Einstein. But it was not a time when even this name could unlock doors quickly. August and September 1939 were months of crisis and war in Europe. The letter was entrusted to Alexander Sachs, a financier and occasional adviser to the President, but it was not until mid-October 1939 that Sachs could get in to see the President.

"Alex, what are you up to?" Roosevelt had demanded genially when Sachs came in. Sachs had an extraordinary answer, not only in Einstein's letter, but also in more recent atomic developments. Roosevelt's interest flagged during the long explanation; he tried to end the whole business by remarking that though it was very interesting, government involvement at the moment seemed premature. Sachs wangled an invitation to breakfast, however, and spent part of the evening calculating how he could get through to the President. When in the morning Roosevelt asked him, "What bright idea have you got now?" Sachs told him about Napoleon's rejection of Fulton when the inventor of the steamship tried to interest him in the idea.

"This is an example of how England was saved by the shortsightedness of an adversary," Sachs went on. The President was quiet a few moments, thinking.

"Alex, what you are after is to see that the Nazis don't blow us up." He called in Watson. "Pa, this requires action."

Action came in fits and starts, and always under the dread apprehension that the Germans might be ahead. Bohr compared the atomic scientists to the "Alchemysts of former days, groping in the dark in their vain efforts to make gold." An advisory committee on uranium was created, with representatives of the Ordnance Departments of both the Army and the Navy, and with Lyman J. Briggs, Director of the National Bureau of Standards, as chairman. The President did not want the initial research and evaluation to be monopolized by one of the services. The committee met with Szilard and Fermi and others but made little progress in the first year. Both the theoretical and operational problems seemed immensely complicated.

Roosevelt did not press the matter. Late 1939 and early 1940 were taken up with the twilight war in Europe. On May 10, 1940 he addressed the Eighth Pan American Scientific Congress in Washington and stated that the "great achievements of science and even of art can be used in one way or another to destroy as well as to create. . . . If death is desired, science can do that. If a full, rich and useful life is sought, science can do that also. . . . You and I, in the long run if it be necessary, will act together to protect and defend by every means at our command our science, our culture, our American freedom and our civilization. . . ." In the audience was a young scientist named Edward Teller. He had not planned to attend, because he disliked politics and considered political speeches a waste of time. But the Netherlands had been invaded that day and the shaken physicist went. Sitting there he concluded that Roosevelt was saying that the duty of scientists was to see that the best weapons would be available for use if necessary, and Teller, who had had serious qualms about devoting himself to weapons, suddenly found his last doubts removed as to whether he should work on the atomic bomb.

The next month the President established the National Defense Research Committee, composed of such luminaries as President James B. Conant, of Harvard, and Karl T. Compton, of the Massachusetts Institute of Technology; and at last extensive research on atomic fission with government funds was begun. Progress was slow. British scientists were also at work and were becoming somewhat more optimistic than their American counterparts. Early in October 1941 Vannevar Bush, Director of the Office of Scientific Research and Development, reported to Roosevelt and Wallace the British view that a bomb could be constructed from U-235 that had been produced by a diffusion plant. Prognostications, he made clear, were still not definite. The President endorsed full interchange with the British and ordered policy considerations to be restricted to a small group composed of himself, the Vice President, Stimson, Marshall, Bush, and Conant. By the eve of Pearl Harbor the President's orders were for full speed ahead. But, as usual, he was taking the experimental approach. If in six months the project was making definite progress, he would make available all the industrial and technological resources of the nation to bring about crash production of the atomic bomb.

By mid-1942 scientists were trying several different methods for extracting the U-235 isotope and plutonium. Harold C. Urey, at Columbia University, was conducting gaseous-diffusion research, physicists at the University of Virginia and the Standard Oil Company were studying the centrifuge method, and Ernest O. Lawrence was directing electromagnetic separation at Berkeley. Scientists at the Metallurgical Laboratory of the University of Chicago, under Fermi, were working on plutonium research and planning to build the world's first nuclear reactor. At this time there was still little to choose among the centrifuge, diffusion, and electromagnetic methods of separating U-235 and the uranium-graphite-pile and uranium-heavy-water-pile methods of producing plutonium. Conant, it was said, had the gambling spirit of the New England pioneers; and so did Roosevelt, who without evident hesitation approved tens of millions of dollars for pilot plants.

When Roosevelt and Churchill met at Hyde Park in June 1942 they apprised each other of their progress with "Tube Alloys," the English code name for the atomic project. Churchill was relieved when the President indicated that the United States would assume the responsibility for development. The project was already outstripping the managerial and governmental resources of the scientists, and in this same month the President ordered the Army to undertake the atomic-bomb program. A new division was created within the Army Corps of Engineers to direct the construction of massive research plants and secret atomic cities. The Manhattan Engineering District was launched in August 1942.

The desperate need for speed gripped the minds of officials and scientists alike. Roosevelt and Churchill knew of the efforts the Germans were making to obtain supplies of heavy water—a sinister term, eerie, unnatural, Churchill felt. Conant, analyzing the imperfect intelligence available, concluded that the Germans might be a year, but not more, ahead of the Allies. "Three months' delay might be fatal," he said.

EIGHT *The State of the Nation*

TWO OF Franklin Roosevelt's traits charmed and puzzled his friends. One was his fascination with European royalty and his willingness to put himself out for its members. The other was his ability to talk at the end of a wearing day and to animate himself through the process of talking. Both these traits were especially noted in the spring and summer months of 1942.

Dispossessed royalty paraded through Washington and Hyde Park almost every week, or so it seemed to the commoners around. The President talked with King Peter about Nazi atrocities in Yugoslavia, presented a submarine chaser to Norway's Crown Princess Martha, and had tea with Queen Wilhelmina at her summer place in Lee, Massachusetts, and invited her over to Hyde Park and to the White House. He treated her as a kind of beloved but crotchety great-aunt; "I'm scared to death of the old girl," he confided to Grace Tully, in a tone of admiration. Wilhelmina got a sub chaser, too, with her name on it.

Rosenman marveled that when Crown Princess Juliana, of Holland, and her husband came in to see the President during a busy speech-writing session, work stopped and Roosevelt talked with his guests as though he had nothing to do. Hassett, with his republican Vermont blood, frowned on the time his chief spent with royalty, but the President seemed to enjoy his role. He did admit to Hassett that the chain of visiting heads of state, especially from Latin America, tired him because of their imperfect knowledge of English. Sometimes they even bored him. But Wilhelmina—nothing was too good for "Minnie," Hassett noted. On her departure for England the President wrote to her that he would do his best "to look after Juliana and the babies."

When Roosevelt this summer spent many weekends at "Shangri-La," a camp in the Catoctin Mountains about sixty miles north of Washington, reporters wondered if he was tired of the demands and semiformality of Hyde Park. Certainly Hyde Park had its shortcomings as a retreat. The President wanted to go back home mainly for a holiday, to have a chance to read, sort out his books, decide on new roads and tree plantings, but he was pursued there by visitors and telephone calls. When he made plans to build a small cottage on Dutchess Hill to "escape the mob," reporters had labeled it his "Dream Cottage," much to his annoyance.

Roosevelt's main reason for favoring Shangri-La during this period was that it could be reached in a two-hour drive from the White House. Arrangements were simple to the point of crudeness there. His cottage had only two baths, one of them his; the other was shared by three bedrooms, and the President laughingly alerted his guests to the fact that the bathroom door did not close securely. Presidential aides roomed in rude pine cabins scattered about the area. The place was staffed by Filipinos borrowed from the *Potomac,* which was now on combat duty.

One rainy Saturday afternoon in the midsummer of 1942 the President left the White House with a small band of companions —the Samuel Rosenmans, Archibald MacLeishes, Grace Tully, his cousin Margaret Suckley, and Secret Service men. The party traveled in four cars whose low White House number plates had been changed to more anonymous digits. The cars moved slowly through the villages, stopping for traffic lights, and were unobserved except when the agents rode on the running board while passing through crowded streets. It was pouring at Shangri-La, too, but Roosevelt seemed not to mind. Wheeled through the cottage, he showed his guests to their rooms and complimented the messmen on their hanging of pictures sent from the White House, adding casually to his guests, "I may make a few changes tomorrow."

"He then sat down in an easy chair in the living-dining room," Dorothy Rosenman noted soon afterward, "and I gave him the box of cheeses, cocktail appetizers and candy we had brought. He had a boyish glee in opening each package within the box, and then told Isaac, the Filipino who is in charge, just when to use each item during the week end. We all sat around chatting—sometimes about matters of importance but mostly about trivialities. The President, Archie and Sam would slide from serious talk to comedy with each other, and the President was thoroughly relaxed. At six o'clock he asked when I would suggest we eat. It was made a question of great moment. I was hungry and suggested some speed. So with much seriousness we all discussed dinner timing, and he finally decided that cocktails would be had at 6:40 and dinner at 7:00, and that he would take a little nap before 6:40. . . ."

Before sitting down to dinner the President asked for his portable radio and listened to the 7:00 P.M. news. He also took a call, with war news, on the direct wire from the White House. "I've just read my newspaper," he said on putting down the receiver.

At dinner the stories began. The guests had heard them before, but relished the retelling—the way their host dwelt on details, his manner of pausing and drawing the story out, the inflection of his voice, above all his zest in being the storyteller. He told a true-life tale about a forger who went from city to city taking the checks of any convenient bank, writing them up, and passing them off. The President had remembered every detail and every city, Sam Rosenman told his wife later. Roosevelt also related an old French story about a barber who supplied delicious veal to the local butcher during the hungry days of the siege of Paris. It seemed that several of the barber's customers were missing. While his lady listeners shivered, the President told in detail how the "veal" was butchered and delivered.

After dinner he worked on his stamps while others read or played cards. He warned people not to play with Grace Tully, because she always won; earlier he had hand-printed and hung a crude sign: VISITORS WILL BEWARE OF GAMBLERS (ESPECIALLY FEMALE) ON THIS SHIP. Tonight Miss Tully won, as usual. Later the President started a detective story. All went to bed about ten.

It had been a very peaceful evening, Dorothy Rosenman reflected. She was a little taken aback by the subjects of Roosevelt's stories. But she thought she knew what had inspired them. That noon, August 8, 1942, two hours before Roosevelt left Washington, six young Nazi saboteurs had been electrocuted in Washington. Roosevelt had commuted the death sentences of two others. His only regret about the six who died was that they had not been hanged.

THE ECONOMICS OF CHAOS

The vast pendulum of war came into a tremulous balance in the early summer of 1942. There was a momentary lull in global battle. The grim submarine war went on in the Atlantic, but was now showing omens of a change of fortune in favor of the Allies. The Japanese, bloated by their conquests and at the same time shaken by their losses at Midway, were moving more slowly, feeling for enemy weaknesses, especially toward the southeast. Here there was conflict. On August 7 Marines invaded Guadalcanal, in the southern Solomons. Later a Japanese task force of cruisers and destroyers raced down to strike the Allied naval forces guarding the Guadalcanal beaches and sank three American heavy cruisers and one Australian.

From Washington the President's naval aide drove to Shangri-La with this jolting news. For a long time he and his chief pored over a large map, while the guests chatted away nearby. Later, at dinner, Roosevelt remarked calmly: "Things are not going so well in the Pacific. There are heavy losses on both sides." He then dropped the subject; soon he was telling long stories again. He was not staking his hopes on any one battle; he would not know for some time whether Guadalcanal was a turning point or merely one more in a long series of delaying efforts.

The President's most urgent front at this point was the battle against inflation at home. In the spring of 1942 he had bluntly told Congress that to "keep the cost of living from spiraling upward"—a phrase he repeated seven times—the nation must "tax heavily," keeping personal and corporate profits at a reasonable rate; fix ceilings on prices paid by consumers, retailers, wholesalers, and manufacturers; stabilize wages and salaries; stabilize farm prices; encourage people to buy war bonds instead of luxuries; ration all scarce, essential supplies; discourage credit and installment buying. "Our standard of living will have to come down," he said. But he rejected the concept "equality of sacrifice," because he believed that a free people, bred to the concepts of democracy, deemed it a privilege to fight to perpetuate freedom. He called, rather, for "equality of privilege."

As summer wore on, however, it was clear that Congress did not quite see its privileges this way. The seven proposals made an impressive package, but the legislative branch was not adapted institutionally for making unified economic policy, the executive branch was not well organized to administer it, and the President was not temperamentally inclined to press for it when the political risk seemed high. Evidently the voters did not welcome a co-ordinated effort except in principle; the clearest popular reaction to the seven-point program was a complaint by each major group that it was sacrificing more than some rival interest.

As usual, tax policy was the hardest to integrate with the rest of the anti-inflation program. In March a committee chaired by Vice President Wallace had recommended 11.6 billion dollars of new taxes, plus a two-billion-dollar increase in Social Security taxes—a total sum that would have soaked up much purchasing power and thus helped stabilize prices, and would have enabled over 40 per cent of war costs to be paid out of current revenue. But Roosevelt and Morgenthau wanted more than fiscal "soundness." They felt deeply that a tax policy could prevent "war millionaires," that a war economy could tolerate and even encourage economic egalitarianism. "Profits must be taxed to the utmost limit consistent with continued production," the President told Congress in presenting his seven-point package. "This means all business profits—not only in making munitions, but in making or selling anything else." If "clever people" found loopholes in the tax laws, he hoped Congress would pass a special tax to thwart them. And he stated flatly that no American ought to have an income after taxes of more than $25,000 a year. This last proposal was dubbed by the New York *Herald Tribune* "a blatant piece of demagoguery," but Frankfurter wrote that Theodore Roosevelt would have said, "Bully."

The administration presented a bold and united front on tax policy, but in fact it was sorely divided. The Wallace committee favored a retail sales tax to raise 2.5 billions; Roosevelt and Morgenthau had long opposed such a tax. Henderson and Federal Reserve Board Chairman Marriner Eccles wanted a compulsory savings policy; Morgenthau much preferred a voluntary savings program. Both sides appealed to the President; Morgenthau demanded that he tell Budget Director Harold Smith to stop undermining Treasury policy.

The President placated both sides. "Well," said Morgenthau philosophically after hearing of the enemy's latest foray at the White House, "I always say when you are doing a tax bill you have got to sleep on the floor so a fellow can't put a knife in your back." Yet administration differences were dwarfed by congressional hostility to major tax increases and tax reform. Morgenthau in March had proposed a heavier and more graduated income-tax schedule but one that would still raise only two-thirds of the revenue recommended by the Wallace committee. This was a concession to congressional feeling, but it did little good.

Roosevelt simply seemed unable to evoke from Congress a sense of urgency about taxes. Morgenthau, partly in order to head off a move on the Hill toward a sales tax, suggested early in May the lowering of personal exemptions from $750 to $600 for single persons and from $1,500 to $1,200 for married couples. Rebuffed by the Ways and Means Committee on his major proposals, the Secretary pinned his hopes on getting any decent kind of bill out of the House and into the Senate, where it would have a better chance.

Roosevelt concurred: "Keep on settin' and no sweatin' and no talkin'," he told Morgenthau. ". . . Just stay put."

Inflationary pressures and threatening shortages made it impossible for the administration to stay put. By midsummer the OPA was staggering along under the double burden of its internal administrative problems and its general unpopularity in the nation. Henderson's people had to keep a host of technicians—lawyers, accountants, and so on—on tap without letting them get on top; they had to staff and run thousands of local rationing boards; they had to issue and enforce a multitude of regulations. One task alone was to apply OPA's General Maximum Price Regulation—"General Max"—to 1,700,000 retailers. By the summer of 1942 the national office was swamped. As in the old New Deal days, the White House was the visible target for complaints about federal interference. "At present we are expected to fill out seventeen forms, reports and questionnaires, a month, to government agencies," a Knoxville foundry operator wrote to "Your Excellency." He went on with a long bill of grievances. "So around and around we go. Rules change faster than replies come from Washington. . . . Is there any hope for relief?"

The main threat to effective price control came from Congress, which felt even more exposed than the President to grass-roots protest. Early in the summer Henderson appealed to the President for help in heading off a move in the Senate to slice OPA's appropriation, require every employee getting more than $4,500 to be confirmed by the Senate, and, in effect, cripple its control of farm-commodity prices. Roosevelt in turn appealed to Wallace, Barkley, and Carter Glass, with some success, but a 100-per-cent-of-parity measure passed the Senate. Henderson warned his chief that the parity provision would mean price increases for bread, packaged cereals, milk, meat—in short, for the staples of millions of families. But there was little Roosevelt could do at the moment in the face of the power structure on Capitol Hill.

For the administration the most trying program was rationing, and of all the rationing tasks the most trying was rubber. Rubber was not only in short supply, but its restriction was a means of limiting the use of automobiles and hence of conserving gasoline, which had been so short on the East Coast as to compel the OPA to start gas rationing there in 1942. Nelson had found on becoming WPB chief early in 1942 that the nation would be practically out of rubber in fifteen months. Although frantic efforts had been made to start a synthetic-rubber program, only one plant was making it —at the rate of 2,500 tons a year. By early summer defense officials were fearing a shortage of several hundred thousand tons.

Pressed by Nelson and Henderson at a meeting early in June to ration gasoline to save rubber, the President seemed to fear the popular reaction and cast about for easier solutions, notably a scrap-rubber-collection campaign. He seemed to lack his usual sure grasp of a policy question.

"Now I suppose I have had as much information on what that scrap rubber is as anybody in the world—anybody, in Congress or out, in a column or out," he told reporters. "And *I don't know*. I don't know who is right. Now here—" pointing to himself, amid laughter—"is the greatest expert on it in the United States, and he doesn't know!" But what Roosevelt did know was how to appeal to the people, and soon he was on the radio describing the rubber shortage in simple, graphic terms and asking people to turn in to the nearest filling station any kind of rubber—old tires, rubber raincoats, garden hose, rubber shoes, bathing caps, gloves. About

450,000 tons were collected in less than a month, but not enough to provide more than a stopgap.

Congress forced the President's hand. Impatient for action, fearful of nationwide gasoline rationing, impressed by the popular demand for czars who could break through the obstacles, the legislature passed a bill establishing a Rubber Supply Agency under a director with wide powers. Roosevelt vetoed the measure, arguing that it would frustrate centralized control under the WPB. But recognizing by now, early August, the need for more drastic action, he announced in his veto message the appointment of a committee of Conant, Compton, and Baruch, chairman, to investigate the problem, after Chief Justice Stone had turned down a similar assignment. "Because you're 'an ever present help in time of trouble' will you 'do it again'?" he wrote to Baruch in longhand—and by enlisting the old promoter of tough remedies, Roosevelt knew that he would get a recommendation for drastic action. So he did: rubber and gas rationing, stepped-up synthetic-rubber programs, and a powerful rubber administrator under the WPB.

At summer's end of 1942 Roosevelt seemed to be losing the battle against inflation. Since April the cost of food exempt from controls had risen at a rate of over 3 per cent a month for wage earners. Surging wage rates were putting heavy pressure on anti-inflation controls. The voluntary bond drive was raising a great deal of money but not enough. And Congress had failed to act on the two measures the President considered central to a stabilization program: taxes and food-price controls.

Roosevelt had wielded his executive power effectively on some anti-inflation fronts, but he had shown little leadership in the politically most sensitive sector of all, especially in an election year—wage control. Lacking clear guidance on wage policy from the White House, the War Labor Board had proceeded on a case-by-case basis. As food prices rose, labor members of the board pressed for bigger wage increases; the employer members resisted, with support from business and farm groups. A long-pending dispute in Little Steel almost broke up the board early in the summer, but the members hammered out a decision that would raise hourly wage rates 15 per cent to compensate for the 15-per-cent rise in the cost of living between January 1941 and May 1942.

Despite howls from both sides, "Little Steel" became the basic formula for disposing of wage disputes. But wage policy was still soft. The War Labor Board could decide only wage rates that came before it in dispute cases; it was always vulnerable to labor or management threats to desert or defy it; and it had little guidance from the White House in handling wage inequities between industries or areas. Lack of set policy in turn put a heavy burden on the President. Again and again in 1942, as in the year before, he had to take time to keep Green and Murray friendly to the administration and at least on speaking terms with each other; to handle barbed issues like double time on Sundays, about which there was strong public feeling; and always to keep a wary eye on the ever-rambunctious John L. Lewis.

Whatever his public posture, the President was not one to deceive himself for long about the economic situation. Aside from all his other sources of information on inflationary troubles, he could always resort to "look-see." He told reporters that on a visit to Hyde Park he drove twelve miles down the Post Road at a steady thirty-five miles per hour; prevented by police (as standard policy) from passing the President, twenty-two cars piled up behind him in that distance. It all showed, Roosevelt went on, that people were driving too fast, using up gasoline, not living up to the request of their President and government. "And we have got to enforce the thing some way."

How could the thing be enforced without laws? Some in the White House, including Rosenman and Sherwood, urged Roosevelt to bypass Congress and carry out his stabilization program through his war powers. The President was sorely tempted. In his electrifying Inaugural Address in 1933, amid numbing economic crisis, he had warned that if Congress did not face up with him to the emergency, he would ask it for broad executive power "as great as the power that would be given to me if we were in fact invaded by a foreign foe." Now he had that kind of power under his war authority. He remarked to reporters that "in the old days, in 1933, when the country was economically on its back, and people's pocketbooks were being hit" he had been able to get measures from Congress at the rate of two or three a week or even one a day, but now that the nation's very existence was threatened he could not get action. Still, the President would not, even in wartime, rely on his war powers. Rather, he relied on an ingenious—and ingenuous—power ploy.

First he lectured and scolded Congress, in a message on September 7, for stalling on taxes and stabilization of the prices of farm products. Its delay "has now reached the point of danger to our whole economy." Then he dramatized that danger in short paragraphs studded with concrete examples of inflation. He talked about the price of pork chops, butter, oranges, sweet potatoes, corn, oats, rye. He warned that wages could not be stabilized unless farm products were. What was needed was an "over-all stabilization of prices, salaries, wages, and profits." Then he sprang his surprise:

"We cannot hold the actual cost of food and clothing down to approximately the present level beyond October first. But no one can give any assurances that the cost of living can be held down after that date.

"Therefore, I ask the Congress to pass legislation under which the President would be specifically authorized to stabilize the cost of living, including the prices of all farm commodities. . . .

"I ask the Congress to take this action by the first of October. Inaction on your part by that date will leave me with an inescapable responsibility to the people of this country to see to it that the war effort is no longer imperiled by threat of economic chaos.

"In the event that the Congress should fail to act, and act adequately, I shall accept the responsibility, and I will act.

"At the same time that farm prices are stabilized, wages can and will be stabilized also. This I will do. . . ."

As usual the President saved his main dramatics for his fireside chat in the evening. He began with the story of an American dive bomber pilot who had promised to lay a bomb on a Japanese flight deck for the "folks back home" and who had died in the Coral Sea doing it. He "hereby and now" awarded him the Medal of Honor.

"You and I are the 'folks back home' for whose protection" the brave pilot had fought and repeatedly risked his life. "How are we playing our part 'back home' in winning this war?

"The answer is that we are not doing enough. . . ."

If Congress did not act, he warned again, he would assume responsibility, to prevent "economic chaos."

"This is the toughest war of all time. We need not leave it to historians of the future to answer the question whether we are tough enough to meet this unprecedented challenge. We can give that answer now. The answer is 'Yes.' "

A few days later a reporter asked the President a question many in Washington were asking: "If by October 1 it appears that your anti-inflation bill is on the way in Congress but has not yet passed, in that case will you wait and give them a chance?"

"What was the first word of that question?" he asked. The reporter mentioned the fatal word "if." Roosevelt would not tip his hand; the only game he would play was his own. He summoned Rayburn back from Texas and asked him to have his flock on hand within a week.

Smarting under the Chief Executive's reprimand and ultimatum, Congress glumly went back to work on an anti-inflation program. Within one week bills were introduced, hearings were held, and measures were reported to both chambers. Once again the farm groups stood like tollkeepers over the legislative roadways; they demanded a recomputation of parity that would mean higher farm prices. Roosevelt publicly denounced the proposal; a presidential veto and assumption of extraordinary economic power seemed in the offing. But Senate moderates concocted a compromise on parity and delegated extensive power to the President to take production costs into consideration. The final measure provided other protection to farmers. Congress passed the bill on October 2, and the President, though not wholly satisfied, signed it the same day.

He had to wait another three weeks for a tax bill, and a disappointing one to boot. The measure would raise only seven billion dollars in new revenues by Treasury estimate. It reduced personal exemptions; lifted the top surtax on individual incomes a little, the top tax on corporate income moderately, and the top excess-profits rate sizably; and it boosted a number of excises on luxuries and scarce goods. Roosevelt had no choice but to sign it; he joked to Morgenthau that he had hardly read it because he could not understand it. The Secretary despaired of ever getting "total war on taxes."

The President had already chosen his man to direct the new stabilization program—Justice James Byrnes, a hardheaded negotiator and operator, whom Roosevelt had appointed to the high court the year before. Liberals were worried by his Southern background and essential conservatism, but Roosevelt was aware of Frankfurter's high opinion of him and impressed by Hopkins's advice that "Jimmy has loyalty and knowledge, judgment and political sense." Byrnes moved into the new east wing of the White House as Director of the Office of Economic Stabilization. Shortly he was telling Hopkins, with a smile, "There's just one suggestion I want to make to you, Harry, and that is to keep the hell out of my business."

THE PEOPLE AT WAR

Four groups had been especially vulnerable during periods of turbulent economic and social change in America—industrial labor, Negroes, ethnic groups, and women. All these groups went through critical transitions during 1942; all established new dependencies on the federal government; all directly or indirectly turned to the President for help.

Women, to be sure, did not seem to be a deprived minority in the war boom of 1942. Besides donning sober uniforms for the women's branches of the military services, they were wearing trousers for war work, and by the middle of the year were pouring into factories, taking over men's jobs, such as driving trucks and running heavy machinery, and bringing home pay checks to swell the family income and civilian spending. Women workers increased by almost two million in the year after Pearl Harbor. The President was impressed by the visual evidence, especially by the large number of women workers he saw on inspection trips. Time and again he recalled seeing women doing a variety of work in the plants he visited.

Booming war employment was boosting income for millions of workers, male and female. National War Labor Board wage decisions were far less important than the enormous war contracts and the heightened competition for labor. Workers and their unions were also winning a bigger voice in production decisions. In April the President shifted all labor-supply functions from the WPB's Labor Division to the new War Manpower Commission, and set up in the WPB a new Labor Production Division as a channel to Nelson for labor information and ideas. Sidney Hillman, now ailing and under criticism from his old union comrades, was eased out of the labor unit; Roosevelt tried to placate him with an offer to serve as special assistant to the President on labor matters, but the union chief, hurt and mystified by the President's seeming loss of confidence in him, preferred to return to his beloved Amalgamated Clothing Workers. The Labor Production Division, under a new chief who had to conciliate both the AFL and the CIO, did not itself have a major role, and indeed encountered considerable criticism from labor, but it helped arouse further union demands for participation in war-production decisions. By the end of 1942 joint labor-management committees were operating in many industries and at many levels.

It was clear that rising wages and a greater union voice in running plants might not outlast the war. The crucial long-run question was whether labor could exploit the war to bolster its organized economic and political power. Left-wing union leaders had claimed in speeches that war would bring a vast union-busting drive and a shift toward the open shop; businessmen had warned of the compulsory unionism of the closed shop. There was a deeper, more philosophical issue: during a time of crisis should the status of unions be frozen for the duration, or did a war of democracies against fascism mean vesting labor with more rights and duties? Before Pearl Harbor, Roosevelt had bluntly warned Lewis and Murray that the "Government of the United States will not order, nor will Congress pass legislation ordering, a so-called closed shop" —but on December 7 federal arbitrators had granted a union shop to Lewis's captive mine workers. The whole disruptive issue had been passed on to the War Labor Board.

During the early months of 1942 the chairman and the three public members of the WLB conducted a search for a formula that would resolve for wartime labor one of the oldest and toughest problems in the Western world: the reconciliation of liberty and order in groups undergoing change and stress. This remarkable quartet—Davis, Morse, Graham, and Professor George W. Taylor—shared Roosevelt's mixture of practicality and lofty idealism. They knew that in the dynamic, expanding productive period of a war economy, as Graham said, union status could not be frozen. But what kind of union status would produce the right balance of flexibility and stability? After much discussion and delay, with the union and employer members contributing both threats and constructive suggestions, the board reshaped an old formula, maintenance of membership, into a new one, maintenance of voluntarily established membership. Under the first, all employees who were members of a union or later became members must stay in the union for the life of the contract, or lose their jobs. Under the second, the same rule prevailed, except that an escape clause would give employees ten or fifteen days to quit the union without penalty before maintenance might take effect. Seemingly a slight change, the new formula provided a compromise to which management and labor reluctantly agreed, provided a practical reconciliation of liberty and security for employees, and was so widely adopted that by war's end it covered almost a third of all workers under union agreement. In the long run it both strengthened and stabilized union power. It was the most brilliant application—some would say the only successful application—of Roosevelt's notion of a moving consensus overcoming a sharply divisive problem.

The President's efforts at a rolling consensus were meeting far less success in another critical sector in 1942. The Fair Employment Practices Committee encountered frustrations and setbacks from its first days. Roosevelt had started it off with a broadly representative six-member board headed by Mark Ethridge, publisher of the Louisville *Courier-Journal,* an old friend and an unusually strong civil-rights advocate for a man born in Mississippi. Murray, Green, David Sarnoff, head of the Radio Corporation of America, Milton Webster, of the Sleeping Car Porters, and Earl B. Dickerson, a Chicago alderman, made up the rest of the board. The committee was slow to get organized and starved for funds; by the time it was transferred from OPM to WPB, its staff included fewer than seven field investigators. Murray and Green proved unable to attend meetings; the President had to appoint alternates. Ethridge aroused a storm among blacks when in Birmingham he defended segregation, at least for Southerners. But the main obstacle was the sheer intractability of the problem: a corporal's guard was trying to breach the citadels of Jim Crow. Training and jobs, for example, were linked in a vicious circle—employers turned away Negroes because they had inadequate training; training classes were closed to Negroes because of an alleged lack of jobs. The United States Employment Service was supposed to refer workers without discrimination, if possible, but not if employers insisted on discriminatory orders; in Southern states the service still maintained segregated employment facilities. AFL craftsmen were hostile. And almost every move of the commission provoked outcries from one side or even both.

In its frustration the FEPC often turned to the President for support, communicating through Marvin McIntyre. On these matters Roosevelt was somewhat unpredictable. He was personally concerned and was quick to respond to specific injustice—for example, when the nonpolitical Negro tenor Roland Hayes and his wife were victims of brutality in a Southern store, and when black troops landing overseas were identified by the War Department as "service troops." But he seemed reluctant to spend any of his own personal political capital to mobilize support for the committee, even within the government, or to give much time to the problem. When Welles opposed public FEPC hearings on discrimination against Mexicans because of their effect south of the border, Roosevelt asked the committee to cut the hearings off. And suddenly in midsummer 1942, without advance warning to the FEPC and against its wishes, he transferred the little agency to Paul V. McNutt's War Manpower Commission and thus cut the presidential apron strings that had been one of the few sources of the FEPC's strength.

All the President's action—and his inaction—on discrimination aroused sharp responses. Eugene ("Bull") Connor, then and for years afterward head of public safety in Birmingham, wrote in to charge that the Employment Service and the FEPC were causing disunity, that venereal disease was the number-one Negro problem, and that the Ku Klux Klan would be revived in opposition. "Don't you think one war in the South, however, is enough?" An equally withering fire descended on the administration from black militants.

It was not surprising, given Roosevelt's fear of any divisive act, that he would shun a frontal attack on discrimination in private enterprises or even in state and local government. His support of Stimson's policies reflected better his personal views. The War Department was proud of the fact that by the spring of 1942 about 10 per cent of registrants under Selective Service were black, several hundred black aviation cadets would soon be in training, and over three hundred Negro officers—including three colonels—shared in the command of five black combat units. But the Army was still segregated except for black troops under white officers—and Stimson believed in this. "The Negro still lacks the particular initiative which a commanding officer of men needs in war," he wrote to a friend. ". . . Also the social intermixture of the two races is basically impossible. . . ."

If a "little group of agitators, led by a man named White," would only keep their hands off, Stimson felt, things would be better. He was pained to discover that MacLeish was planning to speak to Negroes in New York on the discrimination against them in the Army, and that McGeorge Bundy, the son of his close friend and assistant, Harvey Bundy, was helping MacLeish with his speech. After inviting the poet to see him, Stimson told him that he had been brought up in an abolitionist family, and his father had fought in the Civil War, but that the crime of slavery had produced a problem impossible of solution in wartime, that the only thing to do was to be patient and care for individual cases, that the foolish Negro leaders were actually seeking social equality, which was impossible. MacLeish appeared unmoved. Stimson felt secretly that Mrs. Roosevelt was behind MacLeish's activity—the latest example of her "intrusive and impulsive folly," he complained to his diary. But he did not blame *Mr.* Roosevelt, except for letting his Navy shut its doors "absolutely to the Negro race" while making the War Department carry the extra load. The President was more sympathetic to black aspirations than either his War or his Navy Secretary, but his tendency in wartime to look on race relations more as a problem of efficient industrial mobilization than as a fundamental moral problem left policy largely in their hands.

If Stimson seemed weak on Negro rights, within the military circle he was virtually a reformer. Early in 1942 Eisenhower rounded up reports on the "colored troop problem." Not only did army generals in the South and even in multiracial Hawaii oppose the assignment of "colored troops" to their domains, but so also did the Australian government, the President of the Republic of Panama, Governor Ernest Gruening, of Alaska, the government of Bermuda, the British authorities in Trinidad, the South American governments and—absurdity to the point of hilarity—an army colonel advising as to Liberia. Stimson's responses to most of these pleas ranged from "Don't yield" to "Nonsense"; he reminded the Panamanians that the Panama Canal itself was built with black labor; and he asserted that the Southerners would have to get used to Negro troops; but neither he nor anyone else in high command reflected on the implications of the fact that it was *segregated* black units that were being objected to.

For all their troubles, Negroes for once were better off than some other group. This other group was also racial—the Japanese-Americans in the process of being "relocated" from their West Coast homes to inland areas. By the end of spring, Milton Eisenhower, first head of the War Relocation Authority, could report to

Roosevelt that about 81,000 Japanese-Americans were in temporary assembly centers, about 20,000 in permanent relocation centers, another 15,000 had been "frozen" in eastern California, and from 5,000 to 8,000 voluntary evacuees were living precariously in Rocky Mountain states. He also reported that inland governors and attorney generals had fought bitterly the earlier plan of voluntary evacuation on a large scale. Mass meetings had been held, violence threatened, Japanese-Americans arrested. So eleven huge camps had had to be set up to hold 130,000 evacuees, schools and hospitals planned, farms and public works started.

But Milton Eisenhower did not report—and Roosevelt, with all his insight and compassion, could not have grasped—the dismal experience of thousands of evacuees: the sad departure from hard-won homes and farms, the hurry-up-and-wait journey through detention centers to relocation camps, the shock of arrival at Poston or Tule Lake or Gila or some other camp, with its burning heat and numbing cold and clouds of dust, endless barracks with one room to a family, lack of privacy, red tape, boredom—and always the military police and the barbed wire. Not that the President was kept in the dark about the episode. All major decisions were cleared with him; his office received all the information, good and bad. Roosevelt himself termed the centers "concentration camps," as indeed they were. But the psychic cost of the experience was probably beyond his ken, or was simply written off as a sad but necessary casualty of war.

The President might have been more sensitive to the situation if the evacuees had protested vigorously, had demonstrated, gone on strike, fought their guards. But they did not, at this time. The authorities were impressed by their almost cheerful determination to make the best of their lot; their resourcefulness in knocking together tables and benches for their ill-equipped rooms, their quick reconstruction of a semblance of community life through dances, sports, handicrafts, schools. But as the hot months of summer 1942 passed, the mood in some camps changed. The WRA did not live up to its earlier promises or expectations about wages, clothing, garden plots, jobs, and ordinary comforts. Tension rose among the inmates and between them and their Caucasian superiors. There were demonstrations, picket lines, strikes, and beatings of suspected informers.

By fall the very policy that Roosevelt had approved out of military necessity was creating its own military threat. The Office of War Information's chief, Elmer Davis, urged him to speak publicly against anti-Nisei bills in Congress and to authorize loyal American citizens of Japanese descent to enlist in the Army and Navy. "Japanese propaganda to the Philippines, Burma, and elsewhere insists that this is a racial war," Davis reminded the President. "We can combat this effectively with counter-propaganda only if our deeds permit us to tell the truth." At least 85 per cent of the Nisei were loyal Americans, he added. The Navy agreed with this estimate —but still did not want Nisei enlistments.

The contrast between Washington's treatment of Italian- and German-Americans and of Japanese-Americans was revealing. Roosevelt had assured Herbert Lehman, then Governor of New York, that he was "keenly aware of the anxiety that German and Italian aliens living in the United States must feel as the result of the Japanese evacuation of the West Coast." Would Lehman assure them "that no collective evacuation of German or Italian aliens is contemplated at this time"? This was little solace to "Japanese" baking on the flatlands of Colorado—but of keen satisfaction to the Japanese propagandists broadcasting from Manila, Singapore, and Rangoon.

By late summer 1942 the President was giving in to an urge to "go to the country"—an urge as powerful in some politicians as the migratory instinct in the wild goose. He had told Mike Reilly, his bodyguard, that he wanted to travel during the second half of September and he wished to see everything he possibly could from coast to coast. But one thing would be different. He wanted the trip completely off the record until he returned to Washington. He would take along representatives of the three wire services, but that was all. No publicity, no parades, no speeches, he hoped, and if governors and other politicians were to ride with the President they had to be Republicans as well as Democrats.

On September 17 the presidential train pulled out of Washington with the Chief Executive and the First Lady (who went only as far as Milwaukee), a dozen members of the White House staff, the three privileged newsmen—and eight photographers.

The President packed his days as full as if he were running for office. On the first day, overhead cranes came to a sudden stop as the presidential phaeton, its top down, its bulletproof windows up, rolled into the Chrysler Tank Arsenal in Detroit and moved between two huge assembly lines making General Lees, the new all-welded medium tank. Sitting with Eleanor Roosevelt and production officials, the President watched tanks grind through mud and dust on the testing ground; Secret Service agents shuddered as one tank drove straight at the presidential car and lurched to a halt ten feet away. The President shouted, "Good drive!" to the grinning operator. Later in the day he rode with Henry and Edsel Ford down the half-mile assembly line of the enormous Willow Run bomber plant. Next day he inspected the Great Lakes Naval

Training Station, the nation's largest; watched steam turbines and propeller shafts being made at Allis-Chalmers, scene of bitter strikes the year before. In the evening he was in the Twin Cities area for the night shift of a cartridge plant making thirty- and fifty-caliber ammunition, but which had not yet achieved full production. He always arrived unannounced, and sat on the right-hand side of the car, sometimes in back, sometimes in front, smiling, radiant, observant. Plant officials bustled about; ripples of excitement spread as workers stared, then hollered at one another; women peeked while trying to keep their eyes on their machines. As they drove through the plant, Reilly remembered later, the Secret Service men heard such sweet sounds as "Geeze, Mamie, look. It's Roosevelt!"—indicating that the security men had achieved tactical surprise.

No one would later describe the trip with more gusto than the President, who reported first to the press and then in a fireside chat. After leaving the Twin Cities, he said, the party had gone right on to a place called Pend Oreille, in Idaho.

"It's a great lake out there. That and the Coeur d'Alene are the two largest lakes in northern Idaho; and because we have tried, as you know, to disseminate the congestion which has always existed on the east coast and the west coast for Navy facilities, we put this naval training station inland. They had gone into commission five days before I was there, and they already had about a thousand trainees who were coming in at the rate of two or three hundred a day. . . . Then we went on to a place just outside of Tacoma—Fort Lewis—which is one of our principal Army posts on the west coast. We saw a post, which I had known before as a relatively small post, multiplied four or five times in its capacity for troops. . . . Then from there we motored to the Bremerton Navy Yard, and saw wounded ships and wounded men. . . ."

The President and his party took the ferry to Seattle, where he inspected the big Boeing plant and had supper with his daughter, Anna, and her husband, John Boettiger, and their children, Buzzie and Sistie. At Henry Kaiser's Portland shipyards he watched the launching of a ship whose keel had been laid only ten days before. Cries of *"Speech"* rose from the thousands of workers watching. When a portable microphone was pressed into the President's hand, the old campaigner could not resist it.

"You know," he said in a resonant conspiratorial whisper, "you know I am not supposed to be here today." The crowd laughed and cheered. "So you are possessors of a secret—a secret that even the newspapers of the United States don't know. I hope you will keep it a secret. . . ." Merriman Smith, one of the three reporters, who had not yet filed any stories on the trip, was damned if he saw anything to laugh about.

"From there we went down to the Mare Island Navy Yard and saw again a Navy Yard just about three times as big as it ever had been before," the President reported later. "We saw the Jap two-man submarine which had been captured at Pearl Harbor, and we saw one of our own submarines with nine Japanese flags painted on the conning tower.

"From there we went down to the Army embarkation port at Oakland, which is an enormous organization from which a large portion of our supplies of men and materials go out to many parts of the Pacific. . . . Then from there down to Los Angeles, and we saw the Douglas plant at Long Beach, California. . . . Then, from there down to San Diego, we saw the naval hospital, and a lot more wounded men from actions in the Pacific. . . . Then to the naval training center. Then to the old Marine Corps base, Camp Pendleton, and from there to the Consolidated plant, where they are stepping up production all the time. . . ."

Turning east, the President spent most of a day at the ranch of his daughter-in-law Mrs. Elliott Roosevelt, and played with three grandchildren there. He stopped in Uvalde to see his onetime Vice President, John Garner, who had left Washington for good the year before. Pulling up in his little car in front of the Casey Jones Café, Garner strode to the presidential train, swung up the steps, and shouted to the President: "Well, God bless you, sir. I'm glad to see you." The President held Garner at arm's length to survey him. "Gosh, you look well." They talked about local affairs and asked after each other's wife, like old country gentlemen. "How are things going around here?" the President wanted to know. Garner slapped his Texas hat against his leg and roared, "They're one hundred per cent for you." Garner spied Dr. McIntire as he left. "Keep that man in good health," he told him, "and all the rest will take care of itself."

On to the big Southern installations—to Kelly Field, Randolph Field, Fort Sam Houston, to the Higgins Yard in New Orleans, where small boats were building, to Camp Shelby, Fort Jackson, where the Commander in Chief reviewed infantry divisions.

Back in Washington after two weeks and 8,754 miles, the President was in a benign mood about the state of the nation. The people as a whole, he told reporters, had "the finest kind of morale. They are very alive to the war spirit." But he was not happy about the state of the nation's capital. He complained about reporters who discussed military matters without knowing anything about military matters, about inaccurate news reports, especially by columnists and radio commentators, about subordinates in the administration itself who sought publicity by rushing into print about their particular "ism" without having a rounded picture of what the government was doing.

The President waited over a week, until Columbus Day, to report to the nation on its home front. It was a long chatty speech. The main thing he had observed on his trip, he said, was not exactly new—"the plain fact that the American people are united as never before in their determination to do a job and to do it well." He described some of the things he had seen, skillfully interweaving praise for accomplishments and criticism for employers who refused to hire Negroes or women or older people. He announced almost in passing that it would be necessary to lower the existing minimum-age limit for Selective Service from twenty to eighteen. He scorned "typewriter strategists" who were full of bright ideas but little information. He would "continue to leave the plans for this war to the military leaders."

He mentioned the millions of Americans in army camps, naval stations, factories, shipyards. "Who are these millions upon whom the life of our country depends? What are they thinking? What are their doubts? What are their hopes? And how is the work progressing?" He could not really answer these questions on the basis of a two weeks' tour, nor did he try. But perhaps he sensed that the American people were a strange compound of determination to win the war and to avoid its exactions and harshness, of an emotional involvement in the war without wholly understanding it, of constant exposure to war excitement and problems and an effort to elude them.

On the surface the war dominated everything. People were singing "Praise the Lord and Pass the Ammunition," "The Fuehrer's Face," "He's A-1 in My Heart," "I Left My Heart at the Stage Door Canteen," "You're a Sap Mr. Jap." Theater marquees featured *Wake Island, Atlantic Convoy, One of Our Aircraft Is Missing, Torpedo Boat, Remember Pearl Harbor, Flying Tigers.* Practically all big institutional advertising played on the war theme. Even Munsingwear's foundation garments pictured a WAAC saying, "Don't tell *me* bulges are patriotic!" and Sergeant's Flea Powder showed "Old Sarge" exclaiming, "Sighted flea—killed same." The stage was not yet inundated by war plays, but John Steinbeck's *The Moon Is Down* told of heroism in a Nazi-occupied town and Maxwell Anderson's *The Eve of St. Mark* had a remarkable reception on Broadway for a war play.

Some of the promotion and huckstering had a latent radicalism. Pan American Airways ran full-page advertisements presenting answers by John Dewey, Hu Shih, the Archbishop of Canterbury to the question: "What kind of a world are we fighting to create?"; Canterbury's answer was a radical version of the Four Freedoms. Movie documentaries were appearing: *Native Land,* a dramatization of American labor's fight for civil rights; *Henry Browne, Farmer,* a government film on the importance of the Negro to the war effort. The communications media could not always keep up with fast-moving military and ideological developments. Twentieth Century-Fox put out a movie glorifying the Yugoslav Chetniks at a time when General Draja Mikhailovich was losing favor with progressives and the Partisans were winning it. Books were slower to mobilize for war. In the fall of 1942 people were reading Matthew Josephson's *Victor Hugo,* James Thurber's *My World—and Welcome to It,* and Hesketh Pearson's *G.B.S.;* but they were also reading John Scott's *Duel for Europe,* Ethel Vance's *Reprisal,* Herbert Agar's *A Time for Greatness.*

In sum—if one could summarize a vast array of opinions marked by strange combinations of volatility and opaqueness—Americans toward the end of their first year of war seemed emotionally intent on fighting the war but not fully mobilized physically or intellectually to win either the war or the peace to follow. Trying to look at the scene with the detachment she had applied to Samoans and Balinese, anthropologist Margaret Mead feared that Americans were too passive, or at least that the government was treating them as if they were passive. One of the nation's greatest strengths, she wrote this same fall, was in the American *character.* If her definition of this character was hazy, her conclusions went to the heart of the problem of an ill-mobilized nation. As a nation we had to honor our leaders, she granted, as something like ourselves—as part of ourselves. "But if the war should ever come to seem a battle in which Roosevelt and MacArthur and Kaiser are supermen—father figures who do our fighting or our thinking for us while we simply watch the show—then there would be danger, for such an attitude would bring out not the strengths of the American character—but its weaknesses.

"To win this war, we need the impassioned effort of every individual in the country," she continued. ". . . The government must mobilize people not just to carry out orders but to participate in a great action and to assume responsibility. Above all government must tell the truth. . . . It's not that we need victories; but we gotta feel we have victories in us."

She went back to the Puritans for the mixture of practicality and faith in the power of God, for a sense of moral purpose, back to Oliver Cromwell, a Puritan emerging from the Anglo-Saxon tradition—"Put your trust in God, my boys, and keep your powder dry!"

By coincidence the provocative, forty-year-old anthropologist was saying the same thing as the conventional, aging Secretary of War Stimson: the battle against Nazism must be fought with a sense of moral purpose. A moral purpose was exactly what Roosevelt felt he was supplying in his sermonizing speeches. Certainly his personal popularity remained high; the question was whether he was helping people see connections between the lofty, compelling symbols such as Freedom and Democracy and the practical political and economic choices which people could make and which in turn would influence the great decisions of the war.

The most important of these practical choices would come with the congressional elections of fall 1942.

THE POLITICS OF NONPOLITICS

At a press conference some weeks after Pearl Harbor the President had been extolling a new book by Marquis Childs, *This Is Your War.* He quoted approvingly from the jacket blurb: "A pampered nation in the past, America is inexperienced in war." What the country needed was the practical energy of every citizen. "This is your war." Right, said the President.

Could there be a greater concentration of effort on the main problem among various political groups and newspapers, he was asked.

"Yes. Very distinctly. I would say it was about time for a large number of people—several of whom are in this room—to forget politics. It's about time. We read altogether too much politics in our papers altogether. . . . They haven't waked up to the fact that this is a war. Politics is out. Same thing is true in Congress."

Did that include Cabinet members?

It was pretty rare in the Cabinet, said Roosevelt. "Whenever I see any implications of that kind I step on it with both feet."

It was Roosevelt in one of his favorite roles—the high-minded chief of state acting for the whole nation, rising above sordid group and party interests. It was not the first time he had tried to adjourn politics since Pearl Harbor, and it would not be the last. When Democrats gathered at hotel banquet halls across the nation to pay off the party's debt, which survived war and peace, they heard the President discuss the war and denounce "selfish politics" with nary a mention of either the Democratic party or party saints Thomas Jefferson and Andrew Jackson.

The Commander in Chief's nonpolitical posture faced several difficulties from the start. It was not clear just what he meant. Was he against politics in general, or just party politics, or just "selfish" politics? When he publicly called for Congressmen who would "back up the Government," did he mean that they would be tested —even purged—on the basis of support of current war policies of the government only, or even on the basis of their pre-Pearl Harbor support of the administration's foreign policy? Certainly the President could not oppose politics in general in a nation that was proudly flaunting its democratic institutions and processes—including free, regular elections—in a war against totalitarianism. As for selfish politics, everyone was against that—but what was it? Defining what was selfish and unselfish politics was at the heart of the democratic struggle.

Presumably the President was hoping to minimize traditional party politics, for he carefully avoided Wilson's call for a Democratic Congress, and he dismissed as "perfectly silly" a *New Republic* claim that the fall elections would be the most important since the Civil War. Obviously, in wartime the President needed the backing of the two liberal, internationalist parties, the presidential Democrats and the presidential Republicans, for his coalition strategy and war policies. Did he, then, favor a party realignment with all liberals and internationalists in one party, all conservatives and isolationists in the other? Some liberals so concluded and looked eagerly toward an ideological party split. Others were not so sure. Anti-Roosevelt newspapers took advantage of the confusion to hint darkly that the President would cancel the fall congressional elections.

Adjournment of party politics would require the co-operation of the other party. And the Republicans in election year 1942 had no intention of surrendering their monopoly of the opposition. Nor did their leader, Wendell Willkie, whose party position now was even more anomalous than Roosevelt's.

In the weeks after Pearl Harbor the two men had conducted a political minuet. The President offered Willkie a war job as arbitrator under the War Labor Board, and considered him for director of manpower; he did not offer the one job that Willkie doubtless would have accepted—production chief. Willkie suspected that the President had finally appointed a production boss mainly because of his own proddings. The White House announced the offer of the arbitration job before Willkie had had a chance to answer. As for Willkie's demand that MacArthur be brought back to unify the defense effort, Roosevelt told his aides that that was downright silly. Even Winston Churchill stumbled into the strained situation when during his stay in Palm Beach he telephoned Willkie to arrange to see him—only to discover after some conversation that he was talking to Roosevelt. Still, despite all the troubles, Roosevelt and Willkie had a sneaking affection for each other. They met at the White House occasionally and kept in touch through intermediaries.

Whatever the climate at the White House, however, Willkie stuck to his main job as he saw it—constructive criticism. Again and again he demanded that America face up to its postwar obligations, especially the keeping of the peace through international organization. He attacked isolationism, colonialism, race hatred; he joined with Eleanor Roosevelt, La Guardia, Dorothy Thompson, and other notables in founding Freedom House; he denounced the persecution of minorities, though stopping just short of opposing the Japanese relocation program; he took advanced positions on civil rights, civil liberties, colonial peoples, a second front in Europe in 1942. In the four-party battle that survived Pearl Harbor he was lambasting congressional Republicans for their isolationism and conservatism and congressional Democrats for their racism and conservatism.

The absence of a strong, institutionalized opposition party shortened Willkie's reach; it also gave him far greater leeway. Indeed, in the endless Virginia reel of political couplings and cleavings, Roosevelt and Willkie were brought into slightly embarrassing embraces. They met in April to talk, among other things about getting Ham Fish out of Congress. "I did enjoy that little party the other night a lot," Roosevelt wrote to Willkie later, but he admitted that they had not got far on the Fish matter. Willkie later openly opposed the conservative Congressman's renomination. That effort failed, but he also battled and overcame Taft and other congressional Republicans in persuading the Republican National Committee to take a moderately internationalist position at its spring meeting in Chicago, under the very nose of Colonel McCormick. He tried to conduct a "shadow purge" by intervening in Republican primaries against extreme isolationists and reactionaries. He tolerated for a while a short boom for himself as Republican candidate for governor of New York, then firmly stepped on it. Thomas E. Dewey, far more restrained than Willkie, more cautious, was out front for the choice as Republican standard-bearer for the seat Herbert Lehman was vacating.

By summertime hope was rising among some Republican and Democratic liberals that Roosevelt and Willkie might join hands to found a new party, or at least a party coalition, to win the war and organize the peace. The two men seemed agreed on policy; Willkie simply enjoyed a freedom to speak out that was denied the President. Then, on the heels of the 1942 New York Republican convention, Willkie suddenly announced that he was planning to leave the country—and the campaign—to travel around the world. His purposes, he said, were to demonstrate American unity, to "accomplish certain things for the President," and to find out "about the war and how it can be won."

The trip had been Willkie's idea, but the President had seized on it eagerly and fully co-operated. Since Willkie would not be back until shortly before the election, any hope of real collaboration between the presidential parties was gone for 1942 at least. It was easy to see why Willkie wanted to make the trip, but what were Roosevelt's motives? Earlier in the year Eleanor Roosevelt had remarked to her husband that the Democratic party was beginning to creak from disuse. The Republicans creaked more, Roosevelt had said, and would creak even more when he took Willkie into the government. Now the titular Republican leader would be away during the height of the campaign. He was deserting a host of political comrades—men who had fought by his side in 1940 and were running for office two years later—in their hour of need. For weeks he would be the President's personal representative. Did the President want a loyal opposition? Did he hope that the Grand Old Party would creak and creak—and then crumble into the dust?

Certainly the Democracy was creaking. National Chairman Edward J. Flynn, accustomed to good, simple party fights back home in the Bronx, had never fought an election like this one. When he merely tuned up for the fray by suggesting gently that a Republican House would be a disaster, the President repudiated him. The National Chairman was supposed to define issues for the campaign—but what were the issues? Flynn did not even hold the party reins in an off-year election, for oversight of the congressional campaigns was vested in Democratic campaign committees in the Senate and the House. These committees were tied in with the congressional party leadership, however, and had limited funds, few issues on which congressional Democrats agreed, and virtually no control over Democratic candidates for Congress. The only force that might influence such elections from outside was the White House, the only party leader, Roosevelt—but he had adjourned politics for the duration and stressed that winning the war was the only issue. And how could a campaign be fought on that?

Republicans raged at this adjournment by the party enjoying power, and quite understandably. They knew that Roosevelt was too political an animal to rise above partisanship. The White House, indeed, was no place to escape politics. Judges, postmasters, federal attorneys had to be appointed, and around each of these prizes, however small, a fierce little battle was waged, usually under cover but sometimes erupting in charges, countercharges, and headlines. Two of Roosevelt's appointments aroused special wrath—one was Robert E. Hannegan, a St. Louis Democratic organization leader, to be Commissioner of Internal Revenue; the other was a "henchman" of Boss Frank Hague, of Jersey City, to be a federal judge in New Jersey. Even George Norris, Senator from Nebraska, deserted his friend in the White House on the judgeship nomination, crying out in the Senate that the question was whether "one of the most disreputable and demagogic organizations that ever existed will go beyond New Jersey and take in the whole Federal Government." Roosevelt seemed unmoved by this flare-up of old, peacetime politics. When Congresswoman Mary Norton called New Jersey's Governor Charles Edison an arrant hypocrite for opposing Hague on the judgeship matter after seeking Hague's aid earlier—so she claimed—in his own election campaign, Roosevelt sent her a note that was abbreviated even for him: "Dear Mary: You are a grand girl!"

Nor could Roosevelt stay out of politics in his own state and district. The Empire State Democracy prospered under the leadership of Alfred E. Smith, Roosevelt, and Lehman; now it boiled with discord. Jim Farley, still strong with the county leaders, was backing a Democratic party stalwart, Attorney General John J. Bennett, for the gubernatorial nomination. It was clear to the New Dealers in Washington that a Bennett victory in 1942 could mean Farley's dominance over the New York delegation to the national Democratic convention in 1944. A Farley pilgrimage to the White House won from Roosevelt only a grudging promise to announce that he would vote for Bennett, if nominated over Dewey—but "not one word more." Later Roosevelt gave encouragement to New York's junior Senator, Democrat James M. Mead, on the grounds that Bennett would lose and only Mead could get the support of the fusionist American Labor party in New York City as well as a strong vote from upstate. A few days before the convention, however, the President switched again, now telling party leaders that the Mead and Bennett camps had got into such a mess that both had been irrevocably hurt; he now suggested a third candidate, to whom he would be willing to give wholehearted support. This maneuver failed, too, and finally, at the last moment, Roosevelt sent the state convention a letter, via Lehman, stating his first preference for Mead, his second preference for a compromise candidate, and implying his willingness to accept Bennett if he had to.

As usual, Farley had things well in hand and Bennett's nomination went through. The American Labor party, itself sorely divided between garment-union leaders and a militant left wing, repudiated Bennett and nominated its own candidate. Dewey won the Republican nomination easily and faced the happy prospect of a fragmented opposition.

Roosevelt seemed less concerned with these setbacks than with charges that he was spending too much time on politics. When the New York *Herald Tribune* ran a cartoon so implying, he wrote an indignant letter to Mrs. Ogden Reid, a personal friend and wife of the president of the paper. He had acquired over the years the hide of a rhinoceros, he wrote, but there were times when he had to speak to real friends. Actually, the amount of time he had taken from war-work hours to devote to New York politics was exactly zero, he said. He listed the two appointments, one telephone call, and one letter that constituted the totality of his political effort back home. "The total amount of it was not much longer than the very nice visit I had with you the other day—which, by the way, was in 'war' time!"

But time—presidential time—was precisely the resource that had to be invested in politics if the President was to have influence on the election. His old adversary Hamilton Fish was the main case in point. Fish was still one of the few American public men Roosevelt cordially and thoroughly hated. But both the friends and the foes of the Congressman agreed on one thing: Ham put time into his district, which sprawled from the Connecticut line across Dutchess County and the Hudson River into Orange County and over to the New Jersey border. He took time to cover the straw-hat and clambake circuits, to keep in touch with veterans' organizations and Gold Star mothers, to deliver on the gut staples of politics—jobs, favors, recognition. Now in his eleventh term in Congress, he had risen by the seniority ladder to become senior Republican on both the House Rules and the Foreign Affairs Committees—and would

June 10, 1942, C. K. Berryman, courtesy of the Washington (D.C.) *Star*

become chairman of one or both if the Republicans carried the lower house in November.

So Fish was a shining target, but Roosevelt hardly took direct aim. He talked with Willkie and with a few Dutchess County Democratic leaders and showed his library to a Poughkeepsie publisher who had promised that all three of his papers in that city would come out against Fish's renomination. The President had little confidence in the Democratic organization; he felt, indeed, that when the Democrats lacked good men of their own they should combine with enlightened Republicans to choose a Republican. But he took no steps in his own congressional district to carry out this idea. Fish's Republican foes failed to dislodge him in the primary; the Democrats nominated a lackluster candidate, and by fall Roosevelt had lost hope of beating Fish.

In only one state besides New York did Roosevelt openly intervene in 1942, a sharp contrast with his "purge" efforts of four years before. This was the "magnificently justified exception" of Nebraska, where old George Norris, a very special Senator, friend, and progressive, was in the battle of his life against a conservative Republican. Norris's long support of Roosevelt in peace and war—except on patronage—was bringing him abuse as well as support. The President told reporters that he would not change one word of the ringing endorsement he had given Norris six years before, in the Aksarben Coliseum in Omaha: ". . . his candidacy transcends State and party lines . . . one of the major prophets of America . . . a man who has had no boss but his conscience." Roosevelt sent Norris a copy of his re-endorsement, adding, "If this be treason, let every citizen of Nebraska hear about it."

But such eloquence and conviction were in short supply in the congressional elections of 1942. It was a strange contest. During September, at the height of a nationwide election, the heads of the two major parties were cut off from battle—Roosevelt because he was on his blacked-out inspection tour, Willkie because he was still girdling the world. Separation did not make their hearts grow fonder. Willkie talked with Allied and neutral leaders with his usual enthusiasm and expansiveness; he privately advised the President to send wheat to Turkey and publicly urged a second front to help Russia. Willkie was annoyed when he heard in Chungking that Roosevelt had belittled his call for a second front, and annoyed again when the President talked scornfully of "typewriter strategists." Roosevelt tried to make clear that he supported Willkie's mission, was referring only to speculation about the second front, and was simply attacking columnists, but still there was a sharper edge of mutual distrust in their relationship when Willkie returned in mid-October—a feeling that was not wholly dissipated by an amiable meeting at the White House.

All through summer and early fall Hadley Cantril, in Princeton, continued to sample political attitudes for the President. He did not like much of what he found. During the forging of a grand coalition against the Axis, Americans had become a bit less interventionist than before Pearl Harbor. In the midst of a war against Nazism, anti-Semitism seemed more widespread than before the war. Under an administration sympathetic to the Negro, blacks were shifting toward the Republican party in the coming election. Margaret Mead was right—the people wanted their President to be tougher, more demanding of them; they wanted to be told; they wanted it laid on the line.

All this spelled trouble in the fall elections, Cantril warned the President. But he could not be sure he was getting through to Roosevelt, who was still maintaining his nonpolitical posture.

So the campaign, lacking in either dramatic national antagonists or clear-cut issues, meandered on toward the first Tuesday after the first Monday in November. Virtually every candidate in every party backed an all-out war effort, planning for the postwar period, and often even Franklin Roosevelt, at least in his role as war leader. Behind the big consensual symbols politicians stressed little issues, catered to local biases, played up personalities. Political lethargy, reporters found, was rampant. Some Willkie supporters of 1940 crossed party lines to back liberal Democrats, and some New Dealers preferred interventionist Republicans to mediocre Democrats, but the once-heralded party realignment was stalled to the point of nonexistence. There was little suspense about the election outcome. Pundits generally agreed that the Republicans would make gains but not take control of either Senate or House.

"Hope you have a nice election!" a schoolgirl called out to the President after he had voted at Hyde Park Town Hall. It was not to be. In his eve-of-election statement Roosevelt had said nothing about Democrats or Republicans or even about the importance of supporting win-the-war candidates. He merely expressed the hope that people would vote. People would not even do that. The turnout was far below expectations, so the Republican vote was relatively much higher. The GOP picked up forty-four congressional seats and came within a handful of seats, 209 to the Democrats' 222, of winning control of the House. Republicans won nine Senate seats and, more important for the future, several governorships in the biggest states. A sizable band of loyal New Dealers lost their seats without a word of support from the President, for whom they felt they had gone down the line. Ham Fish and most of the other conservative isolationists won easily. The two congressional parties strengthened their hold on Capitol Hill; the presidential Republicans won a couple of potential national leaders in the victories of

Earl Warren in California, who beat the once-formidable Culbert Olson, and Dewey in New York, who outpolled the Democrats and the American Labor party combined. Of the four parties, only the presidential Democrats—Roosevelt's party—lost.

The usual off-year explanations were trotted out and combined with the effect of war conditions: the low vote; the young people, predominantly Democratic, who were off in the war or in war industry; administration toleration of labor excesses; inflation; local problems; gripes. The President was criticized for his hands-off policy. One commentator noted acidly that Wilson had called for a Democratic Congress in 1918 and lost seats in the House and Senate; Roosevelt had not called for anything and lost twice as many.

Cantril's data summed up the hard meaning of the election. Low turnout was the main cause of the Republican gains. The great Democratic potential of low-income voters and younger people had not been mobilized. It was a typical off-year congressional election, hardly influenced by the great issues of war and peace. By staying above the political battle the President had protected his personal standing; but he had not helped the people find a sense of moral purpose or even a sense of direction. He now faced a potent coalition in Congress between congressional Democrats and congressional Republicans.

Roosevelt publicly was mum and privately seemed happy the whole business was over. He was sad about Norris's defeat in Nebraska. So was the lonely old crusader, who was also bewildered. "I can't understand it," he said to friends who came to console him in his Senate office. "I went down to defeat for reasons that even my enemies cannot explain." His remarks were a political dirge for the New Deal in wartime.

NINE *The Flickering Torch*

DURING the bright autumn days of 1942, while Roosevelt was fighting inflation, touring the country, and waiting out an election, he watched the fast-shifting fortunes of war on two distant fronts that soldiers, through sheer doggedness, were making into turning points of history. Despite the mixed reports, the President could write to King George in mid-October that "on the whole the situation of all of us is better in the Autumn of 1942 than it was last Spring, and that while 1943 will not see a complete victory for us, things are on the upgrade while things for the Axis have reached the peak of their effectiveness." One front was Stalingrad; the other, Guadalcanal.

Certainly the Germans felt that they were surpassing the peak of their effectiveness on the great plains between the Don and the Volga during these fall days. Late in August, General Friedrich Paulus's Panzer divisions fought their way into the northern suburbs of Stalingrad; soon the Luftwaffe, in the heaviest strike since the first night's attack on Russia, was pouring incendiaries on the Volga city and sending up such flames that a newspaper could be read at night forty miles away. Like a huge magnet, some death instinct seemed to be drawing German and Russian soldiers to Stalingrad. Having moved from Rastenburg to Vinnitsa, Hitler instructed his generals that "the vital thing now was to concentrate every available man and capture as quickly as possible the whole of Stalingrad itself and the banks of the Volga." On the same day the Russians ordered the citizens of Stalingrad to "barricade every street, transform every district, every block, every house, into an impregnable fortress."

The reports to Roosevelt could hardly convey the horror of Stalingrad—the German forces battering through the ruins to points within a few hundred yards of the Volga; the blazing combat between troops in adjoining buildings, floors, and even rooms as the Russians grappled with the foe within a hand grenade's throw in order to escape Nazi air attack; the tanks firing point-blank at lower floors until houses collapsed, then stalling on the very rubble they had made; a flame thrower flushing out lower stories with fire until the operator himself was hit by an incendiary bullet and turned into a torch; frenzied hand-to-hand struggles in factories, cellars, the grain elevator; the Russian wounded and dying crawling down to the edge of the Volga and groping for a way across; the steady crunch of Russian mortar fire from across the river, omen of victory.

But the President was not long in doubt about the meaning of Stalingrad for the whole war. As the Germans bogged down for days that turned into weeks, it was becoming clear that once again Hitler would be stopped short of his goals on the brink of winter, and that the Anglo-Americans could continue to enjoy their most precious commodity—time.

The full dimensions of Stalingrad would take weeks to become clear even to the Russians, however, and meantime tension and suspicion rose in the Kremlin as the Nazis pressed harder on the whole southern flank and a Russian diversionary effort in front of Moscow failed dismally. In October—the month that Stalin would later concede was the most critical of the whole war—Anglo-Soviet relations fell to a new low. The Soviet press hinted that some British leaders were not entirely free of the taint of Munich. Soviet officials fawned over Willkie, especially after he called for a second front and added that some Allied military leaders might need some "public prodding." He told correspondent Alexander Werth in Moscow that it was taking a terrible risk to postpone the second front until 1943. The Russians did not know that the President had failed to tell Willkie of the plans for North Africa. Willkie left a Moscow aroused to fresh hope by the possibility of a massive second front soon.

The second front that most occupied Roosevelt during these fall days was not in Russia, but in the Solomons, about 1,200 miles northeast of Australia. Here the battle centered on Guadalcanal, a small island the Japanese had occupied as one of a series of steppingstones down which they were moving toward New Caledonia, Fiji, and Samoa in order to reach their supreme goal in the Pacific: cutting the lifelines between the United States and Australia.

Almost everything had been marginal about the Guadalcanal operation from the start. It was not part of a broad strategic counteroffensive, since the main effort was still planned for the Atlantic. Both MacArthur's planners and the Navy commanders had wanted to delay the invasion until a more powerful and cumulative assault could be mounted up the chain of islands, but the Joint Chiefs insisted on a quick counterassault to halt the enemy's southerly advance. Equipment was inadequate, maps faulty, planning amateurish, loading methods primitive. For a time it seemed that the men invading Guadalcanal and neighboring islands might be cut off for good. On August 9, when the Japanese sank four cruisers—including one Australian—and killed over 1,000 sailors, it was one of the worst defeats the American Navy ever suffered. Then the three American carriers pulled out of the area, leaving the amphibious forces "bare-arse," in their commander's phrase. But after quickly seizing a rough airstrip and renaming it Henderson Field, Marines dug in along the north central coast, probed for the enemy, and awaited reinforcements.

The Guadalcanal area had seemed even less likely than Stalingrad to turn into a strategic prize, but, like the Soviet city, it sucked in huge forces intent on bigger goals. Like the soldiers of Stalingrad, too, the Marines after ten weeks still held a narrow strip of land, were backed up against the water, and were facing enemy attempts to drive right through their strip. Otherwise Guadalcanal was a different kind of hell from Stalingrad. Endless tropical rains turned roads, campsites, and the airstrip into a gluey muck. Dysentery, fungus infections, and malaria struck men down by the hundreds; malaria alone sent almost 2,000 to the hospital during October. Night after night Japanese warships, planes, and artillery—including an infuriatingly persistent gun nicknamed "Pistol Pete"—pounded the airfield perimeter and forced sailors and Marines into their rain-filled foxholes. There were shortages of almost everything except a stubborn determination to hang on.

By mid-October Roosevelt was fearful that his troops might be driven out of Guadalcanal. "If we are defeated in the Solomons," MacArthur warned, ". . . the entire Southwest Pacific will be in gravest danger"; he asked that the nation's "entire resources" be diverted to the area. The Navy was locked in fierce battles to hold a line of support. In a series of bloody, old-fashioned sea fights in the "slot" running down from Bougainville to Guadalcanal, and in the eastern Solomons, both sides had suffered cruel losses. The carrier *Wasp* was torpedoed; more cruisers went down; the Japanese lost heavily in transports.

On October 24 the President requested the Joint Chiefs to send every possible weapon to Guadalcanal, even if other areas had to be stripped. At this point Henderson Field had fewer than thirty operational aircraft. Plans were quickly laid for heavy reinforcement, and the Navy kept up the pressure even after the *Enterprise,* the only American carrier in the Southwest Pacific, was knocked out of action. By the end of the naval encounters each side had lost warships totaling about 130,000 tons—the Americans, two carriers and eight cruisers; the Japanese, two battleships and four cruisers—but the Marines and soldiers had hung on to Henderson Field and the coastal strip and were fanning out, ultimately to drive the remaining Japanese off Guadalcanal.

The Japanese spearhead had been blunted. "We have hit the Japanese very hard in the Solomon Islands," Roosevelt cabled to Stalin. "We have probably broken the backbone of the power of their Fleet. They have still too many aircraft carriers to suit me, but soon we may well sink some more of them. . . ." But by this time world attention had shifted to the Atlantic.

THRUST ACROSS THE ATLANTIC

Rarely has an American President commanded a major military enterprise as bizarre, doubt-ridden, and unpredictable as the invasion of Northwest Africa in early November 1942. The attack—now labeled TORCH—was mounted not against his nation's mortal enemy, Germany, but against its oldest ally, France. Its success would turn more on political than military factors. It was opposed by the very generals and admirals who would have to carry it out. It had not even been included in a list of alternatives the Commander in Chief had written out less than four months before the operation.

The targets were French Morocco, Algeria, and Tunisia, forming a huge shoulder of sand and rock mountains that stretched a thousand miles from Casablanca, on the Atlantic, to the Tunisian coast that looked out across the narrow waist of the Mediterranean toward Sicily and the boot of Italy. From the ruins of June 1940 the French had salvaged and desperately clung to two possessions outside France—their Mediterranean fleet and their colonial possessions in Africa. Vichy Frenchmen still ruled imperturbably in Casablanca, Oran, Algiers, Bizerte, Tunis; east of Tunisia the Italians and Germans controlled Tripoli and Cyrenaica, in Libya; and their armies in the summer of 1942 were pressing the British at El Alamein, hardly fifty miles west of Alexandria.

The cast in the forthcoming drama was as remarkable as the plot and the setting. In Vichy: Marshal Henri Pétain, a traditionalist with authoritarian leanings, contemptuous of parliamentary politics of the Third Republic variety, vain, aloof, well disposed toward the United States as long as his regime was not threatened; Pierre Laval, the Premier, who had traversed the parliamentary spectrum from Communism to a fanatical anti-Bolshevism, Foreign Minister under the old regime, now blatantly anti-British, suave to the point of oiliness, "hated, vomited by France," according to one American journalist; Admiral Jean-François Darlan, commander in chief of all land, sea, and air forces under Pétain but more a political animal, smooth, opportunistic, touchy, loyal to the fleet admirals under him, as they were to him, angry at Britain for its humiliating destruction of French warships bottled up in Mediterranean ports. In London: Winston Churchill, relieved that the cross-channel assault had been indefinitely postponed, intent on working with the Americans to make TORCH a brilliant success, but ever keeping a peripheral eye on tempting targets like northern Norway; Dwight Eisenhower, lodged in "Eisenhowerplatz," Grosvenor Square, entrusted by Washington and London with command of the whole enterprise, coping with a thousand problems of supply, organization, personnel, and tactics as he strove to convert the early preparations for "cross-channel" to a plan for Africa; Charles de Gaulle, head of the Free French organization in London, proud, stiff, lofty and vulnerable at the same time, convinced that he embodied the spirit of all anti-Nazi Frenchmen and indeed the honor of France itself. In Northwest Africa: Robert Murphy, in Algiers, the President's political representative, Foreign Service veteran and old Paris hand, who had been organizing in Africa a group of consuls and agents to identify existing Nazi influence and the anti-Vichy potential; Auguste Noguès, Resident General of Morocco, warily friendly to Murphy but dead set on defending his domain against both Germans and Americans; and in the other cities a host of Vichy men who were anti-Nazi but also anti-British and conservative, authoritarian, or even royalist in their views. These men were the main actors, but so labyrinthine were the lines of leadership influence that the actions of a bey or sultan, or a tribe in Morocco or a French warship in Oran, could jeopardize the whole operation. And as in all such undertakings, the stage was full of agents and double agents, adventurers and mercenaries, opportunists and innocents.

TORCH was a project bound to activate and test Roosevelt's skill at deception and surprise and to gratify his flair for the complex and the indirect. Yet he showed a remarkable consistency for over two years in keeping the African option open. He was pressed by liberals to break with the Vichy regime, which seemed so clearly a Nazi tool. He was urged by military advisers to make a surprise attack on the French fleet in order to remove that knight from the chessboard. Even Ambassador Leahy was so disgusted with Darlan for granting military aid to the Germans that he asked to be recalled. The President stuck to his line. He cultivated good relations with Vichy because he wanted at least to keep the French fleet and French Africa out of Nazi hands, and at most he hoped for help from North African French if and when Americans entered Africa.

The President was not averse to letting Hull take most of the brickbats from liberal moralists, but he kept a close eye on policy toward Vichy. He had asked Murphy to send him direct reports from Africa—"Don't bother going through State Department channels"—and Murphy invariably found him knowledgeable about the intricacies of North African politics, economics, and personalities. Month after month—during the long negotiations with Japan, the Atlantic skirmishes with Hitler, Pearl Harbor, the Pacific defeats, the mobilization struggles at home—Roosevelt played his careful hand with Vichy, pressuring here, appeasing there. He recognized that Pétain, fettered and bullied by Hitler, was half impotent, but also that the old Marshal had some bargaining power against all comers, with his fleet and his 100,000 or so troops in Africa. Even Laval's return to power in April 1942—as Vice Chief of State, Foreign Minister, and Interior Minister—brought only Leahy's delayed recall from Vichy, but no basic change in policy.

Roosevelt's dalliance with Vichy meant strain with anti-Vichy Frenchmen, especially the Gaullists, but he was willing to pay this price. It was essential, he told Churchill, that de Gaulle be kept out of the picture and given "no information whatsoever, regardless of how irritated and irritating he may become." He suspected that de Gaulle's headquarters could not keep military secrets. De Gaulle, however, was in good company. "Don't tell anybody in the State Department about this," Roosevelt said to Murphy in discussing invasion plans. "That place is a sieve!" And he was determined above all that TORCH would be an essentially American operation, with the British having a secondary role. His reason was partly that the French would be hostile to the onetime ally who had attacked their fleet and bombed and blockaded their nation. But even more he was intent on making a stunning victory out of TORCH.

It was the first big attack. It would take place just before the congressional elections. It was the President's project, ordered against the advice of his military advisers. It was so politically oriented that a failure would be charged to the politician in chief. It had to succeed.

Success in North Africa was precisely what Roosevelt's soldiers feared would elude them. Marshall warned that the operation would be slow to mount, would turn on hazardous political conditions, would further disperse naval escort—even aside from his main fear of its effect of endlessly delaying a cross-channel second front. King was opposed to North African operations in 1942 partly because of its escort and transportation aspects, partly because it might drain naval strength from the Pacific. Stimson was flatly opposed. At best, he feared, it would be another Gallipoli; the British had lost their nerve. But the President, determined that American troops fight in Europe or Africa in 1942, stuck to his and Churchill's decision for TORCH. Stimson and Marshall and their operations people remained skeptical of the enterprise well into

August, but Marshall dutifully and energetically went about the job of making it succeed.

The military risk alone was formidable. To land on the Atlantic hump of Africa meant taking the gamble of bad weather, especially of the towering rollers that thundered on Casablanca beaches from the Atlantic winds. To land on the more protected beaches of Algeria meant running the heavy risk of a German lunge through Spain to cut the invaders off in Spanish Morocco. To land anywhere in North Africa meant moving thousands of troops across the North Atlantic in waters infested by U-boats, now near their peak strength. TORCH would demand such a mobilization of sea and ground forces as to be a strategic risk, too. Marshall had to reduce eight or nine divisions to such low levels in personnel that at least six months would be needed to restore them to efficiency, and he had "scalped the troops" at home for equipment. The October convoy to Murmansk was suspended partly to help TORCH. British troops in Egypt had to be reinforced by unescorted liners. Even the far-off Pacific felt the drain of naval power.

The political uncertainties vastly compounded the danger. Stalin, no novice in such matters, had expressed some doubts about the political soundness of TORCH. Pétain and/or Darlan might give way under savage threats from Hitler and order resistance to the death against all invaders. Franco might allow Hitler's divisions to plunge down into Africa; he might try to close the Strait of Gibraltar and cut the invasion lifeline; he might open up with his own guns on Gibraltar, which was to be both the command post and the staging area for the operation. Clearly the political and military aspects of the enterprise had to be closely intertwined, but Murphy, who continued to direct the political effort in the field, was wholly ignorant of the conduct of war, and Eisenhower, who recognized the inseparability of political and military factors, felt that politics was the job of politicians, not of soldiers.

The President was not unwilling to keep both the political and the military strings in his hand. Nowhere were the strings so tied together as in decisions on targets and composition of the invading forces. After American and British staff officers became deadlocked on these problems during August, Roosevelt and Churchill stepped in—and promptly came into direct conflict with each other. Their exchanges spelled out their differences—and their talent for dispelling them.

Churchill to Roosevelt, August 27, 1942: "We are all profoundly disconcerted" by the American Joint Chiefs of Staff proposal to throw the weight of the assault against Casablanca. "It seems to me that the whole pith of the operation will be lost if we do not take Algiers as well as Oran on the first day." The crucial thing was to move quickly east to Tunisia before the Germans could reinforce it. Casablanca might easily become an isolated failure. If a choice had to be made between Algiers and Casablanca, Churchill favored attacking the former and dropping the latter.

Roosevelt to Churchill, August 30: "I feel very strongly that the initial attacks must be made by an exclusively American ground force, supported by your naval, transport, and air units. The operation should be undertaken on the assumption that the French will offer less resistance to us than they will to the British." He would need a week after the landing to secure the nonresistance of the French. "Then your force can come in to the eastward." It would take German air and parachute troops at least two weeks to get to Algiers or Tunis. Meanwhile British troops would be ashore, without much opposition, it was to be hoped, and moving east. The landings must be near Casablanca and Oran; possibly there could be a third.

Churchill to Roosevelt, September 1: "We could not contest your wish, if you so desire it, to take upon the United States the whole burden, political and military, of the landings." But would not the British participation be revealed quickly? How would Americans be distinguished from British? "In the night all cats are grey." What if high surf prevented disembarkation on Atlantic beaches? And if a political bloodless victory should go amiss—and the bungled attack on Dakar two years back had been a sad case of cluttering things up with "preliminary conciliatory processes"—would Roosevelt have enough trained forces to do the job directly and simply?

Roosevelt to Churchill, September 3: "Your willingness to cooperate by agreeing that all initial landings will be made by United States ground forces is appreciated." True, British participation would soon be discovered, but this would not have quite the same effect as British forces making the first beach landings. "Bad surf conditions on the Atlantic beaches is a calculated risk." In view of Churchill's urgent desire that Algiers be occupied simultaneously with Casablanca and Oran, he proposed to add Algiers, with 10,000 American troops, if the British could supply the additional forces.

Churchill to Roosevelt, September 3: "We have spent the day looking into physical possibilities." Accepting Roosevelt's general outline, he proposed that Casablanca be reduced by 10,000 or 12,000 troops and the other landings strengthened.

At this point he composed a despairing letter to Hopkins. What was behind all the difficulty? The President's enterprise was being wrecked bit by bit, Eisenhower and his staff officers in London were distressed, every day's delay was helping the Germans forestall the venture.

Roosevelt to Churchill, September 4: "We are getting very close together." He was willing to reduce the Casablanca force by 5,000 men. "Since a similar reduction was made in original Oran assault force, this releases a total of British and United States combat loaders for some 10,000 men for use at Algiers."

Churchill to Roosevelt, September 5: "We agree to the military layout as you propose it. We have plenty of troops highly trained for landing. If convenient, they can wear your uniform. They will be proud to do so." He put away the letter to Hopkins.

Roosevelt to Churchill, September 5: "Hurrah!"

Churchill to Roosevelt, September 6: "O.K., full blast."

He had very good reason, Roosevelt felt, to ask that American troops be the more visible forces on the beaches. Over six months before, Intelligence officials had visited Cantril at Princeton to ask his help in gauging French attitudes toward the Americans and the British. Cantril's new assignment was a challenging one. He would have to gauge likely opposition to, or co-operation with, an American landing without his investigators revealing their goal. Northwest Africa, with its split populations and ethnic diversity, would have been a challenge to the pollster under the most controlled conditions. Opinions of various populations would have to be weighted in terms of their importance in relation to a possible landing. Interviewing could not be straightforward, but would have to be indirect and guarded, for suspicion must not be aroused. Despite all the difficulties, a group of Americans in North Africa under Cantril's absentee direction were able to conduct 142 usable interviews. Although the sample was askew, the returns clearly indicated that an American landing would meet less resistance than an Anglo-American invasion, because of Vichy suspicion of British imperialistic aims and memories of Anglo-French rivalry. The study also led to a proposal that the American voice most known and respected in France—that of Franklin D. Roosevelt—speak to the French in French just after the landing.

The date for the attack was another problem. Originally Roosevelt had set it for some time in October, with October 30 the latest. Discussing TORCH with Marshall, he held up his folded hands in mock prayer and said, "Please make it before Election Day." But the expansion of the operation caused Eisenhower and his colleagues to postpone it until November 8, five days after the election. Roosevelt took the delay gamely. This was a decision that rested with Eisenhower, he told friends, not with the Democratic National Committee. He doubtless had few illusions, however, about an automatic relation between an African landing—which might, after all, fail—and votes for Democratic candidates for Congress. He was probably content to settle for the plaudits he would receive for "rising above politics."

At the moment he was more interested in French African politics. He coached Murphy on the reasons to give the French for the invasion. Murphy must state that information had been received of Axis plans to intervene in French North Africa, that American troops would land to protect French sovereignty and administration, that no change in the existing French administration was planned, that the Americans hoped for and would welcome French assistance—and would guarantee salaries, death benefits, and pensions for French officials who helped the enterprise.

"You will restrict your dealings to French officials on the local level, prefects, and the military," Roosevelt admonished Murphy. "I will not help anyone impose a Government on the French people." Murphy returned to Africa hoping he could enlist General Henri Giraud, who had been captured by the Germans in 1940 and had escaped two years later, to arouse support for the Allies. But he was specifically authorized to negotiate with Darlan if necessary. Churchill said that much as he hated Darlan he would crawl on his hands and knees a mile if Darlan would bring over the French fleet. De Gaulle was to be left completely out of the venture.

Anxiety mounted in Washington and London during the final days. A new battle commander in Egypt, Bernard Montgomery, launched a heavy counterattack against Rommel on October 23, and for a week the armies grappled with each other inconclusively. Battles were also raging in Stalingrad and in the Solomons. Then, from the United States and from the British Isles the vanguard of a fleet of over six hundred ships carrying an assault force of 90,000 men plowed through the Atlantic. The task force of over one hundred ships sailing directly from the United States moved across the Atlantic like a drunken sailor, now pointing toward Dakar, now toward Britain. A British fleet of three battleships, two carriers, and twenty-one cruisers and destroyers covered the Oran and Algiers task forces.

Eisenhower was now at his Gibraltar command post deep in the cold, dripping tunnels of the Rock. So discouraged during previous weeks that he could barely put on a confident mien, he was now having the most anxious night of his whole military career. At the last moment Murphy had asked that the invasion be postponed because political prospects seemed poor, but it was much too late; the vast machinery had long been set in motion. Stimson had spent sleepless hours in bed wondering if Hitler would strike through Spain. Marshall was on edge. Steve Early heard about the invasion just before it started. "Jesus Christ," he said, "why couldn't the Army have done this just before election!"

Roosevelt was at Shangri-La on Saturday night, November 7, with Hopkins and a few friends, as the invasion was starting in the early hours of the morning, African time. He was tense and preoccupied. The telephone rang. Grace Tully answered. It was the War Department. The President's hand shook as he took the receiver. He listened intently, then burst out:

"Thank God. Thank God. That sounds grand. Congratulations. Casualties are comparatively light—much below your predictions. Thank God."

He put down the receiver and turned to the group.

"We have landed in North Africa. . . . We are striking back."

TO WALK WITH THE DEVIL

War is the grand totalizer. The fits of luck and chance that make or break single operations tend to be canceled out in the numberless collisions of vast and extended forces. Roosevelt's luck rose with the military landings in Africa, which evaded almost all the perils that the soldiers had feared, and fell with the political operation, on which he had lavished such effort and thought.

In the early hours of November 8 troops scrambled ashore from a dozen target points along the shoulder of Northwest Africa from south of Casablanca to east of Algiers. Some landings went according to plan, and the troops moved quickly inland against little or no resistance; in other places boats got lost and milled around, soldiers were landed miles from their objectives, and fire fights broke out with the French defenders. But luck prevailed: the Atlantic surf was amazingly calm; the U-boats had been successfully feinted off; the French troops, although quickly rallying to action at some points, suffered from strategic surprise. Key airports and installations fell quickly into Allied hands. And the sheer numbers and spread of invading troops made up for the hasty training and inadequate equipment.

The Commander in Chief was present in his own way. A letter from him to his troops was handed out on all ships just before disembarkation: "Upon the outcome depends the freedom of your lives: the freedom of the lives of those you love. . . ." A few Frenchmen were startled to hear in the early hours the voice of Franklin Roosevelt over BBC London, in French: "My friends, who suffer day and night, under the crushing yoke of the Nazis, I speak to you as one who was with your Army and Navy in France in 1918. I have held all my life the deepest friendship for the French people. . . . I know your farms, your villages, and your cities. I know your soldiers, professors, and workmen. . . . I salute again and reiterate my faith in Liberty, Equality, and Fraternity." He asked the French to aid the invasion. *"Vive la France éternelle!"*

At this point Roosevelt's man in Algiers was appealing to the Frenchmen's "self-interest and national ideals"—and running into trouble. Murphy had planned that as the landings began at

Algiers he would inform the local French authorities that a huge American force was invading Africa and that General Giraud was on hand to take charge. Two things were going wrong early in the morning of the eighth—neither Giraud nor the Allied troops had arrived. And unexpectedly the highest-ranking Frenchman at the moment in Algiers was Admiral Darlan, who was visiting his son, who was ill with polio. Only Darlan could act for Pétain. At first the Admiral was furious when Murphy told him the situation. Apparently the Americans were as stupid as the British, he said. But when Murphy intimated that half a million troops—only a several-fold exaggeration—were descending on the continent, Darlan's indignation gave way to Gallic realism, or at least self-interest. He told Murphy he would co-operate if Pétain approved.

In Vichy, far to the north, the old Marshal received the American Chargé d'Affaires. Roosevelt, "as the Chef d'Etat of the United States to the Chef d'Etat of the Republic of France," had sent him a message. The Germans had "neglected no opportunity to demoralize and degrade your great Nation," Roosevelt said. They were planning to invade and occupy French North Africa and would then threaten the Americas. He was hoping for the co-operation of the French authorities in North Africa. Pétain's answer, composed by Laval and others, was ready for the Chargé. The Marshal had learned of the Allied aggression with stupor and sadness. Roosevelt was attributing false intentions to his enemies. He had always declared he would defend the empire; he would keep his word. The honor of France was at stake.

"We are attacked; we shall defend ourselves; this is the order I am giving." Actually, the Marshal's feelings were far more mixed than his words, but he was as constricted as ever. Shortly, he broke diplomatic relations with the United States—but also authorized Darlan to act in his behalf.

In the fog of politics French officers groped for instructions and order. By midafternoon of the eighth, with Algiers almost surrounded, its coastal batteries overrun, its forts under siege, Darlan agreed to the capitulation of the city. It was different elsewhere. Two cutters with a mixed commando force had stormed Oran harbor before dawn; both had been destroyed, with the loss of all but a handful of the force. Troops made rapid progress ashore at Oran, but the French were resisting and by evening were preparing counterattacks for the next day. The heaviest fighting erupted on the Atlantic beachheads. Noguès, in Casablanca, assumed from first reports that the attack was merely a commando raid; he ordered resistance. After some amateurish landings that produced endless delay and muddle, American troops ran into heavy French gunfire as they pressed into the main cities.

The most dramatic action was a sea battle off Casablanca—"an old-fashioned fire-away Flannagan" between surface vessels, it was called by Samuel Morison, the combat historian present. French warships sortied from the harbor against the big American fleet; *Jean Bart,* the uncompleted French battleship lying immobile in the harbor, spoke with her fifteen-inch guns; American battleships, cruisers, and destroyers poured fire on the hapless French flotilla, sinking or disabling the *Jean Bart* at her berth and a dozen other warships. Among the numerous American sailors winning commendation that day was Lieutenant Franklin D. Roosevelt, Jr., a gunnery officer on a destroyer.

During the following days young Roosevelt's father, who had returned from Shangri-La to the White House, would doubtless have swapped his place for his son's in a simple fire-away Flannagan. Reports from Algiers and Gibraltar were indicating a political situation of mounting complexity and danger. On November 9 Eisenhower's deputy, General Mark Clark, arrived in Algiers, amid a Nazi bombing raid, with the hope of ending hostilities. Giraud arrived, too, with a long-time "promise" from Roosevelt that he would be top man in North Africa. Clark met with Darlan the next day. The American General, like his chief in Gibraltar, abhorred the political aspects of the war. He divided the French leaders into good guys and those he code-named, in reports to Eisenhower, YBSOBS—"yellow-bellied sons-of-bitches." Clark's overwhelming way had its immediate impact; Darlan wanted to wait for more definite orders from Vichy as to a cease-fire, but under Clark's pressure he sent directives in the Marshal's name to Oran and to Morocco, where Noguès ordered a cease-fire just in time to avert a heavy American attack.

It was one thing for Clark, with his bigger battalions, to obtain an armistice, something else to gain Roosevelt's real objective—active French assistance in attacking Germans and Italians to the east. In his continuing negotiations with Clark, Darlan had some high cards: his seeming embodiment of the will and confidence of the Marshal; his influence over the officers, bureaucrats, and *colons* who ran France's African domain; his ability to draw things out in contrast to Eisenhower's desperate need to get Northwest Africa pacified and the French mobilized for the push into Tunisia before the Germans gained a foothold there. The French fleet at Toulon was the big pot in the game. One thing was rapidly becoming clear: American Intelligence had been grievously wrong in thinking that Giraud had strong support, existing or potential, among the French. He was simply dismissed as a *dissident.* Happily Giraud himself came to realize his political impotence and was willing to take military command in Africa under Darlan's headship.

While Clark and Darlan negotiated, Hitler acted with his usual dispatch. Meeting with Laval in Munich, the Führer demanded that Vichy at once make Tunisian ports and air bases available to the Axis. Laval proclaimed his fanatic hostility to Bolshevism—but only the Marshal could grant Hitler's request. The Führer gave immediate orders. At midnight that evening—November 11—motorized German units stabbed across the armistice frontier and swept through southern France without resistance. Italian divisions moved into southeastern France and Corsica. The Axis took steps to fortify Tunisia, even at the expense of Rommel's army retreating west under harrying attacks from Montgomery's desert troops.

Hitler's gulp of the rest of France broke the impasse in Algiers. While Pétain publicly ordered Darlan to continue fighting, the Admiral could claim that the Marshal was acting under duress and in any event was sending out secret orders countermanding his public ones. Negotiations were soon concluded. Eisenhower, who made a brief trip to Algiers, Clark, and Murphy agreed with Darlan, Giraud, and other local French leaders that Darlan would be the political chief and would retain his command of naval forces; the French would actively help liberate Tunisia, and other matters would be left to further negotiations. To the Americans on the scene it seemed to be a safe and sensible arrangement—certainly nothing that could produce an explosion back home.

"Prostitutes are used; they are seldom loved. Even less frequently are they honored." The Darlan deal was only the latest and worst of a long series of concessions and bargains that had weakened and were still weakening democratic resistance. "The United States has only one claim on the allegiance of the peoples of the world: an honest and courageous democratic policy." Africa had produced a "historic clash between two theories of political behavior—the 'quarterback' or opportunist theory, long indorsed by the President, and the theory which insists upon the importance of a thought-out, consistent political line." But what doubtless appeared a reasonable military expedient was proving a costly political blunder. Darlan was America's first Quisling. Appeasement was winning out.

These were the words of Freda Kirchwey, editor and publisher of the *Nation*, but also the sentiments of a host of liberals, idealists, and independents when they got news of the Darlan deal. Walter Lippmann and Dorothy Thompson raised sharp and influential voices. Feeling was even stronger in liberal and left-wing circles in Britain. In both countries opposition developed in high councils of state. Concerned about the effect of the deal on de Gaulle's status and morale, Eden wrangled with Churchill to the point where the Prime Minister shouted, "Well, Darlan is not as bad as de

Gaulle anyway!" In Washington, Stimson was so alarmed at the reaction that he invited his best liberal friends—Morgenthau, Frankfurter, MacLeish—to his home and argued for the military value of the deal. Morgenthau was not placated. He passionately denounced Darlan as a man who had sold thousands of people into slavery, as a violent British-hater; no, the price was too high. The Secretary of the Treasury seemed to Stimson so "sunk" that he was almost for giving up the war. If Frankfurter had any misgivings about the deal, there is no record of his having communicated them to the President.

Stimson performed a bigger service for the President that evening. He heard from Elmer Davis that Willkie was about to address the New York Herald Tribune Forum and to denounce American leaders for promising freedom to the French people and then putting their enslaver in control of them. "Shall we be quiet when we see our government's long appeasement of Vichy find its logical conclusion in our collaboration with Darlan, Hitler's tool?" Reaching his fellow Republican by telephone less than an hour before he was to speak, Stimson implored him to delete the critical passage or otherwise jeopardize the lives of 60,000 soldiers. Willkie lost his temper, denounced Stimson for trying to control his freedom—but after exhausting his reservoir of profanity he agreed to tone down his speech. As delivered, it merely pummeled that battered old punching bag, the State Department. The President listened to Willkie's broadcast and later telephoned Stimson to congratulate him.

By the iron laws of mutual hostility, the more the Americans embraced Darlan in Algiers, the more they alienated de Gaulle in London. The Free French leader, at first exhilarated by the landings in Africa, turned cold toward the invaders as they parleyed with the men of Vichy. He felt that the Darlan deal was politically shortsighted, tactically ineffective, and an American ploy for postwar supremacy. "What remains of the honor of France," he proclaimed, "will stay intact in my hands." He called on Admiral Stark and tendered a one-sentence note: "The United States can pay traitors but not with the honor of France." Stark refused to accept it. Churchill was caught between his desire to sustain the soldiers in the field, his policy of recognizing de Gaulle and working with him, and the revulsion against Darlan among the people and even within his own government. Somehow he managed to back Eisenhower while making clear that the Darlan deal was essentially an American undertaking.

At first Roosevelt seemed unmoved by the furore. He received from Eisenhower a strong cable explaining that if Darlan was repudiated, French armed forces would resist passively and perhaps actively—and the possibility of getting the French Navy out of

Toulon intact and of winning French military assistance in France would be gone. Impressed by this cable, Roosevelt read it to Hopkins with such superb emphasis that it seemed to Sherwood, sitting by, as if he were making a plea for his European commander before the bar of history. But as the tumult over Darlan mounted, Roosevelt was compelled to issue a public justification. "I have accepted General Eisenhower's political arrangements made for the time being in Northern and Western Africa." He understood and approved the widespread feeling that in view of the history of the last two years no permanent arrangement should be made with Darlan. "We are opposed to Frenchmen who support Hitler and the Axis. No one in our Army has any authority to discuss the future Government of France and the French Empire.

"The future French Government will be established, not by any individual in Metropolitan France or overseas, but by the French people themselves after they have been set free by the victory of the United Nations.

"The present temporary arrangement in North and West Africa is only a temporary expedient, justified solely by the stress of battle." It was designed to save lives and to speed the attack on Tunis. He had asked for the abrogation of all laws inspired by Nazi governments or ideologists.

At the same time Roosevelt assured Eisenhower that he appreciated his difficulties, did not question his actions in any way, and that the General could be sure of Roosevelt's complete support—but that Eisenhower should keep in mind:

"1. That we do not trust Darlan.

"2. That it is impossible to keep a collaborator of Hitler and . . . a fascist in civil power any longer than is absolutely necessary." He asked that Darlan's movements be watched and his communications supervised.

Brave words—and yet they masked Roosevelt's sharp disappointment over the political problems in Africa. The operation had been a stirring success militarily, with American casualties amounting to less than 1,500, and a bracing fillip for the people back home, but celebration of this was dimmed by the criticism. When Morgenthau, still depressed after his visit with Stimson, came to the White House to say that North Africa was "something that afflicts my soul," Roosevelt gave him the usual argument of military expediency and went on to quote an "old Bulgarian proverb of the Orthodox Church: 'My children, you are permitted in time of great danger to walk with the Devil until you have crossed the bridge.' " Roosevelt liked the proverb so much he repeated it both to Churchill and to the press, adding to the reporters, "Mind you, this is okayed by the church."

The trouble was that Roosevelt had as little desire to walk with the devil as had the people he led. Rosenman could not remember a time when he was more deeply affected by a political attack, or resented his critics more, especially since so many of them were usually his supporters. At times he refused to discuss the matter at all; other times he read aloud with bitterness some columnist's criticism. It did not help that Stalin later approved the Darlan deal on the ground that military diplomacy must be able to use not only the Darlans but "Even the Devil himself and his grandma." That was doing the Bulgarian one better, but Roosevelt preferred to clothe his policies in idealism, because fundamentally he *was* an idealist.

Still, he was also a practical man, and the final irony of the expedient North African policy was that the expediency failed in major respects. The French did resist initially, causing and sustaining casualties. It was hoped that Darlan could bring over the French fleet in Toulon, but when the Germans closed in on the naval base late in November the French scuttled their fine battleships, cruisers, and destroyers. It was hoped that the French would actively help in the Tunisian campaign, but they proved unwilling or unable to lend decisive assistance. Above all, it was hoped that an early cease-fire would enable the Allies to make a quick thrust into Tunisia, but the Germans got there first, the weather turned foul, and soon the Americans and British were stalled on the Tunisian front. If the Darlan policy had been effective as a way of achieving major short-run military goals, it was far less rewarding, and even probably a handicap, in achieving long-run or even middle-run strategic objectives. Darlan's assassination in Algiers the day before Christmas 1942 relieved Roosevelt of the person but not the problem.

So Roosevelt and his soldiers were left with a gnawing worry about the price that might be paid, impossible to estimate, in disappointment and chagrin among anti-Nazi French inside and outside their country, and among free peoples everywhere who wondered just how far one could walk with the devil, how often, and at what price.

ROOSEVELT: A TURNING POINT?

"The President becomes more and more the central figure in the global war, the source of initiative and authority in action, and, of course, of responsibility." So wrote Hassett in his diary toward the end of November 1942. Hassett, who was as close to his chief as a valet and only a shade less iconoclastic, went on: "A little impatient at delay in offensive against Tunis and Bizerte. 'Why are they so slow?' he queried. But still calm and composed, always at his best, as the first year of the war draws to a close. Still unruffled in temper, buoyant of spirit, and, as always, ready with a wisecrack or a laugh, and can sleep anywhere whenever opportunity affords—priceless assets for one bearing his burdens, which he never mentions. No desire to be a martyr, living or dead."

Buoyancy—this was the quality that struck Roosevelt's staff and friends during the anxious months of planning, waiting, and managing during late 1942. Despite Hassett, he was often ruffled—by reporters, by critics, by delays—but he was quick to recover. As always he found strength in friends, anecdotes, banter, the daily routine of visits, dictating letters, signing documents with the broad-pointed pen he had given Hassett.

And always the darting interest, the instant response, the nimble recovery, the endless curiosity, the quick, almost automatic self-protectiveness. He instructed his naval aide to tell the Navy band that the "Star-Spangled Banner" should be played with fewer frills. He asked his wife to cut down the food bill in the light of the new income-tax law, especially in the large portions served at meals brought up to the study. "I know of no instance where anybody has taken a second help—except occasionally when I do—and it would be much better if I did not take a second help anyway." He wrote to Admiral King, who had informed him primly that he would shortly be sixty-four and hence retirable, "So what old top? I may even send you a birthday present!" (And he did—a framed photograph of himself.) He dunned neighbor Morgenthau for his annual dues ($750) to the Dutchess County Democratic party. He sent his half-niece a transcription of his grandmother's Hyde Park diaries, confessing that neither he nor his niece would have found Hyde Park life sixty years back very exciting. He thanked Fred Allen for sending him a coffee bean, which had ended his anguished coffeeless breakfasts and "made the sun come out"; otherwise he would have resigned as Commander in Chief and taken appointment as a sergeant major in Brazil, where he could have coffee six times a day. He told Ickes, who had invited himself to lunch and threatened to bring his own food, that he would fall into the clutches of the Secret Service and that the President would rather go out to "dine with my old farmer's wife named Jane." He wrote to Herbert Bayard Swope—signing the memo with Grace Tully's initials—that the President would never speak to him again.

"He is affronted and insulted by your suggestion that his French is 'as good' as that of Winston. Furthermore, the President's accent is not only infinitely superior but his French profanity is so explosive that you had better not be within a half mile of him when it goes off." If Swope was such a linguist, he could go to Albania, where the third front was to be established. "Incidentally, a little bird tells us that the pulchritude of the Albanian mountain females is an added attraction. When do you want to shove off?"

He was pleased when Eleanor Roosevelt planned to visit England and he listed people she must see—mainly top royalty. "People whom you should see if they call on you"—more royalty, and a few commoners, including Eduard Beneš, of Czechoslovakia. He wrote letters for her to King George VI and to Queen Wilhelmina. To his wife's query as to whether she should take anything to King George and Queen Mary and to Churchill he replied, *"No."*

On Thanksgiving Day he invited the leaders of his war government—Cabinet members, Army and Navy chiefs, war agency heads, along with the Supreme Court—to worship with him at a special service in the East Room. There he read his Thanksgiving Proclamation. ". . . Yes, though I walk through the valley of the shadow of death, I will fear no evil," the President intoned in a soft, hushed voice. To David Lilienthal, sitting near him, he looked like one of the senior wardens of his little church at Hyde Park, drawing up his eyebrows as he read the words, singing almost soundlessly the "Battle Hymn of the Republic." Afterward he greeted people cheerily, sometimes boisterously, taking their hands in his huge grip, saying a word to their wives like a minister at the church door after the service.

He had much to give thanks for. It looked as though the turning point of the war had at last been reached, he told the Herald Tribune Forum. Despite his annoyance about the flap over Darlan, the weeks after the invasion were a time of solace for the President. "I am happy today in the fact that for three months I have been taking it on the chin in regard to the Second Front and that that is now over," he wrote his old Navy chief, Josephus Daniels. He had the pleasure of sitting back in his chair, puffing contentedly on a cigarette, telling reporters about the long process of planning TORCH, lecturing them mildly on how a second front could not just be bought in a department store, ready-made. He even scored with the columnists. It seemed as though the United Nations had a grand strategy after all, some of them decided, what with American forces drawing the Japanese into the Solomons, the Russians overextending the Germans in the Caucasus, and then the pincers closing on the enemy in Africa. Roosevelt was one of the greatest war presidents, with a grasp of total and global strategy, Major George Fielding Eliot wrote.

If the war seemed at a turning point toward the end of 1942, Roosevelt seemed—a year after Pearl Harbor, two years after his decision for Lend-Lease, halfway through his third term—to be facing a turning point, too. For two years he had been stressing war problems and playing down long-run economic and social issues. He had usually evaded questions about planning for the postwar period. Now, in the first flush of victory, he seemed to be thinking more about future social and economic problems, at home and abroad.

New Dealers had been worried that fall. The town seemed, more than ever, full of big businessmen who now seemed to be running things rather than denouncing things in the Chamber of Commerce Building across from the White House. The President gave an "honorable discharge" to the old Works Progress Administration —symbol of the "Second Hundred Days" of Roosevelt's progressivism at the height of its fervor and turbulence in 1935—and dropped one or two other New Deal agencies. Democratic leaders, according to Washington reporters, were privately conceding that great blocs of labor, farm, and independent votes had gone Republican; the President had lost his political touch, having failed in his two key aims of saving Norris and defeating Dewey; Congress was already in revolt; old New Dealers like Morgenthau, Wallace, and Ickes were unpopular, worn out, fumbling. There were reports—true this time—that Henderson would be out by Christmas.

A sense of defeat hung over Washington, Lilienthal felt—not of military defeat, but of the purposes for which Americans had been told the war was being fought. He sensed a disorganization of spirit, a vacuum at the center that was being filled with reaction, weariness, cynicism. His fears deepened when he went in to see the President in mid-December about some proposals to have lame-duck Senator Norris visit the Tennessee Valley and the Arkansas and other possible river-valley developments, and report back to the President. He suggested that Norris might also report on the possible role of TVA's abroad, where there was intense interest in Roosevelt's experiment.

The President was leery. No, he said, we had better leave the foreign thing out; the other night an NAM speaker had said that the administration had in mind a TVA on the Danube. Lilienthal did not contest the point. He left the White House with a heavy heart. He had heard the stories that the President was interested only in a military victory. "Godamighty"—it was true. One speech before the National Association of Manufacturers—and the man pulled away from the fundamental proposition of America's interest in the welfare of the rest of the world.

Lilienthal had left so that Roosevelt could lunch alone with Norris; then he returned. He seemed to find a changed man. Roosevelt had told Norris that he wanted him to report on the Tennessee Valley project and what it meant to the future of America and to other parts of the world. Lilienthal was elated. He confessed to the President that he had left his office discouraged. Roosevelt leaned back in his chair. He looked as Lilienthal remembered him in the past, when he had fought back against his enemies and usually won. He had, thought Lilienthal, the handsomest fighting face in the world.

"I am going to fight back. I'm not going to take this lying down." Roosevelt had his jaw stuck out. Lilienthal was standing, worried, knowing that Leahy and Marshall were waiting to come in. "I'm really going to *tell* this next Congress." His speech would lay out a program that would give them and the country something to chew on. "Those boys in Guadalcanal and in Africa—does this Congress propose to tell them they are going to come back to fear about jobs, fear about the things a man can't prevent, like accident, sickness, and so on? Well, they will have a chance to go on record about it, to divide on that *political* issue." And as the President got off point after point, he would grin or wink. Lilienthal shook hands to go, but the President was keyed up and went on talking. Lilienthal was aroused, too, and blurted out something he had been aching to say but never expected to have the chance to—that it was when the President took the offensive that the people were with him.

Christmastime came, with parties at Hyde Park for soldiers guarding the Commander in Chief's home; then the President and First Lady returned to Washington for Christmas itself. On New Year's Eve they had their usual small party for close friends, and as usual toasted the United States of America. The company drank to the President; he in turn toasted his wife as the one who made it possible for him to carry on; at his suggestion glasses were raised to friends and family in far-off parts of the world. Then the President offered a new toast: "The United Nations."

PART 3 *Strategy*

TEN *Casablanca*

I AM GOING to fight back," the President had exclaimed to David Lilienthal. "I'm really going to *tell* this next Congress." But as the time for his address to Congress neared, he shifted toward a more conciliatory role, in part because public-opinion studies indicated that people would respond favorably to a co-operative attitude toward Congress. He knew that 1943 would be a transitional sort of year—not one of desperate defense like most of 1942, but not yet the year for all-out attack, and certainly not the year for victory. He had decided it was time to talk about postwar hopes and policies, but he could not forget that the November elections had left him with the biggest Republican–Southern Democratic opposition he had yet faced.

Greeted by two minutes of applause as he made his slow way to the rostrum on January 7, 1943, he launched into a long speech that seemed to play on every note and mood.

He was confident. "The period of our defensive attrition in the Pacific is drawing to a close. Now our aim is to force the Japanese to fight. Last year, we stopped them. This year, we intend to advance." In Europe the main task during 1942 had been to lessen the pressure on Russia by compelling Germany to divert some of its strength west. North Africa had opened up what Churchill had called the "under-belly" of the Axis, the President said.

He was belligerent. "I cannot prophesy. I cannot tell you when or where the United Nations are going to strike next in Europe. But we are going to strike—and strike hard. I cannot tell you whether we are going to hit them"—and here the President bit off the names of possible targets in a rhythmic, mocking tone—"in Norway, or through the Low Countries, or in France, or through Sardinia or Sicily, or through the Balkans, or through Poland—or at several points simultaneously. But . . . we and the British and the Russians will hit them from the air heavily and relentlessly. . . . Yes, the Nazis and the Fascists have asked for it—and—they—are—going—to—get—it."

He was conciliatory. He praised workers, farmers, and even

owners and managers for their war effort. He denied that Washington was a "madhouse"—except in the sense that it was the capital city of a nation that was fighting mad. He apologized for the number of complicated forms and questionnaires. "I know about that, I have had to fill some of them out myself."

He was a bit more apologetic. There had been criticism of the war-production effort and much of it had had a healthy effect, he said. Some production goals had had to be adjusted downward, and others upward; airplane and tank production had fallen short numerically of the 1942 goals. But the over-all record would give no aid and comfort to the enemy. "I think the arsenal of democracy is making good."

Above all, he wanted to talk about the peace. He reminded the Congress of his message on the Four Freedoms two years earlier. Soldiers would not be willing to come home to a bogus prosperity, to slums, or the dole, or selling apples on street corners. "I have been told that this is no time to speak of a better America after the war. I am told it is a grave error on my part.

"I dissent.

"And if the security of the individual citizen, or the family, should become a subject of national debate, the country knows where I stand."

But it was of little account, he went on, to talk of attaining individual security if national security was in jeopardy. "Undoubtedly a few Americans, even now, think that this Nation can end this war comfortably and then climb back into an American hole and pull the hole in after them. But we have learned that we can never dig a hole so deep that it would be safe against predatory animals." The President did not spell out postwar means and ends, but he made clear that he would not repeat the mistake of World War I of seeking a formula for permanent peace based on "magnificent idealism" alone.

And he was eloquent.

"I tell you it is within the realm of possibility that this Seventy-eighth Congress may have the historic privilege of helping greatly to save the world from future fear," he said in closing.

"Therefore, let us all have confidence, let us redouble our efforts.

"A tremendous, costly, long-enduring task in peace as well as in war is still ahead of us.

"But, as we face that continuing task, we may know that the state of this Nation is good—the heart of this Nation is sound—the spirit of this Nation is strong—the faith of this Nation is eternal."

The President submitted a "total war" budget that embodied his big plans. The figures were breath-taking. Current fiscal-year spending was running at seventy-seven billion; in the next fiscal year the federal government would spend one hundred billion dollars. More than ten million people had been added to employment rolls or the armed forces in two and a half years; another six million would be needed during calendar 1943. Sensing Congress's mood the President said that nonwar expenditures had been reduced two billion from the 6.5 billion of fiscal 1939—but "we are fast approaching the subsistence level of government." He called for more taxes, but "I cannot ask the Congress to impose the necessarily heavy financial burdens on the lower and middle incomes unless the taxes on higher and very large incomes are made fully effective." The President asked again for a limitation of $25,000 a year on salaries.

Indeed, beneath the conciliatory Roosevelt was the same old political warrior with his dislike of columnists, carping Congressmen, and conservative critics. He could not help noting that the applause that had repeatedly punctuated his earlier remarks on war policy petered out when he stressed domestic issues toward the end. Congress clearly would be a problem—at least until the next election.

Around this time Roosevelt saw a poem by Howard Dietz, in *PM*, about Clare Boothe Luce, wife of publisher Henry Luce, a playwright, beauty, newly elected Republican Representative from Connecticut, and a recent critic of the administration for trying to fight a "soft war."

> O Lovely Luce—O Comely Clare!
> Do you remember—way back there—
> Holding your lacquered nails aloft,
> "The war we fight," you said, "is soft."
>
> And while the vote hung in the balance
> You turned the trick with all your talents.
> You were the keystone brave and buoyant.
> By Lucifer, were you clarevoyant!
>
> Time marches on. . . .

And so did the verse, for another six stanzas, evoking the gallant deeds of Eisenhower and the rest in the no-longer-soft war. It was a bit crude, and Roosevelt loved it. He had long since fallen out with Henry Luce; only recently he had asked Welles to file a formal protest with Luce on any articles in *Time, Life,* and *Fortune* that "hurt the Good Neighbor policy with Latin America or tend to promote disunity among any of the United Nations. . . ."

"Can't you find a freshman Congressman on our side," he now wrote to McCormack, enclosing the verse, "who will wait his chance until the first time Clare talks and then quote this poem?" But no soldier in the House sprang to answer this summons by the Commander in Chief to perform such an ungallant act.

Two days after his address to Congress the President left for Casablanca.

THE GAMING BOARD OF STRATEGY

"The Axis powers knew that they must win the war in 1942—or eventually lose everything," the President had told Congress in his January 7 message. "I do not need to tell you that our enemies did not win the war in 1942." It was a piece of Rooseveltian understatement, but much of the press in 1943 was not so restrained. The Axis was on the run. It was now only a matter of time. Hitler was licked.

The drop in Nazi fortunes did seem dramatic and irreversible. In October 1942 Hitler had seemed a military colossus. To the east his forces held two vast chunks of Soviet territory, now labeled Reich Kommissariat Ostland and Reich Kommissariat Ukraine. Toward the far southeast his troops had raised the Swastika on Mount Elbrus, the highest alp in the Caucasus, seized the Markop oil fields, and readied their advance toward the Caspian Sea. To the north Norway was occupied, Sweden isolated, Finland militarily allied, and the Nazis were still mauling the Russia-bound convoys in the northern seas. To the west Hitler ruled northern France and even the Channel Islands, and his U-boats and raiders were scoring spectacular successes in the Atlantic. To the south the Mediterranean had become virtually Mare Axeum, and the Balkans were held tight in the German-Italian grip, except for guerrillas, whom Berlin dismissed as bandits. Rommel's forces had awaited orders to advance on Alexandria. Hitler at this point could well indulge the intoxicating thought of pushing through Iran or Egypt—or both—to India and a link-up with Japan.

Then the fall. In four climactic weeks, from Montgomery's counteroffensive during the last days of October and the successful North African landings to the pinching off of Stalingrad in late November as flanking Red Army troops joined forty miles to the west on the Don bend, Hitler's strategy seemed to have collapsed. His own fanatical stubbornness seemed to compound his difficulties. "I won't leave the Volga!" he screamed to his staff, but after a desperate effort to relieve the city, twenty-two German and two Rumanian divisions were left to freeze and die in Stalingrad. He demanded that Rommel hold his coastal strip along the Mediterranean, and his response to TORCH was to prepare to stand in North Africa rather than abandon it. In his hour of need his associates acted like fair-weather friends: Franco looked on blandly while the Americans invaded Africa; the French scuttled their fleet at Toulon; the Turks seemed responsive to Churchill's lures and blandishments. Even the submarine offensive in the Atlantic was taking a turn for the worse by the end of 1942.

Yet, just as the press had exaggerated Hitler's strength in his heyday, they exaggerated his plight after his fall. He was able to consolidate his position on the Eastern Front after Stalingrad, and the insistence of the Americans on invading Africa so far to the west was giving him time to fortify Tunisia. His U-boats would soon be stepping up their Atlantic attack to the point where Roosevelt feared that cross-channel prospects and even the security of Britain were threatened. He had the priceless advantage of holding interior lines of control of the immense land mass he had won.

Then, too, the invasion of Africa had left Hitler with a boon—the realization that the Allies could not invade northern France for some time, and hence the freedom to move troops to the Eastern Front, which to the Führer remained the crucial war. Invasion of Fortress Europe would be hard for his enemies—especially for the Anglo-Americans, who would have to win Africa and then move into the underbelly, which looked far less soft to Hitler than to Churchill. If the Führer's strategy of blitz and annihilation and conquest was now bankrupt, a strategy of dividing and exhausting his enemies might still save the day.

For such a strategy Hitler's strongest weapon was the trait that drove his generals to despair—his merciless determination to deny requests to withdraw, to sack wavering commanders, to make his soldiers stand and die. Thus he could exact the heaviest cost from his enemies. His own resolution and ruthlessness never seemed to waver. During the day he listened, now stonily, now furiously, to the reports from the fronts; dispatched orders on minute tactical matters; berated his aides and his commanders for their stupidity, their cowardice, their refusal to fight to the end and then shoot themselves. In the evening he was more relaxed, sitting around the dinner table with exhausted and often bored officers. Hour after hour his monologues rambled on about Germany's royal family, bureaucrats, industrialists, intellectuals, the Catholic church and all its components—popes, "parsons," Isabella ("the greatest harlot in history")—St. Petersburg, Hungarians, lawyers—all of whom he despised. And about peasant girls, soldiers, Mussolini, babies, and skilled workers, of whom he approved.

Often he talked about his rivals—about Roosevelt, a "half-caste" who behaved like a "tortuous, pettifogging Jew"; about Churchill, the "raddled old whore of journalism," the "unprincipled swine"; about Stalin, "half beast, half giant," "an ascetic who took the whole of that gigantic country in his iron grasp." He talked about the Russian people, whom he loathed; about the English, whom he half hated, half admired; about the Americans, for whom he had contempt mixed with a little fear. And always he returned to the Jews, the root of all evil.

In Moscow the half beast, half giant was savoring, at the start of 1943, only part of the satisfaction that was his due after the Battle of Stalingrad. His troubles seemed to come now from his friends. His comradeship with Churchill had deteriorated sharply since their skittish intercourse in Moscow in August. A galling and ever-present issue was the desperate convoying of supplies around the North Cape of Norway through the Arctic Sea to Murmansk. In September PQ-18 had started out with a huge naval and air escort—a new auxiliary aircraft carrier, destroyers, and a score of torpedo bombers. Although the Soviets dispatched long-range bombers and fighters from their end, only about two-thirds of the merchantmen in this convoy got through. With TORCH coming up, the British had decided they must suspend northern convoying. Churchill so informed Stalin. The latter's reply was crushing in its brevity: Churchill's message had been received. "Thank you."

But the sovereign issue was always the second front. As the Wehrmacht columns lunged toward the Caucasus and coiled around the Volga, Stalin grimly pondered the pledges he thought he had received earlier in the year. His bitterness spilled out for public view in his speech of November 6, 1942, on the twenty-fifth anniversary of the October Revolution. In his usual didactic way he asked and answered questions. "How are we to explain the fact that the Germans were . . . able to take the initiative in military operations this year and achieve substantial tactical successes on our front?" Because the Germans and their allies had been able to muster all their available reserves and shift them to their Eastern Front. But why were they able to do this? "Because the absence of a second front in Europe enabled them to carry out this operation without any risk." He dwelt on the 240 Nazi and satellite divisions fighting on the Russian front. And how many divisions were the British engaging on the Libyan front? "Only four—yes, four—German and eleven Italian divisions."

He went on, ominously: "It is often asked: But will there be a second front in Europe after all? Yes, there will be; sooner or later, there will be. And there will be one not only because we need it, but above all because our Allies need it no less than we. Our Allies cannot fail to realize that since France has been put out of action, the absence of a second front against fascist Germany may end badly for all the freedom-loving countries, including the Allies themselves."

Still, when the Anglo-Americans landed in Africa, the Kremlin could not conceal its pleasure. Stalin wired to Churchill that he was highly pleased with his success in Libya and the successful launching of TORCH. The news was dispatched to the embattled Red Army, with evidently good effect. Later in the month Stalin even sent Churchill birthday greetings. But the sovereign issue remained. Within a week of sending his birthday card, Stalin cabled another message: What was Churchill's answer to his earlier query about the opening of a second front in Western Europe in 1943?

But even in the darkest days before Stalingrad the Kremlin probably was thinking of the implications of the delayed second front for the long run. Russia's shouldering of the burden could pay off later. "To define the direction of the basic blow means to predetermine the nature of operations in the whole period of war, to determine nine-tenths of the fate of the whole war," Stalin had written. "In this is the task of strategy." The reluctance of the West to strike that basic blow could have crucial postwar effects, Kremlin strategists doubtless reasoned. Brooke had noted in Moscow that Stalin was a realist if there ever was one. "Plans, hypotheses, future possibilities, mean nothing to him, but he is ready to face facts, even when unpleasant." And much as he wanted a second front, Stalin, it can be judged, knew that unpleasant facts also bore welcome opportunities.

Winston Churchill had contemplated opportunities of a different sort in the turbulent fall months of 1942. His mind was alive with possibilities, alternatives, contingencies, choices. Would the Nazis break the back of the Red Bear this time? Or, on the contrary, might the Wehrmacht collapse from its own bleeding arteries and open up the Continent for a quick invasion from the West? In either event, might Stalin make a separate peace? Would Montgomery hold, and then beat back the Afrika Korps? Would TORCH bring a secure foothold, and how quickly could the Allies consolidate their position and move east to Tunisia? Would Hitler reinforce his bracketed legions in Africa?

Churchill's eye darted along the Mediterranean, with all its enticing problems and openings. Would Franco intervene? Could Malta hold out? Could Turkey be brought into the war? As the weeks passed, some of his questions were answered by events, but the same events opened up new alternatives. Was Sicily the logical access point to the underbelly? What about Sardinia, even Corsica?

Nor did Churchill lose sight of ROUNDUP—a plan for a relatively early cross-channel attack—as he gazed at the churning events in the Mediterranean. To the chagrin of his military men he suddenly—indeed, while the African landings were proceeding—told his Chiefs of Staff that it would be "most regrettable to make no more use of the success of 'Torch' and Alamein in 1943 than the occupation of

Sicily and Sardinia." "If Africa was going to be used as an excuse to lock up great forces on the defensive," he said, "better not to have gone there at all." Would the Russians be content with "our lying down like this during the whole of 1943, while Hitler has a third crack at them"? He was still for ROUNDUP, though put off until August. But he did not want the Anglo-American armies stuck in North Africa. It was a springboard, not a sofa.

Brooke was appalled at this turnabout. Had not the Americans warned that TORCH would probably preclude ROUNDUP in 1943? The PM "never faces realities," Brooke complained to his diary; "at one moment we are reducing our forces, and the next we are invading the Continent with vast armies. . . . He is quite incorrigible and I am quite exhausted. . . ." Yet the soldiers sensed that their chief's strategic volatility would probably produce another shift in his goals. And they knew that on one matter neither he nor they would ever change their minds: British soldiers must never again go through the stalemate and the blood bath of World War I.

Strategically Churchill focused on one area: Europe—Atlantic Europe, Western Europe, coastal Europe. "I must admit that my thoughts rest primarily in Europe—the revival of the glory of Europe, the parent continent of the modern nations and of civilization," he had written to Eden two weeks before TORCH, during an exchange on postwar plans. "It would be a measureless disaster if Russian barbarism overlaid the culture and independence of the ancient States of Europe. . . ."

In the fall of 1942 Roosevelt was playing an even more improvised game of strategy than Churchill. The former naval person at least had his rough priorities and clear antipathies—notably his bent toward peripheralism and his categorical refusal to risk heavy losses in France. Aside from Atlantic First, Roosevelt had not even these rough guidelines. His reluctance to make a clear strategic commitment was one reason for the bog in which the American military planners were floundering even while the soldiers were planning and executing TORCH.

From Roosevelt's standpoint, however, decision and commitment were impossible while so many imponderables ruled the battle scene. One puzzle was Churchill himself. Over and again the Prime Minister had been warned by the American military, in early and mid-1942, that an invasion of North Africa in the fall of 1942 precluded any heavy cross-channel invasion in 1943. Churchill had seemed to accept this fact cheerfully. Thus it seemed strange that he should reverse himself in the fall and demand of his staff that ROUNDUP be kept alive. Actually his reversal was due to the changed military situation as he perceived it. The pessimism of the American staffs about a cross-channel attack had stemmed, he felt, from fear that Russia would be so crippled by 1943 that Hitler could shift scores of divisions to France and swarm over the Anglo-American invaders. But by fall 1942 it was evident that the Russians were holding their own and would compel the Wehrmacht to husband almost its total strength on the Eastern Front. Churchill had another factor in mind. He feared that a postponement of ROUNDUP would lead to an overdiversion of American troops and war supply to the Pacific. These considerations led him during the fall to call for a reassessment of the whole strategic situation; they did not make him a firm partner of the President in global decision making.

But if Churchill's evolving strategy was not wholly clear to the President, Stalin's was almost opaque. Not that the Chairman's main point was dim; his strident calls for a second front sounded like fire bells in the White House. Other business between Roosevelt and Stalin, however, seemed mired in ambiguity and suspicion. Anxious to bolster the Russians in every way possible except an immediate cross-channel attack, Roosevelt and Churchill had proposed to Stalin that they put a force of bombers and fighters under Soviet strategic command on the increasingly critical Caucasus front. The Kremlin seemed to welcome the idea. The offer was contingent on developments in the Middle East, and especially on the North Africa fronts. When it became necessary to suspend regular convoys to Murmansk, Roosevelt decided that the offer should be made without conditions. "The Russian front today is our greatest reliance," he reaffirmed to Churchill.

Difficulties arose over specific arrangements. The Russians, it developed, for various military and political reasons did not want whole units on Soviet territory; they wanted planes. In mid-December Roosevelt wrote to Stalin that he was not clear as to the state of affairs, but he was still willing to send air units with American pilots and crews, which would operate by units under army commanders but would be under general Soviet command. Stalin replied that the air units were no longer necessary—but would Roosevelt kindly expedite the dispatch of fighters, without crews, under the regular program?

The President encountered similar difficulties, complicated by Soviet neutrality toward Japan, in trying to set up an Alaska-Siberia airplane ferry route. One conclusion seemed inescapable to the frustrated Americans: their Russian comrades were far more interested in bombers than in brotherhood.

By December 1942 several of the imponderables facing Roosevelt had evaporated. The Northwest African foothold had been secured, with Rommel now pulling back toward Tunisia. Spain had stayed neutral. The final effort to drive Axis troops out of Africa was taking longer than expected, but a rough timetable could be set. The Red Army was not only holding but counterattacking. The Japanese were being contained in the Pacific; they were still at peace with Russia. But as some crucial questions and options closed for Roosevelt, others opened up. Did Soviet victories make a cross-channel attack more urgent, or less? Should the Anglo-Americans stand fast on the southern shores of the Mediterranean, where they could protect the east-west sea links, or should they move north? If the latter, where? Try to knock Italy out of the war, or strike farther east, against the Balkans or the Greek isles?

For Roosevelt, tactical developments had outrun strategic decision making. A year after Pearl Harbor he had no definite battle plan. And in the absence of strategic commitments all sorts of other plans, pressures, demands, interests had wider play. The striking example was the Pacific. Despite all the decisions for Atlantic First, by the end of 1942 more than half the American divisions overseas were deployed in the war against Japan. The "limited" offensive moves against the Japanese had brought day-to-day commitments and sudden crises, as in the Solomons, that put heavy pressure on the Washington planners for piecemeal diversions of strength to the Pacific. The pressure was all the heavier in the absence of a set strategic plan that established iron priorities and grimly precluded dispersion.

Clearly strategy making was overdue. "I believe that as soon as we have knocked the Germans out of Tunisia we should proceed with a military strategical conference between Great Britain, Russia and the United States," Roosevelt wrote to Churchill late in November. He proposed that their military chiefs meet with a Soviet delegation in Moscow or Cairo. Churchill agreed on a conference but not of just the military people; Russian generals, he said, would simply refer every major question back to Stalin. And all the Soviet chiefs would do would be to demand a second front. Why shouldn't the heads get together?

After some hesitation Roosevelt agreed. He proposed a meeting in mid-January of the Big Three, accompanied by small military staffs, to take place south of Algiers or in or near Khartoum. "I don't like mosquitoes." He questioned Churchill's idea of Marshall stopping off in London on the way. "I do not want to give Stalin the impression that we are settling everything between ourselves before we meet him. I think that you and I understand each other so well that prior conferences between us are unnecessary. . . ." Roosevelt concluded: "I prefer a comfortable oasis to the raft at Tilsit."

The prospect of a Big Three meeting delighted Churchill. It was the only way of making a good plan for 1943, he wired; at present there was none on the scale or up to the level of events. He still hoped that American and British military staffs could meet in advance, so that there would be some definite plans. "Otherwise Stalin will greet us with the question, 'Have you then no plan for the second front in Europe you promised me for 1943?' "

Roosevelt believed that Stalin would agree to meet, but he was wrong. The dictator said that he could not leave his country during major military operations—and he said nothing about Roosevelt and Churchill coming to the Soviet Union. He was "deeply disappointed," Roosevelt replied; what about March 1? Back came the cool answer: "front matters" would not permit this even in March. Could they not discuss questions by correspondence, Stalin inquired, until they were able to meet? "I think we shall not differ." Stalin must have reflected on the opportunity he was losing to press the second front face to face with the other leaders. "I feel confident," he went on, "that no time is being wasted, that the promise to open a second front in Europe, which you, Mr. President, and Mr. Churchill gave for 1942 or the spring of 1943 at the latest, will be kept and that a second front in Europe will really be opened jointly by Great Britain and the U.S.A. next spring."

Thus Stalin threw the gauntlet into the meeting without even attending it. Roosevelt suggested to Churchill that the two of them confer anyway. England was out as a meeting place "for political reasons." He wanted to get out of the political atmosphere of Washington for a couple of weeks. In Stalin's absence they would need no foreign-affairs people with them, because their work would be essentially military. What about Casablanca as the spot? The military men could precede them by a few days and clear the ground. "Yes, certainly," Churchill answered, "The sooner the better . . ."

At the conference, Roosevelt knew, the British would have a plan and stick to it. Churchill and his chiefs did indeed busy themselves with staff papers that argued strongly for a vigorous follow-up to TORCH, in order to knock Italy out of the war and, they hoped, bring Turkey into it, and to give the Axis no respite. The cross-channel attack would be a basic but long-run project to be conducted by August or September 1943 if conditions permitted. The American planners were busy, too, and came up with their old emphasis on cross-channel first. As a secondary goal—and doubtless as a partial bluff against the British—offensive and defensive operations should be continued against the Japanese in the Pacific and in Burma. The Mediterranean was not even mentioned. In their response a week later the British stuck to their guns.

On January 7, 1943, just before leaving for Casablanca, Roosevelt met with his chiefs for a final planning session. It soon developed that not only were the American and British chiefs still divided, but also the American Chiefs of Staff were not wholly agreed among themselves. King wanted to maintain constant pressure against the Japanese to prevent them from consolidating their conquests. Arnold, as always, stressed air power. Marshall suggested a limited cross-channel operation sometime after July 1943. Roosevelt, still hoping to avoid a definite decision, proposed a compromise that would prepare for operations both in the Mediterranean and across the channel while a commitment was postponed for a month or two. Marshall was unhappy with this notion.

The meeting adjourned with no decision. On the eve of a showdown with the British the Commander in Chief was still evading a strategic commitment.

TOWARD THE UNDERBELLY?

Late Saturday evening, January 9, 1943, Roosevelt, Hopkins, McIntire, and a small party boarded the presidential train at the secret siding near the Bureau of Engraving and Printing. The President was gay and relaxed. He was about to see a new continent, Churchill, combat troops. And he would travel by plane for the first time since his famous flight to the Democratic convention in Chicago in 1932. He would be the first President to fly, the first to leave the United States in wartime, and the first since Lincoln to visit an active theater of war. To take a trip, to enter a war zone, to create precedents—no combination of events could make Roosevelt happier.

On arriving in Miami early on Monday morning, after a long sleepy Sunday chugging through the Carolinas and Georgia, Roosevelt laughed with Hopkins over the realization that the "unbelievable trip" was actually taking place.

Long before dark the Pan American Clipper taxied out of the harbor at Miami and, with Roosevelt and his party strapped in their seats, took off toward Trinidad. The President missed nothing. He asked the pilot to fly over the Citadel in Haiti; scanned the jungle of Dutch Guiana; glimpsed the Amazon where it widens out sharply; noted the merchant ships off the Brazilian port of Belém. Then came the long overnight hop to Bathurst, in British Gambia, where the flying boat landed in the big harbor at the mouth of the Gambia River. Here the cruiser *Memphis* was waiting to berth the President overnight. Hoisted to the deck, the Commander in Chief landed hard on his stern when one of the men carrying him slipped. Next morning the President was driven through the old slaving port of Bathurst to the airport. He noted ragged, glum-looking natives. "Dirt. Disease. Very high mortality rate," he told his son Elliott later.

A Douglas C-54 flew the presidential party from Bathurst over the snow-capped Atlas Moutains and into Casablanca. Mike Reilly and Elliott were waiting. The camouflage was thrown off the ramp, the President was whisked into an armored car, and soon he was driving through a small Eden of green parks and marvelous flowers to the Anfa Hotel, the site of the conference, a high white structure with a nautical shape, wide balconies, and a view of the dazzling blue Atlantic. The hotel and its environs had been converted into a military compound, surrounded by heavy wire, guarded by a zealous armored battalion under the nervous command of General George S. Patton, Jr., and protected further by antiaircraft batteries and radar-equipped British night fighters. The President was installed in a large bungalow. His bedroom, with its drapes and frills, was obviously that of a French lady. Roosevelt looked around and whistled. "Now all we need is the madame of the house." Churchill's bungalow was fifty yards away, and soon the Prime Minister was over for a drink before dinner. Roosevelt invited Churchill and his military chiefs—Brooke, Pound, Mountbatten, Sir Charles Portal—to dine with him and his own chiefs and aides.

The party that night went on until early morning, when an air-raid alarm sounded, lights were doused, and the men sat around the table with their faces lighted by candles. Throughout the evening the talk ran fast and free—talk of war, of families and friends, of Stalin, of the French. It was a relaxed and merry company. But the good cheer was a bit artificial, for earlier in the day the Combined Chiefs at their first meeting had found themselves in flat disagreement over strategy.

It was the same old dispute, but now more urgent than ever. At the first meeting Brooke had spoken for an hour, laying out the British proposals—proposals to clear the North African shore and then capture Sicily, meantime building up strength in England for a cross-channel attack when the time seemed propitious. Then Marshall took a categorical stand for a major cross-channel attack in 1943 and against diversions elsewhere. After lunch Brooke invited King to present the Pacific situation. The Chief of Naval Operations was only too eager to do so, because he felt that the British neglected the other side of the globe. He warned that the Japanese were consolidating their gains and that without greater help Chiang might pull out of the war. He proposed that 30 per cent of the war effort—twice the current proportion, he estimated—go to the Pacific and 70 per cent to the other fronts. The British remarked that this was hardly a scientific way of setting war strategy.

During the conferences over the next few days Marshall doggedly stuck to his proposal of securing Africa and then immediately concentrating on the cross-channel attack. He argued against fighting the war on a day-to-day, opportunistic basis, against taking uncoordinated tactical steps that did not fit in with the "main plot." Every diversion, he contended, acted like a suction pump against the main effort.

The odds were heavily against Marshall. The British Chiefs were united and formidable. They had brought a command ship with ample staffs and communications and had docked her in the harbor as a back-up facility. They had met long and often to unify their position. They had Dill in to brief them on the American outlook. On the eve of the first Combined Chiefs conference they had met with the Prime Minister, who had set out the line he wanted them to follow with the Americans. Roosevelt's corporal's guard of military chiefs and aides, on the other hand, was divided. Whatever their general support for beating Germany before Japan, King could not help being drawn to the Pacific, with its great naval potential, and Arnold to the prospect of building up a huge bomber offensive in the United Kingdom while the cross-channel attack was delayed. All the planners worked amid a quiet, intense competition for scarce war supply. It seemed to one of the British present that the United States Army and Navy had divided the world, with the latter taking the Pacific, and that allocation of resources was a game of grab between the two sides.

Only one man could turn the odds in Marshall's favor—his Commander in Chief. Roosevelt seemed to hold a position midway between Marshall and Churchill, midway between wanting to thrust at the underbelly and thrust across the Channel. While he consistently viewed ROUNDUP as the main effort, his fancy was taken by immediate, opportunistic ventures, especially when Churchill was there to suggest them. In drilling his staff on dealing with the Americans, the Prime Minister had advised them to take plenty of time, to allow full discussions and not to be impatient—"like dripping of water on a stone"—and he would pursue the same tactics with the President. He did, but Roosevelt was hardly adamantine. The British approach had long appealed to him, because it kept major options open, allowed for quick and even cheap victories, might knock Italy out of the war, kept American troops active and moving, and provided the Russians with at least the semblance of a second front. By the fourth day of the conference Churchill could report to his War Cabinet that Roosevelt strongly favored the Mediterranean as the next step. The President did not indicate any less support of ROUNDUP. By taking his middle position he was able to go along with the British, placate Marshall, and assure Eisenhower that he firmly adhered to the basic concept of cross-channel and that he looked on the Mediterranean operation only as support for the main thrust.

After ten days of sometimes heated discussions the Combined

Chiefs presented their agreed-on plan in a full-dress meeting to Roosevelt and Churchill. The plan was an order of priorities. Ironically, at the top of the list was neither the underbelly nor cross-channel, but maintaining security of sea communications in the Atlantic; the ghost of Atlantic First still hovered over the strategists. Second priority was aiding Russia. Third was operations in the Mediterranean—specifically the capture of Sicily. Next came cross-channel, and then the Pacific. The British were elated. They felt they had won almost every point of contention. Brooke was disappointed that the plan made no mention of Italy, but he could console himself with the thought that events would dictate this as the next move, just as the pouring of troops into Africa had made Sicily the next logical step.

The question of command was more easily resolved. Even though his troops were now bogged down in the Tunisian mud, Eisenhower had so impressed both his military associates and his political masters with his capacity to lead and unify an inter-Allied headquarters that there was little question of his retaining top command. Some of the British—especially Brooke—were concerned about his lack of combat experience, but these worries were assuaged when General Sir Harold Alexander was made Eisenhower's deputy, with direct command of combat forces, and Arthur W. Tedder and Sir Andrew Cunningham were given executive command of the air and naval forces respectively. Marshall wanted Eisenhower to be a full general, to rank with the British leaders, but Roosevelt said that he would not promote Eisenhower until he had done some real fighting and knocked the Germans out of Tunisia. However, he soon relented, and Eisenhower got his fourth star.

Roosevelt had hoped that he could avoid political issues at Casablanca and focus on military. But throughout the conference he was entangled with the toughest kind of political problem—French factionalism—and at the end he initiated a doctrine that would have immense political implications.

The specter of de Gaulle had hung over the conference from the start. To much of the French underground, and to partisans of the Free French everywhere, he remained the proud if touchy leader and symbol of French resistance. He was free to enunciate the noble ideals of French patriotism and grandeur while Giraud and other French chiefs in Africa had to make compromises with their Anglo-American conquerors, Vichyites, and military necessity. Eisenhower, handicapped by his political inexperience and by conflicting orders from the State Department, had just given an office to Marcel Peyrouton, an anti-Laval Vichyite. Once again roars of disapproval had sounded in America and Britain. Roosevelt had called Darlan a temporary expedient, and he had now been delivered of Darlan by an assassin; why were he and Churchill, liberal organs protested, still playing with fascist collaborators in the war against fascism?

Sensitive to these outbursts even while pooh-poohing them, Roosevelt felt that the solution was obvious—get de Gaulle and Giraud together at Casablanca and let them hammer out an agreement on the provisional leadership of the fighting French pending the liberation of France, the re-establishment of the French Republic, and a fresh determination of leadership by the French people. It was easy for Eisenhower to produce the "groom," Giraud, but the "bride" in London seemed frigid and unprocurable. De Gaulle had his reasons. He had contempt for the Peyroutons and the whole crew of Vichyites and defeatists. Above all, he wanted to maintain the symbol of French authority and glory, unbroken by the armistice and the Vichy regime, that could protect French interests against both enemies and allies until the time of liberation. He was willing—indeed, had asked—to parley with Giraud separately, but the notion of making a forced visit to an Anglo-American camp to conduct business with another Frenchman deeply offended him.

Roosevelt and Churchill were equally determined that de Gaulle should come to Casablanca. Churchill asked Eden in London to tell the General in effect that if he did not, the President and the Prime Minister would proceed without him and would bypass his movement. Grumbling, de Gaulle came, but he proved as stubborn as ever. In his talks with Churchill and Giraud he was unyielding; he would not deal with Giraud as long as Algiers harbored Vichyite officials, and he wanted top political control, while Giraud as number two could command the reborn French Army. Suspicion of de Gaulle was so strong among the Americans that Mike Reilly and other agents stood outside Roosevelt's room, guns in hand, while de Gaulle poured out his bitterness. Still no agreement.

By now Roosevelt and Churchill were indignant with the tall man. The President told friends that de Gaulle compared himself with Joan of Arc at one moment and Clemenceau the next; this was an exaggeration, but de Gaulle by his very bearing produced caricatures of himself in other leaders' eyes, just as he did in cartoonists' sketches. Yet Roosevelt and Churchill had to admire the Frenchman. The President was taken by a spiritual look in his eyes. Churchill could not help reflecting that this arrogant man, a refugee, an exile from his country under sentence of death, completely dependent on British and American good will, with neither funds nor foothold, still defied all.

During this stalemate there occurred a curious incident. Murphy and his British counterpart, Harold Macmillan, had been hurrying from villa to villa trying to patch up a compromise, to no avail.

Giraud had been willing to sign almost any agreement so that he could concentrate on military matters, but de Gaulle was still adamant. The conference was nearing its end, and Roosevelt and Churchill were worried about returning home with the French still divided and Darlanism still an issue. On the last day of the conference Giraud stopped in to see Roosevelt. He brought two documents that dealt in part with military and economic matters, the product of much earlier discussion, but contained political provisions that promised every facility to Giraud to reunite "all" Frenchmen fighting against Germany and gave Giraud "the right and duty of preserving all French interests in the military, economic, financial and moral plane" until the French people could ultimately set up a constitutional government of their own. The President rapidly looked through these documents and signed them. Thereby he upset the elaborate matrimonial negotiations that he and Churchill had been conducting between Giraud and de Gaulle and he committed Churchill to Giraud without the Prime Minister's approval or even knowledge. Consternation resulted when London and Washington learned of Roosevelt's action later; Churchill had to alter the agreement quietly to restore the balance between the two Frenchmen.

Why had Roosevelt signed the documents? One theory was that he was simply piqued by de Gaulle, but the President had dealt with more exasperating men than the Frenchman without losing his *sang-froid.* Another explanation is more plausible—that the documents were a pressure ploy against de Gaulle, that they constituted the shotgun for the proposed forced marriage—but it is not clear that the bride, the reluctant partner in this match, ever knew of the shotgun. Several at Casablanca had other explanations. They felt that Roosevelt was remarkably gay and lighthearted at the meetings. He seemed to Macmillan in a happy holiday mood; "he laughed and joked continually." Macmillan's feelings might reflect British reserve, but Eisenhower and Murphy also noted independently that the President was lighthearted, even frivolous.

Certainly the President was in a happy holiday mood when after a week of conference duty he was able to get away to visit American troops in the field. He had hoped to be allowed to visit the front, but his military chiefs resisted this notion. The President settled for a 110-mile automobile excursion to Rabat, where he lunched in the open on ham and sweet potatoes with 20,000 soldiers of General Mark Clark's Fifth Army, while a band played "Alexander's Rag-Time Band" and "Deep in the Heart of Texas" against a stiff wind. Afterward he inspected the 9th Infantry Division, where he "felt closer to having tears in my eyes than any other time," he told reporters, because these men were headed toward the front.

Later he motored on to Port Lyautey, inspected the old Moorish fort where French defenders had held out under intense bombardment by the American Navy, and laid wreaths at both the American and the French cemeteries. The President was amused on the trip back by the antics of Reilly and his crew, in the lead jeep, pretending to see planes in the sky or to fall out of their vehicle in order to divert the attention of bystanders from the armed sedan that followed.

Roosevelt seemed in an equally lighthearted mood the following night when he entertained the Sultan of Morocco and the Sultan's son. Dressed in flowing white silk robes, the royal visitors presented their host with a high tiara for his wife—and Elliott was sure that his father winked at him as they both thought of Eleanor presiding over a White House function with this golden object perched atop her hairdo. Churchill was glum at the start, what with the Moslem ban on drinking, and his gloom deepened as the President used the occasion to talk to the Sultan about colonial aspirations toward independence and the end of imperialism after the war. Macmillan felt that the President's performance was provocative, and Murphy worried that de Gaulle might hear of this attempt to woo the royalty of French Morocco.

The Casablanca Conference came to both a climax and a conclusion on the same day, January 24, 1943. During much of the previous night Roosevelt, Churchill, Macmillan, Murphy, and Hopkins had still been trying to frame a compromise formula that both de Gaulle and Giraud would support. In the morning Roosevelt had signed Giraud's documents. Churchill at this point was working on de Gaulle, to no avail. Roosevelt then saw the Frenchman and talked with him in urgent terms, equally to no avail. For a time it was a game of Cox and Box in Roosevelt's villa as the contestants and aides shuttled in and out. By noon Roosevelt had had enough—and reporters and photographers were gathering outside in high hopes of major announcements. After their aides managed to get the two Frenchmen into Roosevelt's villa at the same time, Roosevelt and Churchill put the heaviest kind of pressure on de Gaulle. Finally he agreed to sign a memorandum of unity with Giraud.

At this point Roosevelt acted with his usual nimbleness. What about a picture? The whole party moved out onto the terrace, and the principals sat down in four chairs. Would de Gaulle and Giraud shake hands? The Generals stood up and gingerly held hands while the cameras clicked and whirred and Roosevelt and Churchill looked on with ill-concealed satisfaction. Then the Frenchmen left to compose their communiqué.

It was a typically Rooseveltian performance. Now at Casablanca, as so often in Washington, he had symbolically "locked up" the disputants in a room and forced an agreement. But here, as so often before, the image of unity was more impressive than the substance. That afternoon de Gaulle and Giraud duly put out an eloquent but vague declaration of unity, but the final irony was that after all Roosevelt's talk of the shotgun marriage, no baby was born or even conceived. The Generals parted still in dispute over substance.

With the Frenchmen gone from the courtyard, Roosevelt and Churchill proceeded with the press conference. Roosevelt spoke first. He described the close unity of the Americans and British at the meetings, the determination of the military staffs to give all possible aid to the "heroic struggles of China." Then he paused.

"Another point. I think we have all had it in our hearts and our heads before, but I don't think that it has ever been put down on paper by the Prime Minister and myself, and that is our determination that peace can come to the world only by the total elimination of German and Japanese war power.

"Some of you Britishers know the old story—we had a General called U. S. Grant. His name was Ulysses Simpson Grant, but in my, and the Prime Minister's, early days he was called 'Unconditional Surrender' Grant. The elimination of German, Japanese, and Italian war power means the unconditional surrender by Germany, Italy, or Japan. That means a reasonable assurance of future world peace. It does not mean the destruction of the population of Germany, Italy, and Japan, but it does mean the destruction of the philosophies in those countries which are based on conquest and the subjugation of other people." The other United Nations, he added, felt the same way.

Churchill was surprised. He and Roosevelt had discussed unconditional surrender briefly and he had exchanged views with his War Cabinet, especially on the question of whether Italy should be included. But he did not know that Roosevelt planned to announce it—and announcing it was the crucial step. In explaining his statement somewhat later, the President said that getting de Gaulle and Giraud together had been so difficult it reminded him of Grant and Lee—"and then suddenly the press conference was on, and Winston and I had had no time to prepare for it, and the thought popped into my mind that they had called Grant 'Old Unconditional Surrender' and the next thing I knew I had said it." Actually the doctrine had not been born as spontaneously as Roosevelt implied, for a State Department advisory group had made known to him its consensus view that unconditional surrender should be imposed on Germany and Japan. It was the publicizing of the policy, with its critical implications for grand strategy and political warfare, that surprised Roosevelt's British comrades—and indicated again his euphoric mood at Casablanca.

That euphoria was hardly dimmed in the last hours of Roosevelt's and Churchill's African safari. Churchill insisted that the President drive with him to Marrakesh, which Churchill described as famous for its fortunetellers, snake charmers, and brothels—and for an incomparable view of the Atlas Mountains. So the two men drove 150 miles over the desert, talking shop and touching on lighter matters, while American troops stood at attention along the highway and fighters hovered overhead.

The sun was setting as they reached their villa at Marrakesh. Churchill climbed to the roof to see the evening light on the snow-capped peaks and purple foothills and urged Roosevelt to come up. Servants made a chair with their arms and carried the President up the winding stairs, his legs dangling like the limbs of a ventriloquist's dummy. In the evening the President and the Prime Minister dined with a jolly company of a dozen or so. The two leaders made affectionate little speeches to each other; the President toasted the King; Churchill sang, and Roosevelt joined in the choruses.

"I love these Americans," Churchill remarked to his physician before dinner. "They have behaved so generously." Next morning, in slippers and a bright robe covered with dragons, the Prime Minister drove with the President to the airfield and saw his friend off on the long journey home.

THE FIRST KILL

The President was running a little fever by the time he reached Bathurst and the waiting *Memphis,* but the next day he insisted on taking a trip up the Gambia on a seagoing tug. Once again he was struck by the bad health and living conditions in the British colony; Africa would be a problem for years to come, he told reporters on returning. Next day the President flew to Liberia for lunch with President Edwin Barclay; then he reviewed American Negro troops and was gawked at by natives clustered outside their high grass huts. Then the long flight across the South Atlantic to Brazil, where he conferred at length with President Getulio Vargas on an American destroyer and reviewed troops from a jeep.

He was hollow-eyed and tired by now; the long hours in the air had been distressing, for flying "affects my head just as ocean cruising affects yours!" he wrote to his wife. He was glad to board his train for the trip back to Washington.

By now Stalin had received a message that Roosevelt and Churchill had painstakingly drawn up at the end of the Casablanca Conference. The message told in some detail the plans for the next few months, plans which, "together with your powerful offensive, may well bring Germany to her knees in 1943." Britain and America would keep the pressure on Japan, sustain China, push the Axis out of Africa, clear an effective passage through the Mediterranean, bombard Axis targets in southern Europe, "launch large-scale amphibious operations in the Mediterranean at the earliest possible moment," and step up the bomber offensive from Britain against Germany. Several times the message referred to the paramount objective of re-entering the Continent, but there was no date. This would happen "as soon as practicable."

In the Kremlin, Stalin listened to the translation of this note with a stony face. He turned to Molotov. Had they set a date? No, Molotov ejaculated—not yet, not yet. Stalin remained impassive. He waited out the day, and on January 30 sent thanks to Roosevelt and Churchill for "your friendly joint message" and added: Just when would the concrete second-front operations take place?

Almost two weeks later Churchill replied for Roosevelt and himself. They hoped to expel the quarter-million Axis troops from eastern Tunisia during April, if not earlier. After that they intended to seize Sicily, in July at the latest; after that they would stage an operation in the eastern Mediterranean, probably against the Dodecanese. These operations would take 300,000 or 400,000 men and all the shipping and landing craft in the Mediterranean. The cross-channel attack would come in August or September. There was a slight hedging here. Shipping and assault landing craft would be "limiting factors." And the timing "must of course be dependent upon the condition of German defensive possibilities across the Channel at that time."

Stalin's reply was frosty. It appeared, he said, that operations in Tunisia had been set back to April. But it was now, when the Soviet troops were keeping up their broad offensive, that Anglo-American action in Africa was imperative. And to hammer Hitler from both directions the cross-channel attack must take place much earlier. Stalin here made a hard thrust:

"According to reliable information at our disposal, since the end of December, when for some reason the Anglo-American operations in Tunisia were suspended, the Germans have moved 27 divisions, including five armored divisions, to the Soviet-German front from France, the Low Countries and Germany. In other words, instead of the Soviet Union being aided by diverting German forces from the Soviet-German front, what we get is relief for Hitler, who, because of the let-up in Anglo-American operations in Tunisia, was able to move additional troops against the Russians."

Roosevelt cabled a conciliatory response. He shared Stalin's regret that the Allied effort in North Africa had not gone according to schedule. Heavy rain and poor transportation had been the trouble. He realized the adverse effect of the delay on the common effort and he understood "the importance of a military effort on the continent of Europe at the earliest date practicable in order to reduce Axis resistance to your heroic army." But again there was a slight hedge. The cross-channel attack would go ahead as fast as transportation facilities could be provided.

It was not the best of times for the three leaders. Stalin's troops were exhausted. In a mighty effort they recaptured Kharkov in mid-February, then lost it again as the Soviet counterattack petered out and the front stabilized. Churchill had been stricken with pneumonia after returning from his North African and Mid-Eastern journey. Roosevelt, too, had been ill. And at the time he wrote his February 22 letter, he was undergoing the doleful experience that other chiefs of state had known before him—he had received reports of his troops' first real brush with German ground power.

Hitler had followed through on his decision to reinforce Axis strength in Africa. In December and January Nazi troops and supplies had flowed through Italy and Sicily to the ports and airfields of Bizerte and Tunis. Skimming over the water at 150 feet, Junkers and huge, six-engined Messerschmitts carried in hundreds of tons of war supplies every day. By the end of January 110,000 troops—almost three-quarters of them German—had arrived in Northwest Africa to bolster Rommel's last-ditch stand. The Allies were now paying the price of having secured their rear by landing so far to the west of Tunisia. The Germans jabbed at the British, French, and American troops, and then dug in. By mid-February the British commanded the northern sector, the French the central, and the American II Corps the southern, on an almost straight north-south line, with Axis troops to the east; and the British were advancing along the Mediterranean shore from Tripoli.

It was here in this strange and melancholy land, with its jumble of flattened knolls, low escarpments, open desert, draws, gullies, and cactus, that American soldiers had their baptism of fire. Knowing that the Allies would steadily consolidate their positions, Rommel suddenly struck out at II Corps units on February 14. At last American troops experienced the famed German deployment of tanks, artillery, and dive bombers. They counterattacked bravely but suffered from poor intelligence and communications, faulty map reading, and amateurish deployment—in short, from inexperience. After probing and encircling American forces in a series of hard thrusts, the Germans broke through the Kasserine Pass on February 20. They took thousands of Americans prisoner and destroyed or captured large quantities of weapons. Soon, however, Rommel's forces began to run into bad weather and stiffened Allied defenses; they withdrew back through the Kasserine Pass, taking satisfaction in having knocked the Americans off balance and having disrupted Allied plans farther north. "Hate to disappoint you," Alexander wired to Churchill on February 27, "but final victory in North Africa is not just around the corner."

From the Kremlin, Stalin watched these events narrowly. When Churchill reported to him the "sharp local reverses" of February and hinted that clearing the Axis out of Africa was now hoped for by the end of April, Stalin could not conceal his anger. In mid-March he cabled to Roosevelt and Churchill:

". . . At the height of fighting against the Hitler troops, in February and March, the Anglo-Saxon offensive in North Africa, far from having been stepped up, has been called off. . . . Meanwhile Germany has succeeded in moving from the West 36 divisions, including six armored ones, to be used against Soviet troops." Once again he listed the broken promises of the second front.

". . . I must give a most emphatic warning, in the interest of our common cause, of the grave danger with which further delay in opening a second front in France is fraught. . . ."

"Grave danger." What did Stalin mean? That the Soviet front might collapse before the Anglo-Americans ever got into Europe? That United Nations unity in war and peace might be injured beyond repair? That he might go it alone, militarily and diplomatically? That he might even make a deal with Hitler? Roosevelt and Churchill pondered these questions. Then at the end of March the already glacial relations between Moscow and the West turned even colder when Churchill informed Stalin of another Anglo-American decision.

The trouble lay in the Atlantic. Allied losses by the end of 1942 had exceeded construction by well over a million tons. Heavy gales in the North Atlantic had frustrated the U-boats during the early weeks of 1943, but in March the wolf packs began again to score heavily against the convoys. The most perilous point was the northern reaches of Norway, where the Germans had poised the *Tirpitz,* the *Scharnhorst,* and other warships. Churchill did not dare put his Home Fleet at the mercy of enemy U-boats and shore-based bombers, and he feared that if one or two of his battleships were knocked out of action, the whole command of the Atlantic would be jeopardized.

For the Prime Minister there was only one solution: postpone all convoys to Russia. The President concurred on canceling the scheduled March convoy, but he urged that Stalin not be informed until August or September that all convoys must be suspended. The news would be a heavy additional blow for the Kremlin, he argued, and nobody could be sure of the situation four or five months hence anyway. Churchill waited a week, but after Stalin sent a couple of congratulatory notes about impending Tunisian operations, he manfully decided to break the news. On March 30 he described to Stalin the situation in the North Atlantic and stated that "orders have, therefore, been issued that the sailing of the March convoy is to be postponed." He and Roosevelt were greatly disappointed, he went on. "At the same time we feel it only right to let you know at once that it will not be possible to continue convoys by the northern route after early May, since from that time onwards every single escort vessel will be required to support our offensive operations in the Mediterranean, leaving only a minimum to safeguard our lifelines in the Atlantic." If the attack on Sicily went well and the Atlantic situation permitted, "we should hope to resume convoys in early September." Meantime he and Roosevelt would try to increase the flow of supplies by the southern and Pacific routes.

It was a jolting blow to the Kremlin, and an infuriating one. Postponement of the second front had been serious enough, but the Allies had always contended that at least they would get war supplies to the Russian front, where troops *were* engaging the Germans on a huge scale. Now, to have the crucial northern supply route cut off—and cut off to support a Mediterranean operation that the Kremlin considered at best a feeble substitute for a cross-channel attack, and at worst a means of evading it! Stalin's answer was laconic.

"I regard this unexpected step as a catastrophic cut in the delivery of strategic raw materials and munitions to the Soviet Union by Great Britain and the U.S.A., because the Pacific route is limited in shipping and none too reliable, and the southern route has small clearance capacity, which means that those two routes cannot make up for the cessation of deliveries by the northern route. It goes without saying that this circumstance cannot but affect the position of the Soviet troops."

Even in his bitterness, though, Stalin could not help taking pleasure in North African developments. He had always deprecated plans and contingencies and stressed the need of simply killing and trapping masses of Hitlerites and fascists. And this is what Roosevelt's and Churchill's men were doing by early spring of 1943.

Everything still came hard in Africa. Hitler was determined, now that he had allowed Rommel to withdraw across North Africa, that the Afrika Korps and its reinforcements would make a long and vigorous stand by launching forceful spoiling attacks on Allied positions. He ordered that the rate of supply across the Mediterranean be doubled and even tripled. Early in March Rommel threw four furious attacks against the Eighth Army and lost over two-score tanks to Montgomery's massed antitank artillery. Soon after, the "Desert Fox," ill and dispirited, gave up his command and left for his homeland, never to return to Africa. Later in the month the Eighth Army attacked Axis forces dug in on the Mareth Line, originally a French defense system built to ward off the Italians. Montgomery's frontal attack failed, but New Zealand and other units made a wide flanking movement that routed the foe and forced him to move up toward his Tunisia bastion.

American troops made contact with an Eighth Army patrol in a joyous union early in April. The two armies that had started 2,000 miles apart, Churchill noted, were at last joined together. In an effort to rejuvenate II Corps, which was still licking its wounds from the February setbacks, Eisenhower had put Patton in command. In April, with Patton driving and goading his commanders, II Corps' armored and infantry units tried to push eastward to the sea and thus cut off Axis troops moving up the coast under pressure from Montgomery to the south. Despite Patton's colorful leadership, the attack faltered, and most of the Germans managed to make good their retreat northward. Some in the British command now wanted to send II Corps divisions into rear areas for more training, or at least to parcel them among the more experienced corps, but Marshall and Eisenhower would have none of it. They insisted that the corps be preserved as a unit and given a chance to be in on the final victory, learning the art of battle while it fought. Alexander concurred, but had the whole corps leapfrog north to a new sector adjoining the Mediterranean.

By the end of April Allied troops had compressed German and Italian forces into a shrinking area of northern Tunisia. Escape had been cut off; it was now, as Churchill said, "scrunch and punch." British and American fighters were pouncing on convoys of Axis air transports, bringing down fifty planes one day, fifteen another, thirty another. Hitler's commanders were scouring the Italian coast for small craft and fishing boats, to little avail. Early in May Allied armored troops punched through the German defenses, entered Tunis, and then lunged north to link up with American forces that were overrunning Bizerte. After valiant fighting, the enemy units began to disintegrate. The victors were amazed to see long lines of Germans driving in their own trucks and carts in search of prisoner-of-war cages. Almost a quarter-million prisoners were taken, about half of them German. The victory of Tunisia, Churchill felt, could hold its own with Stalingrad.

Early in April Hitler and Mussolini had met at Berchtesgaden. They were still hopeful. A month later, back in his Eastern Front headquarters, Hitler knew that the African situation was hopeless. He stood by his decision. "Naturally," he said to some officers, "I have tried to reckon whether the undertaking in Tunis, which eventually led to the loss of both men and equipment, was justified. I have come to the following conclusion; by the occupation of Tunisia we have succeeded in postponing the invasion of Europe by six months. More important still, Italy is as a result still a member of the Axis." If he had not stood in Tunisia, he went on, the Allies would have landed in Italy unopposed and pushed up to the Brenner Pass, with German resistance weakened again because of the Russian break-through at Stalingrad. "That would inevitably have led rapidly to the loss of the war."

Stalin could make the same calculation. The capture of Tunisia had taken much longer than his allies had expected, and he could not but consider the implications for the second front. But facts—especially Hitlerites killed—were the main thing, and now the Anglo-Americans were slaying Germans. At the height of the battle he told Churchill he hoped he would capture as much booty as possible, as well as finish off the enemy and take prisoners. At the end he wired to Roosevelt: "I congratulate you and the gallant U.S. and British troops on the brilliant victory which has resulted in the liberation of Bizerte and Tunis from Hitler tyranny. I wish you further success."

ELEVEN *The Administration of Crisis*

"WELL, IT IS now 60 hours since the Old Smiler returned to the White House from his great adventure," William Allen White wrote in his *Gazette* on Roosevelt's return from Casablanca. "Biting nails—good, hard, bitter Republican nails—we are compelled to admit that Franklin Roosevelt is the most unaccountable and on the whole the most enemy-baffling President that this United States has ever seen . . . a certain vast impudent courage. . . . Well, damn your smiling old picture, here it is. . . . We, who hate your gaudy guts, salute you."

Not all the Roosevelt watchers back home were as gallant as the old Kansas Republican. After the first flush of excitement over the President's trip abroad, Washington seemed to revert to its usual condition of guerrilla warfare. Power was so fragmented on Capitol Hill that Congress was able neither to support the President's domestic program wholeheartedly nor to muster support for real alternatives. But Congress could always investigate. The Dies Committee girded itself for further onslaughts against federal bureaucrats. Congressman Howard W. Smith, of Virginia, long a conservative Democratic foe of the President, fished for administrative failures.

Politics seemed to have fallen to a new wartime low of spite and pettiness. The kind of publicity that the President particularly detested was aroused by his provocative nomination early in January of Edward J. Flynn as Minister to Australia. Flynn had been exonerated of the much-publicized charge of having city workers pave a courtyard of his country home with city-owned paving blocks, but the chairman of the third-term campaign was still fair game. Willkie called the nomination crassly cynical. Flynn ran into such heavy weather on Capitol Hill that, by mutual agreement, the President withdrew his nomination. It did not help matters that during the furore over Edward Flynn the movie actor Errol Flynn was undergoing a lurid trial for statutory rape of two teen-agers, or that the other Flynn also was found not guilty.

Some of Roosevelt's friends were as critical of the defense effort as his enemies. "One year after Pearl Harbor," reported a Senate Education and Labor Subcommittee headed by New Deal Senator Claude Pepper, "the Nation looks in vain for a unified program of all-out war production. Each new crisis in production evokes a piecemeal attempt at solution." In the House, the Tolan Committee called for an end to "the drift" in war production. Washington infighting seemed brisker than ever. Czars jousted with czars, army officials with Navy, civilians with soldiers. The manpower program was in a muddle. Senator Vandenberg complained in his diary of a "complete and total lack of authentic liaison between the White House and Congress in respect to war responsibilities."

The President sailed through all these reefs and shoals with his usual outward imperturbability and private annoyance. Editor White watched Roosevelt at a press conference on February 12. "He seemed to be gay, sure of himself, a bit festive at times, informative, indeed illuminating," noted the long-time observer of famous men. He noticed that Roosevelt had grown notably heavier since coming to the White House. But "his growth has not been in paunch. It has been above his navel. His shoulders have widened. His neck and jowls have filled out. His head has taken a new form. . . ." Roosevelt was a vital person, White kept thinking. But that night, sitting after dinner in the new Statler Hotel while Roosevelt gave a Lincoln's Day speech, he felt that in the few hours Roosevelt had grown tired. His voice seemed to lose its fire. In the final sentences his voice dropped, and White could hardly hear him.

White ruminated on Roosevelt's enemies. There were two Republican schools of thought about the President. One "speaks of him trippingly on the tongue as that 'God damn Roosevelt,' short, snappy, and staccato, but without grinding the vocal gears. The other crowd snarls it savagely, adagio, making two words out of God—like Gawud—and two out of damn—like da-yum—growled with heart-pumping scorn and generally with a table-pounding drumbeat. I belong to the lighter, staccato left wing. . . ."

After a year or so of "all-out" war mobilization, though, some in Washington were wondering if the President as Chief Executive was not his own worst enemy.

EMERGENCY MANAGEMENT

In a farsighted move a year and a half before Pearl Harbor, Roosevelt had established the Office for Emergency Management in the Executive Office of the President. The OEM had become a peculiarly Rooseveltian instrument—flexible, informal, adaptable—for spawning, nourishing, and embracing a host of defense units that

Roosevelt could not fit easily into the existing departmental structure and that captured far more public attention than the mother office ever did. The OEM, indeed, later was pushed aside, but the concept and spirit of *emergency management* hung over all the fifty or sixty war agencies that would come to life. The origin of the two words is not clear; probably they were Roosevelt's. Certainly they summed up the curious combination of orderly management and crisis government that characterized his war administration.

That administration never settled down; it never freed itself of the prod and aura of crisis. The rapidly changing battle needs, the stupendous appetite for war production, the ever-shifting impact of science and technology, the zest and combativeness of the chieftains Roosevelt recruited for his war agencies, and the President's own administrative habits kept his regime in almost constant turmoil. Students of public administration would long argue whether the creativity, flexibility, competitiveness, even rugged individualism nurtured by those habits outweighed the wasted effort, faulty coordination, disorder, delays, muddle. The striking fact was that the White House itself, despite its boasts and claims, was never really satisfied with its organization for war, as evidenced by its continual making and breaking of war chiefs and their agencies until the European war was almost over.

On the first anniversary of Pearl Harbor—two and one half years after the United States began its first serious mobilization, in the wake of the fall of France—the administration still faced crises of production. The nation had not achieved the balanced, assured output necessary for its great offensives in the Mediterranean and the Pacific. Production of military airplanes more than doubled from 1941 to 1942 but was still short of the President's call for 60,000 planes; the output of combat planes fell even more below his goals. The navy yards turned out an aircraft carrier and a dozen battleships and cruisers, but the loss of four carriers and five heavy cruisers in 1942 still left fleet strength little greater at the end of 1942 than before Pearl Harbor. Landing-craft output skyrocketed but lagged behind both goals and needs. The production of merchant ships totaled over eight million tons—seven times the 1941 output—but still a million tons short of the President's announced goal—a serious lag considering that the Allies had lost an average of a million tons a month. Somervell admitted to Raymond Clapper on the last day of 1942 that shipment of four hundred tanks to North Africa had cleared out the surplus. Artillery and machine-gun turnout was also short.

The President had been a little defensive about war production in his State of the Union address to Congress in January 1943.

He granted that plane and tank production fell short numerically—"stress the word numerically"—but noted that models were changing, becoming heavier and more complex. The arsenal of democracy, he said, was making good, and he hit out at criticism based on guesswork and malicious falsification. But he remained dissatisfied with war production during early 1943. "The war goes on and on—" he wrote to Beaverbrook in March, "and while I think we are gaining, it is difficult for you and me to curb our impatience, especially when our military and naval friends keep saying that this cannot be done and that cannot be done and this time schedule seems so everlastingly slow to us." A few weeks later Baruch reported that shipbuilding was going well, escort vessels improving, high-octane gasoline coming along better, but aircraft production still lagged. "We are making planes but not as many as we should."

Manpower was a growing problem all through 1943. Manpower! For ten years the Roosevelt administration had struggled to find jobs for workers; now it had to find workers for jobs. Over-all statistics looked good but they concealed serious problems. Unemployment, which was still running at about nine million in mid-1940, fell off to less than a million by mid-1943. In the same span of time womanpower rose from almost fourteen to almost nineteen million. In February, after months of complaints by Congress and the press, Roosevelt called for a minimum wartime work week of forty-eight hours in defense plants and federal agencies; by mid-1943 average weekly hours in manufacturing were about forty-five, though shipbuilders and some others were working sixty hours or more. Turnover and absenteeism, however, continued at alarming rates. The Boeing plant in Seattle, which had 39,000 employees in June 1943, had employed 250,000 people during the previous three years. Labor supply was also uneven across the country. On the West Coast and in the Northeast it reached emergency proportions.

Roosevelt seemed curiously passive about the manpower crisis, which had been predicted months ahead. The War Manpower Commission under Paul McNutt had been unable to cope with the situation in advance, in part because the WPB and the armed services had far more control of the situation than did the commission, in part because the manpower crisis was slower in showing up than rival crises, in part because McNutt neither was a strong chief nor ran a strong agency. The President toyed with a plan to make Ickes Secretary of Labor, with control of manpower, but gave up the idea when people—including Ickes's young wife—warned that the two jobs would be too much for the sixty-nine-year-old Interior chief. Roosevelt seemed far more upset by charges that too many federal civilian employees were receiving deferments than by the broader problem.

"I will make you a good-sized bet," he complained to Harold Smith, "that in the hundreds of Government offices people—young men without a lot of children—are running mimeograph machines or blue-printing machines when the work could just as well be done by women or older men." Manpower was, perhaps, too vast and collective and even impersonal a problem to engage Roosevelt's feelings, which usually seized on specifics close at hand. In the end he kept McNutt as head of manpower. As it turned out, the steps that might have headed off some labor shortages—use of occupation rather than dependency status as the main test in Selective Service, for example, or the placing of war plants and contracts in areas of high labor supply—were not taken when they could have had full effect. Problems were met mainly by improvisation, such as emergency recruitment campaigns and furloughing trained workers from the Army. By mid-1943 the White House was deeply concerned about the growing manpower crisis; by the end of the year it was facing the grim need of national-service legislation.

All these emergencies paled, however, next to the labor ferment of 1943—at least in the crisis management of the White House. "The labor problem is again to the fore—" Roosevelt wrote to Mackenzie King late in the year, "but then scarcely six months have ever gone by since I have been in office, the past ten and a half years, without a 'labor crisis.'" In 1943 hardly a week went by without a crisis. The year had just started when 15,000 coal miners left their jobs in a wildcat strike, and the President had to order them back to work. Walkouts in rubber, plastics, railroads, coal—several times—and a host of other industries followed. So often was Roosevelt forced to order men back to work that the White House lost something of its legitimacy and force as a court of last appeal. Throughout these troubles the administration was under heavy pressure from Congressmen who were worried about their constituents' fuel and other needs—or who saw good fishing in troubled waters.

Bituminous-coal mines became the stormiest battleground. A two-year contract between miners and operators was due to expire in the spring of 1943. John L. Lewis, as truculent and histrionic as ever, was demanding a two-dollar-a-day wage boost in a flat challenge to the President's stabilization program. Lewis had become a towering but isolated figure. His wife had just died; he had broken angrily with Murray; he hated Roosevelt; he was now the villain of the radicals, as once he had been their hero. Having led in the demolition of the old mediation board, he now welcomed his chance to boycott the War Labor Board, which he publicly exhorted to resign and cease casting its "black shadow" over American workers.

Late in April the miners began walking out. "Not as President—not as Commander in Chief—but as the friend of the men who work in the coal mines," the President urged the men to return to the pits.

In the fall of 1940, when Lewis had appealed to his miners to vote against Roosevelt, they had stood by their friend in the White House; now the President was appealing to these same friends to stick to the battle of production—and they were standing by Lewis. The Commander in Chief moved to seize the mines; he, Byrnes, and Sherwood prepared a fireside chat to the people. Even while the President was on his way to the oval office and its microphones, word came that the miners would return to work in two days. The President went ahead with his talk anyway. He spoke in urgent tones.

"A stopping of the coal supply, even for a short time, would involve a gamble with the lives of American soldiers and sailors and the future security of our whole people." He blamed the strike directly on the leaders of the mine workers. "You miners have sons in the Army and Navy and Marine Corps. You have sons who at this

IN THE TEETH OF JOHN L. LEWIS

February 2, 1940, Rollin Kirby, reprinted by permission of the New York *Post* very minute—this split second—may be fighting in New Guinea, or in the Aleutian Islands, or Guadalcanal, or Tunisia, or China, or protecting troop ships and supplies against submarines on the high seas." He cited case after case of miners or sons of miners who had been wounded or decorated. He appealed to the miners' pride: "The toughness of your sons in our armed forces is not surprising. They come of fine, rugged stock. . . ." He concluded: "I believe the coal miners will not continue the strike against their government."

That night, with the miners headed back to work, the President celebrated Byrnes's birthday by throwing a party for those who had worked on the broadcast. The President led in singing "Happy Birthday" and then rendered "When I Grow Too Old to Dream" jointly with his War Mobilizer. Sherwood was the life of the party, dancing and flapping his arms as he sang "When the Red, Red Robin Comes Bob, Bob, Bobbin' Along."

But the speech had been wasted on the wrong occasion. The miners, now back at work, awaited the Labor Board's decision, then struck again when they were denied their pay boost. The summer weeks were full of snarls. Lewis "recommended" that the miners return to work but somehow his order now had less effect. Ickes, who held possession of the pits as Solid Fuels Administrator, bickered with the War Labor Board, which suspected him of making secret deals with Lewis, and demanded that the President order Attorney General Biddle to stop arresting strikers. Congress fretted and thundered—and passed the Smith-Connally bill, restricting labor's right to strike. Roosevelt vetoed the bill, in part because it collided with labor's no-strike pledge, only to have Congress pass it over his veto by wide margins.

The White House was cabled the text of an editorial in the army paper *Stars and Stripes:* ". . . Speaking for the American soldier, John Lewis, damn your coal black soul."

His patience running out, the President ordered Stimson, McNutt, and Selective Service Director General Lewis B. Hershey to waive the age-deferment provisions and start drafting striking miners between thirty-eight and forty-five years old. This was only a temporary expedient. Miners drifted back to work during the summer, then began walking out again in the fall. Once again the President appealed to them; he ordered Ickes to repossess the mines and let the Labor Board offer more money for more work. Most miners returned; some stayed out. But coal troubles badgered the President until well into 1944. It seemed impossible to come to grips with Lewis. Byrnes was convinced that the miners' chief was sabotaging production even when he seemed to be co-operating, and wanted his chief to tell Lewis so, but Roosevelt would not. He knew the limits of his power.

Coal was not the President's only burden. The railroad unions were equally militant and equally hungry for a wage increase, but the circumstances were markedly different. The railroad unions had long held a special relation with the federal government under the Railway Labor Act, with its orderly mediation procedures. When an emergency board recommended an eight-cents-an-hour increase for railroad employees early in 1943, and the Director of Economic Stabilization set it aside, the Chairman of the National Railway Labor Panel, William M. Leiserson, appealed to the President to sustain the emergency board. A deadlock ensued between Leiserson, who had for so long umpired railroad labor disputes that in a later day he would have been dubbed "Mr. Railroad Labor," and stabilization officials. There were continuing appeals to the President. But railroad labor, divided between operating and "non-op" unions and into various crafts, was far less united than the mine workers. After the wage dispute had simmered through the summer and early fall, several of the unions became restive, and Leiserson raised Byrnes's temper by virtually boycotting the economic stabilizers.

Matters came to a head just before Christmas. With the railroad unions threatening to strike, Roosevelt met for hours, day after day, with the parties. Railroad labor split: the chiefs of the trainmen, engineers, and non-ops agreed to White House arbitration, but the heads of the other brotherhoods would not yield despite direct appeals by the President. Two days after Christmas 1943 the President directed Stimson to seize and operate the railroads. Three weeks later the government gave up control after the President had arbitrated the dispute.

On New Year's Eve Marshall had been so concerned by the railroad situation, Byrnes heard, that he considered going on the radio, describing the military aspect, and then resigning. So 1943 had ended on the labor front as it had started—in crisis.

The disputes that had crowded into the White House were complex and varied, but they had one common aspect: resort to the President. The White House became a conciliation office, mediation board, arbitration court, all in one. And it was not well equipped for this function. Pressure, haste, and improvisation in crisis marked its procedures. The President, as usual, maintained his marvelous temper under the stress, but his personal approach exacted its price. Thus when union chiefs were claiming that the President himself had promised them the eight cents, Byrnes had to inform his chief gently that he probably had done so. And the labor crises cut deeply into the President's time, often during periods when great strategic decisions were being shaped.

If Roosevelt depended all too readily on his flair for personal

Franklin D. Roosevelt Library

Hyde Park in the piping days of peace. Franklin D. Roosevelt receiving a medal on his 25th anniversary as an Odd Fellow in Hyde Park Lodge 203, September 16, 1938

United Press International

President Roosevelt in Washington, Lincoln's Birthday, 1940

Franklin D. Roosevelt Lib

Returning to the White House with Mrs. Roosevelt after the third inaugural, January 20, 1941

Franklin D. Roosevelt Library

Roosevelt with Winston Churchill at the Atlantic Charter conference, Argentia, Newfoundland, August 9-12, 1941. General George C. Marshall stands in the middle above.

The President reading the joint resolution by both houses of Congress declaring that a state of war exists with Germany and Italy, December 11, 1941

United Press International

Photo by Heinrich Hoffmann, © 1968 by Christian Wegner Verlag
Reprinted by permission of Harcourt, Brace & World, Inc.

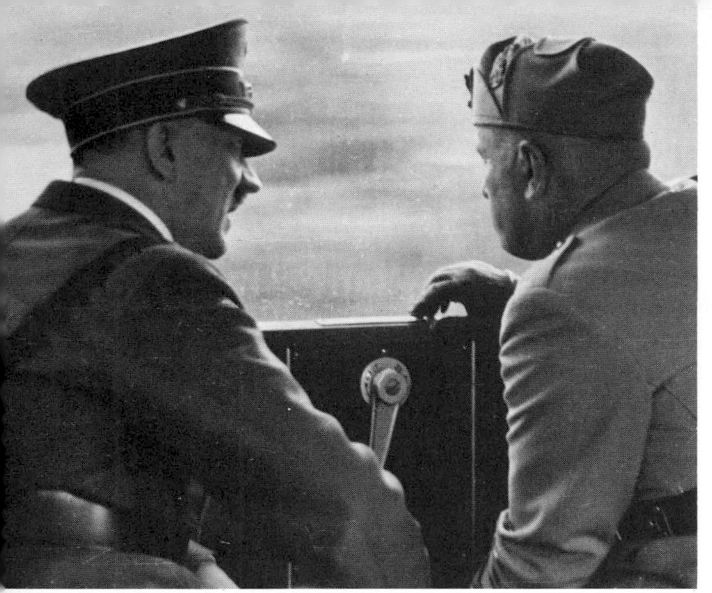

Hitler and Mussolini conferring in 1941

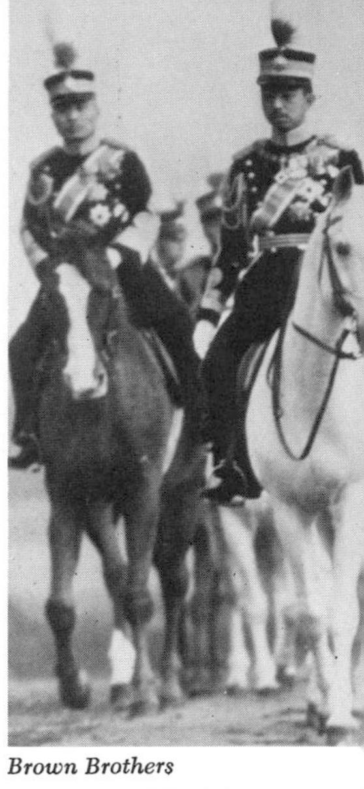

Brown Brothers

Emperor Hirohito of Japan

Joint press conference with Winston Churchill, Washington, D.C., December 23, 1941

United Press Internationa

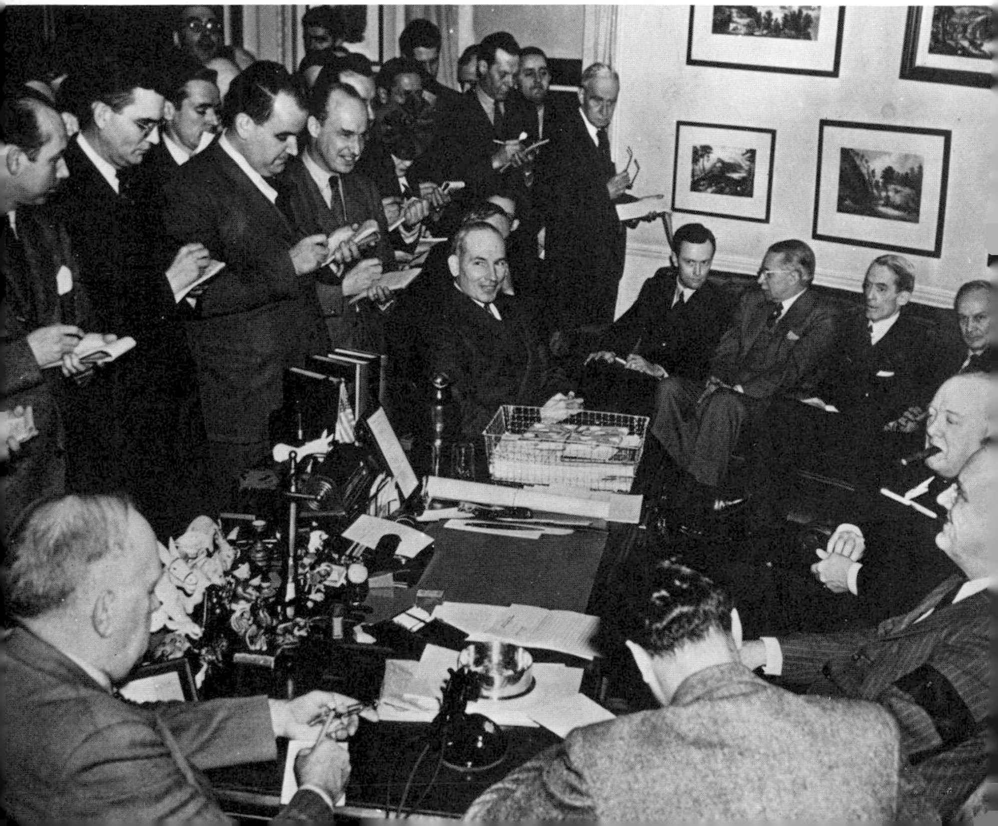

Franklin D. Roosevelt Library

Roosevelt's "secret" war-plant inspection tour: *(Above)* Addressing workers at the Oregon Shipbuilding Corporation, September 23, 1942. Henry J. Kaiser is in the back seat. *(Below)* Inspecting bomber production at the Douglas Aircraft Corporation, Long Beach, California, September 25, 1942

Franklin D. Roosevelt Library

Franklin D. Roosevelt Libra

John Nance Garner visiting Roosevelt aboard the President's inspection-tour train, Uvalde, Texas, September 27, 1942

Lunch in the field: Lt. Gen. Mark Clark, President Roosevelt, Harry Hopkins, Maj. Gen. George S. Patton, Jr., Rabat, Morocco, January 21, 1943

Franklin D. Roosevelt Libra

Forced handshake: Generals Henri Giraud and Charles de Gaulle with Roosevelt and Churchill, Casablanca, January 24, 1943

ranklin D. Roosevelt Library

United States and British military leaders discussing strategy at Casablanca: Adm. Ernest J. King, Chief of Naval Operations; Gen. George C. Marshall, Army Chief of Staff; Lt. Gen. H. H. Arnold, Air Force Chief; Brig. Gen. John R. Deane, U.S. member of secretariat; Brig. Vivian Dykes, British member of secretariat; Brig. Gen. A. C. Wedemeyer, member of War Plans Division; Lt. Gen. Hastings L. Ismay, Chief Staff Officer to Minister of Defence; Vice Adm. Lord Louis Mountbatten, Director of Combined Operations; Admiral of the Fleet Sir Dudley Pound, First Sea Lord; Gen. Sir Alan Brooke, Chief of the Imperial General Staff; Air Chief Marshal Sir Charles Portal, Chief of the Air Staff; and Field Marshal Sir John Dill, chief of the British Mission, Washington

Franklin D. Roosevelt Library

Franklin D. Roosevelt Libra

Roosevelt, en route home from Casablanca, celebrating his 61st birthday aloft, with Adm. William D. Leahy, Harry Hopkins, and Capt. Howard M. Cone, commander of the Boeing Clipper, January 30, 1943

The President with Generalissimo Chiang Kai-shek and Madame Chiang, at the Cairo Conference, November 25, 1943

Franklin D. Roosevelt Libra

'ranklin D. Roosevelt Library

Roosevelt, on the way to the Teheran Conference, in Sicily with Gen. Dwight D. Eisenhower, December 8, 1943

At the Teheran Conference: Harry Hopkins, Stalin's translator, Marshal Stalin, Vyacheslav Molotov, K. Y. Vorishilov

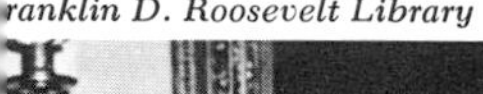

ranklin D. Roosevelt Library

Franklin D. Roosevelt Library

Secretary of State Cordell Hull, Senator James F. Byrnes, and Senator Alben W. Barkley welcome Roosevelt back from Teheran, Washington, D.C., December 17, 1943

Pacific strategy conference, Honolulu: the President with Gen. Douglas MacArthur and Adm. Chester W. Nimitz, July 27, 1944

Franklin D. Roosevelt Librar

Franklin D. Roosevelt Library

Judge Samuel I. Rosenman and Lt. Comm. Howard G. Bruenn, Medical Corps, U.S. Navy, during the President's Hawaiian trip, July 1944

Americans of Polish descent calling on the President at the White House, Pulaski Day, October 11, 1944

Franklin D. Roosevelt Libr

Wide World Photos

President and Mrs. Roosevelt on the campaign trail, New York City, October 21, 1944

Roosevelt after addressing the Foreign Policy Association, with William H. Lancaster, Association Chairman; Secretary of War Henry L. Stimson; Secretary of the Navy James V. Forrestal; UNRRA Director General Herbert H. Lehman, New York City, October 21, 1944

Franklin D. Roosevelt Library

Roosevelt with Fala at Hyde Park, October 22, 1944

United Press International

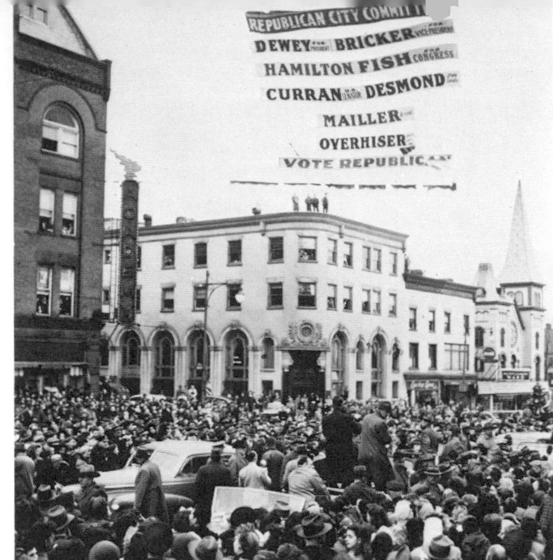

Campaign banner in his political homeland floating above the President's car, Newburgh, N.Y., November 6, 1944

United Press International

Wide World Phot

Roosevelt campaigning with Secretary of the Treasury Henry Morgenthau, Jr., near Hyde Park, N.Y., November 6, 1944

The President, after re-election to a fourth term, with Vice President-elect Harry S Truman and Vice President Henry A. Wallace, making a brief radio address on his arrival in Washington, November 10, 1944

United Press Internatio

Herbert Orth, LIFE Magazine
© Time Inc.

Lucy Mercer Rutherfurd
Painting by Elizabeth Shoumatoff

The President and Mrs. Roosevelt with their thirteen grandchildren, in the White House, January 20, 1945

Franklin D. Roosevelt Library

Franklin D. Roosevelt Librar

The first day of the Big Three meetings at Yalta, February 1945

Roosevelt making a point to Churchill at Yalta

Franklin D. Roosevelt Librar

United Press International

The President reporting to the Congress on the Yalta Conference, March 1, 1945

Roosevelt with the United States delegation to the United Nations founding conference at San Francisco: Rep. Sol Bloom, of New York; Virginia Gildersleeve, Dean of Barnard College; Sen. Tom Connally, of Texas; Secretary of State Edward Stettinius, Jr.; Harold Stassen; Sen. Arthur H. Vandenberg, of Michigan, and Rep. Charles Eaton, of New Jersey, at the White House, March 1945

Franklin D. Roosevelt Library

Franklin D. Roosevelt Library

The caisson bearing President Roosevelt's coffin approaching the Capitol on the way from Union Station to the White House, April 14, 1945

management in handling home-front crises during 1943, those crises were also having an impact on his presidential organization. Under constant pressure the White House was not only expanding, but it was gaining new form and power. Even while the President stuck to his old adminitrative habits, a new executive structure was arising around him.

Changes came by fits and starts. A year after Pearl Harbor, Roosevelt's defense organization was still a public issue. Appointing czars, shoring up the WPB, making Byrnes Economic Stabilization Director—these and other steps did not long satisfy the critics. In Congress the Truman and the Migration Committees continued to call for more centralized authority. A Senate Military Affairs Subcommittee reported that war mobilization was "in crisis." Nelson was under fire for not standing up to the military in the scramble for supplies and production, and the WPB was racked by disputes among its top officials. In the Senate friends of the President sponsored a bill for a super-superagency that would take over and boss a dozen war agencies. Byrnes, struggling with a tide of stabilization problems that cut across bureaucratic empires and their czars, began to lean toward the idea of an office of war mobilization with broad powers to direct the whole war effort.

For a moment the President toyed with a move he had long resisted—to re-establish the WPB as the supreme mobilization agency on the model of the War Industries Board of World War I. And he even decided to appoint the very man, Bernard Baruch, who had headed the earlier board and had the prestige, status, and self-assurance to rebuild and command an agency rivaling the White House in publicity and power. He must have been sorely disturbed by the state of mobilization and the conflicts between and within his war agencies—especially the WPB—to appeal to Baruch. But appeal to him he did, in a letter that frankly admitted that he was "coming back to the elder statesman for assistance." Surprised and pleased, Baruch debated whether he should give up his freedom—as symbolized by his "office" on a Lafayette Park bench—and whether he was physically up to it. He was on his way to New York City to consult his doctor when, as luck would have it, he fell ill, and it was a week before he returned to Washington to tell the President he had decided to accept. Roosevelt, leaning back in his chair and puffing on an uplifted cigarette, greeted him with his usual geniality.

"Mr. President," Baruch began, "I'm here to report for duty." Roosevelt did not reply; he seemed not even to have heard. Baruch knew something had gone wrong. The President said: "Let me tell you about Ibn Saud, Bernie." He chatted a bit about the Mid-East. Then he abruptly stopped talking, excused himself, and departed for a Cabinet meeting. He never again mentioned the WPB post to Baruch. Swallowing his pride, groping for some explanation, Baruch concluded that there must have been intervention by Hopkins, who seemed to Baruch full of the suspicion and self-protectiveness that grip men so close to the throne.

Doubtless Hopkins did influence Roosevelt's change of heart, but a far more important factor also intervened. Both the President and his Economic Stabilization Director were leaning more and more during early 1943 toward the idea of a mobilization office directly under the President rather than in a vast, independent new agency under a new superczar. Byrnes had been working in the east wing for some months and was already dealing with a variety of problems outside his stabilization duties. He proposed a new office of war mobilization with wide powers over war production, allocation, and manpower (except for men in uniform), that he take on this broader role, and that his job as Economic Stabilizer be passed on to Fred M. Vinson, a former Congressman and an old friend.

It was not easy for Roosevelt to go along with this plan. The press had already dubbed Byrnes "Assistant President" and "Chief of Staff"—terms Roosevelt disliked—and throughout his presidency he had resisted sharing his powers with any rival person or office of this sort. On the other hand, he trusted Byrnes. The former Justice was not one to jump onto a white charger and gallop off with the war effort. Long sanded and buffed in the Southern folkways and parliamentary grooves of Capitol Hill, he was cautious, judicious, if narrow-gauged in vision and imagination. He preferred to deal with appeals from clashing agencies rather than to issue plans and commands from on high. He proposed to continue to operate with a tiny staff, headed by Roosevelt's old friend and adviser Benjamin Cohen. Instead of congealing into a whole new bureaucratic layer, his office would co-ordinate policy among the existing war agencies. And he would claim the services of the ablest people—even of Baruch, who gamely continued to advise Byrnes and the White House.

Roosevelt's fight against inflation went on amid crises, controversy, and congressional onslaughts. Exhausted, ill, and bleeding from his political wounds, Henderson resigned as OPA head at the end of 1942. The President replaced him with former Senator Prentiss M. Brown, in the hope of improving the agency's relations with Congress, but, with Henderson out of the way, Congressmen redoubled their efforts to pressure OPA into relaxing price controls and raising price ceilings, at least for their more organized and articulate constituents. Business condemned it for being too tough, labor for being too soft, and even its own officials for lacking direction and drive.

Prices in turn squeezed farmers and workers, whose own income was regulated by agencies other than the OPA. By heavy majorities Congress passed the Bankhead bill, which would bar the deduction of subsidies paid to farmers in the computation of parity prices. Roosevelt was painfully aware that every increase in prices—especially food prices—fueled the drive of militant unions like the Mine Workers to break through the Little Steel wage formula. Proclaiming that nobody had fought harder than he to help farmers get parity prices for their crops, he vetoed the Bankhead bill and a week later issued a dramatic call to "hold the line" on prices and wages. The next day Senators and Representatives deluged the White House with requests to see the President personally; Roosevelt told Watson to pass them on to Byrnes. Philip Murray, the usually soft-spoken union chief, banged on Byrnes's table to drive home his point that unless he could deliver wage increases to CIO members he would be outflanked by Lewis and his Mine Workers. But Roosevelt seemed unmoved by the clamor and the complaints. He had the OPA follow his hold-the-line call with a rollback order that actually shaved the prices of some foods.

The biggest feud within the administration was yet to come. All through the spring of 1943 a dispute was brewing that would erupt into the most spectacular rupture among Roosevelt's crisis agencies. The antagonists were Jesse Jones, Secretary of Commerce and boss of the RFC, and Vice President Henry Wallace, head of the Board of Economic Warfare. Even for Roosevelt's administration the two were gloriously antipodal: Jones, a onetime RFC member under Hoover, taciturn, shrewd, practical, cautious; Wallace, hero of the Lib Labs, dreamy, utopian, even mystical, yet with his own bent for management and power. Jones's distaste for Wallace was less ideological than professional; he could not abide the BEW's speculative practices, its overbuying, its dubious projects. War or no war, the business of the RFC was business. His corporation, Jones announced flatly, "does not pay $2 for something it can buy for $1." Liberals roared over the story—possibly true—that when a fire consumed a New Jersey warehouse filled with tons of precious rubber, Jones remarked, "What's the trouble? It was insured, wasn't it?"

Roosevelt's penchant for overlapping assignments had joined the two men in unholy wedlock. The BEW was empowered to obtain strategic materials from foreign sources through preclusive buying and other methods, but it was not given its own funds, and the RFC remained banker for BEW's foreign activities. BEW ordered RFC to finance the planting in Haiti of Cryptostegia—a rubber project dear to Roosevelt's heart. Jones refused. BEW then asked RFC to finance an experimental rubber project in Africa. Again RFC resisted. For months Jones and Wallace waged an intensive but quiet fight at both ends of Pennsylvania Avenue over the key question of which agency could veto what.

The struggle surfaced during the heat of June 1943. Inflamed by Jones's latest effort to crop his powers, Wallace denounced the Texan for "hamstringing" the war effort. Jones called Wallace's charges hysterical, dastardly, malicious, and false. The President asked Byrnes to "get Henry and Jesse together and harmonize their differences." The two men came to an armistice meeting in Byrnes's office but refused to smoke a peace pipe; Jones would not even speak to the Vice President, and Byrnes feared that he would physically assault him. Within hours the two men were publicly hurling charges back and forth.

Prompted by Byrnes, the President now acted with dispatch. He fired both gladiators from their war jobs by abolishing the BEW, setting up an Office of Economic Warfare under Leo T. Crowley, and switching the Export-Import Bank, the rubber and petroleum agencies, and other dukedoms out of Jones's empire and into the new OEW. To the heads of all federal agencies he dispatched a stern warning that while he recognized the nervous strain they were working under in wartime, if they disagreed among themselves publicly instead of submitting their dispute to Byrnes or himself, "I ask that when you release the statement for publication, you send to me a letter of resignation."

Roosevelt's sternness impressed the country, but his aides were probably more skeptical. They must have doubted that their chief would change his old administrative habits for long. He had issued a similar warning the year before. One assistant, indeed, knew that whatever Wallace's and Jones's transgressions, much of the blame for Washington's civil war lay with the President. Foreign economic policy was a case in point. In February 1943 Budget Director Smith had cautioned his chief that the North African operation had provided a warning signal of "impending breakdowns in our international operations." Item by item Smith described duplication, confusion, disorganization—the division of authority and responsibility among a host of agencies, the muddle over dealing with foreign requirements, the fragmented foreign-aid and subsidy operations in Latin America, the split control of imports and development projects, the tendency of competing agencies to make isolated spot adjustments rather than to follow a comprehensive plan. Smith proposed a basic reorganization and consolidation of agencies.

As usual the President waited for a crisis before acting. As usual he acted by reshuffling people and creating a new agency. Smith contended that whatever the advantage of keen competition of several new agencies during the formative period, a strongly unified foreign administration was now imperative. But whatever Roosevelt's impatience with public brawling, he essentially did not mind—he even welcomed—competition.

"A little rivalry is stimulating, you know," he once said to

Frances Perkins. "It keeps everybody going to prove he is a better fellow than the next man. It keeps them honest too."

Still, war has its own imperatives. At some point at the height of the war the first Chief Executive—the improviser, the disorganizer, the unsettler—gave way to a second. Perhaps it was when he set up the Office of War Mobilization and an "assistant President." Perhaps it was when he confessed, "I get so many conflicting recommendations my head is splitting." The shift was gradual, occurring in his slowly increasing reliance on the White House staff. By the end of 1943 virtually a new system of presidential government had grown out of the makeshift arrangements of old. The foundation had been laid for a powerful Executive Office, a huge war structure, and a vastly expanded social-welfare organization, which were to characterize the presidency for decades to come. During World War II, indeed, the modern presidency was created —and by a man who temperamentally had a decided preference for the White House as it was in the days of Woodrow Wilson or Theodore Roosevelt.

THE TECHNOLOGY OF VIOLENCE

While the demands of war forced the creation of modern presidential government, violence itself was being revolutionized. Modern war had become essentially a warfare of machines, and the weapons rolling off American assembly lines startled even science-fiction writers: radar-guided rockets, amphibious tanks, bazookas, proximity-fused shells, napalm jellied-gasoline flame throwers. Old cavalryman George Patton concluded that "we will have to devise some new method of warfare."

Weapons technology, the imperatives of war, and the improvisations of Roosevelt fitted productively. The speed of weapons development resulted from just those Rooseveltian habits that produced confusion elsewhere: division of authority, overlapping responsibilities, no unified program, changing agencies, improvisation in crisis, and reliance on talented individuals, not orderly administration.

Prewar weapons development had lagged. In the peacetime Army, Marshall told Stimson, the technical services were preeminent because "the fellow that controls the contracts and expenditures . . . is the only one Congress is interested in," and Congress controlled the purse strings. For the Army, cost accounting was more important than weapons development. While Congress cut weapons-research appropriations, Hitler drove thousands of scientists from Europe to America and stirred American scientists to political action. During 1938-40 the National Academy of

Sciences urged a government organization of science to provide the United States with better weapons and techniques. The problem and the forces gravitated toward Roosevelt, the center of power.

After establishing the civilian National Defense Research Committee and appointing Vannevar Bush chairman, the President had requested co-operation from the War and Navy Departments. To the surprise of many, the services eventually complied. Swamped with heavy demands to train pilots, construct tank factories, adapt to jungle, desert, and mountain warfare, the services had little time left for inventing new weapons. The admission of civilians to full-fledged military status, especially for the invention of dramatic new weapons, was a bitter pill, but Stimson and Marshall insisted on co-operation.

At first, the technical services and the scientists merely stayed out of each other's way, for, as Bush found, "basically, research and procurement are incompatible." As the gap between NDRC research and Ordnance procurement grew, however, a crisis threatened: the research tended to be isolated and useless. Prodded by Hopkins, Bush, and Conant, in June 1941 Roosevelt reshuffled agencies and personnel, over the objections of Army Ordnance, the WMC, outside scientists, the OPM, and Ickes, who had a different plan. Though the President created the Office of Scientific Research and Development to bridge the gap between research and production, and shifted Bush from NDRC to the new OSRD, power remained fragmented, and no comprehensive plan emerged. But OSRD and the services learned to compromise their differences.

While NDRC was in its infant stages, Roosevelt had ridden the momentum of public dismay after the fall of France to set up an American-British exchange of secret scientific information. Soon the British arrived in Washington with a black box full of scientific secrets. Five months later, the President reciprocated by sending Conant to London to reveal American developments. A blatant violation of neutrality, the Anglo-American scientific trade provided an early boost to American weapons progress and later helped co-ordinate existing Allied scientific effort. Roosevelt's masterly timing, disrespect for ordained practices, and improvisation gave the speed necessary for American weapons superiority.

In a mimicry of Roosevelt's methods, OSRD achieved military break-throughs in most unmilitary fashion. With no research laboratories of its own, OSRD farmed out research jobs to the universities and industrial laboratories, which in turn garnered scientists from all over the nation; one radiation center had sixty-nine different institutions represented on its staff. The odd mixture of Harvard University and Standard Oil produced the no less odd and no less powerful mixture of soap powder and gasoline called "napalm," which was to ravage almost every major city in Japan. OSRD loosely co-ordinated the research, collaborated with the British, urged new weapons on the Army, and won 99 per cent of its fights with Selective Service over deferments of scientists. On balance the decentralization and loose co-ordination probably gave speed to weapons developments.

As scientists puzzled out new weapons, the military puzzled over how to use them. The airplane was already making old strategies obsolete and forcing commanders to re-evaluate their weapons. By mid-1943, the Navy's most valuable ships were aircraft carriers, the most destructive weapons were air-borne bombs, and the defeat of Germany seemed to rest most heavily on the long waves of American and British bombers. To defeat submarines, the airplane was aided by radar and statistically deduced search patterns; to destroy Germany's most vaunted air weapon—the V-1 rocket bombs—scientists developed SCR-594 ground radar, the M-9 electrical director for antiaircraft guns, and the radio proximity fuse. Soon most of the German missiles would be destroyed in the air. But the record was uneven, as trial and error slowly built up knowledge of how to use the weapons. The thousand-bomber flights were awe-inspiring, as were the mathematically based analyses of photographs of bomb damage, but the actual effect on German military capacity remained to be seen.

Weapons technology had endless built-in problems. Roosevelt and his advisers worried about using the proximity fuse for fear the Germans would copy it. Tank crews found the gyrostabilizers on tank guns too complex and delicate to manage, so disconnected them. All down the line, new weapons created problems of use that the military had to solve in action.

In the spring of 1942, Stimson and Bush recognized the problems and urged Roosevelt to create a Joint Committee on New Weapons and Equipment to bring civilian scientists in at the strategic planning level. Roosevelt acquiesced to the co-ordination, but only at a lower level—under the Joint Chiefs of Staff. This co-ordination was at once not high enough for atomic-bomb planning and too high for most weapons. Civilians were not brought into contact even with staff planners. Co-ordination lagged.

Radar systems were a big exception; they were the best co-ordinated and most useful in combat of all OSRD projects. Some of radar's success traces to Stimson's almost Victorian sense of family. Throughout the war, he was one of the leading exponents of new weapons and techniques, and especially of radar. He had become fascinated by radar through his cousin, Alfred Loomis, a lawyer and pioneer in microwaves. Soon after NDRC was organized,

Loomis was appointed head of a radar section under the Detection and Controls Division. By the spring of 1942, Stimson even had a special personnel consultant for radar and was using his influence and authority to get radar soundly established as a smoothly operating weapon of war.

The British invention of the resonant cavity magnetron, which produced enough power to make possible radar in the microwave region, was the most essential advance. Immediately following the first exchange of scientific secrets, the NDRC, with assistance from British specialists, established the large Radiation Laboratory at MIT for research, design, and construction of radar for short-run use. NDRC scientists subsequently developed 150 different microwave radar systems for ground, air, and sea as requested by the War and Navy Departments for tactical operations. The most powerful radar ever built, the Microwave Early Warning System, developed in 1942, was contained in five trucks and operated by a company of soldiers.

The greatest need in the first year of war was for an effective radar in American planes searching for far-ranging U-boats. The Army installed search radar developed by the Radiation Laboratory in B-24 Liberators and in a group of B-18's, which together helped drive the submarines away from the East Coast. To make possible night bombing of Germany and Japan, British and American scientists invented the Plan Position Indicator and the three-centimeter "Mickey," with glowing radar maps. A Ground Controlled Approach system was contrived by NDRC to direct aircraft landings in bad visibility. The development of a diverse assortment of radar systems, all closely tied to military needs, was OSRD's biggest contribution to Axis defeat. In other areas the scientists, divorced from military weapons, focused simply on dramatic innovations.

OSRD's organizational concentration on developing new weapons led, according to its Deputy Director, Irvin Stewart, to a tendency to place great faith in the weapon or instrument itself, while the importance of the man-instrument combination was relatively slow to be realized. Wars are fought with machines run by men, and while the development of machines spurted forward, the training of their users fell behind. Anyone can throw a Molotov cocktail, but the special skills needed to operate and interpret electronic equipment cannot be produced as quickly as the equipment itself. OSRD developed weapons, the Army trained soldiers, but no one concentrated on the man-weapon combination.

With no central control under Roosevelt of both weapons development and soldier training, an unnoticed revolution took place. America had traditionally relied on hastily drafted civilians to fight its wars, but technical weapons now required professionally trained men. The specialization of weapons demanded combat teams of experts and careful co-ordination between them, a co-ordination not to be learned in two months of basic training. What OSRD's new weapons required was a large, specialized, professional standing army in peacetime in order to fight a war; but a large standing army in peacetime was against American tradition and the Constitution. Fragmented organization meant no responsible agency to deal with such broad problems.

Similar difficulties arose in production. The weapons were as complicated to manufacture as to use, and temporarily converted industries had trouble making them. Only a permanent defense industry could work intensively with the civilian scientists advising and improving on the latest weapon advances. Around the country—at Seattle, Washington, and at Oak Ridge, Tennessee—a military-industrial complex was slowly, almost invisibly, developing. Roosevelt's improvisation speeded the weapons development immensely, yet fragmented authority hampered use, and the lack of a comprehensive, stable agency prevented considerations beyond military expediency from getting a hearing.

ROOSEVELT AS CHIEF EXECUTIVE

To glimpse the titanic military and economic power mobilized by the Roosevelt administration at war's mid-point in 1943, to consider the heavy political forces beating on the White House from the nation and from abroad, to assess the endless problems, appeals, complaints, queries, demands that flowed into the President's office, to recall that for many months after Pearl Harbor the President operated with the help of one talented but ailing deputy, a small, overworked staff, and a shifting array of aides collected from outside the White House—all this is to marvel at the aplomb, the gaiety, the buoyancy, the grace with which Franklin Roosevelt presided over the White House during the years of war crisis. Whatever the muddles and delays, the disputes and outright failures, the President would not duck responsibility. Cartoonists might picture the ship of state lurching and yawing, but no one could doubt who controlled the tiller.

Old Washington hands wondered how he did it. How could one man dominate, even if he did not always control, the dispersed, disorganized, ever-shifting and expanding bureaucracy? How did he remain Chief Executive in fact as well as in title?

The President stayed in charge of his administration by the methods that had seemed to serve him so well in the earlier, prewar years—by drawing fully on his formal and informal powers as Chief Executive; by raising goals, creating momentum, inspiring a personal loyalty, getting the best out of people; by skillful timing, now waiting endlessly while his aides chafed, sometimes moving quickly before his staff was even informed, but usually choosing a time when his target—a foot-dragging agency or bovine official—was most vulnerable; by deliberately fostering among his aides a sense of competition and a clash of wills that led to disarray, heartbreak, and anger but also set off pulses of executive energy and sparks of creativity; by maintaining an extremely wide "span of control"—or at least of attention, encouragement, and intervention; by handing out one job to several men and several jobs to one man, thus strengthening his own position as a court of appeals, as a depository of information, and as a tool of co-ordination; by ignoring or bypassing collective decision-making agencies, such as the Cabinet, and dealing instead with varying combinations of persons from different agencies; by often delving into specific, even tiny matters that some official had assumed were far below or beyond the Chief Executive's reach; by sometimes withholding information, sometimes supplying it, to keep aides and officials in line; by maintaining his own private storehouse of intelligence, drawn from countless letters, memos, gossip, and fed by contending subordinates; by retiring behind the protection of rules, customs, conventions when they served his needs and evading them when they did not—and always by persuading, flattering, juggling, improvising, reshuffling, harmonizing, conciliating, manipulating.

No one saw this Chief Executive more often or more closely than his Budget Director, Harold Smith, who was exasperated as Roosevelt transgressed the orthodox canons of administration even while he gaped with disbelief at his chief's broken-field running. In his diary Smith recorded the range of Roosevelt's interests, his inability to extricate himself from odd details and ideas even at the height of a world war.

March 17, 1943: "The President told me he had a job for me. He tried to find the papers but could not do so. However, he decided to tell me about it. He wants me to investigate the situation with respect to the Government's purchasing the Empire State Building, about which Al Smith has talked to him recently. He . . . had turned the problem over to Jesse Jones, but Jones was getting nowhere with it."

April 9, 1943: ". . . The President did not agree with our recommendation. He made a strong argument that physical fitness and recreation are properly separable, and asked that provision be made in the Office of Defense, Health and Welfare Services for a physical fitness group. . . ."

May 8, 1943: "The President approved the Army budget. . . . I think he proposes to use it as a propaganda instrument in connection with the forthcoming conference concerning military strategy, with the near conclusion of the North African campaign."

June 3, 1943: (The President had just awakened from a short afternoon nap.) "I said I was glad to know that he was following a regimen, since he is one of the most important men today. In passing off my comment, he made a remark to the effect that John L. Lewis apparently did not think he was very important and would be glad to see him out as President. The President said he made a comment—which he thought was a good crack—that he would be glad to resign as President if John L. Lewis committed suicide. . . .

"The President pointed out that mint tea, for instance, would help to satisfy the population of Morocco and Algiers. . . ."

August 31, 1943: "I reminded the President that he had received a letter from his Chief of Staff saying essentially that everything was lovely [in military planning]. I commented that he, the President, knew different. The President suggested that we might continue this correspondence with another memorandum . . . in the vein, 'Now boys, even if you are kidding yourselves, don't try to kid the Commander in Chief. . . .'

"The President commented that the Army was always crying that he did not understand the Army and that he was partial to the Navy. He said, 'You know that I have been tougher with the Navy than with the Army.' I had to admit that was true. Furthermore, he said that he had had more trouble with the Navy in this war than with the Army."

Such was the unconventional Chief Executive as he was known to his subordinates, to conservative critics who castigated him for one-man rule and dictatorial tendencies, and to those who admired him precisely because he did not follow the usual rules of the game and standard principles of orderly administration. But there was another Chief Executive who *had* long been concerned with orderly executive management; who had established New Deal executive or co-ordinating committees and sometimes presided over them; who had set up a host of planning agencies; who had appointed a committee on executive management to shape proposals for more effective presidential direction and control; who had backed most of its proposals against one of the most fanatical counterattacks on Capitol Hill that he had ever encountered; who after the defeat of his first reorganization attempt had won extensive power to reorganize his own Executive Office and submit broader reorganization plans to Congress; who had created the Executive Office of the President and by transferring the Budget Bureau into it had immensely strengthened central presidential control; who had regrouped agencies into more coherent entities, such as the Federal Security Agency; who had secured a continuing authority to reorganize under war-powers acts and had fashioned and refashioned defense and war agencies to his liking.

The two Chief Executives had long lived together in a manner as baffling as Roosevelt's ability to be both party leader and Chief of State, both leader of a popular majority and leader of the people, both conservative—or at least traditionalist—and liberal, both man of principle and man of expediency, without any apparent strain, except on his subordinates. The latter could never be sure which Roosevelt would confront them. By what inner compass or design the President decided to take on any one of these roles—or whether he consciously made decisions about his roles—was never clear even to intimates.

But on one great executive responsibility—the recruitment and positioning of talent—Roosevelt deserved credit by any test of administration. Somehow, as much by some unerring instinct as by observation and insight, the President had made a host of brilliant appointments by mid-war. Hopkins, Hassett, Smith in the presidential office, Stimson, Marshall, Patterson in War, Forrestal in Navy, Elmer Davis in OWI, Henderson and, later, Chester Bowles in OPA, Byrnes and Cohen in OWM, Bush and Conant in war science, Davis and Morse on the War Labor Board, Eisenhower, Nimitz, MacArthur in the field—these men were not only instruments of a President's purpose but also adornments of a public service.

The fate of another adornment of the service, Sumner Welles, at State, poignantly reflected the anomaly of Roosevelt's administrative ways. The President kept Welles on as Undersecretary because he was a superb presidential agent in a vast organization that often seemed beyond the grip of the White House. Hull of course resented the agent and the arrangement; "every department has its thun of a bitch," he told a friend, "but I've got the all-American." Welles's place in Roosevelt's court, along with his hauteur and his brilliance, made for enemies in Washington. And he was vulnerable. Someone spread rumors through Washington that he had made advances to a Negro porter on a train. Roosevelt heard that William Bullitt, long a rival to Welles, was the rumor monger. When the former envoy next came to the oval office, Roosevelt stopped him at the door.

"William Bullitt," he trumpeted, "stand where you are.

"Saint Peter is at the gate. Along comes Sumner Welles, who admits to human error. Saint Peter grants him entrance. Then comes William Bullitt. Saint Peter says: 'William Bullitt, you have betrayed a fellow human being. *You—can—go—down—there.*' " He told Bullitt he wished never to see him again. But he knew that Welles's usefulness was over—and losing a "member of the family" may have accounted for some of Roosevelt's feeling.

Clearly, Roosevelt's administrative ways were hell on his subordinates. Grumbling day after day in his diary and to friends, Stimson spoke for many of his colleagues accustomed to clear-cut delegations of power, orderly staff work, regular channels.

"He wants to do it all himself. . . ." ". . . the poorest administrator I have ever worked under in respect to the orderly procedure and routine of his performance . . ." "I often wish the President wasn't so soft-hearted towards incompetent appointees. . . ." "Today the President has constituted an almost innumerable number of new administrative posts, putting at the head of them a lot of inexperienced men appointed largely for personal grounds and who report on their duties directly to the President and have constant and easy access to him . . . better access to the President than his Cabinet officers have. The lines of delimitation between these different agencies themselves and between them and the departments is very nebulous. . . ." ". . . the Washington atmosphere is full of acrimonious disputes over matters of jurisdiction. . . ."

Oscar Cox complained, too, from his closer vantage point to White House operations, that major policy decisions were going by default, policies were not being swiftly executed, excessive demands were being made on the President's time.

But Roosevelt's enemies found some solace in his methods. Late in 1942 the *Japan Times-Advertiser* editorialized that whatever the congressional clamor for a new unity of command, Roosevelt would never let anyone overshadow him, that he preferred "multi-phased calculations" such as playing one faction against the other and using disunity rather than unity as a means of control, that he was not a military strategist but a public-relations man and hence that America's war organization would not move out of the formative stage. This organizational view of Roosevelt's presidency was duly forwarded to the White House, where it was dismissed, if even noticed, but the criticisms of Roosevelt's executive leadership and management could not be ignored. Indeed, just as Roosevelt's "one-man" administration had become in 1939 a fiery issue that spilled over into the 1940 election, the charge of bungling and mismanagement at the top of the executive branch loomed as a potential issue for 1944.

Most of the critics failed to see that their canons of orderly, "businesslike" administration, clear delegation of power, proper span of control, effective co-ordination, and the other textbook doctrines were not always—or even usually—relevant to the needs of the man in the oval office. For his problem was less one of *management* than of dramatizing goals, enunciating principles, lifting hopes, pointing out dangers, raising expectations, mobilizing popular energies, recruiting gifted aides and administrators, harmonizing disputants, protecting administrative morale. Even crusty Henry

Stimson was not immune to Roosevelt's healing balm. At the height of his annoyance with the President over poor administration, he admitted that a long talk with the President "tended to remove all of the unpleasant feeling which I have gradually been getting into . . . it indicated that his friendship and confidence in me were still unimpaired . . . he was very solicitous about Mabel's health. . . ."

For Roosevelt it was a question of power. When critics charged that he would not make Baruch or some other strong man a superczar because he wanted to hoard his own authority or feared a rival, they were quite right. Partly it was a matter of temperament; as a prima donna, Roosevelt had no relish for yielding the spotlight for long. But mainly it was a matter of prudence, experience, and instinct. The President did not need to read Machiavellian treatises to know that every delegation of power and sharing of authority extracted a potential price in the erosion of presidential purpose, the narrowing of options, the clouding of the appearance of presidential authority, the threat to his reputation for being on top. He grumbled about his own problems.

"The Treasury is so large and far-flung and ingrained in its practices," he told Marriner Eccles, "that I find it almost impossible to get the action and results I want—even with Henry [Morgenthau] there. But the Treasury is not to be compared with the State Department. You should go through the experience of trying to get any changes in the thinking, policy and action of the career diplomats and then you'd know what a real problem was. But the Treasury and the State Department put together are nothing compared with the Na-a-vy. The admirals are really something to cope with—and I should know. To change anything in the Na-a-vy is like punching a feather bed. You punch it with your right and you punch it with your left until you are finally exhausted, and then you find the damn bed just as it was before you started punching."

In no particular did Roosevelt more flagrantly violate the precepts of public administration than in the casual variety of people he was willing to see. He was not easily accessible, but his accessibility was unpredictable. Late in 1943 the young American Chargé d'Affaires in Lisbon, George Kennan, feared that the State Department was making so heavy-handed a demand on Portugal for facilities in the Azores that the pressure might antagonize Salazar and push Franco over to the Nazis. When Kennan tried to take some initiative in assuring Lisbon that the United States would respect Portuguese sovereignty in all Portuguese territory, he was whisked back to Washington. There he was brought to the Pentagon and to a Kafkaesque meeting of Stimson, Knox, Marshall, Acting Secretary of State Stettinius, and other high officials. Kennan was alternately mystified and horrified by the discussion. No one seemed aware of his background reports, interested in his present views, or aware of the facts and the problem. Coolly dismissed from the meeting, he slunk away in despair. But he appealed to his Chief at State, who passed him on to Hopkins, who set up a meeting with the President. Roosevelt jovially waved Kennan to a seat, said he failed to understand how Lisbon could possibly suspect his intentions in the Azores—why, had he not as Assistant Secretary of the Navy personally supervised the dismantling of Azores bases in the *last* war?—and promised to give him a personal letter to take to Salazar. Kennan was elated but puzzled. What about the Pentagon meeting? "Oh, don't worry," Roosevelt said with a debonair wave of his cigarette holder, "about all those *people* over there."

On countless other occasions Roosevelt protected his own purposes by seeing people far down the administrative line. Still, a President's care and nurture of his own power for his myriad ends—winning elections, dealing with friend and foe abroad, protecting the presidential ego, defending the integrity of his position as the chief and only elected federal executive—are not easily and automatically translated into effective war mobilization or national economic power. Certain of his qualities played their part in the countless errors, delays, and wastes in the nation's war effort.

One of these was his ambivalence toward planning itself. In no function were the two chief executives in Roosevelt more at odds with each other. He had long been a planner. He had established numberless planning agencies; he had staffed them well; he had paid attention to their reports. But planning, to Roosevelt, was a sharply limited exercise. It was segmental; he was interested in plans for specific regions, watersheds, industries, not—despite his critics—in "economic planning" or in some grand reshaping of the nation. He was critical of the National Resources Planning Board for indulging in lofty schemes, especially in the economic realm. And Roosevelt's planning was limited in time. Repeatedly he restrained the military from making commitments more than six months or a year ahead. He was also ambivalent toward the administrative canons of unification, co-ordination, integration. He encouraged such tendencies in individual departments, especially in the military, but he resisted unification of the whole executive branch through planning or co-ordinating machinery. He never allowed the Cabinet or the OWM to serve as a collective agency for unified decision making. Over-all co-ordination was glaringly absent in the one area—fiscal and monetary policy—where it was most necessary and potentially effective. The Budget Bureau, under Harold Smith's leadership, was eager to effect a marriage of budgeting and planning—"formal, informal, or of the shotgun type"

—but the bureau never fashioned joint tools for planning, budgeting. and programing as a means of directing and co-ordinating the whole executive branch.

In the absence of strong, comprehensive, long-run planning instruments, Roosevelt's wartime agencies were typically organized to cope with existing, dramatic crises rather than to head off less visible, potentially bigger ones; thus the establishment of a Rubber Director when the rubber supply was collapsing, the Office of Defense Transportation when the railroads seemed about to fail, the fuel and oil czardoms after those commodities were imperiled. Hence Roosevelt's mobilization machinery tended to be more the prisoner of events than the master of them. The most comprehensive control agencies, OES and OWM, never realized their paper potential as means of planning, programing, and control. These agencies were under men—Byrnes and Vinson—who had little authority or temperament for top-level planning, but preferred to deal with disputes batted up by contending agencies, to act on the basis virtually of adversary proceedings, to mediate, negotiate, reconcile, adjust. Roosevelt encouraged them in this. He wanted no superczars in the White House outside of himself.

Nor was the mobilization structure in itself conducive to strong leadership, planning, and control. The agencies and their hundreds of subunits had grown like coral reefs. The pyramid of executive action had been built largely through "layering"—the piling of new agencies on top of others, culminating in the OWM—rather than through planning from the top down. Layering had great merits, but it tended to keep power diffused through the existing levels and it inhibited effective planning and programing from the White House even if Roosevelt had been inclined to it.

These tendencies toward piecemeal, reactive war organization were reinforced by Roosevelt's bent toward dealing with one set of problems at a time rather than establishing priorities across a wide front and over a long span of time. In particular he constantly stressed the importance of "winning the war"—that is, gaining a military victory as quickly and inexpensively as possible—rather than seeking at the same time to gain broader, more complex goals, such as "winning the peace." He did not believe fully in separating the short-run from the long, as indicated by the fact that he was taking up postwar problems and goals long before war's end. But he did so as much for the purpose of keeping his own choices wide and preventing others from capturing and shaping postwar issues—in short, to prevent other persons' planning—as for the purpose of his own long-run planning. And his philosophy permeated his administration and inhibited or enervated long-term planning.

All these administrative tendencies, both institutional and Rooseveltian, toward the immediate, the concrete, the manageable were of the most profound importance in the life of the nation. World War II released social and economic forces that would have enormous impact on American life after the last bomb dropped. Millions of rural people were moving into cities and defense areas; millions of Negroes were leaving the farm, migrating north and west, tasting the delights and miseries, the opportunities and frustrations of city life; millions of women were working in factories and offices for the first time. The explosion of education—from the making of literates to the courses in languages and science—was a revolution in itself. Income, real as well as money, shot up, bringing infinite satisfactions and disappointments. Health, aid to women and children, and other welfare services were immensely expanded. Employment soared; the jobless dropped to an irreducible minimum of dedicated unemployables. Patterns of housing, congestion, employment, opportunity, discrimination were created that would closely affect the nation's social and economic life for decades to come. How much these trends could have been affected by purposeful governmental action at the early stages is hard to say. But to the extent they could be affected, the emphasis on "Dr. Win the War" was bound to enhance the government's short-run *management* only at the expense of long-run *leadership*. The burning cities of 1967 and 1968 were not wholly unrelated to steps not taken, visions not glimpsed, priorities not established, in the federal agencies of 1943 and 1944.

Toward the end of the war a sagacious authority on public administration, Luther Gulick, assessed the whole organization of the war government. The narrowest test of war organization, he wrote, was to muster the nation's maximum resources to destroy the military power of its enemies. But this was an old-fashioned test, he concluded, which ignored long-range and continuing international economic and political problems at home and abroad. He would not apply the second test because the basic continuing elements of war and peace "played little if any role in the war organization of the United States for World War II." On the narrower test of specific war organization he found much to praise and to blame. In part he was disappointed by the failures of planning, programing, and operations—brilliant in spurts, but on the whole not very effective.

Still, Gulick could not but be impressed by the military impact of war organization. Somehow "it worked"—somehow it produced a "mobilization of total national power and a welding together of world military operations beyond the highest dreams of 1939 or 1940 or the greatest fears of Hitler. Those of us who write recipes should taste their pudding!"

TWELVE *The Strategy of Freedom*

FOR MONTHS the President had watched the shining white pantheon rising block by block on a swell of ground beyond the Tidal Basin. From his study window he could see the figure of the third President standing stiff and erect in its austere sanctuary; at night, when the lights were not blacked out, the figure would glow like a beacon. Through the tall columns Thomas Jefferson stared straight at the White House, his face set and stern.

By April 13, 1943 all was in readiness for the dedication of the Thomas Jefferson Memorial on the two hundredth anniversary of his birth. In commemoration, as in life, the Virginian had been able to divide as well as unite people. Bitter controversy had arisen over the design and location of the pantheon. Some had suggested that the memorial be built outside Washington—perhaps out in Virginia somewhere—but Roosevelt had insisted that the shrine be as conspicuous in the capital as the monuments to Washington and Lincoln. The removal of cherry trees had stirred further controversy, which the President had only exacerbated by suggesting that if ladies carried out their threat to chain themselves to the trees, a hoisting device be used to lift the trees and the enchained ladies out of the earth—new holes should then be dug and the trees and the ladies be placed in them—all to be done in a strictly humane manner.

Even on the day of commemoration, controversy continued. The Memorial Commission sponsoring committee included men who had fought bitterly in past years but were united now in tribute: James M. Cox, John W. Davis, Alfred E. Smith, Herbert Hoover, Alf Landon, Wendell Willkie. Their voices were muted on this day, but Republican Senator Edward H. Moore, of Oklahoma, was ready with a speech in which he assailed the New Deal party for paying lip service to Jefferson and charged that Roosevelt's rule was leading to the same outcome as in Germany—Hitlerism. The President prefered to dwell this day on the Jeffersonian ideas and symbols that united Americans: freedom of mind and conscience, inalienable rights, liberty, the end of privilege.

Before a throng that included Mrs. Woodrow Wilson, the President doffed his black cape and stood bareheaded in the sharp breeze that whipped across the water. He had banned silk hats and frock coats from the ceremony "on penalty of being shot."

"Today, in the midst of a great war for freedom, we dedicate a shrine to freedom.

"To Thomas Jefferson, Apostle of Freedom, we are paying a debt long overdue. . . .

"He faced the fact that men who will not fight for liberty can lose it. We, too, have faced that fact. . . .

"He loved peace and loved liberty—yet on more than one occasion he was forced to choose between them. We, too, have been compelled to make that choice. . . .

"Jefferson was no dreamer—for half a century he led his State and his Nation in fact and in deed. I like to think this was so because he thought in terms of the morrow as well as the day—and this was why he was hated or feared by those who thought in terms of the day and the yesterday. . . .

"The words which we have chosen for this Memorial speak Jefferson's noblest and most urgent meaning; and we are proud indeed to understand it and share it:

" 'I have sworn upon the altar of God, eternal hostility against every form of tyranny over the mind of man.' "

''A WORLD FORGED ANEW''

The Presidency, Roosevelt had said shortly before he took office, is pre-eminently a place of moral leadership. He had cited Jefferson as one of the great Presidents who were "leaders of thought at times when certain historic ideas in the life of the nation had to be clarified." When he paid tribute to Jefferson in April 1943 Roosevelt found himself in a dilemma of moral leadership at a time when a profound idea in the life of the planet had to be clarified.

The brightening prospects of victory had produced in early 1943 an eruption of books, articles, speeches, polemics on the question of postwar organization for peace and for security for all nations. On the eve of that year, Henry Wallace had proclaimed, in a national broadcast commemorating the eighty-sixth anniversary of Woodrow Wilson's birth, that it was not Wilson who had failed, but the world. Internationalists in Britain and America hailed the speech. Three days later Wallace called for a world air force to defend the peace. The Vice President had already won liberal plaudits for challenging Henry Luce's proclamation of an "American Century." "The century we are now entering—" Wallace retorted, "the century which will come out of this war—can and must be the century of the common man. . . ."

The most electrifying vision of the future came from no Democrat or socialist but from the leader of the presidential Republicans, Wendell Willkie. Early in 1943 he published *One World,* the tale of his globe-girdling trip of the year before. After reporting his adventures and dialogues in the Middle East, the Soviet Union, and China, Willkie called, in the book, for a war of liberation, for an end to racial imperialism at home and abroad, and for a "council today of the United Nations—a common council in which all plan together . . . a council of grand military strategy on which all nations that are bearing the brunt of the fighting are represented."

An instant hit, *One World* sold a million copies in eight weeks. Willkie's central and most original proposal was that "nothing of importance can be won in peace which has not already been won in the war itself," that during the fighting the United Nations must develop mechanisms for working together after the fighting was over, that the alternative to carefully linked war and postwar planning was "moving from one expediency to another, sowing the seeds of future discontents—racial, religious, political—not alone among the peoples we seek to free, but even among the United Nations themselves." This view—so critical of Roosevelt's whole approach to the problem—Willkie carried to victory rallies throughout the country.

A multitude of other, divergent voices were heard during these days. Thomas Mann warned against political antagonisms between East and West, favored "Americanization of the world, in a certain fundamental moral sense," and urged that his native Germany pass through hard decades of tribulation and atonement. Norman Thomas cautioned against a peace of vengeance. Bertrand Russell called for an international authority with enough force to win any possible future war. CIO President Philip Murray proposed a world federation backed by an international police force. William L. Shirer was dubious about a United Nations police force; solving the German question, he felt, was the key step. Max Lerner predicted that the United States could work with Russia, despite the many hurdles, and warned against being too dogmatic about Soviet boundaries. Colonel McCormick also had a postwar plan—to wit, that Scotland, Wales, and the British Dominions should join the United States as states of the union.

And Roosevelt? As the war progressed he had become more explicit about his postwar ideals and goals. He had definite ideas about the transition period after the war: the world was to be policed by the victorious powers. The Big Four would act as sheriffs. Eventually a true world organization—a successor to the League of Nations—would take over, but the President was vague as to the specifics. During wartime, he told Congress in his State of the Union message, "we should confine ourselves to the larger objectives and not get bogged down in argument over methods and details."

The President's reluctance to get into the hard specifics of postwar security was due in part to his old aversion to making decisions and commitments before he had to. In part it was due to divisions among his advisers. Hull worried about isolationist feelings, urged Roosevelt to dampen down Wallace and others in the administration who were taking an "evangelical" approach to postwar questions. Welles felt that discussions should go ahead within the administration. Hopkins wished that the President would move faster. Certainly the President was happy to see people outside the administration send up trial balloons, as long as the White House was not touched when they were shot down.

Roosevelt's main reason for moving slowly on postwar political questions was probably more intellectual than political. Repeatedly over a quarter of a century he had had to confront the question of world organization, and he had taken about every stand that an internationally minded man could. As a member of the Wilson administration, and later as candidate for Vice President, he had advocated the League vigorously, though his arguments had tended to be somewhat more pragmatic, Wilson's more moralistic. Roosevelt had been tepid about the League during the 1920's, and almost deserted it under the pressure of 1932 nomination politics. As President he had co-operated with League organizations, and he advocated United States membership in the World Court. But, growing more disenchanted with the League during the mid-1930's, he seemed to prefer inter-American security arrangements, as a possible model for the world; and he catered to neutralist feeling. In 1937 he proposed some kind of quarantine for aggressor nations, then hastily dropped the idea, ostensibly because of opposition to it. During the prewar months he leaned toward Anglo-American guardianship of world peace, but later broadened the police force to include Russia and China. To some in 1943 Roosevelt's Big Four police plan was hard to distinguish from a new Holy Alliance. But in supporting some kind of new League, however amorphous, he had come almost full circle since 1918.

How long could the President put off the pressing, concrete postwar issues? He seemed in no hurry; he probably even toyed with the notion that Big Four policing might work so well that it could go on indefinitely. Yet he could hardly evade some of the specific problems, and certainly he did not, in "practical" areas. He helped sponsor global programs in munitions, food, raw materials, trade, and of course military planning. Here he was marvelously concrete, bold, and innovative; here he was making day-to-day decisions that ultimately would influence and even control the political options. But on political planning as such the politician in chief was cautious and halting.

He was not alone. In retrospect the striking quality of the myriad postwar peace proposals of 1943 was their lack of political realism and explicitness. Most of them were not utopian or foolish or shortsighted; they simply failed to relate closely moral ends, political means, and stubborn institutions. Thus the issue of working with Russia after the war was debated on the basis of hope or faith or even history, but few took the trouble to think concretely and imaginatively about specific Soviet experiences, ideology, expectations, and strategies in relation to the moods, optimism, utopianism, and biases of American people in their foreign-policy attitudes, the peculiar machinery through which they made decisions, and the attentive public, patriotic groups, and ethnic voting blocs that closely influenced foreign policy. Thus Michael Straight, a twenty-six-year-old former New Deal junior official, brought out in 1943 a brilliant, eloquent volume, *Make This the Last War*, that marshaled facts of history, economics, resources, production, dependent peoples in ample and glittering array, but turned mushy when it came to the harsh, restricted choices that politicians would confront.

Roosevelt did not enjoy such a privilege. He could orate, dream, aspire, sermonize with the other would-be architects of peace, but he could not ignore such mean facts as, say, the rising controversy over Russia's western borders, significant Polish-American populations in a dozen states, the foreign-policy influence of the Senate and

"IF WE CAN CO-OPERATE FOR WAR, WHY CAN'T WE CO-OPERATE FOR PEACE?"

October 25, 1943, Daniel R. Fitzpatrick, St. Louis *Post-Dispatch* of the Senate Foreign Relations Committee, and the importance of one Arthur H. Vandenberg, Republican Senator from Michigan. Certainly Vandenberg ignored none of these facts. In the spring of 1943 he was busy studying various congressional declarations on postwar security and making clear his own sensitivity to the Polish question. The President could not forget that it was not only bitter-enders like Hiram Johnson and Henry Cabot Lodge, but also Republican moderates—men who were then much like Vandenberg now—who had destroyed Wilson's League.

Still, Hopkins was doubtless justified in complaining to Clapper that his chief was *too* conscious of Congress and of Wilson's failure. The problem was not simply the delay in planning and the failure, despite Willkie's advice, to convert actual war planning and processes into peace machinery and structure. The more serious problem was in the realm of political warfare. The ideal of permanent peace was the single most gripping vision in a world at war. Roosevelt's refusal to put himself at the head of world-wide thinking and planning and building for peace narrowed his chances of competing for world attention and world allegiance with the Nazis and the Communists, who had their own peace plans for a "world forged anew."

On the domestic front the President felt less constraint in planning policy and programs.

People at home and at the front, he had said in his State of the Union address, were "wondering a little about the third freedom—freedom from want." They were expecting after the war to have full employment—to work, to run their farms, their stores, to earn decent wages. "They are eager to face the risks inherent in our system of free enterprise." They did not want undernourishment, slums, or the dole. They wanted assurance against the evils of all major hazards—"assurance that will extend from the cradle to the grave."

"From the cradle to the grave"—these words touched the mood of the day. In England an elderly Oxford don, Sir William Beveridge, had written for the government a report on "Social Insurance and Allied Services." Three hundred pages of small type, loaded with tables, bristling with officialese, the "Beveridge Plan" was nevertheless so explicit and bold a manifesto for "the abolition of want as a practicable post-war aim" that it set off a social-security boom in Britain. An American edition, reproduced photographically from the English, was a quick best seller.

"Frances, what does this mean?" the President asked Miss Perkins as he read newspaper accounts of the plan. "Why does Beveridge get his name on this? Why does he get credit for this? You know I have been talking about cradle to the grave insurance ever since we first thought of it. It is my idea. It is not the Beveridge plan. It is the Roosevelt Plan."

The President was only half joking. He was proud of his fight for Social Security in 1934 and 1935, against one of the most reactionary oppositions in the history of the nation. And perhaps he knew that in his concluding paragraphs Beveridge quoted, as a warranty for his plan, the fifth clause of the Atlantic Charter—which by chance had been signed on the sixth anniversary of the day in 1935 when the Social Security Act became law. On the eighth anniversary—August 14, 1943—the President asked that Social Security be extended to farmers, farm laborers, small businessmen, and the self-employed, and to "the serious economic hazard of ill health."

It was clear, even with the anti-New Deal Congress of 1943, that many a progressive proposal that had failed in the face of the conservative coalition could muster support as a war or veterans measure. Such was the case with the "GI Bill of Rights." The President appointed a committee of educators in November 1942 to frame a program for postwar education and training of veterans. The committee acted more quickly than most such presidential commissions; within a year Roosevelt's recommendations were ready for Congress: federal support for veterans to study up to one year, and "for a limited number of ex-servicemen and women selected for their special aptitudes, to carry on their general, technical, or professional education for a further period of one, two, or three years." The localistic, states'-rights, and religious objections that long had blocked federal support for schooling magically dwindled when it came to helping veterans. The President's proposal of the measure, which was enthusiastically welcomed by Congress, in itself was a tribute to Thomas Jefferson, educator.

When it came to paying for the war and stabilizing the economy, however, the President ran head on into congressional opposition. Most of the legislators seemed to share neither the Jeffersonian concern for equality of sacrifice nor the Hamiltonian doctrine of prudent fiscal management in an economy under stress. In April, Congress terminated the President's authority to limit salaries, by means of a rider attached to a public-debt measure that he was compelled to sign. Roosevelt bitterly attacked the rider, which was aimed mainly against limitation of salaries (including, incidentally, Roosevelt's own) to $25,000 a year. "I still believe that the Nation has a common purpose—" he told Congress, "equality of sacrifice in wartime."

Certainly a large measure of sacrifice was possible. The statistics of the war economy were staggering to a nation raised on Depression scarcities. By mid-1943 war expenditures were reaching the monthly level of seven billion dollars. The national debt would soon be 150 billion. Since the outbreak of war in September 1939 Americans had saved about seventy billions. A third of this was in currency and checking accounts, a third in redeemable or marketable bonds—"liquid dynamite," the Treasury's General Counsel, Randolph Paul, called it. Taxes were running around forty billion a year. The Treasury estimated that income payments to individuals would be over 150 billion for fiscal 1944. Direct personal taxes, at current rates, would skim off about twenty billion, leaving about 130 billion of disposable income. During fiscal 1943 banks had increased their holdings of federal securities by about thirty billion—a key factor in a huge expansion of the total coin, paper money, and checking deposits held by the public.

The President had called for sixteen billion of additional taxes and/or savings in his budget message of 1943. Congressional and public attention had been diverted by a heated dispute in the spring of that year over a scheme of Beardsley Ruml, Treasurer of Macy's, for a pay-as-you-go income-tax plan that would "forgive" all or part of 1942 taxes. Roosevelt favored pay-as-you-go, but he publicly opposed the Senate version of tax forgiveness on the ground that he could not "acquiesce in the elimination of a whole year's tax burden on the upper income groups during a war period when I must call for an increase in taxes and savings from the mass of our people." After the President's intervention the Senate version was narrowly defeated in the House, which then passed a compromise acceptable to the administration.

With the President's main goals of big tax boosts still unrealized, Congress seemed exhausted by its forays against salary limitation and for pay-as-you-go. The administration seemed exhausted, too, and divided. Morgenthau was distressed to hear that War Mobilizer Byrnes and Director of Economic Stabilization Vinson were to have a leading role in tax policy. He protested to Roosevelt, who replied that taxes were part of the whole fiscal situation and that the Secretary and Byrnes should deal directly with each other and not through the President. As Byrnes and Vinson continued to negotiate with tax makers on Capitol Hill, Morgenthau seethed over the role of the Kitchen Cabinet. The pattern was perfectly obvious, he told his staff. The people sitting "over there in the left wing of the White House" were trying to run the show, and if they did they could take the blame, too. They were a bunch of ambitious politicians, maneuverers, finaglers. He told his staff to prepare a direct letter to the President as to who was in charge of tax policy. He wanted it straight from the shoulder.

"AW HEN," the President wrote back. "The weather is hot and I am goin' off fishing. I decline to be serious even when you see 'gremlins' which ain't there."

The President talked with Morgenthau soon after, reassured him as to his primacy in tax policy, and said he wanted twelve billion in new taxes. He advised Morgenthau to put up to Congress various plans that totaled eighteen billion, and let Congress decide on any combination necessary to raise the total. But he would not sign a memorandum to this effect to Byrnes or Vinson. "This is all one big family and you don't do things that way in a family."

This led to a sharp family quarrel early in September when Morgenthau met with the President and Byrnes. Byrnes was pretty bitter and hot, Paul reported; the President tried to stop him a couple of times but Byrnes slugged right on. Who was in charge of tax policy? "I am the boss," Roosevelt said. ". . . We must agree. . . . Then when we agree, I expect you fellows to go in and do the work just like soldiers." Byrnes said he would not work for the bill unless he had a voice in it. He got along with people all right—he got along with Knox and Stimson—but he couldn't get along with Morgenthau. Roosevelt was now aroused. Pounding the table, he insisted again, "I am the boss. I am the one who gets the rap if we get licked in Congress. . . . I am the boss, I am giving the orders."

Despite the raw tempers, Morgenthau and his staff plugged away at new tax proposals and Social Security expansion. For a time the Treasury toyed with the idea, radical in the United States, of including medical insurance under Social Security, but Roosevelt was wary. The people were not ready, he felt. "We can't go up against the State Medical Societies," Roosevelt reassured Senator George, "we just can't do it." Morgenthau concentrated on a tough tax program. Early in October 1943 the Secretary, with the President's blessing, presented the administration's new proposals to Congress. They called for 10.5 billion dollars of additional taxes; four billion of estate and gift taxes, corporate taxes, and excises. Morgenthau also proposed repeal of the victory tax, which would take nine million low-income taxpayers off the tax rolls.

The reaction of most congressional leaders ranged from cool to hostile. The legislators seemed far removed from the new memorial in the Tidal Basin and the egalitarian figure who occupied it.

THE BROKEN PLEDGE

During late 1942 and early 1943 British leaders were concerned less with long-run peace planning than with immediate postwar settlements and arrangements. Anthony Eden had taken the lead in exploring such questions. In February 1943 Churchill suggested to Roosevelt that the Foreign Secretary talk with him on the subject. "Delighted to have him come—the sooner the better," Roosevelt replied. Hull was vacationing in Florida at the time; when Welles told him that the President and he felt that they could carry on the conversations with Eden and hence Hull need not interrupt his vacation, the Secretary took the next train to Washington.

He hardly needed to worry. Roosevelt was even more cautious in approaching immediate postwar arrangements than in long-term planning for peace. The aftermath of Versailles was a constant, nagging reminder to him—a factor as crucial in his thinking as Passchendaele and the Somme were in Churchill's military planning. Roosevelt still preferred to put off making postwar political plans, but increasingly, it seemed, key wartime military decisions had a sharp political edge and crucial postwar implication. So Roosevelt decided to go ahead with Eden, but quietly and tentatively.

Hour after hour Roosevelt and Eden talked together, sometimes with Hull and Halifax, sometimes only with Hopkins, sometimes with a larger company, but never with the military. Roosevelt was still keeping separate the discussion of military and political plans. With Eden he roamed around the globe, but the starting and ending place always seemed to be Russia. What would Stalin want after the war? Eden was sure he planned to absorb the Baltic states into the Soviet Union. This would antagonize American public opinion, Roosevelt felt; since the Russians would be in the Baltic countries when Germany fell, they could not be forced out. He wondered if Stalin would accept a plebiscite, even if a fake one. Eden was doubtful. Perhaps then, Roosevelt said, yielding on this score could be used as a bargaining instrument to get other concessions from the Russians.

The two men agreed that Russia would insist on its prewar boundaries with Finland, and that this was reasonable; they feared that Stalin would demand Hangö, too. But Finland would clearly be a postwar problem, and Poland even more so. The President and the Foreign Secretary agreed that Poland should have East Prussia; Roosevelt added that the Prussians would have to be moved out of the area, just as the Greeks were moved out of Turkey after World War I. This was a harsh method, he granted, but the only way to maintain peace; besides, the Prussians could not be trusted.

The roaming went on. *Serbia:* Roosevelt had long believed that Croats and Serbs had nothing in common and should be separated. *Austria and Hungary:* these should be established as independent states. *Turkey and Greece:* no problem from a geographical point of view. *Belgium:* the President proposed, while Eden listened skeptically, that the Walloon parts of Belgium be combined with Luxembourg, Alsace-Lorraine, and a part of northern France, to make up a new state of "Wallonia." *Germany:* Roosevelt wanted to avoid the Versailles error of dealing with the defeated enemy; he preferred encouraging differences and ambitions that would spring up in Germany and lead toward separatism on the part of major regions. In any event Germany must be divided into several states in order to weaken it. Roosevelt agreed with Hopkins that it was to be hoped that Anglo-American troops would be in Germany in strength when Hitler quit and could prevent anarchy or Communism, but it would be well to work out with the Russians a plan as to just where the armies should stand, especially in the event Germany collapsed before the Americans and British got deeply into France. Hull favored a simpler approach. He hoped that Hitler and his gang would not be granted a "long-winded public trial" but would be quickly shot out of hand.

The major long-run issue was, of course, postwar world organization. Roosevelt and Welles were still emphatic that the United States would not join any independent body such as a European council, but, rather, that all the United Nations should be members of one world-wide body to recommend policies, while representatives of the Big Four and of six or eight regional groupings could make up an advisory council. Real power—especially policing power—should be exercised by the Big Four. Eden was doubtful that China, with its historic instability, could be part of a Big Four; China might well have to go through revolution after the war, he thought. There was some discussion of Asia after the war, but most of it inconclusive. Hopkins guessed that the British were going to be "pretty sticky" about their former possessions in the Far East.

Roosevelt told Churchill and others that he and Eden agreed on 95 per cent of "everything from Ruthenia to the production of peanuts!" Over oysters at the Carlton, Eden told Hopkins he was surprised at the President's intimate knowledge of geographical boundaries. He enjoyed watching the play of Roosevelt's mind, but he had misgivings. There was something almost alarming in the cheerful fecklessness with which the President seemed to dispose of the fate of whole countries. He was like a conjuror, Eden felt, deftly juggling with balls of dynamite whose nature he did not understand.

No conjuring could dispel the lowering clouds over the discussions. What was Stalin's postwar design? Did he plan to dominate eastern and central Europe, establish a belt of satellites, foment revolution, even overrun the whole Continent? Or would he work for peace with the West, in the spirit of the United Nations? Roosevelt was not uninformed, naïve, or incredulous in facing these questions. He was prepared to bargain and demand, resist and compromise, like any good horse trader, in dealing with Moscow's demands.

What the President did not seem to grasp in its fullest implications, however, was the relation between Soviet options and the

April 5, 1943, Carl Rose, *PM*, reprinted by courtesy of Field Enterprises, Inc.

immediate policies that the West was following. He and Eden discussed Soviet plans somewhat abstractly, as though Moscow had already set a definite course, whatever it might be. The two did see the possibility that the Kremlin might be caught between two sets of policies, benign and aggressive; thus Stalin, at the height of his disappointment with the West over the second front, dissolved the Comintern as a gesture of good will toward his allies. But Roosevelt did not fully recognize the implications of immediate military planning for long-run strategic questions.

The burning issue was still the cross-channel invasion. The timing of the invasion had been left so vague at Casablanca that Roosevelt and Churchill agreed at the end of April that they must meet to discuss this and other pressing questions. At this point, though, the President was more interested in seeing Stalin than Churchill. Aware that relations with Moscow had fallen to a new low after postponement of the cross-channel plan and the suspension of northern convoying, Roosevelt reasoned that by talking face to face with Stalin he could take a direct measure of the man, establish a personal rapport, and reassure the Kremlin on Washington's plans and motives. He thought he could satisfy "Uncle Joe" as to cross-channel and other harsh issues. They were both practical men, after all. Certainly he could do better than Churchill.

Roosevelt was scornful of press reports from London that Churchill would be the good broker between Russia and the United States. If anyone was to be a broker, it would be he.

But how was he to get the evasive Stalin to rendezvous? He hit on the idea of emphasizing the importance of his invitation by sending it by a prestigious courier, former Ambassador Joseph Davies, an old favorite with the Kremlin. The letter was carefully composed. He wanted to get away, the President told Stalin, from a big staff conference and the red tape of diplomatic conversation. Therefore "the simplest and most practical method" would be a brief, informal meeting during the coming summer. Where? Africa was too hot, Khartoum was on British territory, and Iceland—"quite frankly," there it would be "difficult not to invite Prime Minister Churchill at the same time." So he proposed either his side or Stalin's side of the Bering Strait. He would take only Hopkins, an interpreter, and a stenographer. He sought no official agreements or declarations—just a meeting of minds.

While Davies flew east to Moscow with the invitation, Churchill and his party were steaming west across the Atlantic on the *Queen Mary*. The liner had been converted into a troopship big enough to carry an American division of 15,000 men; she was fast enough to evade and outrun U-boats. On this trip she was carrying several thousand German prisoners of war, and also some lice picked up on an earlier trip to southern waters. The Germans were sealed off from the VIP's on the top deck, but the bugs were not, and they made life miserable for some of the lower echelon of the upper echelon. But Churchill and his military chiefs were unscathed; day after day, as before, they met, adjusted differences, and prepared a united front for the Washington conference. Churchill warned his soldiers not to appear too keen on any one plan at the conference, for it would simply arouse competing proposals, owing to the "natural contrariness of allies."

Alerted that this formidable task force was bearing down on them, the American chiefs and their staffs resolved that this time they would not be overborne by superior numbers, unity, and staff work, as they felt they had been at Casablanca and earlier conferences. They hoped especially to end the step-by-step opportunism of the past and press on the British a long-term strategy. Preparations were feverish along Constitution Avenue and in the Pentagon, and lines seemed well drawn when Churchill, Dill, Brooke, Pound, Portal, and Ismay held their first meeting with Roosevelt, his Joint Chiefs, and Hopkins in the President's study on May 12. Roosevelt, after gracefully noting the triumphant progress since the last dismal meeting in the White House less than a year before, declared that while it would be desirable to knock Italy out of the war after the battle for Sicily, he shrank from the thought of putting large armies into that country. He favored a strong build-up for a cross-channel attack in the spring of 1944.

Churchill replied for his side. He spoke feelingly of Roosevelt's generosity, at the last White House meeting, when the crushing news of Tobruk's fall had come in. His Majesty's government, he emphasized, stood by the plan for the cross-channel attack, which could come in the spring of 1944 at the earliest, but what in the meantime? Hundreds of thousands of men could not stand idle in the Mediterranean. A strong blow at Italy might knock it out of the war, relieve Russia by forcing Hitler to divert troops from the Eastern Front to replace Italian troops withdrawn from the Balkans, nudge Turkey toward active participation, and allow the seizure of ports and bases necessary for launching assaults against the Balkans and southern Europe.

It was the same old difference of emphasis, timing, and priority. Day after day the Combined Chiefs of Staff met, argued, and adjourned. Marshall, with Roosevelt's backing, was adamant. He feared that once again the suction effect of the Mediterranean would drain away troops and supply and jeopardize cross-channel

"WHAT WORRIES THEM IS WHERE WE'LL MEET NEXT—"

May 14, 1943, © Low, reprinted by permission of *The Manchester Guardian*

BASIC WINSTONESE

plans. King was still pressing for more effort in the Pacific, especially if the British were to have their way in the Mediterranean. Paradoxically, each side felt that the other was undercutting the cross-channel attack—that the British were doing so by diverting to the Mediterranean, the Americans by stressing the Pacific. The British were adamantly against a "premature" cross-channel invasion, with its risk of spilling oceans of blood; the Americans had resolved to resist their ally's strategy of "scatteration" and "periphery-pecking" in the Mediterranean.

The result was a standoff. The British agreed, as first priority, to help mount a "decisive invasion of the Axis citadel," with a target date of May 1, 1944; they also approved an escalating bomber offensive to disrupt and destroy the German military and industrial system and break down the morale of the German people. An emergency cross-channel operation—the old plan named SLEDGEHAMMER—was kept on the books in case of sudden need. In exchange the President and his chiefs agreed to plan further operations in the Mediterranean to knock Italy out of the war. To counter the suction effect, a limit was put on Allied troop strength for the attack on Italy, and seven divisions were slated to be transferred from the Mediterranean to Britain, starting in the fall, to help the build-up there. But Eisenhower would still have twenty-seven divisions in the Mediterranean.

At last a date had been fixed, a rough order of priorities set. Even so, the Americans were uneasy. Churchill did not seem wholly reconciled. And what about Stalin? From his view the only important result of the conference would be wholly negative—postponing a cross-channel invasion until May 1944. Stalin had been furious after the news from Casablanca that the attack had been postponed from spring 1943 to August or September. What would he say now?

This was the question assailing Roosevelt and Churchill as the conference ended. Grimly they sat down together to prepare a letter to their comrade in arms. Hour after hour they wrote and rewrote, sending scrawled passages out to be typed, and then scribbling over the drafts until they were almost illegible. Two of the most gifted expositors in the world at this moment were reduced to stammering schoolboys making a confession. At two in the morning, to Roosevelt's relief, Churchill offered to take the latest draft away with him and "tidy it up" and return it. Both Churchill and Marshall were leaving for Algiers to consult with Eisenhower; Roosevelt agreed that the Chief of Staff could fly with the Prime Minister and work on the statement.

Next day, on the flying boat over the Atlantic, Marshall took the tattered drafts and in two hours wrote a message that aroused Churchill's admiration for its clarity and comprehensiveness. He and Roosevelt approved it unchanged. The President held the message for a week before sending it, signed only by himself. Mostly it was a succinct statement of the whole range of Anglo-American global strategy. But almost hidden in the next-to-last paragraph was the fateful sentence: "Under the present plans, there should be a sufficiently large concentration of men and material in the British Isles in the spring of 1944 to permit a full-scale invasion of the continent at that time. . . ."

By now Davies had returned to Washington with a hopeful report on his meeting with Stalin. Things had started awkwardly, he told the President, who listened eagerly and demanded specifics about Stalin and his comments. Stalin had bluntly reiterated that he could accept neither the African invasion nor the air attack on Germany as equivalent to the second front. He was suspicious of the Americans as well as the British. When Davies urged that if he and Roosevelt met face to face they could together win the war and the peace, Stalin replied tersely, "I am not so sure." It took Davies a long time, he told Roosevelt, to penetrate the suspicion and near-hostility. But he had come back bearing a favorable response to Roosevelt's invitation. Stalin was willing to confer with the President in Fairbanks in July or August.

Roosevelt was elated, but he was apprehensive, too. He had told Stalin about the postponement of cross-channel plans only after Davies had returned. What would Stalin say now? He had not long to wait. "Thank you for the information," Stalin wrote on June 11, in reply to the Roosevelt-Churchill-Marshall message. He then listed item by item all the Anglo-American promises of a second front in 1943. Need he speak of the disheartening impression that this fresh postponement of the second front would produce both among the people and among the Army? The Soviet government could not align itself with this decision—which had been adopted without its participation. Stalin said nothing about the plan to meet in Fairbanks.

Roosevelt now faced a crisis in Soviet-American relations not only over the second front, but also over Poland. Stalin had always been cold toward the Polish government-in-exile in London, headed by General Wladyslaw Sikorski, whom the Kremlin viewed as a bourgeois moderate surrounded by reactionaries and militarists. The Poles had repeatedly appealed to the President on the issue of the 1939 Polish-Soviet boundaries, established when the Russians and the Germans carved up Poland, and on Soviet treatment of Polish nationalists. The President, eager to promote unity within the United Nations camp but always sensitive to the big Polish voting groups at home, had tried to conciliate the London Poles while evading the central issue. On one point he was insistent: there must be no discussion of the Polish-Soviet boundary issue until a later time.

Relations between the Kremlin and the Polish government deteriorated during early 1943 and collapsed in April, with a big assist from the Germans. Goebbels's propagandists suddenly announced that in the Katyn Forest, near Smolensk, there had been found the bodies of thousands of Polish officers shot by the Bolsheviks three years earlier. "Revolting and slanderous fabrications," the Russians charged; the Nazis themselves had committed the monstrous crime. At this point the London Poles, who had always suspected that the Russians were guilty, asked the Red Cross to make an investigation on the spot. Furious over this "collusion" with the Nazis, Moscow broke off relations with Sikorski's government. Stalin so informed Roosevelt.

The President asked Stalin to define his action as a "suspension of conversation" with the Poles rather than a complete severance of diplomatic relations. He doubted that Sikorski had collaborated in any way with the Hitler gangsters but granted that the London Poles had erred in appealing to the Red Cross. "Incidentally," he reminded Stalin, "I have several million Poles in the United States. . . ."

Stalin was unmoved. By now he was seething at his allies. His grievances were many and painful. They had broken off the convoys. They had got bogged down in Africa and let the Red Army take the brunt of the winter fighting. They had never accepted the Polish-Soviet frontier of 1939. They had not broken with Finland. The Soviet government, he felt, had made concession after concession, gesture after gesture. Had he not responded to

Anglo-American wishes in dissolving the Comintern, even though he had sworn on Lenin's tomb never to abandon the cause—Lenin's cause—of world revolution?

And still no second front. To Stalin this was not a question of strategy alone. The blood of his people was at stake. Hundreds of thousands of Russians would perish because the Anglo-Americans would invade Europe in 1944 instead of 1943 or 1942. Millions of civilians would be left that much longer to suffer and die under the Hitlerites. Roosevelt worried about his Poles, but Stalin, too, had a kind of public opinion to consider. The bereaved Soviet families, the millions under Nazi rule, the maimed soldiers—what would they think about Stalin's repeated assurances that the Anglo-Americans were coming? The Marshal—for Stalin had assumed that title during the commemoration of Stalingrad—must have reflected on the seeming obtuseness of the Anglo-Americans about the Soviet need for security on the western borders. For centuries Germans, Poles, Swedes, and others had pillaged their way eastward into Russia across the open plains. From the very start of the war—indeed, during the most desperate weeks in late 1941—Stalin had forthrightly insisted on a western border that would give his nation security. Roosevelt had not responded. In short, the Anglo-Americans would not provide real collective security through a United Nations second front, but neither would they support his efforts to gain security through unilateral action. Were the British hoping that Russians and Germans would exhaust themselves in mortal combat? Was that why they had been so deceitful about when the second front would come? Were they trying to help Russia just enough to keep it in the war, but not so much as to help that country win it? Did they hope that after the war they could pursue the old imperialistic policy of fencing Russia in? Could they even be plotting a separate peace? As long as they delayed the second front they could use it as a threat against Hitler, or as a way of bargaining with him—or his generals—for not attacking. All these dark suspicions must have smoldered in Stalin's conspiratorial mind. He ordered Maisky home from London and Litvinov from Washington. And he cabled to Roosevelt that he could not meet with him.

Twenty years after the end of World War II, historians would hotly debate the questions how and when the Cold War began. Did its origins lie in British and Russian colonial rivalry in the nineteenth century? In Pan-Slavism? In Marxist or liberal ideology? In the Russian Revolution or the Allied counterrevolution? In capitalist neoimperialism? In fascist aggression? In the Nazi-Soviet Pact? In the illusions or broken promises of Yalta? Or in postwar developments?

Most of these forces or episodes doubtless had some part, but perhaps the most determining single factor was the gap between promise and reality that widened steadily during 1942 and 1943. Imperialism, nationalism, revolution, ideology—these are long-standing forces in an unstable world, and can be calculated in advance by practical men. But the striking fact about the Allied postponement of the second front, and about Soviet policy toward Poland, was the contrast between this kind of *Realpolitik* and the promises, pronouncements, and ideals of the United Nations. For a brief shining moment during World War II democratic and Communist nations were united in a euphoria of hope and idealism about how people might live in brotherhood, with common goals, sacrifices, and triumphs. But behind the façade of unity statesmen were pursuing *Realpolitik* and national interest. The resulting cynicism was the breeding ground of postwar disillusion and disunity. The second-front delay far more than any other factor aroused Soviet anger and cynicism. If the Anglo-Americans were planning to land in France in the event that Germany was winning, or in the event that Russia was winning (Operation SLEDGEHAMMER), was not this evidence that the West, whatever its protestations, was following a strategy of letting Russia and Germany bleed each other to death? By mid-1943 the grand coalition was foundering in a welter of broken promises and crushed expectations.

THE KING'S FIRST MINISTER

Nowhere in the world of 1943 did the gap between fact and expectation open so wide and ominously as in China. Nowhere were military reality and Roosevelt's hopes in greater disjunction.

Chiang's problem was almost a caricature of Stalin's. The Chinese, too, awaited a long-promised front—a second or third or fourth front. They, too, felt isolated from the Anglo-Americans, starved for supplies, robbed by Atlantic and Mediterranean needs, put off by promises and excuses, exploited for their vast manpower. Otherwise the Chinese scene was far more somber than the Soviet. Chiang's three hundred divisions still held a sagging front against the Japanese. Prices were still soaring as printing presses turned out billions of fapi; the American loan seemed to have sunk without trace. The Communists, steadily consolidating their northern sectors, offered the peasants just what the Kuomintang could not: stern and demanding but honest village authority; campaigns against landlords, usurers, and other bourgeois devils; participation in local government, collectives, and militias; an ideology of equality, democracy, and freedom. By mid-1943 the Communists controlled 150,000 square miles and about fifty million people.

Roosevelt clung to his high hopes for China's wartime success and postwar greatness even as he stood by his priorities of Europe first, Russia second, and China third. He also knew that aiding China was popular at home. He felt, too, that "China really likes us" and he wanted to sustain the reservoir of good will. He expected China to be a great power after the war and he wanted its friendship. He was proud of his country's record in China and of his own old-time family connections, though he himself had never been there or in any part of Asia. Hopkins said later: "The United States, through the espousal of the 'Open Door Policy,' has an absolutely clean record in China over the years. We must keep it so."

Early in 1943 the President struck a blow for Chinese friendship—a blow that did not cost a single gun or bomber. On February 1 he asked the Senate to ratify a treaty surrendering extraterritorial rights in China. For decades foreigners had resided or done business in China under their own laws and courts, backed by their own gunboats and garrisons, all exempt from Chinese law and taxation. Within eleven days the Senate ratified the treaty and ended an arrangement that was humiliating to the Chinese and embarrassing to wartime America. The British government took similar steps. By their action, declared Chiang, "our Allies have declared their Pacific war aim to sustain the rule of human decency and human right. . . ." Later in the year Roosevelt asked Congress to repeal the Chinese exclusion laws, which had harshly discriminated against Chinese immigration. "Nations, like individuals, make mistakes," the President told Congress. "We must be big enough to acknowledge our mistakes of the past and to correct them." Again the legislators acted quickly and favorably.

Roosevelt's hopes for China were matched by fears. As the Nationalist armies fell back, rumors drifted out of Chungking of a possible separate peace with Japan. Americans in China worried about reports of a considerable trade going back and forth across the Chinese-Japanese lines. Stilwell suspected that Chiang would never pull out and was only bluffing. Roosevelt was not so sure.

Certainly the military situation by early 1943 gave little cause for optimism. Stilwell deplored the rosy picture back home of China's effort. Its army actually was in desperate condition, he reported to Marshall, "underfed, unpaid, untrained, neglected, and rotten with corruption." Still, the hard-bitten General had ambitious military plans for the spring of 1943. He proposed an Allied effort to recapture key areas of Burma and reopen communications from Rangoon to Kunming. British and Chinese forces in India would attack over mountain land from the west, Allied naval forces from the Bay of Bengal to the south. Stilwell would then send thousands of tons of supplies up the Burma Road into Kunming; he would equip and modernize the Chinese armies; he would launch a new offensive to open a seaport in South China or Indochina, thereby gaining further war supply. Thus he would break the siege of China.

Stilwell had planned boldly against the enemy; his troubles lay with his friends and associates. Roosevelt was all for the plan in principle, but he was still giving top strategic priority to Europe, and Churchill was cool to any plan that would drain naval and ground strength from the Mediterranean. Chiang would support the plan only if the Anglo-Americans backed it heavily and soon; otherwise he seemed more interested in it for bargaining purposes. Stilwell's particular nemesis was his fellow general Claire Chennault, Chiang's air adviser and commander of the air force that was still doing valiant work against the Japanese. Chennault had all the self-confidence of the American airman. He assured the President that with 105 fighters, thirty medium bombers, and twelve heavy bombers he could destroy the Japanese Air Force and accomplish the downfall of Japan. Stilwell regarded this plan with a groundman's skepticism, but Chiang favored it as a way of avoiding a huge ground-power commitment he feared he could not deliver.

As usual Roosevelt was caught among the contending forces. Stimson and Marshall strongly supported Stilwell; by the eve of 1943 Chiang was pressing for the Chennault plan and for at least the postponement of the Burma operation. In Congress a platoon of Senators continued to urge more help for China.

At this point the slim, elegant figure of Madame Chiang Kai-shek entered the scene. She had flown to the United States in the fall, protesting to Hopkins on arrival that she had come only for medical treatment but making clear in the same breath that she opposed Europe First, disesteemed Stilwell, liked Chennault, and was suspicious of the Anglos if not of the Americans. By February 1943 she was recovered and in Washington, where she talked with Roosevelt for hours, discreetly lobbied with aides and officials, won a standing ovation from the Senate and shouts of approval from the House. Presented to 172 reporters by Roosevelt with the air of a benevolent uncle, she beguiled the press even as she subtly urged more help for China.

She was an appealing figure in her long black dress, tiny, open-toed pumps, and minute splashes of jade and sequin. She knew how to mix gentle flattery with high strategy. She told Stimson that he had beautiful hands, putting the old man on his guard. Roosevelt was less resistant. He liked to tell friends—in a jocular way but with what Frances Perkins felt was more than a shade of pleasure—how he had asked Madame her impressions of Wendell Willkie in China.

"Oh, he is very charming," she answered.

"Ah, yes, but what did you *really* think?"

"Well, Mr. President, he is an adolescent, after all."

The President could not resist the opening.

"Well, Madame Chiang, so you think Wendell Willkie is an adolescent—what do you think I am?"

"Ah, Mr. President, you are sophisticated."

Madame's visit was perfectly timed, for in late February Roosevelt was facing a crucial choice between the Stimson-Marshall-Stilwell plan for Burma and the Chiang-Chennault plan for air attack. The President, on the advice of Hopkins and Currie, chose the latter. Once again the personal factor weighed heavily in the scales. Roosevelt knew that Stilwell hated Chiang, though even the President could hardly know the extent of the General's contempt for the Generalissimo, which went to the point of referring to him privately as "Peanut." He felt that Stilwell was taking exactly the wrong approach to Chiang.

"All of us must remember," Roosevelt told Marshall, "that the Generalissimo came up the hard way to become the undisputed leader of four hundred million people—an enormously difficult job to attain any kind of unity from a diverse group of all kinds of leaders—military men, educators, scientists, public health people, engineers, all of them struggling for power and mastery, local or national, and to create in a very short time throughout China what it took us a couple of centuries to attain.

"Besides that the Generalissimo finds it necessary to maintain his position of supremacy. You and I would do the same thing under the circumstances. He is the Chief Executive as well as the Commander-in-Chief, and one cannot speak sternly to a man like that or exact commitments from him the way we might do from the Sultan of Morocco." Roosevelt must have sensed that he was overriding the weight of army opinion in stressing in this letter that priority must be given to Chennault's efforts, for he concluded:

"Just between ourselves, if I had not considered the European and African fields of action in their broadest geographic sense, you and I know we would not be in North Africa today—in fact, we would not have landed either in Africa or in Europe!"

Marshall warned his chief that the Chennault tactic was risky. Just as soon as the air assault began to hurt the Japanese, they would attack the air bases and thus there would be a ground battle anyway. But the President wanted to give Chennault a clear chance. He was much impressed by the airman's proposed strategy.

He wanted to respond to Chiang and to Madame. Above all, his strategy of Europe First would not allow much war aid to China in any event, and an attack by air might bring victory cheaply.

The President's disapproval of Stilwell's battle tactics reflected a fundamental difference between the Commander in Chief and the General. Despite his sympathies for the Chinese people, especially the peasants and soldiers, Stilwell advocated a hard-boiled, *quid pro quo* approach to the Kuomintang. Bargaining, pressuring, prodding were the only tactics to use with Chungking. "For everything we do *for* him"—Chiang—"we should exact a commitment *from* him," he wrote to Marshall. If "Peanut" threatened to make a separate peace, call his bluff.

Roosevelt could not allow himself the simplicity of one set tactic. He was following his usual multichanneled approach to a number of goals. He wanted to keep China in the war. He wanted Chiang to cultivate political and economic democracy. He wanted to prepare China for a major postwar role, so that it would become a member of the highest council of world organization and help rally Asians to the new world partnership. He wanted the good will of the Chinese people. And despite his Europe First priority, he wanted to win as quickly as possible in Asia.

Above all, Roosevelt saw China as the kingpin in an Asiatic structure of newly independent and self-governing nations and hence as the supreme example and test of his strategy of freedom. On few points had he been more consistent during the past twenty-five years than on the evil of colonialism. Something of an imperialist in Wilsonian days, he had shifted in the mid-1920's to a more generous and less interventionist policy toward Latin America. As President he had shaped and articulated the Good Neighbor policy, asked Congress to grant Puerto Rico the greatest possible measure of self-government, and advocated legislation that finally became the Philippine Independence Act of 1934.

The American record in the Philippines seemed to Roosevelt, indeed, as proof of his and his nation's commitment to freedom for all peoples. In a radio talk on the seventh anniversary, Novem-15, 1942, of the establishment of the Philippine Commonwealth government, he reminded Americans of the more than thirty years of United States sovereignty, the granting of more and more local self-government, the establishment of a commonwealth with its own constitution, and the plan under way at the time of Pearl Harbor for complete independence in 1946.

"I like to think that the history of the Philippine Islands in the last 44 years provides in a very real sense a pattern for the future . . . a pattern of a global civilization which recognizes no limitations of religion, or of creed, or of race." Roosevelt was surprised that the columnists did not make more of the obvious implications of this for his allies. He lost few opportunities to criticize colonial practices. He told reporters after Casablanca that he had seen different types of colonization in West Africa. "It hasn't been good."

And now, after years of Japanese occupation, the overwhelming number of Filipinos were remaining loyal to the American idea of freedom. Tokyo maintained a strenuous propaganda effort. Quezon warned Stimson that Premier Tojo had visited the Philippines three times, had taken large delegations of Filipinos to Japan, and was offering complete independence. The OWI, working in close collaboration with the Philippine Commonwealth offices in Washington, kept up a counterpropaganda effort, with heavy emphasis on the certainty of Allied victory and hence of liberation and full self-government.

The President viewed the French record in Indochina as an utter contrast with the American record in the Philippines. To him, Indochina was Western colonialism of the worst sort. During 1943 his general anticolonial feeling came to a focus on this strategic area; nor could he forget that this area had served as a crucial issue between Tokyo and Washington in 1941, and as a staging area for Japanese aggression. Again and again Roosevelt made clear that he opposed the return of Indochina to French rule after the war, that he preferred some kind of trusteeship under the United Nations. It was rumored that Roosevelt had a family feeling about Indochina, too—that his hatred for the French there arose from the fact that his maternal grandfather, Warren Delano, had lost a good deal of money in 1867 in Saigon real estate. The truth was simpler. Roosevelt was convinced that Westerners in general and the French in particular had misgoverned their Asian and African colonies. The Indochinese had been so flagrantly downtrodden, Elliott Roosevelt remembered his father saying at Casablanca, that the natives felt that even Japanese rule would be better.

It was one thing for Roosevelt to press his views on the French, who, with the Germans occupying the homeland and the Japanese ruling Indochina, were hardly in a position to resist. It was something else to challenge John Bull himself in the person of Winston Churchill. In the fall of 1942, in response to a demand from Willkie that the United States should take a strong stand against imperialism everywhere, Roosevelt had told his press conference that the Atlantic Charter applied to all humanity. Four days later Churchill had declared, in a speech to the Lord Mayor's dinner, "I have not become the King's First Minister in order to preside over the liquidation of the British Empire."

India was still the great issue. That ancient land still served in

1943 as the acid test of Roosevelt's long-range strategy of freedom for "all humanity" in relation to his immediate need to run a coalition war with his Western allies in Europe. In the wake of the turmoil of 1942 Roosevelt sent his old friend, and Rome hand, William Phillips to India as his personal representative. Arriving in New Delhi in January 1943 with an open mind about the many factions and views in India, Phillips soon grew anxious about the situation and disenchanted with the rigidity of the British Viceroy, the Marquess of Linlithgow, and his government. Week after week Phillips dispatched his gloomy reports to Washington, often writing to Roosevelt directly and at length. Gandhi, in detention, was about to conduct a perilous fast. Nehru and tens of thousands of other Congress party leaders were in jail. Indians had become contemptuous of British promises. The Viceroy, who seemed to be following London's directions to the letter, was unyielding. Behind the emotional solidarity arising from anti-British feeling the Indians were sorely divided, race by race, region by region, class by class. The main cement was Gandhi, who, Phillips wrote to the President, was the "god whom people worship," though a wholly impractical one. Fearing that the Mahatma would die, amid eruptions of terrible violence, Phillips tried to visit him and to indicate American concern with the Indian situation. The Viceroy, a veritable caricature of the Old Tory, objected.

Most alarming was Phillips's report of the rapid decline of Indian faith in Roosevelt, the United States, the Atlantic Charter, the Western idea of freedom itself. He had found on arrival a strong popular feeling that the President of the United States alone could bring influence to bear on the British. By April Phillips was reporting that Indians were coming more and more to disbelieve in the American gospel of freedom for oppressed peoples. The United States was losing its chance to capture the sympathy and allegiance of the Indian people. Not only the conduct of the war but also "our future relations with colored races" were involved. Not only Indians but also other peoples of Asia were coming to regard this war as one simply between fascist and imperialist powers. Could not the President induce the British to make some kind of gesture?

The President could not, or at least would not. The actual issue was a small one—whether Washington would support Phillips in his request for the Viceroy's permission to see Gandhi following his fast, or whether Phillips must ask on his own. The State Department refused such support, so Phillips asked for himself, and the Viceroy turned him down. At the end of April Phillips left for Washington "for consultation"; it was the end of his mission to India.

Two weeks later he talked with Roosevelt. He wanted to pour out his story of a hostile or indifferent India in the future, the lassitude and despair that were gripping the subcontinent, America's right to a voice in Indian affairs in the light of its commitments of men and supplies. He found the President in one of his talkative moods; he felt that he had not got his message through. Roosevelt would not budge. He had tried to pressure Churchill on India the year before and failed. Whatever his private dismay, he would not, in Hull's words, jeopardize the unity of command he and the Prime Minister had established in Europe.

Roosevelt carried this policy to tragic lengths later in 1943. A cyclone and three tidal waves had devastated western Bengal, ruining crops and causing plant disease. By mid-1943 hundreds of thousands of Bengalese were starving; the final toll ran to at least two million—three times the total number of Anglo-American military deaths in World War II. In August 1943 Calcutta officials cabled to Roosevelt desperately begging for cereals and milk powder. They received no reply. In September the President of the India League of America wired to the President asking for help for the famine and for the release of Gandhi, who had survived his fast; the appeal was referred to the State Department.

For a brief moment in mid-war the two Atlantic powers would be able to allocate continents, juggle with whole peoples, grant or renege on the Four Freedoms. But even during 1943 there were ominous indications of stupendous social and economic forces on the rise. Reports were trickling in from intelligence agencies, from newspaper correspondents, including the brilliant Theodore White of the *Time* bureau in Chungking, from famous writers, including Pearl Buck and Agnes Smedley, of the dedication and tenacity of the Chinese Communists, as contrasted with the increasing corruption and lethargy of the Kuomintang. In Indochina, Burma, Indonesia, and other colonial areas nationalist feeling was intensifying not only against the Japanese but also against Western colonialism. Throughout Asia Communist and nationalist forces were glimpsing a supreme opportunity to take over the leadership of the long-simmering rebellion against imperialism and colonialism. These forces, too, had their strategy of freedom.

ROOSEVELT AS PROPAGANDIST

The President's political strategy was soon to face a hard test in Italy. At Casablanca, Roosevelt and Churchill had approved their soldiers' plan to attack Sicily as soon as forces could be deployed after the conquest of North Africa. They hoped that the fall of this island just off the toe of Italy would begin to topple Mussolini's regime. The plan was almost as audacious as TORCH; and the commanders and planners could not even devote full time to fashioning it, since many of them were still engaged in Tunisia. Assault forces had to be gathered from distant areas, including the United States. For the first time a big air-borne operation was planned. Once again the landing-craft shortage complicated planning, but a windfall of LST's and of "ducks," load-carrying amphibious vehicles, made possible a concentrated assault on the southeastern corner of the Sicilian triangle.

On July 10, 1943 Patton's Seventh Army and Montgomery's Eighth Army landed under heavy air protection along the eastern and southeastern plains and beaches of Sicily. The weather was atrocious; paratroopers were blown far from their targets, landing all over southeastern Sicily or falling into the sea. Patton's troops fanned out into the western part of the island toward Marsala and Palermo and then cut back to the east along the northern coast, while the British pushed north toward Mount Etna. The Wehrmacht resisted with its usual resourcefulness, but the invaders, enjoying heavy air superiority and with supporting gunfire from the sea, kept their enemy off balance. Naval gunners were even able to put German tanks under direct fire. Panzer units made a last stand along the saw-toothed ridge shouldering Mount Etna; then the remaining German and Italian forces began a skillful retreat to the mainland across the Strait of Messina. Sicily fell in thirty-eight days, at the cost of 20,000 Allied combat casualties. The Germans lost 12,000 dead and captured; the Italians had 147,000 casualties, mainly prisoners.

The climactic events in the Mediterranean during mid-1943 outshone developments in South Asia and the Pacific. After the seizure of Guadalcanal, MacArthur's troops painfully worked their way up the long ladder of the Solomon Islands that pointed distantly but directly at Japan. In close battles in the gulfs and bays American naval losses were heavy as well as the enemy's. By early fall combined army, naval, air, and Marine operations had secured the central Solomons—though some enemy outposts were simply bypassed—and were moving on Bougainville and the northern Solomons. Five hundred miles west of these steppingstones, American, Australian, and New Zealand troops slowly leapfrogged up the eastern coast of New Guinea toward the Japanese bastion of Rabaul. Capturing or outflanking enemy bases, finding the right mix of amphibious forces, moving inland into mountains and jungles without getting cut off or bogged down—these and other moves took all MacArthur's resourcefulness. By fall his troops were halfway along New Guinea's long northern coast and were threatening to outflank Rabaul.

In Burma fighting ebbed and flowed in small fitful skirmishes, and in the North Pacific, after seizing Attu in a bleak and bitter encounter, the Americans were embarrassed to mount an elaborate invasion of Kiska and find—nothing. The Pacific generally in 1943 was reflecting its lower priority, and it was in Europe that Axis solidarity cracked first.

At Shangri-La, on a bright Sunday afternoon, July 25, the President was working with Rosenman and Sherwood on a fireside chat when Early phoned from the White House to report that he had just heard a news flash on the radio saying Mussolini had resigned. The President seemed surprised but a bit skeptical. His aides eagerly tried to get confirmation—but the officials they talked to were trying to get confirmation from *them.* The President was relaxed. "Oh, we'll find out about it later." The three men then had a leisurely dinner and drove back to Washington. Sherwood marveled that during this whole five-hour period the White House lacked the means of knowing whether an Axis leader had fallen. Shortly, the news was confirmed; much later, the White House learned the details.

The loss of Africa—once the pride of his vaunted new Roman Empire—had brought the Duce near the end of his string. Then came the invasion of Sicily and a summons by Hitler north to a conference. They met in Feltre, in a villa that seemed to the tormented Duce like a crossword puzzle frozen into a house. While Mussolini sat passively in a big armchair Hitler upbraided the Italians for their cowardice and ineptitude in Sicily. But he promised reinforcements and braced Mussolini for a final stand; the voice of history, he said, still beckoned them.

Back in Rome, now under Allied bombing attacks, Mussolini seemed to become more paralyzed as his soldiers retreated and surrendered in Sicily. Disaffection was spreading around him. Members of the Grand Council, which had been moribund for years, demanded a meeting to consider the crisis. This was set for the afternoon of July 24, at the Palazzo Venezia. Expecting trouble, some members arrived at the meeting with concealed weapons and hand grenades, but there was nothing to fear. Mussolini was now a broken man. Long scornful of parliamentary talk and majority rule, he had to sit through six hours of oratory and denunciation, culminating in a vote of 19 to 8 against him. Next afternoon King Victor Emmanuel III received the Duce, dismissed him from office, saw him out the door onto the front steps, where the onetime dictator, unresisting, was whisked into an ambulance and driven off to confinement in a military-police barracks.

The first crack in the Axis had come, Roosevelt exulted. But the hour of triumph plunged him back into political dilemmas.

By chance the Office of War Information had just put out a broadcast quoting a commentator who referred to Victor Emmanuel as that "moronic little king." Next morning Roosevelt saw the comment in the New York *Times* and the following day told reporters that "it ought never to have been done." In his fireside chat he stood staunchly with unconditional surrender. "We will have no truck with Fascism in any way, in any shape," he said. "We will permit no vestige of fascism to remain." But it became evident that the King was staying on his throne and that he was asking Marshal Pietro Badoglio, the Duce's former chief of the Comando Supremo, to become Prime Minister.

Victor Emmanuel, Mussolini's accomplice, to go on as king? Badoglio, the ravisher of Ethiopia, to succeed the Duce? Once again American liberals burst into indignation. Was this a war against fascism, or just against aggression? Badoglio today—and Goering or Goebbels tomorrow? Was the reactionary State Department still running American war strategy? Would Roosevelt deal with a gang of monarchists, clerics, and reactionaries? For such questions Roosevelt was ready at a press conference. The issue was about as meaningful, he said, as the old argument as to which came first, the chicken or the egg.

"When a victorious army goes into a country, there are two essential conditions that they want to meet, in the first instance. The first is the end of armed opposition. The second is when that armed opposition comes to an end to avoid anarchy. In a country that gets into a state of anarchy, it is a pretty difficult thing to deal with, because it would take an awful lot of troops.

"I don't care with whom we deal in Italy, so long as it isn't a definite member of the Fascist Government, as long as they get them to lay down their arms, and so long as we don't have anarchy. Now he may be a King, or a present Prime Minister, or a Mayor of a town or a village. . . .

"You will also remember that in the Atlantic Charter, something was said about self-determination. That is a long-range thing. You can't get self-determination in the first week that they lay down their arms. In other words, common sense. . . ."

The controversy raged on. Roosevelt's political strategy in 1943 was facing two problems. One was the sheer complexity and diffusion of his information and propaganda agencies. Rather than set up a central organization, he had followed his usual policy of establishing parallel agencies with fuzzy but generally overlapping jurisdictions. The military services had psychological-war functions. Robert Sherwood ran the Foreign Information Service under William Donovan, who was Co-ordinator of Information. Roosevelt's old friend Librarian of Congress Archibald MacLeish directed the Office of Facts and Figures. Nelson Rockefeller, Coordinator of Inter-American Affairs, ran his agency, including propaganda, separately from the other offices and insisted on reporting directly to the President. These men, and the journalists, public-relations men, psychological-war experts, and assorted intellectuals they recruited, made up a sparkling array of talent, but they were prone to follow their own bent, compete for funds, and emphasize day-to-day targets of opportunity rather than long-range political warfare.

In mid-1942 Roosevelt had established the Office of War Information under the gifted journalist and radio commentator Elmer Davis, and early in the next year, after the OWI and the Office of Strategic Services disagreed on psychological-warfare policy, the President decided that except for Latin-American operations all domestic and foreign information and propaganda programs should be under OWI. Sherwood later was put in charge of the Overseas Branch of OWI. The Domestic Branch, under a succession of harried directors, ran into heavy congressional opposition. Inflamed by OWI pamphets—especially by an anti-inflation tract, a discussion of Negroes and the war, and a heroic cartoon history of the Commander in Chief—the House of Representatives abolished the Domestic Branch outright and then grudgingly allowed the Senate to save it. Under Davis's gentle direction, the OWI gave more unity to the propaganda effort, but fissures and weaknesses remained. Davis felt that his relations with the President were personally cordial but institutionally unsatisfactory. He even contemplated resigning during the furore over Badoglio. Yet when the smoke cleared away it was evident that the cause of that incident was a lack of understanding of the President's strategy of political warfare.

That was the second main source of trouble in the nation's political war effort. Roosevelt, to be sure, with his gift for political communication, gave a marvelous lift and verve to the propaganda effort; a British expert, Richard Crossman, viewed his and Churchill's speeches as by far the best directives for the propaganda operatives. The problem was the gap between the lofty principles and the day-to-day situations and opportunities. While many political warriors approved of unconditional surrender as an expression of United Nations' determination and unity, for example, they found it unduly constricting in practice. Thus while they were hammering home the importance of complete capitulation, Allied soldiers in fact were making concessions—as in Eisenhower's early terms for an Italian armistice—that greatly eased the stern doctrine.

To undermine and destroy the morale of the population in enemy countries; to kindle hope of liberation and spur resistance in enemy-occupied countries; to win support from the people and thus influence the leadership in neutral countries; to counter enemy attempts to divide the United Nations; to foster understanding of American ideals and practices in Allied countries—these were the major aims of the administration's political warfare. Its message was spread by radio, films, leaflets, posters, press, and all possible media. The enemy was equally active, and far more experienced. Hitler had won power as a master propagandist. He had understood the close link between propaganda and organization. He had concluded that most people were "feminine in nature" and motivated more by feelings than by logic; he had stressed simplicity in propaganda "because the people think primitively"; he did not believe, Z. A. B. Zeman says, "as Jefferson had, that they consisted of individuals capable of directing their own political destinies. . . ." And in Goebbels he had a brilliant and tireless spokesman.

For the Nazi propagandists Roosevelt and his rich, bloated nation were inviting targets. Students at the Hochschule für Politik, a training school for propagandists, had been drilled in the early months of the war on Roosevelt's skill in using the radio and press conferences, his assumption of Woodrow Wilson's role, his moralistic prejudices, his naïve oversimplifications—and, above all, on his hostility to Germany. Americans were Jeffersonian in principle, according to the students' textbook on Roosevelt and public opinion, but in fact he had surrendered control of the country to lobbies, professional politicians, and the press. "In the United States today they preach Jefferson but practice Hamilton: the former stands for the Bill of Rights, equality and liberty, for confidence in the simple man; the latter stands for perpetuated inequality and systematic government which curbs people in the interest of State and capital." In foreign policy, the students were taught, Americans alternated between pacifism and messianism, moralism and economic imperialism.

The Nazi propaganda barrages in 1943 ranged from the standard line that Jewish-capitalist-Communist forces controlled the American government, to the age-old maneuver of trying to divide the Allied opposition. Thus John Bull was trying to bleed America, while the Yanks were out to grab pieces of the British Empire, and the Reds would try to communize their allies after the war. At the front, German leaflets and loud-speakers worked on the GI's war weariness and homesickness. But through all the Nazi propaganda ran a garish anti-Semitic streak. Thus a German cartoon leaflet headed "The Girl You Left Behind" showed rich war profiteer Sam Levy pawing his private secretary, Joan Hopkins, who really loves Bob, but she doesn't know when Bob will come back from the war—and what's a little kiss among friends?

The job of countering such tactics Roosevelt could leave to the propagandists in the field. As propagandist in chief he was responsible for the ideas that would set the direction for the operatives. At that level the central issue between Roosevelt and Hitler by mid-1943 was the meaning and application of the old Jeffersonian issue of liberty, or, in its more modern and positive connotation, *freedom*. For the most part the two adversaries used a different rhetoric of symbols. Hitler exalted Discipline, Authority, the Fatherland, denounced Bolshevism, Internationalism, Plutocracy, and of course the Jews. Roosevelt would not contend for this ground. But the one symbol that had some intrinsic meaning of its own and that also had some universal acceptance on both sides, and hence was fought over by both sides, was Freedom.

Hitler had once interpreted Freedom as essentially lebensraum for Germans, but he steadily shifted its meaning before and during the war years to the freedom for the masses to enjoy security and the good things of life. Freedom in Britain and America he denounced as freedom for the democracies to exploit the world, and the freedom of plutocrats within the democracies to exploit the masses. "If the British declare that they are fighting for freedom, then the British might have given a wonderful example by granting their own Empire full liberty." The symbol of freedom had become world-wide by mid-war. Churchill addressed Americans as fellow workers in the cause of freedom. Stalin in an order of the day to his soldiers stressed that the war was a war for freedom. "The irony of it is," declared a Japanese English-language broadcast late in 1943, "that American men, American arms, American money, are being employed this very minute to rob the people of Asia of their right to live as free men. . . . Americans, who fought the Civil War to liberate the slaves and who think they are fighting this war to free the enslaved people of the world, must find it painful to reflect upon the sad course over which their president is now taking the country." The word was on the lips of colonial peoples, too, though with a special meaning.

Roosevelt repeatedly assailed Hitler's freedom as not freedom to live but simply as freedom for the Nazis to dominate and enslave the human race. The President, who looked on himself as an expert on public psychology, tried to invest the term with relevance to human problems and actual social conditions. "The essence of our struggle today is that man shall be free," he had said a month before Pearl Harbor. "There can be no real freedom for the common man without enlightened social policies. In the last analysis, they are the stakes for which democracies are today fighting." The President developed this theme strongly during the war. But he had a double handicap in the propaganda battle. His war aims and postwar plans were eloquent but so broadly stated that propagandists were often unable to convert them into bread-and-butter policies meaningful to people of other lands. When the President did translate his general principles into specific proposals and then into actual policies—for example, egalitarian tax proposals—he was frustrated by the congressional conservatism, entrenched lobbies, and organized wealth that the Nazis had pointed to. When he called for freedom for colonial peoples he ran hard into his Tory comrade in arms, Winston Churchill. And enemy propagandists pounced on every gap between Roosevelt's creed and the government's acts.

Nor did they need to look very hard. In the early summer of 1943 Los Angeles mobs spilled through Belvedere, Watts, and other American-Mexican districts searching for "zoot-suiters," beating them, stripping them naked before roaring crowds. A week later a fist fight in a Detroit park triggered an orgy of race violence: Negro and white gangs roamed the streets smashing windows, firing Negro homes, tipping cars, looting stores, seizing guns in pawnshops. State troopers were summoned, bars closed, curfews set. Twenty-three died; over seven hundred were hurt. There were racial outbursts in Newark, Mobile, and elsewhere. A black was dragged from a Florida jail and lynched. Tension was increasing in some of the relocation camps.

Students of psychological warfare stress that propaganda is most effective when tied closely to an affirmative and effective program of action. Some enemy propagandists hoped that ultimately racial unrest and class feeling in America could be turned against Roosevelt personally. Certainly he was their favorite target. He was pictured as a dictator, a maker of false promises, a "paralytic cripple" with a warped brain, a tyrant lusting for world hegemony, a "Don Quixote of the present century living in his dreams." His prewar pledge to keep American boys out of foreign wars was relentlessly emphasized. His lofty words against colonialism were mockingly compared with his failure to influence the Atlantic colonial powers. As 1944 approached, it appeared that Roosevelt's promises and performance would be on trial not only at home but also throughout the world.

THIRTEEN *Coalition: Crisis and Renewal*

FOR Roosevelt 1943 was the year of conferences. He had met with Churchill at Casablanca in January, as well as with Giraud and de Gaulle; with Eden in Washington in March; with Churchill and the Combined Chiefs of Staff in Washington in May. During the next six months the Anglo-Americans met so often, and in so many places, that they conducted a kind of traveling strategy conference: Churchill, Marshall, and Eisenhower in Algiers in late May and early June; Stimson and Churchill in London in July; Roosevelt and Churchill at Hyde Park in mid-August; Roosevelt and Churchill and military and diplomatic staffs in Quebec in late August; Roosevelt, Churchill, and military staffs at the White House in September. Then the meetings broadened into a series of global climaxes: Roosevelt, Churchill, and Chiang Kai-shek in Cairo in late November; Roosevelt, Churchill, and Stalin in Teheran at the end of November; Roosevelt and Churchill in Cairo in early December.

No matter how wide his travels, however, Roosevelt seemed never to lose touch with home—his home at Hyde Park. He wrote to his friend Moses Smith that he was horrified at the cost of a tile or wooden silo and urged him to get a secondhand one, and he sent to his superintendent William Plog some Paraguayan gourd seeds with precise instructions for planting them. He called a vestry meeting for his church and offered to conduct the service himself, as he had done, rather unsuccessfully, he admitted, as senior officer present on board ship. He gave a watch to his grandson Buzzie, as he had years earlier to Buzzie's four uncles, and old family books to Sistie; and he worked on family history.

He thought about broader history, too. He wrote to Archibald MacLeish that plans should be made for histories of the war. They should try, he said, "to capture or recapture the public pulse as it throbs from day to day—the effect on the lives of different types of citizens—the processes of propaganda—the parts played by the newspaper emperors, etc. . . . It is not dry history or the cataloging of books and papers and reports. It is trying to capture a great dream before it dies."

When MacLeish indicated that he would like to leave the librarianship of Congress for war work the President answered that that was a coincidence, because *he* was thinking of the time when he would leave Washington and become a librarian at Hyde Park. "But I have the advantage in that, in addition to fussing over books, letters and prints, I shall have plenty of time to plant and harvest Christmas trees and to write scurrilous articles about SOME PEOPLE I KNOW—for publication, of necessity, after I am dead and gone." The Hyde Park property was about to be designated a national historic site, and the President wrote to Ickes that he did not want it named Franklin D. Roosevelt Home, "because it sounds like a home for discarded politicians!"

Neither his home nor his family was immune to wartime politics. When a Republican committeeman from Kansas attacked the Roosevelt sons for being "coddled" and given assignments remote from combat zones, the President was bitter because Minority Leader Joe Martin failed to make any protest on the floor; but he was happy when the Congressman from his son's Texas district read to the House a letter from Elliott stating that "we, as soldiers, don't care whether or how much he disagrees with the President, but for God's sake let us fight without being stabbed in the back for the sake of politics." Hassett noted one day at Hyde Park that when he mentioned to Roosevelt a clambake at Poughkeepsie's Christ Episcopalian Church, whose rector had voted for Ham Fish the previous November, the President mused, "I never got two votes from the crowd"—but added with a smile, "Well, the oak timbers in the roof of the church were cut on this place."

Old friends were passing. Rudolph Forster, who had taken a job at the White House the day after McKinley's first inauguration, died in the summer of 1943, and Marvin McIntyre, who had worked for Roosevelt over a twenty-five-year stretch, at the end of the year. As usual the President expressed his public sorrow and withheld his private grief. Missy LeHand was seriously ill. Eleanor Roosevelt was off to the four corners of the globe, including Australia, New Zealand, and the South Sea islands. The President had at least two heavy illnesses during the year. He told Churchill that he had picked up "Gambia fever" in "that hell-hole of yours called Bathurst," and after he was laid up again in October he complained gaily—again to Churchill—"It is a nuisenza to have the influenza."

THE MILLS OF THE GODS

"We will have no truck with Fascism in any way, in any shape or manner," the President had proclaimed in his July 28 fireside chat. In fact, things were not so simple. The Badoglio government could still negotiate with Hitler for protection. "The war will continue," Rome announced. The Führer, his divisions poised to take the country over, reacted with his usual fury. "Jodl," he exclaimed, "work out the usual order." Panzer troops were to drive into Rome with their assault guns and "oust the government, the king, and the whole crew." And he would rescue his friend Mussolini. "I'll go right into the Vatican," Hitler declaimed. "Do you think the Vatican embarrasses me? We'll take that over right away." He would get hold of the whole diplomatic corps in there—"that rabble . . . that bunch of swine." For the moment, though, he was content to mobilize his division and poise them on the Alpine passes.

Like Darlan nine months before, Badoglio had some strong cards: the Italian fleet, some loyal divisions, a structure of government. He also had—no small matter to Churchill—74,000 British prisoners of war, whom he could send into Nazi hands in Germany. It was the same old dilemma: the President wanted to establish a clear moral principle in dramatizing Axis defeat, extirpating fascism, clearing the slate, but immediate military necessity outweighed all. So he allowed Churchill to play down unconditional surrender, while he negotiated with Badoglio. His liberal critics were still protesting. Some "contentious people," he warned Churchill, were ready to make a row if the Allies recognized Badoglio or the House of Savoy. They were the same people who had "made such a fuss" over Darlan. Roosevelt still feared anarchy in Italy and the number of Allied troops that would be needed to restore order.

It was precisely Roosevelt's and Churchill's concern about social unrest that worried more thoughtful liberals. "Allied public opinion would make no worse mistake," Count Carlo Sforza wrote in the New York *Times,* "than showing itself afraid of the so-called danger of revolution. This fear was the best ally of Hitler and Mussolini during the many years of Chamberlain's blindness. . . ." Alvarez Del Vayo, veteran Spanish antifascist and editor of the *Nation*'s political-war section, complained about the lack of a clear, democratic, antifascist policy. But Roosevelt was concentrating at the moment on military, not political, policy, on the invasion of Italy and the mounting campaign against Germany.

On August 5 Churchill embarked on the *Queen Mary* for a conference in Quebec. That same day he reported to Roosevelt the first peace feelers from Rome. He also passed on alarming intelligence about Italy. As every vestige of Italian rule was swept away, Italy was turning red overnight. Communist demonstrators had been put down by armed force in the northern cities; the middle class had been obliterated, Churchill reported; nothing stood between the patriots rallying around the King and "rampant Bolshevism." The Germans were ready to take over. In these circumstances the King and Badoglio would have to put up a show of fighting the Allies, but this would be only a pretense. "If we cannot attack Germany immediately through the Balkans, thus causing German withdrawal from Italy, the sooner we land in Italy the better."

While Roosevelt and Churchill were exchanging messages about Italy the Prime Minister and his party—the largest yet, including Mrs. Churchill, their daughter Mary, and a staff of over two hundred—were sailing west. As usual intensive staff planning took place en route. After arriving in Halifax August 9 and checking arrangements in Quebec, where ramps had been specially built for the President on the upper floor of the Citadel, Churchill and his daughter traveled to Hyde Park. Detouring to show Mary Niagara Falls, he told local reporters that he had seen the waterfall thirty years before and the principle of the thing still seemed the same. At Hyde Park, Churchill found the President his usual hospitable self, the weather stifling, and Hopkins ailing and fearing that he had lost favor with his chief. But in two days it seemed like old times again. Soon the party moved north to Quebec for the parley.

Once again Roosevelt's military staffs had tried to prepare as carefully for a conference as had Churchill's. The crucial factor, they knew, was the backing their Commander in Chief would give them. Marshall had confronted Roosevelt on the cross-channel issue with all his moral and military authority. Remembering the apparent decision for ROUNDUP the year before, followed by the diversion to North Africa, the Chief of Staff set himself categorically against further peripheralism. Stimson, just back from London, where he had argued about cross-channel plans with Churchill face to face, took an even firmer line with his chief. "We cannot rationally hope to be able to come to grips with our German enemy under a British commander," he told Roosevelt. The shadows of Passchendaele and Dunkerque hung too heavily over the British. They were giving it only lip service, the Secretary said. They still felt that Germany could be beaten by attrition, but that kind of pinprick warfare would never fool Stalin.

Stimson appealed to Roosevelt's sense of history. "We are facing a difficult year at home with timid and hostile hearts ready to seize and exploit any wavering on the part of our war leadership. A firm resolute leadership, on the other hand, will go far to silence such voices. The American people showed this in the terrible year of 1864, when the firm unfaltering tactics of the Virginia campaign were endorsed by the people of the United States in spite of the hideous losses of the Wilderness, Spottsylvania, and Cold Harbor."

If Roosevelt's spine had to be stiffened for the cross-channel decision, Stimson's and Marshall's pressure did the trick. Faced by a firm and united American stand at Quebec, the British were now ready to make the cross-channel pledge, but they still fought for a bigger effort in Italy, in part, they said, as a way to strengthen preparations for the invasion of France. Even so, Churchill argued against any attack in France unless the Allies had clear ground and air superiority. For days the Combined Chiefs debated strenuously about the right mix of forces for the cross-channel build-up and for Italy, with Roosevelt and Churchill each backing his own chiefs. In the end it was agreed that the main Anglo-American effort would be across the Channel, with a target date of May 1, 1944. The Mediterranean effort would be pressed, too, with the aim of knocking Italy out of the war and seizing the Rome area for air bases. And an invasion of southern France—a project Churchill had long resisted and would never fully accept—was planned in connection with the thrust into the north.

The agony of Italy kept obtruding into the quiet rooms overlooking the parapets of the once-embattled fortress. Badoglio was still transfixed between the growing Nazi power north of Rome and the looming Allied invasion of the Italian toe from Sicily. There was a long hiatus while the opposing forces stayed in balance and Badoglio put out frantic peace feelers in Spain and Portugal. The Allies were insisting on unconditional surrender while hinting at easier arrangements later. It was like a dialogue of sleepwalkers, each the victim of his own hallucinations, two historians concluded later: "In the nightmare of the German occupation, Italy gasped, 'Help, I am not free.' After a long pause, the Allies replied, 'Say Uncle.' "

Essentially Roosevelt had wanted Eisenhower to obtain a simple unconditional surrender formally while indicating favorable treatment later, depending on the extent of Italian assistance to the Allies. The British had preferred that the immediate military settlement be related to long-term political arrangements. At Quebec the President went along with the British approach. But military events were already taking control of diplomacy and negotiation. Before dawn on September 3 the British Eighth Army began to stream across the Strait of Messina and onto the Italian mainland. On the same day Italian representatives, after further tortuous negotiations, signed military terms of surrender in an olive grove near Syracuse. It was certain that announcement of this action would bring quick German retaliation, so General Maxwell Taylor slipped into Rome to arrange with the Italian General Staff for a sudden seizure by air-borne troops of the airfields around Rome. He was too late; the Nazis had arrived first with the most. Taylor's air descent was canceled, but the armistice was announced. Italy had surrendered.

Now events accelerated. The Germans began to encircle Rome; the royal family and Badoglio and his officials escaped to Brindisi; Italian fleet units, heavily bombed by the Nazis, made their way to the sanctuary of Malta. Mussolini, who had been moved to a mountain resort in central Italy, was plucked out of confinement by ninety German parachutists, who carried him off to a triumphant reunion with Hitler. Meantime the Allies had launched their climactic blow against Italy.

On September 9 American and British forces landed on a great crescent of beaches at Salerno, about thirty miles south of Naples. Against fierce but scattered opposition the infantry moved across the narrow plain toward the jagged mountains beyond. On the eve of invasion the troops had heard of Italy's surrender, but the Germans had expertly taken over the defense of the area, so the opposition was stiffer than had been expected. Field Marshal Albert Kesselring was relieved that the Allies had not landed closer to Rome; as it was, the invasion was so far south that he was able to clamp a firm grip on the capital area. But Salerno was also far enough south to enable General Mark Clark's Fifth Army to enjoy heavy air cover and to link up with Montgomery's Eighth Army working its way from Taranto and the instep of the Italian boot.

Four days after the landing at Salerno the Germans mustered enough combat power to launch major thrusts against Allied positions and to try to cut in between the landing forces. They almost succeeded. American artillerymen and antitank units, supported by naval gunfire, bore the brunt of the attack, and despite one precipitous retreat the defenders held on to their beachhead. A week after D day patrols from the Fifth Army and the Eighth Army joined hands.

Roosevelt and Churchill had been together at Hyde Park when the battle began. The Prime Minister was ill at ease because he was reminding himself of battles lost over the centuries when generals had failed to press ahead vigorously. He dispatched reminders to the men in the field, while Roosevelt left matters in the hands of Eisenhower and his subordinates. After the fortunes of battle turned, Churchill congratulated Eisenhower: "As the Duke of Wellington said at the Battle of Waterloo, 'It was a damned close-run thing.'" Stalin telegraphed to Roosevelt and Churchill that the landing in the Naples area would considerably facilitate the Red Army's operations on the Soviet-German front. In Italy, Allied soldiers regrouped and began pursuing the enemy north through the narrow defiles between Salerno and Naples. The Germans conducted a slow, hurtful retreat, but on October 1 Allied forces seized Naples.

The successful invasion of Italy opened new military and political opportunities for the President; it also brought military and political dilemmas. Relations with Iberians, French, Yugoslavs, Greeks, Turks, and the peoples along the southern rim of the inland sea were affected by the advances of Allied soldiers up the boot of Italy. Much of Roosevelt's political effort in the months ahead was aimed at enlisting the active support, or at least the passive co-operation, of the Mediterranean nations—nations steeped in age-old enmities and suspicions toward one another and toward the great powers.

On the Mediterranean also lay Palestine, a haven and a dilemma. Of all the opportunities now before Roosevelt the most hopeful and the most tragic was the fate of Europe's Jews. Tens of thousands of them survived perilously in Nazi-occupied Europe, and their escape lines lay mainly across the Mediterranean. During 1942 reports had trickled into the White House of a Nazi decision so appalling that administration officials could not believe them and asked representatives abroad to check and verify. The reports were of Hitler's order for the "final solution" of the racial problem through the wholesale rounding up and systematic murder of all the Jews under Nazi control. The reports were true.

The President had, of course, been concerned about the plight of the Jews ever since Hitler took power in 1933. During the war he had repeatedly attacked the Nazis for their crimes and warned that the guilty, high and low, would be punished. Late in 1942 he announced the plan of the United Nations to establish a commission to investigate war crimes. It was clear, however, that the deterrent effect of these warnings would be small. Tens of thousands of Jews were being murdered every month. Rising popular concern in both Britain and America was demanding quick action. In December 1942 Rabbi Stephen S. Wise, head of the American Jewish Congress, wrote to the President.

"Dear Boss, I do not wish to add an atom to the awful burden which you are bearing with magic and, as I believe, heaven-inspired strength at this time. But you do know that the most overwhelming disaster of Jewish history has befallen Jews in the form of the Hitler mass-massacres." At least two million civilian Jews had already been slain, Wise said. He asked the President to meet with Jewish leaders. At that meeting, just a year after Pearl Harbor, Roosevelt was handed a twenty-page document on the Nazi "Blue Print for Extermination," and he assured the group that the United States would try to save those who might yet be saved and to end the crimes. "The mills of the gods grind slowly," he said. "But they grind exceedingly small."

The wheels not only of justice but also of the Roosevelt administration ground small and slow throughout 1943, to the disbelief and despair of Jewish and other leaders. Some pleaded that the Allies negotiate directly with the Axis powers for the release of Jews, others that the Allies at least relax the blockade to allow the shipment of food and medicines to people in concentration camps and that they persuade the neutral nations to open their frontiers to escaping Jews. The administration was urged to suspend immigration quotas to quicken the flow of refugees. During early 1943 there seemed to be much action on Washington's part, or at least motion; indeed, London and Washington competed for public recognition of their concern for the Jews. But actually the administration moved with wooden legs. At a conference on refugees held in Bermuda in April, American and British delegations agreed on a few expedients and palliatives, but the conference was debarred from pledging funds, committing ships for the transportation of refugees, or promising changes in immigration laws. Reviewing the work of the conference in early May, the President agreed to share with Britain the cost of financing the movement of specific numbers of persons and he approved the setting up in North Africa of temporary depots. But he was emphatically against trying to change immigration laws, he questioned sending large numbers of Jews to North Africa, and he opposed any sweeping promises of relief.

This wariness of the President, rather than his moral indignation, set the pattern of administration policy over the next crucial months. It took the State Department weeks to deal with issues, even to answer letters. And every week lost meant thousands of Jews and others crossed off on Hitler's ghastly calendar of death. In August 1943 the New York *Times* published an "extermination list" detailing, country by country, the 1,700,000 persons who had died from organized murder, the 746,000 who died from starvation or disease. The nation and the administration were shocked, but not into creative action. Roosevelt was helpful in meeting specific situations and spurring emergency rescue efforts, but he seemed unable to face the main problem—the millions of Jewish men, women, and children trapped in the Nazi heartland and headed for the gas chambers.

One reason was the sheer intractability of the problem. Helping to rescue even a few thousand Jews on the rim of the Mediterranean took endless negotiation among local Jewish leaders, the State and Treasury Departments and other United States agencies, neutral nations, relief organizations, and others involved, over money, transportation, relief, housing, Moslem hostility. Getting Congress to modify the immigation laws would probably have been as difficult as Roosevelt anticipated. The fact that so many of the imperiled people abroad and the exhorting leaders at home were Jews made Roosevelt nervous about the reactions of Congress and of some elements among the people. Nor could he, with his heavy military and diplomatic involvement in Moslem Africa, ignore the reverberations there.

But the main reason was Roosevelt's war strategy. The only way to persuade Hitler to relinquish his grip on his victims was by bribing him or by negotiating with him, and Roosevelt flatly opposed this as violating the policy of unconditional surrender. The best way to assist the Jews and other helpless peoples, he believed, was by winning the war as quickly and decisively as possible. Alienating neutrals like Spain, diverting vital shipping from the main task of war supply, arousing false expectations and undue fears, above all, antagonizing Moslems in countries where fighting continued—all that was inconsistent with Roosevelt's single-minded pursuit of military victory.

The same stern priority controlled Roosevelt's approach to "Zion." The President had long taken a cautious but benevolent view of the dream of Palestine as a Jewish homeland, though he felt that the little country was not physically suitable for resettling great numbers of Jews and he flirted with the notion of the Cameroons and later of Paraguay and still later of Portuguese West Africa—Angola—as other havens. By the end of 1942 he was again thinking about the possibilities of Palestine.

"What I think I will do," he told Morgenthau, "is this. First, I would call Palestine a religious country. Then I would leave Jerusalem the way it is and have it run by the Orthodox Greek Catholic Church, the Protestants, and the Jews—have a joint committee run it. . . . I actually would put a barbed wire around Palestine. . . . I would provide land for the Arabs in some other part of the Middle East. . . . Each time we move out an Arab we would bring in another Jewish family. . . . But I don't want to bring in more than they can economically support. . . . Naturally, if there are 90 per cent Jews, the Jews would dominate the government. . . ."

All such thoughts, however, Roosevelt subordinated to war needs, and one great war need of 1943 semed to be peace and stability in the Mid-East. Any time the President touched the issue—even by merely receiving Zionists—he triggered explosive reactions in Egypt or Syria or Saudi Arabia. During 1943 he took steps to get Jewish and Arab leaders to talk with one another, but the War Department was worried about Mid-East repercussions, and at Quebec the President and Churchill decided to postpone any further encouragement of talks between the parties. By fall of 1943 the President was leaning toward a new idea—a trusteeship for Palestine to make it into a real holy land for all three religions, with a Jew, a Christian, and a Moslem as the three trustees. Always confident of his power to persuade on a face-to-face basis, he thought that the ancient, searing enmities of the Middle East could be overcome by negotiation and balm. Meanwhile the Nazi extermination mills ground away.

CAIRO: THE GENERALISSIMO

Reporters had rarely seen the President as wroth as he seemed to be at his press conference of August 21, 1943. He had been asked if he would comment on reports that Stalin had suggested a tripartite conference. No—but he had something else to say, and on the record. A columnist had committed an act of bad faith toward his country; he had damaged the unity of the United Nations and hence the war effort. "I don't hesitate to say that the whole statement from beginning to end was a lie, but there is nothing new in it, because the man is a chronic liar in his columns."

The reporters knew whom and what he meant: Drew Pearson had just written in "Washington Merry-Go-Round" that Cordell Hull "long has been anti-Russian" and had asserted on his radio program that Hull and his chief assistants, "Adolf Berle, Jimmy Dunn, Breckinridge Long, would really like to see Russia bled white—and the Russians know it. . . ." Hull had shown the statements to the President, had labeled them "monstrous and diabolical falsehoods," and had summoned the Soviet Chargé d'Affaires, Andrei A. Gromyko, to his office to repudiate them.

Observers wondered why the administration had felt stung so hard by a seeming pinprick. Pearson was not the first to accuse the administration of trying to let the Russians take the blood bath. The reaction was due mainly to Pearson's timing. By late August 1943, just after Quebec, the President had to confront the fact that his plan for a grand concert of antifascist powers was faltering. Although war supply to Russia had risen sharply during 1943, it was

Why Not Sweep Out?

April 19, 1943, Martin, *PM*, reprinted by courtesy of Field Enterprises, Inc.

attended by numberless grievances and misunderstandings on the Soviet side, and American officials in charge of the long supply lines grumbled that the Soviets were showing little public or private recognition of American efforts. Soviet newspapers kept up a chorus of criticism of their allies' diplomatic and military progress. And neither Churchill nor Roosevelt had yet even met with Chiang Kai-shek.

In the wake of Quebec, Stalin was clearly piqued by one more Roosevelt-Churchill conference deciding matters in his absence. The situation could not be tolerated any longer, he wrote to the President and the Prime Minister late in August. "To date it has been like this: the U.S.A. and Britain reach agreement between themselves while the U.S.S.R. is informed of the agreement between the two Powers as a third party looking passively on." Stalin was referring to negotiations with Italy, but in general he felt shut out of Anglo-American discussions. His complaint was rather baffling, since he had refused to meet with Roosevelt and Churchill earlier. Perhaps at the moment he preferred having a grievance to having a meeting—he could complain that the Russians were taking the brunt of the fighting but were treated as only a half-ally.

Most ominous of all in the fall of 1943 were scattered indications that the Soviets might be seriously considering a go-it-alone strategy. The recall of Maisky and of Litvinov had been sinister reminders of the diplomatic prelude to the Nazi-Soviet Pact of 1939. Throughout 1943 there had been reports of peace feelers by Berlin and Moscow to each other—though on what terms and of how much seriousness were obscure. The Kremlin constantly worried that the Anglo-Americans might make a deal with a non-Hitler German government and leave Russia and Germany to a death struggle. Some Russians now seemed less concerned about the postponement of the cross-channel invasion. Alexander Korneichuk, a Foreign Vice-Commissar, said to Alexander Werth in Moscow: "Things are going so well on our front that it might even be better *not* to have the Second Front till next spring. If there were a Second Front right now, the Germans might allow Germany to be occupied by the Anglo-Americans. It would make us look pretty silly. . . ."

Was Moscow bluffing? Was this subtle blackmail? Or was Russia alternating between two foreign policies, coalition–co-operative and isolationist-aggressive, as conditions seemed to demand? Roosevelt and Stalin both had hard-liners to contend with. The President's were in the administration as well as outside. Some in the Pentagon contended that the Soviets were pursuing their own interest, the only language they understood was force, and Washington should adopt a *Realpolitik,* balance-of-power strategy. William Bullitt earlier in the year had presented to Roosevelt a reasoned, forceful argument that Russia would give no help in the defeat of Japan after the European war, and Britain very little, that Moscow would settle postwar European matters while the United States was still occupied in the Pacific, and hence that Roosevelt should either extract major concessions from Moscow and London or shift his whole strategy to beating Japan first.

Many in the party opposition still argued for Pacific First. Some Republican leaders were rumored to be in secret communication with MacArthur. Others had shifted little from their isolationist positions. Still others, however—most notably Willkie—were taking advanced positions in favor of a firm Anglo-American-Soviet partnership and of United States leadership in a strong postwar security organization. The Republicans held a well-publicized conference on Mackinac Island, in Michigan, as a prelude to platform planning for the presidential campaign of 1944. Some in the congressional party seemed as conservative as ever, but the presidential Republicans, led by Dewey, of New York, Warren, of California, and other governors took a generally internationalist position. It seemed likely that Roosevelt would have to deal with two Republican-party foreign policies, one advanced by the presidential Republicans, the other by the congressional party.

But at the darkest moment of Soviet-American relations a gleam had lighted up a great opportunity. After withdrawing his agreement to meet with Roosevelt in Fairbanks, Stalin had steadfastly refused Churchill's and Roosevelt's invitation to set a new time for all three to meet. He did, however, endorse the idea of a conference of foreign ministers in Moscow, and the exchanges over plans for this meeting seemed to lead naturally, though rather inexplicably, to a cautious acceptance by Stalin of a renewed invitation for a Big Three meeting. The President and the Marshal sparred at length over the place of the conference, with Roosevelt pleading that he could not fly to Teheran because he could not sign or veto congressional bills in the ten days the Constitution allowed him, and Stalin stolidly insisting on the Persian capital. Each hinted that the plan for a conference might founder if he could not get his way, but Stalin won this game of diplomatic "chicken," and Teheran it would be.

Hull's mission to Moscow was a useful testing of the diplomatic waters for the President and something of a triumph for the Secretary. He left Washington with enhanced prestige in the power-conscious capital, for the President had finally asked for the resignation of Sumner Welles, who had continued to vex Hull by his independent dealings with the White House and foreign envoys. Somehow the "gallant old eagle," as Churchill later called Hull, survived the first plane trip of his life, the tortuous discussions, and a Kremlin banquet, and he negotiated coolly, if somewhat long-windedly, with Eden and Molotov over a lengthy agenda. He found that the Russians were mainly interested in a second front and the British in political arrangements for Italy, while he pressed for a declaration of the four nations on general postwar security. He gained Molotov's assent to the American draft; the main issue was less the content—a pledge of consultation and joint action by the big nations to maintain world law and order until a general international-security organization was established—than whether the Chinese should be included in the document and allowed to sign it, as Roosevelt and Hull keenly wished. Molotov finally agreed to this.

On the last night of the conference Hull sat on Stalin's right at a banquet for the delegation in the Catherine the Great Hall of the Kremlin. The Marshal was unusually agreeable, though when Hull tried to induce his host to meet Roosevelt nearer to Washington than Teheran, he turned cool. Then, out of the blue, he made a statement that electrified Hull. The Secretary considered it so important that he notified the President in a message, the first half of which went by Navy code and the second by army code.

SECRET
URGENT

MOSCOW, 2 NOVEMBER 1943

MOST SECRET FOR THE PRESIDENT ONLY FROM HULL.

A MESSAGE HAS BEEN GIVEN ME FROM THE PERSON HIGHEST IN AUTHORITY TO BE DELIVERED TO YOU PERSONALLY IN EXTREME SECRECY. THE MESSAGE PROMISES TO GET IN AND HELP TO DEFEAT THE ENEMY.

REMAINDER FOLLOWS IN ANOTHER CODE.

MOSCOW, 2 NOVEMBER 1943

SECRET

UNNUMBERED. MOST SECRET FOR THE PRESIDENT ONLY FROM HULL.

IN THE FAR EAST AFTER GERMAN DEFEAT (THIS ENDS A MESSAGE IN ANOTHER CODE). PLEASE FLASH ACKNOWLEDGEMENT TO ME AT CAIRO.

We have no record of Roosevelt's response to Hull's message. Perhaps he was as much puzzled as pleased by it. In substance the news was not startling, for Soviet willingness to take on Japan after Germany's fall had long been hinted. But that Stalin should make such a definite and momentous promise in such a casual way, without any bargaining, and to Hull rather than to Roosevelt must have perplexed the President. Doubtless he calculated that such mysteries would soon be solved, for immediately after Hull's triumphant return from Moscow the President would be leaving for a conference with Churchill and Chiang in Cairo, and, it was hoped, for a later rendezvous with Stalin.

Well after dark on Armistice Day, November 11, 1943, the President, Hopkins, Leahy, Watson, and two other aides drove quietly from the White House to the Marine base at Quantico, Virginia. There the party boarded the *Potomac*, which chugged down the quiet river and anchored at the mouth of the Potomac early in the morning. At dawn the President could see the massive silhouette of the battleship *Iowa* five miles distant. Soon the *Potomac* lay alongside the *Iowa*, and the Commander in Chief was hoisted aboard, without fanfare, by a special rigging from the after sun deck of the yacht to the main deck of the dreadnaught.

In his quarters the President found a card stating that his room was Captain's Cabin, he would mess in the Flag Mess, abandon ship in the Lee Motor Whaleboat, and have the entire first superstructure deck, port and starboard, for promenade.

To the new sailor on board, the *Iowa* was a marvel—58,000 tons displacement, 888 feet long, 108-foot beam, 210,000 horsepower, 157 guns, including nine sixteen-inchers, and 2,600 officers and men. Commanding the man-of-war was Roosevelt's former naval aide, Captain John McCrea, who had turned his quarters over to the President and occupied his sea cabin on the navigating bridge. Already on board were Marshall, King, Arnold, and a large staff. Soon the *Iow*a, flanked by destroyers, was pounding through heavy seas, destination Oran. The President met with the Joint Chiefs, rested, braved the squally weather on the flag deck, and in the evening watched movies with his party.

All was routine on the great ship except for one horrifying moment the second day out. From a vantage point just outside his cabin the President was watching the *Iowa* conduct a defense drill. Five-inch guns were setting up a deafening roar when the dreadnaught suddenly swerved, listed heavily, and pulsed up to thirty-one knots. An officer on the bridge two decks above the President leaned over and shouted down, "It's the real thing! It's the real thing!" Hopkins asked Roosevelt if he wanted to go in; the President said, "No. Where is it?" Hopkins rushed to the rail in time to see a huge explosion in the wake of the ship. It was a torpedo that had been accidentally loosed by an escorting destroyer. Admiral King was all for relieving its commander at once, but Roosevelt would not have it, doubtless proceeding on the theory that it would be punishment enough for the poor wretch when he discovered he had almost torpedoed five admirals.

"All goes well and a very comfortable trip so far," the President wrote to "Dearest Babs" a few days later. "Weather good and warm enough to sit with only a sweater as an extra, over an old pair of trousers and a fishing shirt. I don't dare write the route but we should see Africa by tomorrow night and land Saturday morning. . . . It is a relief to have no newspapers! . . ."

Roosevelt said nothing to his wife about the torpedo incident, but perhaps this was the least of the dangers. While he was on the high seas security people discovered that some newspapers were freely reporting the impending meetings. Though it was clear that German planes could attack from Greece or other points, or that Nazi fanatics could make an assassination attempt at any of the President's stopping places, Roosevelt agreed with Churchill not to change plans. After slipping through the Strait of Gibraltar, the *Iowa* put in to Oran, on the old Barbary Coast. Here Roosevelt was greeted by Eisenhower and other theater commanders, and by his sons Elliott and Franklin. Then he went through a strenuous forty-eight hours: flying to Tunis with Ike, driving on to Carthage, where he stayed the night in a villa overlooking the sea; inspecting Elliott's photo-reconaissance wing; viewing the ruins of Carthage and the burned-out tanks, blown-up ammunition dumps, tank traps, and uncleared mine fields of the Battle of Tunisia, and flying along the Nile to Cairo, where he landed Monday morning, November 22.

Churchill had virtually enticed Roosevelt to Cairo with his tales of the lovely villas and gardens in the shadow of the Pyramids, the seclusion, and the desert trips, and he had hardly exaggerated. Churchill met his friend at the airport and escorted him to Ambassador Alexander C. Kirk's large villa, where he was soon settled. It was here over the next few days that he received a stream of visitors like some royal potentate of old: Britons, Egyptians, Greeks, Yugoslavs, Russians, and Chinese.

The Generalissimo and Madame Chiang called at the villa soon after Roosevelt's arrival. The President beheld a small man in a neat khaki uniform, with a serene unwrinkled face below a clean-shaven pate. On the surface Chiang seemed calm, reserved, determined, but as the sessions went by, Roosevelt found him mercurial, defensive, and heavily dependent on his wife. While Churchill chafed and reluctantly gave up hope that the couple could be persuaded to go visit the Pyramids, the President saw Chiang and his wife as often and as privately as he could, and tried to build their trust in him. This effort took all Roosevelt's charm and adroitness, for two cardinal factors were working against the Generalissimo. One was the ebbing confidence in his armies. The other was a fundamental shift in the Pacific situation. As the American fleet expanded west of Hawaii Joint Chief planners were swinging toward the idea that the quickest way to overcome Japan after Germany was by a direct amphibious assault across the central

Pacific and up from the Southwest Pacific. Hence Chiang would before long lose his monopoly of the only feasible route for the main assault on Japan.

But Roosevelt did his best. At dinner with Chiang and Madame the second night of the conference he made clear his view that China should have full membership in the Big Four after the war; he offered China the leading role in the postwar military occupation of Japan—a role Chiang declined—and extensive reparations; he agreed that the four northeastern provinces, Taiwan, and the Pescadores should be restored to China, and that China and the United States would jointly occupy the Ryukyus under international trusteeship; he proposed a vague postwar security alliance between the two nations; as usual he took a strong line against colonialism, even raising the question of Hong Kong.

The couple responded appreciatively to all these rosy hopes and kind gestures, though on Hong Kong the Generalissimo discreetly suggested that the President take up the matter with the British before further discussion. On one question Roosevelt was negative, or at least evasive. Chiang proposed that his nation be allowed to participate either in the Combined Chiefs of Staff conferences or in a new China-U.S. Joint Council. The Combined Chiefs had already considered this question; the Americans were cool, and the British even cooler, toward anything more than inviting the Chinese or the Russians to attend only CCS meetings at which the Chinese or Soviet fronts were under discussion. Central, day-to-day grand strategy would be made by the Anglo-Americans.

The Combined Chiefs had already set this pattern, for they had met that day in Cairo on the formal topic of the role of China in the defeat of Japan but allowed the Chinese military chiefs into the meeting only at the end. Mountbatten and Stilwell were there from their Asia commands to present the theater view. The precise course of all the military deliberations on China during the rest of the Cairo Conference is still not wholly known, but the main lines of contention are clear. Chiang would make a major contribution to a ground operation in Burma only if the Allies promised a big amphibious attack in the Bay of Bengal. Churchill resisted such a commitment because it might jeopardize the major projects he had in mind for the Mediterranean. Roosevelt on the one hand feared such a commitment because of the cross-channel priority; on the other hand he felt that the Chinese effort was lagging badly, that the Allies had not come through on their promises to Chungking, that Chiang must win something from the conference to take back to his people. Churchill stood firm; Chiang wavered; Roosevelt mediated.

"Things have gone *pretty* well," the President wrote to his wife. Even this was a bit of exaggeration. Chiang left with vague promises from Roosevelt of an amphibious operation in the Bay of Bengal and of American equipment for ninety Chinese divisions in the indefinite future. Western strategy was still ambiguous, too; the British, while solemnly pledging loyalty to the invasion of France, were now hedging on the day. OVERLORD, the cross-channel invasion, remained on top of the bill, Churchill said, but should not be such a "tyrant" as to overrule Mediterranean possibilities. As usual the Americans argued against dispersion; as usual King wanted to shift more American power to the Pacific. In a full year of conferences the Anglo-Americans still had not agreed on grand strategy.

Despite these troubles Churchill had never seen the President happier than at the Thanksgiving dinner Roosevelt gave for the Prime Minister, his daughter Sarah, and his own small circle. Propped high in his chair, the President carved two huge turkeys with fine skill. After dinner Sarah danced with the younger men and Churchill with Pa Watson, while Roosevelt watched delightedly from a sofa. The President offered a toast:

"Large families are usually more closely united than small ones . . . and so, this year, with the peoples of the United Kingdom in our family, we are a large family, and more united than ever before. I propose a toast to this unity, and may it long continue!"

It was a fine sentiment on the eve of Teheran.

THE FATES DECIDE.

May 19, 1943, Ernest H. Shepard, © *Punch*, London

TEHERAN: THE MARSHAL

Cairo West Airport, 6:35 A.M., Saturday, November 27, 1943. Mechanics and guards surrounded the "Sacred Cow," standing bulky and dark on the apron. A limousine glided in through the fog; there was a bustle of activity as the President and his party—Hopkins, Harriman, Leahy, Watson, John Boettiger, and a half-dozen others—boarded the plane. Half an hour passed as the pilots waited for the fog to lift; then the "Sacred Cow" lumbered off the runway and roared up through the mist, finally bursting out into the brilliant sunshine. The plane turned east.

Eagerly the President watched the storied lands flow westward beneath him. The plane crossed the Suez Canal, flew over the brown Sinai desert, circled low around Jerusalem and Bethlehem, soared across the Dead Sea and then on to the green valleys of the Euphrates and the Tigris. North of Baghdad the plane turned northeast, picking up the Abadan-Teheran highway as the pilot zigzagged through the mountain passes. The President could see trains and motor convoys loaded with Lend-Lease war supply bound for Russia. The plane flew through a jumble of mountain passes and then landed on a Red Army field a few miles outside Teheran. To the north lay the towering Elburz Mountains, which cut off the Persian capital from the Caspian Sea.

The President was driven to the American Legation, but he stayed there only one night. An assassination plot against the Big Three had been uncovered. Stalin sent word through Harriman that with Teheran infested by Nazi sympathizers and spies, he was concerned about the dangers of an "unhappy incident" while Roosevelt drove back and forth through the city. Would the President be Stalin's guest at the Soviet Embassy? Under the urgings of Reilly and others the President removed to the Russian compound, where he was installed in the main building and was guarded by "servants" whose Lugers could be seen bulging on their hips beneath their white coats. Stalin retired to a smaller house, and Churchill stayed at the nearby British Legation, which had been made part of one big Soviet-British compound.

The President was resting in his new bedroom when Reilly came in to say that the Marshal was on his way over. Roosevelt was quickly wheeled to his big sitting room. Stalin came in slowly, smiling, reached down, and shook hands. The President saw a short man, dignified, relaxed, dressed in a tightly buttoned, mustard-colored uniform with red facings, large gold epaulets on the shoulders, and one medal, a red-and-gold ribbon suspending a gold star. The two interpreters, V. N. Pavlov and Charles E. Bohlen, were the only others present.

"I am glad to see you," the President said. "I have tried for a long time to bring this about." For half an hour the two men chatted. The President led the conversation, touching on the Soviet battle front (Stalin: the Red Army was barely holding the initiative with the Germans having brought up more divisions); Chiang Kai-shek (Stalin: the Chinese soldiers fought bravely but the leadership was poor); de Gaulle (Stalin: de Gaulle acted like the head of a great state but actually commanded little power); the need to prepare Indochina for independence (Stalin: agreed); the need for reform from the bottom in India, "somewhat on the Soviet line" (Stalin: reform from the bottom would mean revolution).

". . . Seems very confident, very sure of himself, moves slowly—altogether quite impressive, I'd say," Roosevelt remarked to his son Elliott later.

The first plenary session got under way directly. Roosevelt had his full diplomatic and military staff with him, except that Marshall and Arnold had been misinformed about the schedule and were still sight-seeing. Churchill, flanked by Eden, Dill, Brooke, Cunningham, Portal, and Ismay sat to the left of the Americans. Stalin had only Molotov and Marshal Kliment Y. Voroshilov flanking him. The men sat around a ten-foot-wide oaken table specially created for the occasion by local carpenters and made round so that no one would sit at the head of the table. But Roosevelt, on the ground that he was the youngest present (and with the prior agreement of the other two), opened the proceedings by welcoming his elders to a family circle whose only object was to win the war. Churchill remarked that this was the greatest concentration of power the world had ever seen; history lay in their hands. Stalin offered a brief welcome, then said, "Let us get down to business."

The President began with a general survey of the war, stressing first his nation's commitment of most of its naval power and of one million men to the Pacific. He sketched out the military plans for China. Then he turned to the cross-channel invasion, which had been delayed, he said, mainly by lack of sea transport. The Channel was such a disagreeable body of water that the attack could not be launched before May 1, 1944.

"We are very glad it was such a disagreeable body of water at one time," Churchill put in. The question, Roosevelt went on, was whether other operations—in Italy, the Adriatic, the Aegean, from Turkey—could make use of Allied forces in Italy, at the possible expense of one to three months' delay for OVERLORD. He and Churchill sought the Marshal's views.

Stalin went straight to the point. The Soviets welcomed American successes in the Pacific. He regretted that the Soviet Union had not been able to help, but its forces were fighting Germany. His strength in the east was enough for defense but would have to be trebled for attack. Once Germany was finally defeated, "we shall be able by our common front to win." Stalin said this casually, without raising his voice; then he abruptly turned to Europe. There, he said, he had over three hundred divisions and the Axis had 260. The Germans at the moment were trying to recapture Kiev with some thirty motorized and tank divisions. As for Italy, that was no place from which to attack Germany proper, for the Alps were an insuperable barrier, as the famous Russian General Suvorov had discovered a century and a half before. The best way to get to the heart of Germany was through northern and southern France. But he warned that the Germans would fight like devils.

Roosevelt and Stalin had now put Churchill on the defensive, but the old warrior rose to the occasion. There was no question, he said, about the cross-channel operation, which would take place in the late spring or early summer. But that was six months away. What could be done in the meantime, after the capture of Rome—which he hoped would take place in January 1944—that would help relieve the Soviet front and not delay OVERLORD by more than a month or two? Could Turkey be persuaded to enter the war? Could help be given to the Yugoslavs? Churchill himself denied any plan to send a large army to the Balkans; it was Roosevelt who, to the surprise of his aides, raised the possibility of an Allied drive at the head of the Adriatic to join with the Yugoslavs and push northeast in conjunction with the Soviet advance west.

So within an hour the positions had been taken: Stalin for an advance into the German heartland, Churchill for wider Mediterranean operations, and Roosevelt—as Churchill later complained—drifting to and fro. The Marshal bluntly opposed Churchill's strategy as undue dispersion and his specific proposals as undesirable. He doubted that Turkey would enter the war except by the scruff of the neck. When Churchill kept arguing for making use of Mediterranean troops after the capture of Rome, Stalin coolly proposed again that the Anglo-Americans invade southern France in advance of OVERLORD. France, he said, was the weakest of all German-occupied areas. The meeting broke up inconclusively.

That evening Roosevelt had Stalin and Churchill and their top aides to dinner at his headquarters. The White House messmen, having moved into a strange kitchen only a few hours before, somehow came up with a dinner for eleven. Postwar Europe was the focus of talk. Stalin coldly wrote off Russia's old enemies. The French ruling class was rotten to the core. Roosevelt said he agreed in part; it would be well to eliminate in any future government of France anyone over forty. Stalin said the Reich must be dismembered and rendered impotent ever again to plunge the world into war. Roosevelt proposed an international trusteeship over the approaches to the Baltic; Stalin misunderstood at first, thought Roosevelt was proposing a trusteeship for the Baltic nations, and absolutely ruled this out.

The President felt ill after dinner and retired early. The atmosphere there became even cooler after he left. Stalin was obviously dissatisfied with Churchill's and Roosevelt's proposals for Germany. He had no faith in the notion of reforming the German people. He did not share the President's view, he told Churchill, that the Führer was mentally unbalanced. He was an able man but not basically intelligent, lacking in culture and with a primitive approach to politics. And the Marshal questioned the unconditional-surrender doctrine, which served merely to unite the German people. Much better to draw up harsh terms and simply tell the Germans to accept them. That would hasten the day of German surrender.

Afterward, back at the British Legation, Churchill was in a black depression. "Stupendous issues are unfolding before our eyes, and we are only specks of dust that have settled in the night on the map of the world." The President had remarked to him, he went on, "You may go at the election, but I shan't." Had the President said much in the conference? someone asked. Churchill hesitated. "Harry Hopkins said that the President was inept. He was asked a lot of questions and gave the wrong answers."

Next day Roosevelt seemed fully recovered. Churchill sent word proposing that they lunch together; to Churchill's dismay Roosevelt declined because he feared Stalin would suspect they were hatching some scheme if they met privately. But after lunch he met privately with Stalin and Molotov. The President wanted to sound out the Russians on postwar organization. He proposed his plan for the Four Policemen with power to deal quickly with threats to peace; a ten-nation executive committee to consider nonmilitary questions; an assembly representing all the United Nations. Stalin doubted that the small nations of Europe would like an organization of the Four Policemen. He doubted that China would be very powerful at the end of the war. He doubted that the United States Congress would agree to American participation in an exclusively European committee which might be able to force the dispatch of American troops to Europe. On the last point Roosevelt agreed; it would take a terrible crisis, he said, for Congress to agree to that. He had envisaged sending only American planes and ships to Europe; Britain and Russia would handle the land armies against a threat to peace. On China, Roosevelt disagreed with the Russian. "After all," he said, "China is a nation of 400 million people, and it is better to have them as friends than as a potential source of trouble."

A brilliant ceremony now intervened. Between rows of towering British and Soviet soldiers in the big conference room Churchill presented Stalin with the Sword of Stalingrad, forged by English craftsmen and given by King George to the "steel-hearted citizens of Stalingrad." His eyes glistening, Stalin raised the sparkling blade to his lips and kissed it, then walked over and showed the weapon to the President, who drew the long blade from the scabbard and held it aloft. His big hands barely covered the hilt. Then he returned the sword to the scabbard with a clang, and it was carried off by an escort.

But no sword of honor could cut through the knotted differences among the three leaders. At the second plenary session, after a report from the CCS reflecting little progress at its morning session, Stalin opened the discussion with an abrupt question:

"Who will command Overlord?"

"It has not been decided," Roosevelt said.

"Then nothing will come out of these operations," Stalin said. Somebody had to be in charge. Once again Churchill launched into a long defense of Mediterranean possibilities; once again the Marshal insisted that they were only diversionary; once again the President referred favorably to Mediterranean alternatives but worried that they might delay OVERLORD unduly—here again was the old suction pump that Marshall had long feared. The President proposed that OVERLORD take place not later than mid-May; Churchill said he could not agree. Roosevelt proposed an *ad-hoc* committee to consider the matter. Stalin balked. What could a committee do that they could not?

"Do the British really believe in Overlord," he asked, "or are they only saying so to reassure the Soviet Union?"

The meeting broke up in disagreement. That evening Stalin was host at a small dinner. He taunted and twitted Churchill, while the President looked on. The Prime Minister, he said, had a secret affection for Germany. He wanted a soft peace. He thought that just because the Russians were a simple people they were also blind. Later in the evening, after innumerable toasts, Stalin returned to his theme. Fifty thousand Germans had to be rounded up and liquidated after the war. Churchill retorted that he and his country would not stand for such butchery. Stalin repeated: "Fifty thousand must be liquidated."

Here the President spoke up. He had a compromise: only 49,000 should be shot. Elliott Roosevelt protested that all this was academic; the soldiers on the field would take care of more than 50,000. At this Churchill rose from the table and stalked out of the room, only to be followed by a grinning Stalin, who clapped his hand on Churchill's shoulder and persuaded him to return.

The conferences went on the next day, Stalin doodling, smoking, scratching words on square-crossed pieces of paper, speaking quietly, arguing bluntly; Churchill glowering behind his glasses, gesticulating with his cigar, lofting into flights of oratory; Roosevelt listening, measuring, interposing, placating. The discussions flowed on, but at some point on November 30, the third day of discussions, the balance swung slowly but inexorably against Churchill and peripheralism. It was partly because the CCS had met in the morning and hammered out a recommendation for OVERLORD, combined with a landing in southern France; partly because Stalin, in a tête-à-tête, had warned Churchill sharply that an Allied failure to invade in May would cause a bad reaction and "feeling of isolation" in the Red Army; partly because Churchill was increasingly hopeful that if the Mediterranean effort had to be subordinated to OVERLORD, Bay of Bengal plans could be subordinated to the Mediterranean. "OVERLORD in May" was confirmed at a "Three Only" (plus interpreters) luncheon shortly thereafter, and at the third plenary session in the afternoon. Stalin promised to launch a major attack from the east at the same time.

That evening Churchill celebrated his sixty-ninth birthday at a dinner for thirty-three at his legation. Roosevelt sat directly on his right, Stalin on his left. Spirits ran high. Roosevelt had learned how to make a small glass last for a dozen toasts. He saluted George VI; Churchill toasted Roosevelt as defender of democracy and Stalin as Stalin the Great; the Marshal saluted the Russian people and American production—especially of 10,000 planes a month. "Without these planes from America the war would have been lost." He ended with a toast to the President. At two in the morning Roosevelt asked for the privilege of the last word.

"There has been discussion here tonight," he said, "of our varying colors of political complexion. I like to think of this in terms of the rainbow. In our country the rainbow is a symbol of good fortune and of hope. It has many varying colors, each individualistic, but blending into one glorious whole.

"Thus with our nations. We have differing customs and philosophies and ways of life. Each of us works out our scheme of things according to the desires and ideas of our own peoples.

"But we have proved here at Teheran that the varying ideals of our nations can come together in a harmonious whole, moving unitedly for the common good of ourselves and of the world. . . ."

The conference might well have ended on this note of harmony, but political questions lay always in the background. At a series of meetings the next day Stalin agreed to help persuade the Turks to enter the war, though he still doubted that they would. He argued for the dismemberment and crushing of Germany. He would demand heavy reparations from Finland and the restoration of the treaty of 1940, with the possible exchange of Petsamo for Hangö. Roosevelt and Churchill jousted with him innocuously on these questions. But Poland, as always, was the pinch, and Roosevelt knew that he would have to come back to it.

With the second front settled, the President decided on a personal plea to Stalin about Poland, but despite his efforts to keep some distance from Churchill, he felt that he had not established personal rapport with Stalin. The Marshal still seemed stiff and unsmiling; there seemed nothing human to get hold of. Roosevelt told Frances Perkins later, doubtless with some embellishment, that he decided to do something desperate.

"On my way to the conference room that morning we caught up with Winston and I just had a moment to say to him, 'Winston, I hope you won't be sore at me for what I am going to do.'

"Winston just shifted his cigar and grunted. I must say he behaved very decently afterward.

"I began almost as soon as we got into the conference room. I talked privately with Stalin. I didn't say anything that I hadn't said before, but it appeared quite chummy and confidential, enough so that the other Russians joined us to listen. Still no smile.

"Then I said, lifting my hand to cover a whisper (which of course had to be interpreted), 'Winston is cranky this morning, he got up on the wrong side of the bed.'

"A vague smile passed over Stalin's eyes, and I decided I was on the right track. As soon as I sat down at the conference table, I began to tease Churchill about his Britishness, about John Bull, about his cigars, about his habits. It began to register with Stalin. Winston got red and scowled, and the more he did so, the more Stalin smiled. Finally Stalin broke out into a deep, heavy guffaw, and for the first time in three days I saw light. I kept it up until Stalin was laughing with me, and it was then that I called him 'Uncle Joe.' He would have thought me fresh the day before, but that day he laughed and came over and shook my hand.

"From that time on our relations were personal, and Stalin himself indulged in an occasional witticism. The ice was broken and we talked like men and brothers."

Less than three hours later Stalin visited the President privately. He had asked the Marshal to come, Roosevelt said, because he wanted to discuss a matter briefly and frankly. It referred to internal American politics. While personally he did not wish to run again in 1944, if the war was still in progress he might have to.

There were in the United States from six to seven million Americans of Polish extraction, he went on, and as a practical man he did not wish to lose their votes. He personally agreed with the Marshal about the need to restore the Polish state, but he would like to see the eastern border moved farther to the west and the western border moved even to the Oder. He hoped, however, that the Marshal would understand that for election reasons he could not participate in any decision at Teheran or even next winter on the subject and he could not publicly take part in any such arrangement at the present time.

Stalin answered that now that the President had explained, he understood.

Roosevelt pushed his luck a bit further. There were many Americans of Lithuanian, Latvian, and Estonian origin, too, he said. Not that the United States would go to war over the question when the Russians reoccupied the three Baltic Republics! But to Americans the big issue would be the right of self-determination. He was personally confident that the people would vote to join the Soviet Union.

Stalin: The three Baltic republics had no autonomy under the last czar, who had been an ally of Britain and the United States, and no one had raised the question of public opinion then and he did not see why it was being raised now.

Roosevelt: The truth of the matter is that the public neither knows nor understands.

Stalin: They should be informed and some propaganda work should be done.

Stalin's "understanding" about Poland seemed to have evaporated by evening. When the President expressed hope that Moscow would proceed to re-establish relations with the Polish government-in-exile, Stalin retorted that the London group was working with the Germans and killing partisans. Of course he wanted friendly relations with Poland—Soviet security was involved—but this was possible only with an anti-Nazi government. Poland could be expanded only at the expense of Germany. The agreement of 1939 had returned Ukrainian soil to the Ukraine and White Russian soil to White Russia.

"The Ribbentrop-Molotov line," Eden put in.

"Call it what you will," Stalin replied, "we still consider it just and right." The three men huddled around State Department maps of central Europe. Of one ethnographic map Stalin remarked contemptuously that Polish statistics must have been used. Discussion went on; Stalin would not budge. By the end of the day—which was the end of the conference—there was no agreement, but there was implicit acceptance of Stalin's demands on borders.

"We came here with hope and determination," the joint Teheran communiqué proclaimed. "We leave here, friends in fact, in spirit, and in purpose." The next morning, December 3, the President flew back to Cairo to meet with Churchill and the Combined Chiefs for the final decisions on grand strategy for 1944.

The most pressing question was Turkey's entrance into the war. The President dispatched John Boettiger to escort President Ismet Inönü to Cairo for final discussions. Over the next three days Roosevelt and Churchill mobilized their combined persuasiveness—along with clear hints about postwar arrangements—to talk Inönü and his colleagues into the war. The Turks were polite, co-operative, concerned, and stubborn. They wanted a commitment of military aid that the straitened Anglo-Americans could not make. So anguished was Inönü as he faced his dilemma that Roosevelt had to admit that if he were a Turk he would need more assurances than were being offered; naturally, he conceded to Inönü, the Turks did not want to be caught with their pants down. Inönü would not make the pledge. Roosevelt seemed unperturbed by the outcome; Churchill gamely swallowed one more setback to his military ambitions in the eastern Mediterranean.

On a far more important matter, however, the Prime Minister won a crucial victory. In Cairo he immediately set himself to induce Roosevelt to renege on his promise to Chiang of a big operation in the Andamans. Churchill had powerful arguments on his side. Stalin's promise to fight Japan after Germany posed the likelihood of a better continental land route into Japan. Operations in the central and Southwest Pacific were opening up other avenues to the enemy homeland. The decision for OVERLORD and ANVIL (the attack through southern France) in May escalated European needs, especially for landing ships. Mountbatten was asking for a much bigger landing force for Southeast Asia than had been expected.

Churchill could see that things were different in this second Cairo meeting. Chiang was no longer present; the crucial decision had been made in Moscow for the second front. Stilwell was in Cairo to speak for Chiang, but "Vinegar Joe" felt at sea amid the big-power politics going on by the Nile.

At first Roosevelt was dead set against withdrawing the promise to Chiang. They had a moral obligation to do something for China, he told Churchill and the Combined Chiefs. Too, he was dubious about putting all the eggs into one basket. Suppose Stalin was unable or unwilling to make good his word; Washington might find that it had forfeited Chinese support without obtaining commensurate help from the Russians. His Joint Chiefs of Staff backed the President; they feared especially that a cancellation of the Andamans thrust would give Chiang an excuse to renege on his promises of land operations and would lead in turn to Chinese withdrawal from the war. Admiral King, feeling especially strongly on the matter, managed to scrounge up enough landing ships for Europe to leave a goodly supply for the Andamans.

But Churchill and his chiefs were determined, and after a day or two of resistance Roosevelt backed down, with the glum acquiescence of most of his chiefs. The President's reasons were partly military: under the Europe First doctrine OVERLORD and ANVIL had to be as secure as possible. Partly they were personal: at Teheran he had sided with Stalin over Churchill on OVERLORD and ANVIL; now he must favor Churchill over Chiang. And there were deepening fears on the part of almost all at Cairo about China's staying power, with or without the Andaman operation.

"I've been as stubborn as a mule for four days but we can't get anywhere," Roosevelt told Stilwell, "and it won't do for a conference to end that way. The British just won't do the operation and I can't get them to agree to it." When Stilwell asked for political guidance on China, the President told anecdotes and mentioned postwar plans. To Chiang, Roosevelt sent a terse wire canceling the Andamans and proposing lesser alternatives. The Generalissimo's answer was as gloomy as feared. The results of the first Cairo Conference had electrified the Chinese people, he cabled. Now this decision at Cairo would dishearten the nation to the point that it might not hold out much longer. The Japanese would deduce that under the Europe First policy the United Nations were now abandoning China to the mercies of Japan's mechanized air and land forces. Yet Chiang seemed to acquiesce in the decision and seemed, indeed, more concerned about his economic than his military problems. He asked simply in his reply for more planes—and for a billion dollars in gold.

One other matter remained to be resolved at Cairo: the command of OVERLORD. This was Roosevelt's decision alone. It had long been expected that Marshall would command the climactic invasion he had so long argued for, and that Eisenhower would return to Washington and take over his post. But Roosevelt could not quite bring himself to make the appointment, even though most of his advisers favored it and Marshall clearly, though diffidently, wanted it. "I feel I could not sleep at night with you out of the country," Roosevelt told his Chief of Staff. It was one of the hardest decisions Roosevelt ever made, Sherwood felt.

Churchill insisted toward the end of the second Cairo Conference that he and Roosevelt motor out and see the Sphinx. For once silent, the two men stared at the brooding features as the evening shadows fell. It was symbolic that Roosevelt thus ended in the company of Churchill alone this year of conferences, just as they had started it together. The two men had had their differences, but in the end they had stood together, even on OVERLORD. Churchill had spent week after week in America, day after day with the President. He had addressed Congress again, attended Cabinet meetings, presided alone—with the permission of the President, who had been in Hyde Park at the time—over a meeting of American and British military and diplomatic chiefs in the White House. He had made no secret—even to Stalin—of his satisfaction at being "half American." He was more papal than the Pope; driving with Roosevelt and his party through Frederick, Maryland, one day he had noticed a sign advertising Barbara Fritchie candy, and while Roosevelt and Hopkins listened in astonishment, he recited a score or so of lines from Whittier's famous poem—"Shoot, if you must, this old gray head. . . ."

Someday there would be a price to pay for the exuberant friendship of the two men. Churchill turned a myopic eye to the teeming masses in Asia; among intimates he could even worry about the Russians breeding like flies and overwhelming the white population of Britain and the United States. His attitude toward China was deeply affected by racial feeling. But in this moment Anglo-American co-operation was at a peak.

Roosevelt left Cairo for home on December 7. He stopped in Tunis, where he greeted Eisenhower with a cheery "Well, Ike, you'd better start packing." He touched down in Malta, where he presented a scroll to the islanders for their heroism. He reviewed troops in Sicily. Then the long return trip on the *Iowa* and a greeting at the south entrance to the White House by the assembled Cabinet. Rosenman had never seen the President look so satisfied and pleased. He also looked tired, but robust and confident. To Stimson, the President said: "I have . . . brought Overlord back to you safe and sound on the ways for accomplishment."

It was Christmastime. The President wanted to be in his own home; for the first time since he became President he celebrated Christmas at Hyde Park. On Christmas Eve he broadcast a report to the people from his own fireside. Mainly it was a long, general, and optimistic survey of the fighting fronts and of his conferences abroad. He announced his selection of Eisenhower to lead an attack from "other points of the compass" along with the stern Russian offensive in the east and the relentless Allied pressure in the south. As for Stalin: ". . . I may say that I 'got along fine' with Marshal Stalin. He is a man who combines a tremendous relentless determination with a stalwart good humor. I believe he is truly representative of the heart and soul of Russia; and I believe that we are going to get along very well with him and the Russian people—very well indeed."

The next day he presided over a family reunion in the old mansion. Seven of his fourteen grandchildren were there, with their mothers. The President watched as gifts were unwrapped, carved the family turkey, and, as always, read Dickens's *Christmas Carol,* skillfully condensing it to hold the attention of the young.

The President was not, however, in a wholly festive mood. Shortly before Christmas he wrote Frankfurter: ". . . I realized on the trip what a dreadful lack of civilization is shown in the countries I visited—but on returning I am not wholly certain of the degree of civilization in *terra Americana.*"

PART 4 *Battle*

FOURTEEN *The Lords of the Hill*

THE PRESIDENT had returned home from Teheran to an embittered capital. All the old simmering issues seemed to be coming to a boil. Joseph Guffey, the aged New Deal war horse, rose in the Senate to castigate the "unholy alliance" of Old Guard Republicans under Joe Pew and of Southern Democrats under Harry Byrd. In reply, his foes threatened to organize a new Southern party that would hold a balance of power between the two major parties. In the House, John Rankin, of Mississippi, pointedly read off the Jewish names of New Yorkers supporting a soldiers'-vote bill. Secretary of Interior Ickes charged over a nationwide radio hookup that the "four lords of the press"—Hearst, McCormick, and the two Pattersons—hated Roosevelt and Stalin so bitterly that they would rather see Hitler win the war than be defeated by "a leadership shared in by the great Russian and the great American."

"There is terrific tension on the Hill," Budget Director Smith noted. "People who have been friends for years are doing the most erratic things." A leading politician said privately: "I haven't an ounce of confidence in anything that Roosevelt does. I wouldn't believe anything he said."

Seldom had race feeling been so conspicuous in the capital. Indignation greeted the news that 16,000 "disloyal" Japanese had rioted at the Tule Lake concentration camp. The Senate killed a federal aid-to-education bill when Republicans adroitly hitched on an antidiscrimination provision. Railroad employers and unions alike defied an FEPC order barring discrimination against Negro firemen. Not since Reconstruction, the *Nation* observed, had sectional feeling run so high in the halls of Congress.

"The President has come back to his own Second Front," Max Lerner wrote. "We shall need to build another bridge of fire, not to link in with our Allies but to unite us with ourselves, and to span the fissure within our own national will."

The center of the storm seemed as calm as ever. He had got the impression on returning that there was a terrible mess in Washington, the President observed mildly to the Cabinet. Nor did he betray any worry. "There he sat," reported the *New Republic's* TRB, "at his first press conference after his five weeks on tour—Churchill sick; inflation controls going all to pot; the Democratic party at sixes and sevens; a rail strike threatened; selfish goals sought by labor and farmers and business; ignoble motives imputed to every public act of every public man; the world a global mess—and there he sat, bland and affable, in his special chair, puffing imperturbably on an uptilted cigarette and welcoming old friends."

Roosevelt was not as imperturbable as he appeared. He was entering the new year like a tightrope walker starting out over Niagara. Monumental questions were hanging in the balance—not only the war economy, his electoral standing with the voters, the cross-channel invasion, the invasion routes to Japan, but also his whole strategy of war and peace. He was following a precarious middle way. He was trying to establish close rapport with Russia and at the same time follow an Atlantic First strategy depending on the closest relations with the British. He was trying to help make China a great nation in war and peace while putting it far down the priority list of military aid and political influence. He was trying to establish a new and better League without alienating the isolationists. He was calling for freedom for all peoples but deferring to the British in India and the Moslems in the Near East. He was demanding unconditional surrender but dealing with Darlans and Badoglios.

He had said that "magnificent idealism" was not enough; neither was manipulation or expediency. How he balanced and interlinked the demands of his faith and the necessities of the moment would be the great test of Franklin Roosevelt in 1944.

A SECOND BILL OF RIGHTS

After seeing soldiers stuck in lonely outposts in Iran and stretched out on hospital cots in Sicily, the President was indignant about the attitudes he found at home—complacent expectations of an early victory, isolationists spreading suspicion about the Allied nations, noisy minorities demanding special favors, profiteers, selfish political interests, and all the rest. He decided to declare war on these elements in his State of the Union message—indeed, to make a dramatic reassertion of American liberalism even at the height of war.

But first he indulged in one of those baffling sidesteps that often had accompanied, and camouflaged, a major Rooseveltian action. To a reporter who had tarried a bit after a press conference the Chief Executive had complained that he wished the press would not use that term "New Deal," for there was no need of a New Deal now. At the next press conference reporters pressed him for an explanation. The President assumed a casual air, as though it was all so obvious; some people, he said, just had to be told how to spell "cat." He described how "Dr. New Deal" had treated the nation for a grave internal disorder with specific remedies. He quoted from a long list Rosenman had put together of New Deal programs. But after his recovery, he went on, the patient had a very bad accident—"on the seventh of December, he was in a pretty bad smashup." So Dr. New Deal, who "didn't know nothing" about legs and arms, called in his partner, "who was an orthopedic surgeon, Dr. Win-the-War."

"Does that all add up to a fourth-term declaration?" a brash reporter asked.

"Oh, now, we are not talking about things like that now. You are getting picayune. . . ."

"I don't mean to be picayune," the reporter went on, "but I am not clear about this parable. The New Deal, I thought, was dynamic, and I don't know whether you mean that you had to leave off to win the war and then take up again the social program, or whether you think the patient is cured?"

The President answered with a confusing analogy of post-Civil

There's an Odd Family Resemblance Among the Doctors

December 30, 1943, C. K. Berryman, courtesy of the Washington (D.C.) *Star*

War policy. Then he insisted again: the 1933 program was a program to meet the problems of 1933. In time there would have to be a new program to meet new needs. "When the time comes . . . When the times comes."

The creator of the New Deal had killed it, the conservative press exulted.

Two weeks later Roosevelt gave the most radical speech of his life. He chose his annual State of the Union message as the occasion. Early in January he had come down with the flu, but he labored over draft after draft while Rosenman and Sherwood sat by his bed. He had not recovered enough to deliver the message to Congress in person, but he insisted on giving it as a fireside chat in the evening for fear that the papers would not run the full text.

The President lashed out at "people who burrow through our Nation like unseeing moles . . . pests who swarm through the lobbies of Congress and the cocktail bars of Washington . . . bickering, self-seeking partisanship, stoppages of work, inflation, business as usual . . . the whining demands of selfish pressure groups who seek to feather their nests while young Americans are dying."

Once again he asked Congress to adopt a strong stabilization program. He recommended:

"1. A realistic tax law—which will tax all unreasonable profits, both individual and corporate, and reduce the ultimate cost of the war to our sons and daughters. . . .

"2. A continuation of the law for the renegotiation of war contracts—which will prevent exorbitant profits and assure fair prices to the Government. . . .

"3. A cost of food law—which will enable the Government (a) to place a reasonable floor under the prices the farmer may expect for his production; and (b) to place a ceiling on the prices a consumer will have to pay for the food he buys. . . .

"4. Early reenactment of the stabilization statute of October, 1942. . . . We cannot have stabilization by wishful thinking. We must take positive action to maintain the integrity of the American dollar.

"5. A national service law—which, for the duration of the war, will prevent strikes, and, with certain appropriate exceptions, will make available for war production or for any other essential services every able-bodied adult in the Nation."

Then came the climax of the address:

"It is our duty now to begin to lay the plans and determine the strategy for the winning of a lasting peace and the establishment of an American standard of living higher than ever before known. We cannot be content, no matter how high that general standard of living may be, if some fraction of our people—whether it be one-third or one-fifth or one-tenth—is ill-fed, ill-clothed, ill-housed, and insecure.

"This Republic had its beginning, and grew to its present strength, under the protection of certain inalienable political rights —among them the right of free speech, free press, free worship, trial by jury, freedom from unreasonable searches and seizures. *They* were our rights to life and liberty.

"As our Nation has grown in size and stature, however—as our industrial economy expanded—these political rights proved inadequate to assure us *equality in the pursuit of happiness.*

"We have come to a clear realization of the fact that *true* individual freedom cannot exist without economic security and independence. 'Necessitous men *are not* free men.' People who are hungry—people who are out of a job—are the stuff of which dictatorships are made."

The President was now speaking with great deliberateness and emphasis. The italics were not in his text, but in his delivery.

"In our day these economic truths have become *accepted as self-evident.* We have accepted, so to speak, a *second Bill of Rights* under which a new basis of security and prosperity can be established for all—regardless of station or race or creed.

"Among these are:

"The right to a useful and remunerative *job* in the industries or shops or farms or mines of the Nation;

"The right to earn enough to provide adequate *food* and *clothing* and *recreation;*

"The right of farmers to raise and sell their products at a return which will give them and their family a decent living;

"The right of every businessman, large and small, to trade in an atmosphere of freedom from unfair competition and domination by *monopolies* at home or abroad;

"The right of every *family* to a decent *home;*

"The right to adequate *medical* care and the opportunity to *achieve* and *enjoy* good health;

"The right to adequate protection from the *economic* fears of old age and sickness and accident and unemployment;

"And finally, the right to a good *education.*

"*All* of these rights spell security. And after this war is won we must be *prepared* to move *forward,* in the *implementation* of these rights, to new goals of human happiness and well-being. . . ."

In its particulars the economic bill of rights was not very new. It was implicit in the whole sweep of Roosevelt's programs and proposals during the past decade; it was Dr. New Deal himself suddenly called back into action. But never before had he stated so flatly and boldly the economic rights of all Americans. And never before had he linked so explicitly the old bill of political rights against government to the new bill of economic rights to be achieved *through* government. For decades the fatal and false dichotomy—liberty *against* security, freedom *against* equality—had deranged American social thought and crippled the nation's capacity to subdue depression and poverty. Now Roosevelt was asserting that individual political liberty and collective welfare were not only compatible, but they were mutually fortifying. No longer need Americans swallow the old simplistic equation the more government, the less liberty. The fresh ideas and policies of Theodore Roosevelt and of Robert La Follette, of Woodrow Wilson and of Al Smith, of the earlier Herbert Hoover and of George Norris, nurtured in days of muckraking and protest, evoked by depression, hardened in war, came to a clear statement in this speech of January 11, 1944.

And this appeal fell with a dull thud into the half-empty chambers of the United States Congress.

"He's like a king trying to reduce the barons," Senator Wheeler had cried out against Roosevelt in the early New Deal years. He himself was the baron of the Northwest; Huey Long, the baron of the South; Roosevelt had once been just a baron, too. Ten years later most of the old barons, including Wheeler himself, dominated the political life of Capitol Hill. But now they were less the lords of regions—except, always, the South—than masters of procedure, evokers of memories, voices of ideology—and contrivers of deadlock.

Power holding on Capitol Hill had changed little since before Pearl Harbor. There was the ancient and ailing Carter Glass, who, with his protégé Harry Byrd, still ran the Virginia Democratic party; Gerald Nye, as forceful, shrewd, and fundamentally isolationist as ever; Bennett Champ Clark, rotund and forensic, a spokesman for veterans; the stocky, smooth-faced Robert La Follette, less isolationist than his father but wary of Roosevelt's foreign commitments; Hiram Johnson, seventy-seven, a true baron of the West, a bit feeble now but still a commanding presence with his noble features and snow-white hair. There were a brace of ambitious Republicans: Robert Taft, already high in the Senate establishment for a first-termer, dry, competent, assured; Arthur Vandenberg, now midway in his long, troubled retreat from isolationism, looking both wise and naïve, with his owlish little features setting off a big round face; the handsome, towering Henry Cabot Lodge, grandson of the great isolationist and a living invocation of the battles of 1919, a soldier who would soon go off to the wars again. There was a handful of vigorous internationalists: Warren Austin, of Vermont, Joseph H. Ball, of Minnesota, Harold H. Burton, of Ohio. Many an internationalist Democrat was there, too: Alben Barkley, Abe Murdock, of Utah, Theodore Green, James E. Murray, of Montana, Harry Truman, and others. But the Democrats were divided in war as in peace. Walter George, Kenneth McKellar, of Tennessee, Theodore G. Bilbo, of Mississippi, William B. Bankhead, of Alabama, E. D. ("Cotton Ed") Smith, of South Carolina, and others were guardians of the South, lords of their committees, and as a group not dependably internationalist.

One way or the other Roosevelt had taken the measure of such men, Republican and Southern Democrat alike. But in early 1944 the rules of the game were different because the stakes had drastically altered. The issue was no longer welfare or domestic reform or economic policy, for which presidential pressure, persistence, and politicking could be counted on to bring a satisfactory if delayed victory. The President's adversaries on the Hill now had the power to deny his supreme ambition—to lead the United States into an effective world-security organization.

Ridden by the memory of Wilson's defeat, Roosevelt had been proceeding all through 1943 with almost fanatical cautiousness on postwar organization. He had let Hull and a group of State Department experts move ahead quietly with planning for postwar peace and security. He had let Willkie and other internationalist Republicans proclaim the postwar security underpinnings of "one world." In Congress the internationalist Democrats were restive. J. William Fulbright, a low-ranking member of the House Foreign Affairs Committee, urged the President to support his resolution favoring international machinery with power adequate to establish and to maintain a just and lasting peace, and for United States participation therein. He had always felt, he wrote, that the President's success had been largely due "to your courage in boldly taking the lead" on troublesome problems. Roosevelt would not take the lead on even such an innocuous resolution, but after conferring with Hull he told Fulbright that he favored action on his resolution if it gained wide backing and if no prejudicial amendments were tacked on it.

As usual Roosevelt's cautiousness was well calculated. His views on postwar organization had developed slowly before Teheran; he still favored Big Four domination and regional security organization. Hull and his State Department planners were strong for one universal organization. Questions were already arising—of a Big Power veto, of the method of representing nations, of a world-security force, of the relation between postwar peace treaties and the establishment of a permanent world organization—questions that aroused disturbing echoes of the controversies that had done the League to death.

Roosevelt wanted to still those echoes. The history-minded President was, indeed, so worried about improper parallels being drawn between 1919 and 1943 that he asked Hull to postpone publication of notes of conversations among Wilson, Lloyd George, and Clemenceau; such notes should not have been made in the first place, he added. He was resolved that any congressional planning for a new League must be very gradual and wholly bipartisan. Above all, discussion must not get bogged down in minor details. But there was considerable feeling in the Senate that specifics were the crucial matter. Willkie Republicans wanted a more explicit plan. When the Senate Foreign Relations Committee reported out the Connally Resolution, calling for United States participation, through its constitutional processes, in the "establishment and maintenance of international authority with power to prevent aggression and to preserve the peace of the world," the President favored an even more general statement.

"Mr. President," he was asked at a press conference late in October 1943, "does the Committee Resolution reported out by the Senate Foreign Relations Committee meet that specification [of generality]?"

"That's the whole trouble," Roosevelt answered. "Now you put your finger right on it. How could I answer that question? I couldn't. Now you are getting down to specific language. You and I could sit down, if we were the dictators of the world, and work out some language that you and I thought was 100 per cent. And then Earl Godwin would come in and give us something that was better."

"Earl Godwin thinks that it does," Godwin said, amid laughter. "Now, if it's just a matter of words, it's sort of silly to take up time—"

"Well," the President interrupted, "I think the Senate has every right to talk about it just as long as they want."

"Exactly, sir, we shouldn't say anything else. But suppose the Senate had adopted the Resolution, which it may at any moment, and you may be over in Europe, will the United States or will the President of the United States feel bound by this kind of Resolution?"

"That's a difficult thing to say. I might not like it."

"Well, it's an expression of the Senate. It isn't the ratification of anything."

The President would not show his hand.

"Well, if the general sentiment is all right that's fine. I have told you what the general sentiment I think ought to be. This country wants to stop war. . . ."

By the end of 1943, however, things were falling into place for Roosevelt. The Republicans at Mackinac had, in the words of

Vandenberg, who had exerted skillful conciliatory leadership, "put down in black and white the indispensable doctrine that Americans can be faithful to the primary institutions and interests of our own United States and still be equally loyal to the essential postwar international cooperations which are required to end military aggression for keeps. . . ." Hull had found in Moscow, as Roosevelt had in Teheran, considerable convergence among the Big Three on postwar security policy. Always flexible on ways and means, the President himself had shifted from a regional emphasis to Hull's universalism.

Roosevelt was also heartened by the the success of international wartime programs and institutions that would undergird postwar co-operation. Lend-Lease, the Combined Chiefs of Staff and its vast Anglo-American supporting and planning machinery, international agricultural and commodity programs, world-wide resource allocation, technical and scientific co-operation—all these activities, and the institutions that embodied and expanded them, appealed to Roosevelt's preference for practical co-operation and progress without labels and controversy. In November he signed an agreement establishing the United Nations Relief and Rehabilitation Administration. "As in most of the difficult and complex things of life," he said on that occasion, "Nations will learn to work together only by actually working together."

By 1944 the time had come to move ahead on more definite postwar security planning. During January the President went over a State Department paper embodying the work of its experts. On February 3 he gave Hull formal word to go ahead with his planning for the United Nations on the basis of the State Department proposals, which would later become, with little change, the administration's proposals to the Dumbarton Oaks Conference. But not for a moment did Roosevelt forget the potential role of the barons on the Hill—or the ambitions and passions that might be aroused by the November elections.

THE REVOLT OF THE BARONS

Despite Roosevelt's talk about keeping issues "out of politics," nothing important could be insulated from the pressures of campaign year 1944. Barkley, Taft, Nye, and a score of other notable Senators would be up for re-election. So would 435 members of the House of Representatives. And so would the President—perhaps. Nothing at this time could have aroused campaign sensitivities more acutely—along with ideological feelings about states' rights, fair play, GI's, the poll tax—than the question of the servicemen's vote.

Late in January the President put the issue directly before Congress. The people, he said, feared that the vast majority of the eleven million servicemen would be deprived of their right to vote in the fall elections. Men stationed all over the world could not comply with the different voting laws of the forty-eight states. A federal absentee-balloting act passed in September was an advance, but a small one; only 28,000 servicemen had voted that year. A bill endorsed by the Senate in December 1943 "recommending" to the states that they pass absentee-ballot legislation was meaningless—a fraud to the servicemen, a "fraud upon the American people." He asked Congress to enact a pending administration bill that would provide for quick and simple voting for federal candidates by name or—if the name of the candidate was still unknown—simply by checking the party preferred.

"Our millions of fighting men do not have any lobby or pressure group on Capitol Hill to see that justice is done for them," the President added pointedly. As Commander in Chief he was expressing their resentment for them. And, admitting that as Chief Executive he had no right to interfere in legislative procedures, as an "interested citizen" he demanded that every member in Congress stand up and be counted in a roll-call vote rather than take cover in a voice vote.

The message hit Congress like a declaration of war. The 1944 campaign was under way, the Commander in Chief himself a likely candidate for President. His face red and his arms flailing, Senator Taft charged that Roosevelt was planning to line up soldiers for the fourth term as WPA workers once were marched to the polls.

Drawing copyrighted 1944 by United Features Syndicate, Inc., reproduced by courtesy of Bill Mauldin

"That's okay, Joe—at least we can make bets."

January 28, 1944, Daniel R. Fitzpatrick, St. Louis *Post-Dispatch*

GOING UP AGAINST SOMETHING

Privately Republicans and Southern Democratic Senators poured out their feelings. "Roosevelt says we're letting the soldiers down," a Senator said. "Why, God damn him. The rest of us have boys who go into the Army and Navy as privates and ordinary seamen and dig latrines and swab decks and his scamps go in as lieutenant colonels and majors and lieutenants and spend their time getting medals in Hollywood. Letting the soldiers down! Why, that son of a bitch . . ."

Roosevelt was the issue. If he would only eliminate himself as a fourth-term candidate, Republican Senator Rufus C. Holman, of Oregon, announced, the bill would pass. Democratic Senator Murdock answered mockingly: "I know it is the prayer in his heart, and it is the prayer in the heart of every other good, old, stand-pat Republican in the United States today . . . that Franklin D. Roosevelt would eliminate himself from politics and give them at least a shadow of a chance to bring in the Grand Old Party again. But I say to them . . . the American people still want Roosevelt." At this the Senate gallery broke into applause and jeers.

Debate took an uglier turn in the House. Southerners feared that a soldiers'-vote act would override the poll tax and enable Negroes to vote. "Now who is behind this bill?" Rankin demanded of the House. "The chief publicist is *PM*, the uptown edition of the Communist *Daily Worker* that is being financed by the tax-escaping fortune of Marshall Field III, and the chief broadcaster for it is Walter Winchell—alias no telling what."

"Who is he?" prompted a conservative Republican.

"The little kike I was telling you about the other day, who called this body the 'House of Reprehensibles.' " No one rose to protest, and after Rankin closed with a quavering appeal to the Constitution and states' rights, scores of Congressmen rose and applauded him.

For weeks the Senate and House worked the bill over, slowly squeezing out its substance. By the time it reached Roosevelt the measure was little more than a shell. The President was so vexed by the confusion and delay wrought by his conservative foes and by the bill's limited scope that he refused to sign it. Under the bill that became law without his signature, 85,000 servicemen voted in the November election by means of the federal ballot, though a larger number—mainly those still in the country—voted via regular state ballots.

David Lilienthal ran into a special brand of Southern racism and reaction. All through the early months of 1944 he was facing congressional inquisitors hostile to the TVA in general and to him in particular. Rankin had been a champion of the TVA—he claimed, indeed, to be its "co-father"—but in the middle of his struggle Lilienthal learned that the Mississippian was threatening to "blow us out of the water" because the TVA had permitted a Negro girl to take an examination for a clerical position. Lilienthal's main threat was not Rankin, but McKellar, an aging spoilsman and probably the most parochial member of the Senate. After baiting Lilienthal for hours before the Appropriations Committee, McKellar told the press that he had the "pledge" of the President that Lilienthal would be gotten rid of. Later, Presidential Assistant Jonathan Daniels lunched with Lilienthal and told him that he had mentioned McKellar's statement to the President, who said that Daniels could tell Lilienthal that the previous spring McKellar had come in with bitter complaints about the TVA Chairman and that the President had replied:

"Well, Kenneth, I have been thinking about getting Lilienthal out of Tennessee myself. I would like to see a Columbia Valley Authority set up in the Northwest, and put Lilienthal in charge of it, since he has done such a good job. But I have never been able to get Congress to pass the bill for a CVA. So if you want to get rid of him, you go back on the Hill and get that bill passed." How much of this was banter, Lilienthal wondered. But he stayed on.

Like other Presidents, Roosevelt found that his dextrous political management and manipulation could not overcome Congress when great political interests and risks were at stake. National-service legislation in 1944 demonstrated the limits of his influences on the Hill. For many months before Teheran he had vacillated on the matter. Stimson pressed him for a strong proposal to Congress, but WMC and WPB officials were cool to the idea. Baruch argued that the best way to mobilize and allocate manpower was by allocating materials; men would shift to high-priority industries to get jobs. His mind set, but tired of the endless debate, Roosevelt, on returning from Teheran, told Rosenman to draft a proposal for a national-service bill for his State of the Union address, but not to tell a soul about it.

Rosenman was aghast. Not even tell Byrnes or McNutt or Stimson or "Bernie," men who had been laboring on the problem? No, said his chief, he did not want to argue about it any more. "I want it kept right here in the room just between us boys and Grace." Byrnes was so indignant when he heard the recommendation over the radio, Rosenman was told, that he stalked into the President's office and bitterly tendered his resignation; Roosevelt talked him out of it. Stimson was equally surprised, but also so delighted that he forgot to be indignant.

Congress was as cool to national-service legislation in early 1944 as it always had been to proposals that united labor and business in opposition. A gulf yawned between the legislators, sensitive to economic pressures, and Stimson, who saw a moral purpose in the bill transcending even the practical needs of war. A national-service law, he told the Congressmen, was a question of responsibility. "It is aimed to extend the principles of democracy and justice more evenly throughout our population. . . ." Congress did not see it that way; the bill died in committee. Roosevelt had finally come around to Stimson's point of view. National service transcended politics, he told Congress. "Great power must be used for great purposes." But he had come to this view late, he had not marshaled his administration behind his position, and he failed to convince the men on the Hill.

The President still met, the first thing on Monday mornings, with the congressional Big Four—Vice President Wallace, Speaker Rayburn, Senate Majority Leader Barkley, House Majority Leader McCormack. Years later Barkley would remember these sessions—Roosevelt sitting in his plain mahogany bed amid a pile of papers, wrapped in an aging gray bathrobe that he refused to give up, puffing on a cigarette through his long uptilted ivory holder, Wallace in turn voluble and quiet, Rayburn laconically sagacious, Barkley himself often speaking for the whole leadership on the Hill.

Late in February 1944 these usually amiable talks took a sharper turn. Even since the previous October, when Morgenthau had presented the President's stiff revenue proposals to the House Ways and Means Committe, the administration bill had been running—more often crawling—a legislative gantlet. The fiscal committees patiently heard scores of special-interest representatives. Most of the nation's press opposed the administration's tax program; the people, as reflected in a Gallup Poll, were as divided as usual. The Ways and Means Committee not only scrapped the Treasury's program, but also barred Treasury officials from attending its executive sessions. Eventually the committee's new bill, which would produce barely two billion dollars, was passed by a lopsided vote in the House. The Senate let the bill go over until the next session. In January the President warned that a realistic revenue law would tax all unreasonable profits, both individual and corporate, and that the tax bill then pending did not begin to meet that test. Undismayed, the Senate passed a bill that would raise only a fraction of the 10.5 billion requested by the President and that bristled with what the administration viewed as inequities and favors to special interests.

Congress, it seemed to Roosevelt, was playing with fiscal dynamite. Treasury men estimated that in the fiscal year 1944 income payments to individuals would amount to 152 billion, and that the amount of goods and services available could absorb only about eighty-nine billion of that figure. While the 1943 tax rate would reduce the difference by twenty-one billion, an inflationary gap amounting to forty-two billion would be left to threaten the nation's stabilization program. War-bond savings and other savings were not expected to reduce this figure enough to forestall the piling up of a dangerous amount of excess income. Taxes were needed for both revenue and stabilization.

The President bespoke his indignation over the tax bill in a bedside conference with the Big Four. All but Wallace urged him to sign it anyway; Roosevelt said he would think it over. A week later he had made up his mind. The administration position had hardened by then. Byrnes originally had favored acceptance of the bill on the ground that if "you asked your mother for a dollar and she gives you a dime" you should go back later for the ninety cents. But Vinson's and Paul's arguments swung Byrnes against the bill; and Morgenthau had glumly concluded that the President should let the bill become law without his signature.

When Barkley and his colleagues arrived for the next Monday conference, the President had his tentative veto message written out. He read it to his silent visitors; then Barkley once again sparred with him on the issues. The President was willing to give way on one or two questions, but he was adamant on what he saw as concessions to special interests. Timber was the main case in point. Barkley argued that it should be taxed as capital gains, since it took fifty years to grow a tree for lumber. He grew trees himself, Roosevelt said. Timber should be treated as a crop and therefore as income when sold.

"Well, Mr. President," Barkley went on, "it's perfectly obvious that you are going to veto this bill and there's no use for me to argue with you any longer about it." Barkley was so depressed that he rode back to the Capitol with Wallace in the latter's limousine without exchanging a word with him. His dismay turned to indignation next day when he saw the text of Roosevelt's veto message. New and searing phrases had been added.

He had asked, the President said, for legislation to raise 10.5 billion dollars over present revenues. Persons prominent in public life—everyone knew he was referring mainly to Willkie—had said that his request was too low. The bill from Congress purported to provide 2.1 billion in new revenues but it canceled out automatic increases in the Social Security tax yielding over a billion and granted relief from existing taxes that would cost the Treasury at least 150 million dollars.

"In this respect it is not a tax bill but a tax relief bill providing relief not for the needy but for the greedy." He listed "indefensible" special privileges to timber and other interests.

"It has been suggested by some that I should give my approval to this bill on the ground that having asked the Congress for a loaf of bread to take care of this war for the sake of this and succeeding generations, I should be content with a small piece of crust. I might have done so if I had not noted that the small piece of crust contained so many extraneous and inedible materials." He went on to condemn Congress for not simplifying tax laws and returns; the people, he added, were not "in a mood to study higher mathematics."

For years Barkley had been ridiculed in the press—especially in *Time*—as a bumbling and spineless flunky of the White House. Now as he read Roosevelt's biting words he felt personally affronted. He had been a liberal long before the New Deal, he reflected bitterly; he had learned his progressivism at the feet of Woodrow Wilson after coming to Washington from Paducah in 1913. He had gone down the line for Franklin Roosevelt's program, he had carried the administration's flag up on the Hill, often with little help from the White House, and now here was this sarcastic message. Barkley had to protect his political situation, too. In Kentucky a Republican trend seemed under way. In the Senate, like other elected leaders before and since, he was caught between members loyal to the President and the anti-Roosevelt Senators clustered in the citadels of power, including the Finance Committee, of which Barkley was a high-ranking member. He checked with his Senate cronies and found them equally aroused. He wanted to denounce the message immediately from the floor, but Chairman George of the Finance Committee was recognized first. Barkley decided to sleep on the matter. Next morning, as he left his apartment he told his wife, an invalid, that he would denounce the President's veto and resign as Majority Leader. "Go to it, I'm with you," she said.

Barkley spoke before packed galleries; he did not disappoint his audience. To keep his Democratic credentials, he began with a crack at Willkie—that "up-to-date Halley's comet darting across the firmament hither and yon to illuminate the heavens with an array of fantastic figures which neither I nor anybody can comprehend." While he talked, his old foe McKellar, who once had refused to speak to him for weeks even though their seats adjoined, ran copy from page boys who were bringing dictated pages from Barkley's office. Barkley went on to rebut Roosevelt's "deliberate and unjustified misstatements" point by point. Roosevelt's effort to compare his "little pine bushes with a sturdy oak, gum, poplar, or spruce . . . is like comparing a cricket to a stallion." The President's comment about tax relief for the greedy is a "calculated and deliberate assault upon the legislative integrity of every Member of Congress. Other members of Congress may do as they please; but, as for me, I do not propose to take this unjustifiable assault lying down." He concluded: "If the Congress of the United States has any self-respect left it will override the veto of the President and enact this tax bill into law, his objections to the contrary notwithstanding." Prolonged applause on the Senate floor, members rising, the reporter noted. Spectators joined in; newsmen dashed from their gallery to their typewriters and telephones.

At this moment Roosevelt was at Hyde Park. He had been quickly informed by Wallace and Byrnes of Barkley's impending speech and resignation—and he appeared to be unconcerned. He told Byrnes to forget it and "just don't give a damn . . ."; he remarked mildly to Hassett that Alben must be suffering from shell shock. Barkley was tired and Mrs. Barkley ill, he said later; it was just a nine-day wonder. When Byrnes pressed him for a conciliatory letter, the President agreed to send one if his War Mobilizer would draft it. Together the President and the former Senator produced a small masterpiece of balm and finesse.

"I sincerely hope," Roosevelt wrote to Barkley, "that you will not persist in your announced intention to resign as Majority Leader of the Senate. If you do, however, I hope that your colleagues will not accept your resignation; but if they do I hope that they will immediately and unanimously re-elect you."

Roosevelt's letter keyed a scenario that had already been planned. Barkley came out of a conference of Senate Democrats to tell reporters, amid exploding flashbulbs, with tears in his eyes, that he had resigned as Majority Leader. He retired to his office while his colleagues deliberated. Suddenly the conference-room door swung open; Tom Connally, resplendent in a long black coat, a boiled white shirt, gold studs, and flowing gray-white hair, burst out, crying, "Make way for liberty! Make way for liberty!" and pushed his way through reporters and cameramen to Barkley's office. A little procession of Senators followed. A few moments later Barkley was triumphantly escorted back to the conference room, where amid cheers and applause he was unanimously re-elected Majority Leader.

The Senate had had its hour. The nation's press was delirious. At last the White House errand boy had turned on his master; at last Congress had revolted against the dictator. More satisfaction was to come. The House overrode Roosevelt's tax veto, 299 to 95; the Senate did the same the next day, 72 to 14. Treasury experts said it was the first revenue act in history to become law over a veto.

The storm, as Roosevelt predicted, blew over in a few days. Barkley, who had seemed self-conscious and uncomfortable as a hero to the Senate barons, wrote the President a cordial note. When he returned to the White House as Majority Leader his role was unchanged. Roosevelt continued to appear undisturbed by the episode. Hassett could detect no bitterness or recrimination—even when the President inspected his Hyde Park timber-cutting operation, which was sending virgin oak direct to shipyards, though possibly it was accidental that photographers were on hand to record the size of the huge trunks. Passage of the tax bill over his veto, Hassett calculated, would save him $3,000 in taxes on his lumbering operations.

Still, things would not be quite the same again. Not only were eight billion dollars of taxes lost, but the orgy of anti-Roosevelt eruptions in Congress and the press left a heavy deposit of bitterness. Western as well as Southern Democratic Senators—Edwin C. Johnson, of Colorado, for one—were coming out publicly against a fourth term. Uneasiness persisted over Roosevelt. Why had he vetoed the bill, knowing he would gain nothing better? And why a veto in such harsh and mocking terms?

The columnists trotted out explanations. It was because Willkie was goading the President, some said, or because Barkley had infuriated him by belittling his Christmas trees, or because some New Dealer—Morgenthau or Byrnes or Rosenman or Paul—was really in control of fiscal policy. But it became evident that Roosevelt had written most of the cutting phrases in the veto message—and this fact helps explain Roosevelt's action. He had come home from a global mission to a squabbling capital. The barons on Capitol Hill in particular—George, McKellar, Rankin, and the rest—seemed to symbolize the parochialism, the selfishness, the greed, the pettiness that Roosevelt felt was undermining the war effort. He himself was less patient, less receptive to advice from congressional spokesman, a bit less sparing of feelings. So his vetoing of the tax and other major bills, and his allowing the soldiers'-vote bill to become law without his signature, dramatized the gap between White House and Congress; but it also would leave the record clear.

And always—for all the politicians—loomed the portent of the fall, the ultimate test by ballot. What would Roosevelt do? At the White House correspondents' dinner, the President threw back his head and roared as Bob Hope gabbed away: "I've always voted for Roosevelt as President. My father always voted for Roosevelt as President. . . ."

THE SUCTION PUMP

It was widely assumed in Washington that Roosevelt would run for a fourth term only if the war was still on by summer 1944.

Many Americans thought the war would be over and won by that time, but the President himself had always been loath to predict an early victory. "We have got a long, long road to go," he told visitors early in March 1944. "We are going to win the war—it is going to take an awfully long time."

The President spoke at a time when the war in Italy—the only active Allied front in the West—was going badly. Inching up the long valleys north of Naples, Mark Clark's Fifth Army and the British Eighth Army, with polyglot elements from other nations, had fought their way through the Germans' winter line and had come up hard against the Gustav Line, anchored in jutting, snow-covered mountains. Here was a soldier's purgatory—rough, brushy terrain cut by gullies and stream beds and flanked by rocky terraces, knife-edge cliffs, broken ridges, all of which favored the defenders. The sunny days of Calabria had given way to weeks of pelting rain and wet snow that turned fields into swamps and quagmires. The drenched, shivering soldiers crouched in foxholes or thigh-deep in swamplands were an ironic symbol. The kind of draining, positioned warfare that Churchill had abhorred in the plains of France was appearing again in the mountains of Italy. When Clark's 36th Division tried to force the Rapido River, south of Cassino, footbridges were blown up by mines or gunfire even while being erected; rubber boats sank under small-arms fire, and the few men who got across were trapped in barbed wire, mines, and machine-gun and shell fire. The 36th took 1,600 casualties in three days—and was not across the Rapido.

Churchill was dismayed but unmoved by the deepening stalemate in Italy. He would not change the Italian strategy, but would adjust other strategy to it. OVERLORD, he professed, still had highest priority, but must everything be subordinated to the "tyranny" of the cross-channel attack? As he saw the problem, the campaign in Italy was the vital counterpart to the main operation in France. He was still critical of the "American clear-cut, logical, large-scale" style of thought. "In life people have first to be taught 'Concentrate on essentials' . . . but it is only the first step. The second stage in war is a general harmony of war efforts by making everything fit together. . . ."

Though still feverish from pneumonia, Churchill had thrown himself into a battle to resuscitate the campaign in Italy. The stagnation on that front was scandalous, he told his Chief of Staff. A ray of hope was that Eisenhower planned an end run—an amphibious flanking attack behind the Germans at Anzio, thirty-eight miles south of Rome, conjoined with a renewed attack on the Gustav Line. Churchill was elated by this plan for a "cat claw." The rub was that fifty-six LST's destined for Britain and

OVERLORD would have to be held in the Mediterranean for the operation. Churchill sent a long, pleading letter to Roosevelt. The Italian battle could not be allowed to stagnate and fester, he insisted. A vast half-finished job could not be given up. The cat claw should decide the Battle of Rome and perhaps even destroy much of Kesselring's army. If this opportunity was lost, the Mediterranean campaign of 1944 would be ruined.

Once again Roosevelt confronted a Churchillian squeeze play in the Mediterranean; once again his Chiefs of Staff and planners worried about the suction pump; once again the President gave in. He did remind the Prime Minister that under the Teheran pledges he could not agree without Stalin's approval to any use of forces or equipment elsewhere that might delay or hazard the success of OVERLORD or ANVIL. "I thank God for this decision," Churchill wired back, "which engages us once again in wholehearted unity upon a great enterprise."

The cat claw struck Anzio on January 22. At first things went well. Undetected by the Germans, American and British assault troops met little resistance and quickly moved several miles inland. Unloading proceeded briskly. At this moment Kesselring's reserves were committed in the battle against the major Allied attack to the south, and for a few intoxicating hours a lunge through to Rome seemed possible. Then came Hitler's order of the day that the Führer expected the "bitterest struggle for every yard" for the sake of political consequences—the defense of Rome. The Anzio "abscess" must be liquidated. Ordering his Gustav Line troops on the defensive, Kesselring skillfully deployed his crack regiments into the Anzio perimeter. German divisions started moving down the boot of Italy. Fearing encirclement if they dashed toward Rome, the invaders fortified their beachhead positions and dug in. The attackers thus became the defenders. In the south the Allies stalled again below the formidable heights of Cassino. Roosevelt told reporters the situation was very tense.

Churchill was appalled at the failure to exploit Anzio. The wildcat hurled onto the shore, he complained later, had become a stranded whale. At least the whale was there to stay; heavy Nazi counterattacks came dangerously close to overrunning the beachhead, but the defenders hung on. It was clear that deadlock once again would grip the Italian front, that more men and supply would be needed, that the suction pump would speed up again. Once again tactics were colliding with strategy. It had been evident for some time that OVERLORD must be postponed until about the end of May. Now the British, who had never been very enthusiastic about ANVIL, were insisting that the planned invasion of southern France be scrapped or put off so that the full Mediterranean thrust would remain concentrated in Italy. German strength would be contained and bled below the Alps.

Roosevelt met with his Chiefs of Staff to consider this major proposal for altering the attack against Fortress Europe. The JCS saw the request as the latest in a long series of British efforts to favor the Mediterranean—efforts that seemed all the more curious now that the soft underbelly had turned out to be so hard. The President was mainly concerned with the political implications. He feared Soviet reaction to a cancellation of ANVIL; he did not want even to raise the matter at this point, when the usual rumors were flying around that Moscow (or Washington, or London) was seeking a separate peace with Berlin. Certainly ANVIL could not be scrapped without consulting Moscow first. The only immediate solution to the problem was to postpone a solution. In London, Eisenhower, ever the adjuster, worked out a formula that favored a further build-up in Italy but kept ANVIL alive.

The President confronted an even more crucial matter of strategy. During the long months of the early Italian campaign doubts had been rising among American military planners, and even more among British, as to the effectiveness of unconditional surrender. American army men at first accepted the presidential declaration without serious question, since it provided a definite, clear-cut goal of defeating the enemy decisively without getting into complex political and psychological problems. By early 1944 it became clear that Nazi propagandists were using the declaration as proof that the Allies were bent on exterminating the German nation and enslaving the German people. Intelligence officers in both London and Washington were becoming more and more doubtful about the doctrine, especially in view of the need to undermine Nazi resistance to the invasion of France. Late in March 1944 the Joint Chiefs of Staff asked the President to retreat from his uncompromising stand and to make clear now that the Allied intention was not to destroy the German people or nation but, rather, the German capacity for military conquest.

The Commander in Chief was adamant. With one eye on possible Soviet reaction to weakening on unconditional surrender, he told his chiefs:

". . . A somewhat long study and personal experience in and out of Germany leads me to believe that German Philosophy cannot be changed by decree, law or military order. The change in German Philosophy must be evolutionary and may take two generations." He was opposed to reconstructing a German state that would undertake peace moves. This might bring a period of quiet, but then a third world war.

"Please note that I am not willing at this time to say that we do not intend to destroy the German nation. As long as the word 'Reich' exists in Germany as expressing a nationhood, it will forever be associated with the present form of nationhood. If we admit that, we must seek to eliminate the very word 'Reich' and what it stands for today."

Of course, the President said to Hull a few days later, there would have to be exceptions, "not to the surrender principle but to the application of it in specific cases." This, he added, was a very different thing from changing the principle. "Germany understands only one kind of language," he told Hull.

The President's harsh attitude toward Germany was not unaffected by a growing burden on the world's conscience. This was the agony of the Jews.

By January 1944 Morgenthau had been pressing Hull for months to move more vigorously on the complex actions needed to save thousands of Jews in their perilous refuges from Rumania to France. He had told Assistant Secretary of State Breckinridge Long to his face that the impression was all around that "you, particularly, are anti-semitic"; Long had denied it. At the turn of the year there was a flurry of activity in the State Department, but when Morgenthau visited Hull on January 11, 1944, he found the old man depressed and perplexed by the refugee situation. Morgenthau asked Randolph Paul to report on the urgency of the situation.

"Report to the Secretary on the Acquiescence of this Government in the Murder of the Jews," Paul entitled his blunt indictment. It began: "One of the greatest crimes in history, the slaughter of the Jewish people in Europe, is continuing unabated." He went on to charge that State Department officials had not only failed to use governmental machinery to rescue Jews from Hitler but also had used that machinery to prevent the rescue of Jews, had hindered private efforts, and had willfully covered up their "guilt."

Morgenthau soon confronted the President with his own version of this report, which he had shortened but not tempered. Paul and John Pehle, the young head of Foreign Funds Control, accompanied their chief to the White House. Roosevelt, Morgenthau later told his staff, "seemed disinclined to believe that Long wanted to stop effective action from being taken, but said that Long had been somewhat soured on the problem when Rabbi Wise got Long to approve a long list of people being brought into this country many of whom turned out to be bad people. . . ." But Morgenthau's anguish and Pehle's specific data impressed the President. The Secretary had brought along the draft of an executive order creating a War Refugee Board to take operations away from the State Department. Roosevelt approved the idea and asked Morgenthau to discuss it with Undersecretary of State Stettinius. Morgenthau did that very afternoon, and Stettinius approved.

Roosevelt acted within the week. He announced the establishment of the War Refugee Board, with Pehle as Acting Executive Director. "It is the policy of this Government," the executive order began, "to take all measures within its power to rescue the victims of enemy oppression who are in imminent danger of death and otherwise to afford such victims all possible relief and assistance consistent with the successful prosecution of the war." Composed of the Secretaries of State, Treasury, and War, and armed with funds and both legal and moral authority, the new board went right to work. It was fearfully late—in many cases too late. But at last the administration was putting some drive and persistence into the vast rescue operation.

Within two months, indeed, Morgenthau could come to the White House with a hopeful progress report. His chief was keenly interested, but even while Morgenthau was talking about refugees, the President was thinking about the implications for Palestine. He was calculating how he could induce the British to promise publicly that if the Refugee Board actually brought Jews out of Europe, London would let them go to Palestine. "You know," the President said to Morgenthau, "the Arabs don't like this thing." Neither did Morgenthau—he was not a Zionist—but he, Stimson, and Pehle persuaded the President to support emergency refugee shelters in the United States. Fearing opposition on the Hill, the President took steps to bring 1,000 refugees from Italy to an emergency shelter in Oswego, New York—and then simply announced his plan to Congress.

"YOUR MOVE, TOJO"

December 14, 1943, © Low, reprinted by permission of *The Manchester Guardian*

The suction pump was still working in the Pacific, too. At the close of the second Cairo Conference Roosevelt and Churchill had initialed a revised plan for defeating Japan. The pivot of strategy would no longer be a mere holding operation around the vast Japanese perimeter, or a counteroffensive based on hopping from one island to the next, or even the long-planned major thrust through Burma and China. The planners now proposed a line of attack as bold and direct as OVERLORD itself—a massive amphibious operation sweeping across the western Pacific, outflanking and isolating big enemy bases, blockading the home islands by sea and air, and then closing in for the final assault. The Pacific advance would be two-pronged. The advance along the New Guinea–Netherlands East Indies–Philippine axis would proceed concurrently with operations to capture the Mandated Islands. The two series of operations would be mutually supported.

Roosevelt was delighted with the plan. Capitalizing on the enormous build-up in supply and troops, it would permit crushing blows against Japan even while the war in Europe continued, and it would meet popular demands for a greater effort in the Pacific. After talking with Eisenhower and Halsey in Washington shortly after the new year began, the President told reporters that the greatest possible pressure would be brought to bear on the European and Pacific theaters simultaneously.

Glittering naval and amphibious feats had made this plan seem feasible. In November 1943 Marines and soldiers under Admiral Spruance had counterattacked on Makin and Tarawa in the Gilbert Islands, now part of the Japanese outer defenses. War had rarely found a lovelier setting—curving ribbons of golden beaches and lowlands and coral reefs embracing placid lagoons, all brushed by warm winds from the encircling Pacific. But embedded under the sand and the rustling palm trees were hundreds of pillboxes built of concrete five feet thick, with roofs of iron rails laid on coconut logs, protected by outer walls of sand and coral ten feet thick. American planes and warships engulfed these tiny islands in flame; amphibious tractors ground toward shore with their machine guns firing; heavily laden Marines and soldiers stormed over the lacerating reefs and closed in on the enemy, only to see the strong points come alive and respond with withering, close-up fire. The only way to win was to advance foot by foot, enfilading pillboxes, pouring automatic fire into gun slits, lofting grenades, poling in TNT attached to long iron pipes, burning Japanese alive in their dugouts or flushing them out and gunning them down. On tiny Tarawa the Marines lost 1,000 dead and killed 3,000 of the enemy.

The Gilberts proved that American troops could capture powerful island bastions once they closed in on them—and that the Japanese Navy could not keep them away. The crucial step was the seizure of control of the central Pacific by Nimitz's fast-growing Navy. By 1944 his carriers and cruisers were ranging almost at will in the vast area. Despite occasional disasters—the carrier *Liscombe Bay* was torpedoed with the loss of over two-thirds of her company—the fleet was big enough to feint widely dispersed attacks and then isolate a target and overwhelm it. In February Nimitz's men seized key islands in the Kwajalein atoll. The Japanese made little effort to counter the heavy onslaught; Imperial Headquarters had decided to let the outlying garrisons conduct delaying actions while the main defense fell back to the perimeter of Timor–western New Guinea–Truk–Marianas. Kwajalein, key point in the atoll, was seized in several days of furious fighting the first week of February; Eniwetok atoll, only 1,000 miles from the Marianas, fell later in the month. The Eniwetok attack had been planned for mid-1944; Spruance had the mobility and the power to accelerate.

The President could be proud of his Navy, Forrestal reported to him during the Kwajalein fighting. The difference in the Navy's teamwork now over 1942 was as of night and day. "It had the most meticulous plan . . . a substantial result at an astonishingly small cost. . . ."

To the south and west Halsey and MacArthur were now accelerating their long climb up the twin ladders of New Guinea and the Solomons. American and Australian troops spent most of late 1943 subduing Japanese forces in southeastern New Guinea; then MacArthur leaped four hundred miles to Hollandia on the northern coast, outflanking 50,000 Japanese in between. Next he hopped another three hundred miles to seize Biak Island. Halsey's forces captured New Georgia during the summer of 1943, gained naval control of the whole northern Solomons area, and he and MacArthur combined forces to seize the Admiralty Islands, bypassing the enemy bastion of Rabaul. Both ladders pointed directly at the Philippines.

In his map room the President studied the great blue charts of the Pacific showing the latest advances and dispositions. He knew that the British Chiefs of Staff were so impressed by his Navy's Pacific operations that they were yearning for British fleet units to help out in the central Pacific and then take their place on MacArthur's left flank. Though no less impressed, Churchill was urging his chiefs to put the main weight of the British effort against Japan not in the Pacific, and not even in Burma and China, but in Sumatra and Malaya, with an eye to the recapture of Singapore. In Asia, too, Churchill wanted an underbelly strategy, with postwar aspects in view. So strongly did he feel, indeed, that he denied even understanding the Pacific plan adopted at Cairo—though he did not deny having initialed it—and this difference between Churchill and his chiefs became so acute during the winter of 1944 that they hinted they might resign.

Roosevelt made his own position clear to Churchill. "My Chiefs of Staff are agreed that the primary intermediate objective of our advance across the Pacific lies in the Formosa–China coast–Luzon area. The success of recent operations in the Gilberts and Marshalls indicates that we can accelerate our movements westward. . . . I have always advocated the development of China as a base for the support of our Pacific advances." Every effort, he went on, must be made to increase the flow of supplies into China, and this could be done only by increasing the air tonnage or by opening a road through Burma. He urged Churchill to give Mountbatten his energetic encouragement in the campaign in Upper Burma.

Roosevelt's letter reflected a continued lowering of earlier American hopes that southern China could become the main base for the final assault on the home islands. As both Stilwell's forces and the British took the offensive in northern Burma during the late winter of 1944, Roosevelt hoped to boost the airlift of supplies over the "Hump" and to push roads and pipelines into China. In personal letters to Roosevelt and Hopkins, Chennault was pleading for more supplies and promising that with them his Fourteenth United States Air Force could sink 200,000 tons of Japanese shipping a month along China's coast.

"To one with your war experience and special mastery of naval strategy," Chennault wrote to Roosevelt, "I need hardly point out that the Japanese position in South-east Asia and the South-west Pacific must soon fall, if Japan has not the shipping and air power to support them." He contended that air attacks on shipping in the months ahead would be far more conclusive than strategic bombing of the homeland.

Roosevelt wrote a warm—and noncommittal—answer. "You are the Doctor," he ended, "and I approve your treatment. Nevertheless, as a matter perhaps of sentimentality, I have had a hope that we could get at least one bombing expedition against Tokyo before the second anniversary of Doolittle's flight. I really believe that the morale effect would help!"

The President shared the high hopes of the time for American air power on both continents. From Britain hundreds of B-17's and B-24's had been striking German targets throughout 1943, focusing on high-priority objectives such as the ball-bearing plants at Schweinfurt and aircraft factories in Regensburg and Bremen. Some of the bombing had been brilliantly effective; other forays had been tragically expensive—as in the loss of sixty out of 228 bombers attacking Schweinfurt in mid-October—and often the Air Force estimates of damage inflicted and enemy planes shot down were grossly exaggerated. This was not merely a public-relations effort; unwittingly inflated reports and hopes reached the Air Force command and the President himself.

By January 1944, indeed, hard-nosed British Intelligence officers were indicating that Goering's fighter force was still increasing. Factories were smashed, workers killed, but the vital machine tools were dragged back into place and made to run again. The Germans were now dispersing their key war plants. This situation boded ill both for deep penetration bombing and for OVERLORD, which would require almost absolute command of the air. "My personal message to you," Arnold wrote to the commanders of the Eighth and Fifteenth Air Forces on New Year's Day, "this is a MUST—is to, *'Destroy the Enemy Air Force wherever you find them, in the air, on the ground and in the factories.'*" The arrival of long-range fighters in early 1944 gave the bombers vitally needed protection over their targets. Late in February the skies cleared over Germany, and 3,300 bombers from the Eighth Air Force and five hundred from the Fifteenth dropped almost 10,000 tons of bombs, with the loss of 226 bombers. Early in March the Eighth bombed Berlin heavily, for the first time. But in the heart of Europe the Luftwaffe was still putting up fierce resistance.

Berlin, Anzio, Kwajalein, Burma—these were but pinpricks compared with the mighty thrusts in the east. In January 1944 the Russians broke the Leningrad blockade. In February and March Soviet troops outflanked several Nazi divisions in the Korsun salient on the Dnieper and in a "mud offensive" pushed toward Rumania. In April they liberated Odessa. The Russians now were killing and capturing Germans by the tens of thousands; their own losses were frightful as always. Stalin, who had politely seized every opportunity to congratulate Roosevelt on Allied successes during 1943, was silent during the early months of 1944. He, too, was waiting for OVERLORD.

FIFTEEN *The Dominion of Mars*

AT THE center of a straining, throbbing nation in arms the White House in the winter of 1944 seemed more tranquil than a decade before. Under a mantle of new snow it showed the quiet of the storm center in its graceful aloofness from the hubbub around it. Visitors, remembering the bustle of grandchildren, ballet dancers, left-wing leaders, politicos, intellectuals, young friends of the Roosevelt children, noted Sistie's and Buzzie's Flexible Flyers standing unused in a litter of miscellany under the portico; the White House, with its pillars peeling a bit at the bottom, even seemed to need a coat of paint.

The people around the President changed but the structure of human relations around him had a kind of fixity. Hopkins was critically ill and out of commission all through the winter and spring, but Leahy partly took his place on military matters and Byrnes on domestic. Eleanor Roosevelt was traveling as much as ever—she was in Brazil on her thirty-ninth wedding anniversary—but Anna had come for a visit in the fall of 1943 and had decided to stay on to help her father. Marvin McIntyre was dead, but in February the President cheerily announced a "court-martial" for the gray, stooped, unflappable Hassett and presented him with a commission as full presidential secretary, dubbing him a "rare combination of Roget, Bartlett, & Buckle." Grace Tully and the other secretaries helped preserve an atmosphere of unhurried efficiency. Fala was four and was given a cake, which he refused to eat for the benefit of the photographers.

Roosevelt still followed his old routine, reading and working in bed until late in the morning, whizzing off in his wheel chair to the oval office, dropping into the map room with Leahy to look over shifting military dispositions noted by flags and pins, seeing callers through the afternoon, dictating his pithy little letters for an hour or so, then returning to the mansion for cocktails and a late dinner. But the pace was a bit slower now, the anecdotes a bit longer, the visitors a bit fewer, the evenings a bit shorter.

On the morning of March 4, 1944 the President observed the

start of his twelfth year in office with a reception for two hundred in the East Room. The old warriors of the New Deal were there and the new warriors of the Pentagon and the Navy. Old Dr. Peabody, now eighty-six, in a full and vibrant voice asked divine help for "thy servant, Franklin" and to "save us from all false choices."

The chief of the warriors was sixty-two and in the winter of 1944 he was ailing and tired. Days after he had recovered from his post-Teheran flu of January he was complaining of headaches in the evening. Those in the White House who saw him the most—especially Anna Boettiger and Grace Tully—became more and more alarmed about his condition. He seemed strangely tired even in the morning hours; he occasionally nodded off during a conversation; once he blanked out halfway through signing his name to a letter, leaving a long scrawl. Finally Anna spoke to Dr. McIntire. The Admiral, an ear, nose, and throat specialist, seemed concerned, too, but curiously resistant to talking with the President. Anna pressed him to speak at least to Eleanor. The upshot was that the President was persuaded to go, on March 27, 1944, to the United States Medical Hospital at Bethesda, Maryland, for a check-up. Lieutenant Commander Howard G. Bruenn, a consultant in cardiology who was in charge of the Electro-Cardiograph Department, was detailed to examine him.

The young Navy doctor was called in so hurriedly that he had no time to look over the President's medical records before greeting his distinguished patient. He quickly felt at ease, though, when Roosevelt came rolling down the corridor in his wheel chair, wisecracking with an old friend and waving genially to the nurses and patients who clustered in the hallways and peeked at him around corners. As the President was lifted to the examining table, he seemed to Bruenn neither disturbed by having to undergo examination nor annoyed by it—indeed, not especially interested in it.

It was Bruenn who was first surprised, then disturbed, and finally shocked as he conducted the examination and then rushed to check the earlier records. Not only was Roosevelt tired and gray of face, slightly feverish, able to move only with difficulty and with breathlessness, and coughing frequently—clearly suffering from bronchitis—but his basic condition was far more serious. Roosevelt's heart, Bruenn found, while regular in rhythm, was enlarged. At the apex, Bruenn found a blowing systolic murmur. The second aortic sound was loud and booming. Blood pressure was 186/108, compared with 136/78 in mid-1935, 162/98 two years later, and 188/105 in early 1941. Since 1941 there had been significant increase in the size of the cardiac shadow. The enlargement of the heart, which was mainly of the left ventricle, was evidently caused by a dilated and tortuous aorta; and the pulmonary vessels were engorged.

Bruenn's findings were grim: hypertension, hypertensive heart disease, cardiac failure.

Emergency conferences were held among McIntire, Bruenn, and other Navy doctors, with Drs. James A. Paullin and Frank Lahey brought in as consultants. It was obvious that the patient must be put on a regimen, but how much could a President—especially *this* President—be expected to follow the ordinary heart patient's routine? One or two weeks of nursing care was suggested, but rejected because of the demands on the President. Bruenn urged that at least Roosevelt be digitalized; there was some resistance, but Bruenn insisted that if that were not done he could take no further responsibility for the case. The doctors finally agreed on a program: digitalis, less daily activity, fewer cigarettes, a one-hour rest after meals, a quiet dinner in the White House quarters, at least ten hours' sleep, no swimming in the pool, a diet of 2,600 calories moderately low in fat, and mild laxatives to avoid straining.

The digitalis seemed to bring good results within three days. When Bruenn examined his patient on April 3, 1944, Roosevelt had had a refreshing ten hours' sleep, his color was good, his lungs entirely clear, and there was no dyspnea on lying flat. The systolic murmur persisted, however, and his blood pressure was still disturbing. He continued to improve during the following days, but Bruenn and his colleagues decided that he needed a real vacation. The President readily agreed to take a long rest in the sun at Bernard Baruch's plantation, "Hobcaw," in South Carolina.

The cardinal issue during these alarming days was who should tell the President about his condition, and in what manner? The doctors agreed that he should be given the full facts, if only to gain his co-operation. But who would tell him? It was soon clear that the President himself would not raise the question; not once did he ask why he had to have the examination or take drugs or get more rest. He simply followed the doctors' recommendations to the extent he could and left the matter there. Bruenn did not feel it his duty to inform the President; he was only a lieutenant commander and was a newcomer to the White House. Everyone evidently assumed that McIntire had the responsibility and would exercise it, but there is no indication that he did. Perhaps he lacked sufficient confidence in his own capacity to pass on such portentous findings to the President, especially if he should be asked difficult questions. Perhaps he sensed that the President would neither accept the significance of the findings nor act on them. Perhaps he realized how fatalistic the President was, or perhaps he realized that no matter how well grounded the findings there was a heavy psychological and political element in the situation, and that a President—especially one with Roosevelt's determination—could not be advised as easily or authoritatively as the ordinary patient. Or perhaps, after all his rosy prognoses of the past, he was simply too timid.

So Roosevelt went off to Hobcaw Barony not knowing that he was suffering from anything more than bronchitis, or the flu. He never asked what were the little green tablets—the digitalis—that he was taking. He wrote to Hopkins that he had had a really grand time there—"slept twelve hours out of the twenty-four, sat in the sun, never lost my temper, and decided to let the world go hang. The interesting thing is that the world didn't hang." He had pleasant visitors—members of his family, and Lucy Rutherfurd. He claimed that he had cut down his drinks to one and a half cocktails per evening and nothing more, "not one complimentary highball or nightcap," and that he had cut his cigarettes down from twenty or thirty a day to five or six. "Luckily they still taste rotten but it can be done." The President did experience a painful gall bladder attack at Hobcaw, but medication relieved the pain and there were no cardiac symptoms.

So it was not really a matter of work. He was tired, Miss Perkins remembered later, and he could not bear to be tired. Grace Tully still worried about the more pronounced tremble of his hands as he lit a cigarette, the dark circles that no longer ever seemed to fade from around his eyes, the slump in his shoulders. Watching Roosevelt at a press conference in March, Allen Drury felt that "subdued" was the only word for the man. The well-known gestures—the quick laugh, the upflung head, the open smile, the intent, open-mouthed, expressionless look when he was listening—all were there, just as they had been in numberless newsreels and photographs. But underneath, Drury detected a certain lifelessness, a certain preoccupation, a tired impatience—whether from work or political opposition, or from age or ill-health, Drury could not tell.

On his Washington stopovers James Roosevelt noted that his father was doing little things—autographing books and digging mementos out of old trunks and boxes for his children and grandchildren—as though he had some feeling of time closing in. Still, the old buoyancy was there, even if it took longer to show. Washington would twitter with gossip that the President was dead or dying, and then he would return from the South or from Hyde Park, refreshed, appearing a bit thin but radiant and vigorous. Visitors kept remarking on how wasted the President's face seemed, but the main reason for his changed appearance was his determination to lose weight—and his success in dropping from 188 pounds to about 165.

Nothing stimulated him more than memories of old times. When Eleanor was told in Curaçao that "Lieutenant" Roosevelt had visited there on an American warship and had been given a goat as a mascot for his ship, she asked her husband, "What have you been holding out on me all these years?"

"I have an alibi," the President wrote in a memo to her. "The only time I was ever in Curacao in my life was in 1904 when I went through the West Indies on a Hamburg-American Line 'yacht.' I was accompanied by and thoroughly chaperoned by my maternal parent.

"I was never given a goat—neither did anyone get my goat!

"This looks to me like a German plot!"

SECRECY AND "SEDITION"

In his diary Stimson was still railing at the President's "one-man government," which helped produce "this madhouse of Washington." In fact, his chief was running the White House much as he had in prewar days, while all around him were rising the huge bureaucratic structures of defense and welfare that would characterize the capital for decades to come.

The apex of the huge structures was the tiny west wing of the White House. Here the old hands, including Steve Early and Pa Watson, served and protected the President. Executive clerks Maurice Latta and William Hopkins sought to keep some control over the documents and messages that flooded into the White House—no easy job given Roosevelt's distaste for set communications channels. The White House office had already begun to spill over into the old State Department Building across the way; administrative assistants—Jonathan Daniels, Lowell Mellett, Lauchlin Currie, David K. Niles, and others—occupied on the second floor a row of offices that they called "Death Row" because of the turnover. The President obtained Blair House, across the street, for putting up distinguished guests. Rosenman was still in charge of the speechwriting team, but he had no team, because Hopkins was in the Mayo Clinic and Sherwood was in London as head of the Overseas Branch of OWI.

Over in the east wing, which was in the final stages of building, Byrnes ran an even smaller shop than Roosevelt's. In a clutter of tiny offices and partitioned cubbyholes—for a time the news ticker was in the men's room—a small staff struggled with the tide of problems relentlessly streaming in from the civilian agencies struggling for funds, authority, manpower, and recognition. Ben Cohen, as incisive and unpretentious as ever, served as his legal adviser; "special adviser" Baruch offered wise, opinionated counsel; Samuel Lubell and a handful of others made up the rest of the full-time staff. Byrnes set up a War Mobilization Committee composed of Stimson, Nelson, and other top civilians. Roosevelt occasionally presided over its meetings—it was the nearest thing he ever had to a war cabinet—but like most of the White House committees it dwindled into innocuous desuetude.

Crowded also into the east wing was Admiral Leahy, with a staff that never numbered more than two or three civilian secretaries and a couple of aides. Unlike Byrnes, he spurned the notion of having a public-relations man, on the grounds that his chief should do all the talking and was better at it anyway. As Roosevelt's personal Chief of Staff, Leahy presided over meetings of the Joint Chiefs of Staff, prepared its agenda, and signed its major decisions, but he did not exert strong leadership on the committee and recognized that important decisions were often made between Roosevelt and individual members of it, especially Marshall. Behind the JCS were banked its supporting agencies: the Joint Deputy Chiefs of Staff, Joint Secretariat, Joint Staff Planners, with its own Joint War Plans Committee, Joint Intelligence Committee, and a host of others.

The third leg supporting the administrative tripod of the White House was the Bureau of the Budget, also located in the old State Department Building. Under Harold Smith's gifted leadership the bureau had moved far beyond its traditional budgetary responsibility and was making ambitious efforts to plan, co-ordinate, and review the whole war administration. With its special access to the west wing and with the talents of men like Wayne Coy, Donald Stone, and Stuart Rice, the Budget Bureau had become the Presiden't biggest single staff resource.

On paper, in form, on an organization chart it all looked so logical—the Chief Executive at the top of the administrative apex, his three "assistant presidents" or chiefs of staff just below him, and then the lines of control and responsibility radiating out to the great bureaucratic workshops along Pennsylvania Avenue and the Mall. In fact, Roosevelt was carrying on the old Rooseveltian tradition of administrative juggling and disorganization. He was no more able in 1944 than in 1940 or 1934 to work through one chief of staff. He had not three, but at least a dozen, "assistant presidents," including Marshall, the more influential Cabinet members, especially Hull and Stimson, war-agency czars Nelson, McNutt, Land, and others. Despite Leahy's and Byrnes's efforts, co-ordination among the "assistant presidents" was sometimes weak. Byrnes and Smith jousted with each other with icy politeness. It was not always clear whether Marshall or Stimson should report to the President on a military matter.

Roosevelt's penchant for secrecy within the administration compounded the whole problem. Even such a primitive matter as communication was not always certain; occasionally messages to Roosevelt were delayed days and even weeks, and generals and admirals learned about a vital White House decision first from the British. Marshall sometimes was unsure which version of presidential statements at Cabinet meetings was correct. And he complained to Byrnes that the JCS had to wait a day or two before learning of important White House decisions.

Hopkins, the only man who had ever really served as assistant president or as an over-all chief of staff, was sorely missed. He was restless to come back but finally aware of his condition. When T. V. Soong asked him for aid on a matter, Hopkins balked. "Tell them I'm sick." But the President seemed in no hurry to have Hopkins back. He ordered him to stay away from the White House until mid-June at the earliest. If he returned before that, Roosevelt warned, he would be extremely unpopular in Washington, "with the exception of Cissy Patterson who wants to kill you off as soon as possible—just as she does me. . . .

"Tell Louise to use the old-fashioned hatpin if you don't behave!"

As Roosevelt's reference to Cissy Patterson suggested, the hostilities between the White House and part of the press continued through the war. Administration officials held confidential "backgrounders" with favored members of the press—columnist Raymond Clapper, Marquis Childs, of the St. Louis *Post-Dispatch*, Turner Catledge, of the New York *Times*, and a few others. The anti-Roosevelt newspapers retaliated by publishing "secret" war information. The President could do little but complain at his press conferences about irresponsible columnists and commentators.

It did seem in early 1944, though, that he was at last bringing to book a group of radical rightists whom he considered guilty of seditious conduct. For weeks he had prodded Biddle at Cabinet meetings: "When are you going to indict the seditionists?" Finally, Biddle did so, but the preliminaries stretched out over months. He put a group of thirty on trial in Federal District Court in Washington. It seemed like a grand rally of all the fanatic Roosevelt haters: Joseph E. McWilliams, head of the Christian Mobilizers, who liked to refer to Roosevelt as the "Jew King"; Mrs. Elizabeth Dilling, author of *The Red Network*; an erratic lady nicknamed "T.N.T." who delighted photographers with her stiff-armed Nazi salutes; James True, said to have received Patent No. 2,026,077 for a "Kike Killer," a short rounded club made also in a smaller size for ladies; Lawrence Dennis, philosopher of fascism; and others ranging from the dotty to the desperate.

The defendants were charged with conspiring to overthrow the government in favor of a Nazi dictatorship and stating that the Japanese attack on Pearl Harbor was deliberately invited by

May 11, 1944, C. K. Berryman, courtesy of the Washington (D.C.) *Star*

Roosevelt and his gang; that the American government was controlled by Communists, international Jews, and plutocrats; that the Axis cause was the cause of morality and justice. The trial got under way amid histrionics but dwindled into endless legalisms and obstructions; it lasted over seven months; the judge died before its conclusion; no retrial was held, and in the end the indictment was ingloriously dismissed. The trial did serve to muzzle "seditious" propaganda, but it also revealed Roosevelt as a better Jeffersonian in principle than in practice.

Perhaps the most bitter anti-Rooseveltian in the spring of 1944 was no seditionist, but Sewell Avery, head of the huge mail-order house Montgomery Ward. For many months Avery had been defying the War Labor Board by refusing to negotiate with the CIO union that had won representation rights. When the union called a strike the President ordered the men to return to work and the company to follow the Labor Board's orders and recognize the union. Avery refused. Normally the War Department would have taken over the plant, but knowing that Stimson was keenly opposed to seizure of a nondefense industry and perhaps glad for a chance to put Jesse Jones on the spot, Roosevelt ordered the Secretary of Commerce to seize and operate the Chicago plant. Jones promptly turned the job over to his Undersecretary, Wayne Taylor, himself a wealthy Chicago businessman. Prodded by Byrnes to go to Chicago and expedite the seizure, Attorney General Biddle flew out, occupied Avery's office, and asked for Avery's co-operation. When Avery refused, saying "to hell with the government," he ordered him taken out.

"You New Dealer!" Avery exploded, using the worst epithet in his vocabulary. A photograph of the portly executive leaning back in two soldiers' arms, his hands folded benevolently over his stomach, hit the front page of hundreds of newspapers. A great hubbub followed. Government by bayonet, one editor termed it.

The President calmly reviewed with reporters "a little history that the country doesn't know," reciting the long story of Montgomery Ward recalcitrance. A lot of people were seeing things under their bed, he complained; having been at Hobcaw Barony he could view the whole thing with some detachment. He did not mention Avery by name. The President's judicious mien had little effect. The company continued its defiance, and later in the year Roosevelt ordered Stimson to take it over. This time the President did not mince words. Montgomery Ward, he said, under Avery's leadership "has waged a bitter fight against the bona fide unions of its employees throughout the war. . . . We cannot allow Montgomery Ward to set aside the wartime policies of the United States Government just because Mr. Sewell Avery does not approve of the Government's procedure for handling labor disputes."

Roosevelt had backed Biddle all the way through. When the Attorney General had to face a special House investigating committee, his chief wrote to him: "Don't let the boys get you down," adding in his own hand, "bite 'em!"

One day during the height of the mobilization effort, Steve Early telephoned Rosenman to say that Mrs. Roosevelt wanted them to talk to a young man about something very important. When Early and Rosenman met with the rather wild-eyed man in Early's office they were astonished when the visitor asked whether the walls were bugged, whether the secretaries ever eavesdropped—and suddenly flung open a door to see if anyone was listening. They were even more astonished when he told them that he worked on atomic energy and told them about the bomb; neither Early nor Rosenman had heard of it. The visitor said he had come because the big corporations in general and Du Pont in particular were taking control of the atomic project in order to monopolize postwar energy. Early and Rosenman could only report the problem—and the visitor—to the War Department.

It was a zany item in the whole complex of secrecy that surrounded the atomic project. It was so secret that Bush's progress reports to Roosevelt were returned, with no copies made even for the White House files. The President withheld knowledge of the project from Hull and from other key decision-making officials. Grace Tully remembered the President saying, around June 1944, "I can't tell you what this is, Grace, but if it works, and pray God it does, it will save many American lives."

The work on the atomic bomb at Oak Ridge, Hanford, and Los Alamos was carried out in utmost secrecy and isolation. Exceptional security precautions were taken. Very few of the 150,000 people employed in the Manhattan Project knew the real purpose of their work. General Leslie R. Groves, head of the project, wanted no communication among scientists working in different sectors, so he enforced a policy of compartmentalization. This policy was virtually ignored, however, in the Los Alamos laboratories, where the free exchange of information was vital and unavoidable. Security officials thoroughly investigated the scientists, censored their mail, listened in on their telephone conservations, forbade them to tell their families the nature of their work, assigned them code names and bodyguards. J. Robert Oppenheimer, Director of Los Alamos and chief recruiter of the glittering assemblage of scientists there, was kept under continuous surveillance by the Army and the FBI.

Secrecy infected every level of government, including Congress. Until 1944 the Manhattan Project had been supported by funds available from various War Department sources, but expenditures were rising so steeply that appropriations had to come directly from Congress. Early in February Stimson, Marshall, and Bush met secretly with Rayburn, McCormack, and Martin and described the program to them in general terms; later they met with Senate leaders. Appropriations were then pushed through a blind Congress without debate. Several Congressmen grew suspicious and proposed to visit the Oak Ridge and Hanford installations; they were headed off by their colleagues and by Stimson and Marshall.

Atomic secrecy strained Anglo-American relations, too. Despite Roosevelt's agreement with Churchill in 1942 on joint conduct of atomic work, a veil of secrecy closed in on the program after the Army took over the Manhattan Project, and by the end of 1942 Roosevelt seemed to support the Army's wish to share no more information with the British than was necessary. At Casablanca, Churchill said that if the exchange of information was not continued Britain would develop the bomb independently, and that would be a somber decision. After Churchill's scientific adviser, Lord Cherwell, told the President in May 1943 that Britain wanted the atomic bomb mainly for military purposes to counteract Soviet might, and was not interested in industrial use of atomic energy, Roosevelt decided in favor of "complete exchange of all information." As a result of a communications mix-up, however, Bush, in England, did not get Roosevelt's instructions and persuaded Churchill to accept a limited interchange of information directly relating to war plans. At Quebec in August the two leaders ratified this agreement in essence and set up an Anglo-American-Canadian policy committee to supervise the joint atomic work of the three nations.

Sharing atomic information with Britain was one thing; with Russia, quite another. In this momentous field the Soviets found themselves once again excluded by the Atlantic partners.

By early 1944 Bohr was arousing sharp concern among his fellow scientists and others about the prospect of a fateful nuclear competition after the war. The Danish physicist did not oppose developing the bomb or even using it in the war, but he was convinced that the enormous power of the atom then being released for destructive purposes offered supreme danger and opportunity after the war. He felt it imperative that before the bomb was ever used the Allies establish international control and inspection of atomic energy to build an open world of friendly international co-operation. Bohr wanted the United States and Britain to approach the Soviets about the matter while Russia was still an ally in order to foster an atmosphere of mutual trust. If the two democracies did not make an early agreement with Moscow, he contended, a suicidal nuclear-arms race was sure to break out after the war.

Bohr won the enthusiastic support of several British officials, including Ambassador Halifax, in Washington, and Sir John Anderson, who was in charge of the British atomic-energy project, as well as Mackenzie King. Introduced to Felix Frankfurter by the Danish Ambassador, Bohr sounded the Justice out cautiously to see if he knew of the project; when Frankfurter obliquely mentioned "X," he saw that he did. Frankfurter knew little about science as such but a lot about the nature and nurture of ideas. He knew, Max Freedman says, that it was repugnant to the ethics and philosophy of scientific research to think of exclusive secrets and of building a barbed wire of security regulations to barricade atomic secrets from the rest of the world. He promised to pass Bohr's views on to the President.

Frankfurter found Roosevelt "worried to death" about the whole postwar atomic problem. The President knew that he and Churchill would have to confront it; he knew about Churchill's fear of sharing secrets with the Russians. Bohr was incredulous when Frankfurter told him that the President wanted him to fly to London and discuss the whole matter with Churchill. While waiting to see the Prime

Minister in London, Bohr received word from an old Russian scientific friend, Peter Kapitza, inviting him to Moscow, where everything necessary for scientific work would be made available. Bohr inferred from this and other items that the Russians knew of the work in the West on the bomb and wanted him to work on fission.

Bohr's meeting with Churchill was a disaster. Busy with the impending invasion of France, the Prime Minister quickly became impatient with Bohr's quiet discursiveness, and the interview ended before Bohr could make his key point. Crushed, he returned to Washington in June and sought out Frankfurter, who promptly reported to the White House. The President was amused that anyone would tackle Churchill in one of his belligerent moods; he said that he would see Bohr. He had not been thrown off by Bohr's long memos, in which the scientist, in contrast to the reporter who makes his key points first and embellishes them, built up a long theoretical background before coming to his conclusions.

Bohr found a different reception in the White House from that at 10 Downing Street. The President greeted him warmly, sat him down next to his gadget-littered desk, told some stories about Churchill and Stalin at Teheran, listened to his views, stated that he generally agreed with them, and sympathized with Bohr's reception by Churchill, adding that the Prime Minister often behaved this way in the face of a new idea. He was confident, the President went on, that atomic power created vast possibilities for good as well as evil, that it would help build international co-operation and even open a new era in history. He seemed to feel that Stalin should be approached on the matter. The President's clear-cut, enthusiastic words elated Bohr—and even more when the President said he would take all this up with Churchill at their forthcoming meeting.

There is no record of Roosevelt's and Churchill's discussion of the bomb at their Hyde Park meeting on September 19, 1944, following their Quebec meeting, but the outcome suggests what happened. The Prime Minister, suspecting that Bohr might be leaking information to Moscow, evidently succeeded in shattering Roosevelt's confidence in the physicist. It was a lugubrious example of what happened when Roosevelt's idealistic impulses and amorphous policy collided with Churchill's narrower, Atlantic-oriented outlook. The *aide-mémoire* issued by the two men spoke with shattering finality.

"1. The suggestion that the world should be informed regarding tube alloys, with a view to an international agreement regarding its control and use, is not accepted. The matter should continue to be regarded as of the utmost secrecy, but when a 'bomb' is finally available, it might perhaps, after mature consideration, be used against the Japanese, who should be warned that this bombardment will be repeated until they surrender.

"2. Full collaboration between the United States and the British Government in developing tube alloys for military and commercial purposes should continue after the defeat of Japan unless and until terminated by joint agreement.

"3. Enquiries should be made regarding the activities of Professor Bohr and steps taken to ensure that he is responsible for no leakage of information particularly to the Russians."

Behind Roosevelt's turnabout was not only his own ambivalence, but also a fundamental change in the *Realpolitik* of the atomic weapon. By the fall of 1944 it was becoming evident that Germany was not succeeding in making the bomb. The terrible fear of the scientists that the Führer would possess the ultimate weapon was dwindling; some scientists were beginning to wonder about their own leaders. The leaders—especially Churchill—were pondering the implications of the weapon being in the hands of the Russians, whom they suspected of conducting atomic espionage. Russia, not Germany, was now the issue. The anti-Hitler coalition was under a new strain.

For the moment the prophetic voice of international science desperately trying to forestall a disastrous nuclear-arms race was cut off from reaching the top levels of the American government. The awesome and deadly new atomic age was being born in secrecy and suspicion, not as a shared adventure in scientific co-operation and world unity, but as a military means of beating the Axis and perhaps containing the Russians. Moscow was reacting with suspicion and espionage. Some notes of Stimson's for a meeting with Roosevelt late in August illustrated the strange combination of idealism and narrow realism that was being brought to bear on S1, Stimson's code name for the atomic project:

"The necessity of bringing Russian orgn. into the fold of Christian civilization. . . .

"The possible use of S1 to accomplish this. . . .

"Steps toward disarmament

"Impossibility of disclosure—(S1)

"Science is making a common yardstick impossible."

THE MOBILIZED SOCIETY

As the President was driven along the streets of Washington he could see the artifacts of a mobilized society. The Mall, with wings and annexes branching out from the drab "temps" of World War I, looked like a vast construction project. Sidewalks were crowded with GI's, sailors, Marines, WAC's, WAAF's, WAVES, soldiers of Allied nations. Not far from the White House was the Stage Door Canteen, in the old Belasco Theatre. Gasoline rationing had cut civilian driving; some government workers rode to their offices on bicycles.

Thousands of girls in their teens and twenties had flocked to Washington; Arlington Farms, across the river, housed 8,000 of them, including 3,300 WAVES, and came to be known as Girl Town. WAC's encamped in the sprawling South Post. Whole agencies had been packed up and moved to other cities—the Rural Electrification Administration to St. Louis, the Farm Credit Administration to Kansas City, the Wage and Hour and Public Contracts Division to New York—but the nation's capital still labored under the housing pressure. Army officers pleaded for apartments, offering bonuses for leads, promising "no pets or parties." Hotels set up cots in dining rooms after mealtime.

Less visible from a presidential limousine but all too clear in the data flowing to the White House from the agencies—from the Pentagon, Isador Lubin's Bureau of Labor Statistics, McNutt's Federal Security Agency, and other offices—were the phenomena of a nation pulsing with fecundity, change, and stress. Despite cutbacks in the output of raw materials, war production was soaring. Early in June 1944 the President reminded a news conference of business-newspaper editors of the "most awful howl all over the country" when he had once asked Congress for 50,000 planes a year. "Couldn't be done—just couldn't be done." Well, he went on, "we are now up to a hundred thousand a year, and we are keeping on going—keeping on making records. American industry has done a lot better than the non-business press thought it could do." The 200,000th United States-financed airplane since July 1, 1940 had just been accepted, Roosevelt added; the first 100,000 had taken 1,431 days to build, the second only 369.

The United States was spending over three hundred million dollars a day on the war. Income—real, disposable, per capita—was soaring to new heights, heading from under $1,000 in 1940 toward almost $1,300 four years later. The total labor force in 1944 was sixty-six million, twelve million over 1940, with women providing five million of the increase. Unemployment had dropped from the eight million of 1940 to 670,000 four years later; the huge lump of Great Depression joblessness had vanished at last. For the first time in history the participation rate (per cent of population over fourteen years employed) rose to over 60 per cent. In 1944 over two-thirds of teen-age boys (fourteen to nineteen) were gainfully employed. One of the biggest jumps in participation was among men sixty-five and over. War had dramatically solved the problem that Roosevelt had struggled with for a decade.

Behind the bounding economic figures was a social panorama etched in hope and anguish. Most evident was the war migration. Eleven million young men and women were uprooted from their communities and sent off to the four corners of the globe; a civilian migration to better jobs was changing the face of the South, the inner cores of major cities, and the industrialized metropolitan outskirts. The war sharply accelerated the decades-old flow of blacks and whites out of the South and into the coastal and inland industrial regions of the North and West. Within metropolitan areas whites were moving to the fringes of the cities, while Negroes settled in the urban cores, where they became more socially visible, economically significant, and politically potent than they had been in the old rural cultures of the South.

Over the frantic protests of the War Manpower Commission, the placement of plants lured workers from their homes, communities, parents, and families to lucrative new jobs. But the migration of able-bodied young men was not enough, for the armed services and industry had an insatiable demand for manpower, and one by one all groups were pulled in. Before Pearl Harbor, Roosevelt and Stimson found that color was no barrier to war usefulness; next, women were urged to work; then the young and the old were summoned, along with the illiterate, the handicapped, the leisured, aliens, students, and finally Japanese-Americans from the concentration camps. The people responded, but the demand was infinite. Even as the participation rate for women climbed over 36 per cent, Roosevelt and Stimson pleaded for drafting women into the Army.

Since for war purposes all bodies were equally necessary, and the war priority was all-powerful, traditional distinctions and ties diminished. The kinship system, never very strong, was virtually dismantled. The demands for young men in the services and on the assembly line lessened their economic dependence on their elders and projected anew the cult of youth. The freedom and importance of young people—almost instant adulthood—sent the marriage rate skyrocketing. The demand for women as economic producers on assembly lines caused a new move toward sexual equality and a de-emphasis on the wife-mother role. Families, separated geographically and functionally, spent less time together. Long overtime hours, migration to job centers, the induction of husbands into the services, and the loss of control by parents over marriage, all weakened family stability.

The equality of bodies virtually destroyed the old yardstick of status, identity, and legitimacy. New income taxes, high wages, and rationing undercut the economic stratification system. Conspicuous consumption was difficult when, for example, yachts were donated to the Navy for shore patrol. The status of jobs in economic sectors changed drastically; the lowly military, political, and governmental jobs suddenly became highly prized. Draft-board regulations made manual labor in factories and on farms more important—and sometimes more rewarding—than the work of salesmen, small businessmen, and college professors. No one planned these changes; few foresaw them.

The hierarchy of age, income, sex—in fact, the whole stratification system—was eroding. From the disorder there gathered, among other forces, a new social energy of black Americans. As a consequence of moving north, blacks became better paid, more educated, better fed and clothed. They were also becoming more frustrated and socially disorganized. Negroes moved into city slum areas as whites departed for the suburbs—and into the hand-me-down housing left behind. Crowding intensified; 60,000 Negroes moved into Chicago areas previously occupied by 30,000 whites. As usual, black income lagged behind white, and many blacks felt more keenly than ever the gap between the egalitarian, antiracist ideals of the war and the pervasive discrimination around them. In May 1944 a clear majority of respondents across the nation told pollsters that whites should have a better chance at jobs than Negroes because whites were superior, or better trained, or more intelligent, or more dependable, or because this was a white man's country.

Negroes by the thousands were now coming into contact with whites in war jobs. And though racial strikes constituted only .00054 of all work stoppages, the confrontation was usually troublesome. After a year of war, OWI reported that "Southern whites who came with the construction crews brought racial attitudes foreign to the community. . . . As a matter of fact, racial tensions actually developed to the acute stage under the influence of these new attitudes. . . ."

In 1943 Ickes wrote to Roosevelt that discrimination, "although it can be nibbled at ineffectively locally, cannot be handled except on a comprehensive national scale. This is not a local question. It is a national one." The Fair Employment Practices Committee and other fragile efforts, however, could not begin to grapple with social resistance and change of this magnitude. The FEPC admitted its impotence in the face of flagrant discrimination by the railroads and the railway unions. The first FEPC report, on defense training by the Office of Education, was suppressed by Roosevelt on the advice of the War Department and Marvin McIntyre. At the urging of the State Department, Roosevelt stopped FEPC hearings on discrimination against Mexican-Americans "for international reasons." When the Office of Education in Washington called on white universities in the South to admit Negro scholars, the Jackson, Mississippi, *Daily News* told it to "go straight to hell. . . . Nobody but an ignorant, fat-headed ass would propose such an unthinkable and impossible action." The South Carolina legislature declared, "We are fighting to preserve white supremacy" in the war, and J. Edgar Hoover reported to Roosevelt that "a good proportion of unrest as regards race relationships results from Communist activities." Two months before Pearl Harbor, Selective Service Director Hershey wrote to Roosevelt, "It is obvious we must sooner or later come to the procedure of requisitioning and delivering men in the sequence of their order numbers without regard to color." After three years of coping with white racism, however, Hershey changed his mind: "what we are doing, of course, is simply transferring discrimination from everyday life into the Army."

Roosevelt was ambivalent. In midwinter 1944 members of the Negro Newspaper Publishers Association met with him for a special press conference. Roosevelt had hardly finished his cheery greetings when John Sengstacke, of the Chicago *Defender,* read a statement. For long moments, while Roosevelt listened, Sengstacke recited grievance after grievance arising from discrimination in jobs, schools, voting, civil rights. Second-class citizenship, he said, violated the Declaration of Independence and the Constitution and hurt the war effort. An awfully good statement, the President commented. He liked to think, he said, that mere association helped things along. But he admitted that "we are up against it." When Chairman Ross of the FEPC suggested facilities for black victims of infantile paralysis at Warm Springs, Roosevelt wrote to his wife, "you can tell Mr. Malcolm Ross that Tuskegee Institute has a whole unit devoted to the care of Negro children," and worriedly asked an aide, "what should I do about this?"

The other race bearing the sting of discrimination in America at the height of the war—Japanese-Americans in concentration camps—also received lukewarm support from the President. In September 1943 Roosevelt had publicly promised, "We shall restore to the loyal evacuees the right to return to the evacuated areas as soon as the military situation will make such restoration feasible." When Stimson admitted to the President in May 1944 that the Army saw no military reason for keeping loyal Japanese in the camps, Roosevelt suggested that he investigate attitudes in California. At a Cabinet meeting Stimson warned that if the Japanese were freed there might be riots and Tokyo would retaliate against American prisoners of war. The President decided that suddenly ending the order excluding Japanese from the West Coast would be a mistake; the whole problem should be handled with the greatest discretion by seeing how many families would be acceptable to public opinion in specific West Coast localities, and by the gradual shifting of one or two families to individual counties throughout the nation. He had found that some Japanese-Americans would be acceptable to Dutchess County. Then it turned out that Ickes, to whose jurisdiction the War Relocation Authority had been transferred early in 1944, favored immediate release; and Hull warned that Tokyo was more likely to react to incidents involving Japanese-Americans in custody than those at large. That put a different face on the problem. By September, Undersecretary of Interior Abe Fortas could report that out of 114,000 evacuees, over 30,000 had been relocated on indefinite leave, 60,000 were in relocation centers and were being released at the rate of 20,000 a month, and over 18,000 were still at Tule Lake and not eligible for relocation.

The old system was gone, replaced by government agencies, and the wartime bureaucracy had but a single standard: military usefulness. Like many institutions, education fragmented under this test. The public schools thrived; working mothers and the move to urban centers sent more six- to fourteen-year-olds into the schools, though there was a drop in high-school attendance. War fervor helped the social-involvement and learning-by-doing emphases of progressivism, which took more control over the public schools. Roosevelt had said, "We ask that every school house become a service center for the home front," and the schools responded with bond drives, courses in Asian geography, and paramilitary school organizations. The boom in public education was only half the story, for colleges and universities were out of a job. Male students and teachers were drafted, women left for factory work; so the colleges stood idle. In 1943-44, liberal-arts graduates were less than one-half and law-school graduates only one-fifth the prewar level. Vannevar Bush estimated to the President that science lost 150,000 college graduates and 17,000 advanced-degree graduates to the war.

Clearly war mobilization meant educational disruption. As protests poured in from college presidents, Roosevelt sought a short-term solution. "Federal participation in this field should be limited, at least for the present, to meeting defense needs," the President said, and asked Stimson and Knox for an immediate study of the fullest use of American colleges for war purposes. By the end of 1943 the Army Specialized Training Program and the Navy V-12 program had used idle college buildings at about five hundred institutions to provide training for about 300,000 men. But as the result of a strong letter from Marshall pleading for young men for the forthcoming invasion of France, the Army cut its program to the bone in early February 1944, and, on Rosenman's advice to the President, the Navy did the same. The war came first; everything else must wait.

Higher education would never return to the prewar system. The drafting of students, the military-training programs, and OSRD weapons research had changed it permanently. Students marched in the Army; the Army marched in the classrooms; science professors improved bombs and medicines in the laboratories. After consultations among Stimson, Smith, Hopkins, Rosenman, and Oscar Cox, Roosevelt, on November 17, 1944, wrote to Bush requesting a program for postwar government subsidy of research and "discovering and developing scientific talent"; from this request evolved the National Science Foundation and the incorporation of universities into a new defense-industry complex. Together with the GI Bill of Rights educational grants, the government subsidies transformed local liberal-arts institutions into centers for national research and vocational instruction. The temporary war-research organizations and the temporary termination of teaching produced a lasting reorganization of education.

The temporary became permanent, the means became ends, as emergency change lasted into the postwar world. Roosevelt himself was responsible for much of the confusion, for he tried artificially to separate war from postwar, temporary crisis from permanent tasks, means from ends. "I am not convinced," he declared, "that we can be realists about the war and planners for the future at this critical time." Yet the future would not wait for peacetime planning; it was growing from the narrowly conceived war organization. Roosevelt demanded the authority to mobilize for war, but he disclaimed responsiblity for planning against the social disruptions brought by mobilization.

With peacetime institutions dismantled, only government organizations could deal with social turmoil. Where government mechanisms persisted into the war period, disruption was transformed into progress. With the Labor Department, the National Labor Relations Board, the War Labor Board, and a host of New Deal agencies agreeing on union policy, union membership during the war jumped more than six million. In 1944 one-quarter of the work force belonged to unions, strikes were a third the prewar level, defense workers received one day of rest in seven, a thirty-minute meal period in the middle of each shift, a vacation period, overtime pay, and a host of other stabilizing and humanizing benefits. Clear policies, established organizations, and the obvious military benefits of good labor relations prevented the turmoil potential in the migrations, conversions of industries, and new entrants to the labor field.

For labor, Roosevelt had a policy and stuck to it; for other social problems there were limited goals and faulty means. In the absence of effective programs, Roosevelt was often confronted by social disruptions that were the product of day-to-day military-industrial decisions. The disruptions were inevitable in a quickly mobilized country, but in the absence of social goals, unrest provoked *ad-hoc* responses seeking vainly to restore prewar arrangements. In housing, the need to shelter millions of black and white war workers thrust the government into deciding for or against segregated housing. In the absence of any social goals, housing agencies decided to abide by prewar "local custom." Migration to defense communities, however, was so massive as to make "local custom" irrelevant; local custom quickly became whatever the government decided. In these communities, the more numerous whites had more political power than the blacks, so cities such as Ann Arbor, Michigan, in which prewar segregation was virtually unknown, received segregated housing, starting a new "local custom" still in force many years later.

Government decisions often aroused even more social unrest when announced goals were sacrificed to political or war expediency. Vacillation and delay in constructing the black Sojourner Truth housing project were one cause of the 1942 race riots in Detroit. Roosevelt's reluctance to restore the Japanese-Americans to their homes helped produce riots at the Tule Lake concentration camp. The President's continual frustration of FEPC work touched off a furore among liberals and blacks. Without goals, without strong organizations to implement social policies, social transformations were uncontrolled.

Organizations have a way of enduring. By refusing to build strong organizations for social policy, Roosevelt insured that the government would not control domestic society. While large residuals of presidential government, the military-industrial complex, and other wartime controls persisted, the dominance of American society by the national government ended with the war. Standards and mechanisms to insure that the social antagonisms enhanced by the war did not tear society apart would have to be a peacetime creation. Some new sources of integration, compounded from the prewar yardstick and the mobilization experience, would have to link together the black cities and the white suburbs of metropolis, the vast military and social-welfare bureaucracies of presidential government, the skyrocketing marriage and divorce rates, the disenchanted students and weapons researchers on campuses. Urban riots, family dissolution, feckless bureaucracy, and campus strife would be the price of not finding such new links.

THE CULTURE OF WAR

". . . There are no two fronts for America in this war," the President had said early in the year. "There is only one front. . . . When we speak of our total effort, we speak of the factory and the field, and the mine as well as of the battleground—we speak of the soldier and the civilian, the citizen and his Government."

Noble words, and perhaps true in the way Roosevelt meant. But in fact there had developed by the third year of war an ambivalence in the American way of war—an ambivalence that would have more significance in the long run than the consensus that the President sought to invoke.

On the one hand Americans were giving massive support to the war. In June 1944 the President reported proudly in a fireside chat that while there were about sixty-seven million persons who had or earned some form of income, eighty-one million parents and children had bought more than six hundred million individual bonds totaling more than thirty-two billion dollars. Americans were growing almost twenty million victory gardens; housewives were canning three billion quarts of fruit and vegetables a year. Boy Scouts, with the motto "Junk the Axis," were tracking down the last remaining worn-out bicycles, old license plates, and scrap metal. In remote towns civil-defense wardens were still manning key buildings with sand buckets and stirrup pumps and scrutinizing the heavens for enemy planes that would never come.

On the other hand there was little indication, as American soldiers came more and more to grips with the enemy, of any deepening or broadening of popular understanding of the meaning of the war. After closely studying American popular attitudes, Jerome Bruner concluded in 1944 that people said that they were fighting for freedom, liberty, and democracy, but that was not why we went to war. "We went to war because our security demanded it." The popular attitude toward the great peace documents of the war, he concluded, was symptomatic. A few weeks after the Atlantic Charter conference some three-fourths of the American people knew that a meeting had taken place and that a charter of some sort had emerged from it. Five months later less than a quarter of the American public said that they had ever heard of the Atlantic Charter. The same was true of the Four Freedoms, he found; only a handful of people would take exception to any of the four points, but they had not become a symbolic rallying cry for the future.

The *Nation* was quick to put the blame on Roosevelt. The American people were asking why we were fighting, and what is our foreign policy. People were asking Roosevelt and Hull this and receiving no answer. There were long, earnest debates as to whether Johnny felt he was simply fighting for Mom and blueberry pie. The "other side" of the war—the black and gray markets, widespread theft of rationing stamps, profiteering—was cited by observers as proof of lack of purpose and faith among the people.

On this score Roosevelt had little patience with his critics. Had he not proclaimed eloquent war aims over and over again? Late in March he stated them once more, and more flatly and succinctly than ever. "The United Nations," he said, "are fighting to make a world in which tyranny and aggression cannot exist; a world based upon freedom, equality, and justice; a world in which all persons regardless of race, color, or creed may live in peace, honor, and dignity." He pointedly read the statement to reporters and added, "Some of you people who are wandering around asking the bellhop whether we have a foreign policy or not, I think that's a pretty good paragraph."

Others wondered. John Dos Passos, exploring wartime Washington, had heard of the quiet and serenity of the White House. He asked a friend who worked there: Did the very stateliness of the place help keep the President out of touch with the country? Was the whole place under a bell glass? His friend thought the President might have lost touch with what real people did and thought and felt. Another man "close to the White House" was more reassuring. Every time the President took a trip, he told Dos Passos, he came back refreshed; perhaps it was a little like the Greek mythical giant who lost strength as soon as he ceased touching the earth. But the President was still seeing old friends—giving them too much time, some felt. Did people hesitate to tell him bad news? The President had a genius for handling that kind of problem.

Later Dos Passos watched the President at a press conference. He noted the two Secret Service men behind the chair, the green lawn sloping down to the great enclosing trees, the President's fine nose and forehead etched against the blue Pacific Ocean on the big globe behind him. Roosevelt was boyishly gay as he described the war, puffing out his cheeks while searching for a word, lifting his eyebrows, scratching the back of his head as he prepared to shoot out an answer. But when the talk turned to strikes and rationing and price control, Dos Passos noted, his manner changed. He became more abrupt, almost querulous. His face took on the sagging look of a man who had been up late at his desk, Dos Passos felt, and had known sleepless nights.

Had the people lost touch with Roosevelt? Dos Passos did not ask this question. The people had no clear way of showing their support or their understanding between elections except through answering questions someone else had framed. So tested, public confidence in Roosevelt as a person and as President was fairly high, but it seemed to turn much more on his experience and competence than on the ideals and war goals he represented. Thus when asked in June the strongest reason for voting for Roosevelt for re-election in 1944, the great majority of voters endorsed his "superior ability to handle present and future situations"; others approved his past record of handling internal affairs; only a handful stressed his personality and general ability. Dr. Win the War did indeed seem to overshadow men's perspectives of their leaders; the long-run goals were still vague in the popular mind.

Ideologies are shaped and hardened in the crucibles of fear and stress. Unlike the British and Russians, Americans as a whole had never had the experience or prospect of fighting for their lives and lands against a foreign invader. Most Americans, even in the darkest days after Pearl Harbor, had never feared a major invasion and certainly not defeat. They had differed only over the question of how long it would take to win, with most expecting victory over Germany within a year or two. But the cause of American optimism and lack of ideology lay much deeper—perhaps in what D. W. Brogan in mid-1944 described as the permanent optimism of "a people that has licked a more formidable enemy than Germany or Japan, primitive North America."

A country has the kind of army its total ethos, institutions, habits, and resources make possible, Brogan wrote. The American Army was the army of a nation whose motto was "Root, hog, or die," of a country that, just as it slowly piled up great economic power as a special kind of corner, piled up military power for a final decisive blow; of a mechanized country of colossal resources and enterprises. "Other countries, less fortunate in position and resources, more burdened with feudal and gentlemanly traditions, richer in national reverence and discipline, can and must wage war in a very different spirit." But Americans were interested not in form but in manpower, resources, logistics; not in moral victories, but in victory.

"Manpower, resources, logistics . . ." The admirals and generals passed through the gates to the White House grounds in their limousines and command cars and strode into Leahy's quarters or into the map room or into the oval office. The military police, walking their hundred-foot beats in their white leggings, belts, and gloves, marched to and from the military installation nearest to the White House, a barracks behind the State Department built in the shadow of the Peace Monument put up after World War I. WAVES, quartered on the Mall, hung up their underthings to dry a stone's throw from the Washington Monument. Encampments stretched alongside the Navy Yard, the Pentagon, the airport. The military dead slept at Arlington.

Unending caravans passed through the city, following occult unit designations posted along the streets. Along the highways and railways north and south of the capital sprawled vast embarkation areas, airfields, dumps, hospitals, depots, encampments, war plants, ports, proving grounds. At the ports of embarkation armies of men and mountains of equipment, clothing, weapons, ammunition were gathered, divided, allocated, paired, and dispatched on aged merchantmen, on Liberty and Victory ships, on converted liners like the *Queen Mary* that could carry a whole division. Overseas, men and munitions were sluiced into more camps and dumps, redistributed, assigned, loaded, shipped to the fronts: artillerymen, engineers, medical corpsmen, storekeepers, cooks, torpedomen, tail gunners, clerks, aircraft spotters, chaplains.

Near the front the manpower and supply routes branched off into corps and division headquarters and dumps, forked off to regiments, twisted along stream beds and jeep roads and mule paths to companies and platoons and squads. At the end of the long road bulging with war supply from the overflowing war plants of America was a thin, irregular line of soldiers with stubby faces, in shapeless fatigues, hardly distinguishable from the earth in which they lived and to which they clung. This was the seemingly fragile shield that held and advanced with tensile force. That force lay not in these few expendables, but in the colossal technology that lay behind the front.

American soldiers were workmen. They did not advance as in a pageant or charge the enemy in splendid array. Occasionally men fought with bayonets and pistols in Hollywood fashion, but for the most part soldiers wormed ahead on their bellies, came up against strong points, manhandled their light weapons into place, poured in fire and explosives; moved on; or if the strong point held, they called up reinforcements, asked for bigger tools, waited, summoned artillery, heavy mortars, planes, directed the holocaust of fire, waited. . . . This was the "cutting edge" of war, glorified by combat reporters, but the Army really moved on the ocean supply routes and the endless lines of trucks clogging the highways.

Behind the front there rose a whole new culture, symbolized more by the quartermaster than the combat soldier. The GI had his own myths and credo, his own humor, his own blasphemy and invective invariably and irrelevantly garnished by one fuckin' expletive, his own press—*Yank* and *Stars and Stripes* and countless unit publications—his own food, clothing, laundries, postal system, schools, recreation, paperbacks, shops, doctors, libraries. Like the soldier himself, all these were Government Issue.

There was no deep gulf between soldiers and civilians, in part because they shared the same ideology or lack of it. The area of consensus among Americans both in and out of the armed forces, investigators found, lay simply in the belief that the Japanese attack on Pearl Harbor meant war. Now they had to win the war to get back to home and blueberry pie. Like the civilians, the soldiers remembered little about the Four Freedoms, had no doubt that their side would win, felt little sense of personal commitment even while, in the soldiers' case, sacrificing years of their lives and sometimes life itself. There was considerable distrust of Russia and some distrust of Britain. The soldiers lacked a consistent rationale by which to justify the war; they lacked a context; the war had no connection with anything that had gone before, except Axis aggression, or would come after it. It had to be fought, to be gotten over quickly so that men could go home.

The Commander in Chief was neither loved nor hated by most soldiers, but simply taken for granted as the top man in charge. He was the only President the younger men had known since the dawn of their political consciousness. A little of the old cynicism remained. Occasionally a vexed soldier would burst out to no one in particular: "Ah *hate* wah. *Eleanor* hates wah. *Sistie* hates wah. . . ." But this was exasperation, not isolationism. By and large there was not much interest in the upcoming national elections. The average GI did not feel that *his* Commander in Chief would be tested at the polls in November. Ernie Pyle reported from Italy that, sure, the average combat soldier wanted to vote, but if there was going to be any red tape he would say nuts to it.

Washington was aware of the problem. The Army searched for Tolstoy's quantity X, "the spirit of the army, the greater or less desire to fight and to face dangers. . . ." Colonel Frank Capra directed a series of films called "Why We Fight," based mainly on Allied and captured enemy newsreels. The films were eloquent, professional, relatively factual; they were required to be shown to all personnel; they provided men with a better knowledge of the prelude to war; they were found to have influenced specific opinions. But they had virtually no effect on general opinions, on commitment and conviction, on ideology. The GI had not ideology, but faith—faith in the rightness of his cause, the iniquity of the enemy, the certainty of victory. He was persuaded mainly by the fact of war, just as the people had been after Pearl Harbor—and just as Roosevelt helped them to be. The GI was a realist, a workman, a practical achiever, just as, in large measure, his Commander in Chief was.

Thus the GI lived and worked and fought and sometimes died in the culture of war. Cutting across it, both at home and abroad, was a curious subculture—scattered enclaves of black soldiers. The Army in 1944 was still segregated; the Navy was lily-white, except for messmen and a few others. Some Negro army outfits had white officers, some had black. Despite their resentment of segregation, Negroes had developed some pride in black combat air and ground units, only to become more indignant than ever in early 1944 when black combat-infantry troops—some of them from famous old Negro outfits—were used for labor service and black pilots were accused of poor combat performance. The Negro press protested; Representative Fish appealed to Stimson; William Hastie, who had resigned as civilian aide on Negro affairs because of despair over the continuing misuse of black troops, wrote to Stimson that the

Secretary had been misled by his own subordinates as to the conversion of Negro combat units into service units.

The White House rarely intervened in the services' handling of Negro matters, but Eleanor Roosevelt passed along complaints, and the known concern of both the President and the First Lady was a brooding presence in Pentagon decisions. Annoyed by both the racists and the Negro "extremists," Stimson believed that "we are suffering from the persistent legacy of the original crime of slavery"; he wanted equal opportunity for both races but not social intermixture. "We have got to use the colored race to help us in this fight and we have got to officer it with white men," he wrote in his diary. ". . . better to do that than to have them massacred under incompetent officers." For Stimson the issue was how best to win the war; but he would not face the question of the potential effectiveness of integrated units. Nor would Roosevelt.

"This war is an ideological war fought in defense of democracy," wrote Gunnar Myrdal in *An American Dilemma,* which appeared in 1944. "In fighting fascism and nazism, America had to stand before the whole world in favor of racial toleration and cooperation and of racial equality."

Roosevelt's position was a mixture of concern, realism, and resignation. When the Negro publishers in their February meeting with him chided him on the treatment of black soldiers, the President answered:

"It is perfectly true, there is definite discrimination in the actual treatment of the colored engineer troops, and others. And you are up against it, as you know perfectly well. I have talked about it—I had the Secretary of War and the Assistant—everybody in on it. The trouble lies fundamentally in the attitude of certain white people—officers down the line who haven't got much more education, many of them, than the colored troops and the Seabees and the engineers, for example. And well, you know the kind of person it is. We all do. We don't have to do more than think of a great many people that we know. And it has become not a question of orders—they are repeated fairly often, I think, in all the camps of colored troops—it's a question of the personality of the individual.

"And we are up against it, absolutely up against it. . . ."

SIXTEEN *The Fateful Lightning*

BY JUNE 4 all seemed ready for OVERLORD. Landing ships built on Lake Michigan and floated down the Illinois River and the Mississippi were packed beam to beam in the ports of southern England. Long ugly LST's constructed in California, their front ends gaping wide like hungry alligators, devoured tanks, trucks, bulldozers. Along pleasant English lanes, under blooming English elms, stood strange amphibious vessels, track to track; barrel-shaped metal containers of ammunition; stacks of bombs; enormous reels of cable; tires, wheels, wooden cases stacked twenty feet high. Rows of Mustang fighters, newly shorn of their protective grease, stood wing to wing on small fields behind the coast. Hundreds of new locomotives and thousands of freight and tanker cars lined the green valleys, waiting to be used in France.

In the dusk mile-long convoys moved down the English roads and disgorged men onto the quays. Soldiers in assault jackets bent under their loads: rifle, life preserver, gas mask, five grenades, a half-pound block of TNT with primacord fuse; and K rations and C rations stuffed into their packs and jackets. The men slowly filed onto the transports and took their positions near their assault craft. The first to land would be the section leader and five riflemen with M-1's; then a wire-cutting team of four men, also with rifles; followed by four search-nose cutters, two Browning automatic rifle teams of two men each, carrying nine hundred pounds per gun; two bazooka teams of two men each; four sixty-millimeter mortarmen with fifteen to twenty rounds; a flame-thrower crew of two men; five demolition men with pole and pack charges of TNT; a medic and the assistant section leader.

The great attack, which had hung in the balance so many times as Roosevelt and Churchill forsook it for Africa, as American admirals drained sea power and landing craft into the Pacific, as Italy insistently sucked in troops, was now itemized and "finalized" and blueprinted on thousands of battle orders, landing schedules, and beach plans. For fifty miles along the Bay of the Seine stretching westward to the Cotentin Peninsula sections of beaches were marked off and code-named—Sword, Juno, Gold, Omaha, Utah. A million and a half Americans, another million British and Canadians, tens of thousands of Norwegians, Danish, French, Belgian, Czech, Polish, and other troops, waited on their landing craft in sealed-off sectors across the south of England, and in supporting areas behind. Nine hundred warships, ranging from PT boats to twenty-six battleships and heavy cruisers, 229 LST's and 3,372 landing craft, and 163 air bases would mount and support the onslaught; 124,000 hospital beds were ready.

The top command post of this massed and balanced power lay in a hazel coppice a few miles north of Portsmouth dockyard, in a nondescript trailer remarkable only for a red telephone for scrambled calls to Washington and a green one for a direct line to 10 Downing Street. This was Eisenhower's headquarters. A mile away was Southwick House, an old country mansion where formal conferences took place; nearby was the caravan of General Montgomery, ground commander of the assault phase. General Omar Bradley's assault headquarters was established near Bristol.

On the far shores waited the Germans. They had long expected an attack across the Channel in the spring of 1944—just when and where they were not sure. Most of the Wehrmacht tactitians anticipated an onslaught between the Seine and the Scheldt; in a flash of intuition Hitler at one point predicted the Cotentin Peninsula as a likely target, but his intuition later flicked up other possibilities. The Führer and his generals had long argued over defense strategy. Demanding "fanatical energy," Hitler had ordered the Atlantic Wall—almost a coastal Maginot Line—to be armed and concreted in order to prevent the invader from gaining a beachhead. He directed his western Commander in Chief, Gerd von Runstedt, to throw the enemy back into the sea by a quick and massive counterattack. Runstedt preferred to rely on the proved tactics of rapid maneuver behind the front, with mobile infantry and powerful armored units deployed to overwhelm the enemy beachheads. Sensing Runstedt's doubts, Hitler had assigned Rommel to the Western Front, with special responsibilities for coastal defense. The old commander of the Afrika Korps would have liked a mobile defense in depth as well, but knowing the air power of the Allies and the poor quality of his troops, many of whom were either young and undertrained or battle weary from service in Russia, he concentrated on beach defenses. By June the Channel beaches were peppered with half a million steel piles, wooden stakes armed with mines, interlocked iron bars, and "Belgian gates," huge slanting gates braced by girders, all connected with barbed wire.

The enemy assault must be liquidated within a few hours,

Hitler demanded. This would prevent the re-election of Roosevelt, who, "with luck, would finish up somewhere in jail." Churchill, too, would be finished, and the Allies would never dare launch another invasion of France.

Only the weather was not ready. When Eisenhower met with his commanders early Sunday morning, June 4, forecasters warned of high winds and heavy cloud. Montgomery was ready to go ahead, but when the others demurred, Eisenhower ordered the operation postponed, even though some ships had to be called back. The prospects improved by evening. For a day or two the weather would be tolerable, though by no means ideal; then it would close in again. The airmen were dubious; Montgomery again said, "Go!" For long minutes Eisenhower agonized. Postponement would bring grave risks, too. How long, he wondered, could he leave the operation hanging on the end of a limb. "I'm quite positive we must give the order. . . . I don't like it but there it is. . . ." Then, "O.K. We'll go."

These words loosed the most formidable amphibious assault the world had ever known. After rendezvousing in a great circle south of the Isle of Wight, warships and transports, landing ships and smaller craft moved in orderly never-ending streams toward the south. Flanking the Utah-bound column was the graceful *Augusta,* with General Bradley in the skipper's cabin occupied by Roosevelt at Argentia. Barrage balloons lofted above the ships on cables guarded the LCI's against enemy air attack. Paratroopers, their faces blackened, sat shoulder to shoulder hugging their parachutes in the transport planes above the Channel. The roar of bombers going out, Edward R. Murrow broadcast from London, was so powerful and triumphant he imagined he heard the strains of the "Battle Hymn of the Republic."

Soon after midnight the paratroopers were floating down in the dark over the low, flat pastures of the Cotentin Peninsula; assault waves were milling around in the launching area and moving toward Utah, Omaha, and the "British" beaches to the east. Warships poured shells and rockets onto beach targets. Boats roared toward the shore; tanks churned through heavy seas, some of them foundering; men waded for hundreds of yards toward the beaches. Some drowned; some were shot down and died in little paroxysms of red foam; some cowered behind obstacles at the water line; some were annihilated as they tried to sprint up the beach. But most made it and dug in under the heavy protection of low bluffs or sea walls, and many of these pressed on.

Roosevelt had spent the weekend with a small entourage at Pa Watson's home near Charlottesville, Virginia. Watching him, Miss Tully felt that every movement of his face and hands betrayed his tenseness. During the weekend he had perused his Book of Common Prayer for a D-day invocation. He returned to the White House Monday morning and that evening went on the air not to pray for the invaders but to salute the fall of Rome, the symbol of Christianity, of authority, and now of Allied victory. He dwelt at length on the degrading effects of fascism as compared to the greatness of the Italian people in both Italy and the United States. But his mind was on the military significance. "One up and two to go!"

And now D day was crowding hard on the event. Even while marking the fall of Rome, Roosevelt had known that ships and troops were streaming across the Channel. He stayed in touch with the Pentagon during the night. At four in the morning the White House operator began waking up staff members with the news. First reports were fragmentary and bewildering, but by the time of his regular press conference in the morning the President was relaxed and even gay. As the correspondents—almost two hundred strong—crowded in, he was joshing with his aides, and Fala was wriggling on his back on the couch.

"Well, I think this is a very happy conference today," Roosevelt began. "Looking at the rows of you coming in, you have the same expression as the anonymous and silent people this side of the desk who came in just before you—all smiles!" He had little definite to report—only that the invasion was up to schedule, "and as the Prime Minister said, 'That's a mouthful.' "

How was the President feeling? "Fine—I'm a little sleepy!"

In the evening he led the nation in prayer. He prayed first for "our sons, pride of our Nation. . . . Lead them straight and true; give strength to their arms, stoutness to their hearts, steadfastness in their faith. They will need Thy blessings. Their road will be long and hard. For the enemy is strong. He may hurl back our forces. Success may not come with rushing speed, but we shall return again and again. . . ." And he prayed also for the people at home, for stout hearts to wait out the long travail and to bear sorrows that might come. "Give us Faith in thee; Faith in our sons; Faith in each other; faith in our united crusade. . . ."

CRUSADE IN FRANCE

Enough things went wrong on D day to lend suspense to the occasion and drama to the retelling. The paratroopers were badly scattered; scores of gliders were shot down or lost their way; on Omaha Beach the invaders ran into unexpected enemy strength and were slaughtered in the water and on the beach; heavy seas slowed operations along all the beaches. But in fact the invasion was not in jeopardy. The long wait until the Germans had been weakened in the east, the stupendous build-up, the elaborate planning by Roosevelt, Churchill, and their military chiefs were now paying off. Strategy was now dominating tactics. By the end of D day, with almost continuous thickets of ships disgorging war power along miles and miles of coast, the immediate issue was all but resolved.

The Germans were not only overwhelmed; they also were deceived, outwitted, and caught flat-footed. Their radar had been so mercilessly shelled that only a handful of radar pieces were operating on the eve of D day, and most of them were foiled by devices that simulated a different landing. The weather that had worried Eisenhower seemed too rough to the enemy to permit amphibious operations. Rommel was not even near the front; he had left on June 5 to visit Hitler at Berchtesgaden. The Führer was so certain that the first landings were a feint that he delayed the dispatch of two Panzer divisions. But even if he had known the date of D day, he could not long have held off the Allies. He had inadequate sea power and air power to challenge the invaders on the Channel or over it. And in the face of massive Allied attacks on railroads, bridges, highways, and marshaling yards, he lacked enough maneuverability to deploy even the forces he had.

The hurricane of fire could be slowed but not stopped. British troops assaulted Caen, which Montgomery now used as the pivot of a great wheeling movement by the Americans to the west. From eastern beaches Canadians moved inland to cut the highway from Caen to the west. The Germans held out tenaciously in the city, which became the center of a furious struggle for weeks. From Utah and Omaha beaches American forces pushed their way slowly south and west in the crucial effort to cut off the Cotentin Peninsula and seize the port of Cherbourg. Progress was agonizingly slow, for this was *bocage* country, where the thick hedges and ditches that enfolded the fields gave ideal protection to the Germans. But the troops inched ahead. Supporting them from the ocean was a continuous relay of ships, which unloaded half a million men in the first ten days. Then storms disrupted the supply lines, but on the Fourth of July Marshall passed on to his chief a report from Eisenhower that the millionth man had just been landed that morning. Slowly the Americans converged on Cherbourg, whose commander had received the usual Hitler order to stand and die, and, after a combined ground-sea attack, broke into the city. The port was found so blasted and mined that it could not be used for weeks. This delay made all the more urgent the two complete artificial harbors—the Mulberries—that were towed across the Channel in huge sections. One Mulberry was torn to pieces in the terrible gales, but the other was properly installed out from the beach and provided a roadstead to receive ocean-going vessels.

All this Roosevelt watched with admiration; he could have no direct part in it. Neither could Churchill, but at least he could visit the beaches. He reported to Roosevelt on his "jolly day": ". . . After doing much laborious duty we went and had a plug at the Hun from our destroyer, but although the range was 6000 yards he did not honour us with a reply. . . . You used the word 'stupendous' in one of your early telegrams to me. I must admit that what I saw could only be described by that word. . . . The marvellous efficiency of the transportation exceeds anything that has ever been known in war. . . . We are working up to a battle which may well be a million a side. . . . How I wish you were here!" The President could only reply that he wished he were, too, and that when he did get over he could land alongside the Quai of Cherbourg.

Roosevelt faced the responsibilities of war if not the experience of it. Hard on the heels of OVERLORD—probably the most impressive combined operation ever conducted by allies—came one of the sharpest disagreements ever between Washington and London. The issue was ANVIL, the invasion of southern France. The Italian suction pump had already delayed ANVIL and robbed it of its original purpose of taking pressure off Eisenhower's forces in the weeks after D day. Eisenhower still wanted ANVIL, in order to bring heavy strength from the Mediterranean up through the Rhone Valley to support his ultimate campaign for the Ruhr. The British flatly opposed shifting divisions from Italy to southern France at a time when Alexander had finally seized Rome and was driving north. Churchill cabled to Roosevelt late in June: "Let us resolve not to wreck one great campaign for the sake of another. Both can be won."

Roosevelt's long reply bluntly answered the British and underscored his strategy for the West.

". . . I agree with you that our over-all strategic concept should be to engage the enemy on the largest scale with the greatest violence and continuity, but I am convinced it must be based on a main effort, together with closely coordinated supporting efforts directed at the heart of Germany.

"The exploitation of 'Overlord,' our victorious advances in Italy, an early assault on Southern France, combined with the Soviet drives to the west—all as envisaged at Teheran—will most certainly serve to realize our object—the unconditional surrender of Germany. . . .

"I agree that the political considerations you mention are important factors, but military operations based thereon must be definitely secondary to the primary operations of striking at the heart of Germany. . . .

"Until we have exhausted the forces in the United States, or it is proved we cannot get them to Eisenhower when he wants them, I am opposed to the wasteful procedure of transferring forces from the Mediterranean to 'Overlord.' If we use shipping and port capacity to shift forces from one combat area (the Mediterranean) to another ('Overlord') it will certainly detract from the build-up of 'Overlord' direct from the United States, and the net result is just what we don't want—fewer forces in combat areas.

"My interest and hopes center on defeating the Germans in front of Eisenhower and driving on into Germany, rather than on limiting this action for the purpose of staging a full major effort in Italy. I am convinced we will have sufficient forces in Italy, with 'Anvil' forces withdrawn, to chase Kesselring north of Pisa-Rimini and maintain heavy pressure against his army at the very least to the extent necessary to contain his present force. I cannot conceive of the Germans paying the price of ten additional divisions, estimated by General Wilson, in order to keep us out of Northern Italy. . . .

"At Teheran we agreed upon a definite plan of attack. That plan has gone well so far. Nothing has occurred to require any change. Now that we are fully involved in our major blow history will never forgive us if we lost precious time and lives in indecision and debate. My dear friend, I beg you to let us go ahead with our plan.

"Finally, for purely political considerations over here, I should never survive even a slight setback to 'Overlord' if it were known that fairly large forces had been diverted to the Balkans."

The military disagreement between the two leaders reflected basic differences over grand political strategy. While denying any strategic interest in the Balkans, Churchill was clearly interested at the least in securing military positions on the Istrian Peninsula that could make possible a major advance against Vienna through the Ljubljana Gap. At the moment, he was less intent on a definite Balkan commitment than in broadening his strategic options, in part as a counter to Soviet power rumbling in from the east. More and more, Churchill had become concerned with postwar political implications. Roosevelt wanted to win the quickest possible military victory; he was worried also about Stalin's reaction to the abandonment of ANVIL and about the political risk he ran at home if people came to feel that the troops and landing craft he had withheld from the Pacific had been used in Europe in a Balkan adventure.

Even after this insistence on the original plan, Churchill appealed again to Roosevelt, and separately to Hopkins, who was now convalescing in his Georgetown home. The Americans remained adamant, partly because they had information from Eisenhower that in the final pinch the British would give in. Grumbling that His Majesty's government would go ahead with the project only under solemn protest, Churchill finally agreed to ANVIL. He visited the Mediterranean at the time of the invasion and could not refrain from boarding a British destroyer to watch the assault troops boating in toward their landing in the Gulf of Saint-Tropez. Having "done the civil" to ANVIL, however, he did not change his mind about its strategic value, even after General Alexander M. Patch's American and French divisions streamed ashore on August 15 over weak opposition and advanced so rapidly north, with the help of the French Resistance, that OVERLORD and ANVIL linked arms within a month of the southern landings. Years later the Prime Minister was still lamenting that the forces in Italy had been denied their chance to disable the Germans and very possibly reach Vienna before the Russians, "with all that might have followed therefrom." Roosevelt and his planners felt that they were thoroughly vindicated by the military success of ANVIL—a success all the sweeter after the doubts of their British comrades.

Just as the descent of his armies onto Africa in the fall of 1942 had confronted Roosevelt with the conflicts of the Mediterranean world, now his forced entry into France made the political problems of Europe more immediate and insistent. Most visible on the horizon was the towering problem of Charles de Gaulle.

Roosevelt's relations with de Gaulle and his Committee of National Liberation had hardly changed since the awkward encounter in Casablanca a year and a half before. Time and again the President insisted that he would not make commitments to the Gaullists that might jeopardize the freedom of the French people to decide their own political fate after their liberation. De Gaulle, certain that he embodied the independent will of the French people, was determined to establish such clear legitimacy before liberation that neither his foes in France nor his reluctant allies outside could gainsay him the role he wished to play. Sheer personal dislike still sharpened the relations between him and Roosevelt. Each viewed the other as a prima donna seeking personal power and the spotlight.

De Gaulle's icy rigidity was a force in itself; it produced a kind of glacial flow that ground down his adversaries even as they resisted. On the last day of 1943 Roosevelt complained to Churchill that "De Gaulle and his Committee have most decidedly moved forward by 'the process of infiltration'—in other words, here a little, there a little." Slowly the General rendered Roosevelt's man Giraud impotent, first by excluding him from any real political power, then by edging him out of the committee, and finally by sacking him as Commander in Chief—all without creating a major clash with the President. Roosevelt had ways of showing his disapproval.

When he turned over a destroyer escort to the French at the Washington Navy Yard, with many a fine reference to the *Bonhomme Richard,* French-American friendship, and all the rest, he pointedly gave it to the French Navy, with not a reference to de Gaulle, the National Committee, or even the French government. In the face of threats from Algiers to repudiate the Allies' planned invasion currency for France, Roosevelt personally went over the scrip's design. He objected to the words "République Française" on the proposed notes and wanted to print in the middle, in color, the French flag supported by the American and British flags on each side. Angrily de Gaulle accepted what he called *"de la fausse monnaie."*

Nothing, indeed, at this point so easily provoked Roosevelt as the issue of de Gaulle. When Eisenhower deferentially suggested that from his information from agents and escaped prisoners of war there seemed to be only two groups, Vichyites and Gaullists, Roosevelt told Marshall that Eisenhower "evidently believes the fool newspaper stories that I am anti-deGaulle, even the kind of story that says that I hate him, etc., etc. All this, of course, is utter nonsense. I am perfectly willing to have deGaulle made President, or Emperor, or King or anything else so long as the action comes in an untrammeled and unforced way from the French people themselves." He cited an example, "which I happen to know about" of an old-time mayor in a little French town in occupied France who was doing a splendid job, but the committee already planned to replace him with an unsuccessful politician who was probably a porch-climbing robber.

How did Eisenhower know that there were only two groups? Roosevelt went on. He had overlooked the biggest group of all—the people who didn't know what it was all about.

"It is awfully easy to be for deGaulle and to cheer the thought of recognizing that Committee as the provisional government of France, but I have a moral duty that transcends 'an easy way.' It is to see to it that the people of France have nothing foisted on them by outside powers. It must be a French choice—and that means, as far as possible, forty million people. Self-determination is not a word of expediency. It carries with it a very deep principle in human affairs." Roosevelt also felt that de Gaulle was on the wane politically.

So on the eve of the supreme adventure of liberating France the Allied relationship with the Free French ranged between acrimony and absurdity. Churchill, who had tried to mediate between Roosevelt and de Gaulle, had invited the Frenchman to be present in England for D day. The General arrived but was so prickly about his real and fancied grievances that a private conference between the two ended in a flat statement by Churchill that if there was a split between de Gaulle's committee and Washington he would almost certainly side with the Americans, and a final remark by de Gaulle that he quite understood that.

Still, with thousands of Anglo-Americans about to pour into France in a grand crusade, it was clear that relations must be patched up. Eisenhower kept insisting that something must be done to cope with the scores of civilian problems that would rise. Through the good offices of the British, de Gaulle and Roosevelt were persuaded to agree to a visit by the General to Washington. To be sure, Roosevelt did not want to take the initiative in inviting him, nor the General the humiliation of asking to be invited, but Downing Street called on all its diplomatic finesse to arrange a meeting with neither an invitation nor an acceptance.

Externally de Gaulle's trip to Washington was a great success. Guns boomed out a salute; the President, his family, and his Cabinet greeted him at the White House; Roosevelt addressed him in French. There followed a round of festivities and ceremonials, capped by a state dinner where Roosevelt not only toasted de Gaulle as "our friend" but lambasted the journalists in Algiers and Washington who made trouble between leaders. The climax of the meeting was Roosevelt's decision to recognize the French Committee of National Liberation as the *de facto* authority in the civil administration of France.

Privately the exchanges were less meaningful. De Gaulle felt that Roosevelt was condescending, even if graciously so, in his long monologues about a future peace based on trust and good will. And Roosevelt, who in his toast to de Gaulle had once again asserted that there were no problems that could not be settled by sitting around the table, must have sensed that the General was impervious to genteel bribes or blarney.

Yet the immediate issue was resolved, and just in time. After cutting and battering through the *bocage* country during July, the American First Army captured Saint-Lô. The new Third Army, under General Patton, then turned one corps into Brittany to mop up and another to move east in a huge wheeling operation linked with the First Army, under General Courtney H. Hodges. Repulsing do-or-die counterattacks ordered by Hitler, the Americans raced east and then turned north to link up with English and Canadian forces, trapping thousands of Germans. The road to Paris was now open. As the Nazis fled and the Resistance began taking over, de Gaulle's troops made their ceremonial entrance into the tumultuous city, and soon the General himself marched down the boulevards before ecstatic throngs.

"The joy that entered the hearts of all civilized men and women,"

Roosevelt announced in Washington, "can only be measured by the gloom which settled there one June day four years ago when German troops occupied the French capital. . . ."

There was joyful news from the east as well. Shortly after D day, Stalin had cabled to Roosevelt that soon the Red Army would renew its offensive, and he hoped that this would be of substantial help to Allied operations in France and Italy. On June 23, the day after the third anniversary of Hitler's invasion of Russia, over a million Red Army troops surged forward across a 450-mile front in Byelorussia. Within a week the Russians had broken through the enemy front in half a dozen places, trapped a huge number of Germans, and captured Minsk; during July the Red Army plunged on, with slowing momentum, destroying a score of German divisions, moving into Poland, and seizing Lublin and Brest-Litovsk.

Once again Roosevelt faced the problem of Poland, but now more urgently than ever. Polish-American editors and politicians in New York and Detroit and other cities were threatening to turn their constituents against Roosevelt in the fall if he failed anti-Communist Poles in their hour of need. Early in June the President held discussions in Washington with Prime Minister Stanislaus Mikolajczyk of the Polish government in London. At a state dinner for the Prime Minister he talked about the problem of borders; he had been looking over sixteen maps that morning, the President said, and they showed that in the last three centuries Poland had included most of Russia and a good part of Germany and Czechoslovakia. "Therefore," he went on, "it is rather difficult to untangle the map of Poland." So he and the Prime Minister had been talking about broader matters, "getting away from the mere questions of whether this town will be on this side of the line or that side of the line."

Roosevelt then sounded Stalin out on seeing Mikolajczyk in Moscow, but the Marshal was cool. A few weeks later Stalin informed Churchill and the President that since the Polish organization in London had turned out to be "ephemeral" and impotent, he was recognizing the new Polish Committee of National Liberation recently formed by Warsaw Poles. He was willing to see Mikolajczyk, but only if he approached him through the National Committee.

Not only did the President fear Stalin's design for Poland and the political reaction in the United States, but also he and Hull were apprehensive that Europe was already veering toward the sphere-of-interest and balance-of-power doctrines that Hull in particular felt had had such iniquitous consequences. The problem was emerging in Poland and, most dramatically, in that classic sphere of interest the Balkans. Halifax had questioned Hull at the end of May on the proposition that London and Moscow reach an agreement that Russia would have a controlling interest in Rumania and the British in Greece. The Secretary responded with a lecture on proper principles of international relations. At the same time Churchill put the matter to Roosevelt as a temporary arrangement.

The President replied that he understood the immediate military necessity but feared that the natural tendency for such decisions to extend to other than military fields would be strengthened by Churchill's action and would result in the division of the Balkans into persisting spheres of influence. Churchill answered that it would be best to follow the Soviet lead in Rumania, considering that neither he nor Roosevelt had any troops there anyway, and that Greece was Britain's old ally. The President reluctantly agreed to a trial of three months, "making it clear that we are not establishing any post-war spheres of interest."

At this time the public relations between Roosevelt and Stalin were at their most cordial. In the spring Russian soldiers and civilians had been grumbling that a second front now would be too easy and too late, but Stalin in his May Day 1944 order gave full credit to Allied operations in Italy and the bombing of Europe. Only a combined blow could smash Hitlerism, he warned. After waiting prudently for a week following D day, the Marshal acknowledged the "brilliant success" of the Allies, adding that "the history of war does not know of an undertaking comparable to it for breadth of conception, grandeur of scale, and mastery of execution."

Privately, attitudes were somewhat different. On the eve of the Allied landing in Normandy, Stalin had received Milovan Djilas, from Tito's headquarters. Urging the Yugoslavs not to frighten London with their Communism, he went on: "Perhaps you think that just because we are the allies of the English that we have forgotten who they are and who Churchill is. . . .

"Churchill is the kind who, if you don't watch him, will slip a kopeck out of your pocket. Yes, a kopeck out of your pocket! By God, a kopeck out of your pocket! And Roosevelt? Roosevelt is not like that. He dips in his hand only for bigger coins. . . ."

PACIFIC THUNDERBOLTS

Strategy in Europe called for mass, focus, unity of purpose, singleness of command. Strategy in the Pacific was prone to dispersion, opportunism, shifting purposes, competing arms and commands.

If as an administrator Roosevelt had long tended to parcel out authority among several subordinates and let them compete with one another, he was now surpassing himself in the Pacific and the Far East. In the great arc stretching ten thousand miles from northeast of Japan to the southwest, Nimitz commanded the northern and central Pacific, MacArthur the Southwest Pacific, and Stilwell and Chennault in the China-Burma-India theater, and each of these pursued his own tactics and relied on his own special combination of services and arms.

The immediate issue lay between Nimitz and MacArthur. As Nimitz's amphibious troops speared into the Gilberts and Kwajalein and Eniwetok, and as his task forces ranged farther and farther west with impunity, the Admiral became more confident of his power to promenade directly across the Pacific to the Marianas, Formosa, and the China coast. Not only would he bypass small island bastions such as Truk, but he saw no reason that troops should run the risk of bogging down in great land masses such as the Philippines. With his carriers achieving greater range, with a growing fleet of supply ships that could provision the Navy at sea, with B-29's building that could fly immense distances, he proposed to leap along a small number of steppingstones on the shortest route to Japan.

MacArthur had rolled the Japanese back over a thousand miles from their farthest penetration; he had routed them on small islands and big ones alike. Above all, he had a promise to redeem —the return to the Philippines. He looked on the Navy plans with a cold eye. A direct attack across the Pacific, he told the Joint Chiefs, would degenerate into a spate of separate sea-borne attacks against positions defended in great depth. Carrier-based aviation could not overcome enemy planes swarming out from big land bases. An attack from his theater, on the other hand, "departs from the base that is closest to the objectives and advances against the most lightly organized portion of the enemy's defenses, effecting a decisive penetration. It is the only plan that permits an effective combination of land, sea, and air power." Heavily defended areas could be bypassed and allowed to fall of their own weight.

Doubtful that the Joint Chiefs would support him, MacArthur proposed that he come to Washington so that he could confront the Pentagon and appeal to the President. For months Roosevelt had held off making the strategic decision; he had not even mediated between the Army and the Navy. The argument and the tentative plans swung back and forth as events blocked certain lines of strategy and unfolded others. Pacific strategy was less the controller of events than the product of them.

And of the enemy. The Japanese Navy had been following a

cautious policy for almost two years, mainly because its carrier groups had been smashed at Midway and replacements eroded away in later encounters, especially in the Rabaul area. But Imperial Headquarters had not lost its will to fight. It was still hoping for the one big naval battle that would decide mastery of the central Pacific. The critical occasion would come when the Americans tried to penetrate the key defense perimeter running from the Mariana Islands through the Palaus and the Vogelkop to Timor. The most opportune situation would be to catch the American Navy when it was conducting an amphibious landing and was tied down to the committed troops.

This decision of the Japanese precipitated one of the great naval battles of the war, for it was precisely the Marianas on which the eyes of King and Nimitz were fixed. The major islands—Guam, Tinian, and Saipan—at the foot of the 425-mile chain were big enough to serve as advance naval and air bases in penetrating the western Pacific. They were 1,600 miles from Tokyo, near enough for the huge B-29's to make a round trip to the enemy homeland with several tons of bombs. And Guam, lost to the Japanese in the dark hours after Pearl Harbor, lay waiting to be liberated. Recognizing the attractiveness of the Marianas to the foe, Imperial Headquarters during early 1944 ordered about 45,000 troops into the islands. Even though American submarines picked off a dozen or more transports and freighters headed for Saipan, drowning about 3,600 troops and sinking the arms and equipment of another 4,000 or 5,000, the Marianas—especially Saipan, with 30,000 troops—were heavily defended by June 1944.

Early that month, while a great invasion force was storming Normandy beaches, another big amphibious force, of over five hundred warships and beaching craft and 125,000 troops, two-thirds of them Marines, was converging on Saipan from bases several thousand miles away. Early on the cool, bright morning of June 15, following heavy but ineffective bombardment by a dozen battleships and heavy cruisers standing six miles out to sea, amtracs packed with Marines churned from the landing ships, clambered over the barrier reefs, and ground up the beaches into the scrubby trees beyond. Despite heavy enfilading fire and much confusion, the Marines were well inland by nightfall, but Japanese counterattacks on D day and the next day were so effective that rosy hopes of capturing Saipan in a few days were soon dashed.

The main counterattack was now forming far out to sea. Admiral Toyoda, from his flagship in the Inland Sea, commanded the Combined Fleet to attack the enemy in the Marianas area and annihilate the invasion force. The Emperor himself warned his soldiers and sailors that "if Saipan is lost, air raids on Tokyo will take place, therefore you absolutely must hold Saipan." Vice Admiral Jisaburo Ozawa commanded nine carriers, five battleships, thirteen cruisers, twenty-eight destroyers, 430 carrier-based aircraft; Admiral Spruance could muster a fleet almost twice as big. On the morning of June 18, exploiting his planes' greater range, Ozawa dispatched wave after wave of bombers and fighters from his carriers against Spruance's battle formations, which were as tightly organized as a Wild West caravan defense, with carriers in the middle protected by a ring of interspersed battleships, cruisers, and destroyers.

Then came the "Great Marianas Turkey Shoot." Ozawa's planes ran into a curtain of fire from the big ships and their protecting Hellcats. Picket destroyers miles away could see Zeroes "falling like plums." The American planes had heavier armor, more firepower, better-trained pilots. Only one of the American surface vessels was even damaged. Ozawa had depended heavily on shore-based aircraft from Guam, but the tables were turned when Spruance sent Helldivers and Avengers over the island and not only smashed planes on the field but also pockmarked it so deeply that Japanese carrier-based aircraft that survived the dogfights crashed on trying to land there. On this day and the next Ozawa lost three carriers, including his own flagship, to American planes and submarines. By the time he took refuge at Okinawa, about four hundred of his carriers' planes had gone down.

Freed from the threat of counterattack, the Marines, now joined by army troops, proceeded with the tedious, bloody advance across Saipan. The days of quick conquests were over; the Japanese were dug into jungles and ridges and were flushed out at a heavy price —a bitter foretaste of battles to come. After three weeks the Japanese, pressed into the northern reaches of the island, were still able to mount a desperate banzai attack that overnight killed or wounded almost 1,000 men in a single army regiment. But this was a last spasm; by July 9 Saipan was "secured." Over 14,000 Marines had been killed or wounded.

Within two weeks Marines and soldiers invaded Guam, which fell after more hard combat, and Marines captured Tinian. The Battle of the Marianas was over; already Seabees and army engineers were clearing great tracts of jungle and cane field for runways that soon would be lofting B-29's toward Japan. Far to the southwest MacArthur had captured Biak and was assaulting Noemfoor, islands off the northern reaches of New Guinea that could serve as steppingstones to the Philippines.

The capture of Saipan would be of the highest importance to future offensives against Japan, Roosevelt cabled to Churchill during the operation. If he regretted that he could not have been with the Prime Minister on his visit to Normandy, the President was consoled by the thought that in a few weeks he would get close to his own war in the Pacific. On July 20, while the national Democratic convention was concluding its proceedings in Chicago, the Commander in Chief, from a high bluff, was watching 10,000 amphibious troops conduct a landing exercise at the huge Navy and Marine Corps base at San Diego.

The next evening Roosevelt and his party—Leahy, McIntire, Rosenman, and aides—boarded the heavy cruiser *Baltimore*, destination Honolulu. Guarded by air patrols and six destroyers, the grim, stripped-down cruiser traveled under wartime conditions, no lights showing. The President read and slept a good deal. The only casualty on the trip was Fala's dignity as a result of the crew's fattening him with tidbits and snipping locks from his hair to send home as souvenirs.

Rows of ships with men standing smartly at attention in their whites greeted the Commander in Chief in Pearl Harbor. Nimitz and a brace of naval and military officers clambered up the gangplank to welcome the President; only MacArthur was missing. After an uneasy delay the President and his party were about to disembark when an automobile siren wailed, a huge open car rolled onto the dock, circled, and drew up at the gangplank—and out stepped MacArthur, in leather windbreaker, creased suntans, and jaunty gold-braided cap. Suddenly summoned from Australia for a military conference with the President—his first meeting with the Commander in Chief in seven years—he had arrived with only one aide and with no reports, plans, maps, or charts, but with a determination to appeal to the highest authority for his plan to redeem the Philippines. The Marianas campaign had not settled Pacific strategy but only sharpened the old dispute.

In a cream stucco mansion overlooking Waikiki's rolling surf Nimitz and MacArthur argued their differences in front of Roosevelt and Leahy. Those differences were sharp but not profound. Tracing distances on a huge chart with a long bamboo pointer, Nimitz once again proposed bypassing the Philippines and moving direct to the attack on Formosa, and MacArthur once again urged the liberation of the Philippines and the bypassing of Formosa. But Navy strategists saw dire problems in assaulting Formosa without securing the Philippine flank, and army planners recognized that it was not a matter of either taking the Philippines or bypassing them, but of which islands in the archipelago to take, in what sequence, on what dates, and with what forces.

In such a situation Roosevelt was at his best, skillfully placating both the Admiral and the General, steering the discussion away from absolutes, narrowing the differences. MacArthur was at his most persuasive with Roosevelt when he took the stand that America had a moral responsibility to redeem its promises to liberate the Filipinos and to free imprisoned Americans. He claimed later that he also told the President—in a private session—that if their Filipino "wards" were left to languish in their agony, "I dare say that the American people would be so aroused that they would register most complete resentment against you at the polls this fall," but that the President had already made his decision, stating: "We will not bypass the Philippines. Carry on your existing plans. And may God protect you."

Roosevelt asked MacArthur to stay on to take a ride with him around the island. With Leahy and Nimitz they drove in an open car through streets lined with saluting servicemen and cheering Hawaiians, while Rosenman and Secret Service men worried about a well-placed bomb. The Commander in Chief reviewed the Army's famous 7th Infantry Division, saw wounded men unloaded from an ambulance plane that had just flown in to Hickam Field from the Marianas, watched a combat team make a simulated attack on a house, and kept remarking on the transformation of Oahu since his visit ten years before, when he witnessed an exercise in which, as he recalled, seven of the twelve World War I tanks broke down, and half the trucks.

At a naval hospital Roosevelt asked to be wheeled through wards occupied by men who had lost arms and legs. He wanted to display himself and his useless legs to these boys who would have to face the same bitterness as he had for twenty-three years, Rosenman wrote later.

After three strenuous days on Oahu the President and his original military party reboarded the *Baltimore* and headed almost due north to Adak. For five days the cruiser plowed north in steadily worsening weather. Cables from Washington and the fighting fronts followed, with reports of heavy fighting and steady progress in France and Italy. And with some grievous news, too—that President Manuel Quezon was dead, a few months short of the planned liberation of his country; that Missy LeHand had finally died after her long illness; that Joseph Kennedy's oldest son, Joe Jr., had been killed in an air attack on German submarine pens.

In Adak the President found intense activity at a nearly completed advance base. He talked to officers and men at the naval air station. "Gentlemen, I like your food. I like your climate." Much laughter. "You don't realize the thousands upon thousands of people who would give anything in this world to swap places with you." Incredulity. It was standing operating procedure in the Aleutians to call the theater the worst iced-over hellhole a man could be stationed in. But here was the Commander in Chief dwelling at length on Alaska as a new frontier for settlement by ex-servicemen after the war. The Alaskan coast, he went on to say, reminded him of the waters off Maine and Newfoundland he had known as a boy. The weather was familiar, too—continuing wind and rain and fog along the Alaskan coast and all the way back to Bremerton.

For the trip back, the President and his party, including Fala, changed to a destroyer, but their weather luck did not change. It was so foul that on the train crossing the country on the way back to Washington Roosevelt dictated a long complaint entitled "Mary Had a Little Lamb—1944 Version," which blamed the Navy for the "low" that had encouraged Admiral McIntire, the President said, to use a new word with almost every sentence.

ROOSEVELT AS COMMANDER IN CHIEF

To observe the superb co-ordination of arms and of units in mock combat, to cause the face of a wounded soldier to light up with surprise and pleasure, to lie in his bunk in the skipper's cabin and feel the engines of the great cruiser strain and pound underneath him, to find Pearl Harbor immensely expanded, with ships and docks back in service, to explore with Nimitz and MacArthur the imposing alternatives in the Pacific—never had Roosevelt assumed the role of Commander in Chief more intensely than in his days in the Pacific. He had not invited Marshall or King or Arnold to take part in the Honolulu conferences; this time the President wanted to deal with his theater commanders alone, except for Leahy. He would be tested in the fall as chief executive and chief politician; he also wanted—indeed, he preferred—to be tested as Commander in Chief.

He relished the title, according to Hull. The Secretary wrote later that at a Cabinet dinner, when Hull was to propose a toast, the President asked him please to try to address him as "Commander in Chief," not as "President." Admiral King wrote, also much later, that a few weeks before the Honolulu meetings Leahy had come to his office and said that the President would like to have King cease using the customary term "Commander in Chief" of both the United States fleet and the Atlantic and Pacific fleets, and to change the designation to commander of each individual fleet. Thus there would be but one Commander in Chief. Was this an order or a request? King asked. It was not even a request, Leahy said, but he knew that the President would like to have it done. King concluded that Roosevelt simply wanted to play up his role in an election year.

But it was more than that. Roosevelt not only assumed the role of Commander in Chief, but he embraced it and lived it. Just as he liked to tell reporters about his own journalistic days (mainly on the *Harvard Crimson*), or farmers that he was a tree grower, or businessmen that he had been in various financial ventures, so he would be a soldier among soldiers. But the feeling of involvement in the military role probably went much deeper; partly because that role was so crucial for a nation at war and partly because he felt keen deprivation at not having seen active service in World War I. He wanted to be a soldier, a professional. It had not been enough to be Assistant Secretary of the Navy during the first war; he had been desperately anxious for service overseas. It was not enough to be President of the United States; he must be symbolically in uniform.

One result was a close rapport between the President and his military chieftains. He often volunteered the observation that he had never overruled his staff. "We haven't had any basic differences," he said, referring to the Joint Chiefs of Staff, "and even haven't had any minor disagreements." This was true only in the narrow sense that the Joint Chiefs may never have come up with a firm and final plan that was flatly vetoed by the Commander in Chief; in fact, he had overridden the advice of military advisers in deciding on the invasion of Africa and in other decisions, and many a showdown was averted because the military men knew the President's views and never allowed disagreements to come to a head. The significant fact is that the President saw such a congruence and even boasted about it. In the occasional real disputes between the President and the Chiefs, he tried to win his way by quiet pressure and maneuver; he would not permit a showdown.

Even when the President felt strongly about an issue for political reasons, he was reluctant to overrule the military. Such an issue was the noncommissioning of Fiorello La Guardia. Son of an army bandmaster, reared on western army posts, proud of his World War I service as an aviator, the Mayor had been eager to join Eisenhower's civil-affairs staff. The "Little Flower" saw a great role for himself in Italy, but in any event he wanted to be in uniform, especially that of a brigadier general.

Roosevelt cabled to Eisenhower asking him to put La Guardia on his staff. Eisenhower agreed but complained to the War Department. Stimson and Marshall intervened at the White House just in time to try to persuade the President not to make La Guardia a brigadier general, but to commission him a colonel and send him to Charlottesville for civil-affairs training. "Eternal vigilance is the price of efficiency in this curious Administration," Stimson grumbled. When McCloy told the Mayor of the decision, La Guardia came to Washington to see Stimson. The Secretary reported to Roosevelt on the interview that had followed.

"1. I told him that there were two lines, of which he could follow either but not both. He could be a soldier or he could be a propagandist. He couldn't do both. The Army does not handle propaganda.

"2. As a friend I strongly advised him to remain in his present pulpit of the mayoralty and to use his influence with Italians from there; that his words would carry much further than if he was a civilian soldier, let alone a make-believe General. . . ."

Roosevelt replied in the stiffest letter he had ever sent a senior Cabinet member.

"Frankly, I think you have this LaGuardia business all wrong.

"I do not agree with your paragraph #1 wherein you told him that he could be a soldier or he could be a propagandist and that he could not be both.

"In view of my knowledge of literally hundreds of officers that you have commissioned out of public life who are neither soldiers or propagandists, I do not see how you could offer him one of the two alternatives. . . .

"I do not like your second paragraph wherein you suggested that he ought not to be a make-believe General. In the strict sense of the word, you have a great many make-believe Generals. . . .

"I do not think that LaGuardia wants 'adventure.' I think that is imputing a motive to him which is not strictly fair to him. Like most people wth red blood, he does hope he can get war service. . . ."

Stimson answered with a long placating letter, but did not retreat an inch. A month later Roosevelt spoke up for La Guardia in a brief conversation with Stimson, though only mildly, and a few months later was still talking to the Secretary about a possible reconsideration. But La Guardia never got his commission.

Even when the President might have had a gust of public feeling behind him he refrained from interfering in military matters. He refused to intervene when an army general, in a much-publicized action, punished soldiers who had "yoo-hooed" at him while he was playing golf. When reporters pressed him to comment on the hubbub over Patton's slapping two soldiers in Sicily, the President reminded them of the story about Lincoln, who had said when informed that his successful commander drank, "It must be a good brand of liquor." Nor did he intervene later when Patton avowed that Britain and the United States would run the world of the future. For a highly political man Roosevelt had shown remarkable restraint in influencing the selection of generals. Even Stimson had granted that his record "was unique in American war history for its scrupulous abstention from personal and political pressure."

At the same time, as Commander in Chief, he did not hesitate to propose specific ideas and changes to the military. He personally authorized the Navy to take extra risks in Atlantic convoying because of the need for emergency tonnage in Africa. He queried King as to whether carrier catapults had been brought into action in Pacific fighting, and Knox and Leahy as to the relative merits of several destroyers as against one heavy cruiser in protecting carriers. He suggested that carriers cope with suicide air attacks by improvising masts and wire on flight decks to be raised and lowered quickly, like barrage balloons. He gave special instructions to both the Army and the Navy about the need to rotate personnel. Yet in making these interventions—especially to the Navy—the Commander in Chief seemed to be acting as a leader of the team rather than as a civilian outsider.

Nor, in contrast to some of his predecessors, did he overturn many sentences following courts-martial. The exceptions are notable. He was vastly amused, in reviewing the dismissal from the Marine Corps of a young second lieutenant, to discover that the young man had simply allowed a sergeant to shoot a "limping" calf for a steak meal, outside the naval reservation at Guantanamo. The President put him on probation for a year—"This man must be taught not to shoot calves"—and seemed surprised that Marine Corps headquarters was distressed. He also put on probation a Navy nurse who had gone absent without leave at Norfolk in order to join her sailor husband for a delayed honeymoon. Hassett pleaded leniency for her. It was arbitrary to refuse her request to join her husband for a honeymoon, he argued. "It was arbitrary for her to go A.W.O.L.," the President countered.

From the start the President had protected his role as Commander in Chief. In appointing Leahy he had made clear that the Admiral would be a leg man, a collector of military advice, a summarizer—"whatever's necessary from the point of view of the Commander in Chief." The reporters did not quite understand. Would Leahy be Chief of Staff to the United Nations strategic command?

"He will be Chief of Staff to the Commander in Chief. . . ."

"He will definitely be chief of staff?"

"To the Commander in Chief," the President put in amid laughter.

"Yes, sir."

"Of the Army and Navy, Mr. President?"

"No. To the Commander in Chief." More laughter.

The President's job description was so predictive of what Leahy would do for the rest of the war that years later the Admiral used it to describe his work at the White House. Perhaps it was not strange that Leahy's assignment remained much the same over the years, for Roosevelt's whole command structure was remarkably stable. He did not hire and fire commanders as Lincoln did. The men who started out with him—Stimson, Marshall, King, Arnold, Leahy—were with him at the end. Only Knox and Stark were missing, the first because of his death, the second a casualty of feeling after Pearl Harbor. Even substituting Marshall for Eisenhower was for the President too much of a disruption of a settled array of relationships.

How, then, did Roosevelt withdraw from this comfortable interplay when political and strategic considerations demanded? The paradox of civil-military relations, William Emerson has pointed out, is that "in the strategic sphere, in all that concerns the structure and deployment of military forces, political leadership must be responsive to technical military opinion and advice, but it must, at whatever cost, shape and direct the military instrument to support and serve its own purposes. 'War,' as Clausewitz pointed out, 'has its own grammar but not its own logic.' " The framers of the Constitution had given the President, as Alexander Hamilton said, "the supreme command and direction of the military and naval forces, as first general and admiral of the confederacy," and events since 1787, including the revolution in war making, had enormously broadened the Commander in Chief's military powers and political responsibilities. He could delegate some of these powers but not, ultimately, the responsibility.

Roosevelt tried to resolve the paradox—to the extent he recognized it—by splitting his military role from his political. As Commander in Chief he left major military planning decisions in the hands of his Joint Chiefs and military planners. His differences with his chiefs over military policy arose not because he was following political objectives and they were pursuing military ones, but because of differing views as to correct military policy. In the months before and after Pearl Harbor he was bent on bringing about that concert of Anglo-American power that would best contain Hitler, while his chiefs were more concerned with husbanding American war production for their poorly equipped forces. The Joint Chiefs themselves were none too united, with Marshall eager to build up ground power in Britain, King naval power in the Pacific, and Arnold air power everywhere. Even so, most of the military disagreements between the President and his chiefs occurred in the early and middle phases of the war. As the war progressed the military thinking of Commander in Chief and Joint Chiefs converged, partly because of their increasing rapport, but mainly because the military build-up and Soviet as well as American military needs now called for the strategy that the Chiefs had long pressed—a central blow at Germany through France.

Meantime Roosevelt pursued some of his political goals separately. He clung tenaciously—almost fanatically—to his unconditional-surrender doctrine in the face of misgivings even among the military. He not only rejected their queries but seemed to reject the very notion that the military had a right to raise them. This seemed a bit odd, since the military would have to apply the doctrine in the first stages of surrender, and since the President's great precedent for the doctrine was a confrontation between two generals.

It was he, the Commander in Chief, who would do the co-ordinating of the political and the military. Such co-ordination called for an almost philosophical detachment in the White House, a capacity to look at things whole, to avoid the dangers of immediacy, opportunism, expediency, piecemeal planning. But to the extent that Roosevelt immersed himself in the role of the soldier and of the Commander in Chief, he was unable to take that balanced and comprehensive view of things that properly arrayed the military against the political, the short-run against the long, the psychological against the operational, the principled against the expedient. And he had no strategic staff in the White House to help him do this. Hopkins had served in this capacity to some degree, but he was too much of an operator like the President, and toward the end too ill and exhausted, to satisfy such a vital need.

Still, if Roosevelt and his fellow soldiers sought victory for its own sake too keenly, it was in part because the American people wanted a simple military victory. For most Americans, as Louis Morton has said, "war was an aberration, a nasty business to be got over with. . . . Postwar politics only complicated the problem and delayed the end. Beat the bully and bring the boys home—that was the American approach to war." And to make military victory the highest goal of the nation, as Morton further suggests, both constricts strategy and overburdens the armed forces.

Roosevelt's role as Commander in Chief contrasted significantly with Churchill's. The Prime Minister met frequently with his Joint Chiefs—often twice a day—and badgered them with chits that went into major details of planning and tactics. As his own Minister of Defence he felt free to communicate directly with theater commanders and to advise them on operations, though generally he left final decisions with the men in the field. Churchill was more disposed than Roosevelt to bring new men into top command positions. Valid or not, his military plans and political goals were closely related. Roosevelt seldom held formal meetings with his Joint Chiefs of Staff, though he was in close touch with them individually and through Leahy. He rarely pressed and never hectored them. The apparent result was considerable autonomy for the JCS, but only within a community of outlook long nurtured between the Commander in Chief and his fellow soldiers in the Pentagon and Navy Building.

Stalin on this score resembled Churchill more than Roosevelt. Major and sometimes minor battle plans were cleared with the Kremlin, though younger generals coming to the top of the heap on the basis of performance won more and more freedom of initiative. Marshal Georgi Zhukov found Stalin clearheaded, businesslike, and willing to be differed with. Stalin, according to Isaac Deutscher, was in effect his own commander in chief, minister of defense, quartermaster, minister of supply, foreign minister, and even his own *chef de protocole*. Neither Stalin nor Roosevelt imposed military dogmas or blueprints on his commanders; both acted as arbiters and adjusters. Stalin's donning of a marshal's uniform bespoke his solidarity with the Red Army, while Roosevelt symbolically donned uniform in becoming a soldier among soldiers.

Hitler prodded and harangued and bullied his generals. He followed operations minutely and intervened daily, sometimes hourly. If Roosevelt occasionally complained that his military planners were conservative and exaggerated the difficulties, Hitler castigated his to their faces as incompetents, cowards, nincompoops, and he sacked generals who retreated in violation of his orders. Hitler made himself Commander in Chief of the Army—"a little matter of operational command," he told General Franz Halder, "something anyone can do"—as well as Supreme Commander of the Armed Forces.

Still, whatever small difficulties the President had with the military could not compare with Hitler's. In July, as it became clear that the Allies were in France to stay, the disaffection among German officers erupted in a plot to kill the Führer. The bomb went off in the conference room at the Wolfsschanze headquarters; Hitler survived.

The President got news of the attempt just before leaving San Diego for his journey to Honolulu on the *Baltimore*. He had a flicker of hope that the German "revolt" might get worse, but reports arrived that Hitler had quickly established control of the situation. Three days before, Premier Tojo had resigned, with his entire Cabinet, on the announcement of the fall of Saipan. Roosevelt could not be dismissed by an Emperor or deposed by ministers or generals. But he was the only military commander who could be sacked by the voters. As his destroyer neared Puget Sound his mind was on the presidential election, which was already well under way.

SEVENTEEN *The Grand Referendum*

THERE IS something both strange and sublime about a great democracy conducting free elections in the midst of total war. Strange because at the very time a people is most unified over its goals and most determined to achieve them it divides into contending parties, mobilizes behind opposing doctrines, and pits gladiator against gladiator in the electoral arena. Sublime because in the act of holding an election a people reaffirms its faith in the democratic process despite all the compelling reasons to suspend it. Even Britain, a seedbed of democratic practice, postponed general elections during World War II, as in the first war.

Some doubted that the nation—or at least Roosevelt—could go through with a wartime presidential election. At a press conference early in February a reporter mentioned rumors in the anti-Roosevelt press that the election would be called off. Roosevelt pounced on him.

"How?"

"Well, I don't know. That is what I want you to tell me."

"Well, you see," Roosevelt said, "you have come to the wrong place, because—gosh—all these people around town haven't read the Constitution. Unfortunately, I have."

An Englishman observing the American scene early in 1944 marveled at the differences in Roosevelt's and Churchill's situations. The Prime Minister had the backing of a united nation, S. K. Ratcliffe noted, while the President moved in an atmosphere of conflict—of political bitterness, industrial discord, racial tension, press opposition, Democratic party defections—and "of an enmity against him so intense and persistent that for a parallel in Britain we would have to go far back."

The White House mail reflected the bitterness. "In conclusion candidate Roosevelt," wrote a Californian, "you are a politician I would not trust; for you use men *to promote your desire for power and more power* and when their usefulness is at an end, they are cast aside, as you double-crossed Al Smith at the 1932 Chicago Convention in your deal with Hearst (whom you now revile),

McAdoo and Garner. Both you and your wife, Eleanor Roosevelt, have done more during your incumbency to promote and stir up class, racial hatreds. . . . May God pardon you." From a New Jerseyite: "The people of the U.S. of America do not like any longer boss rule, nor dictated by a machine. . . ." Of the several hundred persons who wrote in against a fourth term some had specific complaints, some general, but many simply hated Roosevelt.

Many still loved him, or needed him. "Please President Roosevelt don't let us down now in this world of sorrow and trouble. If we ever needed you is now. I believe within my heart God put you here in this world to be our Guiding Star. . . ." Some letters came from organized groups; 6,100 steelworkers signed a petition, "We know that you are weary—yet we cannot afford to permit you to step down. . . ." Few letters dealt with issues, programs, specific goals; here again a gap yawned between great cloudy war aims and peoples' specific needs.

An undercurrent of worry about Roosevelt's health ran through many letters from both friend and foe. From San Diego: "I don't believe in working a good horse to death—so don't try to carry the whole world on your shoulders." From a woman in Brooklyn: " . . . You did many fine and wonderful things for this country, no doubt. . . . Resign, retire to your New York State home rest—and in time enjoy the fruits of your endeavours." One or two advised him to step down and head the peace delegation.

Messages came from Berlin, too. Election year had hardly started when Douglas Chandler, a former Hearst newspaperman who broadcast regularly from Germany under the name Paul Revere, called on his fellow Americans to repudiate the traitor, the charlatan, the weakling in the White House. America, he said, was on the brink of a reign of terror—and, even worse, inflation. "Get that man out of the house that was once white!" Adolf Hitler had cast his ballot early.

AS A GOOD SOLDIER

It might seem that, in theory at least, the most ticklish role in wartime politics would be the opposition's. To conduct a campaign at home against an administration conducting a campaign against the enemy overseas, to agitate and divide the country, to attack the Commander in Chief—politicians might be expected to recoil from such unpopular ventures. But not the pragmatic office seekers of America. By the inexorable calendar of American politics it was election year and hence it was time to smite the party in power, war or no war. By early 1944 the GOP was seething with hope and stratagems, and several men were seeking the Republican nomination.

The most active of these was Wendell Willkie. The 1940 nominee had refused to fade away after his defeat. His global travels, his writings, his calls for strong postwar world organization, his eloquent defense of Negroes and other minority groups, his double-barreled attacks on congressional Republicans and on the Roosevelt administration kept him in the public eye. But by 1944 he was a man without a party. He was still anathema to the congressional Republicans; he had never built a strong grass-roots organization within presidential Republican ranks, and what organized support he had mustered had partly melted away during the war.

Willkie was still a commanding figure, with his big burly frame, shaggy hair, muscular phrases, and blunt assaults on his enemies. But a note of desperate frustration was creeping into his speeches. He lambasted the reactionaries, bigots, and stand-patters in his own party even more bitterly than the racists and reactionaries in the Democratic. Introduced by an industrialist as "America's leading ingrate" to those who had helped him in 1940, he burst out, "I don't know whether you are going to support me or not and I don't give a damn. You're a bunch of political liabilities anyway." He was forever telling Republicans that they could take him or leave him—and many left him. He said all the right things about the Democratic regime—one-man rule, confused administration, self-perpetuation in power—but his criticisms of presidential Democrats seemed to lack the bite and crunch of his attacks on congressional Republicans.

His only hope in 1944, in contrast to his last-minute blitz four years before, was to demonstrate his popularity in a string of primaries. He won a small victory in New Hampshire and then plunged into Wisconsin. He calculated that if he could carry this Midwestern state, with its big German-American population and isolationist tradition, he would have met the crucial test. Day after day before big crowds he lashed his foes—the Chicago *Tribune,* New Deal regimentation, trimmers and poll-takers in his own party—in an exhausting campaign through the cities and towns of Wisconsin. It was like punching air—no other candidate was there to face him. But his lieutenants hoped to win a clear-cut majority of delegates, perhaps even all of them.

The results were clear-cut enough. He won not a single delegate. His leading delegate candidate ran a poor fourth to the top Dewey, MacArthur, and Harold Stassen men. Appalled and played out, Willkie told a crowd that he was quitting the race. He had hoped, he told his startled listeners, that the Middle West, the matrix of so many moral causes, would help produce new leadership. "Perhaps the conscience of America is dulled. Perhaps the people are not willing to bear the sacrifices, and I feel a sense of sickening because I know how much my party could do to make it worthy of its tradition. . . ."

Roosevelt read the results with mixed feelings. Not only did he admire his old adversary in certain ways, but also he had reason to feel uneasy about the two candidates left in the running.

The more notable of these was Douglas MacArthur, Roosevelt's old acquaintance, onetime Chief of Staff, and present subordinate. The President no longer considered MacArthur, along with Huey Long, one of the two most dangerous men in the country, as he had ten years before, but he could not ignore the General. MacArthur was still the darling of the congressional Republicans and the Hearst-McCormick-Patterson press, with their Pacific First strategy, neoisolationist tendencies, and anti-New Deal feelings. While publicly aloof, the General privately was making known his willingness to be drafted. After Vandenberg had shown some interest in MacArthur, the General wrote him an effusive letter intimating that there was much he would like to tell Vandenberg "which circumstances prevent" and asking for the Senator's "wise mentorship." Encouraged and spurred by the General's missionaries to Washington, a small group of conservative Republicans—Vandenberg, publisher Frank Gannett, General Robert E. Wood, of Chicago, former head of America First, among others—quietly fostered MacArthur sentiment. The General made clear that he would

An Odd Twist to an Old Tradition

April 10, 1944, C. K. Berryman, courtesy of the Washington (D.C.) *Star* accept the nomination only if drafted; otherwise he stayed out of the struggle and communicated through intermediaries.

The politicos in the White House watched the boomlet closely. It was clear that MacArthur, if nominated, would campaign for Pacific First; it was possible that he would charge Roosevelt with inadequately preparing the nation for war, with deserting the Philippines and starving the Southwest Pacific theater. The General had repeatedly put himself on record with the Pentagon and the White House about his grievances; his documented appeals would make good campaign material in the fall. But also on record in the White House, in the secret files of the President's naval aide, was the transcript of a discussion between MacArthur and Navy chiefs the day before Pearl Harbor. During this discussion the General had said that he was sure he could defend the archipelago as a whole and that his greatest security was the "inability of our enemy to launch his air attack on our islands." That, too, would make good campaign material in the fall.

For the MacArthur backers everything depended on retaining control of their boom for the General, keeping his name out of the presidential primaries, and timing developments so that he would be summoned to higher duty by the Republican convention. But too many Republicans, desperate to find a candidate who could match Roosevelt's glamour and appeal, crowded onto the small bandwagon. One of these was a Nebraska Congressman who rashly published an exchange of letters with MacArthur in which the Congressman had intemperately attacked the New Deal, and the General had expressed complete agreement with his views and had gone on to refer darkly to the "sinister drama of our present chaos and confusion." The publicity and the ensuing furore pricked the MacArthur bubble; he announced that he did not "covet" the nomination and would not accept it because no high officer at the front should be considered for President.

And then there was one. . . . Thomas E. Dewey had not had to lift a hand while his rivals ran into pitfalls and booby traps. Grandson of a founder of the Republican party in 1854, son of a Republican editor and postmaster in a small Michigan town, he had not only lived a Horatio Alger boyhood, but also at thirteen had nine other boys as his agents peddling the *Saturday Evening Post* and *Ladies' Home Journal*. After graduating from the University of Michigan and from Columbia Law School, he joined a New York law firm in the mid-1920's, practiced obscurely there for six years, then as a mob prosecutor and racket buster won almost instant fame by putting the likes of Legs Diamond and Lucky Luciano behind bars. Dewey was always in a hurry. Elected District Attorney for New York County on the La Guardia ticket in 1937, the next year he took on the redoubtable Herbert Lehman in a race for governor. He lost so narrowly that he was emboldened to seek the Republican presidential nomination in 1940. He led strongly on the early ballots at the Philadelphia convention, only to fall before the Willkie boom. Two years later, with Lehman out of the way, he captured the governorship in a smooth operation.

At forty-two Dewey was a seasoned young professional, with his share of wins and losses. Already he had acquired a reputation for being stiff, humorless, overbearing. With his waxworks mustache and features, his medium height, and his deep baritone he lent himself to cruel remarks: he was the bridegroom on the wedding cake, the only man who could strut sitting down, a man you really had to know to dislike, the Boy Orator of the Platitude. But his adversaries had learned not to underestimate him. He was the clear-cut choice of the Republican rank and file as well as the presidential-party leadership during the early months of 1944. He was running an expert noncampaign. He exuded energy, efficiency, purpose.

The New York Governor had done such a professional job in rounding up delegates, in fact, that he won easily on the first ballot in Chicago. It was a dull convention, enlivened only by Dewey's choice of John W. Bricker, the popular, wavy-haired Governor of Ohio, as his running mate. Bricker was no savant—his mind had been compared to stellar space, a huge void filled with a few wandering clichés—but all agreed that the two men made a strong ticket. And when Dewey, in his acceptance speech, lambasted the Democrats for having grown old and tired and stubborn and

May 18, 1944, C. K. Berryman, courtesy of the Washington (D.C.) *Star*

quarrelsome in office, he made clear the grounds on which he would carry the attack to the Roosevelt administration.

There was little suspense about the Democratic nominee. The President told friends that he wanted to return to Hyde Park "just as soon as the Lord will let me," but by early 1944 there was no doubt in the White House, and little outside, that he would run again, certainly if the war was not yet won. After sparring with reporters for some months, Roosevelt in July handed them copies of a letter to Robert E. Hannegan, now Chairman of the Democratic National Committee, stating that he did not want to continue in the White House after twelve years but that if the convention nominated him and if the people—"the Commander in Chief of us all"—ordered him, as a "good soldier" he would serve.

The big question was his running mate. It was clear that whether the President completed another term or not, the next Vice President would be in a commanding position in 1948. Who was Roosevelt's choice? The President never—not even in 1940—pursued a more Byzantine course than in his handling of this question.

Relations within the top echelons of the Democratic party in early 1944 were reminiscent of the old description of the Massachusetts Democracy as the systematic organization of hatred. Congressional Democrats were threatening to bolt the party, or at least withhold Southern electoral-college votes from the President. Texas and Virginia Democrats were in open revolt. CIO unions and liberal journals, along with a number of people close to Roosevelt, including Eleanor Roosevelt, backed Wallace; most of them opposed Byrnes. A covey of Democratic politicians—Hannegan; Edwin Pauley, Treasurer of the Democratic National Committee; Postmaster General Frank Walker; George E. Allen, Secretary of the National Committee; Boss Ed Flynn of the Bronx—opposed Wallace; so did Pa Watson and Steve Early. Friends of Pauley boasted that the California oil man journeyed from city to city urging local leaders to send reports to the White House about Wallace's unpopularity, and that Pauley had made a deal with Watson that Pa would clear the way into the oval office for anti-Wallace Democrats.

Roosevelt was pursuing his own line. While not discouraging Wallace, he subtly and openly encouraged others. His handling of vice-presidential ambitions in 1944 was much like his crafty, brilliant management of presidential rivalries four years before. At that time he had not only encouraged existing candidates to contend with one another but also had adroitly enlarged the field so that potential opposition would be fragmented and thus more manageable. So in 1944 he tempted Byrnes, who had earlier decided he

May 16, 1944, C. K. Berryman, courtesy of the Washington (D.C.) *Star*

would not try for the job; Hull, who flatly declined; and, by no indication he was out of favor, Vice President Wallace. Word leaked out at various times that the President looked with favor on Barkley, Rayburn, Truman, Winant, Justice Douglas, McNutt, Henry Kaiser, and several others. Wallace was leading in the polls; the President did not help his chances when in May he dispatched him on a mission to Asia, for Roosevelt sometimes sent abroad people he intended to let go.

By early July, with the convention scheduled for Chicago at the end of the month, Roosevelt could not put the matter off much longer. The smoke-filled room of the 1944 Democratic convention took place two weeks early, in the President's sweltering second-floor study, where he met on the evening of July 11 with Hannegan, Walker, Flynn, and others to canvass the field. One by one the names of front runners were lobbed up and smashed down. Byrnes, a Southerner and ex-Catholic, would alienate Negroes, Catholics, and liberals, according to the conventional wisdom of the canvassers. Barkley was too old. Wallace was so clearly anathema to the group that he was hardly discussed. Roosevelt trotted out Douglas's name—he was young, dynamic, he said, and, besides, played a good game of poker—but the others were cool. The talk turned to Truman. Roosevelt liked him for his personal loyalty and legislative support even while running an effective war investigation committee. The others approved his strong partisan background and instincts. He was from the Midwest, from a politically doubtful border state. The President did seem worried about Truman's age and sent someone out to check it, but he wandered away from the subject and it never came up again.

Everybody seemed to want Truman, Roosevelt said with an air of finality. The meeting broke up, but Hannegan, worried that the President might change his mind, got him to pencil a one-line note that Truman was the right man.

How to inform Wallace and Byrnes that Truman had the nod? As usual Roosevelt left this distasteful job to his subordinates. Rosenman and Ickes got hold of Wallace, who had just returned from China. The Vice President was calmly adamant. People were starving to death in Asia by the hundreds of thousands, he told the emissaries; he would talk politics only to the President. At the White House he showed Roosevelt his list of delegate support, his high standing in the polls. Roosevelt seemed to be surprised and impressed. He even discussed possible tactics. And he promised the Vice President a letter of personal endorsement. As he left, the President reached up and put his arm around him. "I hope it's the same team again, Henry."

Byrnes was equally obdurate. When Hannegan and Walker came with the bad news, he insisted on phoning the President at Hyde Park, and he took down the President's answer in shorthand. Was the President allowing people to speak for him?

Roosevelt: "I am not favoring anybody. I told them so. No, I am not favoring anyone."

Why were Hannegan and Walker quoting him as favoring Truman or Douglas?

"Jimmy, that is all wrong. That is not what I told them. It is what they told me." He had not expressed preference for anyone.

Again Byrnes pressed him on the matter.

Roosevelt: "We have to be damned careful about words. They asked if I would object to Truman and Douglas and I said no. That is different from using the word 'prefer.' . . ." He ended by virtually urging Byrnes to run.

By the time the Democrats convened in Chicago they were in a delicious state of confusion. While vice-presidential fever was sweeping the leadership, the delegates milled about in more than the usual state of ignorance. Byrnes had lined up Truman's support so solidly behind his own candidacy that the Missourian was not fulfilling his assigned role as number-one dark horse. Hannegan and his friends were trying to sidetrack Wallace without putting in

Byrnes. Hillman was working hard for Wallace but keeping a line of retreat open to Truman. Ickes was working for either Douglas or Truman—some said just for Ickes. Before the convention started, the President had stopped his train in Chicago on his way to San Diego and complicated things further by reissuing his penciled chit to Hannegan to read as an endorsement of Truman *and* Douglas—either to show he was not trying to run the convention or just to keep things confused.

Wallace's big weapon was a letter Roosevelt had written about him to the convention chairman: "I like him and I respect him and he is my personal friend. For these reasons I personally would vote for his renomination if I were a delegate to the convention." But the letter ended by leaving the matter up to the convention. To some it looked like the kiss of death; others wondered if it might put the Vice President over the top. It might have if Hannegan and his cohorts had not finally broken Truman loose from his pledge to Byrnes. Roosevelt, by now in San Diego, had to do this job, too; after Hannegan had got Truman together with Walker, Flynn, and Chicago boss Edward J. Kelly in a room at the famous Blackstone Hotel and put a call through to the President, Roosevelt demanded: "Have you got that fellow lined up yet?"

The answer was no. Truman still could not believe that the President was supporting him over Byrnes and Wallace.

"Well, tell the Senator," the President said, "that if he wants to break up the Democratic party by staying out, he can; but he knows as well as I what that might mean at this dangerous time in the world. . . ." Convinced at last, Truman asked Byrnes to release him. Wallace led the pack strongly on the first ballot, with Truman, Bankhead, and Barkley following, but the city bosses and the Southern Bourbons converged on the next ballot to put Truman over. Earlier Roosevelt had been routinely renominated; Harry Byrd received eighty-nine votes, virtually all from Southerners, and Farley one. The President had asked for and got a short, mildly New Deal, internationalist platform. He gave his acceptance speech from San Diego over the radio to the delegates sitting in the Chicago Stadium.

"I have already indicated to you why I accept the nomination that you have offered me—in spite of my desire to retire to the quiet of private life. . . .

"I shall not campaign, in the usual sense, for the office. In these days of tragic sorrow, I do not consider it fitting. And besides, in these days of global warfare, I shall not be able to find the time. I shall, however, feel free to report to the people the facts about matters of concern to them and especially to correct any misrepresentations. . . .

"What is the job before us in 1944? First, to win the war—to win the war fast, to win it overpoweringly. Second, to form worldwide international organizations, and to arrange to use the armed forces of the sovereign Nations of the world to make another war impossible within the foreseeable future. And third, to build an economy for our returning veterans and for all Americans—which will provide employment and provide decent standards of living."

The President rarely closed an address by quoting a famous speech, but the peroration of Lincoln's Second Inaugural seemed apt for the occasion:

"With firmness in the right, as God gives us to see the right, let us strive on to finish the work we are in; to bind up the Nation's wounds; to care for him who shall have borne the battle, and for his widow, and his orphan—to do all which may achieve and cherish a just and lasting peace among ourselves, and with all Nations."

A NEW PARTY?

After allowing a decent interval for Democratic convention oratory Dewey resumed his campaign against the tired administration and one-man government. The best way to counter this line of attack, Roosevelt knew, was through action rather than words. His long trip to California, Hawaii, and Alaska was to be testament to a Commander in Chief radiating energy and confidence. But Dewey had a point. So much did depend on that one man. And as the domestic battlelines were forming there were ominous signs that the pressure was too heavy, the body too fragile.

In his railway car in San Diego just before he was to leave to watch the landing exercise, the President was chatting with his son James. Suddenly his face turned white and agonized. "Jimmy, I don't know if I can make it—I have horrible pains." For minutes his father's eyes were closed, his face drawn, his torso convulsed by waves of pain. He refused to let Jimmy cancel his appearance. Then he recovered and was able to leave for the exercise. However serious this episode may have been, it was not reported to Bruenn.

Rumors were spreading. A story circulated even in the White House that the President had had a secret operation at Hobcaw in May. In Hawaii, Roosevelt received word from Hopkins in Washington that an FBI agent in Honolulu had reported to J. Edgar Hoover that the Pacific trip had been canceled because of the President's ill-health. He hoped the report was untrue, Hopkins wired, but if true that some other reason would be given. "The underground is working overtime here in regard to your health." Leahy replied that the President had worked fourteen hours straight the day before and was never in better health, and that the FBI agent should be disciplined for making a false report.

The camera that had projected Roosevelt's radiant face throughout the world could also be cruel. One widely used picture of Roosevelt making his acceptance speech showed a gaunt, shadowed face and a slack, open mouth; Rosenman lamented that Early was not there to prevent that kind of picture from going out, as Early had done in the past.

Perhaps the President missed the feeling of human contact in making his acceptance speech from San Diego; perhaps his mind went back to his dramatic flight to the Chicago convention in 1932 to pledge "a new deal for the American people"; or to the Philadelphia acceptance speech in 1936, when he proclaimed that "this generation of Americans has a rendevous with destiny." Certainly he wanted a live audience for his first appearance back on the mainland after his Pacific trip. He asked Mike Reilly to make arrangements for a speech in the Seattle baseball stadium. Reilly, anxious about security, appealed to Rosenman and Hopkins, who cabled that the President should not be in the position of having crossed the country in one direction in secrecy and then making a speech to a civilian audience on the way back. Why not speak from the deck of his destroyer with its guns as background? The President liked the idea.

To thousands of Bremerton workers jamming the docks—and to a nationwide radio audience—the President gave a chatty travelogue about his Pacific journey. To his aides the talk seemed a near-disaster. The President spoke in the open, against the wind; on the curved deck his braces, which he had been wearing less and less during the war years, were ill-fitting and uncomfortable; his delivery was tepid and halting. Rosenman's heart sank as he sat by the radio and heard the rambling speech.

What Rosenman did not know—and probably Roosevelt himself never knew—is that during the first part of this speech the President was suffering the first and only attack of angina pectoris he had ever had, or would have. Standing just behind him, even Bruenn could not tell what was happening. For about fifteen minutes the oppression gripped Roosevelt's chest and radiated to both shoulders; then the severe pain slowly subsided. Roosevelt told Bruenn right after the talk that he had had some pain; within an hour a white blood count was taken and an electrocardiogram tracing made. No unusual abnormalities were found.

Once again tongues started wagging. Rosenman knew all about the chatter at Washington and New York cocktail parties, about the questions people were asking: Has the master lost his touch? Is he a setup for Dewey's punches? Some of Roosevelt's intimates worried less about this than about Roosevelt's boredom with political detail. He had seemed curiously disengaged concerning the vice-presidential canvassing at the White House. At San Diego he told Jimmy that he didn't give a damn whether the convention chose Douglas or Byrnes or Truman; the important thing was to get on with the war. The Bremerton speech—his first contact with the American people since his acceptance address over three weeks before—he prepared hastily on the destroyer without the help of speech writers. Still, he was not detached about the rumors of his bad health. When Reilly confessed to him that he had allowed reporters to glimpse the President at Hobcaw to counter their taunting claims that he was actually hospitalized in Boston or Chicago, Roosevelt's lips tightened and his eyes glittered. "Mike, those newspapermen are a bunch of God-damned ghouls."

The President's most effective electioneering technique, at least early in the campaign, had always been that of maintaining his presidential posture, above the battle. While activists like Ickes chafed and fretted, while the Republican candidate sought to come to grips with his foe, Roosevelt continued just being President, offering as small a partisan flank as possible for the opposition to bombard.

Being President meant that he could propose and sign popular legislation. In early summer he approved the GI Bill of Rights, which revolutionized the whole approach to the returning soldier. The emphasis was less on a bonus or reward and more on education and individual achievement. Education or training at any level from primary grades to postgraduate would be allowed an ex-serviceman for one year plus the time served in the armed services, up to a total of four years. The bill also provided for a federal guarantee of half of the amount of loans made to veterans to buy or build homes, farms, and business properties; authorized substantial unemployment allowances for jobless veterans; set up machinery to help returning veterans find jobs; and authorized the building of more hospitals. The GI Bill was the capstone of a structure of veterans' benefits fashioned during the war: dependency allowances; mustering-out pay; broad medical care; death and disability pensions; war-risk life insurance; re-employment rights for returning ex-servicemen, and more.

"It gives emphatic notice to the men and women in the armed forces," Roosevelt said in signing the bill, "that the American people do not intend to let them down." It was not the kind of action or statement that presented an inviting target to the Republicans.

Being President meant laying exciting plans for the postwar future. Roosevelt proposed perhaps the most dramatic of these at summer's end when he called for a Missouri River development plan that would be based on the TVA concept that a big river basin contains one river and one set of interrelated problems and opportunities. In spurning a piecemeal legislative program for the basin, the President defied the innumerable groups that clustered around the existing power, recreation, irrigation, transportation, agricultural, and commercial interests in the basin. He called, too, for a study of the Arkansas and Columbia River basins, also with the TVA model in view.

Being President meant upholding the law. In the heat of August the Philadelphia transit system, serving almost a million war workers, came to a halt when motormen quit work because eight black employees had been upgraded to motormen. Strike leaders protested that motormen sat on the same wooden benches between runs and "the colored people have bedbugs." As thousands trudged to work in ninety-seven-degree heat and tension rose in the black enclaves, the President intervened from far out in the Pacific. Under his proclamation the Army took control of the transit system, ordered strikers to return, vainly waited two days for compliance—then moved 8,000 armed soldiers into the city, arrested the strike leaders, warned younger strikers that their draft deferments would be canceled, put two soldier guards behind each complying motorman, got the trolleys rolling again—and protected the Negroes' rights to their jobs.

During these summer months Roosevelt was conducting a curious venture in grand political strategy at home—curious because he ordinarily shunned broad political planning, curious, too, because years later it was still unclear whether he was seriously engaged in fundamental political reform or simply attempting an election ploy.

Certainly the political state of affairs cried out for a major confrontation. By 1944 Roosevelt and Willkie were both badgered and frustrated by the conservative wings of their parties; the presidential Democrats and the presidential Republicans were each under sharp challenge by the opposing congressional party. Roosevelt had been defeated on major legislation, such as taxes, and several of the Southern Democracies were openly defying him. Willkie was so impotent after Wisconsin that he was not even seated as a delegate in the Republican convention, much less invited to speak to the conclave or to testify before the platform committee. He felt more bitter than Roosevelt about his own congressional-party foes. He condemned the postwar international-security plank of the Republican party platform—actually a restatement of the Mackinac formula—as a betrayal of the youth of

America. It was only natural under the four-party pattern of American politics during this period that Willkie seemed to have more friends at the Democratic convention than at the Republican and that there was even some scattered interest in making him Roosevelt's running mate.

One day toward the end of June the President called Rosenman into his office. He said that former Governor Gifford Pinchot, of Pennsylvania—long a leader of presidential Republicans—had had a meeting with Willkie recently and then had come in to see the President. Willkie and Pinchot had talked about the possibility of a new setup in American politics. Roosevelt went on, as Rosenman recalled later, "It was Willkie's idea. Willkie has just been beaten by the conservatives in his own party who lined up in back of Dewey. Now there is no doubt that the reactionaries in our own party are out for my scalp, too—as you can see by what's going on in the South.

"Well, I think the time has come for the Democratic party to get rid of its reactionary elements in the South, and to attract to it the liberals in the Republican party. Willkie is the leader of those liberals. He talked to Pinchot about a coalition of the liberals in both parties, leaving the conservatives in each party to join together as they see fit. I agree with him one hundred per cent and the time is now—right after the election.

"We ought to have two real parties—one liberal and the other conservative. As it is now, each party is split by dissenters.

"Of course, I'm talking about long-range politics—something that we can't accomplish this year. But we can do it in 1948, and we can start building it up right after the election this fall. From the liberals of both parties Willkie and I together can form a new, really liberal party in America."

The President asked Rosenman to go to New York to see Willkie and sound him out on the idea. Rosenman warned his boss that Willkie might interpret the approach as a subterfuge to get him to come out for the President in the election. Roosevelt said that he should explain to Willkie in advance that the project had nothing to do with the coming election.

The two met secretly at the St. Regis—so secretly that Willkie stepped into the bedroom when the waiter served lunch. Willkie was wholly responsive to the idea of a postelection try at party realignment. Both parties were hybrids of liberals and reactionaries, he said. After the war there should be a clear confrontation of liberals and internationalists in one party against conservatives and isolationists in the other. "You tell the President that I'm ready to devote almost full time to this," he told Rosenman. The two men spent most of two hours going over leaders and groups—

labor, racial, and religious groups, small farmers, students, small businessmen, intellectuals, liberal Republicans—who could form the core of a cohesive liberal party. Willkie insisted only that he not see the President until after Election Day.

Roosevelt seemed elated by Rosenman's report of the discussion. "Fine, fine," he said; he would see Willkie at the proper time. But without waiting further, and without telling even Rosenman, he wrote to Willkie on July 13 that he would like to see him when he returned from his trip westward. Willkie did not answer the letter; he preferred to wait. He became even more cautious when word spread that the President had written to him; he suspected a deliberate leak by the White House in order to implicate him in Roosevelt's campaign effort, though he himself had shown the letter to Henry Luce and at least one other friend.

Vast confusion followed as Roosevelt, returning from his Pacific trip, first denied and then admitted that he had asked to see the 1940 nominee. Willkie, backing off, then tried to use former Governor James M. Cox, of Ohio, the Democratic nominee of 1920, to serve as intermediary, but this only confused matters more. The whole question still hung fire when Willkie was hospitalized for heart trouble early in September.

What had happened? Here, Rosenman reflected, were the two most prestigious political leaders in America, two leaders of the world. They were aflame with a great cause—the consolidation of the liberal, internationalist forces in America—that they better than any other men could have conducted with hope of success. And they utterly failed even to begin.

One clue lay in the transformation of Willkie in the last years of his life. The onetime utility tycoon and man of practical affairs had become a passionate ideologue. He had painted his Republican enemies black, calling them reactionary, isolationist, narrow, pathological. He had become aroused not only about isolationism but also about racism at home and abroad. He had read Myrdal and agreed with him that the war was crucial for the future of the Negro, that the race problem was in truth the crisis of American democracy, that the most tragic indignities were those inflicted on Negroes in the armed forces. But above all the author of *One World* was heartsick over what was happening, in the cloying partisan politics of an election year, to the dream of an effective world organization.

And Roosevelt—what was Roosevelt? To Willkie he was the head of a party as unprincipled as the Republican. The New Deal administration he had often charged with tired and cynical expediency, sacrifice of moral principle, misuse of personal power. Toward Roosevelt he was ambivalent; he had criticized him sharply in his preconvention campaigning, partly to keep his Republican credentials; programatically he was much closer to the President than to the congressional Republican leadership. But Roosevelt's opportunism put him off. He was so fed up with pragmatic politicians, he wrote to Gardner Cowles in mid-August, that nothing would induce him to serve under any of them. "I've been lied to for the last time."

Was Roosevelt in effect lying to him? Was the whole thing just an election stratagem? Willkie could not tell. On the one hand, the President had seemed willing to try party realignment only after the election. He would naturally want to win re-election as a step toward realizing a grand new party design afterward. And after all, the President had fought his foes in his own party—and in Willkie's—openly enough; he had even tried to purge conservative Democrats in 1938. But there was a darker side. Roosevelt had put Stimson and Knox in his Cabinet in 1940 without making a sustained effort to win over presidential Republicans. He loved to divide and conquer the GOP at election time. He would be a hard man to work with in overcoming the almost insuperable problems of party realignment. He had put out feelers to Willkie to take other posts; perhaps all these acts were just election gimmicks.

It was hard to say. Better wait until after the election to get really involved, Willkie decided; meanwhile he could put pressure on both candidates and their parties. But on October 8 Wendell Willkie died.

A GRAND DESIGN?

The war would wait for no election, the President had said. Nor would peace. It was Roosevelt's lot that explosive questions of war and peace dominated both his wartime campaigns. In 1940 the problem had been rearming America and aiding Britain but at the same time promising to keep America out of war. In 1944 the problem was America's role in maintaining peace and security after the war was won. The President's management of this problem in 1944—his success in winning a presidential campaign even while the foundations of a controversial postwar organization were being hammered out—was the climactic political feat of his career.

He was still pursuing his idea that nations would learn to work together only by actually working together. Oil, food, education, science, refugees, health—these and many other problems created bridges—and sometimes barriers—between the Allies. UNRRA continued its relief activities under the quiet, devoted leadership of Herbert Lehman; the President's main role was to help win funds from Congress and to define the jurisdictional line between

UNRRA and other relief activities, such as those of the Army and the Red Cross. He took a particular interest in the future of international civil aviation, holding that the air was free but that actual ownership or control of domestic airlines, especially in Latin America, should be in the hands of the governments or the nationals, not of American capital.

Roosevelt generally left the technical aspects of these matters to the corps of presidential advisers and of Civil Service professionals that had risen to peak numbers and talent during the war. But in this election year he kept a careful watch on political implications. No technical problem bristled with more complexities and political dynamite than did international monetary and financial policy.

Planning to prevent postwar monetary chaos had been going on at the Treasury since Pearl Harbor. The chief planner, Harry Dexter White, had long conceived of a United Nations stabilization fund that would enjoin its members both from restrictive exchange controls and from bilateral currency arrangements and would promote liberal tariff and trade policies in order to stabilize foreign-exchange rates; and of a Bank for Reconstruction and Development with enough funds and powers to provide capital for economic reconstruction and relief for stricken people. The British were thinking along somewhat the same lines, though John Maynard Keynes had a far bolder plan, for a Clearing Union that would have no assets of gold or securities but would establish an extensive system of debts and credits making for expansionist pressures on world trade. After endless preliminary discussions a distinguished group of Americans and British, including White and Keynes, in company with Russians, Frenchmen, and others, met amid the meadows and mountains of Bretton Woods, New Hampshire, in July to hammer out agreements.

"Commerce is the lifeblood of a free society," the President wrote in a greeting to the conference. "We must see to it that the arteries which carry that blood stream are not clogged again."

The toughest problems were not economic but political. The members of Congress in the American delegation had to be propitiated. The English feared the postwar supremacy of the American dollar even while having to come to terms with it. The Americans could not go along with the unorthodoxy of Keynes's scheme even though they acknowledged the brilliance, subtlety, economic genius —and occasional insufferability—of the master. The Russians argued stubbornly about their quota of the fund, but Molotov agreed to ease the matter at the eleventh hour. The conference ended with the fund and the bank agreed on, though still needing congressional approval.

Molotov's flexibility raised hopes about future Soviet collaboration with the West. "There are two kinds of people," Morgenthau remarked to Roosevelt later, "one like Eden who believe we must cooperate with the Russians and that we must trust Russia for the peace of the world, and there is the school which is illustrated by the remark of Mr. Churchill who said, 'What are we going to have between the white snows of Russia and the white cliffs of Dover?' "

"That's very well put," Roosevelt said. "I belong to the same school as Eden."

The real test was collaboration in keeping the peace after the war was won. By late August, American, British, and Soviet delegates were hard at work, in the stately Harvard-owned Georgetown residence "Dumbarton Oaks," on the structure of postwar security organization.

The concern of Americans about a new League of Nations had risen to a pitch of both enthusiasm and controversy in the summer of 1944. A host of organizations founded to support a new world order were conducting major publicity campaigns. *Wilson,* an evocative, highly favorable, and somewhat fictional film about the man who had fought for the League, was packing them in at select movie houses across the nation. Over two-thirds of the voters, according to polls, favored the creation of a new international organization and American membership in it. A cross-section of college students took this position by a ratio of almost fifty to one. Heavy majorities favored giving a world organization military power to preserve peace.

A spate of books on world organization appeared in bookshop windows. Sumner Welles, freed of his State Department responsibilities, argued in *The Time for Decision* against reliance on military alliances—none in all human history, he said, had lasted for more than a few short years—and for a United Nations that could enforce peace through an Executive Council of eleven members, including Britain, China, the Soviet Union, and the United States as permanent members. The Council, he said, could act only by unanimous agreement of the Big Four and only by a two-thirds vote of the whole Council. Welles's volume, a Book-of-the-Month Club selection for August 1944, sold almost a half-million copies. Historians and political scientists, including James T. Shotwell, Dexter Perkins, and D. F. Fleming, helped revive the old Wilsonian issues and argued for a new and stronger League. Generally the pundits saw close Big Four unity—especially Soviet-American friendship—as the cornerstone of peace, but they did not always explore the complexity and *Realpolitik* of big-power relations.

"The intellectuals are nearly all with us," Roosevelt wrote to a friend, just as they had been in 1920; he pleaded for a grass-roots effort. Actually the intellectuals were as divided as usual, especially between internationalists and "realists." Theologian Reinhold Niebuhr warned the former against encasing their optimistic view of human nature in leagues and federations; progress could come only after decades of anarchy. Carl Becker wondered *How New Will the Better World Be?*, since national loyalties and power always had been, and always would be, the essence of international politics. William T. R. Fox, of Yale, contended that agreement among the great powers, especially between Russia and the West, was crucial, and that Soviet co-operation was neither to be assumed nor rejected, but *achieved.* In *The Republic,* Charles A. Beard left his fictional internationalist guests speechless after he derided the League of Nations as an effective body and love and morality as ways of running the world. Walter Lippmann's *U.S. War Aims* argued that Wilsonian strictures against nationalism were useless, that "we are not gods," that a world community must evolve slowly from existing nations and communities, that in the middle run the world would be not one but three, with Atlantic, Russian, and Chinese orbits, and that in the short run Washington must boldly co-operate with Moscow, or at least coexist with it.

The books and articles and editorials helped establish the context within which the peace planners worked; so did the presidential campaign. In mid-August Dewey declared that he was deeply disturbed by reports that the Dumbarton Oaks Conference would "subject the nations of the world, great and small, permanently to the coercive power" of the Big Four. A four-power alliance, he said, would be immoral and imperialistic. With Roosevelt's approval, Hull put out a statement denying that any "superstate with its own police forces and other paraphernalia of coercive power" was being thought of; he denied that the Big Four could coerce other nations. Dewey designated his foreign-policy adviser, John Foster Dulles, to meet with Hull, and after three days of long discussion the two men worked out a statement designed to remove the more controversial aspects of postwar organization from the presidential campaign.

The issue that was cleaving the men at Dumbarton Oaks, however, was not the Big Four against the other nations of the world, but the Big Four against themselves. Early in the proceedings Ambassador Gromyko, head of the Soviet delegation, advanced the principle of Big Four unanimity, and he stuck to it all the days following with might and main. The innocuous word cloaked the momentous proposition that assuming the rule of unanimity an aggressive Big Four power could veto Council action intended to protect a smaller nation or—and this aspect was played down—another Big Four power. The Americans had shifted back and forth on the veto question—they could never forget the specter of Senate isolationism—but at Dumbarton Oaks they took the position

February 4, 1944, C. K. Berryman, courtesy of the Washington (D.C.) ***Star***

that a party involved in a dispute, whether a great power or small, should not be allowed to vote on the question. Gromyko flatly opposed any limitation on the veto, as expected, but then he threw a bombshell into the sedate mansion by demanding that all sixteen of the Soviet republics be seated in the new organization.

"My God!" exclaimed Roosevelt when Stettinius told him of the request. He asked the Undersecretary to inform Gromyko that such a proposal—labeled "X matter" to keep it from becoming known—would end the chances of the new United Nations being accepted by the Senate or the American people. Actually, the sixteen-vote proposition seemed so preposterous to Roosevelt that he expected to talk Stalin out of it. The veto was another matter. The more the Anglo-Americans opposed it, the more Gromyko insisted on it. Stettinius, convinced that solving the veto question was crucial to the whole enterprise, decided to bring out his "biggest and last remaining gun." Would the President talk with Gromyko? Would Gromyko, the President asked the Undersecretary, be offended if he received him in his bedroom? Stettinius thought he would be impressed.

It was an odd encounter the next morning between the President in his old bathrobe and the dark, personable young Ambassador. After chatting breezily, Roosevelt turned to the main issue, noting that traditionally in his country husbands and wives in trouble could state their case but not vote on it. He dwelt at length on old American concepts of fair play. Gromyko was pleasant but unyielding. Roosevelt then proposed a cable to Stalin reiterating his argument. That was up to him, Gromyko said. The President sent a friendly but strongly worded cable to the Marshal. Almost a week later the reply came back. The basic understanding was the unanimity of the Big Four. That presupposed no room for suspicion among the major powers. He could not ignore, said Stalin, certain absurd prejudices hindering an objective attitude toward the Soviet Union.

So deadlock had been reached on preserving the peace even as Soviet and Anglo-American troops were winning it. The Russians were still insisting on their sixteen votes. The Dumbarton Oaks meeting adjourned with the shining structure of a new international organization agreed on, but with a dark cloud over the capacity of the great powers to order their own relationships.

In mid-September 1944 Roosevelt and Churchill and the Combined Chiefs met again in Quebec for another conference, this one essentially military. The scene was the same as before, with Roosevelt and Churchill quartered in the Citadel and their staffs in the Chateau Frontenac, perched high on the north bank of the St. Lawrence, but the situation was radically different. Churchill and Roosevelt met as victors. Franklin and Eleanor Roosevelt greeting the Churchills at the station seemed more like the reunion of a happy family than a gathering of world leaders.

Out of ever-increasing solidarity and friendship, Roosevelt said at the start of the conference, had come prospering fortune. Though no one could yet forecast when the war with Germany would end, it was clear that the Germans were withdrawing from the Balkans, and it seemed likely in Italy that they would retire to the Alps. The Russians were at the point of invading Hungary. In the West the Germans probably would retire to the Rhine, which would be a formidable rampart. In Asia, the President went on, the American plan was to regain the Philippines and to control the mainland from there or Formosa, and from bridgeheads that would be seized in China. If forces could be established on the mainland of China, China could be saved.

"Everything we have touched has turned to gold," Churchill summed it up in his own equally favorable review of the situation.

These heady successes helped the conferees debate some of the old issues in relaxed fashion. No longer was the Mediterranean a source of contention; the Americans were willing to leave their troops in Italy until the Germans were defeated or pushed out. Churchill now spoke more freely of Vienna as a key objective, after giving the Germans a "stab in the Adriatic armpit," and the American Joint Chiefs were now less hostile to an amphibious landing on the Istrian Peninsula and even willing to bequeath landing craft to General Wilson for that possibility.

The sharpest turnabout was on Pacific strategy. Gone were the days of trying to limit the diversion of troops and ships to the amphibious attack against Japan; now the British wanted to play their full part. Japan, Churchill told the plenary session, was as much the bitter enemy of the British Empire as of the United States. He proceeded to offer the British main fleet to take part in the major operations in the central Pacific under American command. A detachment could operate under MacArthur if desired, and he also proffered RAF bombers. The Prime Minister knew that King and other admirals were cool to the idea, so he pressed for a showdown while Roosevelt was present. Could he have a definite undertaking about using the British fleet in the main operations against Japan?

"I should like," Roosevelt said vaguely, "to see the British fleet wherever and whenever possible." King said that the matter was being studied.

"The offer of the British fleet has been made," Churchill persisted. "Is it accepted?"

"Yes," the President said.

"Will you also let the British Air Force take part in the main operations?" Marshall answered that not so long ago "we were crying out for planes—now we have a glut."

Evidently the British could not break into the American preserve in the Pacific without a bit of hazing. But Pacific planning still turned largely on the progress of the war in Europe. At the time of the Quebec meeting the Combined Chiefs had high hopes, based on Intelligence estimates, that the Germans would surrender within twelve weeks. Though the President was not so optimistic, it seemed high time to reach final agreement on occupation zones. Roosevelt had long opposed the earlier plan that the British occupy northwest Germany and the Low Countries and the Americans southern Germany, Austria, and France; "I am absolutely unwilling to police France," he had exclaimed. But now at Quebec he changed his mind and approved the original plan, partly because the British agreed that the Americans could control Bremen and its port of Bremerhaven in order to supply their forces.

Long-run policy for Germany was a harsher problem. For weeks Morgenthau, Hull, and Stimson had been debating the treatment of Germany after its surrender. Stimson was willing to punish the

Nazi leaders, destroy the German Army, and perhaps partition Germany into north and south sections and internationalize the Ruhr, but he did not want to destroy raw materials and industrial plant crucial to European recovery. Morgenthau was burning to diminish and fragmentize Germany, dismantle and move out all plants and equipment, close the mines in the industrial heartland, and take control of education and publishing. Hull at times seemed to favor a punitive policy, at other times a softer one, but always a State Department role. Roosevelt talked tough at times—he wrote to Stimson that the Germans should be fed from army soup kitchens for a while—but on policy he wavered among his contending advisers. His central guideline seemed to be that the German people as a whole were responsible for a lawless conspiracy and must be taught a lesson.

Summoning Morgenthau to Quebec, Roosevelt asked him to present his proposals on Germany. As the Secretary spoke, he could hear and see "low mutters and baleful looks" from the Prime Minister. Churchill had never been more irascible and vitriolic, Morgenthau remembered later, as, slumped in his chair, he let loose the full flood of his biting, sarcastic rhetoric. He looked on the Treasury plan, he said, as he would on chaining himself to a dead German. The President sat by saying little. The next day, in a less negative mood—because he wanted Morgenthau's help on Lend-Lease matters, perhaps, or, even more, because he had been persuaded that Britain would gain economically from a deindustrialized Germany—Churchill dictated a statement which he and Roosevelt initialed. It went far in Morgenthau's direction.

"The ease with which the metallurgical, chemical and electrical industries in Germany can be converted from peace to war has already been impressed upon us by bitter experience. It must also be remembered that the Germans have devastated a large portion of the industries of Russia and of other neighboring Allies, and it is only in accordance with justice that these injured countries should be entitled to remove the machinery they require in order to repair the losses they have suffered. The industries referred to in the Ruhr and in the Saar would therefore be necessarily put out of action and closed down. . . .

"The program for eliminating the war-making industries in the Ruhr and in the Saar is looking forward to converting Germany into a country primarily agricultural and pastoral in its character."

Eden, who had flown to Quebec from London, was shocked by the statement. "You can't do this," he exclaimed to Churchill. "You and I have said quite the opposite." A testy quarrel broke out between the two while Roosevelt looked on silently. The Morgenthau plan, it was clear, had an aptitude for dividing people. Stimson had hotly opposed it, Hull would soon turn against it, Churchill eventually would repudiate it, and Roosevelt would quietly back away.

The Quebec Conference, which had opened in a "blaze of friendship," in Churchill's words, closed amicably because of agreed-on military matters. Soon after, Churchill visited Roosevelt at Hyde Park for final discussions. Leahy and others sat by enthralled at lunch the second day while Churchill and Eleanor Roosevelt debated long-run peace strategy—the First Lady contended that peace could best be established by improving living conditions throughout the world, Churchill that it would be kept best by an agreement between Britain and the United States to prevent war if necessary by using their combined forces. Roosevelt was largely silent. He was more interested in the military plans for the short-run than philosophical questions about the long-run.

But even as Roosevelt was bidding Churchill good-by, reports were coming in of German resistance that lowered hopes for victory by year's end and vitiated some of the military planning of the second Quebec Conference.

THE STRANGEST CAMPAIGN

The Presidential Room of the newly built Hotel Statler, in Washington, September 23, 1944. Hundreds of union men, Democratic politicos, and Washington officials pushed back their chairs from their dinner tables. At the head table sat Franklin Roosevelt, flanked by Daniel J. Tobin, of the Teamsters, AFL chief William Green, ship-maker Henry Kaiser. The President was framed by an array of microphones in front of him and a star-spangled curtain behind. Tobin introduced his guest. The room broke into a storm of applause, which died down only to erupt again and again as the President threw his head back and grinned.

Finally the room quieted. There was an air of expectancy. All had heard the rumors of Roosevelt's illness—the pictures from San Diego, the sound of his voice from Bremerton, the long delay while Dewey had campaigned across the nation. Did the old campaigner still have it? During dinner, at a table of Roosevelt's family and friends, Anna Roosevelt Boettiger leaned over and asked Rosenman: "Do you think that Pa will put it over? . . . If the delivery isn't just right, it'll be an awful flop."

Roosevelt began to talk. Then a surprise—he was still sitting down. The first words seemed to come strangely, as though the President were mouthing them.

"Well, here we are—here we are again—after four years—and what years they have been! You know, I am actually four years older, which is a fact that seems to an-*noy some* people. In fact, in the mathematical field there are millions of Americans who are mo-o-o-re than *eleven* years older than when we started to clear up"—now his words quickened and sharpened—"the mess that was dumped into our laps in 1933."

A burst of clapping, shouting, table pounding. Roosevelt proceeded to deride those who attacked labor for three and a half years in a row and then suddenly discovered they really loved labor and wanted to protect it from its friends. The Republicans who approved New Deal laws in their Chicago platform, he taunted, would not recognize those progressive laws if they met them in broad daylight.

"Now, imitation may be the sincerest form of flattery—but I am afraid—I am afraid—that in this case it is the most obvious common or garden variety of fraud.

"Of course, it is perfectly true that there are enlightened, liberal elements in the Republican Party, and they have fought hard and honorably to bring the Party up to date and to get it in step with the forward march of American progress. But these liberal elements were not able to drive the Old Guard Republicans from their entrenched positions.

"Can the Old Guard pass itself off as the New Deal?

"I think not.

"We have all seen many marvellous stunts in the circus but no performing elephant could turn a hand-spring without falling flat on its back."

The President reviewed labor's record, and his own. It was his old New Deal pitch given a new wartime sheen. He recited the statistics of progress, poked fun at the Republicans for trying to play general, denounced labor baiters, and stated that the occasional strikes that had occurred had been condemned by all responsible labor leaders but one. "And that one labor leader, incidentally, is certainly not conspicuous among my supporters."

Roosevelt was in full stride now. Raising and lowering his voice, drawing out his words and sentences, chuckling over some of the more incredible charges of the opposition, he derided Republicans for hating to see workers give a dollar to "any wicked political party" while monopolists gave tens of thousands; chastised them for making it hard for soldiers and sailors overseas and for merchant seamen to vote; reminded his audience of the "Hoovervilles" of 1933; and accused his foes of imitating Hitler's technique of the big lie—especially in the allegation that it was not a Republican but a Democratic depression from which the nation had been saved in 1933.

"Now, there is an old and somewhat lugubrious adage which

says: 'Never speak of rope in the house of a man who has been hanged.' In the same way, if I were a Republican leader speaking to a mixed audience, the last word in the whole dictionary that I think I would use is that word 'depression.' "

By now his listeners in the ballroom were not merely cheering —they were laughing. Anna's fears were stilled. Not only were Roosevelt's lines funny, but he was delivering them with such inflection, emphasis, alternation of deadpan innocence and rolled-up eyes of mock amazement, biting ridicule, and gentle sarcasm that the clapping was drowned in uncontrollable belly laughter.

Then the dagger thrust, planned by Roosevelt long before, the blade lovingly fashioned and honed, now delivered with a mock-serious face and in a quiet, sad tone of voice, rising briefly to indignation.

"These Republican leaders have not been content with attacks —on me, or my wife, or on my sons. No, not content with that, they now include my little dog, Fala. Well, of course, I don't resent attacks, and my family doesn't resent attacks, but"—a pause, and then quickly—"Fala *does* resent them.

"You know—you know—Fala's Scotch, and being a Scottie, as soon as he learned that the Republican fiction writers in Congress and out had concocted a story that I had left him behind on an Aleutian Island and had sent a destroyer back to find him—at a cost to the

October 24, 1944, Eric Godal, *PM*, reprinted by courtesy of Field Enterprises, Inc.

taxpayers of two or three, or eight or twenty million dollars—his Scotch soul was furious. He has not been the same dog since. I am accustomed to hearing malicious falsehoods about myself—such as that old, worm-eaten chestnut that I have represented myself"—he chuckled—"as indispensable. But I think I have a right to resent, to object to libellous statements about my dog."

The President went on for a bit, but he had already answered the big question in the minds of his listeners. In 1940 Roosevelt had said, "I am an old campaigner and I love a good fight." Clearly four years later he still did. This was not one of those speeches that took on importance only in later perspective. It had immediate impact. Reporters traveling on Dewey's campaign train in California heard the speech in the press car and instantly recognized its importance. Dewey felt that the "snide" speech was designed to anger him, and it did. He decided to campaign more aggressively.

After his opening strike the President returned to a stance of nonpartisan Chief Executive for four weeks. His only political speech was a fireside chat urging people to vote and rebutting charges that his administration was Communist-dominated. Meantime his political aides readied final plans. Roosevelt's basic strategy had long been set. As in the past he would appeal to liberal and internationalist Republicans, accuse Dewey of being controlled by his congressional party, and seek to hold the support of his own congressional party, especially in the South, while mobilizing voting power in the big cities.

This strategy was standard and time-tested; more serious was the operational problem. Early in the year, Louis H. Bean, a statistician and political buff, had given to Hopkins, Hannegan, and Hillman a long analysis of voting turnout in relation to Democratic gains and losses. He found that Democratic setbacks in 1942 and 1943 were due not to Republican popularity but to a fall-off in participation. Almost invariably the Democratic percentage shrank with lower participation. This was true in big cities; it was true in less urban areas such as Roosevelt's own Dutchess County. Bean's verdict was conclusive: "Participation . . . is of crucial importance for the Democratic Party in 1944."

The trouble was that the very people who tended to vote Democratic—low-income groups, young people, Negroes, women, ethnic elements—tended also to show the poorest turnout. If the year had been 1936 the President might wage a rousing and militant campaign that would draw at least some of the apathetic to the polls. But in 1944 many people, no matter how concerned, could not vote because they had crossed state lines and were not registered, or were in the service, or were working long hours in remote army bases and war plants. And Roosevelt had no thought of waging an inflammatory campaign during war.

The alternative was to rely on organization, and here, too, the President faced a dilemma. Except in Albany and Chicago and a few other cities the Democratic party was fragmented, locally oriented, or even moribund. By far the strongest national political machine in the summer of 1944 was Sidney Hillman's CIO Political Action Committee. The PAC was organized nationally and regionally and down to ward and precinct committees; it had gifted leadership in Hillman, political and propaganda talent, considerable money, ideas, energy, and conviction.

It was also the main target for Republican attack. Following the Democratic convention—where Roosevelt was said to have had Truman's nomination checked out with the labor leader—"Clear It With Sidney" had become a Republican war cry. CLEAR EVERYTHING WITH SIDNEY was placarded across the nation. "Sidney Hillman and Earl Browder's Communists have registered," voters were told. "Have you?"

The big open Packard, its canvas top down despite the drizzle, drove out onto Ebbets Field and up a ramp. The President of the United States was helped out of the car. Locked in his braces, he stood before a small crowd, doffed his old gray campaign hat, let his blue-black Navy cape fall from his shoulders. He had never seen the Dodgers play, he told the crowd, but he had rooted for them. The rain plastered down his hair and splattered on his pince-nez. He paid a tribute to Senator Bob Wagner—"we were together in the legislature—I would hate to say how long ago"—and asked that he be returned to the Senate. It was pouring by the time he was eased back into the car. He was given a rubdown and dry clothes at a nearby Coast Guard motor pool. Then the ordeal resumed.

Its top still down by the President's order, the limousine led a long cavalcade through Queens to the Bronx, then to Harlem and mid-Manhattan and down Broadway. La Guardia and Wagner sat on jump seats in front of the President; Eleanor Roosevelt was in the procession behind. The cold rain came down relentlessly, drenching the President's upflung arm and sleeve, rolling off his fedora, circling the lines of the grin on his face, seeping into his coat and shirt. Sidecar motorcycles flanked the Packard; guards stood on its running boards; three limousines packed with Secret Service men followed. Hour after hour the procession continued in the downpour. People waited under umbrellas and soggy newspapers to catch a glimpse of the big smile. At his wife's apartment in Washington Square he changed again and rested.

That evening the President spoke to the Foreign Policy Association in the grand ballroom of the Waldorf-Astoria Hotel on Park Avenue. It was a long catchall speech in which he again attacked the congressional Republicans for their isolationist voting, extolled liberal and internationalist Republicans—especially Henry Stimson, who was sitting on the dais—and warned that the likes of Joe Martin and Ham Fish would have controlling power in Congress if the Republicans won. But toward the end he took a stand on the crucial issue of the peace-keeping of the new United Nations.

"Peace, like war, can succeed only where there is a will to enforce it, and where there is available power to enforce it.

"The Council of the United Nations must have the power to act quickly and decisively to keep the peace by force, if necessary. A policeman would not be a very effective policeman if, when he saw a felon break into a house, he had to go to the Town Hall and call a town meeting to issue a warrant before the felon could be arrested.

"So to my simple mind it is clear that, if the world organization is to have any reality at all, our American representative must be endowed in advance by the people themselves, by constitutional means through their representatives in the Congress, with authority to act.

"If we do not catch the international felon when we have our hands on him, if we let him get away with his loot because the Town Council has not passed an ordinance authorizing his arrest, then we are *not* doing our share to prevent another world war. . . ."

The day in New York was a double triumph for the President. His four-hour, fifty-mile drive through the city was his answer to charges of loss of health and stamina. To be sure, anti-Roosevelt newspapers, including the *Daily News,* could run pictures showing him looking tired and worn, with sallow, lined face, but perhaps two million people had seen that uplifted arm and radiant smile. And in his speech that evening he outflanked Dewey on the issue of peace-keeping. Republican Senator Joe Ball, protégé of Harold Stassen, who was still serving in the South Pacific, promptly endorsed Roosevelt on the ground that while Dewey had evaded the issue, Roosevelt had met squarely and unequivocally the central question on which the isolationists had kept America out of the League of Nations.

Six days later Roosevelt carried his campaign to Philadelphia. Once again he toured city blocks for hours in an open car and once again it rained. In the city of brotherly love he talked of war—of his efforts to rebuild the Navy before Pearl Harbor, of the obstruction of the Republicans, of the people who laughed at his call for 50,000 planes a year, of the strategy he had followed in the war, of war supply and logistics and personnel. For once he mentioned his four sons at war: "I can speak as one who knows something of the feelings of a parent with sons who are in the battle line overseas." He promised categorically—in response to charges by Dewey—that servicemen would be returned to their homes promptly after the war—"And there are no strings attached to that pledge."

Two years before, the successful invasion of Africa had not been launched until after the congressional elections. Now Roosevelt's luck returned. On October 21 MacArthur had landed with his troops on Leyte, in the central Philippines, announced on the beach, "I have returned," and asked Filipinos to rally to him and to "follow in His name to the Holy Grail of righteous victory." Roosevelt could not let the opportunity pass. "I think it is a remarkable achievement," he told the throng in Shibe Park, "that within less than five months we have been able to carry out major offensive operations in both Europe and the Philippines—thirteen thousand miles apart from each other.

"And speaking of the glorious operations in the Philippines—I wonder—whatever became of the suggestion made a few weeks ago, that I had failed for political reasons to send enough forces or supplies to General MacArthur?"

He quoted a "prominent Republican orator" as calling "your present Administration" the "most spectacular collection of incompetent people who ever held public office." "Well," said the President, "you know, that is pretty serious, because the only conclusion to be drawn from that is that we are losing this war. If so, that will be news to most of us—and it will certainly be news to the Nazis and the Japs."

The following night Roosevelt spoke from his car in Soldier Field in Chicago. Nobody there that night would ever forget it, Rosenman said later. Over 100,000 people packed the stadium; another 100,000 or more waited outside. A cold wind was blowing in from the lake; Roosevelt's words bounced off the far sides of the stadium and back; but somehow he held the crowd.

It was the strangest campaign he had ever seen, the President said. He quoted the Republicans as saying that the "incompetent blunderers and bunglers in Washington" had passed excellent laws for economic progress; that the "quarrelsome, tired old men" had built the greatest military machine the world had ever known—that none of this would be changed—and "Therefore it is time for a change."

"They also say in effect, 'Those inefficient and worn-out crackpots have really begun to lay the foundations of a lasting world peace. If you elect us, we will not change any of that, either.' 'But,' they whisper, 'we'll do it in such a way that we won't lose the support even of Gerald Nye or Gerald Smith—and this is very important—we won't lose the support of any isolationist campaign contributor. Why, we will be able to satisfy even the *Chicago Tribune*.' "

The President spoke mainly about the economic past and future. He recited the entire economic bill of rights of the previous January. He promised "close to" sixty million productive jobs. He talked about homes, hospitals, highways, parkways, of thousands of new airports, of new cheap automobiles, new health clinics. He proposed that Congress make the FEPC permanent; that foreign trade be trebled after the war; that small business be aided; that the TVA principle be extended to the Missouri, Arkansas, and Columbia River basins. He expressed his belief in free enterprise and the profit system—in "exceptional rewards for innovation, skill, and risk-taking in business."

For Dewey, too, it was a strange campaign. Like his predecessors Willkie and Landon and especially Hoover, he found it impossible to come to grips with his adversary. He had plenty of hard evidence for his charges of mismanagement and red tape and expediency—but words meant little in the face of MacArthur's and Eisenhower's triumphs abroad. He was infuriated by Roosevelt's bringing up the question of enforcing the peace—a question he had understood to be barred from the campaign in the interest of bipartisan unity. He had occasional strokes of luck, such as Selective Service Director Hershey's remark that the government could keep people in the Army about as cheaply as it could create an agency for them when they came out. But Roosevelt was quick to have Stimson shush up Hershey and to make clear his own plans for rapid demobilization.

Dewey's actual position on policy was directly in the presidential Republican tradition—moderate liberalism, moderate internationalism—but the President attacked not the Dewey Republicans but the Taft, Martin, and Fish Republicans. In one speech Roosevelt even turned topsy-turvy one of the oldest and proudest GOP war cries—its stand for stable currency—when he asserted that the "Democratic Party in this war has been the party of sound money," and the Republican party of unsound. To Dewey, as to Hoover, Roosevelt seemed a political chameleon.

FOR YOU ARE THE MAN FOR US

With the polls predicting a close election but with Roosevelt in the lead, Dewey acted more and more like a prosecutor trying to put the President in the dock. And he gravitated more and more toward Communism as the issue. In the final days of the campaign he charged in Boston that to perpetuate himself in office for sixteen years his opponent had put his party on the auction block, for sale to the highest bidder. The highest bidders were the PAC and the Communist party. Roosevelt had pardoned Earl Browder, he said, in time to organize the fourth-term election. "Now the Communists are seizing control of the New Deal, through which they aim to control the Government of the United States." By now Democratic leaders were telling Rosenman and Sherwood that the President must answer the charges—the voters feared Communism more than Nazism or fascism.

Roosevelt had long disliked Dewey; now his attitude had become one of "unvarnished contempt." Bringing his campaign to a climax in Boston three days before the election, he met Dewey's charges with ridicule.

"Speaking here in Boston, a Republican candidate said—and pardon me if I quote him correctly—that happens to be an old habit of mine—he said that, quote, 'the Communists are seizing control of the New Deal, through which they aim to control the Government of the United States.' Unquote.

"However, on that very same day, that very same candidate had spoken in Worcester, and he said that with Republican victory in November, quote, 'we can end one-man government, and we can forever remove the threat of monarchy in the United States.'

"Now, really—which is it—Communism or monarchy?

"I do not think that we could have both in this country, even if we wanted either, which we do not.

"No, we want neither Communism nor monarchy. We want to live under our Constitution which has served pretty well for a hundred and fifty-five years. And, if this were a banquet hall instead of a ball park, I would propose a toast that we will continue to live under this Constitution for another hundred and fifty-five years.

"Everybody knows that I was reluctant to run for the Presidency again this year. But since this campaign developed, I tell you frankly that I have become most anxious to win—and I say that for the reason that never before in my lifetime has a campaign been filled with such misrepresentation, distortion, and falsehood. Never since 1928 have there been so many attempts to stimulate in America racial or religious intolerance.

"When any politician or any political candidate stands up and says, solemnly, that there is danger that the Government of the United States—your Government—could be sold out to the Communists—then I say that that candidate reveals—and I'll be polite—a shocking lack of trust in America. . . ."

Al Smith had died early in October, and to the Irish of Boston the President cited the lesson of Al Smith:

"When I talked here in Boston in 1928, I talked about racial and religious intolerance, which was then—as unfortunately it still is, to some extent—'a menace to the liberties of America.'

"And all the bigots in those days were gunning for Al Smith. . . .

"Today," he told the roaring, partisan crowd, "in this war, our fine boys are fighting magnificently all over the world and among those boys are the Murphys and the Kellys, the Smiths and the Joneses, the Cohens, the Carusos, the Kowalskis, the Schultzes, the Olsens, the Swobodas, and—right in with all the rest of them—the Cabots and the Lowells."

It had been in Boston in 1940 that the President had made his famous pledge to the mothers of America that their sons would not be sent into any foreign war. He would retract nothing now.

"I am sure that any real American—any real, red-blooded American—would have chosen, as this Government did, to fight when our own soil was made the object of a sneak attack. As for myself, under the same circumstances, I would choose to do the same thing—again and again and again. . . ."

On the day before the election, the President talked in the frosty open air to his "neighbors" on both sides of the Hudson. Election eve he gave a radio broadcast to the nation, ending with a prayer composed by Bishop Angus Dun, of Washington. Election Day he voted, along with forty million other Americans; like some of them he had trouble with the voting machine, and a mild oath floated out from behind the curtain.

In the evening the old ritual was followed in the mansion above the Hudson: the dining-room table was cleared, tally sheets and pencils laid out, the big radio and the news tickers turned on. Leahy sat with the President; Eleanor welcomed guests and staff—the Morgenthaus, the Watsons, Sherwood, Rosenman, Early, Hassett, Grace Tully—who clustered in the library. From the start, the President was calm and confident—well poised, unexcited, courteous, and considerate as always, Hassett noted. Once again, after a few ambiguous returns, the big Eastern and urban states began to fall solidly in line for the President. Shortly after eleven the torchlight parade arrived with fife and drum. The President talked quietly from the portico about election nights in the old days, when people would come in farm wagons for a Democratic celebration.

Dewey did not concede until after 3:00 A.M. Only then did the President go upstairs to bed. In the corridor he turned to Hassett and said: "I still think he is a son of a bitch."

The ballots were still being counted across the nation. Some Negroes had, "on this little note," passed their votes to Mr. Franklin D. Roosevelt because they were not allowed into their polls. One vote had been received in the White House in the form of a letter from a black woman in Pittsburgh:

"I have all way believed
That when God put you in the White House
He shore did no that you were the right
Man for the poor people.
I have never got anything
When the other party was in.
Only when you became Prest. did I get
What was do for the poor person.
Dear Mr. Roosevelt
No matter what the other partie say
I am all way for you . . .
So I am praying to the Good Lord above
That he will take good care of you
And put you back in the White House
For as long as you live
For you are the man for us."

EIGHTEEN *The Ordeal of Strategy*

THERE WAS a great flutter in Union Station as the President's train pulled in three days after the election. Truman, Stimson, Wallace, and other notables climbed aboard to welcome the conquering hero back to the capital. The Police Band sounded "Hail to the Chief" with ruffles and flourishes. It was like New York all over again. Despite the driving rain the President ordered the top put down; Truman and Wallace squeezed in with him, while young Johnnie Boettiger sat grandly in front. Outside, in Union Plaza, 30,000 people waited in the downpour. The car stopped and a panel of microphones was slid across the President's lap. He would always remember this welcome home, he told the crowd.

"And when I say a welcome home, I hope that some of the scribes in the papers won't intimate that I expect to make Washington my permanent residence for the rest of my life!"

Behind police motorcycles a long sleek line of limousines paraded up Pennsylvania Avenue. A half-dozen bands played. Over 300,000 people, including federal employees given time off and children let out of school, craned their heads and applauded as the presidential car went by. Soon after reaching the White House the President was greeting the staff, receiving congratulations from officials, and holding a press conference. He had no news, he said, except that he had underestimated his electoral votes. A reporter asked: "Mr. President, may I be the first to ask if you will run in 1948?" The President laughed with the others at the hoary old question.

It was a time of sweet victory. Not only had he beaten Dewey by 432 electoral votes to 99, but he had won the big Northeastern states, half the Midwest, including Illinois and Michigan, and all the West except Wyoming and Colorado. Only the Plains states had gone solidly for Dewey. The President's strength in Congress had been boosted. Formidable isolationists or conservatives had fallen: Gerald Nye, James J. Davis, of Pennsylvania, Guy Gillette; and leading Senate stalwarts, including Bob Wagner, Claude Pepper, Elbert Thomas, of Utah, Scott Lucas, of Illinois, Lister Hill, of

STUDY IN SELF-RESTRAINT

Alabama, and Alben Barkley, had kept their seats. There were some attractive new faces both in the Senate—Brien McMahon, of Connecticut, Fulbright, of Arkansas, Wayne Morse, of Oregon—and in the House—Helen Gahagan Douglas, California New Dealer; Emily Taft Douglas, of Chicago, wife of a University of Chicago economics teacher named Paul Douglas, then serving in the Marines; Adam Clayton Powell, of New York, who claimed to be the first Negro Congressman from the East. Once again Roosevelt had won out against the great majority of the nation's newspapers; not only the Hearst-Patterson-McCormick-Gannett press, but also Henry Luce's *Life* and a number of internationalist journals had supported Dewey. And once again he had beaten John L. Lewis in the mine leader's own precincts in Pennsylvania and West Virginia.

Above all, he had won the referendum of 1944 for American participation in a stronger United Nations. The "great betrayal" of 1920 would not be repeated. He had strengthened his own hand for future negotiations. Congratulations flowed in from abroad—from Churchill, Stalin, Mao Tse-tung.

Physically, the campaign had taken its toll. At times Roosevelt had completely disregarded his rest regimen; he had had to be strenuously active for long periods of time. He seemed more tired than ever after the election; his appetite was poor, his color only fair. But Bruenn found that his blood pressure was actually lower when he was out on the hustings, and when he examined the President two weeks after the election he found that his lungs were clear, the heart sounds were clear and of good quality, there were no diastolic murmurs. Roosevelt's blood pressure was 210/112.

Politically, the victory concealed some weaknesses. The Republicans had been defeated, but not the two congressional parties; the "unholy" coalition of conservative Democrats and Republicans would still largely control Congress, at least on domestic affairs. Roosevelt's popular-vote margin of 3.6 million votes out of 48 million cast was the narrowest since Wilson's hairline victory over Hughes in 1916. In retrospect it would seem remarkable that a forty-two-year-old governor with experience in neither war nor diplomacy could come so close to toppling a world leader at the height of a global war. Most important, events in eastern Europe were threatening to erode the very premises on which Roosevelt had won the election and made solemn commitments to the American people.

EUROPE: THE DEEPENING FISSURES

Europe was trembling with hope and fear, change and convulsion. As the Germans were driven out of France and Greece and the vast areas overrun by the Red Army, tormenting political problems flared up in their wake. Roosevelt had hoped to postpone politics until after the war was won, but political problems would not wait—especially those of eastern Europe.

For months now, Poland had linked war and politics, ancient quarrels and future hopes, Chicago ward bosses and Kremlin strategists. On the prompting of Roosevelt and others, Stalin saw Mikolajczyk in Moscow early in August, only to urge the "émigré group" to come to terms with the Committee of National Liberation, the Lublin Poles. The two Polish groups met and failed to agree. By this time Roosevelt was facing heightened election pressure from Polish-American groups at home. In Washington and on his campaign trip to Chicago he promised representatives of the Polish-American Congress that the principles of the Atlantic Charter in general and the integrity of Poland in particular would be protected.

The torment of Warsaw foreshadowed future calamity. When Soviet troops neared the Polish capital at the end of August, underground forces mainly loyal to the London Poles struck at the Germans from houses, factories, and sewers. In moments the city was engulfed in a bitter street-to-street battle. In the next few days, as the fighting became more and more desperate, the Warsaw Poles begged for help from Churchill, who persuaded Roosevelt to send with him a joint message to the Marshal.

"We are thinking of world opinion if the anti-Nazis in Warsaw are in effect abandoned. We believe that all three of us should do the utmost to save as many of the patriots there as possible. We hope that you will drop immediate supplies and munitions to the patriot Poles of Warsaw, or will you agree to help our planes in doing it very quickly? We hope you will approve. The time element is of extreme importance."

A shocking reply came from Stalin:

"Sooner or later the truth about the handful of power-seeking criminals who launched the Warsaw adventure will out. Those elements, playing on the credulity of the inhabitants of Warsaw, exposed practically unarmed people to German guns, armour and aircraft. The result is a situation in which every day is used, not by the Poles for freeing Warsaw, but by the Hitlerites, who are cruelly exterminating the civil population. . . ." Stalin promised, however, that his troops would try to repulse German counterattacks and renew their offensive near Warsaw.

Stalin's mounting temper stemmed partly from frustration. His troops had in fact been forced back from Warsaw by savage German counterattacks. The Warsaw Poles had not co-ordinated their plans with him; he suspected they were trying to force his hand. He did not want American and British airmen poking around his rear bases, especially at the very time his forces were pulling back. But he was moved by colder calculations. By now he was fully sponsoring the Lublin Poles. He did not propose to help liberate Warsaw from the Nazis only to leave it in the hands of bourgeois Poles who were the pawns of London and Washington. Better to let the Warsaw elements destroy themselves by their foolhardy action.

In a last try Churchill asked Roosevelt to agree to a joint message that implored Stalin to allow Allied aircraft to land behind the Russian front after dropping war supply to the beleaguered Poles; privately Churchill suggested to Roosevelt that if Stalin did not reply they ought to send the planes and "see what happens." Roosevelt would not go along on this. Distressed though he was by Stalin's attitude toward the Warsaw tragedy, he feared that pressure on Moscow would jeopardize more important long-range military co-operation with Russia, especially in the Far East. In mid-September Stalin finally relented and allowed bombers to drop some supplies. But it was too late; resistance was nearing an end.

A quarter of a million Warsaw Poles were dead; most of the city was in ruins. Somehow Roosevelt managed to resist Churchill's and Mikolajczyk's importunities about Warsaw at the same time he was holding his own with Polish-Americans in the election campaign. He even asked Churchill to hush up any controversial announcement about Poland until after Election Day. Two weeks after the election, when former envoy Arthur Bliss Lane urged him to demand of Moscow that the independence of Poland be maintained, and added that if the country was not strong when it had the biggest Army, Navy, and Air Force in the world it never would be, the President asked sharply, "Do you want me to go to war with Russia?"

In despair Mikolajczyk appealed directly to Roosevelt. He was being pressed to accept the Curzon Line without any reservations, he cabled. The Poles would feel terribly deceived and wronged if after all their efforts and sacrifices they were faced with the loss of nearly one-half their territory. "I retain in vivid and grateful memory your assurances given me in the course of our conversations of June, last, in Washington, pertaining particularly to Lwow and the adjacent territories." For the last six hundred years Lwow had been a Polish city no less than Cracow and Warsaw. Would the President not throw his decisive influence into the scales by appealing to Stalin?

The President sent Mikolajczyk an evasive reply, adding that Harriman would discuss the question of Lwow with the Polish leader privately. A few days later, caught between the Allies' caution and his associates' militancy, but with his warm feeling for Roosevelt evidently undiminished, Mikolajczyk resigned. This left Roosevelt and Churchill with no leader of the London Poles who could serve as a bridge to Moscow and the Lublin Poles. Playing for time, Roosevelt in mid-December appealed to Stalin not to recognize the Lublin group before the three leaders met in January.

The Marshal was unbending. The polish *émigré* government, he said, was a screen for criminal and terrorist elements who were murdering officers and men of the Red Army in Poland. Meantime the Polish National Committee—the Lublin group—was strengthening and expanding the Polish government and Army and carrying out agrarian reform in favor of the peasants. The Soviet Union, he went on, was a border state to Poland and was carrying the main brunt of the battle for its liberation. The Red Army had to have a peaceful and trustworthy Poland to its rear as it fought into Germany. If the Lublin Poles transformed themselves into a provisional government, the Soviet government would have no reason not to recognize them.

He was disturbed and deeply disappointed by this message, Roosevelt responded to Stalin. "I must tell you with a frankness equal to your own that I see no prospect of this Government's following suit and transferring its recognition from the Government in London to the Lublin Committee in its present form. This is in no sense due to any special ties or feeling for the London government." There was simply no evidence that the Lublin Committee represented the people of Poland. "I cannot ignore the fact that up to the present only a small fraction of Poland proper west of the Curzon Line has been liberated from German tyranny, and it is therefore an unquestioned truth that the people of Poland have had no opportunity to express themselves in regard to the Lublin

Committee. . . ." Would Stalin not wait for the three of them to meet?

Stalin's reply was terse. The London Poles were disorganizing things and thus aiding the Germans. Roosevelt's suggestion to postpone was "perfectly understandable to me" but he—Stalin—was powerless. The Presidium of the Supreme Soviet of the USSR had already notified the Lublin Poles that it intended to recognize the provisional government of Poland as soon as it was formed.

It was interesting to see, Churchill scornfully cabled to Roosevelt, that the "Presidium of the Supreme Soviet of the USSR" had now been brought up into the line.

During these months of fall 1944 Roosevelt and Churchill were only superficially united in their attitude toward Stalin. At the climax of the coalition effort the two Western leaders were divided over strategy for dealing with Russia, with Communism in general, and indeed with all the forces of change erupting in the wake of the Nazi armies.

Churchill was trying to play a close game of *Realpolitik* with the Marshal. Journeying to Moscow early in October, he and Eden had hardly sat down with the Russians in the Kremlin when he decided on a quick gambit. Stating that London and Moscow must not get at cross-purposes in the Balkans, he pushed across the table to Stalin a half-sheet of paper with a simple, stark list giving Russia 90 per cent predominance in Rumania and 75 per cent in Bulgaria, Britain 90 per cent in Greece, and dividing Yugoslavia and Hungary fifty-fifty between Russia and the West. Stalin had paused only a moment, then with his blue pencil made a large tick on the paper and passed it back to Churchill.

There had been a long silence. The paper lay in the middle of the table. Then Churchill said: "Might it not be thought rather cynical if it seemed we had disposed of these issues, so fateful to millions of people, in such an offhand manner?" He proposed to burn the paper. "No, you keep it," said Stalin.

This was precisely the kind of high-level trading over spheres of interest that had worried Roosevelt about a Churchill-Stalin meeting. He had had Harriman attend the meetings, but his Ambassador to Russia had no power to commit the President. So the crucial matters—the veto, Poland, Germany, Far Eastern strategy—were put off until the three leaders could meet.

If *Realpolitik* united Churchill and Stalin, it divided Churchill and Roosevelt. An acrimonious dispute flared over Italy between Washington and London early in December when the British informed Premier Ivanoe Bonomi that the appointment of Count Sforza, a symbol of antifascism to many liberals and leftists, would be unacceptable. Winant was instructed to inform the Foreign

Office that Washington regretted this intervention in an internal Italian political crisis, especially without prior consultation. Incensed, Churchill made it known to Washington that he considered Sforza a dishonorable intriguer and mischief-maker and that he felt entitled to tell the Italians this "because we have been accorded command in the Mediterranean, as the Americans have command in France, and therefore we have a certain special position and responsibility." He had an added grievance: he felt that he had done his best to ease the Italian situation for the President, especially before the presidential election.

When the State Department put out a critical press release about British policy in Italy, Churchill went into a towering rage. He dispatched a cable to Roosevelt that Sherwood later described as the most violent outburst in all their correspondence. He reminded Roosevelt of all his past support on the Darlan affair and other issues. Roosevelt, who was at Warm Springs at the time and feeling rather detached from the rumpus, deplored any offense that the press release might have given but firmly reminded the Prime Minister that Italy was still "an area of combined Anglo-American responsibility" and that the British had acted on their own in blocking Sforza.

One reason for Churchill's anger was the obvious implication for Greece of Washington's failure to support him in Italy. Armed with Stalin's agreement that he could control this sphere and with Roosevelt's acquiescence in temporary British predominance, Churchill was determined that his nation's ancient ally in the eastern Mediterranean would not become a political void and hence prey to E.L.A.S., the strong Communist and guerrilla movement there. After the Germans pulled out, E.L.A.S. had made a bid for power in Athens, only to become locked in a struggle with British troops quickly sent in by London. Liberal and leftist groups in Britain and the United States flared up at what seemed a British ploy to enthrone reaction and to kill those who had fought the Nazis most zealously.

Intent on his mission of saving Greece from Communism, Churchill was bitter over the lack of sympathy in Washington. It almost seemed to him that outside the War Cabinet his only solid supporter was Stalin, who was saying nothing about Greece. Churchill was furious when a message in which he instructed the British general in Greece not to hesitate to shoot rebels if necessary leaked out in the American press, evidently through the State Department. At this juncture Roosevelt sent him a long, almost benevolent letter stating that he was sorry about Churchill's difficulties in Greece but he could not stand with his old friend there. "Even an attempt to do so would bring only temporary value to you, and would in the long run do injury to our basic relationships." Roosevelt made a number of specific suggestions—including, promise a regency instead of the return of the King—that Churchill found utterly useless. For the Prime Minister the only recourse was more troops, which eventually did put down E.L.A.S.

More troops. In Greece and Poland and elsewhere troops were becoming the arbiters of strategy. Were they to shape the new world as they had the old?

Harriman's answer was yes—at least before he sat in on Churchill's conference with Stalin. In mid-September he had informed the White House that relations with the Russians had taken a startling turn in the last two months. On issue after issue they were silent or indifferent or obstinate. Their attitude seemed to be that it is "our obligation" to help Russia and accept its policies because "she had won the war for us." Unless Washington took issue with this policy, Harriman warned, Russia would become a world bully.

Hull asked Harriman to spell out his views further. On reflection Harriman seemed more temperate—or ambivalent. Stalin, he said, seemed to have two strings to his bow—friendliness toward the West, and suspicion and hostility to it. The Russian people craved peace; they wanted the close Allied relations to continue after the war; Stalin could not disrupt the alliance without causing grave concern among the Russian people. On the other hand the Soviet leaders keenly felt the backwardness of their country; they were unduly sensitive and suspicious; and powerful elements close to the Marshal would insist on independent action where Russian security was strongly affected.

Practically, this meant, Harriman said, that Moscow would often take unilateral action; would block consideration by a United Nations security council of any question close to its national interests; would insist on shaping its own relations with neighboring states. Harriman's advice was ambivalent, too—meet the Russians more than halfway, but "oppose them promptly with the greatest of firmness" when they seemed to "go wrong."

All this left it to Roosevelt to decide when he should oppose the Russians, or when he should yield and release—it could be hoped—the potential for friendship and good will that even his hardheaded Ambassador saw in the Russian people.

CHINA: THE EDGE OF THE ABYSS

In the Far East Roosevelt was facing a sharp and ominous contrast by the fall of 1944 between the brilliant military advances scored in the Pacific and the political-military stalemate on the land mass of Asia.

The invasion of Leyte challenged the imperial high command

even more blatantly than had Saipan. The Philippines shielded the vital lifelines across the South China Sea; they formed huge steppingstones for the American assault on Formosa, the Chinese coast, on Japan itself. Once again, as in the Marianas, Japanese naval chiefs planned a combined attack on the task forces guarding the American amphibious forces. As MacArthur's infantry deepened the beachhead on Leyte, Japanese striking forces moved toward the central Philippines from the Singapore area and from Japan. Defending the Leyte waters were the Seventh Fleet, commanded by Admiral Thomas C. Kinkaid, who was under MacArthur, and the Third Fleet, under Bull Halsey, who was responsible to Nimitz's command post thousands of miles away at Pearl Harbor.

The enemy's big counteroffensive began on October 23. The largest Japanese fleet, under Vice Admiral Takeo Kurita, with two superbattleships and a dozen cruisers, advanced directly across the Sibuyan Sea toward San Bernardino Strait, only to meet such fierce attacks by submarines and carriers that after two days it turned about and started back west. To the south another Japanese fleet, under Vice Admiral Shoji Nishimura, ran into a perfectly planned ambush in the Surigao Strait and was almost annihilated. A third and smaller enemy fleet sortied down from the Inland Sea, not to fight, but to lure Halsey's big force north and thus leave the landing forces unguarded. Halsey, burning to come to grips with what he thought was the main enemy carrier strength, and persuaded that Kurita's force was manageable if not beaten, steamed north to meet the enemy head on.

An epic of confusion and gallantry followed. Kurita's fleet, battered but still formidable, turned back east to go for the unprotected invasion ships. Not one of the major Japanese fleets knew just what the others were doing. Halsey was about to close with the northern enemy fleet when he turned about to help block Kurita's move. Too late—Kurita was already pounding the little collection of escort carriers and destroyers that lay between him and Leyte. Kurita's battleships and heavy cruisers were just about to catch and sink the lightly armored American ships when he suddenly broke off the action for fear that Halsey's big fleet would catch *him*. But Halsey had managed to steam three hundred miles north and three hundred miles south without engaging the main enemy forces.

In Washington the President jubilantly summoned reporters to his office. He had received a report from Admiral Halsey, he announced, that "the Japanese Navy in the Philippine area has been defeated, seriously damaged and routed by the U.S. Navy in that area." Statistics later told the tale—the Japanese lost 306,000 tons of combat ships, including three battleships and ten cruisers in the Battle of Leyte Gulf, and the Americans 38,000. And behind the statistics, aside from brilliant seamanship and bad communications, was the ever-expanding industrial power and naval technology of the United States.

On the dusty plains of China, on the other hand, and in the jungles of Burma, the infantryman was still king, especially when assisted by aerial knights who could leap over obstacles. In the early months of 1944 the Japanese struck with their infantry forces against two vulnerable areas, India and China. Tokyo's strategy was as much political as military—to divide the people and destroy the governments of the two most populous nations in the world.

In Burma the Japanese attacked along the coast of Arakan in an effort to outflank a British advance south, only to be outflanked in turn and then repulsed as Mountbatten supplied his troops by air. The enemy then advanced on the Imphal Plain to the northwest; here again the British used gliders and air-borne troops skillfully to hold the attack. The approaches to India were secure, at least for a time. Roosevelt sent Churchill his congratulations on "an epic achievement for the airborne troops, not forgetting the mules." To the east, Stilwell, who had left CBI theater headquarters to assume command in the field, deployed Chindits, Chinese, and Americans to capture the airfield at Myitkyina and hence safeguard the lifelines to China.

These heroic efforts soon were overshadowed by the successes Tokyo was scoring in its other great military-political effort. By late spring strong Japanese spearheads were cutting through disorganized Chinese resistance in Honan to seize control of Hankow-Canton communications and threaten Chennault's advance air bases. Ambassador Clarence E. Gauss cabled that Chungking had been thrown into despair. Chinese peasants, he reported, were even turning on the Kuomintang troops. Stilwell, arriving in Chungking from his Burma headquarters early in June to resume his duties as commander of American troops, Chief of Staff to the Generalissimo, and trainer of his armies, shifted Hump tonnage to Chennault, but he feared that on the ground there was nothing to stop the Japanese.

The melting away of Chiang's troops before enemy ground attacks realized Roosevelt's worst fears about China. More than anyone, other than the Generalissimo himself, he bore responsibility for the diversion of men and war supply to China. He had personally sponsored Chennault's efforts. He particularly had encouraged the Generalissimo, exhorting and persuading but not demanding or cajoling or really bargaining. Churchill had been skeptical of the effort in China; others had urged the White House to get tough with Chungking, but the President, sensitive to the tangle of military problems and political disloyalties surrounding Chiang, had insisted that he be treated as an ally, as chief of state, and indeed as one of the Big Four.

And now after all his patient efforts in China, Roosevelt's strategy seemed to be crumbling. The President's tone with the Generalissimo took on an edge of sharpness. "The extremely serious situation which results from Japanese advances in Central China," he radioed on July 6, "which threatens not only your Government but all that the United States Army has been building up in China, leads me to the conclusion that drastic measures must be taken immediately if the situation is to be saved." He asked Chiang to put Stilwell in full command, under himself, of all Chinese forces. He added that he knew how Chiang felt about Stilwell, but the future of all Asia was at stake.

Chiang replied that he agreed in principle but asked for a delay, for "Chinese troops and their internal political conditions are not as simple as those in other countries"; he also asked Roosevelt to send a personal representative to help adjust relations between Stilwell and himself. The President agreed and chose Major General Patrick J. Hurley, an Oklahoma Republican, corporation lawyer, Secretary of War under Hoover, negotiator between Mexico and expropriated American oil companies, more recently a roving diplomat for the President, a towering picture-book general with considerable experience of almost everything except China. As Hurley proceeded to China, the Japanese were pressing on. In mid-September Stilwell cabled to Marshall that "the jig is up in South China."

It was not, seemingly, in northern China. Armed with instructions from Roosevelt, Hurley plunged into the trackless problem of helping bring a settlement between the Kuomintang and Mao Tse-tung's Communist regime. He arrived at a time when American officials in China were at last seeing Chinese Communism firsthand. On Roosevelt's prompting, Vice President Wallace had persuaded Chiang in June to allow embassy and army officers to visit Yenan, the Communists' capital, for personal observations and talks. The visiting Americans, liberated from the drift and demoralization of Chungking, felt that they had come into a different country and were meeting a different people. From Mao down, the officials impressed them with their cordiality, directness, and lack of show. There were few police in Yenan, no beggars, no desperate poverty, the observers reported to Chungking and Washington. Morale was high. People were serious, busy, organized, confident. Even Hurley seemed to become drawn into Yenan's intoxicating atmosphere of discipline and dedication.

The Communists did not conceal their interest in the United States and its President. They bombarded their visitors with questions. Might America swing back to isolationism and let China "stew in her own juice"? Was it really interested in democracy? Did it realize that Chiang was in no way representative of China, that even Hitler had a better claim to power? Much depended on Roosevelt—was he going to be re-elected? Chairman Mao, in a fine humor after dancing gaily with his wife, sat down next to an American second secretary during a lull and talked about the possibility of a Kuomintang-Communist compromise. He thought Roosevelt would not put any pressure on Chungking until after the election because he would not want to stir up Chiang's supporters.

"We will wait," Mao added. "We have had a long training in patience." Laughingly he asked about Roosevelt's chances of re-election.

Roosevelt at the moment was far more worried about the Generalissimo than about the Chairman or even perhaps his own re-election chances. As the Japanese pressed on in eastern China, and as Chiang showed no signs of reorganizing and reforming his government, or seeking unity with the Communists, the President decided on a firmer hand. In a stinging cable to Chiang he said that China was facing the disaster he had feared. Chiang would have to assume personal responsibility for what was happening.

"I have urged time and time again in recent months that you take drastic action to resist the disaster which has been moving closer to China and to you." He and Churchill had just decided at Quebec, he went on, to accelerate operations to open the land line to China. "The action I am asking you to take" was "at once placing General Stilwell in unrestricted command of all your forces."

It fell to Stilwell to deliver this message personally to the Generalissimo. Vinegar Joe could not resist a surge of pleasure in presenting to his chief the kind of near-ultimatum that for months he had wanted Washington to send. "I handed this bundle of paprika to the Peanut and then sank back with a sigh," he wrote happily in his diary. "The harpoon hit the little bugger right in the solar plexus, and went right through him. It was a clean hit, but beyond turning green and losing his power of speech, he did not bat an eye. He just said to me, 'I understand.' "

For Stilwell it was but a brief moment of triumph. The Generalissimo was stung by the handling of the message as well as by its content; a subordinate had thrust upon him an ultimatum. Stilwell must go, he hold Hurley; he was unfitted for the vast, complex, and delicate duties of the new command. He had never been able to get along with the Generalissimo. Chiang would tolerate him no longer.

So the gauntlet was thrown at Roosevelt's feet. Marshall urged him to stand behind Stilwell. It was a last chance to appeal to liberal, reformist, or even Communist elements in China. But here Roosevelt hesitated. Expressing his surprise and regret to Chiang, he agreed that Stilwell be relieved as Chiang's chief of staff but asked that he be placed in direct command of Chinese troops in Yunnan and Burma. Chiang refused. He stood by his original demand that Stilwell be relieved of all his offices and replaced. And now Roosevelt submitted. Stilwell would be brought home. Clearly no American general would take over-all command of the armed forces of Nationalist China. There would be no basic reorganization of the Chinese Army, no fundamental social reform, no pressure on Chiang to make a settlement with the Communists—and probably no real drive against the Japanese in South China. By November 1944 Roosevelt's China strategy seemed to be in ruins.

ROOSEVELT AS GRAND STRATEGIST

Why did Roosevelt reverse his China strategy at the critical moment? Stilwell's answer was simple: the Commander in Chief was a weak and procrastinating politician, an "old softy" who had refused to bargain with Chiang, who knew little about China, and who was probably ill, to boot. The truth, as usual, was not so simple. Roosevelt, with his sensitivity to personalities, doubtless felt that he was responding mainly to Chiang's insistence on his prerogatives as chief of state, to Stilwell's crusty individualism and inability to get along with Chiang, Mountbatten, or Chennault, to the views of Hurley, who was siding with the Generalissimo against Stilwell. But his main reason for ending pressure on Chiang stemmed from his basic Chinese strategy.

Since Pearl Harbor, Roosevelt had been pursuing two aims in China: to strengthen it as the central base for the final attack on Japan, and to treat it as a great power that would be a bulwark of Asian stability and democracy after the war and a focus of American co-operation with Asia. While the first aim was a matter of military need and the latter of long-run hopes, the two goals meshed. By sending men, munitions, and money to China he was strengthening its postwar as well as its war role; by including China as one of the Big Four, by bringing it into summit conferences such as that at Cairo, he was bolstering Chungking's legitimacy, giving it a greater claim on war supply and on participation in military decisions.

Roosevelt sharply modified his first goal during 1944. As Chiang's armies melted away before the Japanese ground attack, as Chennault not only failed to break up that attack but also lost his advance air bases, as Chiang refused to undertake drastic reforms of his government and army command, and—most important by far—as American amphibious forces hopped across the Pacific with ever-growing power and momentum, the President lost hope that China would constitute the main springboard for the climactic assault on the home islands. Stalin's promise to take on the Japanese armies in Manchuria sometime after Hilter's fall, along with the anti-Japanese and pro-American attitude of the Yenan Communists, made Chiang's role even less vital. In telling the Generalissimo twice in October that the ground situation in China had deteriorated so sharply that he no longer wanted an American officer to take command of Chiang's forces under the Kuomintang, Roosevelt was not only venting his frustration, but he was signaling his changed military policy, and he was demonstrating once again that essentially military considerations dominated his basic strategy.

The shift in military policy, however, was not accompanied by a shift in political. Faced with his failure in China, Roosevelt had a choice of only two fundamental alternatives. He could continue or even accelerate his military effort in China and try to persuade or compel Chiang to produce basic reforms, thus giving the government the military basis for its aspirations as a great power; or he could scale down his political goals for China at the same time he scaled down his military ones. In fact, the President tried to do both and ran the risk of succeeding in neither. He kept talking to and about China as a great power even while he was giving higher and higher military priorities to other theaters.

This separation of strictly military and operational from broad political or strategic considerations in Asia exemplified Roosevelt's approach to the European situation, too. Europe First had been his firm priority from the start, regardless of political-military implications for Asia. And in planning strategy in Europe he and Stimson and Marshall had put it to the more politically minded British that the invasion of France was the quickest, cheapest, and surest means of defeating Germany. Churchill had struggled to plant Allied influence in the Balkan area, only to give in to Roosevelt's insistence on nourishing the invasion of France even at the expense of the Allied effort in northern Italy. In the fall of 1944, as Allied troops pressed to the border of Germany, the American emphasis on a focused, massed military effort, regardless of political considerations, seemed vindicated.

Other examples of Roosevelt's setting military over political priorities could be cited—his cautious approach to rescuing the Jews of Europe, his handling of the occupation zones in Germany, his withholding of atomic information from the Russians—but his absolute insistence on unconditional surrender seemed to some at the time and to many in retrospect as the clearest example of his subordination of long-run political concerns to immediate military ones. The practical purposes of unconditional surrender were to allow the Allied commands to concentrate on winning a total military victory over Germany, to strengthen the anti-Hitler military coalition by insuring that neither Russians nor Anglo-Americans would negotiate for a separate peace, and to help insure that the Russians would live up to their promise to join the war against Japan. Neither Churchill nor Stalin supported the doctrine with Roosevelt's determination, but each gave it lip service while seeking to modify it to meet particular situations.

If military strategy, in Samuel Morison's words, is the art of defeating the enemy in the most economical and expeditious manner, Roosevelt must rate high as a military strategist. As Commander in Chief he husbanded military resources in both the Atlantic and the Pacific until the enormous power, industrial and technological, of the nation could be brought to bear on the military scene. Despite endless temptations to strike elsewhere he stuck firmly to an over-all strategy of Atlantic First, and in Europe, despite the diversions of Africa and Italy, he and his military chiefs finally delivered the full weight of the Anglo-American effort into France. He helped gain a maximum Soviet contribution to the bleeding of German ground strength and brought Allied troops into the heart of Germany at just the right time to share in and claim military victory; he found the right formula for getting the most militarily from the Russians without letting them, if they had so wished, occupy the whole continent. And if he was deliberate and single-minded in Europe, where victory demanded consistency and continuity of effort, he was opportunistic and flexible in the early stages of the Pacific war. He shifted from a strategy of depending on China and Formosa as huge bases for ground forces to stepped-up island-hopping by amphibious forces. Compared with Soviet, German, and even British losses, and considering the range and intensity of the effort and the skillful and fanatical resistance of the enemy, American casualties in World War II were remarkably light.

He had been an architect of military victory. Well could the Commander in Chief boast in his Navy Day campaign talk in Philadelphia on October 27, 1944, that, since Navy Day a year before, the Army, Navy, and Air Force had participated in no fewer than twenty-seven landings in force on enemy-held soil and that "every one of those 27 D-Days has been a triumphant success." Until the final days of 1944 Roosevelt never met a major military defeat after the setbacks of Pearl Harbor, the Philippines, Kasserine Pass, and in the Pacific during the first fifteen months of the war.

But grand strategy—achieving the nation's broad and enduring goals by marshaling its full military, diplomatic, economic, and psychological resources—puts a much harsher test to a Commander in Chief.

Grand strategy requires not only putting ends before means, political goals before military, long-run aims before immediate successes. It is not merely, in the Clausewitzian sense, the subordination of war to diplomacy, and diplomacy to politics. It is the marshaling of a series of plans and decisions in every relevant area of a nation's life—war, diplomacy, economics, popular opinion, domestic politics—in such an order that power and action can be mobilized persistently and widely behind a people's enduring principles and goals, that the instrumental ends and means—governmental policies, military decisions, institutional patterns—be continually readapted in the light of the wider purposes being served, and that the goals and principles be reassessed in the light of those ends and means. The language of grand strategy is the language of priorities. The priorities serve and structure a nation's ideology.

It has become conventional to see Roosevelt as a master pragmatist or opportunist or improviser who waged war without political ends in mind, or who at least subordinated his ends to his means and made a mess of the former, or even of both. The dichotomy was not this simple.

Roosevelt had political goals; few leaders in history, indeed, have defined them with more eloquence or persistence. He expressed these goals most broadly and simply in the Four Freedoms—freedom of speech, freedom of religion, freedom from fear, freedom from want—a bit more extensively in the Atlantic Charter, and at great length in a host of pronouncements, campaign speeches, press releases, fireside chats, letters, and conversations. The Four Freedoms, he said, were the "ultimate stake," perhaps not immediately attainable throughout the world, "but humanity does move toward those glorious ideals through democratic processes." Those freedoms would be realized through the more specific aims of the Atlantic Charter—the end of territorial aggrandizement, the right of all peoples to choose their own form of government, the free and fair sharing of raw materials, international collaboration to raise living standards, abandonment by nations of the use of force. Serving these goals in turn were a host of still more concrete policies and institutions: Big Power unity and co-operation, the complete eradication of Nazism, general disarmament, a United

Nations with power to enforce the peace, and a variety of international agencies and arrangements for specific purposes in education, transportation, relief, refugees, and many other fields.

It is said that while Roosevelt stated noble ultimate ends and appropriate instrumental ends and generally believed in them, he ignored or compromised them when an immediate purpose or advantage could thereby be achieved, that he was supremely subject to what Alfred Vagts has called the vice of immediacy. He decided in favor of the invasion of North Africa, for example, without fully grasping its inevitable effect of delaying the cross-channel attack on Germany; and he "walked with the devil" in the person of Darlan and Franco and Badoglio without seeing the implications for democratic principle and morale. Too, in 1942 he could urge on Smuts that the United Nations not adopt a hard-and-fast strategic policy for 1943 until 1942 operations were concluded. And he could tell Churchill, in perhaps the most revealing phrase of all, that the "political considerations you mention are important factors, but military operations based thereupon must be definitely secondary to the primary operations of striking at the heart of Germany."

The sharpest indictment of Roosevelt on this score concerns unconditional surrender. It has been ably argued that this policy, on which he insisted to the end and which was gleefully exploited by Goebbels, may well have hardened the resistance of the German people and of the Wehrmacht, discouraged the resistance to Hitler inside the armed forces and without, prolonged the war, and caused unnecessary loss and bloodshed, and that all of this was at variance with Roosevelt's goals. Yet unconditional surrender is a prime example of how the standard indictment of Roosevelt can be turned around and can require a closer look at his grand strategy.

Unconditional surrender flatly contradicts the usual argument that Roosevelt was pragmatically and opportunistically concerned with immediate specific results at the expense of the more general and long run. It was fully apparent to the President, as to his friends and critics, that the Nazis could exploit unconditional surrender to stiffen resistance to the Allies. Indeed, the President's own Chiefs of Staff had advised him to modify the doctrine for military reasons. The Commander in Chief not only insisted on unconditional surrender, but he also resisted Machiavellian notions that he modify the doctrine publicly and later apply it in fact. Roosevelt's ultimate insistence on a direct attack on Germany, whatever the military cost, as compared to a strategy of encirclement or attrition, his decision to recover the Philippines largely for symbolic reasons despite practical military arguments for bypassing them, his own warning to Senators that there could be no sharp division between political and military matters are other examples of his willingness to subordinate immediate military advantage to broader goals.

The real point is less Roosevelt's simple separation of political ends and military means than his capacity to marshal his means of all kinds–military, institutional, propagandistic, diplomatic, and indeed political–in support of his most fundamental objectives. His failures lay in linking the ends and the means. Thus he was banking on Soviet popular as well as governmental confidence in the willingness of the Big Four to share and sacrifice together, yet he agreed to a long delay in the cross-channel attack. He wished to recognize the potential role of the several hundred million Chinese people but made Chungking a poor third in the allocation of military assistance, and he was unwilling to apply the political pressure that was the only conceivable way to bring about military and possibly political and economic reforms in China. He was deeply concerned about colonialism and expressed strong views to the British about India in particular, only to draw back when Anglo-American collaboration seemed threatened. Even when Churchill appealed to him in 1944 for some ships after an ammunition ship had exploded in Bombay Harbor sinking vessels loaded with 36,000 tons of grain, Roosevelt refused to divert shipping from military needs.

Roosevelt was a practical man who proceeded now boldly, now cautiously, step by step toward immediate ends. He was also a dreamer and sermonizer who spelled out lofty goals and summoned people to follow him. He was both a Soldier of the Faith, battling with his warrior comrades for an ideology of peace and freedom, and a Prince of the State, protecting the interests of his nation in a tumultuous and impious world. His difficulty lay in the relation of the two. The fact that his faith was more a set of attitudes than a firmly grounded moral code, that it embraced hope verging on utopianism and sentiment bordering on sentimentality, that it was heavily moralistic, to the point, at least in the view of some, of being hypocritical and sanctimonious–all this made his credo evocative but also soft and pasty, so that it crumbled easily under the press of harsh policy alternatives and military decision.

Roosevelt's moral credo was a patchwork of attitudes and instincts about honor, decency, good neighborliness, *noblesse oblige*. It was often hard to translate these attitudes and instincts into clear directives, operative programs, specific policies. His mind rejected comprehensive plans and long-run programs. He shrank from set institutional arrangements because these tended to freeze rather than invigorate end-means relations. Trumbull Higgins has said of Roosevelt that when his "dichotomies could not be resolved by the great political magician himself, they were left to circumstance." But Roosevelt's lofty dreams and his parochial compromises not only collided with one another; they also inflated the importance of each other, for the higher he set his goals and the lower he pitched his practical improvisations, the more he widened the gap between the existing and the ideal and raised men's expectations while failing to fulfill them.

Roosevelt's views of atomic secrecy are a case in point. All his instincts were toward trusting people, toward sharing, toward fostering the community of learning. Churchill had aroused his fears and suspicions at Hyde Park about the Soviet quest for atomic information, but when members of the scientific community became less alarmed about the German threat and more alarmed about the dangers of secrecy, and when scientists brought influence to bear in the White House during the fall of 1944, the President may have drifted back toward his original instinct of putting some trust in the Russians and restricting the use of the bomb. Alexander Sachs got in to see him in December and claimed later that Roosevelt agreed that the first step should be a nonmilitary demonstration of the bomb observed by international scientists and clergymen, following which a warning would be given, specifying the time and place of an imminent nuclear attack, thus permitting civilians to escape. But he never did instruct Stimson to carry out such a plan, and he took no step toward sharing the secret with the Russians. He talked about the global brotherhood of science and the ability of all peoples to work together for peace, but between the idea and the reality, between the conception and the creation, fell the shadow.

If Roosevelt was both realist and idealist, both fixer and preacher, both a prince and a soldier, the reason lay not merely in his own mind and background, but also in his society and its traditions. Americans have long had both moralistic and realistic tendencies, the first strain symbolized by Wilson, the second by the tough-minded men—Washington, Monroe, the two Adamses—who directed the foreign policy of the republic in its early years. No modern American statesman could fail to reflect this dualism. If Roosevelt's values were a bit overblown and vaporous, they were developed against a background of liberal values and internationalist impulses so widely shared and diluted as to provide little ideological support for politicians and parties. To some extent Roosevelt succumbed to the classic dilemma of the democratic leader: he must moralize and dramatize and personalize and simplify in order to lead and hold the public, but in doing so he may arouse false hopes and expectations, including his own, the deflation of which in the long run may lead to disillusionment and cynicism.

American foreign policy in particular has been shaped by two diplomacies, as Russell Bastert has argued—one diplomacy of short-run expediency and manipulation, of balance of power and sphere of interest, of compromise and adjustment, marginal choices, and limited objectives, and another diplomacy—almost an antidiplomacy—of world unity and collective security, democratic principle and moral uplift, peaceful change and nonaggression. Then, too, the institutional arrangements in Washington—the separation of decision making between the State Department and the Pentagon, and in their lines of access to the President, the absence from the White House of a staff that could integrate diplomacy and military policy, the institutional gaps in Congress among legislators specializing in military, foreign, and domestic policies, and indeed the whole tendency in Washington toward fragmented policy making—all reinforced the natural tendency of the President to compartmentalize.

All great nations, all world leaders exhibit such dichotomies; everything depends on the actual combinations. Stalin, for all his ruthless opportunism, was so consistently intent on the long-run, or at least middle-run, goal of postwar Soviet security that in the darkest days after Hitler's assault he would not barter or gamble on matters relating to that security. He was, like Roosevelt, a brilliant tactician, an actor and even a dissimulator; like Roosevelt he was a master of timing, of the art of "dosage"—measuring out pressure to what the traffic could bear—and of waiting and watching as well as striking out quickly; like Roosevelt he was superb in playing his adversaries off against one another. But Stalin far more than Roosevelt linked his wartime decisions to a strategy for long-run security, a strategy to which he adhered with steel-like tenacity. He had in abundance the defects of his virtue. Insecure, suspicious, parochial, he was so imbued with an essentially old-fashioned and brutal *Realpolitik* that he could never claim the impact on mass opinion and ideals of a Lenin, a Gandhi, or even a Roosevelt.

As a grand strategist Churchill was a more subtle study. Not lacking in his own canons of honor and responsibility, he embodied a diplomatic and military tradition that had helped Britain, in protecting its tiny isles against the colossi on the Continent, to practice all the black arts of diplomacy deplored by Hull and the other Wilsonians. He was, in truth, the Whig aristocrat of the eighteenth century that Harold Laski called him during the war. He had the aristocrat's saving compassion for the miserable, but he also had the Whig's fatal incomprehension of the tumultuous forces gushing out of the revolutions in Russia and China and elsewhere. Compared with Roosevelt's, his vision was long but narrow; he could see the relation between wartime strategy and postwar balances of power in Europe, but he could not imagine the surge of masses of people in Asia or Africa. Like Roosevelt he was an opportunist and improviser in his approach to grand strategy, but he lacked the comprehensive principles that gave at least a general direction and focus to Roosevelt's day-to-day decisions. He himself, as he once wrote admiringly of Lloyd George, "surveyed the problems of each morning with an eye unobstructed by preconceived opinions, past utterances, or previous disappointments and defeats," and in the wartime kaleidoscope of shifting values and prodigious events, his strategy drew from intuition and insight rather than long-run purpose and settled goals. Versatile, fertile, vigorous, he lacked the steadiness of direction, the comprehensiveness of outlook, the sense of proportion and relevance that mark the grand strategist. And his strategy was Western-oriented; Roosevelt at least glimpsed the explosive energy lying dormant in the billion people of Asia, especially when that energy was released and focused by the call of freedom that the antifascist leaders were trumpeting throughout the world.

Such, at least, was a possible judgment toward the end of 1944, and if history is written by the survivors, Roosevelt would not have the opportunity of Churchill and even of Stalin to vindicate himself in later years. But Roosevelt, like Churchill, would have argued that all the long-run plans of mortal men are subject to the caprices of chance and conflict, that, in sum, events control strategy—and in the dying days of 1944 a sudden, cruel event was being readied on the quiet Western Front.

CHRISTMAS 1944

After his triumphal return to Washington, the President had worked steadily to catch up on postponed business. Hassett, still smarting from election attacks on the tired, quarrelsome old men, noted that while his boss had been laboring like a Trojan, young Dewey had been resting for a fortnight in a suite at a posh vacation resort. Late in November, though, Roosevelt journeyed through a leaden rain with a retinue of secretaries, aides, and doctors to take a long Thanksgiving rest at Warm Springs, his first extended visit there since Pearl Harbor.

As usual, his work load followed him. Shortly after the election, Hull had announced his decision to retire, and all the President's persuasiveness could not induce him to stay on until January 20 to round out "our Third Term," as Roosevelt called it. The President chose Stettinius to succeed him. Though earnest and agreeable, the former Undersecretary could not ease the eternal tension between White House and State Department. When Stettinius submitted a mixed bag of nominations for assistant secretary—including Joseph

Grew, James Dunn, Nelson Rockefeller, and Archibald MacLeish—the President signed the documents without enthusiasm, stating to Hassett that MacLeish was the only liberal in the lot. He wrote to the Librarian of Congress that he was thrilled that MacLeish was staying on in Washington, even if it meant jumping from one mausoleum to another.

The other appointments raised the hackles of old New Dealers, and the reporters were waiting to pounce on the President when he returned to Washington late in December. The redoubtable May Craig asked:

"Mr. President, this is a contentious question, but I would like a serious answer."

"You would find it awfully hard to get, May."

"There's a good deal of question as to whether you are going right or left politically, and I would like your opinion on which way you are going."

"I am going down the whole line a little left of center. I think that was answered, that question, eleven and a half years ago, and it still holds."

"But you told us a little while ago," another reporter said, "that you were going to have Dr. Win-the-War and not Dr. New Deal."

"That's right."

"The question is whether you are going back to be Dr. New Deal after the war—"

"No, no. No. Keep right along a little to the left of center, which includes winning the war. That's not much of an answer, is it?"

"No," said May Craig amid laughter.

"However, you have broken the ice, May."

"Mr. President," someone asked, "if you are going down a little left of center, how does that match with the six appointments you sent up to the Hill on the State Department?"

"Very well."

"Would you call them a little left of center?"

"I call myself a little left of center. I have got a lot of people in the Administration—oh, I know some of them are extreme right and extreme left, and everything else—a lot of people in the Administration, and I cannot vouch for them all. They work out pretty well, on the whole. Just think, this crowd here in this room—my gracious, you will find every opinion between left and extreme right."

The President showed remarkable aplomb at this press conference considering the reports that had just been coming in from the European front. Three days before, the Germans had struck with power and ferocity in the Ardennes and broken through the light Allied defenses there. It was Hitler's supreme gamble in the west.

He had lost over three million officers and men by the end of autumn 1944; he had suffered over a million dead, wounded, and missing during the summer of 1944 alone; his cities were in ruins; he still felt the effects of the bomb attempt on his life. Finland had broken with Germany in September; Bulgarians and Rumanians were switching sides to Russia. But the Führer still carried a paper strength of ten million men and at least three hundred divisions and brigades, over forty of them armored, and Himmler scoured the country for another twenty-five divisions. Hitler won the grudging support of his generals for a "grand slam" that would re-create the spectacular days of 1940.

Anxiously Roosevelt and Leahy followed the attack on the wall charts in the map room, as the Germans encircled Bastogne and Saint-Vith and drove on west toward the great supply dumps. Not only was the counteroffensive—rapidly coming to be called the Battle of the Bulge—a stunning tactical blow, but it symbolized the military plight of the West at the end of 1944. Even before the attack, Churchill had warned Roosevelt that "we have definitely failed to achieve the strategic object which we gave to our armies five weeks ago." Allied bombing of Germany was rising to a peak, but so was German war production, as indicated by the great supplies that the Wehrmacht had stored for the attack.

The reports from the Bulge were still gloomy, aside from the valiant defense of Bastogne and other points, when Roosevelt entrained from Washington for Christmas at Hyde Park. His spirits improved as his grandchildren took over the mansion and gifts were piled high in the living room. Elliott was there, with his new wife, Faye Emerson. Christmas Eve the President spoke to the nation, dwelling on the soldiers who were far from home. He also sat in his old rocker next to the fireplace and began his annual reading of *The Christmas Carol.* Halfway through, a three-year-old grandson suddenly noticed a gap in the President's lower jaw, where he had neglected to insert his false tooth. Fixing the President with his gaze he cried out, "Grandpère, you've lost a tooth!" The President smiled and kept on reading, but when the young man advanced on him and asked, "Did you swallow it?" the President laughed and closed the book.

"There's too much competition in this family for reading aloud."

"Next year," said Elliott's wife, "it'll be a peacetime Christmas."

"Next year," said Eleanor Roosevelt, "we'll *all* be home again."

PART 5 *The Last Hundred Days*

NINETEEN *The Supreme Test*

BERLIN IN January 1945 lay in ruins under a relentless day-and-night bombing. Whole blocks had collapsed in rubble, which burned and smoldered for days. The vast columned Chancellery was half destroyed, its concrete roof smashed through, its imperial halls seared by fire and explosion. To an undamaged wing of the Chancellery Hitler returned in mid-January from his command post in the west; from here, in a conference room with deep leather chairs and thick carpet, the Führer directed his dying battalions. During bombings he moved to a huge concrete shelter in the Chancellery garden.

By now his pale, puffy face, stooped shoulders, shuffling gait, and slack left arm and trembling hand made him look like an old man, but he had lost none of his fanaticism. There was an indescribable flickering glow in his eyes, a visitor noted; when crossed, he raised his fists and shouted his rage. But he still was talking strategy. By now his great counteroffensive to the west had failed. In the east, 180 Soviet divisions opened an attack on a vast front stretching from the Baltic to the Carpathians. The Führer's only remaining hope was that the unnatural coalition against him would crack, as the Bolsheviks tried to possess the Balkans and the Middle East, the Americans tried to take over British possessions, and the English tried to strengthen themselves in the Mediterranean. "Even now," he told his generals, "these States are at loggerheads, and he who, like a spider, sitting in the middle of his web, can watch developments, observes how these antagonisms grow stronger and stronger from hour to hour. . . ."

Moscow was now far behind the front. People were flocking to ballet and concert halls. Almost every night hundreds of guns roared out their victory salutes; some evenings fireworks burst over Red Square for hours, lighting up the huge gold stars on the Kremlin towers. No longer did Stalin have to attend to the details of battle; the strategy was set for the capture of Germany. In response to a plea from Churchill, the Marshal stepped up preparations for a winter offensive that might take some of the pressure off the German lunge into the Ardennes. Despite bad weather the Red Army attacked, and Churchill thanked Stalin for his "thrilling message" reporting the offensive. Soon Stalin boasted in an order of the day that his winter attack had thwarted the German winter offensive in the west.

London, peppered for months by flying bombs, was still under fire from long-range rocket bases in Holland. The people were now in their sixth year of war. Churchill, after spending Christmas in Athens coping with the civil strife there, returned to London to confront the deepening cleavage between Russia and the West over Poland. A meeting with Stalin seemed more imperative than ever. It was clear that the Marshal was adamant against leaving his country, so Churchill and Roosevelt glumly agreed on Yalta as a meeting place. The Prime Minister, elated when Roosevelt decided to go by sea to Malta and thence by air to the Crimea, cabled that he would be waiting on the quay. "No more let us falter. From Malta to Yalta. Let nobody alter!"

In Los Alamos the lights burned late in the laboratories; thousands of Oppenheimer's scientists and technicians labored in their tiny sectors of the vast project. On the next to last day of 1944 Groves informed Marshall: "It is now reasonably certain that our operations plans should be based on the *gun type bomb,* which, it is estimated, will produce the equivalent of a ten thousand ton TNT explosion. The first bomb, without previous full scale test which we do not believe will be necessary, *should be ready about 1 August 1945.* The second one should be ready by the end of the year and succeeding ones . . . at intervals thereafter . . . the *509th Composite Group, 20th Air Force has been organized and it is now undergoing training* as well as assisting in essential tests. . . ." Stimson underscored the key words in presenting the report to Roosevelt within hours after Marshall received it.

Tokyo was ablaze during the first hours of January 1945 from the bombings of B-29's that were now making regular runs from the Marianas. As the Emperor returned from family prayers he could smell smoke drifting across the gardens of the Imperial Palace. Only the day before he had sharply questioned Prime Minister Kuniaki Koiso about the setbacks on Leyte. What measures were being taken to retrieve the situation? Imperial Headquarters, unable to reinforce the outlying islands or pull troops back because of American air and naval attacks, began to prepare for a last-ditch stand in Japan. Air Forces were instructed to indoctrinate their pilots in the kamikaze spirit of death-dealing self-sacrifice.

A peace group was arising around the Emperor, but the Army was still in control of the war. The peace party feared that Communism might spread from North China to Japan if political chaos developed in the wake of military defeat. The Americans were insisting on unconditional surrender. What to do? The Emperor showed Prince Konoye a verse he had once written:

"Sublime is the moment
When the world is at peace
And the limitless deep
Lies bathed in the morning sun."

"THE ONLY WAY TO HAVE A FRIEND . . ."

In Washington the White House came to life as Franklin Roosevelt returned from Hyde Park and swung into the typically heavy January work load of the American President—the budget, the annual message to Congress on the state of the union, the legislative program, major appointments. He had also to prepare for his fourth inaugural—and make plans for his climactic meeting with Churchill and Stalin.

It was time, too, to gauge public attitudes toward the great international issues that were coming to a head. Cantril's reports in January 1945 were worrisome. He had discovered, he informed the White House and the State Department, a significant decline since the previous June in public confidence that the President and other officials were successfully handling the nation's interests abroad, though support personally for Roosevelt remained high. There had also been a decrease, he reported, in the appreciation and knowledge of Britain's own war effort. Over twice as many Americans now felt that Britain was fighting mainly to keep its power and wealth as felt it was fighting to preserve democracy. The Russian war effort rated much higher in public attitudes.

Cantril's summary of opinion on postwar organization carried a sharp warning to the President. Although the vast majority of Americans now favored a strong international organization necessarily dominated by the big powers, their outlook was a mixture of expediency and idcalism. Without roots in any broad or long-range conception of self-interest or extensive knowledge, internationalist opinion had little intellectual basis and was hence prone to fickleness and skepticism as events occurred that did not fit into the framework of idealism. "With opinion uncrystallized and with people generally disinterested in the mechanics needed to achieve lasting peace, there is little doubt that they expect and desire strong leadership and would support the policies and mechanics the President felt necessary to achieve the ideals he has expressed—particularly if the reasons for proposed steps were made clear."

Roosevelt had little time to ponder such implications in January

1945. Events great and small crowded in on him. At the first Cabinet meeting of the new year Stettinius announced that the Russians had recognized the Lublin committee as the Polish government. Stimson stated that even though the Germans were making probing attacks at the head of the Bulge, the Allies were continuing to exert pressure at the bases of the enemy salient and would not be diverted from this basic tactic. Forrestal reported on battleship repairs on the West Coast, Byrnes on shipping problems, Jones on a patent question, Ickes on the "truculent" John L. Lewis and on the waste of electric power. When the Secretary of the Interior also discussed the future government of Pacific islands, Forrestal suggested solemnly that Ickes be made King of Polynesia, Micronesia, and the Pacific Ocean area.

The stunning setback in the Bulge still hung heavy over Washington even as Montgomery, Bradley, and their comrades slowly pressed in on the flanks of the salient to pinch off its head. An even greater national effort seemed necessary. After Stimson and Forrestal jointly wrote to the President early in January requesting a national war-service law—promptly dubbed a "work or fight" bill—in order to achieve total mobilization of manpower, he promptly asked Congress for the measure not only on the ground of mobilization but also to assure the fighting men that the nation was making its total effort and to warn the enemy that he could not get a negotiated peace. The President also asked Congress for legislation to use the services of the four million 4-F's. The President's budget for fiscal 1946 proposed only a moderate decline from the prodigious spending of 1945—a clear indication of the administration's expectation of a long, hard war against Japan.

The President's message on the state of the union ran to 9,000 words; it was the longest such message he had ever sent Congress. It was as though he wanted a culminating speech that would cover all that he had been fighting for during the past twelve years, all that he had promised the people in his last campaign, all that he hoped for the future. The message was far too long for Roosevelt himself to read; he gave a shorter version as a fireside chat in the evening. In his message he defended his Europe First strategy, praised the campaign in Italy, expressed his confidence in Eisenhower's leadership, warned against enemy propaganda and agents seeking to divide the grand coalition, called for a "people's peace," invoked the Atlantic Charter, demanded a strong and flexible United Nations, and again proposed a second bill of rights, promising new proposals on social security, health, education, taxation.

"This new year of 1945 can be the greatest year of achievement in human history," his message concluded.

"Nineteen forty-five can see the final ending of the Nazi-Fascist reign of terror in Europe.

"Nineteen forty-five can see the closing in of the forces of retribution about the center of the malignant power of imperialistic Japan.

"Most important of all—1945 can and must see the substantial beginnings of the organization of world peace. . . ."

As usual, Cabinet members submitted their resignations; as usual, he rejected them—all but one. On Inauguration Day he sent Secretary of Commerce Jesse Jones a letter that reached a new high for combined frankness and dissimulation. "Dear Jesse," he began.

"This is a very difficult letter to write—first, because of our long friendship and splendid relations during all these years and also because of your splendid services to the Government and the excellent way in which you have carried out the many difficult tasks during these years.

"Henry Wallace deserves almost any service which he believes he can satisfactorily perform." Though not on the ticket himself, he had worked hard for the cause. Wallace had decided he wanted Commerce and he should have it. "It is for this reason only that I am asking you to relinquish this present post for Henry." But the President said he was very proud of all that Jesse had done.

"During the next few days I hope you will think about a new post—there are several Ambassadorships which are vacant—or about to be vacated. I make this suggestion among many other posts and I hope you will have a chance, if you think well of it, to speak to Ed Stettinius. . . ." A battle instantly broke out in the Senate.

Secretary Perkins tried to resign, too—and she really seemed to mean it. Roosevelt kept putting her off. She suggested possible successors—Byrnes, Winant, and others—but with no response from the White House. Finally, on the eve of Inauguration Day, she went to the President after a Cabinet meeting.

"Don't you think," she said, as she later remembered, "I had better get Early to announce my resignation right now? I'll go in and write out the announcement."

"No," he said, "Frances, you can't go now. I can't think of anybody else. Not now! Do stay there and don't say anything. You are all right." Then he pressed his hand over hers and said in a voice filled with exhaustion:

"Frances, you have done awfully well. I know what you have been through. I know what you have accomplished. Thank you."

Rumors spread in Washington that the Roosevelt administration was falling apart—that Byrnes and Morgenthau were feuding over tax matters, that Hopkins had blackballed Ben Cohen as counselor to the State Department, that Rosenman was about ready to quit. As usual the stories were exaggerated, but there was trouble enough for the President. He could not escape even the trifling disputes. When Lilienthal wrote a piece for the New York *Times Magazine* entitled "Shall We Have More TVA's?" and answered predictably with a resounding yes, Ickes told his chief that "that master propagandist" was trying to force the President's hand. "I cannot sit quiet longer under his covert attacks," which "are aimed principally at me." Wearily Roosevelt asked Jonathan Daniels to handle the matter and "try to keep Lilienthal from getting Ickes mad."

Frances Perkins had known Roosevelt a long time; she had followed him through his physical as well as political ups and downs. She had put little stock in the stories about his physical decline. But at that Cabinet meeting the day before the inauguration she was struck by his appearance. His face was thin, his color gray, his eyes dull, his clothes too big for him. Still, he seemed gay and happy. It was only at the end of the meeting two hours later that she felt he had the deep-gray color of a man who had long been ill; he supported his head with his hand; his lips were blue; his hand shook. Yet so strong was Roosevelt's recuperative power that next day Leahy, who had seen the President day after day, found no decline in his physical condition, and Lilienthal thought he looked well.

Weeks before Election Day Roosevelt had checked on the history of presidential inaugurations and found that on more than a dozen occasions, especially in the earlier years, Presidents had taken the oath of office elsewhere than on the Capitol steps. Gleefully he told the press a week after the election that while Senator Byrd—the head congressional economizer—and his committee had appropriated $25,000 for the inauguration, "I think I can save an awful lot of money. . . . I think I can do it for less than $2000." The ceremonies would take place on the south portico of the White House.

Would there be a parade? a reporter asked.

"No. Who is there here to parade?"

Saturday, January 20, 1945, was a cold day with a gray sky. Several thousand people stood on the hard-packed snow on the White House lawn. The Marine Band in resplendent red uniforms struck up "Hail to the Chief." The President moved through the crowd on the portico with his slow, locked-knee motion to his chair. He sat there with no cape or coat. Then his son James and a Secret Service man leaned over him; he wrapped his arms around their necks, and they raised him, stiff-legged, until he could grasp the edge of the speaking lectern; then he lowered his arms, calmly nodded to Jimmy, shook hands with Truman, and turned to face Chief Justice Stone. The President gazed at the crowd, at the thin layer of snow on the Ellipse, then lifted his eyes to the Washington Monument and to the Jefferson Memorial beyond. He repeated the oath clearly and firmly after the Chief Justice. Then he spoke.

". . . We Americans of today, together with our allies, are passing through a period of supreme test. It is a test of our courage—of our resolve—of our wisdom—of our essential democracy.

"If we meet that test—successfully and honorably—we shall perform a service of historic importance—of historic importance which men and women and children will honor throughout all time. . . ."

The President was speaking quietly, with occasional emphasis.

"We shall strive for perfection. We shall not achieve it immediately—but we still shall strive. We may make mistakes—but they must never be mistakes which result from faintness of heart or abandonment of moral principle.

"I remember that my old schoolmaster, Dr. Peabody, said—in days that seemed to us then to be secure and untroubled, 'Things in life will not always run smoothly. Sometimes we will be rising toward the heights—then all will seem to reverse itself and start downward. The great fact to remember is that the trend of civilization itself is forever upward; that a line drawn through the middle of the peaks and the valleys of the centuries always has an upward trend.'

"Our Constitution of 1787 was not a perfect instrument; it is not perfect yet. But it provided a firm base upon which all manner of men, of all races and colors and creeds, could build our solid structure of democracy.

"And so today, in this year of war, 1945, we have learned lessons —at a fearful cost—and we shall profit by them.

"We have learned that we cannot live alone, at peace; that our own well-being is dependent on the well-being of other Nations, far away. We have learned that we must live as men and not as ostriches, nor as dogs in the manger.

"We have learned to be citizens of the world, members of the human community.

"We have learned the simple truth, as Emerson said"—and here the President spoke very slowly and rhythmically and with great emphasis—" 'The only way to have a friend is to be one.'

"We can gain no lasting peace if we approach it with suspicion and mistrust—or with fear. We can gain it only if we proceed with the understanding and the confidence and the courage which flow from conviction. . . ."

THE KING OF THE BEARS

Just two weeks later, as its fighter escort circled overhead, the "Sacred Cow" touched down on the icy runway of the Soviet airport of Saki in the Crimea. Molotov, Stettinius, and Harriman climbed aboard to greet the President and his party. When Churchill landed in his plane a little later, Mike Reilly helped his boss into a jeep. With the Prime Minister plodding along at his side and a crowd of service cameramen walking backward as they shot their pictures, the President moved slowly in his jeep to a guard of honor. The soldiers stood frozen to attention, their commander holding his sword in front of him like a great icicle. The band played the "Star-Spangled Banner," "God Save the King," and the "Internationale."

To Churchill's physician the President looked old and thin and shrunken in his big cape as he stared at the guard, his face drawn and his mouth open. But once he was transferred to a limousine, with Anna at his side, and moving toward Yalta, ninety miles distant, Roosevelt watched everything with lively interest—the endless line of guards, many of them young girls with Tommy guns; the gutted buildings and burned-out tanks; and later the snow-covered mountains through which the caravan threaded its way before descending to the coast of the Black Sea. Soon the President was installed in Livadia Palace, a fifty-room summer place of the czars overlooking gardens filled with cypress, cedar, and yew trees.

From the terrace of the palace the President could look north to a striking panorama of mountains overlooking the shore line. One of these mountains resembled a huge bear hunched over with its mouth in the sea. A Crimean legend had it that this was the king of the bears and that years ago a beautiful young girl had been abandoned on the shore and had been adopted by the king and brought up by the bears. Then a prince had sailed from across the sea and had fallen in love with the girl and had taken her away in his ship. Desperately the king had put his mouth down to drink the sea dry and rescue the girl from the stranded boat, and he had drunk and drunk. . . .

Many of his countrymen felt, when Roosevelt arrived in Yalta early in February 1945, that the Russian bear was gorging itself on neighboring lands and waters in a ferocious quest for security and power. The President shared this fear. He did not arrive in Yalta with any misapprehension of the appetite or the ambitions of the bear. He made the trip as a supreme act of faith in his own capacity to evoke the best in a friend and ally, to reach agreement on immediate issues, to build a new world order that would assign the old ways of international relations—spheres of influence and balances of power and war itself—to the scrap heap.

"I am inclined to think that at the meeting and the Prime Minister I can put things on level than they have been for the past two or had written to Harold Laski a few days before le

He was staking everything on the face-to-face Stalin; he knew that the trip itself would be an begged the Marshal to meet with him in Scotlan Malta or Athens or Cyprus or anywhere else in the ranean, but Stalin pleaded illness this time and was as ever about leaving his homeland. After crossing the ...tic on the *Quincy,* he had spent a day at Malta, where he lunched with Churchill, Eden, and Stettinius and conferred with the Joint Chiefs and the Combined Chiefs, and then had flown overnight to Saki. All the reports of Yalta were unfavorable—the buildings had been left empty of everything but lice, the nearest airfield was more than an hour away, Allied communications ships could not go there because of mines and had to be stationed in Sevastopol—but nothing could deflect Roosevelt from his aim to meet with Stalin.

The time seemed ripe for great achievements around the peace table, and so did the company that gathered at Yalta. Victory over Germany was clearly in sight. By the end of January the Russians had invested Budapest, captured Warsaw, overrun East Prussia, and fanned out toward Stettin, Danzig, and the lower reaches of the Oder; the Allies had recovered from the Battle of the Bulge and were mobilizing for a great push eastward, meanwhile maintaining heavy air attacks despite bad weather. In the Far East American troops were closing in on Manila. To Yalta had come the politicians who had forged the grand coalition and the soldiers who were executing the destruction of Nazi Germany. In Roosevelt's party were the old hands, including Hopkins, Leahy, and Marshall, and also some faces new to Big Three conferences—Stettinius, Byrnes, the State Department's Alger Hiss, a specialist in international organization, Admiral Land, General Somervell, and even Boss Ed Flynn of the Bronx. With Churchill were Eden and Clark Kerr, Britain's Ambassador to Russia, and the usual big assemblage of soldiers and sailors, and the gifted permanent officials Sir Alexander Cadogan and Sir Edward Bridges. With Stalin were Molotov, Vishinsky, Maisky, and Gromyko.

The discussions would range across the globe, remake a good part of the map, and reshape the structure of world power. But Roosevelt, for all his wide interests and darting intelligence, was focusing on three questions on the eve of Yalta: Poland, Soviet participation in the Pacific war, and the new United Nations organization. Each of these in turn would embody the harshest choices and dilemmas for his statecraft: the relation of foreign omestic politics, of immediate military needs to long-time considerations, of opportunistic compromise to lofty hopes the postwar comity of nations.

For Roosevelt the new international organization was by far the most important issue on the Yalta conference table. There was no question about an organization being established; the question was how much power it would have and how that power would be organized. Early in December Roosevelt had urged on Stalin that the great powers exercise moral leadership by agreeing that on procedural matters all parties to a dispute should abstain from voting, but Stalin had flatly insisted on the principle of great-power unanimity. Harriman cabled an explanation of why the Soviets were demanding the right to veto consideration by the proposed council of all matters, even peaceful procedures. The main reason, he said, was simply their suspicion of other nations.

It was this kind of pervasive suspicion the President was determined to overcome in private, face-to-face meetings with the Soviet leaders. Stalin and Mototov had hardly arrived at Livadia Palace in their big black Packard on the opening day of the conference, February 4, and sat down in the former Czar's dark-paneled study when the President was telling them how struck he was by the extent of German destruction in the Crimea. He was more bloodthirsty toward the Germans than he had been a year ago, he said, and he hoped that the Marshal would again propose a toast to the execution of 50,000 officers of the German Army. Everyone was more bloodthirsty than a year ago, Stalin said. After discussing military developments, Roosevelt asked about Stalin's meeting with de Gaulle; Stalin seemed mainly impressed by France's military weakness. Roosevelt told his old yarn about how de Gaulle had compared himself to Joan of Arc and Clemenceau.

He would now tell the Marshal something indiscreet, the President went on, since he would not wish to say it in front of the Prime Minister, namely that the British for two years had had the idea of artificially building up France into a strong power that could maintain troops on the eastern border to hold the line long enough for Britain to assemble an army. The British were a peculiar people, he said, and wished to have their cake and eat it. Stalin did not disagree. The mildly anti-British exchanges must have seemed to Roosevelt an auspicious start to his effort to establish personal rapport with Stalin.

Roosevelt and the two Russians proceeded directly to the first plenary meeting, which was devoted wholly to a military review by the generals and admirals. At a small dinner given by the President in the evening, Stalin was in good humor, as was Churchill, who even toasted the proletarian masses of the world.

But as Stalin drank his vodka, covertly mixing it with water, and rose to dozens of toasts, he spoke in favor of great-power supremacy so vehemently that to Eden his attitude seemed grim, almost sinister. Nor was the Marshal to be disarmed by pleasantries. When Roosevelt, at the height of the conviviality, mentioned to him that he and Churchill called him Uncle Joe, Stalin flared up in anger. Molotov smoothed things over. Later, after Roosevelt and Stalin left, the others discussed the unanimity problem in the new world organization. Churchill was inclining to the Russian view, he said, and promptly fell into a stiff argument with Eden, who feared the reaction of the smaller nations.

It was an ill-boding start for Roosevelt's supreme aim at Yalta. To make things worse, the Soviet leaders were still requesting sixteen votes in the proposed Assembly. When Stettinius presented the detailed American proposals for the new organization at the third plenary session, Stalin was at his most surly and suspicious. He baited Churchill over the possibility that Egypt in the Assembly might demand the return of the Suez Canal. He implied broadly that the Anglo-Americans were ganging up on him. He said that his colleagues in Moscow could not forget how at the instigation of the French and British the League of Nations during the war with Finland had expelled the Soviet Union and isolated it and crusaded against it. Roosevelt sat through all this patiently, intervening only to insist that Big Three unity was the keystone to an international system.

The next day Molotov suddenly shifted and declared Roosevelt's voting proposals acceptable. Then almost in the same breath he mentioned the request at Dumbarton Oaks for sixteen seats for the Soviet republics. He would now be satisfied with the admission of three or even two of the republics—Ukrainian, White Russian, and Lithuanian. They had borne the greatest sacrifices of the war.

Even while expressing his pleasure at the shift, Roosevelt recognized the dilemma he faced. "This is not so good!" he wrote on a chit to Stettinius. He had come to Yalta planning to reject the sixteen-seat request, a proposal that would offend both the idealists and the cynics at home. Now the Russians were reducing this to two extra votes, and accepting his voting plan for the world organization. It was the moment for a gesture on his part, but he feared accepting the two extra votes. For a while he kept talking in order to delay a showdown, until Hopkins noticed Stalin's impatience—or was it annoyance?—at Roosevelt's failure to reciprocate.

During the next twenty-four hours Roosevelt was under heavy pressure from outside—and perhaps from inside himself—to endorse the two extra seats for the Soviet Union. The British, with an eye to their own empire and dominions, were siding with the Russians.

Stettinius seemed sympathetic to the idea. Clearly any further delay or division might imperil the whole dream of a United Nations. If he moved now he might get the whole conference held by late April in the United States. At the next plenary meeting he endorsed the two extra votes, but only on the understanding that later the United Nations conference itself would grant the votes, with Big Three support.

"TAKE ME IN, MISTER?"

Roosevelt's concession disturbed Byrnes and Leahy. The war mobilizer reminded his chief how the opponents of the League of Nations had contended that London, because of the dominions, would have five votes in the League Assembly to Washington's one. He and Flynn later persuaded the President to request British and Russian support for an extra two votes for the United States if needed. Churchill and Stalin both said they would agree to the request if made.

The three leaders were in a mood of self-congratulation when they dined at Stalin's Yusupov Palace a few hours after the initial agreement on extra seats. Stalin toasted Churchill as the bravest governmental figure in the world, as the leader of a nation that had stood alone against Germany at a time when the rest of the world was falling flat on its face before Hitler. Churchill saluted Stalin as the leader of the nation that had broken the back of the

German war machine. Stalin then toasted Roosevelt as a man whose country had not been seriously threatened but who had had perhaps a better concept of national interest than any other leader, especially in supplying war aid. Roosevelt, in replying, said he felt the atmosphere of the dinner was that of a family, as were the relations among the three countries.

Stalin was in an expansive, almost philosophical, mood. He was talking too much, like an old man, he said. "But I want to drink to our alliance." It must not lose its character of intimacy and frankness.

"In an alliance the allies should not deceive each other," Stalin continued. "Perhaps that is naïve? Experienced diplomatists may say, 'Why should I not deceive my ally?' But I as a naïve man think it best not to deceive my ally even if he is a fool. Possibly our alliance is so firm just because we do not deceive each other; or is it because it is not so easy to deceive each other . . . ?

The bleak specter of Poland hung over the conference even as the men of Yalta celebrated the brave new world they were building. It had long been agreed by the Big Three that the war-racked nation would be picked up like a carpetbag and set down a few hundred miles to the west, satisfying Russia's appetite, penalizing Germany's, and, it was hoped, taming Poland's. The product of cynical partition and hopeful re-creation, of *Realpolitik* and romanticism, Poland epitomized the ancient ways of princes even as it roiled and divided the three leaders.

Roosevelt was under no illusion about Soviet plans for Poland. Stalin had recognized the Lublin Poles in the face of the President's and the Prime Minister's most urgent pleas for delay. As the conference met, the Red Army was completing Poland's liberation—and occupation. The question was how much representation for non-Communist Polish elements could be extracted from a nation that controlled every precinct, viewed liberals and conservatives as bourgeois exploiters, if not fascists, and was absolutely determined to protect the Red Army's rear and its own future frontiers.

Roosevelt decided to be relatively flexible about Poland's new borders—which in any event had been essentially determined by the Red Army's advance and by understandings at Teheran and elsewhere—but to insist on a democratic, independent, and viable Polish government.

"I should like to bring up Poland," Roosevelt said at the third plenary meeting. "I come from a great distance and therefore have the advantage of a more distant point of view of the problem. There are six or seven million Poles in the United States." As he had said at Teheran, he went on, in general he favored the

Curzon Line. "Most Poles, like the Chinese, want to save face."

"Who will save face," Stalin interrupted, "the Poles in Poland or the émigré Poles?"

"The Poles would like East Prussia and part of Germany," Roosevelt went on. "It would make it easier for me at home if the Soviet Government could give something to Poland." He hoped that Marshal Stalin could make a gesture and give Poland Lwow and the adjacent oil lands. Stalin was silent.

"But the most important matter is that of a permanent government for Poland. Opinion in the United States is against recognition of the Lublin government on the ground that it represents a small portion of the Polish people. What people want is the creation of a government of national unity to settle their internal differences. A government which would represent all five major parties"—Roosevelt named them—"is what is wanted. It may interest Marshal Stalin that I do not know any of the London or of the Lublin government. Mikolajczyk came to Washington and I was greatly impressed by him. I felt that he was an honest man. . . ."

Churchill backed the President. "I have made repeated declarations in Parliament in support of the Soviet claims to the Curzon line, that is to say, leaving Lvov with Soviet Russia. I have been much criticized and so has Mr. Eden by the party which I represent. But I have always considered that after all Russia has suffered in fighting Germany and after all her efforts in liberating Poland her claim is founded not on force but on right. In that position I abide. But of course if the mighty power, the Soviet Union, made a gesture of magnanimity to a much weaker power and made the gesture suggested by the President we would heartily acclaim such action.

"However," he continued, "I am more interested in the question of Poland's sovereign independence and freedom than in particular frontier lines. I want the Poles to have a home in Europe and to be free to live their own lives there. . . . This is what is dear to the hearts of the nation of Britain. This is what we went to war against Germany for—that Poland should be free and sovereign. Everyone here knows . . . that it nearly cost us our life as a nation." He went on to plead for the establishment at the conference of a new interim government of Poland pending free elections. "His Majesty's Government cordially support the President's suggestion and present the question to our Russian allies."

Stalin asked for a ten-minute intermission. He came back well primed.

"The Prime Minister has said that for Great Britain the question of Poland is a question of honor. For Russia it is not only a question of honor but of security. . . . During the last thirty years our German enemy has passed through this corridor twice. This is because Poland was weak. It is in the Russian interest as well as that of Poland that Poland be strong and powerful and in a position in her own and in our interests to shut the corridor by her own forces. The corridor cannot be mechanically shut from outside by Russia. It could be shut from inside only by Poland. It is necessary that Poland be free, independent and powerful. . . ." Then Stalin turned to the Curzon Line and Churchill's appeal for modifications.

"The Prime Minister thinks we should make a gesture of magnanimity. But I must remind you that the Curzon line was invented not by Russia but by foreigners . . . by Curzon, Clemenceau and the Americans in 1918-1919. Russia was not invited and did not participate. . . . Lenin opposed it." Stalin was speaking with more and more heat. "Some want us to be less Russian than Curzon and Clemenceau. What will the Russians say at Moscow, and the Ukrainians? They will say that Stalin and Molotov are far less defenders of Russia than Curzon and Clemenceau. I cannot take such a position and return to Moscow."

By now Stalin was standing. "I prefer that the war continue a little longer and give Poland compensation in the west at the expense of Germany." As for the government, the Prime Minister had said that he wanted to create a Polish government here. "I am afraid that was a slip of the tongue. Without the participation of Poles we can create no Polish government. They all say that I am a dictator but I have enough democratic feeling not to set up a Polish government without Poles." As a military man he wanted peace and quiet in the wake of the Red Army. The Lublin government could maintain order, while the agents of the London government had already killed 212 Russian soldiers.

"The military must have peace and quiet. The military will support such a government and I cannot do otherwise. Such is the situation."

There was a pause, and Roosevelt suggested adjournment. During the next three days the President and the Prime Minister and their foreign secretaries waged a tough and concerted campaign to win concessions from the Russians on Polish independence. The President informed Stalin bluntly that he would not recognize the Lublin government "as now composed" and that if the three leaders could not agree on Poland they "would lose the confidence of the world." Churchill told him that the Lublin group did not represent even one-third of the people and he feared arrests and deportations of underground leaders. He contended that 150,000 men of the Polish Army on the Italian and Western fronts would feel betrayed if the London government was brushed aside. He noted acidly that in Egypt, "for example," whatever government held an election won the election. To which Stalin replied that Egyptian politicians spent their time buying each other off, but this could not happen in Poland because of the high rate of literacy there.

Step by step Roosevelt and Churchill exacted paper concessions from the Russians: that the Lublin government be "reorganized on a broader democratic basis" with the inclusion of democratic leaders from within Poland and without; that free and unfettered elections be held soon—perhaps within a month—on the basis of open suffrage and secret ballot; that leaders such as Mikolajczyk could take part in them. What was really at stake, however, was not the general formula but how much opportunity Washington and London would have in fact to influence the reorganization of the government and monitor the conduct of the elections. Even on this score Stalin conceded that Harriman and Kerr could consult with Lublin and non-Lublin leaders in Moscow, but the manner of holding and policing the elections was obscure.

"Mr. President," said Leahy, when he saw the compromise formula, "this is so elastic that the Russians can stretch it all the way from Yalta to Washington without even technically breaking it."

"I know, Bill—I know it. But it's the best I can do for Poland at this time."

The best he could do . . . Doubtless Roosevelt knew already that the Polish compromise would be the most criticized part of the Yalta agreement, but he could hardly have sensed that it would be the heart of the later charges of betrayal, "sellout," and near-treason. If he had known this, though, he would probably have taken the same basic position. He had reached the limit of his bargaining power at Yalta. His position resulted not from naïveté, ignorance, illness, or perfidy, but from his acceptance of the facts: Russia occupied Poland. Russia distrusted its Western allies. Russia had a million men who could fight Japan. Russia could sabotage the new peace organization. And Russia was absolutely determined about Poland and always had been. If the Big Three broke up at Yalta, the President knew, he would lose the great opportunities that lay ahead—for him to win Soviet co-operation by his personal diplomacy and friendliness, and for the United Nations to draw Russia over the years into the comity of nations.

Roosevelt also knew that Poland was a crucial issue not only in itself but also as a bellwether of Communist ambitions in eastern Europe. Fearing the erosion of Western influence, he had taken the lead in drawing up a proposed Declaration on Liberated Europe upholding, on the principles of the Atlantic Charter, "the right of all peoples to choose the form of government under which they will live," pledging Big Three assistance in holding free elections, and providing that the three governments would establish joint machinery when necessary to carry out these aims. The declaration, which evoked little British or Soviet opposition, was much on Roosevelt's mind as Polish elections were being discussed. Poland, he said, would be the first application of the declaration.

"I want this election in Poland to be the first one beyond question," he said. "It should be like Caesar's wife. I did not know her but they say she was pure."

"They said that about her," Stalin remarked, "but in fact she had her sins."

ASIA: THE SECOND SECOND FRONT

The President seemed so frail, his face so thin and transparent, at Yalta that his friends watched him narrowly for any signs of decline. Eden thought him vague and loose the first evening, and Lord Moran wrote him off as a dying man. Yet the Americans who worked with him closely at the conference—Byrnes, Stettinius, Leahy, Harriman—felt that he handled matters effectively and even skillfully. The main formal sessions came late in the afternoon, a time of day when Roosevelt's strength had typically been at low ebb during the past year, but he conducted himself well in the discussions, even on technical matters on which he was not well briefed, and even though he had the added burden of presiding. He did not speak out as eloquently as Churchill or as bluntly or cogently as Stalin, but he was generally quick, alert, articulate, and even witty. When Churchill, in defending his imperial stand, added that he had sent his arguments to Wendell Willkie, the President shot back, "Was that what killed him?"

Nor was Roosevelt ill during these February days in the Crimea, in the sense of the later charge of the "sick man at Yalta." He worked hard through the day, even though he could not always take his afternoon rest. A cough kept him awake intermittently during the first few nights, but he complained of no cardiac or other pain, and Bruenn found his lungs clear and his heart and blood pressure unchanged. There were no electrocardiographic changes. Bruenn did become concerned, however, at what seemed to be a whipsawing of the President by the English; it seemed that Eden would take him on in the morning, and Churchill, who would sleep until noon, would take over in the afternoon. The evening banquets lasted until late at night. On February 8, after an especially difficult discussion of the Polish problem, his color was gray, and for the first time his blood pressure showed *pulsus alternans.* Although his lungs and heart were good, Bruenn insisted on no visitors until noon and more rest. Within two days his appetite was excellent and the *pulsus alternans* had disappeared.

Eden conceded later that Roosevelt's seeming ill-health did not alter his judgment. He marveled, indeed, that the President not only kept up with Churchill in the round of formal and informal conferences, but also found time to conduct a whole separate enterprise at Yalta—negotiations with Stalin over the Far East.

It was not until the fifth day that the subject of Soviet entrance into the Pacific war came up between Roosevelt and Stalin. They were meeting privately except for Harriman, Molotov, and the interpreters. Churchill and Eden were not there, nor the American military. Stalin said that he would like to discuss the political conditions under which the Soviet Union would enter the war against Japan. He added that he already had discussed the matter with Harriman.

Roosevelt remembered only too well that discussion of mid-December, for Harriman had relayed it to him with some urgency. Stalin had gone into the room next to his office in the Kremlin, Harriman reported, and brought out a map. The Marshal had said that the Kurile Islands and lower Sakhalin should be returned to Russia in order to protect the approaches to Vladivostok. He had drawn a line around the southern part of the Liaotung Peninsula, including Port Arthur and Dairen, and stated that the Soviets wished again to lease these ports and the adjacent area. The Marshal had added that he wished to lease the Chinese-Eastern Railway running from Dairen to Harbin and beyond but—in answer to a pointed question of Harriman's—he averred he had no intention to impair the sovereignty of China in Manchuria.

Since then the whole matter had been anxiously discussed by Roosevelt and a small group of advisers. Churchill was leaving the matter largely in the President's hands. All agreed that the matter must be settled at Yalta.

There would be no difficulty whatsoever, the President said now, in regard to the southern half of Sakhalin and the Kurile Islands going to Russia at the end of the war. As for a warm-water port in the Far East, the Marshal would recall that they had discussed the matter at Teheran, and that he, the President, had suggested that Russia be given the use of a warm-water port at the end of the south Manchurian railroad. He had not yet had an opportunity to discuss the matter with the Generalissimo and hence could not speak for China. The Russians could obtain the use of the port either by outright leasing from the Chinese or by Dairen being made a free port under some kind of international commission; he preferred the latter because of the relation to the question of Hong Kong. He hoped that the British would give Hong Kong back to China and that it would then become an internationalized free port. Churchill, he added, would have strong objections to that.

Stalin then raised the question of Soviet use of the Manchurian railways. He described the extensive network the czars had used. Roosevelt said that, again, he had not talked with Chiang but the alternatives were to lease under direct Soviet operation or to set up a commission composed of one Chinese and one Russian. Stalin stated that if his conditions were not met it would be difficult for him and Molotov to explain to the Soviet people why Russia was fighting Japan, a nation that, unlike Germany, had not threatened the very existence of the Soviet Union. But if the political conditions were met the people would understand. Stalin did not register the infinite satisfaction he must have felt in turning the Anglo-Americans' favorite argument—public opinion—back upon them.

This easy, almost casual sparring between Roosevelt and Stalin at once reflected and concealed felt national interests and long-run volcanic forces. The President and his military chiefs had long agreed that the invasion of Japan would be immensely costly and that Soviet intervention on the Asiatic mainland was imperative. Even with Russian participation, the military planners estimated, the war in the Pacific would last eighteen months after Germany surrendered; without Russian aid the war might last indefinitely, with unbearable losses. It was also understood that the Red Army would take part once it had the chance to deploy troops to the east; Stalin had made this clear—even volunteered it—over and over again. The Russians' eagerness to fight Japan in order to protect their postwar interests was so clear, and their promises so definite, that some, including Eden, argued that Roosevelt need make no concessions to Stalin; Moscow would make war anyway.

But Stalin—and probably Roosevelt, too—knew that the fact of Soviet participation was not the vital point. It was the timing and strength of the intervention that were crucial. And here both leaders acted against a background of the harshest kind of *Realpolitik*. Doubtless Stalin knew his lesson better than Roosevelt did because he had learned it under the most excrutiating circumstances. In 1939, after years of fearing a coalition of capitalistic and fascist nations against Russia, he had cut the Gordian knot—and fractured his own ideological credibility—by the pact with Hitler on Poland. But hardly had the deal been concluded when the Kremlin strategists went through agonies of suspense. What if Hitler inveigled Russia into claiming its half of Poland prematurely and they got involved in fighting Poles before the Poles were ready to be beaten? Even worse, what if Hitler made peace with Warsaw and left the Russians to fight all the Poles and even France and Britain? Then when the Wehrmacht came crashing through the Polish defenses, Stalin's fears were transmuted into a nightmare. What if the advancing Nazis did not stop at the agreed-on line or—unthinkably—at the Polish-Soviet border?

Things had turned out all right—Hitler was a man of honor, at least among thieves—and the Kremlin felt it had won its gamble when the Germans ended the Polish campaign locked in combat with Britain and France. But fears rose again in Moscow when the Nazis overcame France. Would the West now make a separate peace with Hitler at the expense of Russia? Britain did not—but worse was to come. The German attack on Russia robbed Stalin of his scales-tipping power. After all his frantic efforts he was at the mercy of the West, which could time its re-entry onto the Continent for its own advantage, not Russia's. This the Anglo-Americans did.

Now—at Yalta—the tables were turned. The Marshal had his allies just where they had had him for three long years. He could intervene whenever he wished—and his timing would turn on political as well as military factors.

So the man who faced Roosevelt across the table in Livadia Palace was schooled in the art of offering and delaying assistance. The President, too, was quite aware of the application of this art to the Pacific, if only because his military chiefs were. They stressed the need for Russia to attack in Manchuria at least three months before the planned invasion of Kyushu; they also saw the Soviet advantage in waiting to attack the Japanese until American troops invaded Kyushu and forced Tokyo to pull troops off the Asiatic mainland. It was the strategy of the European front stood on its head. It was the second second front.

Casting its shadow across these calculations was the two-headed giant China. Despite his deepening disappointment over Chiang's efforts, the President clung to his long-term hopes for a free, democratic, and friendly China. He wanted to win Moscow's support for Chungking and to discourage Russian intervention in China's affairs. To reach his twin goals of Japan's defeat and China's survival, Roosevelt had to induce Stalin to do things that the Marshal had no overpowering desire to do—to join in the war against Japan at a time that would be more advantageous for his allies than for himself, and to support a "bourgeois" regime that was at odds with his ideological comrades in Yenan.

Clearly Stalin held by far the stronger hand. Roosevelt's best cards were that he could legitimize the Marshal's demand for Pacific real estate and Manchurian railways and ports and that he was the most likely of the Big Three to induce Chiang to go along. But to do the latter he had to gain Soviet backing for Chiang.

Roosevelt was disturbed by Stalin's ambitions in Manchuria. Toward the end of the conference he had Harriman ask Stalin and Molotov to agree that Port Arthur and Dairen be free ports and that the Manchurian railroad be operated by a joint Chinese-Soviet commission. Stalin did so, except that he insisted Port Arthur must be a naval base and had to be leased. He granted that Chiang's concurrence was necessary—he preferred that Roosevelt ask Chiang for it—but demanded in return that the Generalissimo agree to the *status quo* in Manchuria. To all this Roosevelt agreed—and also to the need for secrecy. The matter of informing Chiang was postponed on the ground that no secret was safe in Chungking—and Stalin did not want Tokyo to get wind of his plan and then strike the first blow. Above all, he did not want his careful timing to be spoiled.

The Russians did not ask for as much at Yalta as their power in Asia would have enabled them to gain on their own. Churchill made no objection to the deal when Stalin talked to him near the end of the conference. Eden objected to it because of the secrecy of the whole thing, but the Prime Minister overrode his Foreign Secretary for the reason that British authority in the Far East would suffer if they were not signatories to the agreement.

So by the time of their final dinner meeting at Yalta, on February 10, 1945, the Big Three seemed in broad agreement. Churchill happily presided over the affair at his villa, the reception hall of which had been closely searched and locked by Red Army soldiers before Stalin arrived. The Prime Minister offered a toast to the King, the President, and the President of the Supreme Soviet. In his reply Roosevelt spoke of the time in 1933 when his wife had gone to a country town to open a school. On a classroom wall there had been a map with a great blank space for the Soviet Union—and the teacher had told the First Lady that it was forbidden to speak of this place. He had then decided to open negotiations to establish diplomatic relations with Moscow, the President said. After more toasts he told another story that illustrated how hard it was to have any prejudices, racial, religious, or other, if you really knew people. Stalin said this was very true. Churchill and Stalin discussed British politics; the Marshal thought his friend would win the next election because Labour could not form a government and Churchill was more to the left than the socialists anyway. Churchill remarked that Stalin had a much easier political task, since he had only one party to deal with; the Marshal agreed with this. Switching subjects, Stalin said that the Jewish problem was a difficult one; he had tried to establish a national home for the Jews in an agricultural area but they had stayed there only two or three years and then scattered to the cities.

The President said that he was a Zionist and asked if Stalin was one. Stalin said he was one in principle but there were difficulties.

At this point Zion seemed to be on Roosevelt's mind. When Stalin walked over to him at the dinner to ask if he could stay longer at the conference, Roosevelt said that he had three kings waiting for him. The President was willing to stay longer but he was eager to get through the tedium of official drafting of communiqués and agreements and to try his hand at personal diplomacy with the three monarchs, Farouk, of Egypt, Ibn Saud, of Saudi Arabia, and Haile Selassie, Emperor of Ethiopia. While the three foreign ministers wrestled with the final conference protocol, Roosevelt motored to Sevastopol, touring the battlefield of Balaklava on the way, stayed overnight on the conference communications ship, and then flew to an Egyptian airfield near Ismailia and boarded the *Quincy*, anchored in Bitter Lake.

To Hopkins what followed seemed a lot of horseplay, and much of it was. The Commander in Chief donned a huge black cape and seated himself on the forward gun deck to receive his royal visitors. Young Farouk came aboard in his admiral's uniform; Roosevelt urged him to raise more long-staple cotton and presented him with a twin-motored transport. Selassie, a dignified small man in a huge army coat and cap, discussed the disposition of Italian possessions in North Africa with the President; he received four command and reconnaissance cars. The whole affair seemed to reach a peak of peacockery when Ibn Saud hove to in full regalia on the deck of an American destroyer, which had picked him up at Jidda along with his rugs, sheep, awnings, charcoal-cooking buckets, holy water, and a retinue of royal relatives, guards, valets, food tasters, and servers of ceremonial coffee.

Anna Boettiger was nowhere in sight when the monarch came aboard the *Quincy*. The President had told his daughter, Mike Reilly said later, with perhaps a trace of blarney, that the King of Arabia would not allow women in his presence on such occasions and had added, "By the way, those women he does see, he confiscates. . . ."

After the two chiefs of state agreeably discussed oil and reforestation, Roosevelt moved the discussion toward Palestine. At once the balmy atmosphere turned frigid. The President asked the King to admit some more Jews into Palestine, indicating it was such a small percentage of the total population of the Arabian world; he was shocked when Ibn Saud said no. The King went into a monologue about how the Jews had made the countryside bloom only because of millions from American and British capitalists, how the Palestine army of Jews was not fighting Germans but Arabs, how the Arabs would take up arms before yielding further. The President, Hopkins wrote shortly after, seemed not to comprehend fully what Ibn Saud was saying and brought up the question two or three times more, and each time the King was more emphatic. Still, the King got his present, an airplane.

The *Quincy* proceeded through the Suez Canal to Alexandria, where Churchill, who had made a quick trip to Athens to assay the stormy Greek situation, came aboard with his daughter Sarah and son, Randolph, for a family lunch with Roosevelt, Anna, Hopkins, and Winant. To Churchill, the President seemed placid and frail, with a slender contact with life. Roosevelt had admitted in a note to his wife earlier that he was exhausted "but really all right." And now, en route to Algiers, he wrote to "Dearest Babs":

"Headed in the right direction—homeward!

"All well, but still need a little sleep.

"A *fantastic* week. King of Egypt, ditto of Arabia and the Emperor of Ethiopia! Anna is fine and at the moment is ashore in Algiers. Give John and Johnnie my love. I hope to come to Washington when you say you are going to be there—one of those 8 days.

"Devotedly

"F.D.R."

Roosevelt and Hopkins had left Yalta in a mood of satisfaction and optimism, and the heady alliance with the potentates did not dim the euphoria. But as the *Quincy* steamed westward through the Mediterranean the mood changed. Pa Watson had been hospitalized by the ship's surgeon on leaving the Crimea, and inexplicably did not improve. Roosevelt had invited de Gaulle to meet him in Algiers, and the General huffily declined. Hopkins was ailing on arrival in Algiers and decided to fly home to avoid the long sea trip. Roosevelt was annoyed because he had wanted Hopkins to help him with his report on Yalta during the return voyage. Luckily he had already summoned Rosenman to meet him at Algiers for the trip.

Two days out of Algiers Pa Watson died of acute congestive heart failure and a cerebral hemorrhage. The President seemed unusually depressed, and exhausted. For days Rosenman could not get him to work on his report to Congress and the people. He would stay in bed most of the morning reading books he had brought with him and looking over documents. After lunch in his cabin he sat with Anna on the top deck in the sun, reading or just smoking and staring off into space. He seemed to show some of his old-time gaiety and animation only at cocktail time and at dinner.

After gliding through semitropical seas the *Quincy* ran into rough weather between Bermuda and the Chesapeake capes. It put into Newport News on February 27, 1945, and the President went directly to the White House. Adolf Berle, who had taken a rather hard line toward the Russians, went around to see him. Roosevelt threw his hands up and said:

"I didn't say it was good, Adolf, I said it was the best I could do."

TWENTY *With Strong and Active Faith*

TWO DAYS later the doorkeeper of the House of Representatives bawled out word of the President's arrival, Congressmen and packed galleries stood and applauded, and then quieted to a hush as the President of the United States was rolled to the well of the chamber in an armless wheel chair and seated in a red plush chair in front of a small table. Eleanor and Anna Roosevelt looked down from the gallery; Princess Martha, Baruch, Halifax were there; Vice President Truman and Majority Leader McCormack presided at the dais behind; arrayed in a row of chairs immediately in front of the President were members of his Cabinet. In the rows just beyond were members of the United States Senate, one-third of whom could thwart Roosevelt's carefully laid plans for postwar organization and peace.

"I hope that you will pardon me for an unusual posture of sitting down during the presentation of what I want to say," the President began, "but I know that you will realize that it makes it a lot easier for me in not having to carry about ten pounds of steel around on the bottom of my legs; and also because I have just completed a fourteen-thousand-mile trip." Then he added lightly and quickly: "First of all, I want to say, it is good to be home."

"It has been a long journey. I hope you will also agree that it has been, so far, a fruitful one."

Slightly stooped over the table, the President was talking in a flat tone, sometimes slurring his words and stumbling a bit over his text, which he followed with his forefinger. Occasionally he raised his voice for emphasis, but the ringing rhetoric of old was gone. His voice had lost its timbre, Acheson felt; it was an invalid's voice. Friend and foe noted his lean, set face, his trembling hand as he reached for a glass of water.

"Speaking in all frankness, the question of whether it is entirely fruitful or not lies to a great extent in your hands. For unless you here in the halls of the American Congress—with the support of the American people—concur in the general conclusions reached at a place called Yalta, and give them your active support, the meeting will not have produced lasting results."

It was a long rambling speech, with little that was new to his listeners. He had not been ill for a second, he said, until he arrived back in Washington and heard all the rumors that had spread in his absence. He talked at length about plans for Germany, reiterating that unconditional surrender would not mean the destruction or enslavement of the German people, describing the four occupation zones, and promising the destruction of the Nazi party, militarism, and the German General Staff, "which has so often shattered the peace of the world."

The President ad libbed over and over again, to Rosenman's despair; his voice almost gave way at one point; and throughout there was a repeated tiny faltering in his emphasis, as though his mind could not sustain its grip on the speech. But toward the end his flagging voice took on an edge of desperate conviction.

"The Conference in the Crimea was a turning point—I hope in our history and therefore in the history of the world. There will soon be presented to the Senate of the United States and to the American people a great decision that will determine the fate of the United States—and of the world—for generations to come. . . .

"No plan is perfect. Whatever is adopted at San Francisco will doubtless have to be amended time and time again over the years, just as our own Constitution has been. . . .

"Twenty-five years ago, American fighting men looked to the statesmen of the world to finish the work of peace for which they fought and suffered. We failed—we failed them then. We cannot fail them again, and expect the world to survive again.

"The Crimea Conference . . . ought to spell the end of the system of unilateral action, the exclusive alliances, the spheres of influence, the balances of power, and all the other expedients that have been tried for centuries—and have always failed.

"We propose to substitute for all these, a universal organization in which all peace-loving Nations will finally have a chance to join. . . ."

EUROPE: THE PRICE OF INNOCENCE

Victory—and an end to power politics. It was a time for hope. Allied forces were converging on the Rhine; Cologne was under direct attack; to the south American troops pushed into Trier. The whole German defense structure west of the Rhine was crumbling. On the Eastern Front the Red Army was streaming across the Oder hardly fifty miles from Berlin; other troops had turned north toward the Baltic to cut off Danzig.

Peace would break out soon; could it be secured? A conference had been called to meet at San Francisco on April 25 to frame the charter for the United Nations Organization. The President had chosen a bipartisan delegation, including Vandenberg and Stassen, to represent the United States. He looked forward to going there as host, he told reporters, just to say "howdy do." The general response to the Yalta Conference seemed favorable, though Senator Wheeler called it a "great victory for Stalin and Russian imperialism" and the old isolationist press charged a sellout of the Atlantic Charter. Cantril reported that the conference had raised hopes for a long-time peace and that Americans were impressed both by Big Three co-operation and by the way the administration was handling American interests abroad. Even the Polish arrangements were accepted. Cantril did report colossal public ignorance about the actual decisions at Yalta, but the more informed seemed the more satisfied.

Then, in just one month, while Roosevelt looked on dismayed and almost helpless, everything seemed to come unhinged.

Again Poland was the engine of conflict, just as it had been in 1939 and before. The three leaders had agreed at Yalta that Molotov, Harriman, and Kerr would serve as a commission in Moscow to supervise the reorganization and broadening of the provisional Polish government. Crucial matters were left to the commission, such as what Poles should be initially consulted, whether the Lublin (now the Warsaw) Poles should constitute the core of the new government, with the other elements serving as window dressing, or whether the provisional government should be totally reorganized into a broad-based, coalition, antifascist regime. The underlying question was whether Moscow would control Poland.

Churchill knew the line that the Russians would take if he pressed them. Stalin would remind him that Moscow had not intervened in Greece; why should the British interfere in eastern Europe? Hence Churchill had to pitch the issue at a higher level and to do this he needed Roosevelt's support. But the President seemed at first curiously unresponsive to elaborate British formulas to protect the non-Communist Polish elements; Churchill felt that he was not getting through to him. Time was running short, he saw, for every day the Kremlin and the Warsaw Poles seemed to be fastening their grip on the country. On March 13 Churchill cabled to Roosevelt:

". . . Poland has lost her frontier. Is she now to lose her freedom? . . . I do not wish to reveal a divergence between the British and the United States Government, but it would certainly be necessary for me to make it clear that we are in presence of a great failure and an utter breakdown of what we settled at Yalta. . . ."

Stalin seemed so rigid about Poland that Washington and London observers speculated that the Politburo was forcing a strong line on him. But the Marshal had not shifted ground. He had agreed to the Polish formula at Yalta because Churchill and Roosevelt were always talking about public opinion and he was willing to help them appease it with a formula. If Western public opinion was not satisfied with the formula, it should be re-educated. The blood of Soviet soldiers had been shed prodigiously to liberate Poland. Did Churchill and Roosevelt really think he would allow in Warsaw a bourgeois-dominated government that would threaten the Red Army's rear today and Soviet frontiers tomorrow?

All through March the President had been putting off Churchill's proposal that the two of them join in a stiff note to Stalin. Finally he decided to move on his own. On March 29 he cabled to Stalin that the high hopes and expectations raised by Yalta among the peoples of the world were in danger of being crushed. "Having understood each other so well at Yalta I am convinced that the three of us can and will clear away any obstacles which have developed since then." He could not understand the Russian insistence on preserving the Warsaw government. "I must make it quite plain to you that any such solution which would result in a thinly disguised continuation of the present Warsaw regime would be unacceptable. . . ."

Roosevelt was suffering from another bitter disappointment when he sent this letter. He had learned from the State Department that Ambassador Gromyko would head the Soviet delegation to the San Francisco conference—Molotov would not attend. For a second-rank official to represent Russia at the founding conference, on which Roosevelt had set his hopes, struck him as a veiled attack on the nascent organization. He appealed to Stalin to let Molotov come for at least the vital opening sessions; he warned of world reaction otherwise. Stalin was adamant; public reaction, he said, could not decide such matters.

The President had a public-opinion problem of his own at this point. After conceding the Soviet Union two extra Assembly votes at Yalta and winning Churchill's and Stalin's consent to two extra for the United States, Roosevelt abandoned the latter notion but kept the extra Soviet votes secret, possibly because he hoped he could talk Stalin out of them before San Francisco. Inevitably the story leaked out. An outburst of anger followed on Capitol Hill, and the President was left on the defensive.

Physically, Roosevelt seemed at a low ebb. He had again begun to work late into the evening. He complained of not being able to taste his food. But once again Bruenn found his basic condition unchanged: his heart size was unchanged, there were no cardiac symptoms, the systolic murmur had not changed. For the moment even the blood pressure values were somewhat lower. But few around him, medical or lay, could doubt that the election and then Yalta and now the crisis over Poland were taking their toll of his strength and vitality.

At the grand climax of coalition warfare, with German resistance buckling, everything seemed to be deteriorating politically: Russia and the West were at odds; even Churchill and Roosevelt exchanged some stiff messages as they groped for a way to deal with the Bear; the San Francisco Conference itself seemed flawed by power politics and compromise. "My God, what a mess Europe is in!" Eden said to Harold Nicolson. "What a mess!"

Observers were asking what had gone wrong. Internal tensions in the Kremlin? Anti-Soviet attitudes in the West? Stalin's paranoia? Churchill's old anti-Communism? Roosevelt's fatigue, or his utopianism? Or simply the utter hopelessness of such ancient problems as Poland?

Few saw the main source of friction—the internal dynamics of a coalition in the process of losing the enemy that had united ideologically diverse partners—until an obscure event set off an illuminating blaze of fear and suspicion.

Early in March General Karl Wolff, SS commander in Italy, secretly met in Zurich with Allen Dulles, OSS chief in Switzerland, to explore the possibilities of some kind of German surrender in Italy. Eleven days later there was a second exploratory meeting. Churchill realized that the Kremlin might be suspicious of a separate military surrender in the south, which would enable the Anglo-American armies, he admitted later, to advance against lessened opposition as far as Vienna and beyond, or even toward Berlin or the Elbe, so he ordered that Moscow be informed. Molotov already knew of the "negotiation" and demanded to be told why the Russians had not been invited to take part. He suspected not just a misunderstanding, "but something worse."

The answer lay partly with the Combined Chiefs. They did not want the Russians to be part of the early stages of the parley. The meetings, they contended, were preliminary, mainly about mechanics; no political matters would be discussed; if the Russians took part the meetings would be protracted, a great opportunity might be lost, more Allied soldiers would die.

He had to support officers in the field, Roosevelt told Stalin, when there was a possibility of forcing the surrender of enemy troops. As a military man the Marshal would understand this, he added. "There can be in such a surrender of enemy forces in the field no violation of our agreed principles of unconditional surrender and no political implication whatsoever."

Stalin's answer reflected all the fears and suspicions that were gripping the strategists in the Kremlin. Talks with the enemy, he said, were permissible only if they did not give the Germans opportunity to use the negotiations to cause German troops to be switched to other sectors—above all, to the Soviet sector. That was why he wanted Russians present at even the preliminary negotiations. The Germans had already taken advantage of the talks to shift three divisions from northern Italy to the Soviet front. What had happened to the agreement at Yalta to hold the enemy on the spot and to prevent him from maneuvering? The Red Army was living up to this, he said, but Alexander was not. The Red Army was encircling Germans and exterminating them. Were the Germans in the west opening their front to the Anglo-Americans?

Indignantly Roosevelt denied all these charges. There had been no general negotiations. Lack of Allied offensive operations in Italy was due mainly to transfer of Allied forces to the Western Front. The shift of German troops antedated all the surrender talks. The trouble, he concluded bitterly, was due to Germans trying to sow suspicion between the Russians and the West. Why let them succeed?

Instead of placating Stalin, Roosevelt's message—and his continued protestation of innocence—brought to a pitch the pent-up distrust felt by the men in the Kremlin. Why were the Allies insisting on the Swiss talks in the face of Soviet objections? What were they trying to hide? Was it simply a stratagem to permit Hitler to transfer even more troops to the east? Were the Anglo-Americans maneuvering to subdue the Communists and leftist elements in northern Italy, as they had in Greece? Were they still aspiring to get to Trieste—or even Vienna—before the Russians? Would they engulf whole sectors of Germany while the Nazis held back the Red Army? Or were there even more diabolical plans on foot? All these suspicions spilled over into Stalin's reply to Roosevelt.

"You affirm that so far no negotiations have been entered into. Apparently you are not fully informed." His military colleagues had information that negotiations did take place whereby Germany would open the front to the Anglo-American troops and let them move east, in exchange for easier armistice terms. This was why those troops were advancing into the heart of Germany almost without resistance. He saw the advantage for the Anglo-Americans, but why conceal this from the Russians?

"And so what we have at the moment is that the Germans on the Western Front have in fact ceased the war against Britain and America. At the same time they continue the war against Russia, the ally of Britain and the U.S.A."

It was the most brutal message Stalin had ever sent Roosevelt;

it was also the most portentous. The surrender discussions had incited the fear that had dominated Soviet strategy for over a decade—the fear that the fascist and capitalist powers would combine against Russia. Everywhere Stalin looked events seemed to be conspiring in that direction: the shift of German troops to the east; the furious defense by the Hitlerites of obscure towns in the east while they yielded big cities to the Anglo-Americans in the west; the mysterious discussions with Wolff in Switzerland, and the stubborn refusal to let the Russians take part. And always there was the secret Allied development of an atomic weapon. Roosevelt was the tool of Churchill—the same Churchill who had tried to strangle the Bolshevik Revolution at birth.

Once again Roosevelt responded indignantly. He had received his message with astonishment, he told Stalin. He asked the same trust in his own truthfulness as he had always had in the Marshal's. Could the Russians believe that he would settle with the Germans without Soviet agreement? It would be a tragedy of history if, just as victory was within their grasp, such lack of faith should prejudice the entire undertaking after all the colossal losses.

"Frankly," he concluded, "I cannot avoid a feeling of bitter resentment toward your informers, whoever they are, for such vile misrepresentations of my actions or those of my trusted subordinates."

There could be no question now—the edifice of trust and good will and neighborliness that Roosevelt had shaped so lovingly was crashing down around him. The same Stalin who was making these horrendous accusations was practicing power politics in Poland, withholding Molotov from San Francisco, and doubtless planning to use the veto to disrupt the United Nations. And Roosevelt was innocent of Stalin's charges; he had neither the will nor the capacity to indulge in labyrinthine maneuvers at this point. But his innocence had a dangerous edge. He was being tripped again by his old tendency to compartmentalize military and political decisions. Because to him military negotiations need not have political implications, he did not see what Stalin saw: that any discussion with the enemy, on any kind of time schedule, inevitably created certain political possibilities and blocked others.

For a moment Stalin sensed that he might have gone too far in upbraiding the President. He assured Roosevelt that he did not question his trustworthiness, but then he repeated all his arguments. Time was running out. Stalin's latest message on Poland was dated April 7, 1945.

ASIA: NEVER, NEVER, NEVER

Brilliant Allied victories amid deteriorating coalition politics—that was the strategic plight of Asia, too, in the late winter of 1945.

In mid-February a fast carrier force under Spruance slipped through thick weather to a point seventy miles from the Japanese coastline and sent several hundred bombers over Tokyo. It was the first naval attack on the capital since Doolittle's raid. Next day a huge amphibious force appeared off Iwo Jima, a tiny island which, with its three airfields, flat surface, and steep mountain at one end, was like a stationary aircraft carrier seven hundred miles from Japan. On D day—February 19—seven battleships and an armada of cruisers and destroyers smashed the beach areas with the most concentrated prelanding bombardment of the Pacific war. The defenders had mainly fortified the higher ground inland, however, and as soon as the bombardment lifted and the assault craft hit the beaches, the Marines were pinned there under withering fire. The attackers held on and began the bloody business of blowing and burning out deep underground strong points. Over 6,000 Marines died during the next five weeks of cave-to-cave fighting, along with virtually all the 21,000 defenders. Kamikazes sank an escort carrier and crippled the fleet carrier *Saratoga*.

Iwo Jima proved that the American Navy could seize enemy territory within a few hundred miles of the Japanese mainland and thus thrust its line of steppingstones almost to the heartland; it also demonstrated that the enemy could exact a fearful price for a few square miles of volcanic ash. Roosevelt, returning from Yalta, could feel vindicated in paying a price for Soviet participation in the Asian war.

It was this same price, however, that was causing unrest in Chungking during the weeks after Yalta. Rumors were circulating through the capital that the independence of China had been gravely compromised by a deal between Roosevelt and Stalin. Hurley felt he must return to Washington to ascertain from the President his long-range plans for China. He left in mid-February, with General Albert C. Wedemeyer, who had succeeded Stilwell as Chiang's Chief of Staff.

Hurley had other reasons to see his chief. After a promising start, his mediation between the Nationalists and the Communists had collapsed. In November he had won Yenan's adherence to a five-point agreement providing for "unification of all military forces in China for the immediate defeat of Japan" and for a new coalition government "of the people, for the people, and by the people" that would control all the military forces in the country, including the Communist. Triumphantly Hurley had brought to Chungking not only the draft agreement, but Chou En-lai himself to take part in the negotiations, only to be accused by the Nationalists of having been sold a bill of goods. To agree to a coalition government, the Generalissimo said, would be to acknowledge total defeat. In return he offered a three-point proposal that would recognize the Communists as a legal party in exchange for control by the Nationalist government of the Communist armed forces. The Communists turned this down flat on the ground that they were simply being asked to surrender. The indefatigable Ambassador managed to persuade the two sides to resume talks. All in vain. The distrust was too deep.

"China is in a dilemma," Stettinius summed it up to the President early in January. "Coalition would mean an end of Conservative Kuomintang domination and open the way for the more virile and popular Communists to extend their influence to the point perhaps of controlling the Government. Failure to settle with the Communists, who are daily growing stronger, would invite the danger of an eventual overthrow of the Kuomintang. . . ."

Hurley had troubles of his own. He had become convinced that the Foreign Service officers in China not only held different views from his own but also were sabotaging his relations with the State Department. He was certainly right on the first point. In contrast to the Ambassador, who liked Chiang, had confidence in the long-run survival and improvement of his government, and, with Wedemeyer, came to believe he was making a fair fight against the enemy, the China hands, who had had far more opportunity to observe, deemed Chiang and the Kuomintang ineffective, corrupt, reactionary, insensitive to the misery around them, incapable of reform, and not only unable to fight the Japanese but also unwilling to do so because they were hoarding their men to fight the Communists after the war. Late in February the Chargé d'Affaires at Chungking reported to Stettinius that American aid to the Nationalists was threatening to drive Yenan closer to Russia, that China was headed toward a disastrous civil conflict, and that Washington should deal directly with and aid Yenan. This message arrived at the State Department while Hurley was in Washington and led to a confrontation between Hurley and officials of the Far Eastern office.

So it was an indignant Ambassador who reported to the President. Just what happened when he went to the White House twice during March is not wholly clear. He said later that he wanted a showdown with the Commander in Chief but "when the President reached up that fine, firm, strong hand of his to shake hands with me" and Hurley found in his hand a "loose bag of bones" and saw the wasted face, he lost some of his nerve. Apparently the President was in better shape than he looked, for he scoffed at Hurley's worries and stated vigorously that he had not surrendered the territorial integrity or political independence of China. "You are seeing ghosts again." He was loath to let Hurley have the Yalta documents on the Far East, but Hurley insisted on seeing them, and in a later meeting the Ambassador felt—or so he testified later—that the President seemed less confident about the agreements and had decided that Hurley should see Churchill and Stalin to discuss them. The President stuck to the basic policy of giving military aid only to Chiang, but he urged Hurley to continue to conciliate the Communists and he approved representation for Yenan on the Chinese delegation to the San Francisco Conference. Hurley left the White House satisfied that he had been thoroughly sustained in his fight with the young China hands.

Thus passed a last opportunity for Roosevelt to abandon his China strategy. Yet despite all the illusions that dominated American thinking about China it was not ignorance or stupidity or illness that was the prime source of Roosevelt's continuing gamble on Chiang. It was a combination of utopian hopes for the possibility of Chinese unity, stability, progress, and democracy, Western-style, and of hard-nosed military planning to minimize American casualties in the conquest of Japan.

Hurley had hardly left Washington for his trip to London and Moscow when Americans were once again reminded of the need for Soviet help in the final struggle. On April 1 Marine and army divisions swarmed ashore on Okinawa, the largest island in the Ryukyus and a threshold to the East China Sea. It was the most daring move in the Pacific campaign, for Okinawa lay only four hundred miles east of the China coast and barely 350 southwest of Kyushu itself. The invaders had an April Fool's surprise when they met little resistance the first day. But during the following week, as the infantry pushed south through choppy terrain, they encountered the most formidable defenses in their Pacific experience. Losses mounted appallingly as hardened Marines and soldiers ground their way through endless mazes of mutually supporting strong points.

Several hundred Japanese aircraft from the home islands also attacked the invaders. Most were shot down, but enough kamikazes slipped through to cause heavy losses, especially among destroyers and picket ships. Twenty-two of the first twenty-four suicide crashes were effective. Clearly Japanese fanaticism was intensifying as the Americans drove closer to Kyushu and Honshu. More sharply than ever the Commander in Chief and the men in the Pentagon confronted the question: If a few Japanese divisions and a handful of suicide planes could exact such a price in defending an outlying island, what would happen when the Americans attacked the heartland?

By early April it seemed likely that the atomic bomb would be finished in time to use against Japan if not against Germany. Would this make the difference? Scientists were becoming more and more worried about the prospects of dropping the bomb on civilians, the lack of international control of information, the still-pervasive secrecy. Bush and others were pressing Stimson to support a general pooling among nations of all scientific research to prevent secret plans for weapons, but Stimson wanted to give the Russians information about the weapon only on the basis of a "real" *quid pro quo*. He seemed to draw back a bit after a long talk with his aide, Harvey Bundy, during which the two went "right down to the bottom facts of human nature, morals and government," Stimson noted in his diary, but the Secretary was still divided between continuing secrecy and international sharing and control. So was Roosevelt, who wanted to put off a decision until the first bomb was tested. Einstein wrote a letter to the President introducing Leo Szilard, who raised the portentous atomic questions of the future. This time Roosevelt did not respond.

Early in April Bohr returned to the United States and prepared for the President a new memorandum against atomic secrecy and distrust. He asked Halifax and Frankfurter how the statement could be brought to the President's attention. The Ambassador and the Justice decided to discuss the matter in the privacy of Washington's Rock Creek Park. They planned to meet on April 12.

Wedemeyer, as well as Hurley, visited the White House in March—characteristically Roosevelt had his two China lieutenants in separately—and he was even more disturbed than the Ambassador by Roosevelt's drawn face and drooping jaw. But on one point at least the President was clear and emphatic. He was going to do everything possible to grant the people of Indochina their independence from France. He instructed Wedemeyer not to hand over any supplies to the French forces operating in the area.

Independence for Indochina had become a near-obsession of the President's during the past year or two. He told Stalin at Yalta that he had in mind a temporary trusteeship for Indochina, but that the British wished to give it back to France, since they feared the implications of a trusteeship for their own rule in Burma. De Gaulle, he said, had asked for ships to carry Free French forces to Indochina. Was he going to get them? Stalin asked. The President answered archly that he had been unable to find any ships for de Gaulle.

Indochina seemed to engross the President on the way home

from Yalta. For two whole years, he told reporters, he had been terribly worried about that country. He recounted his Cairo talk with Chiang, who had said that the Chinese did not want Indochina but that the French should not have it. Roosevelt had proposed the temporary trusteeship idea, he told reporters. "Stalin liked it. China liked the idea. The British don't like it. It might bust up their empire. . . ." Wilhelmina, he went on, was planning to give Java and Sumatra independence soon, New Guinea and Borneo only after a century or two. The skulls of the New Guineans, the Queen had explained, were the least developed in the world.

Churchill, a reporter remarked, seemed opposed to a policy of self-determination. He had said that the Atlantic Charter was not a rule, just a guide. He seemed to be undercutting it. The President agreed.

"The Atlantic Charter is a beautiful idea," he said. Did he remember the speech, a reporter asked, that Churchill had given about not being made prime minister to see the Empire fall apart?

"Dear old Winston will never learn on that point. He has made his specialty on that point. This is, of course, off the record."

The most significant sentence in these remarks was, perhaps, the last one. Roosevelt would not make a public issue of colonialism. It would only make the British mad, he said. "Better to keep quiet just now." He could not forget an incident at Yalta. Stettinius had begun to discuss trusteeships under the new world charter when Churchill broke in, exclaiming that he did not agree with a single word. His phrases spilling out in spurts of anger, he shouted that as long as he was prime minister the British Empire would not be put into the dock. He would never yield a scrap of his country's heritage. Roosevelt had intervened only to ask that Stettinius be allowed to finish his statement; the Secretary was not talking about the British Empire. Churchill had subsided ungraciously, muttering, "Never, never, never."

Roosevelt would tease Churchill to his face about his colonies; he would joke or complain about Churchill's imperialism with Stalin and others; but he would not directly confront the Prime Minister. He was serious about the trusteeship idea, telling Hurley at their March meetings that United Nations trusteeships would be set up at the forthcoming San Francisco Conference. But such a policy required the concurrence of Britain and France and perhaps other colonial nations, and Roosevelt gave little indication that he was ready to challenge the other Atlantic powers. Indeed, since his talks with de Gaulle in July 1944 he seemed also to be veering toward more recognition of the French interest in Indochina, especially if de Gaulle lived up to his promises about giving Indochina representation within a postwar French federal system.

Even more important in the whole situation was Roosevelt's Atlantic First strategy, which in early 1945, as China weakened and the Soviets seemed to grow more chauvinistic, seemed likely to be as important after the war as it had been during it. Caught between these forces, Roosevelt left Indochina in a political void. He merely provoked Churchill and de Gaulle without accomplishing anything specific.

The President had anticolonial ideals; what he lacked was a carefully conceived strategy to carry them out, given the global strategic considerations and the checkered and volatile politics of Southeast Asia. Great possibilities were open in the early months of 1945. Roosevelt's anticolonialism, his sponsorship of the Atlantic Charter, his support of Philippine independence were well known to nationalistic and revolutionary leaders in Burma and India, in Indonesia and Indochina. So was America's own revolutionary past. When Ho Chi Minh was drawing up a manifesto of independence he asked an American friend for the language of the great declaration of 1776. Roosevelt was not willing to launch a crusade against colonialism or to risk the kind of public confrontation with the Atlantic powers that would have captured for him the allegiance—or at least the rapt attention—of the colonial peoples of Asia.

Rather, he felt that his stated goals combined with his personal influence with Wilhelmina and King George and even Churchill and de Gaulle would be enough to resolve the issue when the fighting was over. So it was not necessary to frame comprehensive programs and detailed policies, especially since it was hard to calculate all the factors in advance, and the war had to be won first anyway. He would attend to it at the right time. It was not the lack of personal convictions but the easy assumption that he would be around to translate them into decision and action, along with the shadowy dominance of Atlantic First, that flawed Roosevelt's anticolonial credo at the beginning of spring 1945.

"THE WORK, MY FRIENDS, IS PEACE"

If events abroad were reaching one of the great climacterics of history, domestic affairs by the spring of 1945 were following their own tepid cycle. In the wake of the President's challenging pronouncements of January the committees of Congress assumed command of the legislative process with their ancient weapons of discussion, dilution, and delay. The manpower bill, after passing the House, slowly bled to death in the Senate as victories abroad blunted the spur of emergency. Wallace was finally confirmed as Secretary of Commerce, but only after a bitter struggle in the Senate—and only after the big federal lending agencies were separated from Commerce so that the former Vice President could not "control" billions in loans. Congressional investigators of subversive activities conducted feckless little witch hunts. The Senate rejected Roosevelt's nomination of Aubrey Williams, former National Youth Administrator, as head of Rural Electrification. John L. Lewis threatened another coal strike.

Not for years had the President's legislative fortunes seemed at such a low ebb. The Republican and Democratic congressional parties were collaborating smoothly. Roosevelt, however, seemed hardly aware of the congressional situation; in any event he was not going to invite a quarrel with the legislators over domestic matters at a time when he needed Republican and conservative support for his foreign policies, especially for American leadership in the new international organization.

His administration ran on with the momentum of twelve years of liberal activism. He urged renewal and strengthening of the Trade Agreements Act. He asked for an inquiry into guaranteed annual-wage plans. He received ambassadors, awarded medals, discussed jobs with Democratic politicos.

He seemed to be dwelling in the past and the future, as well as the present. "I still say, thank God for those good old days and for old and tried friends like you," he wrote to a Dutchess County friend who had remarked that it was a long step from the size of apple barrels—an issue in Roosevelt's 1912 campaign—to meeting Churchill and Stalin and perhaps deciding the fate of the world. He was looking forward to his trip to San Francisco in April and to England later in the spring with his wife. And by late March he could relax about military prospects in Europe. When he told Frances Perkins of his projected trip to England and she protested that it was still too dangerous, he put his hand to the side of his mouth and whispered: "The war in Europe will be over by the end of May."

Both Anna Boettiger and Grace Tully were quietly trying to conserve the President's strength until he could get some rest at Warm Springs. Both were perplexed by his sudden changes in appearance. So were the reporters, who were watching him closely. At the White House correspondents' dinner, Allen Drury noted how old and thin and scrawny-necked he looked when he was wheeled in, how he stared out at the crowded tables as though he did not see the people, how he failed to respond to the blare of trumpets and to the applause.

Then he suddenly came to life, Drury noted, and began to enjoy himself. The notables of Washington were there, including Leahy and Marshall, Byrnes and Ickes and Biddle and Morgenthau, Justices Douglas and Jackson, Senators Ball and Morse and Austin;

and Vice President Truman, with a handkerchief carefully folded so that the four corners showed. Danny Kaye performed, and Jimmy Durante and Fanny Brice. Everyone watched the greatest performer of all—how he steadily drank wine and smoked his uplifted cigarette, how he leaned forward with his hand cupped behind his ear to hear a joke repeated as laughter welled up in the room, how his booming laughter rang out—but then a few moments later simply sat at the table with an intent, vague expression on his face, while his jaw dropped and his mouth fell open.

But he lasted out the evening and gave a talk at the end. It was about Humanity, he said—"We all love Humanity, you love Humanity, I love Humanity. . . ." And in the name of Humanity he would give them a headline story—"I am calling off the press conference for tomorrow morning."

The applause rang out as he was shifted back to his wheel chair, Drury noted in his diary, "and just before he went out the door he acknowledged it with the old, familiar gesture, so that the last we saw of Franklin Roosevelt was the head going up with a toss, the smile breaking out, the hand uplifted and waving in the old, familiar way."

The usual crowd clustered around the little Warm Springs station as Roosevelt's train pulled in on Good Friday, March 30, 1945. Something seemed different this time as Roosevelt's big frame, slumped in the wheel chair, seemed to joggle uncontrollably as he was rolled along the platform. A murmur drifted through the crowd. But the President drove his own car to the Little White House atop the hill.

That evening Hassett suddenly blurted out to Bruenn that the President was slipping away. Hassett admitted that he had been maintaining a bluff to the family and even Roosevelt himself, but he felt there was no hope for him. His feeble signature—the bold stroke and heavy line of old were gone, or simply faded out. Bruenn cautiously granted that Roosevelt was in a precarious condition, but said it was not hopeless if he could be protected from emotional and mental strain. That was impossible, Hassett said. He and Bruenn were on the verge of emotional upset.

But after a few days in the warm Georgia sun Roosevelt's gray pallor changed and some of his old vitality returned, though the level of his blood pressure had become extremely wide, ranging between 170/88 and 240/130. The news from Europe was exciting: American, British, and Canadian troops were encircling the Ruhr, spearing northwest toward Hannover and Bremen, driving ever deeper into the heart of Germany. Reports were also coming to Washington of the many thousands of civilian deaths in the fire bombings of Japanese and German cities; it is doubtful that Roosevelt understood the enormity of the civilian losses, which would compare with the effects of the later atomic bombings.

Stalin's harsh messages were forwarded to Warm Springs. Roosevelt was disturbed but not depressed by his deteriorating relations with the Kremlin. Unlike Churchill, who at the time foresaw the darkness ahead, as he said later, and moved amid cheering crowds with an aching heart, Roosevelt was sure that things would be put aright. He tried to calm the troubled waters. The Swiss incident was fading into the past, he cabled to Stalin; in any event there must not be mutual distrust. He urged on Churchill that the Soviet problem be minimized as much as possible; things would straighten out. He added:

"We must be firm however, and our course thus far is correct."

The President seemed more concerned with Asia than with Europe during these early April days. He was pleased with the news of the sudden fall of the Japanese Cabinet in the wake of the invasion of Okinawa. President Sergio Osmeña was back from the Philippines to report on the terrible destruction in Manila. The President talked with reporters in remarkable detail about conditions in the Philippines, economic problems, needed American assistance. It was the President's 998th press conference.

He was especially determined that there be no change in plans for immediate independence for the Philippines. It depended only on how quickly the Japanese were cleared from the islands. He would set an example for the British and the other colonial powers. He wrote to his old chief, Josephus Daniels, that he would like independence to go into effect in August and to be present himself, but he feared he might have to be in Europe for a conference about that time.

On the afternoon of April 11 the President dictated the draft of a speech for Jefferson Day.

"Americans are gathered together in communities all over the country to pay tribute to the living memory of Thomas Jefferson—one of the greatest of all democrats; and I want to make it clear that I am spelling that word 'democrats' with a small *d*. . . ."

The President paid a traditional tribute to Jefferson as Secretary of State, President, and scientist. Then he continued:

"The once powerful, malignant Nazi state is crumbling. The Japanese war lords are receiving, in their own homeland, the retribution for which they asked when they attacked Pearl Harbor.

"But the mere conquest of our enemies is not enough.

"We must go on to do all in our power to conquer the doubts and the fears, the ignorance and the greed, which made this horror possible. . . .

"Today we are faced with the preeminent fact that, if civilization is to survive, we must cultivate the science of human relationships—the ability of all peoples, of all kinds, to live together and work together, in the same world, at peace.

"Let me assure you that my hand is the steadier for the work that is to be done, that I move more firmly into the task, knowing that you—millions and millions of you—are joined with me in the resolve to make this work endure.

"The work, my friends, is peace. More than an end of this war—an end to the beginnings of all wars. Yes, an end, forever, to this impractical, unrealistic settlement of the differences between governments by the mass killing of peoples.

"Today, as we move against the terrible scourge of war—as we go forward toward the greatest contribution that any generation of human beings can make in this world—the contribution of lasting peace, I ask you to keep up your faith. I measure the sound, solid achievement that can be made at this time by the straight edge of your own confidence and your resolve. And to you, and to all Americans who dedicate themselves with us to the making of an abiding peace, I say:

"The only limit to our realization of tomorrow will be our doubts of today. Let us move forward with strong and active faith."

EPILOGUE *Home-coming*

WARM SPRINGS on Thursday morning, April 12, 1945, was sunny and pleasant. Dogwood and wild violets bloomed along the road to Pine Mountain. There, at his favorite picnic spot, friends of Franklin Roosevelt were preparing a barbecue for the late afternoon; the smells of honeysuckle and stewing beef and chicken mingled in the soft Georgia air. A wooden armchair was set out for the guest of honor under a wisteria-laden oak tree, whence he could gaze at the greening valley below.

Down in the valley, in his corner bedroom in the Little White House, the President was sitting in bed reading the Atlanta *Constitution;* the big-city newspapers from the north had been delayed by bad weather in Washington. The headlines reported American troops fifty-seven miles from Berlin and 115 miles from the Russians; a big fleet of super-Forts had bombed Tokyo in daylight. Roosevelt looked up from his paper at the sound of chatter in the kitchen. He called out to Lizzie McDuffie, who was dusting the living room. What were they talking about? Lizzie came to the door. Mr. Roosevelt had always had time to talk with her, to answer her questions.

"Well, Mr. Roosevelt, do you believe in reincarnation?" Did *she* believe in it? he countered. She didn't know, Lizzie said, but if there was such a thing she wanted to come back as a canary bird.

"A *canary bird!"* The President looked at her two-hundred-pound frame, threw his paper down, and burst out laughing. Lizzie McDuffie would never forget that scene: the President with his head thrown back, his eyes closed, laughing and exclaiming—as she had heard him do a hundred times—"Don't you love it? Don't you *love* it?"

When Hassett reached the Little White House around noon with the delayed mail pouch, Roosevelt was sitting in the living room in his leather armchair chatting with his cousins Margaret Suckley and Laura Delano and with Mrs. Winthrop Rutherfurd. Two years before, Lucy Mercer Rutherfurd had commissioned a portrait painter, Elizabeth Shoumatoff, to do a water color of the President; recently he had asked the artist to paint another picture of him as a gift to Lucy's daughter. Madame Shoumatoff came in while Roosevelt was signing a sheaf of appointments and awards Hassett had put before him—signing them as usual with a wide flowing pen, so that Hassett had to spread them out to dry. The usual banter followed about putting out Hassett's laundry. One document was a bill just passed by Congress to continue the Commodity Credit Corporation and increase its borrowing power. The President signed it with a flourish, telling the ladies, "Here's where I make a law."

Hassett looked on disapprovingly as the painter set up her easel, measured Roosevelt's nose, asked him to turn back and forth. His boss looked much too weary for all this, he felt. He collected the signed documents and departed, leaving the President with some papers to read while he was being sketched. The room was quiet now. The artist continued her work, but the President became so intent in his reading that he fell out of his pose. She used the time to fill in colors. At one o'clock the President looked at his watch.

"We've got just fifteen minutes more." The houseboy was setting the dining table on the other side of the room. Margaret Suckley continued to crochet, Laura Delano to fill vases with flowers. Lucy Rutherfurd watched the President. He made a little joke and looked into her smiling face. He lit a cigarette and studied his papers.

The fifteen minutes were almost up when the President raised his left hand to his temple, dropped it limply, then raised and pressed it behind his neck. He said very quietly: "I have a terrific headache." Then his arm dropped, his head fell to the left, his body slumped. A call went out to Dr. Bruenn, who had been sunning himself at the pool. When Bruenn arrived, the President was still slumped in his chair; only with difficulty was the heavy, inert body carried into the bedroom. The President's breathing stopped, then started again in great snoring gasps. Bruenn sheared away his clothes; injected papaverine and amyl nitrate; and telephoned Admiral McIntire in Washington. Madame Shoumatoff had already left with Mrs. Rutherfurd. Hassett arrived and knew the end was near when he heard the awful labored breathing. Grace Tully sat quietly in a corner, her lips moving in prayer. The minutes ticked by; the breathing grew more tortured; then it stopped. Bruenn could hear no heart sounds. He injected adrenalin into the heart muscle. No response. At 3:55 P.M. Bruenn pronounced him dead.

Grace Tully walked into the bedroom, kissed the President lightly on the forehead, then walked out onto the porch and stood there wordless and tearless. The reporters were summoned from the barbecue on Pine Mountain. They swept into the little house. Hassett was standing near the center of the living room. "Gentlemen," he said quietly, "it is my sad duty to inform you that the President of the United States is dead. . . ."

The news came to Churchill in his study at 10 Downing Street just before midnight; for a long time he sat stunned and silent, feeling as though he had been struck a physical blow. In Moscow, Harriman was awakened at 2:00 A.M.; he drove to the Kremlin to see Stalin, who seemed moved and preoccupied by the news as he held the envoy's hand for a long moment, saying nothing. In Chungking, the Generalissimo received the news as he began eating breakfast; he left the meal untouched and retired for mourning. In Japan, an announcer for Radio Tokyo read the death bulletin and unaccountably presented some special music "in honor of the passing of a great man."

In Berlin, the news came to Goebbels on the steps of the Propaganda Ministry just after a bombing attack. His exultant face could be seen in the light of the flames from the burning Chancellery across the Wilhelmplatz. He had been telling the Führer and others that Germany would be saved at the eleventh hour by an unexpected event, just as Frederick the Great had been saved by the death of the Czarina two centuries before. He called for champagne and telephoned Hitler, who was in his deep bunker.

"My Führer! I congratulate you. Roosevelt is dead. It is written in the stars that the second half of April will be the turning point for us. This is Friday 13 April. It is the turning point!"

FREEDOM'S ONCE-BORN

Next morning the army band and a thousand infantrymen from Fort Benning, black streamers flying from their colors, led the hearse between lines of helmeted paratroopers down the curving red clay road through the Warm Springs Foundation. Behind came Eleanor Roosevelt in an open car, Fala at her feet. At Georgia Hall patients in wheel chairs waved farewell to the friend who had presided at their Thanksgiving dinners and swum with them in the warm pool. Graham Jackson had waited at the barbecue to play his accordion for the President; now, his face a map of anguish and disbelief, he stepped out from the columned portico and rendered "Going Home."

Its drums beating a steady, deadened roll, the procession wound down to the little railroad station. The heavy, flag-draped coffin was handed through a window into the rear car of the presidential train. There it rested on a pine box so low that only the top of the casket could be seen through the windows. Four servicemen stood

Today's Army-Navy Casualty List

Washington, Apr. 13.—Following are the latest casualties in the military services, including next-of-kin.

ARMY-NAVY DEAD

ROOSEVELT, Franklin, D., Commander-in-Chief, wife, Mrs. Anna Eleanor Roosevelt, the White House.

Navy Dead

DECKER, Carlos Anthony, Fireman 1c. Sister, Mrs. Elizabeth Decker Metz, 16 Concord Pl., Concord, S. I.

guard. The train started imperceptibly and began rolling down the track to Atlanta.

Eleanor Roosevelt sat in the presidential lounge car. The afternoon before, she had been at the White House when word came from Warm Springs that her husband had fainted;. Admiral McIntire, in Washington, advised her to go ahead with a speaking engagement so that people would not be alarmed. She had done so, with her unquenchable sense of duty, only to be called back to the White House and told the definite news. She had had time to ask Harry Truman, "Is there anything we can do for *you?*"; to send a message to her four soldier sons, "He did his job to the end as he would want you to do." Then she had flown south with Early and McIntire.

While the train rolled through the gently billowing land of west central Georgia—his adopted state, Roosevelt called it—the world was trying to adjust to the death of the President. Almost everywhere the first reactions had been shock, incredulity, grief, and fear. Now it was time for second thoughts. Editorialists struggled to capture the nature of the man, the meaning of his life, the measure of the loss.

It was no easy task, for even those who knew Roosevelt best agreed that he was a man infinitely complex and almost incomprehensible. On such a relatively simple matter as his behavior toward fellow human beings he oscillated; like all men, he was both generous and vindictive, but it was Roosevelt's mixture of the two qualities that was so baffling. Even now, friends of Al Smith were remembering how Roosevelt had befriended him during the war years and tried to bail out his Empire State Building, even though the "Happy Warrior" had scathingly attacked the New Deal. But Henry Luce, who had not treated the President ungently, was suddenly and arbitrarily barred by the White House from touring the Pacific Theater; he would hate Roosevelt to his dying day. The President could get along with anyone he wanted to, from Stalin to MacArthur to Huey Long to the man in the street; people in Warm Springs remembered the time he was driving his little car through the town and had stopped and waved over a Negro walking by; how the "colored man was scared, scraping his feet and all. . . . Then, first you know, he was leaning on the President's automobile, throwing his arms around like he was talking to anybody." Yet people as different as Jim Farley and Dean Acheson felt that he condescended—that he conveyed, Acheson felt, much of the attitude of European royalty.

South of Gainesville, Georgia, black women in a cotton field saw the train coming and fell to their knees in supplication. It was remarkable, this human touch of the President's, but sometimes his charm had an edge of coquetry and pretense. Marshal Sir William Sholto-Douglas, of the RAF, remembered how Roosevelt had greeted him with a lecture on Scottish history and the achievements of the Douglases, told how he had a Scottish grandmother himself, and so on. Douglas sensed an indefinable flaw in his manner; he felt that he was witnessing some kind of performance—still, he was moved to the point that tears came to his eyes, and Roosevelt, he confessed later, nearly had him eating out of his hand. Jesse Jones, just fired from the administration, told a reporter that the President was a hypocrite and lacking in character but "you just can't help liking that fellow."

Along with all his democratic manner and instincts he had that curious interest in royal and noble personages and doings. He told a friend, rather improbably, that he had been hurt in England after the first war when he had not been invited to Buckingham Palace. In a different vein, and most curiously, he allowed and even encouraged Adolf Berle to call him "Caesar" in addressing the President in private. Berle, who was always bemused by the irony of power, was still calling him this the last time he saw Roosevelt, just after Yalta. Did the President derive from the term some curious satisfaction that outweighed the risk of his enemies discovering it and gleefully publicizing it—or did he tolerate Berle's fun because he enjoyed imagining what they would do if they *did* find out about it?

Night came, and the funeral train—blacked out except for the ghostly, half-lit rear coach—wove slowly back and forth through the

Carolina piedmont. Looking out from her berth at the countryside her husband loved, Eleanor Roosevelt glimpsed the solemn faces of the crowds at the depots and crossroads. The train would arrive in Washington eighty years to the day after Lincoln was shot. Eleanor remembered Millard Lampell's poem "The Lonesome Train":

"A lonesome train on a lonesome track,
Seven coaches painted black. . . .
A slow train, a quiet train,
Carrying Lincoln home again. . . ."

The train wove back and forth but always returned to a bearing on north. Perhaps it was in Roosevelt's home that the main clues to his character lay. William James, borrowing from Cardinal Newman, spoke of the "once-born," those who easily fitted into the ideology of their time, and of those "sick souls" and "divided selves" who went through a second birth, seizing on a second ideology. Roosevelt was one of the once-born. His identity was formed in a stable and harmonious family; he moved securely and surely from the pedestal of the only child of doting parents into the wider but equally untroubled environments of Hyde Park, Groton, and Harvard friendships. If his loving references to his Hyde Park home were not revealing enough of his sense of identity and of roots, his habit all through his presidency of reducing policies and programs to terms of home and family would have betrayed his thinking; thus the Good Neighbor policy, the Big Four constables or policemen, the Lend-Lease "garden hose"; his idea that new institutions like the United Nations must toddle like a child for a few years before gaining strength; his repeated references to heads of state sitting around the table like members of the same family, or like neighbors, and his suggestion on at least one occasion that the best way to keep peace in a family—he was referring to de Gaulle and the other Frenchmen—was to keep the members of the family *apart*.

With an assurance undergirded by this sense of identity, Roosevelt moved from Groton and Harvard into the muckraking decade of Theodore Roosevelt, into the simmering politics of the Hudson Valley, into the reformist and idealistic mood of the Wilson years. It was with this assurance, sometimes bordering on arrogance, that he could confront and overcome his domestic adversaries of the 1930's—and do so without personal hatred for a Huey Long, a Carter Glass, a Norman Thomas, an Al Smith, or a Wendell Willkie. He reserved his hatred for people in his own social world, such as Hamilton Fish, who he felt had betrayed him; as they did for him.

He embraced the ideology of freedom not with the demonic passion of the true believer who possesses a creed and ends up being possessed by it, but with the easy assurance of a man who slowly fashions his political faith, borrowing from the thinkers and political leaders of the day, reshaping his ideas as he undergoes new experiences and lives through changing times—and hence can, when necessary, keep his distance from its possessive demands. He overcame his adversaries not only because he outwitted and outmaneuvered and outstayed them, but also because he outsermonized and outmoralized them. Only a man deadly serious and supremely self-assured could have spent the time Roosevelt did appealing to old-fashioned moralisms of home and school, the Golden Rule and the Ten Commandments as interpreted by Endicott Peabody, the maxims of freedom as practiced by Wilson and Al Smith, the "simple rules of human conduct to which we always go back," as he said in 1932. So certain was he of the rightness of his aims that he was willing to use Machiavellian means to reach them; and his moral certainty made him all the more effective in the struggle. He used the tricks of the fox to serve the purposes of the lion.

People in northern Virginia and Washington felt they had never known such a lovely spring. On the warm and windless morning of Saturday, April 14, the lilacs and azaleas were in full bloom. The funeral train rolled through woods spattered with showers of dogwood, crossed the Potomac, and pulled into Union Station. Thousands waited outside in the plaza, as they had so often before. Anna, Elliott, and Elliott's wife entered the rear car; President Truman and his Cabinet followed. Then the soldier's funeral procession began—armored troops, truck-borne infantry, the Marine band, a battalion of Annapolis midshipmen, the Navy band, WAC's, WAVES, SPAR's, women Marines, then a small, black-draped caisson carrying the coffin, drawn by six white horses, with a seventh serving as outrider. Army bombers thundered overhead.

"It was a processional of terrible simplicity and a march too solemn for tears," William S. White wrote, "except here and there where someone wept alone. It was a march, for all its restrained and slight military display, characterized not by this or by the thousands of flags that hung limply everywhere but by a mass attitude of unuttered, unmistakable prayer."

In front of the White House the coffin was lifted from the caisson while the national anthem was played, carried up the front steps, and wheeled down a long red carpet to the East Room. Here where Lincoln had lain, banks of lilies covered the walls. The President, Cabinet members, Supreme Court justices, labor leaders, diplomats, politicians, agency heads crowded into the room and spilled over into the Blue Room. At the close of his prayer, Bishop Dun paused and quoted from the First Inaugural: ". . . Let me assert my firm belief that the only thing we have to fear is fear itself. . . ."

Eleanor Roosevelt rose and left the room; then the others filed out. Later, upstairs, she came into Anna's room, in anguish. She had heard in Warm Springs, from a relative, about Lucy Rutherfurd's visits; she had heard that Lucy had been with her husband when he died. Her daughter must have known of this; why had she not told her? Mother and daughter confronted each other tensely. Then, as always, Eleanor Roosevelt steadied herself. She returned to the East Room, had the casket opened, and dropped in some flowers. Then the casket was sealed for good. Later in the evening the funeral cortege went back to Union Station. Crowds still lined the avenues. The presidential train, with seventeen cars filled with officials and politicians, pulled out before midnight.

DEMOCRACY'S ARISTOCRAT

The train had brought Roosevelt's body up through Virginia, the land of Washington and Jefferson; now, from the capital all the way to Hyde Park, he would be following the route of Abraham Lincoln's last journey, and people would be thinking of the strange parallels between the two—the sudden, unbelievable deaths, the end for each coming in the final weeks of terrible wars, the same April dates—and of things that seemed to be more than coincidence. Both men had been perplexing combinations of caution and courage, of practicality and principle; both had taken their countries into war only after *faits accomplis* had allowed it; both had acted for black Americans only under great pressure.

Through the long night, under weeping clouds, the train moved north, through Baltimore to Wilmington to Philadelphia. And everywhere it was as it had been eighty years before:

> "When lilacs last in the dooryard bloom'd. . . .
> With the waiting depot, the arriving coffin, and the somber faces,
> With dirges through the night, with the thousand voices rising strong and solemn. . . ."

After all his delays and evasions, Lincoln had won standing as a world hero, through emancipation and victory and martyrdom, but Roosevelt—what kind of hero was Roosevelt? Some close observers felt that people exaggerated Roosevelt's political courage. Clare Boothe Luce remarked that every great leader had his typical gesture—Hitler the upraised arm, Churchill the V sign. Roosevelt? She wet her index finger and held it up. Many others noted Roosevelt's cautiousness, even timidity. Instead of appealing to the people directly on great developing issues and taking clear and forthright action to anticipate emergencies, he typically allowed problems to fester and come to a head in the form of dramatic issues before acting with decision. He often took bold positions only to retreat from them in subsequent words or actions. He seemed unduly sensitive to both congressional and public opinion; he used public-opinion polls much more systematically than was realized at the time, even to the point one time of polling people on the question of who should succeed Knox as Secretary of the Navy (Stassen lost). His arresting speeches gave him a reputation as the fearless leader, but he spent far more time feinting and parrying in everyday politics than in mobilizing the country behind crucial decisions.

Around 2:00 A.M. the train crossed into New Jersey, the state where Woodrow Wilson had plunged into politics as a reformer, while young Roosevelt, impressed, watched from Hyde Park and Albany. Old Wilsonians later had compared Roosevelt unfavorably to the great idealist who had gone down fighting for his dream. Roosevelt, too, had watched that performance—had been part of it—and had drawn his conclusions from it. Sherwood remembered him sitting at the end of the long table in the Cabinet room and looking up at the portrait of his onetime chief over the mantelpiece; the tragedy of Wilson, Sherwood said, was always somewhere within the rim of his consciousness.

"The tragedy of Wilson . . ." There were some who said that this was merely a personal tragedy for the man and a temporary tragedy for the nation and the world, that the prophetic warnings of the great crusader had been vindicated so dramatically by the collapse of the balance of power twenty years later that Wilson's very defeat had made possible American commitment to a new international organization. Roosevelt did not share this view. He had no wish to be a martyr, to be vindicated only a generation later. He believed in moving on a wide, short front, pushing ahead here, retreating there, temporizing elsewhere, moving audaciously only when forces were leaning his way, so that one quick stroke—perhaps only a symbolic stroke, like a speech—would start in his direction the movement of press and public opinion, of Congress, his own administration, foreign peoples and governments. All this he could do only from a position of power, from the pulpit of the presidency. To gain power meant winning elections; and to win elections required endless concessions to expediency and compromises with his own ideals.

Projected onto the international plane this strategy demanded of Roosevelt not only the usual expediency and opportunism but also a willingness to compromise with men and forces antagonistic to the ideals of Endicott Peabody and Woodrow Wilson. Again and again, self-consciously and indeed with bravado, he "walked with the devil" of the far left or far right, in his deals with Darlan and Badoglio, his toleration of Franco, his concessions to Stalin. Yet this self-confessed, if temporary, companion of Satan was also a Christian soldier striving for principles of democracy and freedom that he set forth with unsurpassed eloquence and persistence.

Did he then not "mean it"? So Roosevelt's enemies charged. It was all a trick, they said, to bamboozle the American people or their allies, to perpetuate himself in power, or to achieve some other sinister purpose. But it seems clear that Roosevelt did mean it, if meaning it is defined as intensity of personal conviction rooted in an ideological commitment. "Oh—he sometimes tries to appear tough and cynical and flippant, but that's an act he likes to put on, especially at press conferences," Hopkins said to Sherwood. "He wants to make the boys think he's hard-boiled. Maybe he fools some of them, now and then—but don't ever let him fool you, or you won't be any use to him. You can see the real Roosevelt when he comes out with something like the Four Freedoms. And don't get the idea that those are only catch phrases. *He believes them. . . .*"

Roosevelt, like Lincoln and Wilson, died fighting for his ideals. It might have been more dramatic if he had been assassinated by an ideological foe or had been stricken during a speech. But his decisions to aid Britain and Russia, his daring to take a position before the 1944 election against the Senate having direct power over America's peace-enforcing efforts in the proposed Council of the United Nations, his long, exhausting trips to Teheran and Yalta, his patient efforts to win Stalin's personal friendship, his willingness to go out on a limb in his belief that the United States and the Soviet Union could work together in the postwar world—all this testified to the depth of his conviction.

Yet he could believe with equal conviction that his prime duty was to defend his nation's interests, safeguard its youth, win the war as quickly as possible, protect its postwar economy. With his unconquerable optimism he felt that he could do both things—pursue global ideals and national *Realpolitik*—simultaneously. So he tried to win Soviet friendship and confidence at the same time he saved American lives by consenting to the delay in the cross-channel invasion, thus letting the Red Army bleed. He paid tribute to the brotherly spirit of global science just before he died even while he was withholding atomic information from his partners the Russians. He wanted to unite liberal Democrats and internationalist Republicans in one progressive party but he never did the spadework or took the personal political risks that such a strategy required. He yearned to help Indians and other Asiatic peoples gain their independence, but not at the risk of disrupting his military coalition with Britain and other Atlantic nations with colonial possessions in Asia. He ardently hoped to bring a strong, united, and democratic China into the Big Four, but he refused to apply to Chungking the military resources and political pressure necessary to arrest the dry rot in that country. Above all, he wanted to build a strong postwar international organization, but he dared not surrender his country's substantive veto in the Council over peace-keeping, and as a practical matter he seemed more committed to Big Four, great-power peace-keeping than he did to a federation acting for the brotherhood of all mankind.

"I dream dreams but am, at the same time, an intensely practical person," Roosevelt wrote to Smuts during the war. Both his dreams and his practicality were admirable; the problem lay in the relation between the two. He failed to work out the intermediary ends and means necessary to accomplish his purposes. Partly because of his disbelief in planning far ahead, partly because he elevated short-run goals over long-run, and always because of his experience and temperament, he did not fashion the structure of action—the full array of mutually consistent means, political, economic, psychological, military—necessary to realize his paramount ends.

So the more he preached his lofty ends and practiced his limited means, the more he reflected and encouraged the old habit of the American democracy to "praise the Lord—and keep your powder dry" and the more he widened the gap between popular expectations and actual possibilities. Not only did this derangement of ends and means lead to crushed hopes, disillusion, and cynicism at home, but it helped sow the seeds of the Cold War during World War II, as the Kremlin contrasted Roosevelt's coalition rhetoric with his Atlantic First strategy and falsely suspected a bourgeois conspiracy to destroy Soviet Communism; and Indians and Chinese contrasted Roosevelt's anticolonial words with his military concessions to colonial powers, and falsely inferred that he was an imperialist at heart and a hypocrite to boot.

Roosevelt's critics attacked him as naïve, ignorant, amateurish in foreign affairs, but this man who had bested all his domestic enemies and most of his foreign was no innocent. His supreme difficulty lay not in his views as to what *was*—he had a Shakespearian appreciation of all the failings, vices, cruelties, and complexities of man—but of what *could be.* The last words he ever wrote, on the eve of his death, were the truest words he ever wrote. He had a strong and active faith, a huge and unprovable faith, in the possibilities of human understanding, trust, and love. He could say with Reinhold Niebuhr that love is the law of life even when people do not live by the law of love.

It was still dark when the train drew into Pennsylvania Station. New York had been alive with rumors that Jack Dempsey or Frank Sinatra or some other celebrity had died, too. At the time of Roosevelt's funeral service in the White House, New York City news presses stopped rolling, radios went silent, subway trains came to a halt, police held up traffic. In Carnegie Hall the Boston Symphony Orchestra, under Serge Koussevitzky, played Beethoven's "Eroica" Symphony. Roosevelt's train paused for a time at the Mott Haven railroad yards in the Bronx, then moved across Hell Gate and up the New York Central lines on the east bank of the Hudson—the route that Roosevelt had taken so often before.

LAST TRIBUTE

Newspapers were still reporting people's reactions around the world—still reporting the shock, incredulity, and fear, but above all the sense of having lost a friend. In Moscow, black-bordered flags flew at half mast; Soviet newspapers, which invariably printed foreign news on the back page, published the news of Roosevelt's death and his picture on page one. The theme of the editorials in Russia was friendship. Many Russians were seen weeping in the street. The *Court Circular* of Buckingham Palace broke ancient precedent by reporting the death of a chief of state not related to the British ruling family; Roosevelt would have been pleased. In Chungking, a coolie read the wall newspapers, newly wet with shiny black ink, and turned away muttering *"Tai tsamsso liao"* ("It was too soon that he died"). "Your President is dead," an Indian said to a passing GI, "a friend of poor. . . ." Everywhere, noted Anne O'Hare McCormick, the refrain was "We have lost a friend."

It was this enormous fund of friendship on which Roosevelt expected to draw in carrying out his hopes for the postwar world. He expected to combine his friendships with captains and kings and his standing with masses of people with his political skills and the resources of his nation to strengthen the United Nations, maintain good relations with the Soviets, help the Chinese realize the Four Freedoms, discourage European colonialism in Asia and Africa. But all depended on his being on deck, being in the White House.

The train threaded its way along the curving tracks on the bank of the Hudson, passing the towering palisades across the river—High Tor, Sugar Loaf, Storm King. At Garrison, opposite West Point, men removed their hats just as they had done at Garrison's Landing eighty years before. Then Cold Spring, Beacon, Poughkeepsie, on the bank of the Hudson, the river of American politics.

Around the world men who had known Roosevelt were struggling to phrase their eulogies. Churchill was preparing a tribute for Parliament, but he would say nothing more cogently than his Teheran toast to Roosevelt as a leader who had "guided his country along the tumultuous stream of party friction and internal politics amidst the violent freedom of democracy." Ivan Maisky would remember him as a statesman of very great caliber, with an acute mind, a wide sweep in action, vast energy, but in the end essentially bourgeois, flesh of the flesh of the American ruling class. John Buchan felt that he had never met a man more fecund in ideas; Robert Sherwood found him spiritually the healthiest man he had ever known; Henry Stimson called him an ideal war commander in chief, the greatest war President the nation had ever had. Young Congressman Lyndon Johnson, grieving over the news of the death of his friend, said Roosevelt was the only person he had ever known who was never afraid. "God, how he could take it for us all!"

A second-rate intellect, Oliver Wendell Holmes had called him, but a first-rate temperament. To examine closely single aspects of Roosevelt's character—as thinker, as organizer, as manipulator, as strategist, as idealist—is to see failings and deficiencies interwoven with the huge capacities. But to stand back and look at the man as a whole, against the backdrop of his people and his times, is to see the lineaments of greatness—courage, joyousness, responsiveness, vitality, faith. A democrat in manner and conviction, he was yet a member of that small aristocracy once described by E. M. Forster—sensitive but not weak, considerate but not fussy, plucky in his power to endure, capable of laughing and of taking a joke. He was the true happy warrior.

VOYAGER'S RETURN

"All that is within me cries out to go back to my home on the Hudson River," Roosevelt had said nine months before. The train, still hugging the riverbank, crossed from Poughkeepsie into Hyde Park. It was Sunday, April 15, 1945, a clear day, the sky a deep blue. Tiny waves were breaking against the river shore where the train slowed and switched off into a siding below the bluff on which the mansion stood. Cannon sounded twenty-one times as the coffin was moved from the train to a caisson drawn by six brown horses. Standing behind was a seventh horse, hooded, stirrups reversed, sword and boots turned upside down hanging from the left stirrup—symbolic of a lost warrior.

Following the beat of muffled drums the little procession toiled up the steep, winding, graveled road, past a small stream running full and fast, past the ice pond, with its surface a smoky jade under the overhanging hemlocks, past the budding apple trees and the lilacs and the open field, and emerged onto the height. In back of the house, standing in the rose garden framed by the hemlock hedge, was a large assembly: President Truman and his Cabinet and officialdom of the old administration and family and friends and retainers, a phalanx of six hundred West Point cadets standing rigidly at attention in their gray uniforms and white crossed belts. Behind the coffin, borne now by eight servicemen, Eleanor Roosevelt and her daughter, Anna, and her son Elliott moved into the rose garden.

The aged rector of St. James Episcopal Church of Hyde Park prayed—". . . earth to earth, ashes to ashes, dust to dust." Raising his hand as the servicemen lowered the body slowly into the grave, he intoned:

> "Now the laborer's task is o'er,
> Now the battle day is past,
> Now upon the farther shore
> Lands the voyager at last. . . ."

A breeze off the Hudson ruffled the trees above. Cadets fired three volleys. A bugler played the haunting notes of Taps. The soldier was home.

ACKNOWLEDGMENTS

THIS SECOND volume on Franklin D. Roosevelt, like my first, has had to be an exercise in collective scholarship because of the enormous scope and complexity of both the materials and the problems analyzed. I thank warmly the following, who served as my research associates and who labored with me, and without me, for long days in the records, and made major substantive contributions: Mrs. John W. Baer, of Annapolis, who worked in the Washington, D.C. collections and had an appreciative eye for significant data; Douglas D. Rose, who conducted research primarily at the Franklin D. Roosevelt Library, discussed major research and substantive problems with me, worked out significant theoretical approaches to several questions, wrote drafts of several sections of chapters (as indicated in the chapter bibliographies), criticized drafts of my own chapters, and did all this with style, wit, wisdom, and a dash of iconoclasm; and Stewart Burns, who did research and writing on scientific and other aspects of war mobilization, drafted sections on these aspects, as noted elsewhere, and, despite his keen aversion to all things military, brought detachment as well as insight to the questions he studied. Sally Burns also assisted on research, especially on data relating to Roosevelt's health; and Kate Rose helped on research and brought pungency and good humor to her reviews of my manuscript.

From his broad and penetrating knowledge of American diplomatic history, Russell H. Bastert, of Williams College, made criticisms of my manuscript, as did John Morton Blum, of Yale, from his masterly studies of the Roosevelt and earlier presidencies. Robert C. L. Scott, of Williams College, brought to bear on my draft his versatility and fine judgment on history. Forrest Pogue, writer of authoritative studies of World War II generalship, made numerous suggestions for improving the manuscript. I am grateful to these busy men for sharing their knowledge and judgment so generously.

A. A. Foursenko, Institute of History, Leningrad; Martin Gilbert, Merton College, Oxford; Kurt Tauber, Williams College; and Gordon Wright, Stanford University (formerly Cultural Attaché, American Embassy, Paris), assisted me in arranging interviews with historians and others in the Soviet Union, Great Britain, Germany, and France, respectively. With these four scholars, too, I enjoyed substantive discussions of World War II historiography.

Mrs. Anna Roosevelt Halsted assisted me in gaining access to important materials bearing on her father's presidency. Paula Levine (Mrs. Richard

Lewis Gaines) helped me locate data at the Williams College and other libraries. Paul W. Streicker conducted research at the Franklin D. Roosevelt Library, concentrating on tabulating and interpreting public-opinion data. Professor Benedict J. Duffy, Jr., M.D., of the Tufts University School of Medicine, and Dr. James A. Halsted advised me on the interpretation of data bearing on Roosevelt's health.

Pamela L. Buck made special translations from the Russian, and Gisela C. Dittmer from the German.

My editor at Harcourt Brace Jovanovich, William B. Goodman, was knowledgeable, demanding, and compassionate; Roberta Leighton edited the manuscript with her usual grace and skill.

All these people I thank; I thank, above all, my most beloved and constructive critic, Joan Simpson Burns.

GENERAL BIBLIOGRAPHY

Research on Franklin D. Roosevelt's first two presidential terms, and on his earlier years, must be undertaken largely at the Franklin D. Roosevelt Library (FDRL). Research on the war years requires, as well, the use of a great many other libraries and archives, though FDRL still remains primary. The difficulty in consulting records on a man and presidency of such enormous scope was matched only by the unvarying helpfulness of archivists and librarians, whether American, British, or Russian. Of great help, too, were the bibliographies of the period, of which I will mention only two here: Louis Morton, "Sources for the History of World War II," *World Politics,* Vol. XIII, April 1961, pp. 435-453; and William J. Stewart, compiler and editor, *The Era of Franklin D. Roosevelt* (Hyde Park, N.Y.: The Franklin D. Roosevelt Library, 1967), especially pp. 960-1278, an extensive bibliography of periodical and dissertation literature.

At the Roosevelt Library, the collections of which I described briefly in *Roosevelt: The Lion and the Fox,* pp. 490-491, I have used many of the sets of papers that were useful for the first volume: President's Personal File (PPF), Official File (OF), President's Secretary's File (PSF), Press Conferences (PC), the Harry L. Hopkins Papers (HHP). For this volume, the Hopkins Papers have continued to be indispensable, as have the following: President's Map Room Papers (PMRP), PSF Safe File, Oscar Cox Diary, Harold Smith Diary, and many others that are noted in the chapter bibliographies. The major files are subdivided into numerous separate files, organized by name or subject.

Other major collections or archives I have used are:

1. The Manuscript Division, Library of Congress: papers of Henry H. Arnold, Raymond Clapper, Joseph E. Davies, Felix Frankfurter, Cordell Hull, Frank Knox, Henrietta Nesbitt, George W. Norris, Robert Patterson, Francis B. Sayre, Laurence A. Steinhardt, William Allen White, Wendell L. Willkie; and diaries of Clapper, Mrs. Nesbitt, and William D. Leahy.

2. Transcripts of interviews, Oral History Project, Columbia University: Harvey H. Bundy, John Carmody, Thomas C. Hart, Gardner Jackson, Arthur Krock, Herbert Lehman, William Phillips, Norman Thomas, and others.

3. National Archives, especially the records of the State Department and of the Army. The State Department records are a useful supplement to, and check on, the invaluable compilation *Foreign Relations of the United States.* The Army records are too vast and variegated even to be sum-

marized here; they are referred to in the chapter bibliographies, as are the State Department records.

4. Henry L. Stimson Diary and Papers, Yale University Library: these two sets of documents are rich in factual material, Stimson's day-to-day observations, and more formal records; they are indispensable to a study of the war administration.

5. Other important sources: Harry S. Truman Library; Princeton University Library (Forrestal Papers); Brandeis University (David Niles Papers, through the courtesy of A. L. Sachar); Widener Library; in Great Britain: the British Museum, the Foreign Office Library, the Imperial War Museum; in the Soviet Union: the Moscow State Library. I thank the personnel of all these institutions for their unfailing courtesy.

In conversations that were not so much formal interviews as attempts to look back at the period through the eyes of participants, I have had the benefit of the views of: Lord Avon (Anthony Eden), V. Berezhkov, Adolf A. Berle, David Bruce, Randolph Churchill, Ernest Cuneo, Jonathan Daniels, Thomas E. Dewey, Morris Ernst, Anna Roosevelt Halsted, Mrs. Harold L. Ickes, Archibald MacLeish, Ivan Maisky, Samuel I. Rosenman, Grace Tully.

Writing of so international a figure as Roosevelt during his leadership of a world coalition imposes on the historian a special responsibility to understand the perspectives of historians in other countries. I greatly appreciated the opportunity to discuss aspects of the war period, especially of grand strategy, with the following persons:

In Britain: H. C. Allen and his colleagues at the Institute of United States Studies; D. N. Dilks, London School of Economics; John Ehrman; Michael Howard, then of the University of London; Arnold Toynbee, Chatham House; D. C. Watt, Chatham House.

In France: Jean Baptiste Duroselle; André Fontaine.

In Germany: Waldemar Besson, University of Konstanz; Ossip Flechtheim, Free University of Berlin; Andreas Hillgruber, University of Freiburg; Hans-Adolf Jacobsen, Bonn University; Jurgen Röhwer, Library for Contemporary History, Stuttgart; and Hermann Graml, Lothar Gruchmann, and Thilo Vogelsang, Institute for Contemporary History, Munich.

In the Soviet Union: Youri L. Kouznets, Leningrad University; Georgi A. Arbatov, A. A. Gromyko, N. N. Yakovlev, and their colleagues at the Institute of the United States of America; V. Berezhkov (Stalin's interpreter), *New Times;* historians at the Institute for Soviet-American Relations; Professor Silachov and his colleagues at the History Department, Moscow State University; G. Deborin, Marx-Lenin Institute. I also benefited immeasurably from lengthy exchanges of views that I had with members of the Institute of History, Soviet Academy of Sciences, in both Leningrad and Moscow, when I lectured there in 1963. I thank all the above scholars for their hospitality and courtesies.

Ernest Cuneo, Morris Ernst, and Samuel I. Rosenman not only counseled me at length on aspects of the war period, but also supplied me with personal documents. The late Hadley Cantril, of Princeton, generously lent me his extensive notebooks, consisting of the results both of the polls he conducted and of other polls, and of his correspondence with the many persons through whom the results and conclusions were channeled to the President. The Roper Public Opinion Research Center at Williams College assisted me in obtaining and interpreting public-opinion data. The staff of the Williams College Library was, as always, helpful and obliging.

CHAPTER BIBLIOGRAPHIES

The following abbreviations are used in citations in the chapter bibliographies:

AR	Army Records, National Archives
FDRL	Franklin D. Roosevelt Library, Hyde Park, New York
FRUS	*Foreign Relations of the United States,* Washington, D.C., cited by year and volume except for special-subject volumes, which are cited by title
HHP	Harry Hopkins Papers, Franklin D. Roosevelt Library
HSTL	Harry S. Truman Library, Independence, Missouri
LC	Library of Congress, Washington, D.C.
NA	National Archives, Washington, D.C.
NYT	The New York *Times*
OF	Official Files, Franklin D. Roosevelt Library
OHP	Oral History Project, Columbia University
PC	Press Conferences, Franklin D. Roosevelt Library
PHA	*Pearl Harbor Attack,* see Basic Book List
PL	Elliott Roosevelt (ed.), *F.D.R.: His Personal Letters* (New York: Duell, Sloan and Pearce, 1950), Vol. II
PMRP	President's Map Room Papers, Franklin D. Roosevelt Library
PPA	Samuel I. Rosenman (ed.), *The Public Papers and Addresses of Franklin D. Roosevelt,* Volumes 1941–1944-5 (4 vols., New York: Harper & Brothers, 1950). Cited by year volume covers
PPF	President's Personal File, Franklin D. Roosevelt Library
PSF	President's Secretary's File, Franklin D. Roosevelt Library
SD	State Department

Books cited in the chapter bibliographies were published in New York City unless otherwise noted. When the author's last name alone is used, the full citation will be found either in the Basic Book List, if that author has been cited in more than one chapter, or in the chapter bibliography. Thus the Basic Book List contains names of only those works cited in more than one chapter. An author's name with a superior number (Pogue [1]) is used when the Basic Book List contains more than one book by that author; the list provides the key to the particular book. In most cases where documents have been faithfully reproduced in published secondary sources I have cited the latter for the sake of readier accessibility to the reader.

BASIC BOOK LIST

Acheson, Dean, *Present at the Creation* (New York: W. W. Norton & Company, Inc., 1969)

Allen, George E., *Presidents Who Have Known Me* (New York: Simon and Schuster, Inc., 1950)

Arnold, Henry H., *Global Mission* (New York: Harper & Brothers, 1949)

Asbell, Bernard, *When F.D.R. Died* (New York: Holt, Rinehart & Winston, Inc., 1961)

Barkley, Alben W., *That Reminds Me* (Garden City, N.Y.: Doubleday & Company, Inc., 1954)

Barnard, Ellsworth, *Wendell Willkie* (Marquette, Mich.: Northern Michigan University Press, 1966)

Baruch, Bernard M., *Baruch: The Public Years* (New York: Holt, Rinehart & Winston, Inc., 1960)

Baxter, James Phinney, 3rd, *Scientists Against Time* (Boston: Little, Brown and Company, 1946)

Berezhkov, Valentin, *Teheran, 1943* (Moskva: Izdatel'stvo agentstva pechati novosti, 1968)

Biddle, Francis, *In Brief Authority* (Garden City, N.Y.: Doubleday & Company, Inc., 1962)

Bloom, Sol, *The Autobiography of Sol Bloom* (New York: G. P. Putnam's Sons, 1948)

Blum, John Morton, *From the Morgenthau Diaries* (Boston: Houghton Mifflin Company). Vol. II, *Years of Urgency, 1938-1941* (1965): Blum[1]. Vol. III, *Years of War, 1941-1945* (1967): Blum[2]

Bohlen, Charles E., *The Transformation of American Foreign Policy* (New York: W. W. Norton & Company, Inc., 1969)

Bradley, Omar N., *A Soldier's Story* (New York: Henry Holt & Company, Inc., 1951)

Bryant, Arthur, *Triumph in the West* (London: William Collins Sons & Co. Ltd., 1959): Bryant[1]

—, *The Turn of the Tide* (Garden City, N.Y.: Doubleday & Company, Inc., 1957): Bryant[2]

Buchanan, A. Russell, *The United States and World War II* (2 vols., New York: Harper & Row, 1964)

Bullock, Alan, *Hitler: A Study in Tyranny* (New York: Harper & Brothers, 1953)

Burns, James MacGregor, *Roosevelt: The Lion and the Fox* (New York: Harcourt, Brace and Company, 1956)

Bush, Vannevar, *Science: The Endless Frontier* (Washington, D.C.: National Science Foundation, 1945)

Butler, J. R M., *Grand Strategy*. Vol. II, September 1939-June 1941 (London: H. M. Stationery Office, 1957)

Butow, Robert J. C., *Tojo and the Coming of the War* (Princeton, N.J.: Princeton University Press, 1961)

Buttinger, Joseph, *Vietnam: A Dragon Embattled* (2 vols., New York: Frederick A. Praeger, Inc., 1967)

Byrnes, James F., *All in One Lifetime* (New York: Harper & Brothers, 1958)

Cairo-Teheran: Foreign Relations of the United States. The Conferences at Cairo and Teheran 1943 (Washington, D.C.: U.S. Government Printing Office, 1961)

Cantril, Hadley (ed.), *Public Opinion 1935-1946* (Princeton, N.J.: Princeton University Press, 1951)

Celler, Emanuel, *You Never Leave Brooklyn* (New York: The John Day Company, Inc., 1953)

Churchill, Winston, *The Second World War* (Boston: Houghton Mifflin Company, 1948-1953). Vol. I, *The Gathering Storm* (1948): Churchill[1]. Vol. II, *Their Finest Hour* (1949): Churchill[2]. Vol. III, *The Grand Alliance* (1950): Churchill[3]. Vol. IV, *The Hinge of Fate* (1950): Churchill[4]. Vol. V, *Closing the Ring* (1951): Churchill[5]. Vol. VI, *Triumph and Tragedy* (1953): Churchill[6]

Ciano, Galeazzo, *The Ciano Diaries,* Hugh Gibson, ed. (Garden City, N.Y.: Doubleday & Company, Inc., 1946)

Civilian Production Administration, *Industrial Mobilization for War.* Vol. I, *Program and Administration* (Washington, D.C.: Bureau of Demobilization, 1947)

Clark, Alan, *Barbarossa: The Russian-German Conflict, 1941-45* (New York: William Morrow & Co., Inc., 1965)

Cline, Ray S., *Washington Command Post: The Operations Division* (Washington, D.C.: Office of the Chief of Military History, 1951)

Coit, Margaret L., *Mr. Baruch* (Boston: Houghton Mifflin Company, 1957)

Connally, Tom, *My Name Is Tom Connally* (New York: Thomas Y. Crowell Company, 1954)

Correspondence Between the Chairman of the Council of Ministers of the U.S.S.R. and the Presidents of the U.S.A. and the Prime Ministers of Great Britain During the Great Patriotic War of 1941-1945 (Moscow: Foreign Languages Publishing House, 1957). Vol. I, *Correspondence with Winston S. Churchill and Clement R. Attlee: Correspondence*[1]. Vol. II, *Correspondence with Franklin D. Roosevelt and Harry S. Truman: Correspondence*[2]

Craven, Frank C., and James L. Cate, *The Army Air Forces in World War II* (7 vols., Chicago: University of Chicago Press, 1948-1958)

Current, Richard N., *Secretary Stimson* (New Brunswick, N.J.: Rutgers University Press, 1954)

Dallin, David J., *Soviet Russia's Foreign Policy, 1939-1942* (New Haven, Conn.: Yale University Press, 1942)

Daniels, Jonathan, *The End of Innocence* (Philadelphia: J. B. Lippincott Co., 1954): Daniels[1]

—, *Washington Quadrille* (Garden City, N.Y.: Doubleday & Company, Inc., 1968): Daniels[2]

Davis, Nuel Pharr, *Lawrence and Oppenheimer* (New York: Simon and Schuster, Inc., 1968)

de Gaulle, Charles, *War Memoirs.* Vol. II, *Unity* (New York: Simon and Schuster, Inc., 1959)

Deakin, F. W., *The Brutal Friendship: Mussolini, Hitler and the Fall of Italian Fascism* (New York: Harper & Row, 1962)
Deane, John R., *The Strange Alliance* (New York: The Viking Press, 1947)
Deborin, G., *The Second World War* (Moscow: Progress Publishers, n.d.)
Deutscher, Isaac, *Stalin, a Political Biography* (London and New York: Oxford University Press, 1949)
Divine, Robert A., *Roosevelt and World War II* (Baltimore: The Johns Hopkins Press, 1969)
Djilas, Milovan, *Conversations with Stalin* (New York: Harcourt, Brace & World, Inc., 1962)
Drury, Allen, *A Senate Journal, 1943-1945* (New York: McGraw-Hill Book Company, 1963)
Eccles, Marriner S., *Beckoning Frontiers* (New York: Alfred A. Knopf, Inc., 1951)
Eden, Anthony (The Earl of Avon), *The Eden Memoirs: The Reckoning* (London: Cassell & Co., Ltd., 1965)
Ehrman, John, *Grand Strategy* (London: H. M. Stationery Office). Vol. V (1956): Ehrman[1]. Vol. VI (1956): Ehrman[2]
Ehrenburg, Ilya, *The War: 1941-45* (Cleveland: The World Publishing Company, 1965)
Eisenhower, Dwight D., *Crusade in Europe* (Garden City, N.Y.: Garden City Books, 1948)
Fairchild, Byron, and Jonathan Grossman, *The Army and Industrial Manpower* (Washington, D.C.: Office of the Chief of Military History, 1959)
Farago, Ladislas, *The Broken Seal* (New York: Random House, Inc., 1967)
Fehrenbach, T. R., *F.D.R.'s Undeclared War* (New York: David McKay Co., Inc., 1967)
Feis, Herbert, *The Atomic Bomb and the End of World War II* (Princeton, N.J.: Princeton University Press, 1966): Feis[1]
—, *The China Tangle* (Princeton, N.J.: Princeton University Press, 1953): Feis[2]
—, *Churchill—Roosevelt—Stalin* (Princeton, N.J.: Princeton University Press, 1957): Feis[3]
—, *The Road to Pearl Harbor* (Princeton, N.J.: Princeton University Press, 1950): Feis[4]
Flynn, Edward J., *You're the Boss* (New York: Collier Books, 1962)
Flynn, John T., *The Roosevelt Myth* (New York: The Devin-Adair Co., 1948)
Foreign Relations of the United States, 1940-1945 (Washington, D.C.: State Department Series). Cited by year and volume, except for major subject volumes, which are cited in Basic Book List and in chapter bibliographies by subject title—*i.e., Malta-Yalta.*
Forrestal, James, *The Forrestal Diaries,* Walter Millis, ed. (New York: The Viking Press, 1951)
Frankland, Noble, *The Bombing Offensive Against Germany* (London: Faber & Faber Ltd., 1965)

Freedman, Max (annotator), *Roosevelt and Frankfurter: Their Correspondence, 1928-1945* (Boston: Little, Brown and Company, 1967)

Friedländer, Saul, *Pius XII and the Third Reich* (New York: Alfred A. Knopf, Inc., 1966): Friedländer[1]

—, *Prelude to Downfall: Hitler and the United States, 1939-1941* (New York: Alfred A. Knopf, Inc., 1967): Friedländer[2]

FRUS–Japan: *Foreign Relations of the United States.* Vol. II, *Japan: 1931-1941* (Washington, D.C.: State Department, 1943)

Führer Conferences on Matters Dealing with the German Navy (Washington, D.C.: Office of Naval Intelligence, 1947)

Fuller, J. F. C., *The Second World War* (London: Eyre & Spottiswoode (Publishers) Ltd., 1948)

Garland, Albert N., and Howard McGraw Smyth, *Sicily and the Surrender of Italy* (Washington, D.C.: Office of the Chief of Military History, 1965)

Gowing, Margaret, *Britain and Atomic Energy, 1939-1945* (London: Macmillan & Co. Ltd., 1964)

Green, Constance McLaughlin, Harry C. Thomson, and Peter C. Roots, *The Ordance Department: Planning Munitions for War* (Washington, D.C.: Office of the Chief of Military History, 1955)

Greenfield, Kent Roberts, *American Strategy in World War II: A Reconsideration* (Baltimore: The Johns Hopkins Press, 1963): Greenfield[1]

—, (ed.), *Command Decisions* (New York: Harcourt, Brace and Company, 1959): Greenfield[2]

Grew, Joseph C., *Turbulent Era,* Vol. II (Boston: Houghton Mifflin Company, 1952)

Groves, Leslie R., *Now It Can Be Told* (New York: Harper & Brothers, 1962)

Gunther, John, *Roosevelt in Retrospect* (New York: Harper & Brothers, 1950)

Gwyer, J. M. A., and J. R. M. Butler, *Grand Strategy,* Vol. III (London: H. M. Stationery Office, 1964)

Hammer, Ellen J., *The Struggle for Indochina* (Stanford, Calif.: Stanford University Press, 1954)

Harrison, Gordon A., *Cross-Channel Attack* (Washington, D.C.: Office of the Chief of Military History, 1951)

Hassett, William D., *Off the Record with F.D.R.* (New Brunswick, N.J.: Rutgers University Press, 1958)

Heinrichs, Waldo H., Jr., *American Ambassador* (Boston: Little, Brown and Company, 1966)

Hewlett, Richard G., and Oscar E. Anderson, Jr., *The New World* (University Park, Pa.: The Pennsylvania State University Press, 1962)

Higgins, Trumbull, *Hitler and Russia* (New York: The Macmillan Company, 1966): Higgins[1]

—, *Winston Churchill and the Second Front, 1940-1943* (New York: Oxford University Press, 1957): Higgins[2]

Hinsley, F. H., *Hitler's Strategy* (Cambridge: Cambridge University Press, 1951)

Hitler, Adolf, *Secret Conversations, 1941-1944* (New York: Farrar, Straus and Young, 1953). Cited as *Hitler's Secret Conversations.*

Howard, Michael, *The Mediterranean Strategy in the Second World War* (London: George Weidenfeld & Nicolson Limited, 1968)

Howe, George F., *Northwest Africa: Seizing the Initiative in the West* (Washington, D.C.: Office of the Chief of Military History, 1957)

Hull, Cordell, *The Memoirs of Cordell Hull,* Vol. II (New York: The Macmillan Company, 1948)

Hurd, Charles, *Washington Cavalcade* (New York: E. P. Dutton & Co., Inc., 1948)

Ickes, Harold L., *The Secret Diary of Harold L. Ickes.* Vol. III, *The Lowering Clouds* (New York: Simon and Schuster, Inc., 1954)

Ike, Nobutaka (ed.), *Japan's Decision for War* (Stanford, Calif.: Stanford University Press, 1967)

Industrial Mobilization for War, see Civilian Production Administration

Ismay, Hastings, *The Memoirs of General Lord Ismay* (New York: The Viking Press, 1960)

Jacobsen, H. A., and J. Rohwer (eds.), *Decisive Battles of World War II: The German View* (New York: G. P. Putnam's Sons, 1965)

Janeway, Eliot, *The Struggle for Survival* (New Haven, Conn.: Yale University Press, 1951)

Japan 1931-1941: Foreign Relations of the United States (Washington, D.C.: Government Printing Office, 1943), 2 vols.

Johnson, Donald Bruce, *The Republican Party and Wendell Willkie* (Urbana, Ill.: University of Illinois Press, 1960)

Josephson, Matthew, *Sidney Hillman: Statesman of American Labor* (Garden City, N.Y.: Doubleday & Company, Inc., 1952)

Jungk, Robert, *Brighter Than a Thousand Suns* (New York: Harcourt, Brace and Company, 1958)

Keitel, Wilhelm, *The Memoirs of Field-Marshal Keitel* (London: William Kimber & Co. Ltd., 1965)

Kennan, George F., *Memoirs, 1925-1950* (Boston: Little, Brown and Company, 1967): Kennan[1]

—, *Russia and the West Under Lenin and Stalin* (Boston: Little, Brown and Company, 1961): Kennan[2]

Kennedy, J., *Asian Nationalism in the Twentieth Century* (London: Macmillan & Co. Ltd., 1968)

Kimmel, Husband E., *Admiral Kimmel's Story* (Chicago: Henry Regnery Co., 1955)

King, Ernest J., and Walter Muir Whitehill, *Fleet Admiral King* (New York: W. W. Norton & Company, Inc., 1952)

Kirby, S. Woodburn, *The War Against Japan* (London: H. M. Stationery Office, 1965)

Kolko, Gabriel, *The Politics of War* (New York: Random House, Inc., 1968)

Langer, William L., and S. Everett Gleason, *The Undeclared War* (New York: Harper & Brothers, 1953)

Lash, Joseph P., *Eleanor Roosevelt: A Friend's Memoir* (Garden City, N.Y.: Doubleday & Company, Inc., 1964)

Leahy, William D., *I Was There* (New York: McGraw-Hill Book Company, 1950)

Liddell Hart, B. H., *The German Generals Talk* (New York: William Morrow & Co., Inc., 1948)

Lilienthal, David E., *The Journals of David E. Lilienthal,* Vol. I, *The TVA Years, 1939-1945* (New York: Harper & Row, 1964)

Long, Breckinridge, *The War Diary of Breckinridge Long,* Fred L. Israel, ed. (Lincoln, Neb.: University of Nebraska Press, 1966)

Lord, Russell, *The Wallaces of Iowa* (Boston: Houghton Mifflin Company, 1947)

MacArthur, Douglas, *Reminiscences* (New York: McGraw-Hill Book Co., Inc., 1964)

MacGregor-Hastie, Roy, *The Day of the Lion* (New York: Coward-McCann, Inc., 1964)

Macmillan, Harold, *The Blast of War* (London: Macmillan & Co. Ltd., 1967)

Maisky, Ivan, *Memoirs of a Soviet Ambassador. The War: 1939-43* (New York: Charles Scribner's Sons, 1968)

Malta-Yalta: Foreign Relations of the United States. The Conferences at Malta and Yalta 1945 (Washington, D.C.: U.S. Government Printing Office, 1955)

Matloff, Maurice, *Strategic Planning for Coalition Warfare, 1943-1944* (Washington, D.C.: Office of the Chief of Military History, 1959)

Matloff, Maurice, and Edwin M. Snell, *Strategic Planning for Coalition Warfare, 1941-1942* (Washington, D.C.: Office of the Chief of Military History, 1953)

McNeill, William Hardy, *America, Britain, & Russia: Their Co-operation and Conflict, 1941-1946* (London: Oxford University Press, 1953)

Meskill, Johanna Menzel, *Hitler & Japan: The Hollow Alliance* (New York: Atherton Press, 1966)

Military Situation in the Far East. Hearings before the Committee on Armed Services and the Committee on Foreign Relations, 82nd Congress, 1st Session (Washington, D.C.: U.S. Government Printing Office, 1951)

Moore, Ruth, *Niels Bohr, the Man, His Science, & the World They Changed* (New York: Alfred A. Knopf, Inc., 1966)

Moran, Lord (Sir Charles Wilson), *Churchill: The Struggle for Survival, 1940-1965, Taken from the Diaries of Lord Moran* (Boston: Houghton Mifflin Company, 1966)

Morgenthau Diary: Morgenthau Diary (China), Vol. II, prepared by the Subcommittee to Investigate the Administration of the Internal Security Act and Other Internal Security Laws, Committee on the Judiciary, United States Senate, 89th Congress, 1st Session (Washington, D.C.: U.S. Government Printing Office, 1965). Cited as *Morgenthau Diary* (China).

Morison, Elting E., *Turmoil and Tradition* (Boston: Houghton Mifflin Company, 1960)

Morison, Samuel Eliot, *History of United States Naval Operations in World War II* (Boston: Little, Brown and Company). *The Battle of the Atlantic* (1947): Morison[1]. *Operations in North African Waters* (1947): Morison[2]. *The Rising Sun in the Pacific* (1948): Morison[3]. *Coral Sea, Midway and Submarine Actions* (1950): Morison[4]. *The Invasion of France and Germany* (1957): Morison[5]

Morton, Louis, *Strategy and Command: The First Two Years* (Washington, D.C.: Office of the Chief of Military History, 1962)

Mosley, Leonard, *Hirohito, Emperor of Japan* (Englewood Cliffs, N.J.: Prentice-Hall, Inc., 1966)

Myrdal, Gunnar, *An American Dilemma* (New York: Harper & Brothers, 1944)

Nazi Conspiracy and Aggression (Washington, D.C.: Office of United States Chief of Counsel for Prosecution of Axis Criminality, 1946), Vols. 1-24

Nelson, Donald M., *Arsenal of Democracy* (New York: Harcourt, Brace and Company, 1946)

Nicolson, Harold, *Diaries and Letters*. Vol. II, *The War Years, 1939-1945* (New York: Atheneum Publishers, 1967)

Novick, David, Melvin Ashen, and W. C. Truppner, *Wartime Production Controls* (New York: Columbia University Press, 1949)

Osgood, Robert E., *Ideals and Self-Interest in America's Foreign Relations* (Chicago: University of Chicago Press, 1953)

Paul, Randolph E., *Taxation for Prosperity* (Indianapolis: The Bobbs-Merrill Co., Inc., 1947)

Pawle, Gerald, *The War and Colonel Warden* (New York: Alfred A. Knopf, Inc., 1963)

Payne, Robert, *Chiang Kai-shek* (New York: Weybright & Talley, Inc., 1969)

Pearl Harbor Attack. Hearings before the Joint Committee on the Investigation of the Pearl Harbor Attack, 79th Congress (Washington, D.C.: U.S. Government Printing Office, 1946). Cited as PHA

Perkins, Frances, *The Roosevelt I Knew* (New York: The Viking Press, 1946)

Pogue, Forrest C., *George C. Marshall*. Vol. II, *Ordeal and Hope, 1939-1942* (New York: The Viking Press, 1966): Pogue[1]

——, *The Supreme Command* (Washington, D.C.: Office of the Chief of Military History, 1954): Pogue[2]

Range, Willard, *Franklin D. Roosevelt's World Order* (Athens, Ga.: University of Georgia Press, 1959)

Reilly, Michael F., *Reilly of the White House* (New York: Simon and Schuster, Inc., 1947)

Reston, James, *Prelude to Victory* (New York: Alfred A. Knopf, Inc., 1942)

Reynaud, Paul, *In the Thick of the Fight* (New York: Simon and Schuster, Inc., 1955)

Rigdon, William M., *White House Sailor* (Garden City, N.Y.: Doubleday & Company, Inc., 1962)

Rogow, Arnold A., *James Forrestal* (New York: The Macmillan Company, 1963)

Romanus, Charles F., and Riley Sunderland, *Stilwell's Command Problems* (Washington, D.C.: Office of the Chief of Military History, 1956): Romanus and Sunderland[1]

—, *Stilwell's Mission to China* (Washington, D.C.: Office of the Chief of Military History, 1953): Romanus and Sunderland[2]

—, *Time Runs Out in CBI* (Washington, D.C.: Department of the Army, 1959): Romanus and Sunderland[3]

Roosevelt, Eleanor, *This I Remember* (New York: Harper & Brothers, 1949)

Roosevelt, Elliott, *As He Saw It* (New York: Duell, Sloan & Pearce, Inc., 1946)

Roosevelt, James, and Sidney Shalett, *Affectionately, F.D.R.* (New York: Harcourt, Brace and Company, 1959)

Rosenman, Samuel I., *Working with Roosevelt* (New York: Harper & Brothers, 1952)

Ross, Malcolm, *All Manner of Men* (New York: Reynal & Hitchcock, Inc., 1948)

Rothstein, Andrew (tr.), *Soviet Foreign Policy During the Patriotic War.* Vol. I, June 22, 1941–December 31, 1943 (London: Hutchinson & Co. (Publishers) Limited, n.d.): Rothstein[1]

—, *Soviet Foreign Policy During the Patriotic War: Documents and Materials.* Vol. II, January 1, 1944–December 31, 1944 (London: Hutchinson & Co. (Publishers) Limited, 1946): Rothstein[2]

Rukeyser, Muriel, *One Life* (New York: Simon and Schuster, Inc., 1957)

Schmidt, Paul, *Hitler's Interpreter,* R. H. C. Steed, ed. (London: William Heinemann Ltd., 1951)

Schoenbrun, David, *The Three Lives of Charles de Gaulle* (New York: Atheneum Publishers, 1966)

Shaplen, Robert, *The Lost Revolution* (New York: Harper & Row, 1965)

Sherwood, Robert E., *Roosevelt and Hopkins* (New York: Harper & Brothers, 1948)

Shirer, William L., *The Rise and Fall of the Third Reich* (New York: Simon and Schuster, Inc., 1960)

Smith, Gaddis, *American Diplomacy During the Second World War* (New York: John Wiley & Sons, Inc., 1965)

Snell, John L., *Illusion and Necessity* (Boston: Houghton Mifflin Company, 1963)

Snyder, Louis L., *The War: A Concise History, 1939-1945* (New York: Dell Publishing Co., Inc., 1960)

Somers, H. M., *Presidential Agency* (Cambridge, Mass.: Harvard University Press, 1950)

Sontag, Raymond James, and James Stuart Beddie, *Nazi-Soviet Relations* (Washington, D.C.: U.S. Government Printing Office, 1948)

Stalin, J., *The Great Patriotic War of the Soviet Union* (New York: International Publishers Co., 1945)

Steinberg, Alfred, *The Man from Missouri* (New York: G. P. Putnam's Sons, 1962)

Stilwell, Joseph W., *The Stilwell Papers* (New York: William Sloane Associates, Inc., 1948)

Stimson, Henry L., and McGeorge Bundy, *On Active Service in Peace and War* (New York: Harper & Brothers, 1948)

Stouffer, Samuel A., *The American Soldier,* Vol. I (Princeton, N.J.: Princeton University Press, 1949)

Sulzberger, C. L., *A Long Row of Candles* (New York: The Macmillan Company, 1969)

Tansill, Charles Callan, *Back Door to War* (Chicago: Henry Regnery Co., 1952)

Taylor, Telford, *Sword and Swastika* (New York: Simon and Schuster, Inc., 1952)

Teller, Edward, and Allen Brown, *The Legacy of Hiroshima* (Garden City, N.Y.: Doubleday & Company, Inc., 1962)

Timmons, Bascom N., *Jesse H. Jones* (New York: Henry Holt & Company, Inc., 1956)

Trevor-Roper, H. R. (ed.), *Blitzkrieg to Defeat: Hitler's War Directives, 1939-1945* (New York: Holt, Rinehart & Winston, Inc., 1965)

Tsou, Tang, *America's Failure in China, 1941-50* (Chicago: The University of Chicago Press, 1963)

Tugwell, Rexford G., *The Democratic Roosevelt* (Garden City, N.Y.: Doubleday & Company, Inc., 1957)

Tully, Grace, *F.D.R. My Boss* (New York: Charles Scribner's Sons, 1949)

Ulam, Adam B., *Expansion and Coexistence* (New York: Frederick A. Praeger, Inc., 1968)

The United States at War, see War Records Section

United States Relations with China. Department of State Publication 3573, Far Eastern Series 30 (Washington, D.C.: U.S. Government Printing Office, 1949)

Vandenberg, Arthur H., Jr. (ed.), *The Private Papers of Senator Vandenberg* (Boston: Houghton Mifflin Company, 1952)

Viorst, Milton, *Hostile Allies* (New York: The Macmillan Company, 1965)

Walker, Turnley, *Roosevelt and the Warm Springs Story* (New York: A. A. Wyn, Inc., 1953)

War Records Section, Bureau of the Budget, *The United States at War* (Washington, D.C.: Committee of Records of War Administration, 1946)

Warlimont, Walter, *Inside Hitler's Headquarters* (New York: Frederick A. Praeger, Inc., 1964)

Warner, Geoffrey, *Pierre Laval and the Eclipse of France* (New York: The Macmillan Company, 1969)

Watson, Mark Skinner, *Chief of Staff: Prewar Plans and Preparations* (Washington, D.C.: Office of the Chief of Military History, 1950)

Wedemeyer, Albert C., *Wedemeyer Reports!* (New York: Henry Holt & Company, Inc., 1958)

Welles, Sumner, *The Time for Decision* (New York: Harper & Brothers, 1944)

Werth, Alexander, *Russia at War, 1941-1945* (New York: E. P. Dutton & Co., Inc., 1964)

White, Theodore H., and Annalee Jacoby, *Thunder Out of China* (New York: Williams Sloane Associates, Inc., 1946)

White, William S., *Majesty and Mischief* (New York: McGraw-Hill Book Company, 1961)

Whitney, Courtney, *MacArthur: His Rendezvous with History* (New York: Alfred A. Knopf, Inc., 1964)

Williams, William Appleman, *The Tragedy of American Diplomacy* (New York: Dell Publishing Co., Inc., 1962)

Willkie, Wendell L., *One World* (New York: Simon and Schuster, Inc., 1943)

Willoughby, Charles A., and John Chamberlain, *MacArthur, 1941-1951* (New York: McGraw-Hill Book Company, 1954)

Wilson, Theodore A., *The First Summit* (Boston: Houghton Mifflin Company, 1969)

Wohlstetter, Roberta, *Pearl Harbor: Warning and Decision* (Stanford, Calif.: Stanford University Press, 1962)

Woodward, Llewellyn, *British Foreign Policy in the Second World War* (London: H. M. Stationery Office, 1962)

Wright, Gordon, *The Ordeal of Total War* (New York: Harper & Row, 1968)

Yakovlev, Nikolai N., *Franklin Roosevelt—chilovek i politik* (Moskva: Mezhdunarodnoye otnosheniye, 1965)

Young, Roland, *Congressional Politics in the Second World War* (New York: Columbia University Press, 1956)

Yu Te-jen, *The Japanese Struggle for World Empire* (New York: The Vantage Press, Inc., 1967)

Zhukov, Georgi K., *Marshal Zhukov's Greatest Battles,* Harrison E. Salisbury, ed. (New York: Harper & Row, 1969)

PROLOGUE

Election night account: NYT, Nov. 6, 1940, pp. 1-2; Lash, pp. 191-193; Eleanor Roosevelt, "My Day," Nov. 7, 1940. Roosevelt's comments on the election: Rosenman, p. 236; to Lash: Lash, p. 194. Roosevelt dictated a letter to Henry Luce denying that pencils were laid out, his necktie loosened, etc., but he did not send it; see Robert T. Elson, *Time Inc.* (Atheneum, 1968), pp. 443-444; I have corresponded with Judge Samuel I. Rosenman on the matter and believe that *Time* and the above sources were essentially accurate. The President spoke later in the evening to a second group that assembled; some accounts refer to both meetings. Roosevelt's fears of "fifth column" activity: Roosevelt to King George, Nov. 27, 1940, PSF, Diplomatic Corr., Great Britain, 1933-45, King and Queen, Box 7. Roosevelt to Attorney General, June 18, 1940, enclosing clippings from Eleanor Roosevelt, OF 4022; see Friedländer[2], pp. 97-101, 152-155. Purported ties between elements of the Republican party and fascist elements: HHP, Box 297, "Confidential Political File—Corr.—Misc."

Nazi plans re the United States: copy of confidential memorandum from Alexander Kirk to State Department, left with Missy LeHand, June 17, 1940, PSF, Diplomatic Corr., Germany, 1934-41. See, generally, Niles Papers, especially N5.211, N5.44 (1940); Alton Frye, *Nazi Germany and the American Hemisphere* (New Haven: Yale University Press, 1967), especially pp. 136, 142, 150.

Hyde Park. Sara Roosevelt's remark about her son: NYT, Nov. 6, 1940, p. 2. Contemporary attitudes toward, and bafflement by, Roosevelt: Charles Hurd, NYT *Magazine,* Jan. 19, 1941, p. 3. Eleanor Roosevelt comment to Lash: Lash, p. 203; Vandenberg, p. 5. Roosevelt's affair with Lucy Mercer: Daniels[2], chap. 6; confidential source. Noddle-Fala exchange: PPF 1, Dec. 23, 1940; see also Roosevelt to Eleanor Roosevelt, PPF 2, April 9, 1941. Joan Erikson on Eleanor Roosevelt: Erik H. Erikson, *Gandhi's Truth* (Norton, 1969), p. 127.

London. This material is drawn largely from Churchill[2], pp. 23, 375-376, 553; I have consulted also Ismay; Walter Henry Thompson, *Assignment: Churchill* (Farrar, Straus, 1955); Pawle; Moran, pp. 321-322. Churchill's Dec. 8, 1940 letter to Roosevelt is quoted in full in Churchill[2], pp. 558-567. A document that reflects administration views of the time as to ways of aiding Britain is E. S. Land to Roosevelt, "Proposed British Shipbuilding in the United States," Dec. 2, 1940, OF 99.

Berlin. For the general background to the events of fall 1941, see Shirer; Telford Taylor, *The Breaking Wave* (Simon and Schuster, 1967); Bullock; Frederick L. Schuman, *The Nazi Dictatorship* (Knopf, 1935). Quotations from Hitler's speeches are from Raoul de Roussy de Sales (ed.), *My New Order* (Reynal & Hitchcock, 1941), pp. 871-873, 873-899. Taylor; Schmidt; *Hitler's Secret Conversations;* and *Führer Conferences* are sources of private statements on Hitler. Molotov-Ribbentrop exchange in the bomb shelter: Berezhkov (Molotov's interpreter) to author, Moscow, May 6, 1969.

Tokyo. Tokyo's reaction to the election results: NYT, Nov. 7, 1940, p. 9. Description of the imperial ceremony: Hugh Byas, *Government by Assassination* (Knopf, 1942), chap. 5; Ambassador Joseph C. Grew's diary, *Ten Years in Japan* (Simon and Schuster, 1944), pp. 352-353; but see Heinrichs, pp. 367-369. For the historical and general background to Japanese politics and policy, see Butow. Ike is an indispensable source of records of the 1941 policy conferences in Tokyo. Ruth Benedict, *The Chrysanthemum and the Sword* (Boston: Houghton Mifflin, 1946), probes deeply into Japanese values and culture patterns. On more immediate events prior to fall 1941, see Langer and Gleason, chaps. 1 and 2; Hull, Vol. I; Heinrichs, chaps. 18-19; Mosley. The "Green Light" message is in Grew, pp. 1224-1229; see also Heinrichs, pp. 317-318. On various views within the administration: Morgenthau to Roosevelt, "Petroleum Situation in Japan," Aug. 14, 1940; Stimson to Roosevelt, Oct. 12, 1940; Knox to Roosevelt, Oct. 23, 1940; Sayre to Roosevelt, Nov. 13, 1940; Eleanor Roosevelt to Roosevelt, Nov. 12, 1940; Roosevelt to Eleanor Roosevelt, Nov. 13, 1940—all in FDRL. Grew's letter of Dec. 14, 1940 to Roosevelt and Roosevelt's reply are quoted in Grew, pp. 359-363.

Washington. On Roosevelt's daily schedule and life, see Tully; Sherwood; Reilly. The source of Roosevelt's statement to Lothian is Blum[1], p. 199; of Hull's statement to Latin-American diplomats, Hull, p. 824. Roosevelt's parking-shoulders crack: PC 697, Nov. 26, 1940; PPA, 1940, p. 584. Hopkins's comment on Roosevelt's Lend-Lease germinations: Sherwood, p. 224. Earlier origins of his Lend-Lease ideas: see Land to Roosevelt, Nov. 29, 1940, FDRL; Eccles, pp. 348-349; Churchill[2], p. 567; Ickes, p. 367; Blum[1], pp. 98, 211; Freedman, pp. 573-574. The Lend-Lease press conference: PC 702, Dec. 17, 1940; PPA, 1940, pp. 604-615. The German reaction: NYT, Dec. 21, 1940, p. 6; Dec. 22, 1940, p. 1. Writing of the Dec. 29 speech: Sherwood, p. 227. The speech itself is in PPA, 1940, pp. 633-644; film excerpts are in NA. Grew's reaction: *Ten Years in Japan,* pp. 357-358. See, generally, Clapper Papers (Diaries, 1940-1942), Box 9, LC, for this period.

CHAPTER ONE

Rosenman, p. 262 ff., and Sherwood, p. 231, describe Roosevelt's preparation of his annual message to Congress; for the result, see PPA, 1940, pp. 663-672; and for one reaction, Freedman, p. 577. Roosevelt's earlier reference to the "5th" freedom is in PC 658, July 5, 1940; PPA, 1940, p. 285. The Inaugural Address of 1941: PPA, 1941, pp. 3-6; see also PL, pp. 1111, 1117. Rosenman reports the President's misgivings about the reception of the speech: Rosenman, p. 271.

The New Coalition at Home. Cantril, pp. 756-758, provides a most useful listing over time of responses to the question "If you were voting today, would you vote for or against Roosevelt?" The responses are broken down by geographical section, economic status, and other categories. The Republican Senator was Vandenberg: Vandenberg, p. 10. Dr. McIntire's comment on Roosevelt's health: NYT, Jan. 19, 1941, p. 36. I have described the historical development and structure of Roosevelt's party coalition of 1941 in *The Deadlock of Democracy* (Englewood Cliffs, N.J.: Prentice-Hall, 1963). Noses: Roosevelt to Glass, PSF, U.S. Senate Folder, Box 58. Banning of Hamilton Fish: Roosevelt to Sherman Minton, March 1, 1944, PSF, Minton Folder, Box 52. Stimson: Stimson and Bundy; Elting E. Morison; Current. There is no adequate biography of Knox, and most of the other key civilian figures in defense have not had the biographies they deserve; but see Rogow's probing *James Forrestal.* On Ickes, see *The Secret Diary of Harold L. Ickes.* Much of Frances Perkins's personality emerges in her sparkling *The Roosevelt I Knew.* On Southern politics in the South and on Capitol Hill, see V. O. Key, Jr.'s brilliant *Southern Politics* (Knopf, 1949).

On the nature of public opinion on foreign policy, see Cantril Notebook I; Cantril, pp. 971 ff.; I have had some of these measures broken down with the assistance of the Roper Public Opinion Research Center, at Williams College. The two standard works on organized isolationists and interventionists are Wayne S. Cole, *America First* (Madison, Wis.: University of Wisconsin Press, 1953), and Walter Johnson, *The Battle Against Isolation* (Chicago: University of Chicago Press, 1944). How closely in touch the White House was with William Allen White and his committee is indicated in William Allen White Papers, Box 317, LC. On the committee generally, see Clapper Papers (Diaries, 1940-1942), Box 9, LC. On the background of attitude and mood, see Selig Adler, *The Isolationist Impulse* (Collier Books, 1961), and Manfred Jonas, *Isolationism in America, 1935-1941* (Ithaca, N.Y.: Cornell University Press, 1966). See Gabriel A. Almond's path-breaking *The American People and Foreign Policy* (Praeger, 1960) on moods in American public opinion toward foreign-policy making. Roosevelt's meeting with Willkie: Sherwood, pp. 233-234. HHP, Box 298, contain some public-opinion data.

Lend-Lease: The Great Debate. Preparation of Lend-Lease legislation: Cox Diary, Jan. 6, Feb. 13, 1941, FDRL. The text of Wheeler's speech is in *Congressional Record,* Vol. 87, Pt. 10 (Appendix), A178-179; Roosevelt's reply, PC 710, Jan. 14, 1941; PPA, 1940, pp. 711-712. Blum[1], pp. 211-222, and Langer and Gleason, pp. 254 ff., provide accounts of the Lend-Lease debate; there is some relevant material in HHP, Box 296. On Stimson's dilemma, see Elting E. Morison, p. 518, and Current, pp. 148-149. Testimony is taken from the House and Senate hearings: "To Promote the Defense of the United States," Hearings before the Committee on Foreign Affairs, House of Representatives, 1941; and before the Committee on Foreign Relations, United States Senate (on S. 275), Jan.-Feb. 1941, Pts. 1-4. See also Osgood, pp. 417-420.

Cole and Johnson describe the role of the two big isolationist and interventionist organizations. State Department, Box 28, FDRL, throws light on Roosevelt's reaction to the debate.

"Speed—and Speed Now." Roosevelt's indignation session: Sherwood, pp. 265-266; see also Rosenman, p. 273. Speech to the White House correspondents: PPA, 1941, pp. 60-69. On the general background of defense mobilization, see *The United States at War* and *Industrial Mobilization for War*. The press conference on the new defense-production setup is in PPA, 1940, pp. 684-685. On some of the problems of early 1941, see Janeway; the Stimson quotation on aluminum is from Janeway, p. 240. See Ickes, on other defense problems, especially oil and power. Press conference on the Dunn report: PC 722, Feb. 28, 1941. Baruch's role and relation to Roosevelt: Baruch; Coit. On Baruch's advice on defense production, see these works and Baruch to Roosevelt, PPF 88, Dec. 20, 1940, and Clapper Papers (Diary, May 19, 1941), LC. Stimson's "sting of responsibility" comment: Blum[1], p. 272; see the same, p. 273, for Morgenthau's view on defense organization.

PM's story on the New York derelicts is in the edition of Jan. 21, 1941, pp. 1, 12-13; see this newspaper and the liberal weeklies *The Nation* and *The New Republic* for reports on social conditions during the mobilization period. The findings of Gunnar Myrdal and his associates were reported in the magnificent *An American Dilemma;* see pp. 420 and 421 for examples of the plight of Negroes in the Army. Josephson provides full coverage of Hillman's defense role. Strike situation in early 1941: War Department Memo (n.d.), PSF, Strikes Folder. Allis-Chalmers: Patterson to Roosevelt, April 3, 1941, PSF, Strikes Folder.

Roosevelt's White House. The account of John Gunther's interview is taken from his sensitive and knowing *Roosevelt in Retrospect,* pp. 24, 27; I have both paraphrased and quoted it. Sherwood's description and memories of the White House: Sherwood, pp. 203 ff. The most revealing book on Eleanor Roosevelt in the White House is Lash; see also Alfred Steinberg, *Mrs. R: The Life of Eleanor Roosevelt* (Putnam, 1958); Eleanor Roosevelt; Tully; Roosevelt and Shalett. Roosevelt on Hopkins: Sherwood, pp. 2-3; on Hopkins in the White House: Ickes, p. 471; Blum[1], p. 231; Stimson Diary and Papers. Baruch's comment on Hopkins was made to Raymond Clapper: Clapper Papers, Cont. 23, Jan.-Feb. 1942 Folder, LC.

Moley's and Corcoran's departures from the presidential limelight: Raymond Moley, *After Seven Years* (Harper, 1939); Freedman, pp. 577-578. Many items in PL indicate Roosevelt's capacity to deal with day-to-day problems and to indulge in small jokes; see, for example, PL, pp. 1092, 1100, 1148; also Rosenman to author. The call for diaper service is recorded for history in Henrietta Nesbitt's Diaries, Feb. 16, 1941, LC.

CHAPTER TWO

Churchill and Roosevelt exchange on repair of British ships: Langer and Gleason, p. 424; PL, p. 1137. On Roosevelt's policies toward Vichy, Madrid, Athens, etc., see Hull; Leahy, chaps. 2-4; Churchill[3], pp. 130-131. Langer and Gleason is especially useful for its detailed studies of the diplomatic background to the events of early 1941. Ickes's denunciation of the State Department: Ickes, p. 473; see Ickes also for occasional criticism of Roosevelt's failure to act more decisively, and for indicating Frankfurter's view. Stimson's comment: Stimson Diary, April 22, 1941. The President's discussion on the flux of public opinion with the press: PC 737, April 22, 1941; and on defeatism: PC 738, April 25, 1941; PPA, 1941, p. 132. His letter to Norman Thomas, May 14, 1941, is in PL, p. 1156. For day-to-day attitudes of American and other officials, see Clapper Papers (Diaries, 1941), LC. Pacific Theater background: "Admiral Hart's Narrative of Events, Pacific Theatre, Leading Up to War," PMRP, Naval Aide's Files (no box number).

Hitler: The Rapture of Decision. Hitler's Rheinmetall-Borsig speech, Dec. 10, 1940: Raoul de Roussy de Sales (ed.), *My New Order* (Reynal & Hitchcock, 1941), p. 889. Churchill's comments on Hitler can be found in his works. Studies of Hitler's personality are legion; I have used especially Shirer; Bullock; Trevor-Roper; Erik H. Erikson, *Young Man Luther* (Norton Library, 1962), pp. 105-110; Jochen von Lang, *Adolf Hitler: Faces of a Dictator* (Harcourt, Brace, 1969). Hitler's strategic decisions of late 1940 and early 1941: Sontag and Beddie, pp. 258-259, 260; *Führer Conferences,* 1941; Hinsley; other sources cited in Prologue notes; interviews with German and Soviet historians. Hitler's strictures against the Russians and the Jews are quoted in *My New Order,* p. 973. His message to Mussolini is in Sontag and Beddie, p. 353. The Führer's relations with his generals are reflected in *Hitler's Secret Conversations;* Taylor; and in Keitel and other memoirs by his generals. Shirer, p. 1080, and Keitel, p. 138, indicate Hitler's reaction to the change of government in Belgrade. Hitler's

Russian strategy: Hinsley, chap. 6; Warlimont, chap. 3; Liddell Hart, chap. 13. Warlimont, p. 161, is the source of the description of the officers' meeting with Hitler; and Bullock, p. 652, of the Führer's comment on kicking down the Russian door.

Churchill: The Girdle of Defeat. Churchill's estimate of the situation, winter 1940-41: Churchill[2], p. 626. His note to Roosevelt on a possible invasion: Churchill[3], p. 26. His vignette of Hopkins, *ibid.,* p. 24. Bryant[2] is a useful source for a more professional view of Britain's situation during this period; see also Eden; Ismay. On the question of diversion from Africa to assist the Greeks, see the above sources. Brooke's comment is in Bryant[2], p. 198; see also Ismay, p. 199. Churchill's questioning message to Eden: Churchill[3], p. 70. The House of Commons debate is quoted from 371 *H.C. Debates,* 5th session, May 1941, pp. 871, 880, 927, 937. Roosevelt's letter to Churchill on the Near Eastern situation: Churchill[3]. Churchill's increasing emphasis on the need for full American intervention: *ibid.,* pp. 160, 274, 283, and his flat call for participation, *ibid.,* p. 235. The Prime Minister's description of his relations with the Americans: 371 *H.C. Debates,* May 7, 1941, p. 945. Forrestal on Churchill's private attitude and expectations of American involvement: Clapper Papers (Diary, May 15, 1941), LC.

Konoye: The View Toward Chungking. Grew's comment on the possibility of a Japanese attack on Pearl Harbor: Grew, p. 1233 (Jan. 27, 1941). Indispensable sources on Japan's strategic planning during this period are Butow, p. 204 and *passim;* and Yale C. Maxon, *Control of Japanese Foreign Policy* (Berkeley: University of California Press, 1957), pp. 150, 153-154, and *passim.* Roosevelt's comment on Matsuoka's trip is in PL, p. 1125 (Feb. 19, 1941). Hitler-Matsuoka negotiations: Sontag and Beddie, pp. 289 ff.; Schmidt, pp. 226 ff.; *Nazi Conspiracy and Aggression,* Vol. IV, pp. 526 ff. Schmidt, p. 231, stresses Hitler's emphasis to Matsuoka on the uncertainty of Nazi-Soviet relations. Text of Japanese-Soviet agreement: Dallin, pp. 164-165. On Chinese-American relations in 1941, extensive background is provided by PSF, China, 1941-44, and by *Morgenthau Diary* (China), Vol. I, which reprints large sections of Morgenthau's diary, including transcripts of his conferences with his staff.

The Yangtze River description is from Agnes Smedley, *Battle Hymn of China* (Knopf, 1943). Chiang at this time: White and Jacoby, pp. 122-129; Tsou, chap. 2; Payne, pp. 233 ff. On Chiang's relations with the Chinese Communists during this period, see Lawrence K. Rosinger, *China's War Time Politics, 1937-1944* (Princeton, N.J.: Princeton University Press, 1945), pp. 38-39 and *passim.* Appointment of Lattimore: Currie to Roosevelt, May 6, 1941, PSF, China, and other correspondence, Box 4. For Chiang's comments and views generally, see his *Resistance and Reconstruction* (Harper, 1943) and *The Collected Wartime Messages of Generalissimo Chiang Kai-Shek,* Vol. 2 (1940-1945) (John Day, 1946), compiled by the Chinese Ministry of Information. U.S.-Chinese relations generally, during early 1941: PSF, Currie Folder, Box 45.

Roosevelt: The Crisis of Strategy. Roosevelt to Grew: Heinrichs, p. 328. Roosevelt's note to Knox about the "dear, delightful" Navy officers: PSF, Navy Department, Box 20, Dec. 23, 1940. Background of army planning and strategy: Cline, chaps. 1 and 2. Navy: King and Whitehill. On the more immediate background, see Matloff and Snell, chaps. 1-3. Admiral Stark's strategic appreciation of Nov. 1940: PSF, Navy Department, Box 20, Nov. 4, 1940. The characterization of Plan Dog as the first attempt to deal with American military strategy as a whole is from Matloff and Snell, p. 25. Pogue[1], p. 127, among others, notes Roosevelt's noninvolvement openly in the early planning; see also Divine, chap. 2. Marshall: Pogue[1], pp. 22-23 and *passim;* Sherwood, pp. 164-165; Robert Payne, *The Marshall Story* (Englewood Cliffs, N.J.: Prentice-Hall, 1951), chap. 16. The President's general directive of Jan. 16, 1941 is quoted in Watson, pp. 124-125. Roosevelt's editing of the directive: Watson, p. 373. On the discussions and agreements of the British-American staff, see Matloff and Snell, chap. 3; the plan to concentrate American naval efforts in the eastern Atlantic is spelled out in Knox to Roosevelt, March 20, 1941.

Roosevelt's elaborate and cautious preparations for American trusteeship of Greenland are reflected in documents in PSF, Greenland, Memorandum, Stimson and Knox to Roosevelt, April 22, 1941, and his reply to them of April 30, 1941; and in PSF, Denmark, which includes Roosevelt's correspondence with Hull on the wording of his appeal to the King of Denmark, April 14, 15, and 18, 1941. Implications of a Pacific First strategy: Feis[3], pp. 45-47.

Harriman's description of the atmosphere of London: Sherwood, p. 276. Roosevelt's aid to Britain: HHP, Box 305; also Roosevelt to Churchill, March 25, 1941, SD 811.6363/38 1/2. Roosevelt's humorous exchange with the press: PC 735, April 15, 1941; PPA, 1941, pp. 113 ff. The President's highly significant statement about convoying leading to war: PC 712, Jan. 21, 1941. Knox's claim about cleaning up the Atlantic is quoted in Langer and Gleason, p. 445. Roosevelt's and Marshall's views on Hawaii are indicated in Pogue[1], pp. 135-136. Stimson's comments on convoying to Roosevelt: Stimson and Bundy, p. 369. Ickes's view of Roosevelt's approach: Ickes, pp. 466, 470, 485, 538; Morgenthau's views: Blum[1], pp. 253-254 and *Morgenthau Diary* (China). Iowa farmers: Wallace to Roosevelt, May 26, 1941, PSF, Box 59. Hopkins's position: Clapper Papers, May 19, 1941, LC. Frankfurter's position: Freedman, pp. 599-602. The croquet game incident is reported in Ickes, p. 510; I infer that Hull went on with his game only from Ickes's word "interrupt." Stimson's boa constrictor quotation: Elting E. Morison, p. 518. The Stimson outburst "Keep on walking": Stimson and Bundy, pp. 370-371.

Stalin: The Twist of Realpolitik. Stalin stated his preference for political arithmetic over algebra to Eden at their conference in Moscow, Dec. 1941: Eden, p. 251. Munich as catalyst: Kennan[2], pp. 321-329. Molotov's comments on *Realpolitik* and on Russian-American relations are quoted in Werth, pp. 51-52, 94; on the latter see also Currie to Roosevelt, May 8, 1941, FDRL. Churchill[3], pp. 357 ff., describes his warnings to Stalin of the impending German invasion. Matsuoka described to Hitler his meeting earlier with Stalin: Sontag and Beddie, pp. 296-297. Soviet-American economic relations: Hull, pp. 971-972; Acheson, p. 34. Stalin's send-off of Matsuoka is described in Langer and Gleason, pp. 354-355; Dallin, p.

346; Werth, p. 121; the reported words vary but the meaning is similar in these sources. Stalin's information and policies before the invasion: Ulam, pp. 303-313; Deborin, pp. 148-150; Werth, pp. 120-126. Stalin's important speech of May 5, 1941 to the officer graduates, with its implication that Russia might have to take the initiative against Germany in the future, is quoted in Werth, pp. 122-123; Werth compiled this quotation from several Russian oral sources several weeks later, but all his sources, he states, agree on Stalin's having made the statement about possibly taking the initiative. I have discussed this speech with Berezhkov and Soviet historians. The Tass statement and the exchange between the German Ambassador and Molotov are quoted in Werth, pp. 125, 127. Alan Clark's *Barbarossa* presents a graphic picture of the initial German advance; see also Werth. Stalin's near-collapse: Zhukov, pp. 11-12, 33; Werth, pp. 315-316. Hitler's on-the-eve message to Mussolini is in Ciano, p. 369; Churchill's broadcast, in Churchill[3], p. 371; and Stalin's broadcast, in Werth, pp. 162-165. Ilya Ehrenburg, pp. 10-11, describes hearing the speech.

CHAPTER THREE

Roosevelt's letters to Bailey, to the Congressman (James F. O'Connor), and to Bruce Barton: respectively, PL, p. 1154, May 13, 1941; PL, p. 1159, May 19, 1941; PPF 7550, May 19, 1941; see also Roosevelt to Norman Thomas, May 14, 1941, PL, pp. 1156-1157. Watson's memo to Roosevelt, May 16, 1941, on foreign-policy opinion: PL, p. 1158; see also Cantril, pp. 1061, 1128, 1162; OF 857; PPF 4721; PSF, Post-War Planning Folder, Box 54; Cantril Notebook I; PSF, Public Opinion Folder, Box 54. Ickes's warning to Roosevelt about Hitler and incidents: Ickes to Roosevelt, May 24, 1941, PSF, Box 73. Differences within the administration on policy are fully covered in Langer and Gleason, pp. 458 ff.; Sherwood, pp. 295-298, which also describes the writing of the speech declaring a full emergency, and Roosevelt's reaction to the reaction. *Bismarck* episode: Sherwood, p. 295; Rosenman, p. 283. The speech: PPA, 1941, pp. 181-194. The press conference the following morning: PC 745, May 28, 1941. Roosevelt's first reaction to *Robin Moor* sinking: Roosevelt to Hull and Welles, June 11, 1941, SD 195.7 Robin Moor 12 1/2, NA. On the mood of spring 1941, see Clapper Papers (diaries of that time), LC.

Atlantic First. Churchill's speech on the German invasion of Russia: Churchill[3], p. 372. On earlier British-Soviet relations, see Werth, p. 162; Butler, pp. 544 ff.; Eden, p. 263; Dallin, chap. 11; FRUS, 1941, Vol. I, pp. 155, 164, 167, 176. American relations with Russia and lack of confidence in that country's holding out against the Wehrmacht: Hull, pp. 971-973; Langer and Gleason, pp. 530-531; PHA, Pt. 14, p. 1336; see also Divine, pp. 79-84. Roosevelt's dislike of Oumansky: Ickes, p. 569. Roosevelt's response to the invasion: Sherwood, pp. 303-311; Kennan[2], pp. 352-355. State Department declaration of June 23: FRUS, 1941, Vol. I, pp. 766-768; see also Welles, p. 171. The Roosevelt-Oursler exchange, June 25, 1941: PPF 2993. Davies's reports from Moscow: George Fischer, "Genesis of the United States–Soviet Relations in World War II," *The Review of*

Politics, July 1950, pp. 363-378. Administration view that the best way to help Russia would be to step up aid to Britain: Cox to Hopkins, June 23, 1941, Cox Diary, FDRL. Pressure on Roosevelt to step up the Atlantic war: Sherwood, pp. 303-304; PHA, Pt. 16, pp. 2175 ff.; Ickes, pp. 549 ff.; Harriman to Roosevelt, April 24, 1941, HHP, Box 305. Roosevelt's operations orders for Atlantic escorting: PHA, Pt. 5, pp. 2293-2295. Operational orders on Iceland: Stark to Hopkins, June 17, 1941, with accompanying copy of instruction from the Chief of Naval Operations to the Commanding General, First Marine Brigade (Provisional), June 16, 1941, PSF, Iceland. Churchill on Iceland: Churchill[3], p. 138. Morison[1], p. 79, and King and Whitehill, pp. 343-344, note some of the more specific operational choices in escorting ships. See, generally, PSF, Navy, Box 21, 1941. Hitler's refusal to escalate in the Atlantic: *Führer Conferences,* June 24, 1941, p. 1; July 10, 1941, pp. 3, 8, 9; Shirer, pp. 1149-1153; Schmidt, p. 231.

Roosevelt's citing of Sandburg on Lincoln on strategy: PC 662, Aug. 19, 1941; PPA, 1941, p. 329. Roosevelt to Ickes on shortage of naval ships: PSF, Ickes Folder, July 1, 1941; see also PPA, 1941, p. 280. The exchanges between Hull and Nomura are exhaustively documented in *FRUS-Japan;* for the stiff Hull oral statement, June 21, 1941, see *ibid.,* p. 485. Long throws some light on Hull and internal State Department relationships. Events in Tokyo during this period: Ike, pp. 60, 65-66, 78-90, 97, 98, 101; see also Konoye's retrospective account in PHA, Pt. 20, pp. 3995-3997. Roosevelt's action on Indochina: FRUS, 1941, pp. 527-530; see also PPA, 1941, pp. 279-280. Roosevelt's comment on the "knock-out" fight in Tokyo is from the letter to Ickes cited above. Ickes's comment on the "noose" policy, July 27, 1941: Ickes, p. 588. Stimson's comment was in a handwritten note in the margin of a report to him by Robert Patterson, on the Cabinet meeting of July 18, 1941 attended by Patterson, in Stimson Papers. Grew's comment: Grew's diary, quoted by Langer and Gleason, p. 654. Mosley, pp. 206-209, describes some of the activities of the moderates in or close to the Emperor's circle during this period.

Russia Second. On the fighting in Russia, see the graphic accounts in Werth, Pt. 2, and Clark, chaps. 3-4; and in the North Atlantic, Morison[1], chap. 4. Military estimates of the prospects of Russian survival: Stimson to Roosevelt, June 22, 1941, quoted in Sherwood, pp. 303-305; Churchill[3], pp. 393-394, 398, 402. Churchill[3], pp. 457-458, is also the source of the account of his exchange with Maisky. On Roosevelt's "expedient" approach to Russia, see Fischer, cited above. Langer and Gleason, p. 542, has a roundup of congressional reactions to the German-Soviet hostilities. Raymond H. Dawson, *The Decision to Aid Russia, 1941* (Chapel Hill: University of North Carolina Press, 1959), offers an excellent compilation of interventionist and isolationist reactions to the Russo-German war, as well as a balanced account of the relations of foreign policy and domestic politics following this event. Conflicting advice to Roosevelt: Pogue[1], p. 158; Sherwood, pp. 306-307. Popular attitudes toward Russia as reported to Roosevelt: Cantril to Roosevelt, July 3, 1941, PSF, Public Opinion Polls; see also Cantril Notebook I.

Hopkins's mission to Moscow and reports on his talks with Stalin: Sherwood, chap. 15; HHP, Box 298. Roosevelt on Wheeler: Roosevelt to

Frankfurter, July 25, 1941, Freedman, p. 611. Roosevelt's exasperation over lagging aid to Russia: Ickes, pp. 592-593; Blum[1], p. 264. Morgenthau telephone call to Cox: Cox Diary, Aug. 2, 1941, FDRL. See Paul Carell, *Hitler's War on Russia* (London: Harrap, 1964).

Government as Usual. The press-conference exchange on the defense effort: PC 733, April 8, 1941; PPA 1941, p. 90. Price control: PSF, Rowe Folder, Box 56; Harvey C. Mansfield and Associates, *A Short History of OPA* (Washington, D.C.: Office of Price Administration, 1947); see also Smith Diary, March 18, 1941, FDRL. Lilienthal notes the policy divisions within hierarchies of defense agencies. Josephson, p. 545, and Ickes, pp. 535-536, describe the Cabinet discussion of labor problems. PPA, 1941, pp. 205-208, has the President's statement and executive order seizing the North American Aviation Co. plant. For the White House and labor disputes generally, see PSF, Strikes Folder, Box 56. Reports to the White House from the scene of the strike: Grady to Patterson, June 9, 1941, and Patterson to Roosevelt, June 12, 1941, OF 407-B. Reaction to the plant seizure: special compilation and analysis conducted for this book by Paul Streicker, at FDRL, OF 407-B, Boxes 20-24. On the White House reaction to congressional calls for restrictive labor measures, see Hillman to Roosevelt, June 24, 1941 (on the Vinson bill), PSF, Strikes Folder. Discussion of dollar-a-year men: PC 735, April 15, 1941; PPA, 1941, p. 116. The state of the defense program in early 1941 is reflected in Smith Diary, FDRL; McCloy to Stimson, May 21, 1941, Stimson Papers; *The United States at War,* p. 81; Nelson, pp. 275 ff.; see also Truman Committee hearings, cited below. Keynes: Clapper Papers (Diary, May 17, 1941), LC. The private report to Roosevelt, July 15, 1941, initialed rwh, is in War Department Folder, FDRL. The origins of the Truman Committee are described in Donald H. Riddle, *The Truman Committee* (New Brunswick, N.J.: Rutgers University Press, 1964), chap. 1, and in Steinberg, chap. 22; the proceedings are in "Investigation of the National Defense Program," Hearings before a Special Committee Investigating the National Defense Program, 77th Congress, 1st Session, and later sessions; the Connally comment is at p. 1325. Roosevelt's earlier preparations for congressional investigations: Roosevelt to Stimson, Knox, Knudsen, Hillman, March 6, 1941, PSF, OPM Folder, Departmental. The Lippmann comment is from his "Today and Tomorrow" column, a copy of which is in the Stimson Papers; see also *Time* and the liberal weeklies for criticism of Roosevelt's leadership during this period. The Lilienthal comparison with 1933: Lilienthal, p. 321. The struggle over extension of Selective Service is well described in Pogue[1], pp. 145-157; Langer and Gleason, pp. 568-574. See Stimson and Bundy, pp. 376, 378; Pogue[1], pp. 149, 153, 155-156; Vandenberg, pp. 13-15, for criticism of Roosevelt's leadership in the fight. I. F. Stone's comment: *The Nation,* Sept. 6, 1941, pp. 194-195. See Stone's *Nation* articles generally for brilliant studies of defense mobilization. See Somers for later developments.

"Federal Disbursements for Defense," PSF, OPM Folder, is a useful one-page summary of major defense spending in 1940 and early 1941. Smith Diary, July 15, 1941, FDRL, describes a conference, same date, of Morgenthau and congressional tax leaders with the President; see also

Roosevelt to Representative Robert Doughton, July 31, 1941, PSF, Box 47, "C" File; PSF, Tax Folder, Box 57. Alpheus Thomas Mason, *Harlan Fiske Stone* (Viking, 1956), pp. 563-574, authoritatively describes Stone's appointment. Roosevelt memorandum to Jones on appointments is dated April 30, 1941, with enclosure, James Rowe to Missy LeHand, April 25, 1941, PSF, Rowe Folder. Louis Ruchames, *Race, Jobs, & Politics* (Columbia University Press, 1953), includes a well-documented treatment of the background of Executive Order 8802; see PPA, 1941, pp. 233-235, for text of the order. OF 391 provides useful correspondence on this subject; on Roosevelt's attitude, see, especially, Roosevelt to McIntyre, June 7, 1941. Eleanor Roosevelt to "Steve" (Early), Aug. 8, 1935: PPF 1336. For a typical Roosevelt letter to civil-rights leaders during the later prewar years, see Roosevelt to Arthur B. Spingarn, June 14, 1940, PPF 1336. On the march on Washington, see Wayne Coy to Roosevelt, June 16, 1941, OF 391; and E.M.W. (Watson) to Roosevelt, June 24, 1941, PSF, Watson Folder.

Rendezvous at Argentia. General sources on the Argentia Conference: FRUS; Wilson; H. V. Morton, *Atlantic Meeting* (Dodd, Mead, 1943), the last an account of the public events by a British observer on the *Prince of Wales.* Roosevelt's departure for his Atlantic trip: Roosevelt to Sara Delano Roosevelt, Aug. 2, 1941, PL, pp. 1196-1197. A log was kept of the whole trip, entitled "Narrative," n.d., 16 pp., PSF Safe File. On personalities and other aspects of the trip: Roosevelt and Shalett, pp. 334-337; King and Whitehill, pp. 331-333; Reilly, pp. 117-124; Tully, pp. 246-247. Preparations and expectations for the conference: Sherwood, p. 358; Pogue[1], p. 142. Account of Churchill's report on the war: Elliott Roosevelt, pp. 28-31. The Sunday services are described in Churchill[3], pp. 431-432; King and Whitehill, p. 335; Sherwood, p. 353; Morton, chap. 10; they were well covered by films, which are in NA. Military and diplomatic discussions and results: FRUS, 1941, Vol. I, pp. 354-356, 358; Churchill[3], pp. 438-442; Gwyer and Butler, pp. 125-130; Pogue[1], pp. 142-145; Watson, pp. 400-406; Matloff and Snell, p. 55.

Roosevelt on postwar planning: Roosevelt to Berle, June 26, 1941, PSF, State Department, 1941, Box 28. Churchill's early draft of the Atlantic statement: FRUS, 1941, Vol. I, p. 355. Churchill-Roosevelt discussions of the charter: Sumner Welles, *Where Are We Heading?* (Harper, 1946), p. 11. Discussions of postwar organization: FRUS, 1941, Vol. I, p. 363; Churchill[3], p. 437. Postwar trade: Hull to Roosevelt, Aug. 23, 1941, 740.0011 ER 1939, SD. The note on "Adelai Stevenson" (sic) in the log is from the "Narrative," cited above, p. 16. Frankfurter's tribute: Frankfurter to Roosevelt, Aug. 18, 1941, Freedman, pp. 612-613; cf. Kolko, pp. 242-245.

CHAPTER FOUR

Senate discussion of the Atlantic meeting: *Congressional Record,* Vol. 87, Pt. 7, Aug. 12-Oct. 20, 1941; Langer and Gleason, pp. 689-690, reports major press reaction. Roosevelt's exchange with the press on the charter: PC 761, Aug. 16, 1941; PPA, 1941, p. 322. Data on popular reaction to the meeting and to 1941 events generally: Roper Center, AIPO #237, May 20, 1941; #238, May 29, 1941; #240-K, June 24, 1941; #241-T, June 1941; #245, Aug. 1941; #248-K, Sept. 17, 1941. These are comparable to Cantril, pp. 1162-1163, with small differences in the "Don't know" categories and others. Transmission of data to White House: Hadley Cantril, "Summary Interpretation of Latest Results," July 3, 1941, PSF, Public Opinion Polls. Stimson to Roosevelt on leadership: Stimson Diary, June 30, 1941. Stimson-Roosevelt exchange on strategic requirements: Roosevelt to Stimson, July 9, 1941; Stimson to Roosevelt, Sept. 23, 1941, PSF, Stimson Folder. Times Square poll: Harold Lavine, *The Nation,* Aug. 30, 1941, pp. 179-180. A Soviet view of the background of Pearl Harbor: N. N. Yakovlev, esp. Pts. II, III.

The Winds and Waves of Strife. Roosevelt's warning to Tokyo: Churchill[3], p. 446; Hull, pp. 1018, 1229; Long, p. 215. The President's conference with Nomura: *FRUS—Japan,* pp. 554-555; Hull, p. 1019. Reception of the warning by the Japanese: Hull, p. 1019; *FRUS—Japan,* p. 555; Langer and Gleason, pp. 697 ff.; PHA, Pt. 15, p. 1682. Roosevelt to Churchill on the former's warning, Aug. 18, 1941: FRUS, 1941, Vol. IV, p. 380. Proposed Roosevelt-Konoye conference: Butow, pp. 234-235, 245; Ike, pp. 112-124; Grew, pp. 1301-1302. Japanese note of Aug. 28: *FRUS—Japan,* pp. 573-575; Ike, pp. 124-126. Nomura on Roosevelt's reception of note: PHA, Pt. 17, p. 2794. Grew's change of outlook: *FRUS—Japan,* p. 565; FRUS, 1941, Vol. IV, pp. 382-383; Heinrichs, pp. 340-343; Grew, pp. 1310-1312 (slight differences in the same texts are due to paraphrasing). Roosevelt-Nomura conference of Sept. 3, 1941: *FRUS—Japan,* pp. 588-589. Liaison conference meeting of Sept. 3: Ike, pp. 32, 130; Butow, pp. 249-250; Butow, at p. 250, cites problems of translation; I have used his translation. Conference of Konoye and military chiefs with Hirohito: PHA (Konoye testimony), Pt. 20, p. 4004; Mosley, pp. 214-215; Ike, p. 133; Butow, pp. 254-255. Imperial Conference of Sept. 6: Ike, pp. 134-163; Butow, p. 258; Mosley, p. 220; PHA, Pt. 20. p. 4005; versions of the Emperor's poem differ slightly.

The *Greer* incident: Gerard E. Hasselwander, "Der US-Zerstörer 'Greer' und 'U 652' am 4, September 1941," *Marine-Rundschau,* Heft 3, 1962, pp. 148-160, a thorough account; PSF, Navy Department, Box 21, 1941; Beardall to Roosevelt, Sept. 9, 1941, enclosing copy of dispatch, Senior Officer Present Afloat, Iceland, to Chief of Naval Operations, Sept. 6, 1941, FDRL; FRUS, 1941, Vol. IV, pp. 93 ff.; Churchill[3], p. 493. Death of Sara Delano Roosevelt: Rosenman, pp. 290-292; Sherwood, pp. 370-372; Watson-Hassett memorandum, PPF 8, Sept. 19, 1941. Mackenzie King to Roosevelt, Nov. 10, 1941: PSF, Canada Folder. Churchill's diversion of destroyers after American assumption of full convoying: Churchill[3], p. 517. Knox speech to American Legion is quoted in Langer and Gleason, p. 746. Roosevelt's "shoot on sight" speech: PPA, Sept. 11, 1941, pp. 384-392. Hitler's reaction: *Führer Conferences,* Sept. 17, 1941, pp. 33, 37-40. American public opinion: Cantril, pp. 1128-1129. Roundup of press opinion: Langer and Gleason, p. 751.

The Call to Battle Stations. General sources on Pearl Harbor attack and its background: PHA; Wohlstetter; Farago; Yakovlev. Forestry Service transfer: Ickes, p. 626. Plans for a Key West fishing retreat: Sherwood, p.

378. Roosevelt's health: Ross McIntire, *White House Physician* (Putnam, 1946); and other references cited in chap. 15 notes below. Main source for Japanese-American relations, late 1941: *FRUS—Japan;* FRUS, 1941, Vol. IV; Feis[3]; Grew; PHA; Butow; Ike; Hull. On relations with China: Hull, pp. 1005, 1024; Grew, pp. 1279, 1355; Matloff, p. 63; Feis[4], p. 276; Butow, p. 595; *Morgenthau Diary* (China), pp. 364-365, 377-379, 547-548; FRUS, 1941, Vol. IV, pp. 396, 435, 436-441; Hull to Roosevelt, Aug. 19, 1941, PSF, China Folder, 1941-1944. Continuing negotiations with Japan: PHA, Pt. 20, pp. 4423-4427; *FRUS—Japan,* pp. 656-661, 662-663, 685; Grew, p. 1272 and *passim.* Evidence of faulty perception or communication: Clapper Papers (Diary, Nov. 18, 21, 1941), LC; *FRUS—Japan,* pp. 612, 619, 631, 687; Konoye, in PHA, Pt. 20, pp. 4005, 4006; FRUS, 1941, Vol. IV, pp. 412 419, 423; Wohlstetter. *Kearny* incident: Morison[1], pp. 92-93; PSF, Navy Department, Box 21, 1941, Roosevelt's Navy Day speech, Oct. 27, 1941: PPA, 1941, pp. 438-444. For an authoritative German account of the *Kearny* episode, see Jürgen Rohwer, "Der Kearny-Zwischenfall," *Marine-Rundschau,* Heft 5, 1959, pp. 288-301.

Roosevelt's dire warning, Oct. 9, 1941, of a Russian-type plight for Americans if Hitler won in Europe: PPA, 1941, p. 411. Roosevelt's empty bag of tricks: Sherwood, p. 383. Indications that Japan would attack British or Dutch or Russian territory, not American: Wohlstetter, chap. 5 and *passim;* Farago, pp. 288, 290, 307-308, 350; Yakovlev, Pt. III. American reluctance to fight for Kra Peninsula, etc.: Sherwood, p. 429; these views are corroborated by polling data received at the White House and indicating that respondents were strong for helping Britain and the Philippines but not Singapore or Australia; Russell Davenport to Hopkins, July 10, 1941, HHP, Box 298. Shift on defense of the Philippines: Watson, pp. 438-444; Matloff and Snell, pp. 67-68. Shifting attitudes on policy toward Japan: Cantril, p. 975. Roosevelt's cautious handling of aid to Russia: Raymond H. Dawson, *The Decision to Aid Russia, 1941* (Chapel Hill: University of North Carolina Press, 1959), chaps. 7-10. Press and political reaction to Roosevelt's comments on religion in Russia: Dawson, p. 260. Taylor mission to Vatican: Myron C. Taylor (ed.), *Wartime Correspondence between President Roosevelt and Pope Pius XII* (Macmillan, 1947); Roosevelt to Taylor, Sept. 1, 1941, PSF, Italy Folder; Taylor memorandum summarizing views of Monsig. Tardini, Sept. 20, 1941, PSF, Vatican Folder; see also *The Holy See and the World War,* Vol. V (Rome, 1969). Stalin's comments to Churchill about lack of clarity in British-Russian relations: Churchill[3], pp. 528-529.

A Time for War. Liaison conference, Nov 1, 1941: Ike, pp. 208-239; Mosley, pp. 202-204. Proposals A and B: Ike, p. 204; Butow, pp. 322-323; texts: Ike, pp. 209-211. Imperial Conference, Nov. 5, 1941: Butow, p. 325; Ike, pp. 208-239; Mosley, pp. 230, 240. Roosevelt-Nomura discussions, Nov. 10, 1941: Sherwood, p. 420; Stimson Diary; PHA, Pt. 11, pp. 5420, 5431. Cabinet meeting next day: Stimson and Bundy; PHA, Pt. 11, pp. 5420, 5432; Hull, p. 1058. Roosevelt offer to Nomura to expedite exploratory discussions: *FRUS—Japan,* pp. 715-719. Roosevelt discussions with Nomura and Kurusu, Nov. 17, 1941: *FRUS—Japan,* pp. 740-743; Freedman, p. 623. Report on Chiang's fears: Currie to Hull, Nov. 25, 1941, 711.93/481-1/2SD. Hull's denunciation of Proposal B: Hull, p. 1070. Roosevelt's truce offer, c. Nov. 17, 1941: PHA, Pt. 14, p. 1109; on dating of same, see Langer and Gleason, p. 872; Feis[4], p. 312. Hull's changes: PHA, Pt. 14, pp. 1110-1115. Roosevelt to Churchill, Nov. 24, 1941, on the proposal: PL, p. 1246; Churchill's response: PHA, Pt. 14, p. 1300. Stimson to Roosevelt on Indochina: PHA, Pt. 11, p. 5434; see also PPA, 1941, p. 510; Blum[1], p. 330. Hull to Stimson on "washing his hands of it": PHA, Pt. 11, p. 5422. Japanese liaison conference, Nov. 29, 1941: Ike, pp. 260-262. Imperial Conference, Dec. 1, 1941: Ike, pp. 262-283. Mussolini on Roosevelt is quoted in Langer and Gleason, p. 925. Roosevelt to Hirohito: PPA, 1941, pp. 511-513.

Morison[3], pp. 83 ff., pictures the Japanese training and preparations for Pearl Harbor. Roosevelt's fatalistic statements: Blum[1], p. 391; Smith Diary, Dec. 6, 1941, FDRL. My interpretation of Roosevelt's strategic state of mind as of late fall 1941: PL; PHA, Pt. 11, pp. 5438-5441; Lilienthal (Hu Shih conversation with Roosevelt, morning of Dec. 7, 1941), pp. 505-506; Sherwood, p. 428 (Roosevelt's complaints later to Hopkins about Hull—complaints I believe also directed at himself); Yakovlev, Pt. III; Raymond A. Esthus, "President Roosevelt's Commitment to Britain to Intervene in a Pacific War," *Mississippi Valley Historical Review,* June 1963, pp. 28-38; F.W.F.S. Birkenhead, *Halifax* (London: Hamilton, 1965), pp. 529-530; George E. Morganstern, *Pearl Harbor* (Devin-Adair, 1947), chap. 3, pp. 599-603; see also Langer and Gleason; Woodward, pp. 186-187. Roosevelt's request for Asia-Pacific bases: Hull to Winant and to Johnson (Canberra), FRUS, 1941, Vol. I, pp. 573-575. Roosevelt on Japan's strategy: PPA, 1941, p. 501; *FRUS—Japan,* p. 772; Sherwood, p. 428. Roosevelt's receipt of first thirteen parts: PHA, Pt. 10, pp. 4659-4671; Sherwood, pp. 426-427; Smith Diary, Dec. 6, 1941, FDRL; Farago, pp. 352-354.

Rendezvous at Pearl. Pearl Harbor attack: primarily, Morison[3], chap. 5; Walter Lord, *Day of Infamy* (Holt, 1957); Kimmel. Knox's reception of news: Morison[3], p. 101. Hopkins's remark: Sherwood, p. 431. Hull's statement to the Japanese envoys: Hull, p. 1096. Churchill's reaction to the news of Pearl Harbor: Churchill[3], pp. 604-605; John G. Winant, *Letters from Grosvenor Square* (Boston: Houghton Mifflin, 1947), p. 199; I have described Churchill's reaction wholly on the basis of his later recollection. Roosevelt's reaction and early events in his study: Tully, pp. 254 ff.; Farago, pp. 378-379; Stimson Diary; PHA, Pt. 11, pp. 5438-5439; Lilienthal (Hu Shih's remembrance), p. 507; Biddle, p. 206; NYT, Jan. 24, 1943, VII, p. 3; interview with Eleanor Roosevelt, New York *Post,* Dec. 7, 1961, p. 57. Evening meeting: Perkins, pp. 379-380; Sherwood, p. 433; Ickes, pp. 622-665; Blum[2], p. 1; Biddle, p. 206; Stimson Diary; PHA, Pt. 11, p. 5439, Pt. 19, p. 3503; PL, p. 1252. PHA, Pt. 19, pp. 3503-3507, has transcript of the congressional conference with the President, evening of Dec. 7, 1941. Scene outside White House: Richard L. Strout, *Christian Science Monitor,* Dec. 8, 1941, p. 3; and other periodicals. Military reports arriving at White House: PSF, Philippines Folder, 4-41, especially Marshall telephone calls forwarding MacArthur messages of Dec. 7 (9:00 P.M.), Dec. 8, Dec. 9

(Washington time). Roosevelt to Murrow: Alexander Kendrick, *Prime Time* (Boston: Little, Brown, 1969), pp. 239-240.

CHAPTER FIVE

Roosevelt's feeling of anguished relief and attitude toward security arrangements after Pearl Harbor: Tully, pp. 256 ff.; Eleanor Roosevelt, p. 237; Perkins, pp. 379 ff.; Hurd, p. 265. Churchill's immediate action: Churchill[3], pp. 610-611. Churchill's "harem" remark: Bryant[2], pp. 225-226. Roosevelt's press conference and fireside chat of Dec. 9, 1941: PPA, 1941, pp. 516-530. White House arrangements: Eleanor Roosevelt, p. 237; Blum[2], pp. 1-2; Rosenman, p. 310. Hitler's strategic reaction to Pearl Harbor: Meskill, pp. 40-47; Warlimont, pp. 208-209; Ciano, p. 416; Hinsley, pp. 186-188; Bullock, pp. 661 ff.; Shirer, pp. 1155 ff.; Friedländer[2], pp. 270-271. I have discussed the Japanese-Soviet aspect of Hitler's decision with German and Soviet historians. Hitler's war address: Shirer, pp. 1173 ff.; Gordon W. Prange, *Hitler's Words* (Washington, D.C.: American Council on Public Affairs, 1944). A useful general source on major 1942 diplomatic episodes is Joseph E. Davies Papers, 1942 Folders, Box 11, LC.

A Christmas Visitor. Immediate defense efforts after Pearl Harbor: Marshall to Stimson, Dec. 9, 1941, PSF, War Department Folder; Pogue[1], p. 235; Matloff, pp. 82-83. The memorandum on Roosevelt's World War I experience is G.G.T. to S.T.E., Dec. 11, 1941, PL, pp. 1255-1256; internal evidence indicates strongly that this was composed by Roosevelt. On Roosevelt's earlier defensiveness about his World War I role, see Burns, pp. 65-66. Roosevelt's call for a conference to draft a basic wartime labor policy, and warning about strikes, Dec. 11, 1941: PPA, 1941, pp. 533-534; his remarks to the management-labor conference: *ibid.,* pp. 558-562. Miss Perkins's observation of him at this point: Perkins, p. 368. Eleanor Roosevelt's reaction to her sons going off to war: Lash, p. 262. Churchill's arrival in Washington and installation in the White House: Sherwood, pp. 442-443; Reilly, p. 125; Churchill[3], pp. 662-663; Eleanor Roosevelt, pp. 242-243. The Roosevelt-Churchill Christmas Eve ceremony, PPA, 1941, pp. 593-595; Sherwood, p. 443.

Churchill's concern about a possible shift in U.S. strategy: Churchill[3], pp. 641-643. Washington's position on strategy: Pogue[1], p. 266; Matloff and Snell, p. 99, and references contained therein. The British plan for North Africa: Churchill[3], pp. 663-665; Gwyer and Butler, pp. 353-354. Gwyer and Butler, pp. 354-357, has a full report on the Anglo-American military discussion; see also Pogue[1], p. 268; Stimson Diary, Dec. 21, 1941. Stimson's role: Stimson Diary, Dec. 20, 1941; and "Memorandum of Decisions at White House," Dec. 21, 1941, Stimson Papers. Churchill's view of the American approach to strategy: Churchill[3], p. 673; see also Gwyer and Butler, pp. 350, 358; McNeill, pp. 102-108; and for a dissenting British view of Churchill's plan: Bryant[2], p. 236. The question of unified command: Sherwood, p. 455; Gwyer and Butler, p. 368; Pogue[1], p. 276. Diversion of MacArthur-bound forces to the British: Stimson Diary, Dec. 25, 1941; Pogue[1], pp. 265-266. Dill's report on the American command setup to Brooke: Bryant[2], p. 234. Wavell appointment: Churchill[3], p. 673; Bryant[2], p. 235; Gwyer and Butler, p. 370; Sherwood, p. 457; Moran, p. 18. Combined command structure: British proposal, Gwyer and Butler, p. 372; Roosevelt's handwritten modifications: Sherwood, p. 469; see also Matloff, p. 125. On the War Department's early support for a "Supreme War Command" to be established in Washington, see "Memorandum of Decisions at White House," Dec. 21, 1941, Stimson Papers. Admiral King: King and Whitehill, chap. 29; Rogow, pp. 102-105. Wilson's comment: Moran, pp. 23-24.

Senior Partners, and Junior. Roosevelt's negotiations with Litvinov over a religion clause: Sherwood, pp. 448-449; Hull, p. 1120. Churchill[3], pp. 682-683, relates Roosevelt's alleged effort to save Litvinov's soul; see also Lash, p. 266. Formulating the Charter of the United Nations: Hull, chap. 81; Sherwood, pp. 449 ff. (with text showing Russian amendments); Churchill[3], pp. 666, 683-685; Lash, p. 270; McNeill, pp. 94-102; Davies Papers, May 1942 Folder, Box 11, LC. Text of the Charter: PPA, 1942, pp. 3-4; Rothstein[1], p. 114. Lash, p. 271, quotes Churchill on "four-fifths of the human race."

Relations with China; Roosevelt to Morgenthau, Jan. 9, 1942, PL, p. 1270; PSF, Diplomatic Corr., China, 1933-1943; Blum[2], pp. 87-102; Currie to Roosevelt, Sept. 13, 1941, PSF, Currie Folder. Attitudes of Pacific allies: Matloff, pp. 87-96; Roosevelt to Marshall, Jan. 9, 1942, PL, p. 1271; Roosevelt to Berle, Jan. 29, 1942, PL, p. 1281. Lash, p. 268, relates the exchange among Churchill, Hopkins, and Roosevelt on Russia. Stalin's complaints about war supplies: Stimson Diary, Nov. 24, 1941. Eden-Stalin discussions: Eden, pp. 289 ff. (with texts of some of the exchanges); Churchill[3], pp. 694 ff.; see also Gwyer and Butler, pp. 319-325. Churchill to Eden on likely postwar considerations: Churchill[3], p. 696. Washington reaction: Hull to Roosevelt, May 5, 1942, PSF, Hull Folder. Stalin's earlier interest in American troops on his front: Sherwood, pp. 342-343. Later Soviet attitudes and developments: Eden, p. 300; Churchill[3], pp. 627-628; Russian Correspondence, AR, 4557-31, Dec. 15, 1941; see also Roosevelt to Currie, and attached cable, Dec. 12, 1941, PSF, China, Box 4. Hoped-for Soviet intervention against Japan: Stimson Diary, Dec. 10, 1942; Gerow to Marshall, Dec. 17, 1941 (marked "Not Used"), AR, 4557-32 (but see Stark to Roosevelt, Dec. 13, 1941, AR, 4557-32); see also Matloff, p. 239, and sources cited therein; *Correspondence*[2], pp. 17-18. MacArthur's advice: MacArthur to Marshall, Dec. 10, 1941, AR, 4544-26. Roosevelt on Stalin: Lash, pp. 262, 267, 268. Roosevelt to Mrs. Churchill on Churchill: Sherwood, p. 478.

The Sinews of Total Victory. Roosevelt's State of the Union message, Jan. 6, 1942: PPA, 1942, pp. 32-42. Mobilization situation after Pearl Harbor: Matloff and Snell, p. 108; Hopkins to Roosevelt, Jan. 2, 1942, HHP, Maritime Commission Folder; Frankfurter to Roosevelt (with enclosed memorandum), Dec. 17, 1941, Freedman, pp. 628-632; Roosevelt to Land, Feb. 21, 1942, PSF Safe File.

The mobilization situation pre-Pearl Harbor: Novick *et al.*, pp. 83 ff.; *Industrial Mobilization for War,* pp. 181 ff. Lubin reports: PSF, Currie Folder, Box 45. Influences close to the administration for reorganized production machinery: Stimson to Roosevelt, Jan. 7, 1942, PSF, Stimson Folder; Frankfurter letter cited above; Smith Diary, LC. Baruch: Clapper Papers, Personal File, Cont. 23, LC. Knudsen shift: E. M. W. (Watson) to Roosevelt, Dec. 8, 1941, with Wallace memorandum, PSF, Wallace Folder; Sherwood, pp. 475-476; Smith Diary, Jan. 12, 13, 16, 1942, LC. For Stimson's general view, see his letter to Roosevelt cited above. Frankfurter's praise: Frankfurter to Roosevelt, Jan. 17, 1942, Freedman, pp. 643-644. Labor's attitude toward union security: Harry A. Millis and Royal E. Montgomery, *Organized Labor* (McGraw-Hill, 1945), p. 695. Captive mine labor situation: John L. Lewis to Roosevelt, Nov. 19, 1941, PSF, Strikes Folder; William H. Davis to Roosevelt, Nov. 22, 1941, PSF, Strikes Folder. An appraisal of labor leadership of the time: Frankfurter to Roosevelt, March 20, 1942, Freedman, pp. 652-654. Origins of White House labor-management conference: Lubin to Roosevelt, Nov. 6, 1941, PSF, Strikes Folder. Interest-group concerns in price-control policy-making are amply reflected in "Hearings before the Committee on Banking and Currency," House of Representatives, on H.R. 5479, 77th Congress, 1st Session. I have used my dissertation, "Congress and the Formation of Economic Policies," Harvard University, 1947, chap. 4, "The Emergency Price Control Act of 1942," in connection with the price-control situation of early 1942. Roosevelt's statement on signing the Emergency Price Control Act, Jan. 30, 1942: PPA, 1942, pp. 67-70.

CHAPTER SIX

Eleanor Roosevelt reports her husband's remark about all being killed except Miss Perkins: Eleanor Roosevelt, p. 249. Roosevelt's White House life: PSF, Eleanor Roosevelt Folder, Box 55. Stimson saw the President's map room: Stimson Diary, April 12, 1942. Roosevelt and Lucy Mercer Rutherfurd: Daniels[1], chaps. 11, 13; Clapper Papers, Nov. 3, 1942, Box 23, LC; confidential sources. Detailed accounts of Roosevelt's weekend trips to Hyde Park: Hassett, pp. 1-81. Roosevelt's veto of Eleanor's proposal to make Hyde Park a convalescent home: PL, p. 1283, Feb. 9, 1942. Hassett, pp. 26-28, and Lash, pp. 271-275, picture Roosevelt's March (26-30) 1942 weekend at Hyde Park; the Lash diary item evidently refers to the same weekend.

Defeat in the Pacific. For the Japanese plan of attack, see Morton, pp. 103 ff., and Butler, Vol. 3, Pt. II, pp. 293 ff., both of which make extensive use of Japanese sources. MacArthur's initial reports to Washington: see references for chap. 4. Morison[3] describes the American naval defeats feelingly. Kirby, *The War Against Japan,* Vol. I, *The Loss of Singapore* (London, 1957), chaps. 10, 11, 12, 14, 17, 20, narrates in detail the British retreat in Malaya. Churchill[4], pp. 5-6, 8, provides documentation of his exchanges with the Australians; on later developments, see Hopkins to Roosevelt, March 25, 1942, PSF, Australia; Freedman, pp. 650-651, 654-655. Early American planning on the Philippines: Pogue[1], pp. 238-239; see also Stimson and Bundy, p. 396; Stimson Diary, Dec. 14, 1941; and "Our Preparations for Supporting MacA," handwritten, Stimson Papers. Churchill's feelings about the Chinese: Churchill[4], p. 135; on the Chiang-Wavell issue, see also Butler, pp. 410-412; Stimson Diary, Dec. 29, 1942, and Dec. 30, 1942. Wavell's comment on American sentiment toward China: Churchill[4], pp. 134-135.

Louis Morton, *The Fall of the Philippines* (Washington, D.C.: Office of the Chief of Military History, 1953), is a richly detailed study with emphasis on military operations. Broader questions of command: MacArthur; Whitney; and Willoughby and Chamberlain, which describes the command situation and differences from the MacArthur perspective; and Pogue[1]; Stimson and Bundy; Morton, *Fall of the Philippines,* from the Washington viewpoint. See Lewis H. Brereton, *The Brereton Diaries* (Morrow, 1946), for somewhat different views, and John Hersey, *Men on Bataan* (Knopf, 1943), and Carlos P. Romulo, *I Saw the Fall of the Philippines* (Doubleday, 1943), for close-ups of the combat. The early write-off of the Philippines as a strategically defensible theater is indicated in Pogue[1], pp. 239 ff.; Stimson Diary, Dec. 24, 1941; and Morton, *Strategy and Command,* pp. 187 ff. MacArthur's feeling of security against air attack: report of conference of MacArthur and others, Manila, Dec. 6, 1941, PMRP, Naval Aide's file, Warfare, Philippine Islands, Box 17. On the White House interpretation of Roosevelt's Philippine message, see Whitney, p. 29, and NYT, Dec. 29, 1941, pp. 1, 6; Dec. 30, 1941, p. 1. The Quezon message: MacArthur, pp. 138-139; Stimson Diary, Feb. 9, 11, 1942; the texts of Roosevelt's messages to MacArthur and Quezon are in Stimson and Bundy, pp. 400-403; see also PSF, Interior. Richard H. Rovere and Arthur Schlesinger, Jr., *The MacArthur Controversy* (Farrar, Straus, 1965), discusses the episode and puts the MacArthur–War Department relationship in a wider perspective. MacArthur's reports and proposals to Washington: MacArthur to Adjutant General, Dec. 23, 1941; MacArthur to Marshall (no. 201), Feb. 4, 1942; MacArthur to Marshall (no. 297), Feb. 16, 1942; MacArthur to Marshall (no. 344), Feb. 22, 1942; Marshall's main response: Marshall to MacArthur, Feb. 8, 1942—all in PSF Safe File, Philippines, Feb. 8, 1942. See also Frank Sayre to Roosevelt, Jan. 26, 1942, PSF, Philippine Folder. This file also contains communications on relations with Quezon and on the evacuation from the Philippines.

This Generation of Americans. Roosevelt's standing in the polls: relevant polls in PSF, Box 54; see also Cantril, pp. 756, 1174-1175. Press support: study by James S. Twohey Associates, cited in *PM,* Feb. 27, 1942. "Sinking" of the Japanese "battleship": Morison[2], p. 180, n. 33, which indicates the difficulty of identification. Attacks on Hopkins: *Time,* Jan. 5, 1942, pp. 16-17; Sherwood, p. 517. *Social Justice* attacks are from facsimiles of articles in *PM,* Feb. 20, 1942. Roosevelt's attitude toward his old-time adversaries: Rosenman, p. 6. Joseph Kennedy's nonappointment: PL, pp. 1289-1290; see also PL, p. 1383; Richard J. Whalen, *The Founding Father* (New American Library, 1964). Stimson and Lindbergh: Stimson Diary, Dec. 21, 1941, Jan. 12, 1942; see also Stimson Papers, Jan. 9, 1942, Jan. 13, 1942. Roosevelt on Washington as a rumor factory, Feb. 17, 1942: PPA, 1942, p. 102. Roosevelt on the "Cliveden Set" and its associates: PSF, Vatican Folder, Box 19; Hassett, p. 19; PL, pp. 1301-1302. Cissy Patterson's "undies": Ernst to Roosevelt, March 20, 1942, Ernst Papers; Roosevelt to Ernst, March 23, 1942, PL, p. 1300. Roosevelt's Washington's Birthday speech, Feb. 23, 1942: PPA, 1942, checked against recordings. Japanese shelling: Sherwood, p. 504. Roosevelt on personal leadership: Roosevelt to Leffingwell, March 16, 1942, and to Mary Norton, March 24, 1942, PL, pp. 1298-1299, 1300; see also Roosevelt to Josephus Daniels, July 30, 1942, PPF 86. Elmer Davis remark: PL, p. 1298.

The background and events of the Japanese evacuation have been brilliantly researched by scholars with various perspectives: Dorothy Swaine Thomas and Richard S. Nishimoto, *The Spoilage* (Berkeley: University of California Press, 1946); Morton Grodzins, *Americans Betrayed* (Chicago: University of Chicago Press, 1949); Jacobus tenBroek, Edward N. Barnhart, Floyd W. Matson, *Prejudice, War, and the Constitution* (Berkeley: University of California Press, 1954); Stetson Conn, "The Decision to Evacuate the Japanese from the Pacific Coast," in Greenfield[2]. The last, part of the U.S. Army history program, makes full use of government records. White House records on this subject are relatively scanty; see Thomas D. Campbell to Roosevelt, March 12, 1942, and attached memorandum, Campbell to John McCloy, Feb. 25, 1942 and March 7, 1942, OF 133; and for an example of Roosevelt's differentiation between Japanese and Caucasian aliens, see Roosevelt to Stimson, May 5, 1942, OF 4849. Biddle's experience with Roosevelt on civil-liberties matters: Biddle, pp. 166 ff., 207, 238.

The War Against the Whites. The poem "Remember December Eighth" is from Mosley, p. 270. The Japanese army and nationalist reaction: F. C. Jones, *Japan's New Order in East Asia* (Oxford University Press, 1957), pp. 362-363. The central role of Japan in the co-prosperity sphere: Otto D. Tolischus, *Through Japanese Eyes* (Reynal & Hitchcock, 1945), pp. 86, 87. Roosevelt's and Churchill's first exchange on the Indian question: Churchill[4], p. 209; Moran, p. 33. Frankfurter's views: Frankfurter to Roosevelt, July 9, 1942, enclosing Frankfurter to Stafford Cripps, July 9, 1942, Freedman, pp. 664-667. Feeling in the Senate on British imperialism in India: Robert M. La Follette, Jr., to Roosevelt, Feb. 20, 1942, PSF, Senate Folder. Mixed administration attitudes: Clapper Papers, Cont. 23, Jan.-Feb. 1942 Folder, LC. Roosevelt's concern that the Indians would not rally in defense of their country: FRUS, 1942, Vol. I, p. 604. Churchill to Harriman on Indian incapacity for defense: *ibid.,* pp. 608, 612. Roosevelt to Churchill, March 10, 1942, on American experience with confederation: *ibid.,* pp. 615-616. Johnson on Indian situation: *ibid.,* pp. 626 ff. Hopkins's view: *ibid.,* p. 629. Churchill to Cripps on coming home: Churchill to Roosevelt, April 11, 1942, *ibid.,* p. 633. Roosevelt to Churchill, April 11, 1942, urging postponement of Cripps's departure: *ibid.,* pp. 633-634. Churchill's reply to Roosevelt: *ibid.,* pp. 634-635. Indian Ocean situation: messages in HHP, Box 305. Roosevelt to Marshall on putting Hopkins to bed: Sherwood, p. 531.

Willkie on the U.S. Navy: *Time,* March 9, 1942, pp. 9-10. Roosevelt on the Navy's lack of enterprise: Stimson Diary, Dec. 28, 1941. Knox's exchange with Churchill: Churchill[3], p. 667. Morison[2], chaps. 11-21, and

Morison[3], chaps. 1-9, provide a graphic portrait of the triumphs and tribulations of American naval power in the Pacific during the early months of the war. Doolittle raid: PMRP, Box 15; Arnold to Roosevelt, April 21 and 22, 1942, Arnold Papers, Box 45, LC. The Battle of the Coral Sea and Midway: Morison[3]; Morton; Mitsuo Fuchida and Masatake Okumiya, *Midway: The Battle That Doomed Japan* (Annapolis, Md.: United States Naval Institute, 1955), with a useful foreword by Admiral Spruance; Walter Lord, *Incredible Victory* (Harper, 1967); Masatake Okumiya and Jiro Horikoshi, *Zero!* (London: Transworld Publishers, 1958), pp. 144 ff. The "Shangri-La" exchange is reported in Hassett, pp. 40-41, and I have quoted Morison[3], p. 76, on the Japanese as Oriental disciples of Mahan. Roosevelt message to MacArthur about approaching Japanese fleet: PSF, Australia, Box 1. On the fall of Corregidor, see Jonathan M. Wainwright, *General Wainwright's Story* (Garden City, N.Y.: Doubleday, 1946).

CHAPTER SEVEN

Roosevelt and inflated battle reports: Roosevelt to Churchill, March 17, 1942, PMRP; compare Morison[3], p. 389; see also Emmons to Marshall, June 7, 1942, on AAF role at Midway, HHP, Box 308; report from Western Defense Command, June 12, 1942, PSF Safe File. Hitler's directive: Directive No. 41, April 5, 1942, Führer Headquarters, text in Trevor-Roper, pp. 116-121. Hitler on Middle Eastern prospect: Hinsley, chap. 10. Stalin's May Day proclamation: Stalin, p. 54. Litvinov on second front: *Time,* March 9, 1942, p. 9. Background of strategic planning: Pogue[1], p. 304; Matloff and Snell, pp. 177 ff.; Marshall to Roosevelt, quoted in Sherwood, p. 519. Stimson on taking initiative: Stimson to Roosevelt, March 27, 1942, PSF, Stimson Folder. White House conference of April 1, 1942: Marshall to Roosevelt, n.d., Marshall Folder, PSF Safe File; see also Pogue[1], p. 306; Sherwood, pp. 518 ff.; Matloff, pp. 183 ff. Roosevelt's "cigarette-holder gesture": Pogue[1], p. 306. Roosevelt's developing views on second front: PMRP, Spring 1942. Stimson on the memorable meeting: Stimson Diary, April 1, 1942. Roosevelt to Churchill on the planned Hopkins-Marshall trip: Churchill[4], p. 314. Reports of conference to Roosevelt: Marshall to Roosevelt (via McNarney), April 12, 1942, PSF, Marshall Folder. Churchill's position on war plans: Bryant[2], pp. 286 ff.; Sherwood, pp. 523 ff.; Moran, pp. 38-39; Churchill[4], pp. 317 ff., quoted from p. 322.

Reprise: Russia Second. Background of policy on military aid to Russia: AR, 4557-32 to AR, 4557-38 (Dec. 1941 to Feb. 1942). Conferences: Roosevelt to Stalin, April 12, 1942, *Correspondence*[2], pp. 22-23; Roosevelt to Churchill, March 18, 1942, PMRP. Molotov's accoutrements: Eleanor Roosevelt, pp. 250-251. Soviet-British peace treaty: Rothstein[1], pp. 158-160. Roosevelt-Molotov discussions: FRUS, 1942, Vol. III, pp. 566 ff.; Sherwood, pp. 557-576, which includes notes by Samuel H. Cross, interpreter, as well as by Hopkins. On Molotov's stop-over in London earlier, see Clapper Papers (Diary, March 24, 1943), LC. Roosevelt's concern about Russian front: Sherwood, pp. 568, 569. Text of second-front statement: Sherwood,

p. 577; Rothstein[1], pp. 166-167 (slight variation). Roosevelt on his relations with Molotov: Roosevelt to Winant, June 17, 1942, PL, p. 1329. Churchill to Molotov on second front: Gwyer and Butler, pp. 596-597; Churchill[4], pp. 341-342. Molotov report in Moscow: Werth, pp. 382-384. Churchill on keeping the President on the rails: Bryant[2], p. 320. Churchill at Hyde Park: Pawle, p. 167; Churchill[4], pp. 376-377. Receipt of news of Tobruk fall: Ismay, p. 255; Bryant[2], p. 329; Churchill[4], p. 383. Marshall's reaction: Pogue[1], p. 333; Marshall to Roosevelt, July 10, 1942, AR. Stimson and Marshall on second front: Stimson to Roosevelt, July 15, [1942], PSF, Stimson Folder; Elting E. Morison, pp. 586-587. Discussions in England and Roosevelt's shift: Sherwood, pp. 606-612. On second front generally: Berezhkov, Pt. II; Deborin, chap. 10; McNeill, pp. 178-201; Kolko, pp. 14-20; Maisky, Pt. 4; Davies Papers, Jan.-Nov. Folders, Boxes 11-12, LC; Clapper Papers, 1942, LC.

Roosevelt to Churchill on latter's forthcoming meeting with Stalin: Sherwood, p. 616. Churchill's trip to Russia: Churchill[4], p. 475. Stalin on diversions from Soviet front: *Correspondence*[2], p. 28 and *passim*. Stalin's refusal to accept second-front postponement: *Correspondence*[1], p. 56. Churchill-Stalin discussions in Moscow: Churchill[4], pp. 472-502; Sherwood, pp. 617-622. Reports from the front: A. I. Yeremenko, *Stalingrad Notes of the Front Commander* (Moscow, 1961), p. 87, as cited by Ulam, p. 337. See Ulam, pp. 328-338 and generally, on this period. Roosevelt's message to Stalin after the conference: Sherwood, p. 622. Implications of second-front strategy: Williams, pp. 209-229.

Asia Third. Hopkins on "white man's burden": Sherwood, p. 578. Indian political situation: M. S. Venkataramani and B. K. Shrivastava, "The United States and the 'Quit India' Demand," *Indian Quarterly* (New Delhi), April-June 1964, pp. 101-139, and sources cited therein; see also FRUS, 1942, Vol. I, pp. 663 ff., 685 ff. Gandhi-Chiang meeting: Payne, pp. 243-244. Gandhi to Chiang, June 25, 1942: PSF, China.

Chiang to Roosevelt, July 25, 1942: FRUS, 1942, Vol. I, pp. 695-698. British position on India: FRUS, 1942, Vol. I, pp. 703-705; further correspondence of principals: *ibid.*, pp. 703, 705, 713, 714-715, 716; see also Hull, pp. 1486-1490; Roosevelt to Ickes, Aug. 12, 1942, PPF 3650. See, generally, PSF, Diplomatic Corr., China, 1933-43; FRUS, 1942, *China*. American military turn to the possibility of Pacific First: Stimson Diary, July 10, 1942; Dill to Churchill, July 15, 1942, Churchill[4], pp. 439-440; Sherwood, p. 594; King and Whitehill, pp. 398-399; Marshall to Roosevelt, May 9, 1942, Arnold Papers, Box 45, LC; see also Morison[5], p. 13. Roosevelt's response: PMRP, Box 13; Stimson Diary, July 15, 1942; Sherwood, p. 605; Morison[5], p. 13 n.; Churchill[4], pp. 440-441. MacArthur's pressing for second front in Asia: PMRP, Naval Aide's File, S.W. Pacific, Box 17.

The Long Arms of War. Führer Conferences, p. 80, records Hitler's new interest in submarine warfare. Estimates and reports of ship losses from submarine and raider attacks must be treated with care; I have used Richard M. Leighton and Robert W. Coakley, *Global Logistics and Strategy, 1940-1943* (Washington, D.C.: Office of the Chief of Military History,

1955), pp. 206 ff.; see also Hinsley, pp. 204 ff. The early difficulties of the Navy and Army in the antisubmarine offensive: McNarney to Marshall, April 14, 1942, PMRP; see also Morison[1], chaps. 6, 10; Craven and Cate, Vol. I, chap. 15. Roosevelt's PBY suggestion: Roosevelt to King, April 21, 1942, PL, p. 1311. Roosevelt's response to the slow Navy mobilization: Sherwood, p. 499; Hopkins's report from London, *ibid.,* p. 528. Land's labor proposal: Land to Roosevelt, March 13, 1942, PSF, Maritime Commission Folder. Janeway on energy and efficiency: Janeway, p. 250.

Lagging war production, spring 1942: Roosevelt to Nelson, May 4, 1942, copy to Arnold, Arnold Papers, Box 45, LC. Roosevelt and Army expansion goals: Roosevelt to Harold Smith, June 8, 1942; Roosevelt to Marshall, June 10, 1942, PSF, War Department Folder. Nelson's status: Nelson to Somervell, May 21, 1942, PSF, War Production Board; see, generally, *Industrial Mobilization for War,* chap. 2; *The United States at War,* chap. 5 (also the source, p. 113, of the quotation on the disappearing balance in the production program); Nelson, chap. 19. Anglo-Saxon basis of the Munitions Assignments Board: Leighton and Coakley, p. 252. Roosevelt and aid to Russia: Blum[2], pp. 81, 82, 85; see also Roosevelt to Stimson, April 11, 1942, PSF, Stimson Folder.

The Alchemists of Science. Of the abundant literature on the early development of the atomic weapon, especially relevant to Roosevelt's role are Baxter; Churchill[4], Bk. 1, chap. 22; Groves; Moore. Einstein's letter, Aug. 2, 1939: text in Teller and Brown, pp. 10-12. Sachs's meeting with Roosevelt: Jungk, pp. 109-111. Bohr on the "Alchemysts": Freedman, p. 732. Roosevelt's speech to Pan American scientists, May 10, 1940: PPA, 1940, pp. 184-187; Teller and Brown, pp. 12-13. Different types of research: Baxter, pp. 433-436. Roosevelt-Churchill discussion, June 20, 1942: Churchill[4], pp. 377-381. Conant on time factor: Baxter, p. 434. Stewart Burns helped in research and drafting of this section.

CHAPTER EIGHT

Texts of Roosevelt's communications with Wilhelmina, and of his toast to her: PSF, Netherlands File. Rosenman on Wilhelmina: Rosenman, p. 338. On Roosevelt's hospitality to royalty in previous years, see, for example, Roosevelt to Princess Juliana, June 6, 1941, PSF, Netherlands Folder. Hassett's observations: Hassett, pp. 88, 91, 92-93, 104, 133. Roosevelt to Wilhelmina, Aug. 21, 1942, on caring for Juliana: PL, p. 1340. "Shangri-La": Hassett, pp. 113-115. Roosevelt on problems at Hyde Park: Roosevelt memorandum, Dec. 9, 1942, PL, pp. 1378-1380. August 8, 1942 trip to Shangri-La: Dorothy Rosenman, in Rosenman, pp. 351-355, excerpt from p. 352. Gambling caution: Tully, pp. 20-21. Roosevelt and the Nazi saboteurs: Hassett, pp. 97, 98; see also Biddle, pp. 327-328, 330, 331.

The Economics of Chaos. Roosevelt on the situation in the Pacific: Rosenman, p. 353; PC 857, Nov. 6, 1942; PPA, 1942, pp. 445-447. Roosevelt's anti-inflation proposals to Congress, April 27, 1942: PPA, 1942, pp. 216-224; Eccles, Pt. 6, chap. 4. Reaction to his stabilization program:

see roundup of opinion in *PM,* May 3, 1942, p. 12. Tax proposals, April 27, 1942: PPA, 1942, pp. 220-221. New York *Herald Tribune* comment is quoted in Paul, p. 301; Theodore Roosevelt's presumed "bully" in Freedman, p. 657. Friction between Morgenthau and Smith: Smith Diary, FDRL; Blum²; Rosenman, p. 357. Morgenthau on writing tax bills: Blum², p. 38. Roosevelt to Morgenthau on standing pat: Blum², p. 42; see also Smith Diary, June-July 1942, FDRL. The Knoxville foundry operator's complaint: J. W. Keller to Roosevelt, June 12, 1942, OF 327. Politics of price control: McIntyre to Roosevelt, June 30, 1942, with memorandum, Henderson to Roosevelt, n.d.; Henderson to Roosevelt, July 17, 1942, OF 327; Henderson to Roosevelt, July 10, 1942 (telegram), FDRL; Roosevelt to Wallace and others, July 11, 1942, OF 4403. Rubber situation: Nelson, p. 292; Smith Diary, June 5, 1942, FDRL; Charles Michelson to Roosevelt, n.d., but evidently mid-1942, OF 56-B; Nelson, p. 304 (misdated). Roosevelt on the scrap-rubber situation: PC 831, June 9, 1942; PPA, 1942, p. 265; Smith Diary, Aug. 6, 1941, FDRL. Stone to Roosevelt, July 20, 1942, Freedman, pp. 663-664. Roosevelt to Baruch, July 29, 1942, PL, p. 1334. The rubber program: PPA, 1942, pp. 319-322. See, generally, J. Joseph Huthmacher, *Senator Robert F. Wagner and the Rise of Urban Liberalism* (Atheneum, 1968), chap. 16.

Extent of Roosevelt's personal, *ad-hoc* involvement in labor problems and crises: see documents in OF 407, 1942. Roosevelt on pleasure driving: PC 846, Sept. 11, 1942. Preparation of stabilization speech of Sept. 7, 1942: Rosenman, pp. 356-360; Sherwood, p. 631. Roosevelt on the response of Congress in 1933: PC 848, Oct. 1, 1942; see also Clapper Papers, Cont. 23, LC. Fireside chat, Sept. 7, 1942: PPA, 1942, pp. 368-377. Exchange with reporter over possible congressional rejection: PC 846, Sept. 11, 1942. Recall of Congress: Roosevelt to Rayburn, Sept. 6, 1942, PL, p. 1346. Farm policy and politics: *The United States at War,* pp. 267-270; Young, pp. 95-98. Roosevelt and Morgenthau on tax legislation: Blum², p. 51. Frankfurter on Byrnes: Freedman, pp. 660-661, 670-671; Hopkins on Byrnes: Hopkins to Roosevelt, Sept. 29, 1942, HHP, Box 317. Byrnes to Hopkins: Sherwood, p. 634.

The People at War. Roosevelt on the women's diffidence, Oct. 12, 1942: PPA, 1942, p. 420. For intra-administration views of labor-management production efforts, see Hillman to Roosevelt, Feb. 18, 1942; Addes to Nelson, Dec. 15, 1942; Nelson to Addes, Dec. 28, 1942, OF 407; see also OF 4451 (Requisitioning). Hillman's situation: Frankfurter to Roosevelt, March 20, 1942, Freedman, pp. 652-654; Josephson, pp. 577-586; *Industrial Mobilization for War,* pp. 246-248, 265-266; Nelson, chap. 16. The new union security formula: J. M. Burns, "Maintenance of Membership: A Study in Administrative Statesmanship," *Journal of Politics,* Feb. 1948, pp. 101-116. As an interesting possible example of Roosevelt's influence on maintenance-of-membership policy, see Roosevelt to Wayne Coy, Dec. 30, 1941, OF 407. FEPC: OF 4245 G, Box 3, has correspondence and other documents on initial FEPC appointments; on later developments, see OF 93 and 4245 G, which includes data on transfer to War Manpower Commission; Smith Diary, FDRL. Stimson's private views: Stimson to

Alfred E. Stearns, Jan. 30, 1942, Stimson Papers; Stimson Diary, Jan. 24, 1942. Rejection of Negro units: Eisenhower to Marshall, March 25, 1942, with marginal comments by Stimson, Arnold Papers, Box 44, Folder 127, LC. Japanese-American relocation situation: Milton Eisenhower to Roosevelt, June 18, 1942, OF 4849. Roosevelt's term for the camps: PC 853, Oct. 20, 1942. Situation in the camps: Dorothy Swaine Thomas and Richard S. Nishimoto, *The Spoilage* (Berkeley: University of California Press, 1946), pp. 38, 40, 45. Propaganda aspect: Elmer Davis to Roosevelt, Oct. 2, 1942, OF 197. Navy attitude: J. H. Newton to Knox, Oct. 15, 1942, OF 4849. German- and Italian-Americans: Roosevelt to Herbert Lehman, June 3, 1942, PPF 133; see also enclosure, unsigned, n.d., but presumably Luigi Antonini to Lehman.

Roosevelt's defense tour: HHP, Box 333, includes planned itinerary; the President's reports to press, Oct. 1, 1942, and public, Oct. 12, 1942, are in PPA, 1942, pp. 384-396, 416-426. The trip itself: Merriman Smith, *Thank You, Mr. President* (Harper, 1946), pp. 50-56; *Time,* Oct. 12, 1942, pp. 15-17. Margaret Mead's book was *And Keep Your Powder Dry* (Morrow, 1942); quotations from pp. 161, 167, 174. On the problems of the mobilization effort and the mood of the people, early 1942: Reston, especially chaps. 2, 3, 7, 11.

The Politics of Nonpolitics. Roosevelt's comments to the press on forgetting politics: PC 811, March 13, 1942; see also PC 803, Feb. 6, 1942; PPA, 1942, p. 80. Liberal hopes for party realignment: *PM,* Feb. 8, 1942, p. 11. Roosevelt-Willkie relationship: Smith Diary, Feb. 14, 1942, LC (Smith mistakenly cites the Labor Relations Board); Barnard, p. 325. Roosevelt and Willkie's trip abroad: Roosevelt to Marshall, July 31, 1942, PSF, Willkie; see also PL, pp. 1336, 1341-1342; PPA, 1942, pp. 334-335.

Roosevelt to Mary Norton, June 1, 1942: PL, p. 1328. Bennett candidacy in New York: Roosevelt to Flynn, Aug. 14, 1942, PSF, N.Y. State, Political Folder; see also Hassett, pp. 104-106. Roosevelt and Hamilton Fish: Hassett, pp. 86, 94. Norris candidacy: PPA, 1942, p. 433; Roosevelt's earlier endorsement, Oct. 10, 1936: PPA, 1936, pp. 431-432; see, generally, Norris Papers, LC. Roosevelt to Norris, Oct. 22, 1942: PL, p. 1357. Willkie trip: Willkie to Roosevelt, Sept. 10, 1942, PSF, Willkie; Clapper Papers, Oct. 30, 1942, Cont. 23, LC. Roosevelt on "typewriter strategists": PC 849, Oct. 6, 1942; Barnard, pp. 361, 375-377. Cantril data: Cantril Notebook I, pp. 12, 14, 30-32; Cantril to Anna Rosenberg, July 24, Aug. 3, Aug. 17, Sept. 1, 1942, *ibid.* General election situation: Kenneth Crawford, in *PM,* Oct. 5, 1942, p. 3; Clapper interview of Hull, Nov. 23, 1942, Clapper Papers, LC. Election Day at Hyde Park: Hassett, p. 133. Norris's reaction to his defeat: *The Nation,* Nov. 14, 1942, p. 497.

CHAPTER NINE

Roosevelt to King George, Oct. 17, 1942: PL, p. 1354. Stalingrad: Werth, Pt. V; Zhukov, chaps. 9-10; Clark, chaps. 11-12. Stalin on Oct. 1942 as low point: Werth, p. 484. Willkie in Moscow: Werth, p. 485; Davies Papers, Box 12, LC. Guadalcanal: S. E. Morison, *The Struggle for Guadalcanal* (Boston: Little, Brown, 1949); John Miller, Jr., *Guadalcanal:*

The First Offensive (Washington, D.C.: Office of the Chief of Military History, 1949). For estimates of the situation by naval authorities in Washington during the battle: Clapper Papers, Nov. 6, 1942 (Adm. King); Nov. 10, 1942 (Adms. Ghormley and Horne), LC. Roosevelt on low point of Guadalcanal operation: Roosevelt to Queen Wilhelmina, Oct. 17, 1942, PL, p. 1355; Roosevelt to Churchill, Oct. 19, 1942, PL, p. 1356. MacArthur's warning: MacArthur to Marshall, Oct. 17, 1942, PMRP, Box 17. Roosevelt to Joint Chiefs on reinforcing Guadalcanal: Roosevelt to Leahy, King, Marshall, and Arnold, Oct, 24, 1942, PMRP, Box 17. Roosevelt to Stalin on situation in Solomon Islands: Sherwood, p. 658, and, in paraphrased form, *Correspondence*[2], p. 40.

Thrust Across the Atlantic. The history of the political-military invasion of North Africa has been well served by historians and participants. General background and significance: William L. Langer, *Our Vichy Gamble* (Knopf, 1947); Robert Aron, *Histoire de Vichy* (Paris: Librairie Arthème Fayard, 1954); Geoffrey Warner, *Pierre Laval and the Eclipse of France* (Macmillan, 1969); Paul Farmer, *Vichy Political Dilemma* (Columbia University Press, 1955); Kolko, pp. 64-67; Maisky, pp. 278-289; Woodward, chap. 10. Military operations: I. S. O. Playfair and C. J. C. Molony, *The Mediterranean and Middle East,* Vol. IV, *The Destruction of the Axis Forces in Africa* (London: His Majesty's Stationery Office, 1966); Howe; Morison[2]. Participants' reports: Macmillan; Robert Murphy, *Diplomat Among Warriors* (Doubleday, 1964); de Gaulle, chaps. 1-3; Eisenhower; Mark W. Clark, *Calculated Risk* (Harper, 1950); Harry C. Butcher, *My Three Years with Eisenhower* (Simon and Schuster, 1946). On de Gaulle and North Africa, see also Viorst. Strategic aspects of invasion: Fuller, pp. 240-243. On United States relations with Vichy, see Roosevelt-William D. Leahy correspondence, ABCD File, FDRL. For a detailed estimate of the Vichy situation by Leahy, see Leahy to Roosevelt, Nov. 22, 1941, ABCD File, FDRL. See, generally, Davies Papers, Nov. 2-15, 1942 Folder, Box 12, LC.

Misgivings about the North African enterprise: Marshall to Leahy and King, 8/17/42, WDCSA/381 Torch, AR; Arnold to Hopkins, Sept. 3, 1942, Arnold Papers, Box 43, LC; Matloff, pp. 236-239, 290; Bryant[1], pp. 403-406; OCS 21384-3, AR; Stimson Diary, Box 39; Stimson and Bundy, p. 426. Repercussions of TORCH on other theaters: Pogue[1], p. 410; Bryant[2], p. 407. Stalin's doubts on political aspects: Sherwood, p. 618. Murphy's military knowledge: Murphy, p. 103. Eisenhower's political grasp: Eisenhower, pp. 100, 109. Background of planning: OCS 21384-3, AR. Churchill-Roosevelt exchange in the planning of TORCH: Churchill[4], pp. 530-543; Bryant[2], pp. 398-403. Key quotes have been taken from the full messages. Measuring opinion in Africa: Hadley Cantril, "Evaluating the Probable Reactions to the Landing in North Africa in 1942: A Case Study," *Public Opinion Quarterly,* Fall 1965, pp. 400-410. Roosevelt to Marshall on timing of invasion: Pogue[1], p. 402. Roosevelt's instruction to Murphy: Murphy, pp. 102, 106. Murphy's relations with French leaders: Murphy, p. 118. French African political situation: McNeill, pp. 203-209. Anxieties on the eve of invasion: Stimson Diary; Pogue[1], pp. 398, 416; Langer, p. 354.

Eisenhower's earlier discouragement: Eisenhower to Marshall, Oct. 10, 1942, 381 Torch, AR. Early's remark: conference with Marshall, Nov. 15, 1942, Clapper Papers, LC. Roosevelt's reception of the news of the landing: Tully, p. 264.

To Walk with the Devil. Reflections on the "luck" of the African enterprise, by an old military observer: J. C. Smuts (writing from Chequers) to Roosevelt, Nov. 15, 1942, PSF, Union of South Africa. Roosevelt's letter to troops: copy in PSF, War Department File. Roosevelt's broadcast in French: Butcher, p. 174; PPA, 1942, pp. 451-452; Morison[2], p. 71; see also Frankfurter to Roosevelt, April 16, 1942, Freedman, p. 656. Exchange of messages between Roosevelt and Pétain: PPA, 1942, pp. 455-457; see also Leahy to Welles, Nov. 5, 1942, 740.001 EW 1939/25712, SD; Warner, chap. 10. Casablanca "fire-away Flannagan": Morison[2], p. 91. Generally, on the landings, see Morison[2] and Howe. Roosevelt's "promise" to Giraud: McNeill, pp. 205, 246-247, and sources cited therein. The American military and politics: Butcher, p. 165; Mark Clark, pp. 107, 121, 133, 138. Darlan's situation: Clark, pp. 109-110, has part of the transcript of the Clark-Darlan exchange. Roosevelt to Churchill on Giraud and Darlan, Nov. 11, 1942: 740.0011 EW 1939, SD. See, generally, volumes cited in notes for previous section of this chapter. Marshall's and Eisenhower's defense of Darlan dealing: conference with Marshall, Nov. 15, 1942, Clapper Papers, LC.

Freda Kirchwey quotation: *The Nation,* Nov. 21, 1942, pp. 529-530; *ibid.,* Nov. 28, 1942, pp. 559-560. Churchill to Eden on de Gaulle: Eden, pp. 350-351; see also Nicolson, pp. 262-267. Stimson and the liberals: Stimson Diary, Nov. 16, 1942, Box 41; Blum[2], pp. 148-150; Freedman, p. 681. Stimson's call to Willkie: Stimson, *ibid.*; Barnard, pp. 391-394. De Gaulle and the Darlan deal: Viorst, p. 124. Churchill and North African politics: Churchill[4], pp. 639-640. Roosevelt's military calculations: Langer, pp. 359-360; Sherwood, p. 651. Military losses in invasion: Howe, p. 173. Churchill on the critics: Churchill[4], p. 641. Military advice to Roosevelt to deal with Darlan: Marshall to Roosevelt, n.d.; Marshall to Roosevelt, Nov. 26, 1942, both in 381 Torch, AR. Morgenthau's complaint to Roosevelt: Blum[2], pp. 150-151. Roosevelt on walking with the Devil: he quoted the saying slightly differently each time; I have used his comment to the press conference, Nov. 17, 1942, PPA, 1942, p. 479. Stalin and *his* proverb: Sherwood, p. 651. A later critique both of the dealings with Vichy in North Africa and of Langer's treatment of them: Louis Gottschalk, "Our Vichy Fumble," *Journal of Modern History,* March 1948, pp. 47-56. Later military developments, North Africa: Howe.

Roosevelt: A Turning Point? Hassett on Roosevelt: Hassett, p. 145. Roosevelt on the "Star-Spangled Banner" without frills: Roosevelt to Capt. John L. McCrea, Aug. 31, 1942, PL, p. 1343. Roosevelt on second helps: Roosevelt to Eleanor Roosevelt, Oct. 7, 1942, PL, p. 1352. Roosevelt and King: King and Whitehill, p. 412. Hyde Park diaries: Roosevelt to Mrs. Theodore Douglas Robinson, Nov. 19, 1942, PL, pp. 1368-1369. Dining with Ickes: Roosevelt to Ickes, Dec. 4, 1942, PL, p. 1376. Coffeeless breakfasts: Roosevelt to Fred Allen, Dec. 28, 1942, PPF 8275. Roosevelt's French:

Grace Tully to Herbert Bayard Swope, Dec. 1, 1942, PL, pp. 1374-1375 (the memorandum was obviously written by Roosevelt himself). Eleanor Roosevelt's planned trip to Great Britain: Roosevelt to Eleanor Roosevelt, Oct. 16, 1942, PL, pp. 1353-1355. Roosevelt at Thanksgiving service: Lilienthal, pp. 562-563. Roosevelt on the second front: Roosevelt to Josephus Daniels, Nov. 10, 1942, PL, pp. 1362-1363. George Fielding Eliot on Roosevelt as strategist: *Time,* Dec. 7, 1942, p. 21. Lilienthal at the White House: Lilienthal, pp. 566, 570-572. New Year's Eve gathering: Sherwood, p. 665; Rosenman, p. 365.

CHAPTER TEN

Roosevelt on telling off Congress: Lilienthal, p. 571. Preparing message to Congress: Rosenman, p. 366. Public opinion favoring conciliation: Cantril Notebook I, pp. 90-96. The address, Jan. 7, 1943: PPA, 1943, pp 21-34. Roosevelt and Clare Boothe Luce: PL, pp. 1390-1391. Roosevelt to McCormack, n.d.: PL, p. 1389. Roosevelt and Henry Luce: Roosevelt to Welles, Dec. 28, 1942, 811.917 Time/128, SD.

The Gaming Board of Strategy. Quotation from President's 1943 message to Congress, Jan. 7, 1943: PPA, 1943, p. 22. Hitler on leaving the Volga: quoted in Shirer, p. 1210. On Hitler's strategic situation: Higgins; Warlimont; Trevor-Roper; Shirer. Atlantic sinkings: Roosevelt to Marshall and to King, March 18, 1943, PMRP, Naval Aide's File, Box 31. Stalin to Churchill on suspension of convoys: *Correspondence*[1], p. 72. Stalin's public questioning of second-front absence: Stalin, pp. 61, 64; Werth, p. 491. Stalin on war progress in Africa: *Correspondence*[1], p. 75; Werth, p. 491. Stalin on "basic blows": quoted in Higgins, p. 149, from Raymond Garthoff, *Soviet Military Doctrine* (Glencoe, Ill.: The Free Press, 1953), p. 130. Brooke on Stalin as strategist: Bryan[2], pp. 460-465; see also Churchill[4], p. 582. Churchill on plans for after Africa: Churchill[4], pp. 649-650. Churchill on Europe: Churchill[4], p. 562.

Roosevelt's lack of strategic commitment: Roosevelt to Churchill, Nov. 11, 1942, 740.0011 EW 1939/25495 1/3 CF, SD. Churchill's awareness that TORCH precluded ROUNDUP in 1943: Churchill[4], pp. 648, 656. (I am using ROUNDUP here to include the build-up—BOLERO—as well as the actual cross-channel attack.) Issue of Allied planes for Caucasus: *Correspondence*[2], pp. 36 (Roosevelt to Stalin, Oct. 9, 1942), 44 (Roosevelt to Stalin, Dec. 16, 1942), 45 (Stalin to Roosevelt, Dec. 18, 1942); see also Matloff, pp. 329-346. Actual, compared with planned, distribution of American military strength, end of 1942: Matloff, pp. 357-360; see also Maisky, pp. 352-353. Planning for Big Three or Big Two conference: Churchill[4], pp. 662-665 (Roosevelt to Churchill, Nov. 26, 1942; Churchill to Roosevelt, Nov. 26, 1942; Roosevelt to Churchill, Dec. 3, 1942; Churchill to Roosevelt, Dec. 3, 1942); *Correspondence*[2], pp. 42-45 (Roosevelt to Stalin, Dec. 2, 1942; Stalin to Roosevelt, Dec. 6, 1942; Roosevelt to Stalin, Dec. 8, 1942; Stalin to Roosevelt, Dec. 14, 1942). Churchill and second front: Maisky, pp. 351-353. Preparations for Casablanca Conference: Stimson Diary, Jan. 7, 1943; Churchill[4], p. 671; Matloff, pp. 376, 379-380. On specific aspects of cross-channel, see Harrison, pp. 32-38. Roosevelt's continued indecision: Sherwood, p. 671; Churchill[4], p. 664; Matloff, p. 363.

Toward the Underbelly? Roosevelt's trip to Casablanca: Sherwood, pp. 671-674; Roosevelt to Eleanor Roosevelt, Jan. 13, 1943, PL, p. 1393; Elliott Roosevelt, p. 75; Reilly, chap. 14. Roosevelt at Casablanca: Elliott Roosevelt, p. 66; PL, pp. 1393-1394; Reilly, pp. 149-151; and works cited below. Military conferences at Casablanca: Matloff, pp. 19-36; King and Whitehill, pp. 416-417; Bryant[2], p. 446. Churchill's instructions to the British military chiefs: Bryant[2], p. 445. Roosevelt-Churchill conferences: Sherwood, pp. 674-675; Churchill[4], p. 676; Eisenhower, p. 163; Bryant[2], pp. 454, 458-459. Eisenhower's appointment: Sherwood, pp. 677-678; Bryant[2], pp. 454-455; Ismay, pp. 288-289.

French politics and personalities at Casablanca: Sherwood, pp. 675-686; Churchill[4], pp. 680-682; Macmillan, pp. 255-256; de Gaulle, chap. 3; Eden, p. 363. Roosevelt's conference with de Gaulle: Reilly, pp. 157-158; Sherwood, p. 685. Roosevelt's and Churchill's personal feeling about de Gaulle: Churchill[4], p. 682. Roosevelt and Giraud's documents: Arthur Layton Funk, "The 'Anfa' Memorandum: An Incident of the Casablanca Conference," *Journal of Modern History,* No. 3, September 1954, pp. 246-254, and documents cited therein; see also Macmillan, pp. 256-260; Stimson Diary, Feb. 3, 1943. Roosevelt's seeming lightheartedness at Casablanca: Macmillan, p. 259; Murphy, p. 165; Eisenhower, p. 161; Elliott Roosevelt, chap. 4; Stimson Diary, Feb. 3, 1943. President's trip to Rabat: Elliott Roosevelt, pp. 105-107; PPA, 1943, pp. 45-47, 61-62; Reilly, p. 160; PPA, 1943, pp. 57-58. Roosevelt's dinner party for the Sultan: Murphy, pp. 172-173; Macmillan, pp. 250-251; Elliott Roosevelt, pp. 109-112. "Reconciliation" of Giraud and de Gaulle: Macmillan, p. 253; Moran, p. 89; PPA, 1943, p. 84; Sherwood, pp. 693-694; these accounts differ in minor details. Announcement of unconditional surrender: PPA, 1943, p. 39; Sherwood, p. 696; Churchill[4], pp. 686-687; see also Macmillan, pp. 263-264; Ismay, p. 290; cf. Deborin, pp. 296-297. Early staff work on unconditional surrender: Department of State, *Postwar Foreign Policy Preparation,* Dept. of State Publication 3580, General Foreign Policy Series 15, 1950, p. 127. Roosevelt's and Churchill's trip to Marrakesh: Churchill[4], pp. 694-695; Moran, p. 90.

The First Kill. Roosevelt's return trip to the United States: PC 876, Feb. 2, 1943; PPA, 1943, pp. 55-62; Roosevelt to Eleanor Roosevelt, Jan. 29, 1943, PL, p. 1395. Roosevelt-Churchill message to Stalin: *Correspondence*[2], pp. 51-52 (message received Jan. 27, 1943). Stalin's reception of message: Feis[3], p. 114; William H. Standley and Arthur A. Ageton, *Admiral Ambassador to Russia* (Chicago: Regnery, 1955), p. 327. Further exchanges: *Correspondence*[2], pp. 54-55, 55-56, 56-57. Battle of Tunisia: Howe, chaps. 20-24; Churchill[4], p. 764. American defeat: Martin Blumenson, *Kasserine Pass* (Boston: Houghton Mifflin, 1967). Further Stalin-Roosevelt-Churchill exchanges: *Correspondence*[1], pp. 99-102, 105-106; *Correspondence*[2], pp. 58-59.

Roosevelt to Churchill on informing Stalin about suspension of convoys: Churchill[4], pp. 752-753. Churchill to Stalin: *Correspondence*[1], pp.

110-111. Stalin's answer: *Correspondence*[1], p. 112. Linking of Eighth Army and American troops: Churchill[4], p. 771. Shift of II Corps north: Eisenhower, p. 177; Howe, Pt. 6. Churchill on results of Tunisia: Churchill[4], p. 780; on "scrunch and punch": Nicolson, p. 291. Hitler on his African strategy: quoted in Warlimont, p. 314. Stalin's congratulations on Tunisia: Stalin to Churchill, April 12, 1943, *Correspondence*[1], p. 117; Stalin to Roosevelt, May 8, 1943, *Correspondence*[2], p. 64.

CHAPTER ELEVEN

William Allen White on Roosevelt: quoted from Emporia *Gazette* in *Time,* Feb. 22, 1943, p. 53; March 8, 1943, p. 12. Vandenberg on White House–Congress liaison: Vandenberg, p. 33.

Emergency Management. Establishment of Office for Emergency Management: PPA, 1940, pp. 624-625. War production: *The United States at War,* chaps. 5-7; Clapper Papers, Cont. 23, Dec. 31, 1942, LC; PPA, 1943, p. 26; Roosevelt to Beaverbrook, March 24, 1943, PL, p. 1416; Baruch to Roosevelt, PPF 88, May 10, 1943; see also *Industrial Mobilization for War,* pp. 604-608. Manpower: *The United States at War,* pp. 431-432; Harold Smith memoranda, Nov. 23, 1942, Dec. 4, 1942, and Roosevelt to Smith, Nov. 19, 1942, Smith Diary, FDRL; Hassett, p. 160. Labor developments: Roosevelt to Mackenzie King, Nov. 1, 1943, PL, p. 1462. John L. Lewis: Saul Alinsky, *John L. Lewis* (Putnam, 1949); James A. Wechsler, *Labor Baron* (Morrow, 1944). Roosevelt's response: Byrnes, p. 180; Rosenman, p. 380; PPA, 1943, pp. 190-197; extensive material in OF 407-B, Box 29; see especially Ickes to Roosevelt, July 9, 1943, July 17, 1943; Roosevelt to Ickes, July 11, 1943; Biddle to Roosevelt, July 11, 1943. Attitudes of coal miners: Cantril to Lubin, "How the Miners Feel," March 21, 1943; Cantril Notebook II. Byrnes's birthday celebration: Byrnes, p. 181. *Stars and Stripes* editorial: Kirk to Hull, June 16, 1943, with text, OF 407-B. Drafting of miners: Roosevelt to Stimson *et al.,* June 21, 1943, Stimson Diary; Roosevelt to Davis, Nov. 8, 1943, and earlier draft proposals by Byrnes, OF 407-B. Railroad labor troubles: OF 407-B and OF 4451; see, especially, Leiserson to Roosevelt, June 29, 1943, Oct. 13, 1943; Vinson to Roosevelt, July 5, 1943, Dec. 20, 1943; Byrnes to Roosevelt, Oct. 21, 1943; see also Byrnes, pp. 198-202. Marshall's threat to resign: Byrnes, p. 201; his biographer, Forrest Pogue, is dubious about this report.

Senate subcommittee report on production: Senate Committee on Military Affairs, "Report of Subcommittee on War Mobilization," 78th Congress, 1st Session, May 13, 1943. Baruch's near-appointment: Baruch, pp. 314, 318; Byrnes, p. 174; Sherwood, p. 700; Rosenman to Roosevelt, May 24, 1943, PSF, Rosenman; Stimson Diary, Feb. 16, 1943, Feb. 22, 1943; Cox Diary, June 6, 1943, FDRL. Roosevelt's veto of Bankhead bill, April 2, 1943: PPA, 1943, pp. 135-142; Byrnes, pp. 177-178. Jones-Wallace imbroglio: Byrnes, pp. 192-194; *The United States at War,* pp. 421-425; Smith to Roosevelt, Feb. 6, 1943, March 3, 1943, Smith Diary, FDRL; Cox to Hopkins, July 12, 1943, Cox Diary, FDRL. For the Jones and Wallace views respectively: Timmons, chap. 28; Lord, pp. 496-514; PC 890, April 9,

1943. Roosevelt ban on public disputes: PPA, 1943, pp. 299-300. 1942 plea: White House statement, Aug. 20, 1942, 111.018/114 1/2, SD. Roosevelt on administrative rivalry as technique: Perkins, pp. 380-387. Roosevelt on conflicting recommendations: Smith to Roosevelt, Nov. 8, 1943, quoting Roosevelt memorandum of Sept. 14, 1942, Smith Diary, FDRL.

The Technology of Violence. This section was drafted by Douglas Rose and Stewart Burns in collaboration with the author. The warfare of machines: Baxter, p. 395. Patton on new weapons: Baxter, p. 236. Marshall on peacetime army: Marshall to Stimson, Stimson Papers, April 18, 1944. Hopkins as idea buffer: Washington *Post* "Parade Publications," Oct. 31, 1943. Creation of NDRC: Baxter, pp. 14-16; Irvin Stewart, *Organizing Scientific Research for War* (Boston: Little, Brown, 1948), pp. 5-7. Civilian-military co-operation: Green, Thomson, and Roots, pp. 216-219, 226-232. Bush on incompatibility: Baxter, p. 12. Creation of OSRD: Baxter, pp. 124-135; Stewart, p. 36; Fulton to Roosevelt, July 1, 1941, PPF 7656; Hopkins to Roosevelt, Roosevelt to Coy, May 20, 1941; Coy to Roosevelt, June 13, 1941; Bush to Watson, July 10, 1941, OF 4482; Ickes to Roosevelt, Aug. 19, 1940, Feb. 7, 1941; Knudsen to Roosevelt, Feb. 18, 1941; Smith to Roosevelt, March 17, 1941; Ickes to Roosevelt, April 11, 1941, OF 2240. American-British scientific exchange: Baxter, pp. 119-123. OSRD operating methods: Stewart; Baxter, pp. 21, 129.

Bombing effectiveness: Stimson Diary, Dec. 13, 31, 1944; Stimson and Bundy, pp. 465-469. Reluctance to use the proximity fuse: Stimson Diary, Oct.-Nov.-Dec. 1944. Problems of weapons use: Green, Thomson, and Roots, pp. 512-515. Co-ordination of science and military: Baxter, pp. 28-32; Stewart, pp. 325-329. Stimson and radar: Stimson and Bundy, pp. 464-470; Baxter, pp. 136-157. Stewart on faith in instrument: Stewart, p. 328. Problems of man-instrument combination: Stewart, pp. 325-328; Green, Thomson, and Roots, pp. 515-517.

Roosevelt as Chief Executive. Excerpts from Smith Diary are by dates indicated. More orthodox aspects of Roosevelt's administrative record: Barry Dean Karl, *Executive Reorganization and Reform in the New Deal* (Cambridge: Harvard University Press, 1963). Roosevelt's assumption of different roles: Burns. For shrewd comments on Roosevelt as chief executive in the broadest, political sense, see Richard E. Neustadt, *Presidential Power* (Wiley, 1960), which also throws light on Roosevelt's war leadership; see especially pp. 214-215.

Stimson on Roosevelt as administrator: Stimson Diary, Jan. 23, 1943, Feb. 3, 1943, March 28, 1943, May 4, 1943; Stimson to Burlingham, March 13, 1943, Stimson Papers, Box 400; Stimson to Horner, May 7, 1943, Stimson Papers, Box 401; see also (for Hull's views) Blum[2], pp. 241-242. Cox's criticism: Cox to Lubin, Oct. 12, 1942, Cox Diary, FDRL. For a measured critique just after Pearl Harbor on the implications of the British and French war administrative experience for the United States, see Frankfurter to Roosevelt, Dec. 17, 1941, with enclosure, Freedman, pp. 628-632; see also Cox's call for a war secretariat in diary item cited above. *Japan Times-Advertiser* comment on Roosevelt as chief executive: FCC recording, from Domei transmission in English, OWI, Oct. 1, 1942,

FDRL. Roosevelt on controlling the Treasury, etc.: Eccles, p. 336. Kennan's visit to Washington: Kennan[1], pp. 145-161; memo on War Department meeting, Nov. 2, 1943, PSF, Portugal. Stettinius to Roosevelt, Nov. 8, 1943, PSF, Portugal; for different perspectives, see Hull, pp. 1335-1344; Stimson Diary, Nov. 2, 1943, Nov. 9, 1943. Roosevelt's reluctance to make military manpower or spending commitments more than a year ahead: Roosevelt to Smith, June 8, 1942; Roosevelt to Marshall, June 10, 1942; Roosevelt to Stimson and Marshall, Aug. 11, 1942, Smith Diary, FDRL; PSF, War Department Folder. Harold Smith on budgeting and planning: Smith Diary, Aug. 31, 1943, pp. 6-7, FDRL. "Layering" and the Office of War Mobilization: Somers. Roosevelt hating to fire: Smith Diary, Sept. 26, 1941, FDRL; Flynn, p. 226. Gulick observations: Luther Gulick, "War Organization of the Federal Government," *American Political Science Review,* Dec. 1944, pp. 1166-1179.

CHAPTER TWELVE

The main records of the building of the Thomas Jefferson Memorial: OF 1505. See Roosevelt to Daniel C. Roper, Dec. 27, 1937, OF 1505, Box 1; see also PPF 5319 and OF 4077 for Roosevelt's intense personal interest in the planning and building of the memorial. Roosevelt and the cherry-tree ladies: Hassett, p. 19. Moore speech: NYT, April 14, 1943, p. 16. Roosevelt's warning against silk hats: RB to Watson, March 24, 1943, OF 1505, Box 2. His address, April 13, 1943: PPA, 1943, pp. 162-164; Edith Helm Papers, Cont. 9, 1943, LC.

"A World Forged Anew." Roosevelt on the presidency as a place of moral leadership: NYT, Nov. 13, 1932, VIII, p. 1. Wallace on the century of the common man: Lord, pp. 492, 494-496. Willkie: quotations from Willkie, pp. 178, 178-179. Other views: roundups in *PM,* Dec. 11, 1942, Jan. 5, Jan. 11, 1943, March 16, March 31, 1943, April 14, 1943. Development of Roosevelt's views on world security and organization: Range; PPA, 1943, pp. 5, 30, 87; Roosevelt to Norris, Sept. 21, 1943, PL, pp. 1446-1447; Burns, pp. 318-319, 523-524; Clapper Papers, Cont. 23, interview with Hopkins, Feb. 11, 1943, LC; Robert A. Divine, *The Illusion of Neutrality* (Chicago: University of Chicago Press, 1962). Administration views: Clapper Papers, Cont. 23, interview with Welles, Nov. 19, 1942; interview with Hull, Nov. 23, 1942, LC; Vandenberg, p. 43 (April 7, 1943 diary notation); see also Burns, chaps. 4, 7, 13, 19, and *passim.* Roosevelt on role of Big Four: PC 916, Sept. 7, 1943; PPA, 1943, p. 376. Roosevelt on concrete postwar arrangements: Roosevelt to Hull, April 9, 1943, 800.50/626, CF, SD Files, NA; see, generally, Kolko, chap. 11. Straight's book: Michael Straight, *Make This the Last War* (Harcourt, Brace, 1943). Vandenberg's views: Vandenberg, pp. 39, 43, 45, 47-48, 50. Hopkins on Roosevelt's caution: Clapper interview with Hopkins, Feb. 11, 1943, Clapper Papers, LC.

State of the Union address, Jan. 7, 1943: PPA, 1943, pp. 30-31. Beveridge plan: William Beveridge, *Social Insurance and Allied Services* (Macmillan, 1942); for a contemporary report, see Richard Lee Strout, "The Beveridge Report," *The New Republic,* Dec. 14, 1942, pp. 784-786.

Roosevelt on the "Roosevelt plan": Perkins, p. 283. Popular attitudes toward expanded Social Security: Cantril Notebook II, pp. 64-73. GI Bill of Rights: PPA, 1943, pp. 449-453. Rider ending Roosevelt's authority to limit salaries: PPA, 1943, pp. 157-160. Tax situation generally: Paul, pp. 144-145. Roosevelt on tax forgiveness, May 17, 1943: PPA, 1943, pp. 209-210. Congressional action: Young, pp. 130-136. Morgenthau and Roosevelt on tax struggle: Blum[2], pp. 64-70; Paul, pp. 145-147. Roosevelt on the administration as one big family: Blum[2], p. 68. Roosevelt on medical insurance: Blum[2], p. 72.

The Broken Pledge. Roosevelt to Churchill on talks with Eden: FRUS, 1943, Vol. III, pp. 1-3. Hull's return to Washington: Hull, p. 1213. Roosevelt on postponing discussion of immediate postwar arrangements: Clapper Papers, Cont. 23, Feb. 11, 1943, LC. Roosevelt on announcement of his discussions with Eden: FRUS, 1943, Vol. III, p. 5. Roosevelt-Eden discussions: FRUS, 1943, Vol. III, especially pp. 13-18, 25-26, 35, 36, 39; Eden, pp. 373, 377; Sherwood, pp. 707-720. Roosevelt on results of discussions: Churchill[4], p. 738; PC 888, March 30, 1943; PPA, 1943, pp. 133-134. Eden on Roosevelt as conjuror: Eden, pp. 373-374. Questions about Stalin's postwar plans: FRUS, 1943, Vol. III; Eden, p. 373. Davies mission to Moscow: Davies Papers, Box 13, LC. Roosevelt's invitation to Stalin: *Correspondence*[2], pp. 63-64. Journey of Churchill and party to the United States: Ismay, p. 294; Churchill[4], p. 788. U.S. Joint Chiefs' preparation: Stimson Diary, May 12, 1943; Matloff, p. 69. The Washington discussions in May are well covered in Stimson Diary, May 1943; Churchill[4]; Sherwood; Brooke; Ismay; see Ismay, pp. 296-298, for an excellent summary of the British and American approaches.

Roosevelt's and Churchill's letter to Stalin: Churchill[4], pp. 812-813; *Correspondence*[2] (received June 4, 1943), pp. 67-69. Davies in Moscow: Sulzberger, p. 213. Davies's report to Roosevelt: Davies Papers, June 3, 1943, LC. Stalin's letter agreeing to meet in July or August: *Correspondence*[2], p. 66 (Stalin indicated the place—Fairbanks—orally through Davies). Stalin's response to postponement of second front: Stalin to Roosevelt, June 11, 1943, *Correspondence*[2], pp. 70-71. Polish-Soviet developments: FRUS, 1943, Vol. III, pp. 329, 362, 373-374, 396. Major items on diplomatic correspondence between the Polish government and the President are in PSF, Poland; see also Werth, Pt. 6, chap. 6; Churchill[4], pp. 757-761; and for the Polish case, Bronislaw Kusnierz, *Stalin and the Poles* (London: Hollis & Carter, 1949). Roosevelt's attempt to conciliate Stalin: Roosevelt to Stalin, *Correspondence*[2], p. 61. Stalin's reactions and reflections: *Correspondence*[1] and *Correspondence*[2]; Maisky, pp. 351, 361, 362; Deutscher, pp. 478-479; Ehrenburg; Berezhkov, Pt. II. Origins of the Cold War: Williams, especially chap. 6; D. F. Fleming, *The Cold War and Its Origins* (Doubleday, 1961); Louis J. Halle, *The Cold War as History* (Harper, 1967); John Lukacs, *A History of the Cold War* (Doubleday, 1961); Paul Seabury, *The Rise and Decline of the Cold War* (Basic Books, 1967); André Fontaine, *History of the Cold War* (Pantheon, 1968).

The King's First Minister. Roosevelt's attitude toward China: Sherwood; Blum[2]; see especially *Morgenthau Diary* (China), p. 658; Sherwood, p. 925. Chiang on the end of extraterritorial rights: quoted in Feis[2], p. 62. Roosevelt on repeal of exclusion laws, Oct. 11, 1943: PPA, 1943, pp. 427-428. Rumors of Chinese separate peace with Japan: Feis[2], p. 61. Stilwell's skepticism: Romanus and Sunderland[2], chap. 7. Stilwell on Chinese military condition: Romanus and Sunderland[2]. Chennault's plan and assurances to Roosevelt: Claire Lee Chennault, *Way of a Fighter* (Putnam, 1949), pp. 212-214, quoted in Romanus and Sunderland[2], pp. 252-253. Madame Chiang Kai-shek's visit to the United States: Sherwood, pp. 660, 706-707; *Time,* March 1, 1943, pp. 9-10, 23-26; PC 881, Feb. 19, 1943; PPA, 1943, pp. 100-108; Stimson Diary, May 4, 1943; Perkins, p. 74; Eden, p. 377. Roosevelt to Marshall on dealing with Chiang, March 8, 1943: quoted in Romanus and Sunderland[2], pp. 279-280. Marshall's reply, March 16, 1943, is quoted in Romanus and Sunderland[2], pp. 280-282. See, generally, Woodward, chap. 24.

Stilwell on calling Chiang's bluff: Romanus and Sunderland[2], p. 278. Roosevelt's anticolonial views: Foster Rhea Dulles and Gerald E. Ridinger, "The Anti-Colonial Policies of Franklin D. Roosevelt," *Political Science Quarterly,* March 1955, pp. 1-18. The administration's views of the U.S. record in the Philippines: Hull, p. 1491; Clapper interview with Hopkins, Feb. 11, 1943, Clapper Papers, LC; PPA, 1942, p. 474; Clapper interview with Wallace, Dec. 7, 1942, Cont. 23, Clapper Papers, LC. Roosevelt's criticism of Western colonial record, following Casablanca Conference: PC 879, Feb. 12, 1943; PPA, 1943, p. 86. Philippine wartime developments: Stimson Diary, Aug. 12-Sept. 5, 1943; Elmer Davis to Roosevelt, June 24, 1943, OF 400 P.I. Indochina: Hull, p. 1596; Eden, p. 378; Stilwell, p. 246; see, generally, Bernard B. Fall, *The Two Viet-Nams* (Praeger, 1963); Buttinger. Reference to Roosevelt's grandfather in Indochina: Fall, p. 453. Roosevelt on French colonialism in Indochina: Elliott Roosevelt, p. 115; Hull, p. 1597. Question of Free French representation on Pacific War Council: 740.0011 Pacific War/3648, SD, NA. Roosevelt on Atlantic Charter: PC 855, Oct. 27, 1942; PPA, 1942, p. 437. Phillips-Roosevelt and Phillips-Hull exchanges: FRUS, 1943, Vol. IV, pp. 178-222; specific quotations or references are from pp. 190, 207, 211, 222, 215, 220-222; see also William Phillips, *Ventures in Diplomacy* (Boston: Beacon Press, 1952), chap. 22; Hull, p. 1491; Vandenberg, pp. 52-53; Nicolson, p. 295; interview with Hull, Nov. 23, 1942, Clapper Papers, LC. Roosevelt and the Indian famine: M. S. Venkataramani, "The Roosevelt Administration and the Great Indian Famine," *International Studies* (New Delhi), Jan. 1963, pp. 241-264. Appeal to Roosevelt: Sirdar J. J. Singh to Roosevelt, Sept. 29, 1943, 845.48/333, SD, NA. Nationalist developments in Indonesia: George McTurnan Kahin, *Nationalism and Revolution in Indonesia* (Ithaca, N.Y.: Cornell University Press, 1952), chap. 4.

Roosevelt as Propagandist. Battle of Sicily: Garland and Smyth; Samuel Eliot Morison, *Sicily-Salerno-Anzio* (Boston: Little, Brown, 1954), chaps. 4-10; Eisenhower, pp. 200-206; Hanson Baldwin, *Battles Lost and Won* (Harper, 1966), chap. 6; Fuller, pp. 260-264. Roosevelt's receipt of the news of Mussolini's fall: Sherwood, pp. 741-742; Rosenman, pp. 383-384. Roosevelt on OWI broadcast about Italian King, July 27, 1943: PPA, 1943, p. 323. Mussolini's fall: F. W. Deakin, Bk. IV, which has extensive quotations from the council proceedings; see also MacGregor-Hastie, chap. 8. Roosevelt's fireside chat after Mussolini's fall, July 28, 1943: PPA, 1943, pp. 326-336. Roosevelt on dealing with Italians: PC 912, July 30, 1943; PPA, 1943, pp. 344-345. Background of development of information and propaganda agencies: Reston, pp. 199-215; PPA, 1942, pp. 274-283; PPA, 1943, pp. 118-121; *The United States at War,* chap. 8. Cantril critique of OWI, circa Dec. 1942: Cantril Notebook I, pp. 60-61; Philleo Nash interview by Mrs. Sharp, "Historical Appraisal on O.W.I., World War II," Jan. 9, 1942, HSTL. Elmer Davis's appointment and adventures as director: Frankfurter to Roosevelt, March 12, 1942, Freedman, p. 651; Elmer Davis Correspondence, Box 1, 1943, LC; Elliott Roosevelt, pp. 137-138; Smith Diary, Aug. 25, 1943, FDRL; Harold Smith to Roosevelt, Feb. 5, 1943, Smith Diary, FDRL; George Creel to Davis, Aug. 4, 1942, Davis Correspondence, LC. Unconditional surrender and psychological warfare: Ernest K. Bramsted, *Goebbels and National Socialist Propaganda, 1925-1945* (East Lansing: Michigan State University Press, 1965), p. 309; William E. Daugherty and Morris Janowitz, *A Psychological Warfare Casebook* (Baltimore: Johns Hopkins Press, 1958), pp. 260, 263, 273 ff., 278; Murray Dyer, *The Weapon on the Wall* (Baltimore: Johns Hopkins Press, 1959), pp. 32, 47; Garland and Smyth, pp. 268-278. Generally, on the strategy of freedom: Reston, chaps. 1, 3.

Allied propaganda aims, as in Italy: Hammond to AC of S, OPD, Oct. 27, 1942, OPD Torch, AR. Nazi propaganda: FDRL has transcripts of translated Nazi radio broadcasts, which were sent on to the White House, some marked for special attention of the President. See, generally, Z. A. B. Zeman, *Nazi Propaganda* (Oxford: Oxford University Press, 1964); Alexander L. George, *Propaganda Analysis* (Row, Peterson, 1959); Paul M. A. Linebarger, *Psychological Warfare* (Washington, D.C.: Infantry Journal Press, 1948). Zeman quotation is from Zeman, p. 6. Excerpts from Hochschule text, 1939, are in FDRL. The Nazi cartoon leaflet is reprinted in Linebarger, pp. 138-139. The struggle over freedom as a symbol: J. M. Burns, "The Roosevelt-Hitler Battle of Symbols," *Antioch Review,* Fall 1942, pp. 407-421. Roosevelt statement on freedom and social progress, Nov. 6, 1941: PPA, 1941, p. 476. Japanese propaganda is quoted in Daugherty and Janowitz, pp. 431-432. Roosevelt on himself as an expert on public psychology: Roosevelt to Basil O'Connor, May 16, 1939, PSF, Box 53. Relation of propaganda and deed: Daugherty and Janowitz, pp. 19, 44; Dyer, p. 104. Roosevelt as target: Daugherty and Janowitz, pp. 436-437. Roosevelt and Hitler compared as propagandists: Ralph K. White, "Hitler, Roosevelt, and the Nature of War Propaganda," *Journal of Abnormal and Social Psychology,* April 1949, pp. 157-174. See, generally, H. G. Nicholas, "Roosevelt and Public Opinion," *The Fortnightly,* May 1945, pp. 303-308.

CHAPTER THIRTEEN

Hyde Park matters: Roosevelt to W. Russell Bowie, Feb. 6, 1943, PL, p. 1399; Roosevelt to Moses W. Smith, June 10, 1943, PL, p. 1428; Roosevelt to William A. Plog, June 11, 1943, PL, p. 1429; Roosevelt to Curtis Roosevelt Dall, Feb. 19, 1943, PL, pp. 1402-1403; Roosevelt to Eleanor

Roosevelt Dall, April 8, 1943, PL, p. 1419. Library matters: Roosevelt to Archibald MacLeish, June 9, 1943, PSF, MacLeish Folder; Roosevelt to Ickes, Oct. 29, 1943, PL, p. 1461. Roosevelt on Joe Martin: Roosevelt to Fritz G. Lanham, March 9, 1943, PL, pp. 1407-1408. Roosevelt on Poughkeepsie Episcopalians: Hassett, p. 204. Roosevelt on his two illnesses: Roosevelt to Churchill, March 17, 1943, PL, p. 1413; Roosevelt to Churchill, Oct. 25, 1943, Churchill[4], p. 314.

The Mills of the Gods. "No truck with fascism" pledge, July 28, 1943: PPA, 1943, p. 327. Hitler on his plans for Rome: quoted in Shirer, p. 1298. British prisoners of war in Italy: Churchill[5], p. 59. Roosevelt on dealing with any Italian leaders except Fascists: PC 912, July 30, 1943; PPA, 1943, pp. 344-345. Sforza on fear of revolution: NYT, July 30, 1943, p. 3. Del Vayo on lack of democratic policy: *The Nation,* Aug. 21, 1943, p. 211. Churchill on radical tendencies in Italy: Churchill to Roosevelt, Aug. 5, 1943, Churchill[5], pp. 99-100. PMRP, Naval Aide's File, Italy and Sicily, Box 13, include extensive documentation on the Italian surrender; see, especially, Murphy to Roosevelt, Nov. 6, 1943. Churchill's trip to Niagara Falls and Hyde Park: Churchill[5], p. 82. Marshall's and Stimson's strictures to Roosevelt before Quebec Conference: Matloff, pp. 211-213; Stimson and Bundy, pp. 436-438; Stimson Diary, Aug. 10, 1943. Quebec Conference: Matloff, pp. 220-230; Bryant[2], pp. 575-586; Churchill[5], pp. 83-85; Sherwood, pp. 745-749. Leahy Diary, LC. Garland and Smyth provide a detailed account of the Italian surrender; the "say Uncle" quotation is from p. 444. Churchill[5], chap. 6, offers a good short picture of the developments. Battle of Salerno: *Salerno* (Washington, D.C.: War Department, 1944); Eisenhower, chap. 10; Churchill[5], pp. 142-149; Garland and Smyth, pp. 521, 523. Stalin's message of congratulation: Stalin to Churchill and Roosevelt, Sept. 10, 1943, *Correspondence*[1], p. 162.

Roosevelt's wartime concern for Jewish victims of Nazism, Oct. 25, 1941: PPA, 1941, p. 433; Aug. 21, 1942: PPA, 1942, p. 329; July 30, 1943: PPA, 1943, p. 338. Establishment of commission to investigate crimes, Oct. 7, 1942: PPA, 1942, p. 410. Of the extensive published material on Roosevelt and the European Jews, see, especially, Arthur D. Morse, *While Six Million Died* (Random House, 1967), and published and unpublished materials cited therein; and review of Morse by John M. Blum, *The New Republic,* Feb. 17, 1968, pp. 30-32. Wise to Roosevelt is quoted in Morse, pp. 26-27. Bermuda Conference: FRUS, 1943, Vol. I, pp. 134-250. Roosevelt on the conference: Roosevelt to Hull, May 14, 1943, FRUS, 1943, Vol. I, p. 179. Background of British and American policy on refugees: Hull to Roosevelt, n.d., but probably late Feb. 1943, with enclosures on British policy, FDRL; see also materials in SD, NA, 1943. Roosevelt and Zion: Range, pp. 152, 156-157; Blum[2], pp. 207-208; Hull, pp. 1531-1534, 1536.

Cairo: The Generalissimo. Drew Pearson incident: PC 915, Aug. 31, 1943; Hull, p. 1253; Hull to Roosevelt, Aug. 30, 1943, Hull Papers, Box 52, LC. Stalin's pique: Stalin to Roosevelt and to Churchill, Aug. 22, 1943, *Correspondence*[2], p. 84; *Correspondence*[1], pp. 138 ff. I have discussed with Soviet historians why Stalin did not meet with Roosevelt and Churchill to press his second-front demands, rather than complaining about exclusion, but the explanation remains elusive. Diminished Soviet interest in the second front: Long, pp. 320-322, 331; Sherwood, p. 734; Stimson Diary, Nov. 10, 1943; Matloff, pp. 285-286, 303, and references therein; Leahy Diary, Oct. 7, 1943, LC; Werth, p. 747. *Realpolitik* attitude in the War Department: Matloff, pp. 287-288. Reports of peace feelers: Nicolson, pp. 277, 309, 345; Leahy Diary, Aug. 11, 1943, LC; see also Ulam, p. 333; McNeill, p. 324 and citations. Bullitt's strategic alternative: Bullitt to Roosevelt, May 12, 1943, PSF, Bullitt Folder. For a different (and somewhat later) view, see Kennan[1], pp. 211, 218 ff. Mackinac Island conference: Vandenberg, pp. 55-61. Proposed foreign ministers' and Big Three meetings: Roosevelt to Stalin, Sept. 6, 1943; Stalin to Roosevelt, Sept. 8, 1943; Roosevelt to Stalin, Sept. 11, 1943; Stalin to Roosevelt and to Churchill, Sept. 12, 1943; Roosevelt to Stalin, Oct. 14, 1943; *Correspondence*[1], pp. 89, 90-91, 92-93, 94, 100-101; Hull, pp. 1292-1296. Hull mission to Moscow, including Chinese adherence to the four-nation declaration: FRUS, 1943, Vol. I, pp. 513-781; Hull, chaps. 92-94; Eden, chap. 10. Stalin's statement about Soviet intervention against Japan following defeat of Germany: FRUS, 1943, Vol. I, p. 686; Hull, pp. 1310-1311; FRUS, *Cairo-Teheran,* p. 147; PMRP, Box 210; text also in Hull Papers, Box 52, LC. Previous Soviet indications of willingness to join war against Japan: Harriman statement, *Congressional Record,* Vol. 97, Pt. 14, Aug. 27, 1951, pp. 5410-5416; Deane, p. 226; Leahy, p. 147.

Roosevelt's trip to Cairo: FRUS, *Cairo-Teheran;* Leahy Diary, LC. Torpedo incident: FRUS, *ibid.,* pp. 279-280; King and Whitehill, p. 501; Sherwood, p. 768; NYT, March 16, 1958, p. 52 (recollections of the erring destroyer's officer of the deck at the time). Roosevelt to Eleanor Roosevelt en route, Nov. 18, 1943: PL, p. 1469. Precautions for the trip: Churchill[5], pp. 326-327; Eisenhower, pp. 220-221; Green to Matthews, Nov. 18, 1943, PMRP, Folder 3, Box 17. Churchill on Cairo: Churchill[5], p. 316. Roosevelt's exchanges with Chiang: FRUS, *Cairo-Teheran,* Nov. 23, 1943, pp. 322-325; Leahy Diary, Nov. 23, 1943, LC; see also Elliott Roosevelt, pp. 142, 163-166. The Chinese and the CCS: FRUS, *ibid.,* pp. 305-307, 325, 337, 379-380, 390, 748. The theater view: FRUS, *ibid.,* pp. 316-322; Stilwell, p. 245. The strategic dilemma: Churchill[5], p. 328; Matloff, pp. 347-352. Roosevelt to Eleanor Roosevelt on the conference, Nov. 21, 1943: PL, p. 1470. Roosevelt's promise to Chiang on Bay of Bengal operations: Matloff, p. 350. Thanksgiving dinner: Churchill[5], p. 341; Elliott Roosevelt, pp. 159-160.

Teheran: The Marshal. Roosevelt's trip from Cairo to Teheran: "Log," FRUS, *Cairo-Teheran,* pp. 459-460; Leahy, p. 202; Reilly, pp. 176-177; Leahy Diary, Nov. 27, 1943, LC. Arrangements in Teheran: FRUS, *ibid.,* pp. 463-464; Reilly, pp. 177-179. Assassination plot: Laslo Havas, *Hitler's Plot to Kill the Big Three* (Cowles, 1969); Viktor Yegorov, "The Plot Against Eureka," in *Soldiers of Invisible Battles* (Moscow: 1969); Yakovlev, Pt. II; Berezhkov, Pt. I. Roosevelt's first meeting with Stalin: FRUS, *ibid.,* pp. 483-486; Elliott Roosevelt, p. 176; see also PPA, 1943, p. 558. First plenary session: FRUS, *ibid.,* p. 487; Arnold, p. 465. The bulk of the remainder of this section is drawn from FRUS, *Cairo-Teheran;* Ehrman[1], chaps. 4-5; Yakovlev; Bryant[1], pp. 68-101; and Berezhkov, Pts. II-V. The FRUS minutes were drawn from two prime sources: a record kept by Bohlen, the interpreter; and Joint Chiefs of Staff Minutes. FRUS, *Cairo-Teheran,* pp. xi-xxi, explains the scope and limitations of the official records of Cairo and Teheran. Stalin on future Soviet intervention against Japan: FRUS, *ibid.,* pp. 489, 499-500; Ehrman[1], p. 173. Roosevelt's interest in operations at the head of the Adriatic: FRUS, *ibid.,* pp. 489, 499, 503; Sherwood, p. 780. Turkish situation: FRUS, *ibid.,* 505; Churchill[5], p. 355. Roosevelt's illness after first dinner: Eden, p. 427; Leahy Diary, Nov. 28, 1943, LC; Moran, p. 150. Stalin on unconditional surrender: FRUS, *ibid.,* p. 513; Sherwood, p. 783; the Minutes suggest that Roosevelt may have left the after-dinner discussion by the time Stalin mentioned unconditional surrender; Roosevelt later stated to Hull that the matter had not been raised at Teheran in his presence: Roosevelt to Hull, Dec. 23, 1943, PSF, Hull Folder, pp. 2-43. Churchill quoting Hopkins on Roosevelt: Moran, p. 150. Roosevelt's private meeting with Stalin: Churchill[5], p. 363; Sherwood, p. 784; Moran, p. 146. Sword of Stalingrad ceremony: King and Whitehill, pp. 519-520; Arnold, pp. 467-468; Elliott Roosevelt, pp. 180-182; Perkins, p. 85. Roosevelt's toast: FRUS, *ibid.,* p. 585; Arnold Papers, Box 42, LC; Yakovlev, Pt. II.

Roosevelt to Perkins on playing up to Stalin: Perkins, pp. 83-85; Berezhkov emphasizes Roosevelt's rapport with Stalin and popularity with the Soviet delegation. Roosevelt to Stalin on Polish situation: FRUS, *ibid.,* pp. 594-596; later discussion of Poland: *ibid.,* pp. 596-604, 837-838. Teheran in summary: Smith, chap. 4. Teheran communiqué and declaration: PPA, 1943, p. 533; drafts are in OF 4675 (Teheran Conference). Roosevelt on Turkish point of view: FRUS, *ibid.,* p. 698, 713. Change of plans for Bay of Bengal: FRUS, *ibid.,* p. 706; Ehrman[1], pp. 183-193; Stilwell, pp. 251-255; Sherwood, p. 801; Elliott Roosevelt, p. 207. Chiang's response: Chiang to Roosevelt, received Dec. 9, 1943, in Romanus and Sunderland[1], pp. 74-75; also in PMRP, Box 210, Sextant. Eisenhower's appointment: Sherwood, p. 803; Stimson Diary, Dec. 16, 17, 1943; Churchill[5], pp. 413 ff.; Eisenhower, pp. 235-236. Visit to Sphinx: Churchill[5], p. 419; Film 208 UN 82, NA. Churchill's rendition of "Barbara Fritchie": Sherwood, p. 729; Churchill[4], pp. 795-796. Churchill on Russians: Arnold, p. 474. Roosevelt's return trip: Stimson Diary, Dec. 17, 1943; Film 208 UN 82, NA; Rosenman, p. 411. Roosevelt's Christmas Eve address: PPA, 1943, pp. 553-562. Roosevelt on lack of civilization: Roosevelt to Frankfurter, Dec. 23, 1943, Freedman, p. 709.

CHAPTER FOURTEEN

Quotations and references are, respectively, to Smith Diary, Dec. 11, 1943, FDRL; leading politician, *Time,* Dec. 20, 1943, pp. 13-15; *The Nation,* Dec. 18, 1943, pp. 720-723. Max Lerner, *PM,* Dec. 20, 1943, p. 2; TRB, *The New Republic,* Dec. 27, 1943, p. 914.

A Second Bill of Rights. Roosevelt's mood on returning from Teheran:

Rosenman, p. 421. Roosevelt's post-press conference remark on no need for a New Deal: *Time,* Jan. 3, 1944, p. 14; his remarks at the next press conference on Dr. New Deal and Dr. Win-the-War: PC 929, Dec. 28, 1943; PPA, 1943, pp. 569-575 (checked against PC transcripts, indicating only slight differences). State of the Union address, Jan. 11, 1944: preparation: Rosenman, pp. 417-427; Freedman, pp. 715-717; text: PPA, 1944, pp. 32-42 (checked against recording of radio address as given, which varied slightly in wording and emphasis). The economic bill of rights as culminating concept in American ideological development: James MacGregor Burns, *Presidential Government* (Boston: Houghton Mifflin, 1965), chap. 7, and works cited therein.

Wheeler on the barons: cited in Burns, *Roosevelt,* pp. 341-342. State Department planning on postwar security organization: Harley Notter, *Postwar Foreign Policy Preparation* (Washington, D.C.: Department of State, 1949), chaps. 8-10. Fulbright Resolution: Fulbright to Roosevelt, June 26, 1943, SD, NA; Hull, pp. 1262-1263. Roosevelt's cautiousness on postwar security planning: Hull to Roosevelt, Sept. 9, 1943; Roosevelt to Hull, Sept. 16, 1943, PSF, Hull Folder, 2-43. Roosevelt's colloquy with reporters, Oct. 29, 1943: PC 924; PPA, 1943, pp. 460-461. Vandenberg on Mackinac conference: Vandenberg, p. 59. United Nations Relief and Rehabilitation Administration: PPA, 1943 (Nov. 9, 1943), p. 503; see also PC 926, Nov. 9, 1943. Go-ahead to Hull on planning: Hull, p. 1649.

The Revolt of the Barons. Roosevelt and the servicemen's vote: message to Congress, Jan. 25, 1944, PPA, 1944-45, pp. 53-60; congressional reaction: Drury, pp. 45, 60-61; *Congressional Record,* Vol. 90, Pt. 1, Jan. 26, 1966, pp. 706-740, 745 ff.; *Time,* Feb. 7, 1944, p. 13. Legislative action: PPA, 1944-45, pp. 111-116. Lilienthal's trials: Lilienthal, pp. 627, 630, 632. National service law: Stimson and Bundy, pp. 483-484; PPA, 1944-45, p. 39 (State of the Union message, Jan. 11, 1944); Rosenman, pp. 421-424.

Background of tax bill: Paul; Blum[2], chap. 2; J. M. Burns, "Congress and the Formation of Economic Policies," chap. 5, "The Revenue Act of 1943" (Ph.D. dissertation, Harvard University, 1947). Byrnes quoted in Blum[2], p. 75. Barkley's role: Barkley, chap. 12; interview with Alben W. Barkley, Reel 5, Side 1, HSTL. Roosevelt's veto message, Feb. 22, 1944: PPA, 1944-45, pp. 80-83. Congressional reaction: Drury, pp. 87-91. Barkley's speech: *Congressional Record,* Vol. 90, Pt. 2, Feb. 23, 1944, pp. 1964-1966. Roosevelt's reaction: Roosevelt to Mackenzie King, Feb. 28, 1944, PSF, Canada, 1-44; Byrnes, pp. 211-212; Hassett, pp. 235-236; Roosevelt to Sherman Minton, March 1, 1944, PSF, Box 52. Roosevelt's letter to Barkley: PSF, Senate Folder, 4-40. Barkley's resignation and redesignation: Drury, pp. 91-93. Roosevelt's timber-cutting and taxes: Hassett, p. 237. On the considerable comment at the time on Roosevelt's approach to Congress, see, especially, James Wechsler, *PM,* Feb. 27, 1944, p. 3. Bob Hope's comment: *Time,* March 13, 1944, p. 12.

The Suction Pump. Roosevelt on the long road ahead, March 8, 1944: PPA, 1944-45, pp. 99-100. The strategic situation in the Mediterranean: Ehrman[1], chaps. 6-7; Matloff, chap. 18. Churchill's view: Churchill[5], pp. 426-427, source of quotation, p. 429. Roosevelt-Churchill exchange on

Anzio, Dec. 28, 1943: Churchill[5], pp. 440-441. General developments in Italy: W. G. F. Jackson, *The Battle for Italy* (Harper, 1967), pp. 182-201. German reaction to Anzio: Marshall to Roosevelt, Jan. 28, 1944, PMRP, Naval Aide's File, Box 13. Roosevelt on Anzio situation: PC 935, Feb. 11, 1944. Churchill on same: Churchill[5], p. 488. Question of abandoning or postponing ANVIL: Matloff, pp. 416-426; Ehrman[1], pp. 241-242. Unconditional surrender: Matloff, pp. 428-432; retrospective statement by Eisenhower, NYT, Dec. 21, 1964, p. 6; Hull, pp. 1574-1582; Roosevelt to Joint Chiefs of Staff, April 1, 1944, quoted in Matloff, p. 431. Roosevelt to Hull on not making exceptions, April 5, 1944: Hull, p. 1577. Roosevelt to Hull on Germans, April 1, 1944: Hull, p. 1576. Roosevelt and the plight of the Jews: Blum[2], pp. 220-221; cf. Hull, pp. 1538-1540; Long, pp. 334-337. Roosevelt on Long: quoted by Morgenthau in Blum[2], p. 221; see also Arthur D. Morse, *While Six Million Died* (Random House, 1967), pp. 90-97 (Morse later interviewed Pehle). Creation of War Refugee Board, Jan. 22, 1944: PPA, 1944-45, pp. 48-50. Roosevelt on Palestine: Blum[2], pp. 224-227. Emergency refugee shelters: Roosevelt to Congress, June 12, 1944, PPA, 1944-45, pp. 168-171.

The Pacific plan is well laid out in Ehrman[1], pp. 421-423. Army operations in Makin and Kwajalein are described in Philip A. Crowl and Edmund G. Love, *Seizure of the Gilberts and Marshalls* (Washington, D.C.: Office of the Chief of Military History, 1955); also American Forces in Action Series, *Makin* (Washington, D.C.: U.S. Government Printing Office, 1946). Tarawa: Robert Sherrod, *Tarawa* (Duell, Sloan & Pearce, 1944); James R. Stockman, *The Battle for Tarawa* (Washington, D.C.: Historical Section, Marine Corps, 1947). Admiralties: American Forces in Action Series, *The Admiralties: Operations of the 1st Cavalry Division* (Washington, D.C.: U.S. Government Printing Office, 1945). Churchill on the Pacific plan: Ehrman[1], pp. 439, 448. Roosevelt's position: Roosevelt to Churchill, Feb. 25, 1944, Churchill[5], pp. 561-562; Leahy draft is in PMRP, Box 14. Chennault's views: Chennault to Roosevelt, Jan. 26, 1944; Chennault to Hopkins, Feb. 8, 1944, Pacific File, FDRL. Roosevelt's response: Roosevelt to Chennault, March 15, 1944, Pacific File, FDRL. Background of development of air power and operations in Europe: Craven and Cate, Vol. II, chaps. 20-21; Vol. III, chaps. 2-3; Arnold, chap. 26. Inflated reports: Craven and Cate, Vol. II, p. 711; Arnold Papers, Boxes 43, 45, LC; Noble Frankland, *The Bombing Offensive Against Germany* (London: Faber and Faber, 1965), chap. 2. British intelligence reports: Craven and Cate, Vol. II, p. 708; see also United States Strategic Bombing Survey, cited in Fuller, p. 225.

CHAPTER FIFTEEN

Noel F. Busch, *What Manner of Man?* (Harper, 1944), pp. 12-17, describes the President in the White House in early 1944. The President's health during this period and earlier and later: main source is a detailed and informed manuscript by Dr. Howard G. Bruenn (the heart specialist who attended Roosevelt during the last year of the President's life),

"Clinical Notes on the Illness and Death of President Franklin D. Roosevelt," pp. 1-30, based on Dr. Bruenn's records and observations. Also consulted: W. G. Eliasberg, "How Long Was Roosevelt Ill Before His Death?," *Diseases of the Nervous System,* Nov. 1953, pp. 323-328; Noah D. Fabricant, "Franklin D. Roosevelt's Nose and Throat Ailments," *The Eye, Ear, Nose and Throat Monthly,* Feb. 1957, pp. 103-106; Rudolph Marx, "FDR: A Medical History," *Today's Health,* April 1961, pp. 54 ff.; James A. Halsted, "F.D.R.s 'Little Strokes'—A Medical Myth," *Today's Health,* Dec. 1962, pp. 53 ff.; Ross McIntire, *White House Physician* (Putnam, 1946); review of Hugh L'Etang, *The Pathology of Leadership* (London, 1969), in *Medical World News* (especially on Roosevelt's rumored malignant melanoma). On Roosevelt's health, see, generally, Hassett; Tully; Reilly; Perkins; Jonathan Daniels interview, HSTL; Edith Helm Papers, LC; Herman E. Bateman, "Observations on President Roosevelt's Health during World War II," *Mississippi Valley Historical Review,* June 1956, pp. 82-102; see also John T. Flynn, pp. 368, 412. On Roosevelt's health especially during 1944: Hassett, pp. 233, 242; Perkins, pp. 389-390; Tully, pp. 273-274. Roosevelt at his press conference: Drury, pp. 107-108. Roosevelt at Hobcaw, and afterward: Roosevelt to Hopkins, May 18, 1944, Sherwood, pp. 6-8; Hassett, p. 241; Roosevelt and Shalett, p. 347. Curaçao incident: Eleanor Roosevelt to Roosevelt, April 4, 1944; Roosevelt to Eleanor Roosevelt, April 5, 1944, PPF 1063.

Secrecy and "Sedition." Stimson's comment: Stimson Diary, March 15, 1944, May 23, 1944. White House arrangements: Jonathan Daniels interview, pp. 16, 22, 23, 35, 63, HSTL. Blair House: Roosevelt to Hull, Aug. 28, 1942, FW 110.12/326 SD. Byrnes office: Somers, pp. 51-60; Byrnes. Leahy office: Leahy, p. 97. Budget Bureau: Smith Diary, FDRL. Roosevelt-Marshall channels of communication: Cline, pp. 105-106. Hopkins on his condition: Sherwood, p. 805. Roosevelt on Hopkins's return to Washington: Sherwood, p. 6. Administration "backgrounders" (or "seminars") for reporters: Clapper Papers, LC. Publication of "secret" war information: Biddle, pp. 248-251. Background of sedition trial: Biddle, chap. 15; the trial itself is vividly described in *Time* (especially May 1, 1944, pp. 17-18) and in *PM*. Montgomery Ward episode: Stimson Diary, April 4, 1944, May 1, 2, 1944; Biddle, pp. 311-324; PPA, 1944-45, May 9, 1944, pp. 122-125, Dec. 27, 1944, pp. 446-452; Timmons, pp. 343-345.

The White House visitor: interview with Jonathan Daniels, April 13, 1969; see also Moore, p. 323; Hewlett and Anderson, p. 203. Secrecy: Tully, pp. 265-266; Davis; Groves. Keeping atom secret from Congress: Bush to Bundy, Feb. 24, 1944; transcript of telephone conversation, Stimson and Representative Andrew J. May, Nov. 27, 1943, Stimson Papers. Sharing atomic information with Britain: Gowing, chaps. 4-5; Groves, pp. 125-137; Sherwood, p. 704; with Russia: Hewlett and Anderson, pp. 268, 329-330. Bohr's views: Moore. Bohr to Roosevelt, July 3, 1944: Freedman, pp. 728-735. Frankfurter to Roosevelt, Sept. 8, 1944: *ibid.,* pp. 735-736. Frankfurter's views: *ibid.,* pp. 723-728; Freedman cited, p. 724. Bohr's interview with Churchill: Gowing, pp. 354-355; Moore, pp. 342-344; with Roosevelt: Moore, pp. 348-350. Roosevelt-Churchill conference: Leahy, p. 266; Moore, pp. 351-353. *Aide-mémoire* of Sept. 19, 1944: Moore, p. 353; text is from Gowing, p. 447. Indications that Germans were not building the bomb: Churchill[6], p. 148; Stimson Diary, Dec. 13, 1944. Stimson's notes on meeting with President: Stimson Papers, Aug. 23, 1944.

The Mobilized Society. The author and Douglas D. Rose collaborated in research and writing for this section. Roosevelt on building planes: PC 956, June 9, 1944; PPA, 1944-45, pp. 165-166. Data and description of social and economic changes is drawn largely from research conducted by Douglas D. Rose at the Franklin D. Roosevelt Library and at the University of Minnesota. Urban crowding: Davis McEntire, *Residence and Race* (Berkeley: University of California Press, 1960), chap. 3. Whites' attitudes toward Negro job opportunity: Cantril, p. 510. Racial stoppages: FEPC statement, n.d., OF 4245 G, Box 5. OWI report, Dec. 9, 1942: OF 4245 G O, OWI Box 13. Ickes on discrimination as a national question: Ickes to Roosevelt, July 7, 1943, OF 6, 1943. Suppression of FEPC report: Cramer to Roosevelt, July 3, 1942; Patterson to Roosevelt, July 14, 1942; Roosevelt to McIntyre, July 17, 1942; McIntyre to Cramer, July 17, 1942; OF 4245 G, Box 3. FEPC Mexican-American hearings stopped: Welles to Roosevelt, June 20, 1942, continued to July 31, 1942; McIntyre to Roosevelt, OF 4245 G, Box 3. Jackson *Daily News* is quoted in *PM,* March 20, 1944, p. 3. South Carolina legislature declaration, March 31, 1944: OF 93. Hoover report on Communism: FBI report sent to Daniels, Aug. 22, 1944, OF 4245 G, F-H-L Box 10. Hershey on requisitioning and discrimination: Hershey to Roosevelt, Oct. 4, 1941, OF 93; War Department communication, Selective Service 6142, see OF 93 B, Sept. 18, 1944. Visit of members of the Negro Newspaper Publishers Association: PC 933, Feb. 5, 1944; PPA, 1944-45, pp. 66-70. Roosevelt on Negroes at Warm Springs: Ross to Eleanor Roosevelt, Jan. 25, 1944; Roosevelt to Eleanor Roosevelt, Jan. 31, 1944; Roosevelt to Daniels, Feb. 7, 1944, OF 93. Roosevelt promise of Japanese-American return: press letter to the President of the Senate, Sept. 10, 1943, OF 4849, 1942-1944, Box 1. Japanese-American situation: Stimson Diary, May 17, 1944, May 26, 1944; Roosevelt to Stettinius and Ickes, June 12, 1944; PL, pp. 1517-1518; Hull to Roosevelt, June 16, 1944, OF 4849; Fortas to Roosevelt, Aug. 25, 1944, OF 4849.

School attendance: I. L. Kandel, *The Impact of the War Upon American Education* (Chapel Hill: University of North Carolina Press, 1948), pp. 85-88. Roosevelt requests schools as service centers: Roosevelt message to National Institute on Education and the War, Aug. 28, 1942, OF 6 G. On curriculum: *What the Schools Should Teach in Wartime,* NEA pamphlet, OF 107, Box 8. On idle colleges: report to Roosevelt, July 30, 1943, OF 5182; Bush, p. 7. ASTP and V-12 programs and cuts: OF 25 NN, 1943-45, especially Patterson to Rosenman, Jan. 27, 1944; Rosenman to Roosevelt, Feb. 21, 1944; Marshall to Roosevelt, Feb. 22, 1944. Roosevelt on limited federal school participation: Roosevelt to Pepper, Nov. 12, 1942, OF 107, Box 8. Roosevelt's request of War and Navy Departments for a study of use of colleges for war purposes: PPF 7886, Oct. 15, 1942. Roosevelt's request of Bush for postwar science program: PPA, 1944-45, Nov. 17, 1944, and note; Cox Diary, Oct. 24, 1944, FDRL; draft letter to

Hopkins, Oct. 18, 1944; Cox to Hopkins, Nov. 9, 1944, with proposed Roosevelt letter to Bush; Smith Diary, Daily Record, March 19, 1945, FDRL. See Kandel on war and education in general. Roosevelt on planning for future: Roosevelt to Embree, March 16, 1942, OF 93. Union and labor changes: Executive Order 9240, OF 15. E. J. Burtt, *Labor Markets, Unions, and Government Policies* (St. Martin's, 1963), pp. 15, 94, 99, 273. Ann Arbor housing segregation: Emmerich to McIntyre, Feb. 16, 1943; McIntyre to McNutt, March 4, 1943; McIntyre to Blandford, March 29, 1943, OF 63, Box 16.

The Culture of War. Roosevelt on the existence of one front: State of the Union message, Jan. 11, 1944, PPA, 1944-45, p. 42. Citizen participation in the war: "Review of the Progress of the War," fireside chat by the President, June 12, 1944, PPA, 1944-45, p. 173. American attitudes toward the meaning of the war: Jerome S. Bruner, *Mandate from the People* (Duell, Sloan & Pearce, 1944), pp. 27-29. *The Nation* criticism of Roosevelt: *The Nation,* April 1, 1944, p. 381. Roosevelt's summary of war goals, March 24, 1944: PPA, 1944-45, p. 103. Roosevelt's answer to critics, March 24, 1944: PPA, 1944-45, p. 109. Dos Passos' observations: John Dos Passos, *State of the Nation* (Boston: Houghton Mifflin, 1944), pp. 181, 215-223. Roosevelt's electoral standing: Cantril, pp. 627, 631, 632, 634, 635, 762-763. Brogan on American people at war: D. W. Brogan, "The American Way in War," *Harper's,* May 1944, pp. 491-499.

The Washington scene: Hurd, chap. 24. This section is based in part on personal observation by the author, as a government employee in Washington and Denver, 1942-43, and as an infantryman and combat historian, 1943-45. Civilian and servicemen attitudes toward the fact of war: Stouffer, chap. 9; see also John M. Blum, "The G.I. in the Culture of the Second World War," *Ventures,* Spring 1968, pp. 51-56. Infantrymen's attitude toward soldiers' vote: Ernie Pyle, *Brave Men* (Holt, 1944), p. 137. "Why We Fight" films and their impact: Stouffer, pp. 461-468. Negro soldiers: Fish to Stimson, Feb. 1, 1944, *Congressional Record,* Vol. 90, Pt. 8, pp. A659-A660; Hastie to Stimson, Feb. 29, 1944, text in Ulysses Lee, *The Employment of Negro Troops* (Washington, D.C.: Office of the Chief of Military History, 1966), pp. 478-479; see Lee generally for a well-documented and significant treatment of this subject. Attitude of black troops toward discrimination: Stouffer, pp. 502-503. Stimson's views generally: Stimson and Bundy, p. 461; Stimson Diary, Jan. 27, 1944. Myrdal on the ideological war: Myrdal, p. 1004. Roosevelt on problems of Negro servicemen: special conference for Negro Newspaper Publishers Association (full text in FDRL), Feb. 5, 1944, PPA, 1944-45, pp. 66-67. See, generally, Mina Curtiss (ed.), *Letters Home* (Boston: Little, Brown, 1944).

CHAPTER SIXTEEN

Supply background to the invasion of France: Roland G. Ruppenthal, *Logistical Support of the Armies,* Vol. I, *The European Theatre of Operations* (Washington, D.C.: Office of the Chief of Military History, 1953). The British scene before the invasion: Pogue[2]; Churchill[5], p. 596; Cornelius Ryan, *The Longest Day* (Simon and Schuster, 1959); Morison[5]. On the final meetings, see Pogue[2], p. 170, n. 23. Enemy estimates and plans: Trevor-Roper, pp. 149-153, 164-165; B. H. Liddell Hart (ed.), *The Rommel Papers* (Harcourt, Brace, 1953), p. 465; Warlimont, pp. 407-408; Friedrich Ruge, "The Invasion of Normandy," in Jacobsen and Rohwer, pp. 317-349. Hitler on Roosevelt: Liddell Hart, cited above, p. 465. The cross-channel attack: Harrison; Morison[5]; see also Churchill[6]; Eisenhower; Bradley, among other accounts and memoirs. Murrow's broadcast: Edward R. Murrow, *In Search of Light* (Knopf, 1967), p. 81. Roosevelt prior to D day: Tully, p. 265; Hassett, p. 248. Press conference on morning of D day: PC 954, June 6, 1944; PPA, 1944-45, pp. 154-160; see original transcript, FDRL, for slightly expanded coverage.

Crusade in France. Harrison describes operations in Normandy through the fall of Cherbourg. Eisenhower on the millionth man to land: Marshall to Roosevelt, July 4, 1944, PMRP, Box 23. Churchill's visit to the war: Churchill[6], p. 15. Roosevelt's response: Roosevelt to Churchill, June 19, 1944, PMRP, Box 23. Differences over grand political strategy: see the able discussion in Ehrman[1], pp. 249, 255; see also Ehrman[1], pp. 345-367; Matloff, pp. 466-475. Churchill's "solemn protest": Ehrman[1], p. 356. Churchill to Roosevelt on ANVIL, June 28, 1944: Churchill[6], pp. 63-64. Roosevelt's response, June 29, 1944: Churchill[6], pp. 721-723. On composition of latter message, and on Roosevelt's information that the British ultimately would give way on Trieste, see Leahy to Roosevelt, June 30, 1944, PMRP, Box 23. ANVIL landings: Morison[5], chap. 16. Churchill's inspection: Churchill[6], p. 100.

Roosevelt's relations with de Gaulle, 1943 and early 1944: de Gaulle; FRUS, 1943, Vol. II; FRUS, 1944, Vol. IV; Viorst, chap. 11; Schoenbrun, chap. 5, which includes extensive documentation. Roosevelt on de Gaulle's "infiltration": Roosevelt to Churchill, Dec. 31, 1943; PL, p. 1474. Presentation of destroyer escort, Feb. 12, 1944: PPA, 1944-45, pp. 70-72. French currency: Blum[2], pp. 166-177; Nicolson, p. 377. Roosevelt to Marshall on de Gaulle: Roosevelt to Marshall, June 2, 1944 (in answer to Marshall to Roosevelt, May 17, 1944, enclosing Eisenhower to Marshall, n.d., including Eisenhower message for Roosevelt), FDRL. On Roosevelt's attitude toward de Gaulle around the time of D day, see also Blum[2], p. 168; Stimson and Bundy, p. 551. Churchill–de Gaulle exchange at this time: Churchill[5], pp. 629-630. Preliminaries to de Gaulle's visit to Washington: Viorst, p. 207; Hull, p. 1432; memorandum and correspondence, June 27, 1944, Stimson Papers. Roosevelt's toast to de Gaulle, July 7, 1944: PPA, 1944-45, pp. 194-196; see also de Gaulle, pp. 265-275. Roosevelt on liberation of Paris, Aug. 24, 1944: PPA, 1944-45, pp. 240-241. Stalin on Soviet military plans: Stalin to Roosevelt, June 7, 1944, *Correspondence*[2], p. 145. Roosevelt's toast to Mikolajczyk, June 7, 1944: PPA, 1944-45, pp. 160-163. Poland: Roosevelt to Stalin, June 19, 1944; Stalin to Roosevelt, July 23, 1944, *Correspondence*[2], pp. 146, 152-153. Spheres of interest: Hull, pp. 1451-1452; Roosevelt to Churchill, June 11, 1944; Churchill to Roosevelt, June 11, 1944; Roosevelt to Churchill, June 13, 1944, all in Churchill[6], pp. 75, 75-77. Stalin's May Day order: Werth, pp. 842-843. Stalin's comments on Churchill and Roosevelt: Djilas, p. 73.

Pacific Thunderbolts. Strategic situation in the Pacific, 1944: Matloff, chap. 20; Ehrman[1], chap. 11; S. E. Morison, *New Guinea and the Marianas* (Boston: Little, Brown, 1953), chap. 1. Differences between MacArthur and Navy: King and Whitehill; Whitney; Willoughby and Chamberlain. MacArthur's strategy as quoted: Whitney, p. 120. Japanese naval situation: Morison, *ibid.*, pp. 10-14. Strategic value of Marianas: Morison, *ibid.*, pp. 157-158. Japanese plans and injunctions in the Marianas: Morison, *ibid.*, p. 221; Philip A. Crowl, *Campaign in the Marianas* (Washington, D.C.: Office of the Chief of Military History, 1960), p. 117. The "Great Marianas Turkey Shoot": Morison, *ibid.*, chaps. 14-16. Capture of Saipan: Carl W. Hoffman, *Saipan: The Beginning of the End* (Washington, D.C.: Historical Division, U.S. Marine Corps, 1950); Crowl, chaps. 3-12; see also Edmund G. Love, *The 27th Infantry Division in World War II* (Washington, D.C.: Infantry Journal Press, 1949). Guam: O. R. Lodge, *The Recapture of Guam* (Washington, D.C.: Historical Branch, G-3 Division, U.S. Marine Corps, 1954); Crowl, chaps. 15-20 (on army operations). See, generally, Jeter A. Isely and Philip A. Crowl, *The U.S. Marines and Amphibious Warfare* (Princeton, N.J.: Princeton University Press, 1951); Earl S. Pomeroy, *Pacific Outpost: American Strategy in Guam and Micronesia* (Stanford, Calif.: Stanford University Press, 1951); Clark G. Reynolds, *The Forging of an Air Navy* (McGraw-Hill, 1968); Robert Sherrod, *On to Westward! War in the Central Pacific* (Duell, Sloan & Pearce, 1945).

Roosevelt to Churchill on importance of capture of Saipan, June 19, 1944: PMRP, Box 23. Trip to Oahu and arrival: Rosenman, pp. 456-457; Leahy, pp. 249-250; Rigdon, pp. 115-116. MacArthur's arrival: Rigdon, p. 116; Rosenman, pp. 456-457; Whitney, p. 123. Data on the conferences is sketchy; see Matloff, p. 482; Leahy Diary, July 28, 29, 1944, LC; Leahy, pp. 250-251; Whitney, pp. 123-125; Willoughby and Chamberlain, pp. 233-236; Robert L. Eichelberger, *Our Jungle Road to Tokyo* (Viking, 1950), pp. 165-167. MacArthur on Philippines and Roosevelt's re-election: Whitney, p. 125. Roosevelt's tour of Oahu: Rosenman, p. 458; PPA, 1944-45, pp. 206-212; Films 2594-72, 208 UN 116, NA. Aleutians and trip back: Leahy, pp. 253-254; PPA, 1944-45, pp. 213-216. Reports received at sea: PMRP, Box 23. Roosevelt on the "low" that followed the ship, Aug. 14, 1944: PL, pp. 1527-1529. Roosevelt's follow-up letters to MacArthur and to Nimitz: Rigdon, pp. 121-123.

Roosevelt as Commander in Chief. Roosevelt's wish to be called Commander in Chief: Hull, p. 1111; King and Whitehill, p. 567; there is no reference to the episode by King, or in Leahy or Leahy Diary. Roosevelt's desire to be considered a soldier: GGT (but undoubtedly Roosevelt) to S.T.E. (Early), Dec. 11, 1941, PL, pp. 1255-1256. Roosevelt on not overruling his military advisers: address to Advertising War Council Conference, March 8, 1944, PPA, 1944-45, p. 99; see also Sherwood, p. 948. Noncommissioning of La Guardia and La Guardia background: Arthur Mann, *La Guardia: A Fighter Against His Time* (Philadelphia: Lippincott, 1959); Stimson and Roosevelt: Stimson Diary, March 27, 30, April 6, 7, 9, 10, May 3, 1943; Charles Burlingham to Stimson, March 28, 1943, with copies of Burlingham–La Guardia correspondence; Stimson to Burlingham, March 30, 1943; Stimson to Roosevelt, April 6, 1943; Roosevelt to Stimson, April 8, 1943; Stimson to Roosevelt, April 12, 1943; all in Stimson Papers, Box 400; Roosevelt to Stimson, Oct. 15, 1943, PL, p. 1456. On later developments: Roosevelt to Stimson (unsigned), Sept. 29, 1944, PMRP, Box 12; Hopkins to Roosevelt, Sept. 30, 1944, HHP. Roosevelt on Patton: PC 927, Dec. 17, 1943; PPA, 1943, p. 552. Second Patton incident: Pogue[2], pp. 164-166. Stimson on Roosevelt's nomination of generals: Stimson to Roosevelt, April 12, 1943, Stimson Papers, Box 400; see Rawleigh Warner to Mrs. Frank Knox, March 29, 1949, Knox Papers, LC. Roosevelt's technical advice, respectively: Roosevelt to Acting Cominch, Feb. 23, 1943, PMRP, Naval Aide's File, Logistics; King to Roosevelt, July 17, 1942; Roosevelt to Knox, Aug. 12, 1942; Roosevelt to Leahy, Sept. 16, 1942, all three in PMRP, Naval Aide's File, General Corr., 1942-45, Box 31; Wilson Brown to King, Nov. 27, 1944, PMRP, Box 15; Roosevelt to Stimson and Knox, Sept. 20, 1943, PL, pp. 1443-1444; see also Roosevelt to Land, Sept. 14, 1942, U. S. Maritime Comm., FDRL. Calf shooting: PC 948, May 6, 1944; PPA, 1944-45, pp. 119-120. The AWOL WAC, July 2, 1944: Hassett, pp. 257-258.

Exchange with reporters over Leahy's status: PC 836, July 21, 1942; Leahy, p. 97. Paradox of American civil-military relations: William Emerson, "Franklin Roosevelt as Commander-in-Chief in World War," *Military Affairs,* 1958, pp. 181-207 (this excellent article has been of great assistance in this analysis, especially on the question of the change over time in the extent of Roosevelt's disagreements with his military advisers); see also Greenfield[1], pp. 41 ff.; Neustadt, pp. 214-215. War as an aberration for Americans: Louis Morton, "National Policy and Military Strategy," *Virginia Quarterly Review,* Winter 1960, pp. 10, 11. See also the excellent essays in Greenfield[2] for implications for Roosevelt as Commander in Chief. Churchill as Commander in Chief: see his volumes, especially the documents and appendices; also Morison[5], p. 12. Stalin as Commander in Chief: Deutscher, p. 466; Zhukov. Roosevelt on military planners' occasional conservatism: Matloff, p. 211. Hitler as Commander in Chief: Shirer, p. 1134; see also almost any of the memoirs of German generals. Roosevelt on officers' plot against Hitler: Roosevelt to Eleanor Roosevelt, July 21, 1944, PL, p. 1525; Roosevelt to Stalin, July 21, 1944, *Correspondence*[2], pp. 150-151.

CHAPTER SEVENTEEN

Suspension of presidential election: PC 934, Feb. 8, 1944, PC Transcripts. Discord in America: S. K. Ratcliffe, "America's Crucial Year," *Contemporary Review,* April 1944, p. 198. Letters to Roosevelt: these are drawn from a wider selection made by Paul Streicker in Aug. 1966 from a large collection in OF 4166. Chandler is quoted in *PM,* Jan. 27, 1944, p. 16.

As a Good Soldier. Willkie's 1944 nomination campaign: Barnard, chaps. 20-21; Johnson, chap. 7. Willkie's speech to industrialists: Johnson, pp. 250-251. His statement after defeat: Johnson, p. 280. MacArthur's campaign: Vandenberg, pp. 75-89. For Roosevelt's earlier view of MacArthur, see Tugwell, p. 349; Jonathan Daniels, *The Time Between the Wars* (Doubleday, 1966), p. 207. MacArthur's discussion with naval officers prior to Pearl Harbor: Report of Conference, PMRP, Manila, Dec. 6, 1941. Naval Aide's File, Warfare, Philippine Islands, Box 17; see also Forrestal, pp. 17-18. Published material on Dewey is slight; for the pre-1944 period, see Stanley Walker, *Dewey: An American of This Century* (McGraw-Hill, 1944), a campaign biography. Dewey's acceptance speech: *ibid.*, pp. 344-350.

Roosevelt on not running for a fourth term: Leahy, p. 239; Roosevelt to Patrick H. Drewry, March 7, 1944, PL, pp. 1499-1500. Roosevelt on running for a fourth term: Roosevelt to Hannegan, July 11, 1944, PPA, 1944-45, pp. 197-198. Personal memoirs and accounts of preconvention Democratic party politicking are numerous; see, for example, Rosenman, chap. 22; Blum[2], pp. 280-281; Byrnes, chap. 13; Barkley, pp. 188-191; Allen, chap. 10; Lord, pp. 526-537; Josephson, pp. 616-625; Steinberg, chap. 24; Tully, pp. 275-277. Roosevelt's handling of 1940 nomination rivals: Burns, pp. 411-412. Roosevelt's handling of vice-presidential ambitions: Tully to Roosevelt, July 11 and 13, 1944, PSF, Box 54; Blum[2], pp. 280-281; Byrnes, pp. 219-222; Krock interview, Oral History Project, p. 90. July 11 conference with party leaders: Allen, pp. 127-128; Rosenman, pp. 443-445; Byrnes, pp. 221-222. Wallace's response: "Report from Senator Guffey," July 11, 1944, PSF, Wallace Folder; Lord, p. 529. Byrnes's response: Byrnes, pp. 223-224. Roosevelt's personal statement for Wallace: Roosevelt to Samuel D. Jackson, July 14, 1944, PPA, 1944-45, pp. 199-200. Roosevelt's pressure on Truman: Rosenman, p. 451; Steinberg, p. 213. Roosevelt's acceptance speech, July 20, 1944: PPA, 1944-45, pp. 201-206.

A New Party? Roosevelt's spell of pain in the railroad car: Roosevelt and Shalett, pp. 351-352; Roosevelt to Eleanor Roosevelt, July 21, 1944, PL, p. 1525. Rumors of Roosevelt's ill-health: Daniels interview, p. 42, HSTL; Reilly, pp. 195, 196; Moran, p. 242. FBI agent's report: Hopkins to Roosevelt, July 28, 1944; Leahy to Hopkins, July 28, 1944, PMRP, "Trip to Pacific Theatre," Box 23. On pictures of Roosevelt giving his acceptance speech, see Rosenman, p. 453. Arrangements for Seattle speech: Roosevelt to Reilly, PMRP, Box 23; see also Reilly, pp. 191, 193-194. Aides' reaction to the talk: Rosenman, pp. 461-462; Reilly, p. 194; Tully, pp. 277-278. Roosevelt's physical condition: Bruenn Ms. (see notes, chap. 15 above); Rigdon, p. 130. Roosevelt's seeming boredom with political detail: Roosevelt and Shalett, p. 351. Roosevelt on "ghoulish" newspapermen: Reilly, pp. 196-197. Signing of GI Bill of Rights, June 22, 1944: PPA, 1944-45, pp. 180-185. Missouri Valley Authority, Sept. 21, 1944: PPA, 1944-45, pp. 274-278; see also PC 980, Nov. 14, 1944; PPA, 1944-45, pp. 419-422.

Willkie's views after Wisconsin: Wendell L. Willkie Papers, Speech Material Cont., LC; Johnson, chap. 9. Willkie's support in the presidential Democratic party: Barnard, p. 478. Joseph Barnes, *Willkie* (Simon and Schuster, 1952), pp. 367-371, has rounded up the rumors of Willkie as a possible Roosevelt running mate; see also Roosevelt to Norris, July 17, 1944, PL, p. 1522, which indicates that Roosevelt had a role in feelers put out to Willkie even though he implies he had not. "Leaking" of Roosevelt's letter: Barnard, p. 482. So secretive were both Roosevelt and Willkie about their preliminary negotiations over party realignment that documentary sources are limited; see, however, Roosevelt to Willkie, July 13, 1944, PL, p. 1520; Roosevelt to Willkie, Aug. 21, 1944, PL, pp. 1531-1532; and Willkie statements and correspondence in Barnes and Barnard. Rosenman, chap. 24, offers the fullest and most firsthand report of Roosevelt's actions. Hassett, p. 255, confirms that Roosevelt saw Pinchot on June 29, 1944.

A Grand Design? Specialized international co-operation: Myron Taylor to Roosevelt, n.d.; Roosevelt to Taylor, June 5, 1944, PSF, Myron Taylor Folder, Vatican; Berle to Roosevelt, May 19, 1944; Roosevelt to Berle, May 20, 1944, PSF, Hull Folder, 2-44. Bretton Woods: Stettinius to Roosevelt, Feb. 29, 1944, with enclosures; Roosevelt to Byrnes, March 6, 1944; Byrnes to Roosevelt, March 10, 1944, FDRL; Blum², chaps. 5-6; Roy F. Harrod, *The Life of John Maynard Keynes* (St. Martin's, 1963), chap. 13. Roosevelt's message to conference: Blum², p. 257; see also PPA, 1944-45, pp. 138-140. Popular attitudes toward postwar international organization: Cantril, pp. 908-910. Congressional role: Young, pp. 191-196. Background and basic documents on Dumbarton Oaks: Robert A. Divine, *Second Chance* (Atheneum, 1967); Welles; FRUS, 1944, Vol. I, General, pp. 614-923. Roosevelt on the intellectuals is quoted in Divine, p. 167. Daily progress reports submitted to Roosevelt by Stettinius are in FDRL and included in FRUS. Dewey criticism and response: Hull, pp. 1686-1699. Soviet stand on veto: FRUS, *ibid.*, pp. 738, 742, 748, 750, 766, 777; see Kolko, pp. 272-274. Roosevelt-Gromyko meeting: FRUS, *ibid.*, pp. 784-787.

Second Quebec Conference: Ismay on the Churchills' and Roosevelt's reunion: Ismay, p. 373. Roosevelt's and Churchill's estimate of the situation: Churchill⁶, pp. 153-154; Ehrman¹, p. 509. Adriatic strategy: Ehrman², p. 511; Matloff, p. 510; Churchill⁶, pp. 155-156. Churchill's offer of fleet: Churchill⁶, pp. 154-155; Ehrman¹, p. 518; King and Whitehill, p. 569; Ismay, p. 374. Expectations of German defeat: Matloff, p. 508. Allied zones: Ehrman², p. 515; Blum², pp. 330, 372; Stimson Papers. Morgenthau plan: Blum², chap. 7; Churchill⁶, pp. 156-157; Morgenthau-Churchill confrontation: Blum², pp. 373-374; Moran, pp. 190-193; McCloy notes, Sept. 20, 1944, Stimson Papers. Roosevelt-Churchill statement: Blum², p. 371. Churchill-Eden exchange: Blum², p. 371; Eden, p. 476. On Roosevelt's backing away from Morgenthau plan, cf. Eleanor Roosevelt, pp. 334-335. Stimson's reaction: memorandum, Sept. 5, 1944, Stimson Papers. Hyde Park days: Leahy, p. 265; see also Hassett, pp. 271-272.

The Strangest Campaign. Anna Roosevelt Boettiger on her father's Teamsters' talk: Rosenman, p. 478. Teamsters' Union speech, Sept. 23, 1944: PPA, 1944-45, pp. 284-292, read against recordings of speech. Dewey's reaction: *Time,* Oct. 2, 1944, pp. 22-23; *PM,* Sept. 25, 1944, p. 12; interview with Dewey, April 11, 1969. Vote analysis: Bean to Lubin and Hopkins, Feb. 4, 1944, FDRL; see earlier study of turnout by Cantril, April 26, 1943, Cantril Notebook II, pp. 50-63. Role of PAC: Joseph Gaer, *The First Round* (Duell, Sloan & Pearce, 1944), which includes documents and leaflets; Josephson, p. 631. Negro vote: Cantril Notebook IV, p. 97.

Campaign tour of New York: Hassett, pp. 278-282; Reilly, pp. 198-199; Eleanor Roosevelt, pp. 336-338; Film 2757-14, NA. Other campaign speeches are from PPA, 1944-45. Silencing Hershey: memorandum of talk with Roosevelt, Oct. 3, 1944, Stimson Papers. MacArthur's announcement: Whitney, p. 158. Chicago speech: Rosenman, p. 496; Hassett, p. 286. Communism as issue, and Boston speech: Sherwood, p. 829; Reilly, p. 197; Roosevelt and Shalett, p. 353; Hassett, pp. 277, 287; Forrestal, p. 13; *Time,* Nov. 27, 1944, p. 18. Election Day and night: Hassett, p. 293; Leahy, pp. 277-278; Leahy Diary, Nov. 7, 8, 1944.

For You Are the Man for Us. Roosevelt's comment on Dewey to Hassett, election night: Hassett, p. 294. Roosevelt's notes, election night: PSF, Box 54. Letter from black woman in Pittsburgh (lines broken, from prose form of letter, by author): OF 4166, Fourth-term Corr., letter dated Nov. 1, 1944. Votes written in to Roosevelt: Susie Phillips to Roosevelt, Oct. 10, 1944, OF 93.

CHAPTER EIGHTEEN

Roosevelt's return to Washington after the election: Hassett, pp. 295-296. His speech, Nov. 10, 1944: PPA, 1944-45, pp. 418-419. Press conference: PC 979, Nov. 10, 1944. Congratulations from Stalin and Mao, respectively: Stalin to Roosevelt, Nov. 9, 1944, *Correspondence*[2], p. 168; Mao to Hurley, Dec. 16, 1944, FRUS, 1944, Vol. VI, pp. 740-741. Election figures: Svend Petersen, *A Statistical History of the American Presidential Elections* (Frederick Ungar, 1963), Tables 35-42.

Europe: The Deepening Fissures. Basic U.S. policy toward Poland, especially future economic reconstruction: Stettinius to Roosevelt, Oct. 31, 1944, with enclosed report "Reconstruction of Poland," FDRL. Polish-American pressures: Arthur Bliss Lane, *I Saw Poland Betrayed* (Indianapolis: Bobbs-Merrill, 1948), pp. 58-62; Stettinius to Roosevelt, on "Resolution of Polish American Democratic Organization of Chicago," Jan. 4, 1945, Poland Folder, 1-45, FDRL. Roosevelt-Churchill correspondence with Stalin on Warsaw: Roosevelt and Churchill to Stalin, Aug. 20, 1944; Stalin to Roosevelt and Churchill, Aug. 22, 1944, *Correspondence*[2], pp. 156, 157; Churchill to Roosevelt, Aug. 24, 1944, Sept. 4, 1944; Roosevelt to Churchill, Aug. 24, 1944, Aug. 26, 1944, Sept. 5, 1944, Churchill[6], pp. 136-144. Stalin's general attitude and policy on Warsaw situation: Werth, pp. 873-883; Deborin, pp. 370-374; Ulam, pp. 361-363; Hull, p. 1446; FRUS, 1944, Vol. IV, p. 1013. Roosevelt's view: above citations and Hull, pp. 1448-1449. Churchill "hushing up" Poland for Roosevelt: Churchill to King George, Oct. 16, 1944; Roosevelt to Churchill, Oct. 22, 1944, Churchill[6], pp. 239, 242. Lane and Roosevelt exchange: Lane, pp. 64-67. Mikolajczyk appeal to Roosevelt, Oct. 26, 1944: *Malta-Yalta,* pp. 207-209; Roosevelt to Mikolajczyk, Nov. 17, 1944, *ibid.,* pp. 209-210; memo, Stettinius to Roosevelt, Nov. 15, 1944, *ibid.,* p. 209. Roosevelt's appeal to Stalin and Stalin's answer, Dec. 16, 1944 and Dec. 27, 1944, respectively:

Malta-Yalta, pp. 217-218, 221-223; Stalin's further message and Roosevelt's response, Dec. 30, 1944 and Jan. 1, 1945, *ibid.,* pp. 224-226; see also *Correspondence*[2], pp. 175-184. Churchill to Roosevelt, Jan. 6, 1945: *Malta-Yalta,* p. 226.

Churchill-Stalin agreement on spheres of interest: Churchill[6], pp. 226-228; see also Harriman reports, FRUS, 1944, Vol. IV, pp. 1003-1024. Harriman's presence at Churchill-Stalin meeting: Roosevelt to Churchill, Oct. 4, 1944, Churchill[6], pp. 219-220. Dispute over Italy: *Malta-Yalta,* pp. 266 ff., 430 ff.; Sherwood, pp. 838-839. Churchill's "easing" of Italian situation before presidential election: Churchill to Halifax, Dec. 4, 1944, *Malta-Yalta,* pp. 267-269. Greek situation: Churchill[6], chap. 18; Eden, chap. 14; Sherwood, pp. 839-843; Roosevelt to Churchill, Dec. 13, 1944, Churchill[6], pp. 299-301. Harriman's reports on Soviet policy and attitudes: Hull, p. 1459; FRUS, 1944, Vol. IV, pp. 988-990, 992-998.

China: The Edge of the Abyss. On Chinese developments generally during 1944, see Tsou, Pts. 1-2; FRUS, 1944, China, Vol. VI; Kirby, Vol. IV; Kolko, chap. 10; Stilwell, chaps. 10-11; Romanus and Sunderland[3], chap. 1; White and Jacoby; OPD 384 (China), AR. Battle for Leyte Gulf: King and Whitehill, pp. 576-580; S. E. Morison, *Leyte* (Boston: Little, Brown, 1958); Forrestal, pp. 19-20; E. B. Potter and Chester W. Nimitz (eds.), *Triumph in the Pacific* (Englewood Cliffs, N.J.: Prentice-Hall, 1963), chap. 5. CBI developments: Romanus and Sunderland[3], chaps. 4-6; Churchill[5], p. 566. Churchill's skepticism of Chinese possibilities: Churchill[5], pp. 560-561. Roosevelt-Chiang exchanges on military situation: Romanus and Sunderland[1], pp. 383-384. Stilwell's report on situation: *ibid.,* p. 435. Internal problems of China: Smith, pp. 48-52, 94-98.

Reports on Mao's regime: Gauss to Hull, Aug. 26, 1944, enclosing report by Second Secretary John S. Service, FRUS, 1944, China, Vol. VI, pp. 517-520; see also *ibid.,* pp. 551-556, 559-567. Attitude and questions of Communist leaders: *ibid.,* p. 606; Oct. 10, 1944, pp. 637-638; see also White and Jacoby, pp. 240-241. Roosevelt to Chiang on the developing disaster: text in Romanus and Sunderland[1], pp. 445-446. Stilwell's presentation of the climactic message: Stilwell, p. 333. Final developments: Roosevelt to Chiang, Oct. 5, 1944, FRUS, 1944, China, Vol. VI, pp. 165-166; Chiang to Roosevelt, Oct. 9, 1944, *ibid.,* pp. 166-167; also Chiang to Hurley, Oct. 10, 1944, *ibid.,* pp. 167-170; Roosevelt to Chiang, Oct. 18, 1944, Romanus and Sunderland[1], pp. 468-469. Many of Roosevelt's messages to Chungking were drafted in the War Department; see OPD 384, AR.

Roosevelt as Grand Strategist. Stilwell's view of Roosevelt: Stilwell, chap. 11. Roosevelt's aims in China: Tsou, pp. 33-34, 123-124; Romanus and Sunderland[1], pp. 59, 457-458; Gauss to Hull, Aug. 9, 1944, FRUS, 1944, China, Vol. VI, pp. 139-140. Roosevelt to Chiang on deteriorating military situation: Roosevelt to Chiang, Oct. 5, 1944, Oct. 18, 1944, Romanus and Sunderland[1], pp. 459, 468-469; see PC 960, July 7, 1944, 2-3, 8, for a much earlier indication of Roosevelt's awareness of both the deterioration of Chinese resistance and the role of bombing. Unconditional surrender: address by Roosevelt to White House Correspondents' Association, Feb.

12, 1943, PPA, 1943, pp. 79-80; see also PC 962, July 29, 1944; PPA, 1944-45, pp. 209-211; Hull, chap. 113; Anne Armstrong, *Unconditional Surrender* (New Brunswick, N.J.: Rutgers University Press, 1961), especially chap. 2. Grand strategy defined: S. E. Morison, *Strategy and Compromise* (Boston: Little, Brown, 1958), pp. 5-6; Greenfield[1]; Fuller; B. H. Liddell Hart, *Strategy: The Indirect Approach* (Praeger, 1954), pp. 335-336, 362; Urs Schwarz, *American Strategy: A New Perspective* (Doubleday, 1966), chaps. 2, 3, and preface by Henry Kissinger.

View of Roosevelt as military pragmatist or opportunist: Matloff, pp. 3-4; Divine, chap. 4. Roosevelt on Four Freedoms as ultimate stake: PPA, 1941, p. 66; see also Range. Military and civilian ends and means: William T. R. Fox, "Civilians, Soldiers, and American Military Policy," *World Politics,* April 1955, pp. 402-418. Roosevelt quoted on priority for military policy: Roosevelt to Smuts, Aug. 3, 1942, PL, p. 1337; Roosevelt to Churchill, June 29, 1944, Churchill[6], Appendix, p. 721. A critical treatment of Roosevelt's unconditional-surrender policy is Armstrong; see also Paul Kecskemeti, *Strategic Surrender: The Politics of Victory and Defeat* (Stanford, Calif.: Stanford University Press, 1958); Louis J. Halle, "Our War Aims Were Wrong," NYT *Magazine,* Aug. 22, 1965, pp. 13 ff., and, for a more favorable view, John L. Chase, "Unconditional Surrender Reconsidered," *Political Science Quarterly,* June 1955, pp. 258-279. Widespread recognition of the impact of unconditional surrender on German resistance: Vandenberg, p. 91; Liddell Hart, memorandum of July 1943, quoted in Armstrong, p. 155; Matloff, pp. 428-432; see also Snell, pp. 115 ff. Roosevelt's warning to Senators about separating military and political problems: Forrestal, p. 23. Bombay Harbor incident: Ehrman[1], pp. 466-468. Atomic developments, fall 1944: Jungk, chap. 11; Stimson Diary. Higgins on Roosevelt: Higgins[2], p. 141. The two diplomacies: Russell H. Bastert, "The Two American Diplomacies," *The Yale Review,* Summer 1960, pp. 518-538; see also Acheson, pp. 15-16. Stalin and the art of "dosage": quoted in Kennan[2], p. 248. Churchill as grand strategist: Liddell Hart, in A. J. P. Taylor and others, *Churchill: Four Faces and the Man* (London: Penguin, 1969), pp. 155-202; see also, in the same collection, J. H. Plumb, "The Historian," pp. 119-151, on Churchill's response to mass popular attitudes and change; this essay is also the source of Churchill on Lloyd George, p. 144. On Churchill and the tides of change, see also Liddell Hart in *ibid.,* pp. 196-199; Churchill[6], p. 351; Moran, p. 265. On certain aspects of the three leaders' views, see McNeill, pp. 366-368. Roosevelt and Wilson compared: Osgood, pp. 410-411. A book on grand strategy for "the freedom of men," which Roosevelt was reported to have read (Clapper Diary, June 1, 1942, LC), is H. J. Mackinder, *Democratic Ideals and Reality* (Holt, 1919).

Christmas 1944. Dewey's vacation: Hassett, p. 299. Hull's resignation: Roosevelt to Hull, Nov. 21, 1944, PL, pp. 1554-1555; Hull, pp. 1715-1719. State Department nominations: Hassett, pp. 303-304; Roosevelt to MacLeish, Dec. 1, 1944, PL, pp. 1558-1559. Press conference, Dec. 19, 1944: PC 984; PPA, 1944-45, pp. 436-437; Drury, pp. 305-307. News from the Bulge: Leahy, p. 282. Battle of the Bulge: John Toland, *Battle* (Random

House, 1959); Eisenhower, chap. 18; Churchill[6], Bk. 1, chap. 17; Hugh M. Cole, *The Ardennes: Battle of the Bulge* (Washington, D.C.: Office of the Chief of Military History, 1965); Hasso von Manteuffel, in Jacobsen and Rohwer, pp. 391-418; and, on a different aspect, "Did Stalin Betray Us in the Battle of the Bulge?," *American Legion Magazine,* Jan. 1968, pp. 6-13, 48. Churchill on the failure of the strategic objective: Churchill[6], p. 268. Allied bombing: Cole, p. 5; Craven and Cate. Vol. III, chap. 6. Christmas at Hyde Park: Christmas Eve talk to the nation, Dec. 24, 1944, PPA, 1944-45, pp. 444-445; Elliott Roosevelt, pp. 226-227.

CHAPTER NINETEEN

Berlin in Jan. 1945: Hans Rumpf, *The Bombing of Germany* (Holt, 1962); Hans-Georg von Studnitz, *While Berlin Burns* (Englewood Cliffs, N.J.: Prentice-Hall, 1964). Hitler at this time: Warlimont, pp. 495-497; Bullock, pp. 759-765; Shirer, pp. 1417-1418. Moscow and Stalin: Werth, pp. 951-952; Deborin, pp. 408-411; Kennan[1]. Churchill to Stalin, Jan. 6, 1945, *Correspondence*[1], p. 294; Stalin to Churchill, Jan. 7, 1945, *ibid.,* pp. 294-295; Churchill to Stalin, Jan. 9, 1945, *ibid.,* p. 295. Trip to Yalta: Churchill[6], pp. 337-338. Atomic-bomb development: Groves to Marshall, Dec. 30, 1944, *Malta-Yalta,* pp. 383-384; Stimson Diary, Dec. 31, 1944. Hewlitt and Anderson, pp. 333-335. Tokyo: Kirby, pp. 226, 230-232.

"The Only Way to Have a Friend . . ." Public attitudes toward Roosevelt and foreign events: Cantril Notebook VI, Dec. 1944, Jan. 1945; Cantril, p. 763; see also Stettinius to Roosevelt, Dec. 30, 1944 and Jan. 6, 1945, memoranda on public-opinion trends based on the Cantril reports, State Department Folder and Stettinius Folder, FDRL. Cabinet meeting, Jan. 5, 1945: Forrestal, p. 21; Stimson notes, Stimson Papers. National war-service legislation: Stimson memorandum for Diary, Dec. 23, 1944, Stimson Papers; Stimson and Forrestal to Roosevelt, Jan. 3, 1945, FDRL; Rosenman, pp. 514-516; Drury, pp. 332, 338. Message on the state of the union, Jan. 6, 1945: PPA, 1944-45, pp. 483-507. Jesse Jones dismissal: Roosevelt to Jones, Jan. 20, 1945, PL, pp. 1566-1567 (carbon of original in State Department Folder, 2-45, FDRL). Question of Perkins resignation: Perkins, pp. 391-394; Roosevelt to Perkins, Jan. 22, 1945, PL, p. 1569. Rumors of administration dissension: *Time,* Jan. 15, 1945, pp. 18-19. Ickes's troubles: Ickes to Roosevelt, Jan. 13, 1945; Roosevelt to Daniels, Jan. 22, 1945, PSF, Daniels Folder, Box 47; Lilienthal, p. 680.

Roosevelt's appearance: Perkins, pp. 391, 393; Leahy, p. 290; Lilienthal, p. 676. Early plans for inauguration: PSF, Inauguration File, Aug. 16, 1944; later plans: PC 980, Nov. 14, 1944; PPA, 1944-45, pp. 422-424; see also Inauguration File cited above on specific plans for the ceremonies; and Edith Helm Papers, 1945, LC, with inauguration lists and plans, and letters from Roosevelt and Eleanor Roosevelt to Helm, both dated Jan. 22, 1945. The ceremony: Lilienthal, p. 675; Acheson, p. 102; *Time,* Jan. 29, 1945, pp. 18-19; Dorothy Parker, *PM,* Jan. 22, 1945, p. 2. The address: PPA, 1944-45, pp. 523-525, checked against recordings.

The King of the Bears. Major documentary sources on Yalta: *Malta-*

Yalta, 1945, which not only is a remarkably full report of the major general and many of the smaller "private" meetings, but also often provides two or three different sets of minutes for the same meeting, thus allowing the historian to compare; Stettinius; Churchill[6], Bk. 2, chaps. 1-4; Rothstein[2]; *Correspondence*[2], pp. 187-193. Many of the participants described the discussions in their memoirs. Of the many works on the conference, John L. Snell (ed.), *The Meaning of Yalta* (Baton Rouge: Louisiana State University Press, 1956) is useful; Williams, chap. 6, is perceptive. Roosevelt's trip to Yalta and arrival: *Malta-Yalta,* p. 549; Reilly, p. 212; Rigdon, pp. 138-146; Elliott Roosevelt, pp. 236-271; Moran, p. 234; Edward J. Flynn, pp. 202 ff. Roosevelt's appearance: Moran, p. 234; Churchill[6], p. 344. King of the Bears: legend narrated to author by citizen of Yalta, May 1963. Roosevelt on forthcoming meeting: Roosevelt to Laski, Jan. 16, 1945, PL, pp. 1565-1566. Roosevelt's pre-Yalta urging on Stalin of provisions for voting under international organization: *Correspondence*[1], pp. 173-174. Harriman on Soviet demand for veto, Dec. 28, 1944: *Malta-Yalta,* pp. 64-66. Roosevelt's initial meeting with Stalin and Molotov: *Malta-Yalta,* pp. 570-573. President's dinner: *Malta-Yalta,* p. 589; Stettinius, pp. 111-116; Eden, p. 512. Stalin as "Uncle Joe": Stettinius, p. 115; Churchill[6], p. 393. Extra votes for the U.S.S.R. in the new Assembly: *Malta-Yalta,* pp. 663-667, 672-677; Stettinius, p. 174; Sherwood, p. 856. Later developments: Stettinius, pp. 193, 195-196; *Malta-Yalta,* pp. 737, 966-967; Churchill[6], pp. 359-360; Byrnes, pp. 40-41; Leahy, p. 310. Stalin's dinner: Churchill[6], pp. 361-363; *Malta-Yalta,* pp. 797-799.

Immediate background on Poland: "Poland: Government and Boundaries" (preconference State Department study), *Malta-Yalta,* pp. 202-236. Roosevelt's raising of the issue at Yalta: *Malta-Yalta,* p. 677; further discussion and letters: *ibid.,* pp. 727 ff., 776 ff., 846 ff., 883. Leahy's reaction: Leahy, pp. 315-316. Proposed text of Declaration on Liberated Europe: *Malta-Yalta,* pp. 862-863. Roosevelt on purity of elections: *ibid.,* pp. 853-854. On Poland generally: Smith, chap. 8 and *passim;* Snell, *The Meaning of Yalta,* pp. 14-19 and *passim.* See also John T. Flynn, pp. 388-389.

Asia: The Second Second Front. Roosevelt's health at Yalta: Bruenn Ms. (see chap. 15 notes); Churchill[6], p. 477; Moran, p. 242; Nicolson, p. 435; Byrnes, pp. 23, 40; Leahy, pp. 313, 321; Stettinius, p. 73; Harriman testimony, *Military Situation in the Far East,* p. 3330; Edward Flynn, p. 203; John T. Flynn, chap. 14. Roosevelt's reference to Willkie: *Malta-Yalta,* pp. 854, 856. Eden on Roosevelt's separate negotiations: Eden, p. 513. Roosevelt-Stalin discussion of political conditions for Soviet entrance into the Pacific war: *Malta-Yalta,* pp. 768-770. Harriman's earlier report to Roosevelt on his discussion with Stalin, Dec. 15, 1944: *ibid.,* pp. 378-379. American military policy on Soviet intervention: Harriman testimony, p. 3332; *Malta-Yalta,* pp. 361 ff., 367, 593-594, 757-760; Stettinius, p. 92; Snell, *The Meaning of Yalta,* p. 137. Notion that Russia would enter war in any event: Eden, p. 511. Stalin's experience with unreliable partners in coalition politics: Ulam, pp. 280-284. Desire of American military for Soviet intervention and awareness of problem of timing: Forrestal, pp. 51,

55; Snell, *The Meaning of Yalta,* pp. 147-148; Deane, pp. 223-226; Tsou, p. 244; Rigdon, pp. 157-158. Louis Morton, "Soviet Intervention in the War with Japan," *Foreign Affairs,* July 1962, pp. 653-662, clearly sees the problem of timing; see also sources cited therein. Roosevelt's worry about Soviet ambitions in the Far East: *Malta-Yalta,* pp. 894-895. Extent of Soviet claims in the Far East in relation to its military power: Tsou, pp. 245-246, 259. Eden's reservations: Eden, p. 513; see also Churchill[6], pp. 388-390. Churchill's dinner at Yalta: *Malta-Yalta,* pp. 921 ff.; Churchill[6], pp. 390-393; Stettinius, pp. 272-278.

Winding up Yalta: *Malta-Yalta,* pp. 924-925; Byrnes, p. 22. Roosevelt receives the three monarchs: Leahy, pp. 325-327; Reilly, pp. 216-223; Sherwood, p. 872; PPA, 1944-45, p. 558; Rigdon, chap. 10. Churchill's visit to Roosevelt at Alexandria: Churchill[6], p. 397. Roosevelt to Eleanor Roosevelt, Feb. 18, 1945: PL, p. 1571. Decline of euphoria: Sherwood, p. 870; Rosenman, p. 526. Watson's death: Bruenn Ms. (see chap. 15 notes). Trip home across Atlantic: Rosenman, pp. 522-524. Roosevelt's comment to Berle: Berle to author, Aug. 8, 1969.

CHAPTER TWENTY

Roosevelt's address to Congress on his trip to Yalta, March 1, 1945: PPA, 1944-45, pp. 570-586, as corrected against recordings; Rosenman, pp. 527-528; Drury, pp. 371-373; Acheson, p. 103.

Europe: The Price of Innocence. Planning for San Francisco Conference: Roosevelt to Stettinius *et al.,* Feb. 28, 1945, PPA, 1944-45, pp. 565-566; Vandenberg, pp. 94, 172-175; *Correspondence*[2]. Reaction to Yalta: N.Y. *Journal-American,* Feb. 14, 1945; N.Y. *World-Telegram,* Feb. 13, 1945; N.Y. *Daily News,* Feb. 14, 1945; Vandenberg, chap. 9; Cantril to Roosevelt and to Stettinius, March 13, 1945, Cantril Notebook VI. Churchill on likely Soviet reaction: Churchill[6], p. 420. Churchill to Roosevelt on Polish crisis, March 13, 1945: Churchill[6], p. 426. Motivation for Kremlin line: Stettinius, p. 309; Rosenman, p. 539; Ulam, p. 379; *Correspondence*[2]. Churchill pressure on Roosevelt: Churchill[6], Bk. 2, chap. 6. Roosevelt to Stalin on Polish situation, March 29, 1945 (received April 1, 1945): *Correspondence*[2], pp. 201-204. Molotov nonattendance at San Francisco Conference: Roosevelt to Stalin, March 24, 1945, PL, p. 1577; Stalin to Roosevelt, March 27, 1945, *Correspondence*[2], pp. 199-200. Extra votes in Assembly for the United States: Roosevelt to Stalin, Feb. 10, 1945; Stalin to Roosevelt, Feb. 11, 1945, *Correspondence*[2], pp. 191-192; later developments: Tully, pp. 356-357; Rosenman, pp. 540-541; Drury, pp. 401-402; Vandenberg, pp. 159-163; Grew to Roosevelt, March 22, 1945, United Nations Conference Folder, FDRL.

Eden comment: Nicolson to Victoria Sackville-West, March 1, 1945, Nicolson, p. 439. Dulles-Wolff episode: Feis[3], chap. 61; Allen Dulles, *The Secret Surrender* (Harper, 1966); Deborin, pp. 431-432. Churchill on advantage of separate military surrender: Churchill[6], pp. 441, 444-445; see also Churchill to Eden, March 24, 1945, Churchill[6], p. 442. View of Combined Chiefs of Staff: Feis[3], pp. 584 ff. Roosevelt-Stalin exchange on matter: *Correspondence*[2], pp. 198-213; see also Ulam, p. 381; Kolko, pp. 375-379; Deborin, pp. 431-432.

Asia: Never, Never, Never. Iwo Jima: Kirby, pp. 235-240; Yu Te-jen, pp. 250-253; S. E. Morison, *Victory in the Pacific* (Boston: Little, Brown, 1962). Hurley's trip to Washington and rumors in Chungking: Hurley testimony, *Military Situation in the Far East,* pp. 2883-2885. Draft agreement between Nationalists and Communists: *Military Situation in the Far East,* pp. 3669-3679. Summary of China's dilemma: Stettinius to Roosevelt, Jan. 4, 1945, Feis[2], pp. 219-220. Hurley's disagreement with Foreign Service officers in China: *ibid.,* pp. 260-264; *United States Relations with China,* pp. 87-92; Hurley testimony, pp. 3255-3257. Hurley meetings with Roosevelt, March 1945: Hurley testimony, pp. 2883-2885, 2887, 2906; Feis[2], pp. 265, 272; Hassett, pp. 321, 326; Tsou, p. 298. Postwar testimony on China must be treated with caution; but see Harriman testimony, *Military Situation in the Far East,* pp. 3335-3342. Battle of Okinawa: Roy E. Appleman, James M. Burns, Russell A. Gugeler, and John Stevens, *Okinawa: The Last Battle* (Washington, D.C.: Department of the Army, 1948); Morison, cited above; Yu Te-jen, pp. 254-264. For its effect on military thinking, see Churchill[6], pp. 626, 627-629. Stimson on giving Russians information: memorandum, Dec. 31, 1944, Stimson Papers. Later atomic-bomb developments: Stimson Diary, Feb. 13, Feb. 15, March 5, March 15, 1945; Moore, p. 362; Freedman, p. 726; Hewlett and Anderson, pp. 339-340, 342.

Wedemeyer's meeting with Roosevelt: Wedemeyer, p. 340; *Military Situation in the Far East,* pp. 2293-2567. Policy toward Indochina: Hull, pp. 1596-1599; Eden, p. 378; Arthur H. Schlesinger, Jr., *The Bitter Heritage* (Boston: Houghton Mifflin, 1967) and works cited therein. Roosevelt to Stalin on Indochina: *Malta-Yalta,* p. 770. Roosevelt's trusteeship idea: PPA, 1944-45, pp. 562-563. Press conference discussion: *ibid.,* pp. 562-564. Churchill at Yalta on the Empire: *Malta-Yalta,* pp. 844, 856, 858; Byrnes, p. x; Moran, pp. 244-245. Roosevelt's position on trusteeship issue, March 1945: Hurley testimony, *Military Situation in the Far East,* pp. 2890-2891 (testimony of June 21, 1951). Declaration of Independence as exemplar: Shaplen, p. 29.

"The Work, My Friends, Is Peace." Legislative situation: Drury, p. 408 and *passim.* Guaranteed wage plans and Trade Agreements Act renewal: PPA, 1944-45, pp. 592-593, 595-600. Roosevelt on the good old times: Roosevelt to Morgan Hoyt, Feb. 28, 1945, PL, p. 1572. Roosevelt on ending of war in May: Perkins, p. 396. Roosevelt at the dinner of the White House Correspondents' Association, March 22, 1945: Drury, pp. 388-390. Military situation in Europe: John Toland, *The Last 100 Days* (Random House, 1966).

Hassett to Bruenn on Roosevelt's health, March 30, 1945: Hassett, pp. 327-328; Bruenn Ms. does not mention this incident. Churchill on deteriorating relations with Russia: Churchill[6], p. 456. Roosevelt's efforts to quiet the situation: Roosevelt to Stalin, (received April 13, 1945), *Correspondence*[2], p. 214; Roosevelt to Churchill, April 12, 1945, Churchill[6], p. 454. Philippine independence: Sergio Osmeña to Roosevelt, March 31, 1945, Philippines Folder, 1-45, FDRL; PC 998, April 5, 1945;

PPA, 1944-45, pp. 607-610; see also Sayre Papers, Box 7, LC; Hassett, p. 330; Early to Stimson, April 11, 1945, White House Correspondence–Stimson, AR. Undelivered Jefferson Day speech: PPA, 1944-45, pp. 613-616; Hassett, p. 333; Rosenman, p. 551.

EPILOGUE

For the sake of continuity, some of the ideas and language used in the epilogue to the first volume of this biography have been used or expanded in this epilogue. Asbell, chaps. 1-3, has recounted Roosevelt's death in detail and with sensitivity; see also Hassett, pp. 333-338; Reilly, pp. 229-234; Tully, pp. 361-366. Roosevelt-McDuffie exchange: Asbell, pp. 7-9. Churchill's reaction to the news: Churchill[6], p. 471; Stalin's: Sulzberger, p. 253; Chiang Kai-shek's: NYT, April 13, 1945, p. 10; Goebbels's: Shirer, pp. 1440-1441. Other foreign reaction: Nicholas Halasz, *Roosevelt Through Foreign Eyes* (Princeton, N.J.: Van Nostrand, 1961), pp. 308-319.

Freedom's Once-Born. Departure from Warm Springs: Walker, pp. 300-302; Asbell, chap. 12. Luce's feeling about Roosevelt: John Kobler, *Luce: His Time, Life, and Fortune* (Doubleday, 1968), pp. 122-123. Acheson on Roosevelt's condescensions: Dean Acheson, *Morning and Noon* (Boston: Houghton Mifflin, 1965), p. 165. Sholto-Douglas and Roosevelt: William Sholto-Douglas, *Years of Command* (London: Collins, 1966), pp. 230-231. Jones on Roosevelt: George Dixon, Washington *Times-Herald,* Feb. 1, 1945. Roosevelt and Buckingham Palace: John M. Carmody interview, OHP, 607.

"The Lonesome Train": Millard Lampell, "The Lonesome Train," a musical legend, Decca Records, 1949; Asbell, chap. 15. Concept of the "once-born": William James, *The Varieties of Religious Experience* (Longmans, Green, 1935), p. 199, as cited and interpreted in Erik H. Erikson, *Young Man Luther* (Norton, 1962), pp. 41, 117. Roosevelt's references to home and family in connection with policy matters are too numerous to be listed; some examples can be found in Range, p. 62; Churchill[6], p. 216; PL, p. 1380. William White on the funeral in Washington: quoted in Asbell, p. 170. Funeral service in the White House: Biddle, p. 360; Lilienthal, p. 693. Eleanor Roosevelt's confrontation of Anna: confidential source.

Democracy's Aristocrat. Clare Boothe Luce on Roosevelt's cautiousness: Kobler, p. 121. Poll on choice of new Navy Secretary: Cox Diary, May 1, 1944, FDRL. "Meaning it": Erikson, *Young Man Luther,* pp. 208-210. Hopkins on Roosevelt's commitment: Sherwood, p. 266; see also White, pp. 75-76, 87-88. Roosevelt's belief in the brotherly spirit of science: PPA, 1944-45, p. 615. Roosevelt on dreaming dreams: Roosevelt to Smuts, Nov. 24, 1942, PL, pp. 1371-1372. Roosevelt to MacLeish, June 9, 1943: PSF, MacLeish Folder. Niebuhr on love and life: Reinhold Niebuhr, *Christianity and Power Politics* (Scribner, 1940), chap. 1; see also Osgood, pp. 381-383.

New York City rumors: *PM,* April 13, 1945, p. 9. Reactions abroad are from *Time,* April 23, 1945, p. 27; *Life,* April 23, 1945, pp. 30, 32; NYT, April 14, 1945, p. 14. Lincoln's trip: Carl Sandburg, *Abraham Lincoln: The War Years* (Harcourt, Brace, 1939), Vol. IV, chap. 76. Individuals' views of Roosevelt: Maisky, pp. 286-287; Churchill[6], Bk. 2, chap. 9; Arnold Papers, LC. Buchan: Janet Adam Smith, *John Buchan* (London: Rupert Hart-Davis, 1965), p. 405. Sherwood: Sherwood, p. 882. Lyndon Johnson: *Life,* April 23, 1945, p. 32. Stimson: Stimson to Eleanor Roosevelt, April 16, 1945, Stimson Papers. See also William S. White, pp. 12-15. The final sentences in this section are from Burns, p. 477. See, generally, Allen.

Voyager's Return. Roosevelt on returning to Hyde Park: Roosevelt to Hannegan, PPA, 1944-45, pp. 197-198. Hyde Park burial service: Asbell, chap. 18; and contemporary accounts.

INDEX

NEW HANOVER COUNTY PUBLIC LIBRARY
3 4200 00182 7274